THE UNHERALDED TRIUMPH

THE JOHNS HOPKINS UNIVERSITY
STUDIES IN HISTORICAL AND POLITICAL SCIENCE
102d Series (1984)

THE UNHERALDED TRIUMPH

City Government in America, 1870–1900

Jon C. Teaford

THE JOHNS HOPKINS UNIVERSITY PRESS
Baltimore and London

© 1984 by The Johns Hopkins University Press
Printed in the United States of America

The Johns Hopkins University Press, Baltimore, Maryland 21218
The Johns Hopkins Press Ltd., London

Library of Congress Cataloging in Publication Data

Teaford, Jon C.
  The unheralded triumph, city government in America,
1870–1900.

  Includes bibliographical references and index.
  1. Municipal government—United States—History—19th
century.   2. Municipal services—United States—History—
19th century.   I. Title.
JS323.T427   1983   352′.00724′0973   83–12082
ISBN 0–8018–3062–1
ISBN 0–8018–3063–X (pbk.)

Contents

Tables

Acknowledgments

Among those aiding in the preparation of this work was Professor James Oakes of Princeton University who offered useful suggestions for its improvement. Joyce Good and Grace Dienhart deserve thanks for overseeing the typing of the manuscript. I am also indebted to the libraries of the Ohio State University and the University of Illinois, which proved so valuable at every stage of the project. Parts of chapters 4 and 5 previously appeared in the *American Journal of Legal History*, July 1979 and July 1981, respectively, and I thank the editors for their willingness to allow the reprinting of this material.

THE UNHERALDED TRIUMPH

1 TRUMPETED FAILURES AND UNHERALDED TRIUMPHS

In 1888 the British observer James Bryce proclaimed that "there is no denying that the government of cities is the one conspicuous failure of the United States."[1] With this pronouncement he summed up the feelings of a host of Americans. In New York City, residents along mansion-lined Fifth Avenue, parishioners in the churches of then-sedate Brooklyn, even petty politicos at party headquarters in Tammany Hall, all perceived serious flaws in the structure of urban government. Some complained, for example, of the tyranny of upstate Republican legislators, others attacked the domination of ward bosses, and still others criticized the greed of public utility companies franchised by the municipality. Mugwump reformer Theodore Roosevelt decried government by Irish political machine hacks, the moralist Reverend Charles Henry Parkhurst lambasted the reign of rum sellers, and that pariah of good-government advocates, New York City ward boss George Washington Plunkitt, also found fault, attacking the evils of civil service. For each, the status quo in urban government was defective. For each, the structure of municipal rule needed some revision. By the close of the 1880s the litany of criticism was mounting, with one voice after another adding a shrill comment on the misrule of the cities.

During the following two decades urban reformers repeated Bryce's words with ritualistic regularity, and his observation proved one of the most-quoted lines in the history of American government. Time and again latter-day Jeremiahs damned American municipal rule of the late nineteenth century, denouncing it as a national blight, a disgrace that by its example threatened the survival of democracy throughout the world. In 1890 Andrew D. White, then-president of Cornell University, wrote that "without the slightest exaggeration . . . the city governments of the United States are the worst in Christendom—the most expensive, the most inefficient, and the most corrupt."[2] Four years later the reform journalist Edwin Godkin claimed that "the present condition of city governments in the United States is bringing democratic institutions into contempt the world over, and imperiling some of the best things in our civilization."[3] Such preachers as the Reverend Washington Gladden denounced the American city as the "smut of civilization," while his clerical colleague Reverend Parkhurst said of the nation's municipalities: "Virtue is at the bottom and knavery on top. The rascals are out of jail and standing guard over men who aim to be honorable and law-abiding."[4] And in 1904 journalist Lincoln Steffens stamped American urban rule with an indelible badge of opprobrium in the corruption-sated pages of his popular muckraking exposé *The Shame of the Cities*. Books, magazines, and newspapers all recited the catalog of municipal sins.

Likewise, many twentieth-century scholars passing judgment on the development of American city government have handed down a guilty verdict and sentenced American urban rule to a place of shame in the annals of the nation. In 1933 a leading student of municipal home rule claimed that "the conduct of municipal business has almost universally been inept and inefficient" and "at its worst it has been unspeakable, almost incredible."[5] That same year the distinguished historian Arthur Schlesinger, Sr., in his seminal study *The Rise of the City*, described the development of municipal services during the last decades of the nineteenth century and found the achievements "distinctly creditable to a generation . . . confronted with the phenomenon of a great population everywhere clotting into towns." Yet later in his study he returned to the more traditional position, recounting tales of corruption and describing municipal rule during the last two decades of the century as "the worst city government the country had ever known."[6] Writing in the 1950s, Bessie Louise Pierce, author of the finest biography to date of an American city, a multivolume history of Chicago, described that city's long list of municipal achievements but closed with a ritual admission of urban shortcomings, citing her approval of Bryce's condemnation.[7] Similarly, that lifelong student of American municipal history, Ernest Griffith, subtitled his volume on late-nineteenth-century urban rule "the conspicuous failure," though he questioned whether municipal government was a greater failure than state government.[8]

Historians such as Schlesinger and Griffith were born in the late nineteenth century, were raised during the Progressive era, and early imbibed the ideas of such critics as Bryce and White. Younger historians of the second half of the twentieth century were further removed from the scene of the supposed municipal debacle and could evaluate it more dispassionately. By the 1960s and 1970s, negative summations such as "unspeakable" and "incredible" were no longer common in accounts of nineteenth-century city government, and historians professing to the objectivity of the social sciences often refused to pronounce judgment on the quality of past rule. Yet recent general histories of urban America have continued both to describe the "deterioration" of city government during the Gilded Age and to focus on political bosses and good-government reformers who were forced to struggle with a decentralized, fragmented municipal structure supposedly unsuited to the fast-growing metropolises of the 1880s and 1890s. Some chronicles of the American city have recognized the material advances in public services during the late nineteenth century, but a number speak of the failure of the municipality to adapt to changing realities and of the shortcomings of an outmoded and ineffectual municipal framework. Sam Bass Warner, Jr., one of the leading new urban historians of the 1960s, has characterized the pattern of urban rule as one of "weak, corrupt, unimaginative municipal government."[9] Almost one hundred years after Bryce's original declaration, the story of American city government remains at best a tale of fragmentation and confusion and at worst one of weakness and corruption.

If modern scholars have not handed down such damning verdicts as the contemporary critics of the 1880s and 1890s, they have nevertheless issued evaluations critical of the American framework of urban rule. As yet, hindsight has not cast a golden glow over the municipal institutions of the late nineteenth century, and few historians or political scientists have written noble tributes to the achievements of American municipal government. Praise for the nation's municipal officials has been rare and grudging. Though many have recognized the elitist predilections of Bryce and his American informants, the influence of Bryce's words still persists, and the image of nineteenth-century city government remains tarnished. Historians have softened the harsh stereotype of the political boss, transforming him from a venal parasite into a necessary component of a makeshift, decentralized structure. Conversely, the boss's good-government foes have fallen somewhat from historical grace and are now typified as crusaders for the supremacy of an upper-middle-class business culture. But historians continue to aim their attention at these two elements of municipal rule, to the neglect of the formal, legal structure. They write more of the boss than of the mayor, more on the civic leagues than on the sober but significant city comptroller. Moreover they continue to stage the drama of bosses and reformers against a roughly sketched backdrop of municipal disarray. The white and black hats of the players may have shaded to gray, but the setting of the historian's pageant remains a ramshackle municipal structure.

Nevertheless, certain nagging realities stand in stark contrast to the traditional tableau of municipal rule. One need not look far to discover the monuments of nineteenth-century municipal achievement that still grace the nation's cities, surviving as concrete rebuttals to Bryce's words. In 1979 the architecture critic for the *New York Times* declared Central Park and the Brooklyn Bridge as "the two greatest works of architecture in New York . . . each . . . a magnificent object in its own right; each . . . the result of a brilliant synthesis of art and engineering after which the world was never quite the same."[10] Each was also a product of municipal enterprise, the creation of a city government said to be the worst in Christendom. Moreover, can one visit San Francisco's Golden Gate Park or enter McKim, Mead, and White's palatial Boston Public Library and pronounce these landmarks evidence of weakness or failure? Indeed, can those city fathers be deemed "un-imaginative" who hired the great landscape architect Frederick Law Olmsted to design the first public park systems in human history? And were the vast nineteenth-century water and drainage schemes that still serve the cities the handiwork of bumbling incompetents unable to cope with the demands of expanding industrial metropolises? The aqueducts of Rome were among the glories of ancient civilization; the grander water systems of nineteenth-century New York City are often overlooked by those preoccupied with the more lurid aspects of city rule.

A bright side of municipal endeavor did, then, exist. American city governments could claim grand achievements, and as Arthur Schlesinger, Sr., was willing to admit in 1933, urban leaders won some creditable victories in the struggle for improved services. Certainly there were manifold shortcomings: Crime and poverty persisted; fires raged and pavements buckled; garbage and street rubbish sometimes seemed insurmountable problems. Yet no government has ever claimed total success in coping with the problems of society; to some degree all have failed to service their populations adequately. If government ever actually succeeded, political scientists would have to re-tool and apply themselves to more intractable problems, and political philosophers would have to turn to less contemplative pursuits. Those with a negative propensity can always find ample evidence of "bad government," and late-nineteenth-century critics such as Bryce, White, and Godkin displayed that propensity. In their writings the good side of the municipal structure was as visible as the dark side of the moon.

Thus, observers of the late-nineteenth-century American municipality have usually focused microscopic attention on its failures while overlooking its achievements. Scoundrels have won much greater coverage than conscientious officials. Volumes have appeared, for example, on that champion among municipal thieves, New York City's political boss William M. Tweed, but not one book exists on the life and work of a perhaps more significant figure in nineteenth-century city government, Ellis Chesbrough the engineer who served both Boston and Chicago and who transformed the public works of the latter city. Only recently has an admirable group of studies begun to explore the work of such municipal technicians who were vital to the formulation and implementation of public policy.[11] But prior to the 1970s accounts of dualistic conflicts between political bosses and good-government reformers predominated, obscuring the complexities of municipal rule and the diversity of elements actually vying for power and participating in city government. And such traditional accounts accepted as axiomatic the inadequacy of the formal municipal structure. Critics have trumpeted its failures, while its triumphs have gone unheralded.

If one recognizes some of the challenges that municipal leaders faced during the period 1870 to 1900, the magnitude of their achievements becomes clear.

The leaders of the late nineteenth century inherited an urban scene of great tumult and stress and an urban population of increasing diversity and division. During the midcentury, thousands of Roman Catholic immigrants from Ireland and Germany had flooded American metropolitan areas, threatening the traditional Protestant dominance and igniting sharp ethnic conflicts. Riots between the native-born and immigrants flared in Philadelphia during the 1840s; the anti-immigrant Native American Party assumed control of both Philadelphia and Baltimore in the 1850s; and New York City's Draft Riots of 1863 pitted Irish against blacks in the nation's bitterest and most destructive urban uprising. The melting pot was coming to a boil, and yet throughout the 1870s, 1880s, and 1890s, waves of newcomers continued to enter the country, including more and more representatives of the alien cultures of southern and eastern Europe. To many in 1870, social and ethnic diversity seemed to endanger the very foundation of order and security in the nation, and municipal leaders faced the need to maintain a truce between Protestants and Catholics, old stock and new, the native business elite and immigrant workers.

The rush of migrants from both Europe and rural America combined with a high birth rate to produce another source of municipal problems, a soaring urban population. New York City, Boston, Baltimore, and Philadelphia were dynamic centers, expanding rapidly and increasing their populations at a rate of 30 percent to 40 percent each decade. Chicago, on the average, doubled in population each decade between 1870 and 1900, and elsewhere, growth rates of 50 percent or 60 percent were not unusual. During the last thirty years of the century, the nation's chief cities absorbed thousands of acres of new territory to accommodate this booming population, and once-compact cities sprawled outward from the urban core. This expansion and sprawl produced demands for the extension of services and the construction of municipal facilities. The newly annexed peripheral wards needed sewer lines and water mains; they required fire and police protection; and residents of outlying districts expected the city to provide paved streets and lighting. Municipal governments could not simply maintain their services at existing levels; instead, they had to guarantee the extension of those services to thousands of new urban dwellers.

Improved and expanded municipal services, however, required funding, and revenue therefore posed another challenge for city rulers. Municipalities markedly extended their endeavors during the midcentury, purchasing waterworks, creating paid fire brigades, establishing public school systems, and forming modern police forces. To pay for this, taxes rose and municipal indebtedness soared. Taxpayer revolts were common as early as the 1850s, with angry citizens in New York City, Chicago, Philadelphia, and Milwaukee complaining of public extravagance and corruption and already urging a more frugal, businesslike administration of municipal government. Inflation in the 1860s and economic depression in the 1870s exacerbated the financial problems of the city, leading to heightened cries for retrenchment. And throughout the 1880s and 1890s city governments faced the difficult problem of meeting rising expectations for services while at the same time satisfying demands for moderate taxes and fiscal conservatism. This was perhaps the toughest task confronting the late-nineteenth-century municipality.

During the last three decades of the century, American city government did, however, meet these challenges of diversity, growth, and financing with remarkable success. By century's close, American city dwellers enjoyed, on the average, as high a standard of public services as any urban residents in the world. Problems persisted, and there were ample grounds for complaint. But in America's cities, the supply of water was the most abundant, the street lights were the most brilliant, the parks the grandest, the libraries the largest, and the public transportation the fastest of any place in the world. American city fathers rapidly adapted to advances in technology, and New York City, Chicago, and Boston were usually in the forefront of efforts to apply new inventions and engineering breakthroughs to municipal problems. Moreover, America's cities achieved this level of modern service while remaining solvent and financially sound. No major American municipality defaulted on its debt payments during the 1890s, and by the end of the century all of the leading municipalities were able to sell their bonds at premium and pay record-low interest. Any wise financier would have testified that the bonds of those purported strongholds of inefficiency and peculation, the municipal corporations, were far safer investments than were the bonds of those quintessential products of American business ingenuity: the railroad corporations.

Not only did the city governments serve their residents without suffering financial collapse, but municipal leaders also achieved an uneasy balance of the conflicting forces within the city, accommodating each through a distribution of authority. Though commentators often claimed that the "better elements" of the urban populace had surrendered municipal administration to the hands of "low-bred" Irish saloonkeepers, such observations were misleading. Similarly incorrect is the claim that the business and professional elite abandoned city government during the late nineteenth century to decentralized lower-class ward leaders. The patrician, the plutocrat, the plebeian, and the professional bureaucrat all had their place in late-nineteenth-century municipal government; each staked an informal but definite claim to a particular domain within the municipal structure.

Upper-middle-class business figures presided over the executive branch and the independent park, library, and sinking-fund commissions. Throughout the last decades of the nineteenth century the mayor's office was generally in the hands of solid businessmen or professionals who were native-born Protestants. The leading executive officers were persons of citywide reputation and prestige, and during the period 1870 to 1900 their formal authority was increasing. Meanwhile, the legislative branch—the board of aldermen or city council—became the stronghold of small neighborhood retailers, often of immigrant background, who won their aldermanic seats because of their neighborhood reputation as good fellows willing to gain favors for their constituents. In some cities men of metropolitan standing virtually abandoned the city council, and in every major city this body was the chief forum for lower-middle-class and working-class ward politicians.

At the same time, an emerging body of trained experts was also securing a barony of power within city government. Even before the effective application of formal civil service laws, mayors and commissioners deferred to the judgment and expertise of professional engineers, landscape architects, educators, physicians, and fire chiefs, and a number of such figures served decade after decade in municipal posts, despite political upheavals in the executive and legislative branches. By the close of the century these professional civil servants were securing a place of permanent authority in city government. Their loyalty was not to downtown business interests nor to ward or ethnic particularism, but to their profession and their department. And they were gradually transforming those departments into strongholds of expertise.

The municipal professional, the downtown business leader, and the neighborhood shopkeeper and small-time politico each had differing concepts of city government and differing policy priorities. They thus represented potentially conflicting interests that could serve to divide the municipal polity and render it impotent. Yet, during the period 1870 to 1900, these elements remained in a state of peaceful, if contemptuous, coexistence. Hostilities broke out, especially if any element felt the boundaries of its domain were violated. But city governments could operate effectively if the truce between these elements was respected; in other words, if ward business remained the primary concern of the ward alderman, citywide policy was in the hands of the business elite, and technical questions were decided by experts relatively undisturbed by party politics. This was the informal détente that was gradually developing amid the conflict and complaints.

Such extralegal participants as political parties and civic leagues also exerted their influence over municipal government, attempting to tip the uneasy balance of forces in their direction. The political party organization with its ward-based neighborhood bosses was one lever that the immigrants and less affluent could pull to affect the course of government. Civic organizations and reform leagues, in contrast, bolstered the so-called better element in government, the respected businessmen who usually dominated the leading executive offices and the independent commissions. Emerging professional groups such as engineering clubs and medical societies often lent their support to the rising ambitions and growing authority of the expert bureaucracy and permanent civil servants. And special-interest lobbyists like the fire insurance underwriters also urged professionalism in such municipal services as the fire department. Municipal government was no simple dualistic struggle between a citywide party boss with a diamond shirt stud and malodorous cigar and a good-government reformer with a Harvard degree and kid gloves. Various forces were pushing and pulling the municipal corporations, demanding a response to petitions and seeking a larger voice in the chambers of city government.

State legislatures provided the structural flexibility to respond to these demands. The state legislatures enjoyed the sovereign authority to bestow municipal powers and to determine the municipal structure, but when considering local measures, state lawmakers generally deferred to the judgment of the legislative delegation from the affected locality. If the local delegation favored a bill solely affecting its constituents, the legislature usually ratified the bill without opposition or debate. This rule of deference to the locality no longer applied, however, if the bill became a partisan issue, as it occasionally did. But in most cases authorization for new powers or for structural reforms depended on the city's representatives in the state legislature, and each session the state assemblies and senates rubber-stamped hundreds of local bills. Thus, indulgent legislators provided the vital elasticity that allowed urban governments to expand readily to meet new challenges and assume new responsibilities.

Local delegations, however, responded not only to the requests of the formal rulers of the city—the board of aldermen and the mayor; they also considered the petitions of extralegal agencies eager to obtain favors and reforms. Recourse to the state legislature became an alternate route for those seeking action, a detour around the obstruction of city authorities. Indeed, many believed that the right to appeal to state lawmakers created too much flexibility in the governmental system. Early advocates of municipal home rule therefore sought to block this avenue and to create a less flexible system, but before 1900 those favoring a more rigid, less adaptable structure won few victories. In most states, then, the legislatures responded readily to urban demands, perhaps too readily, and lawmakers tinkered endlessly with the governmental mechanism.

Even so, this process of perpetual adjustment resulted in a mechanism that succeeded in performing the job of city government. Municipal leaders adapted to the need for experts trained in the new technologies and hired such technicians. Moreover, downtown businessmen and ward politicos, the native-born and the immigrants, Protestants and Catholics, loosened the lid on the melting pot and reduced the boiling hostility of the midcentury to a simmer. The cities provided services; they backed off from the brink of bankruptcy; and the municipal structure guaranteed a voice to the various elements of society in both immigrant wards and elite downtown clubs.

Why, then, all the complaints? Why did so many critics of the 1880s and 1890s indulge in a rhetoric of failure, focusing on municipal shortcomings to the neglect of municipal successes? Why was municipal government so much abused? The answer lies in a fundamental irony: The late-nineteenth-century municipal structure accommodated everyone but satisfied no one. It was a system of compromise among parties discontented with compromise. It was a marriage of convenience, with the spouses providing a reasonably comfortable home for America's urban inhabitants. But it was not a happy home. The parties to the nuptials tolerated one another because they had to. Nevertheless, the businessman-mayors and plutocrat park commissioners disliked their dependence on ward politicians, whom they frequently regarded as petty grafters, and they frowned upon the power of the immigrant voters. Likewise, the emerging corps of civil servants was irked by interference from laypersons of both high and low status. And the plebeian party boss opposed efforts to extend the realm of the civil servants who had performed no partisan duties and thus merited no power. None liked their interdependence with persons they felt to be unworthy, incompetent, or hostile.

Enhancing this dissatisfaction was the cultural absolutism of the Victorian era. The late nineteenth century was an age when the business elite could refer to itself as the "best element" of society and take for granted its "God-given" superiority. It was an age when professional engineers, landscape architects, public health experts, librarians, educators, and fire fighters were first becoming aware of themselves as professionals, and with the zeal of converts they defended their newly exalted state of grace. It was also an age when most Protestants viewed Catholics as papal pawns and devotees of Italian idolatry, while most Catholics believed Protestants were little better than heathens and doomed to a quick trip to hell with no stops in purgatory. The late nineteenth century was not an age of cultural relativism but one of cultural absolutes, an age when people still definitely knew right from wrong, the correct from the erroneous. The American municipality, however, was a heterogeneous polyarchy, a network of accommodation and compromise in an era when accommodation and compromise smacked of unmanly dishonor and unprincipled pragmatism. Municipal government of the 1870s, 1880s, and 1890s rested on a system of broker politics, of bargaining and dealing. Yet Parson Weems's panegyric of George Washington, a figure of unbending morality, had molded the political conscience of nineteenth-century American school children, and on reaching adulthood these Americans still believed in the ideal of the great statesman who could not tell a lie. Although the prefix *poly* and the term *relativism* were alien to the guiding principles of the nineteenth century, they are basic to any description of urban government in that era.

Some leaders of the period could, without troubled conscience, act as broker and bargainer, and these figures thrived in urban politics. For example, the high-born Mayor Carter Harrison, Sr., of Chicago, was a master of municipal government and a pragmatic politician who seemed to enjoy the heterogeneity of his city. Likewise, in New York City the low-born Tammany boss Richard Croker commanded his motley metropolis, though he was unable to master the mechanism sufficiently to prevent the ouster of his organization twice in a decade. And a number of high-minded gentlemen seemed capable of playing the game of politics and winning the mayoral office, though they might turn to reform periodicals and lambaste in print the very system they exploited. Still, the idea of reaching an accommodation with grafters, saloonkeepers, and other social pariahs seemed reprehensible, especially among the upper middle class. Through its control of executive offices and independent commissions, the upper middle class was usually the dominant force within city government, and America's municipalities proved especially effective in providing services for that class, with its devotion to flush toilets, public libraries, and suburban parks. No other group, however, proved more hostile in its attacks on the existing system of municipal rule. Though often effective, city government was, according to upper-middle-class critics, almost always dishonorable.

Late-nineteenth-century urban government was a failure not of structure but of image. The system proved reasonably successful in providing services, but there was no prevailing ideology to validate its operation. In fact, the beliefs of the various participants were at odds with the structure of rule that governed them. The respectable elements believed in sobriety and government by persons of character. But the system of accommodation permitted whiskey taps to flow on the Sabbath for the Irish and for Germans, just as it allowed men in shiny suits with questionable reputations to occupy seats on the city council and in the municipal party conventions. The ward-based party devotees accepted the notions of Jacksonian democracy and believed quite literally in the maxim To the victor belong the spoils. But by the 1890s they faced a growing corps of civil servants more devoted to their profession than to any party. Although new professional bureaucrats preached a gospel of expertise, they still had to compromise with party-worshiping hacks and the supposedly diabolical forces of politics. Likewise, special-interest lobbyists such as the fire insurance underwriters were forced to cajole or coerce political leaders whom they deemed ignorant and unworthy of public office. Each of these groups worked together, but only from necessity and not because they believed in such a compromise of honor. There was no ideology of heterogeneous polyarchy, no system of beliefs to bolster the existing government structure. Thus late-nineteenth-century city government survived without moral support, and to many urban dwellers it seemed a bargain with the devil.

Twentieth-century historians also had reasons for focusing on urban failure rather than urban success. Some chroniclers in the early decades accepted rhetoric as reality and simply repeated the condemnations of critics such as Bryce, White, and Godkin. By the midcentury greater skepticism prevailed, but so did serious ills. In fact, the urban crisis of the 1960s provided the impetus for a great upsurge of interest in the history of the city, inspiring a search for the historical roots of urban breakdown and collapse. Urban problems were the scholars' preoccupation. Not until the much-ballyhooed "back-to-the-city" movement of the 1970s did the city become less an object of pity or contempt and more a treasured relic. By the late 1970s a new rhetoric was developing, in which sidewalks and streets assumed a nostalgic significance formerly reserved to babbling brooks and bucolic pastures.

The 1980s, then, seem an appropriate time to reevaluate the much-maligned municipality of the late nineteenth century. Back-to-the-city euphoria, however, should not distort one's judgment of the past. Instead, it is time to understand the system of city government from 1870 to 1900 complete with blemishes and beauty marks. One should not quickly dismiss the formal mechanisms of municipal rule as inadequate and outdated, requiring the unifying grasp of party bosses. Nor should one mindlessly laud municipal rule as a triumph of urban democracy. A serious appreciation of the municipal structure is necessary. How did it work? Who was in charge? What did it achieve?

I THE STRUCTURE OF URBAN RULE

2 NEIGHBORHOOD POWER: THE CITY COUNCIL

In 1800 a visitor to Philadelphia or New York City would have discovered municipal power concentrated in the city council, or board of aldermen; the municipal legislature was virtually the government of these cities. One hundred years later an observer of America's major cities would have found the aldermen and city councils objects of disdain and ridicule, stripped of their former powers and inferior to the mayor and executive commissioners in their authority to determine basic municipal policy. In 1890 an exasperated *New York Tribune* editorialized that "the name 'alderman' has become such a byword that it ought to be blotted from the municipal dictionary," and a reform-minded academic of the 1890s agreed that the "honored historical name of alderman" had assumed "a stigma of suspicion and disgrace."[1] Indictments of nineteenth-century city government repeatedly singled out the municipal council as chief villain. Toward the end of the century, the punishment for the council's perfidy was a loss of stature. No change in the formal structure of municipal government was so marked as the seeming decline of the city council as molder of the urban future. Whereas the council began the century as the premier element in city government, by the 1890s some were asking whether municipal legislatures served any useful purpose.

Yet the change represented not so much a decline in authority as a shift in focus. Although the city council of the late nineteenth century may have played a more limited role in formulating policy of citywide significance than it had previously, it continued to serve a vital function. It survived as the voice of the neighborhoods, the means by which the fragments of the metropolis could win concessions and favors from the ever-more-powerful executive offices of city government. It was the channel through which constituents won exemptions or licenses and neighborhoods obtained pavements, sewers, or water mains. This was its chief role during the last decades of the century. Aldermen of the 1880s and 1890s were masters of the microcosm and not overseers of the macrocosm. They were big men at the corner saloon but small fry when compared with the bankers and brokers downtown.

This shift in focus reflected the changing realities of nineteenth-century urban rule. The American city of the Gilded Age was not a structural dinosaur lumbering stupidly across the urban landscape, unable or unwilling to adapt or survive. Rarely have lawmakers revised and reformed a government structure so often as did the framers of nineteenth-century municipal charters. Charter amendments were frequent, and structural tinkering was constant. Both formally and informally, the municipal structure adjusted to the social and technological environment, and as it adapted to the world of the 1880s and 1890s the role of the city council narrowed and became more sharply defined.

Three factors influenced the change in the alderman's role. First, the perceived decline in the social standing of aldermen caused those members of the chambers of commerce or the reform leagues who wrote the municipal charter proposals to favor a shift in authority. As foreign-born representatives of working-class wards came to enjoy a prominent voice on the city council, and as reports of bribed aldermen became increasingly prevalent, the framers of the municipal structure allocated less power to the déclassé council. Second, technological advances and expanding municipal responsibilities led to a transfer of authority from the council to special-purpose commissions or executive departments. As municipalities invested in waterworks, sewerage systems, professional fire and police brigades, parks, and libraries, lawmakers perceived a need for specialized, expert administration and guidance by individuals with citywide constituencies. The amateur, general-purpose municipal council, whose members represented geographically defined wards and often reflected the working-class attitudes of those wards, seemed ill-equipped to supervise the esoteric technology of water supply or to chart the cultural destinies of libraries. Third, the emerging geographical heterogeneity of the city heightened the need for neighborhood representatives and bolstered the alderman's function as ward advocate at the same time that his hold over citywide policy was weakening. By 1900 American cities included a mass of disparate neighborhoods with different social and ethnic orientations and diverse transportation, paving, and drainage needs owing to differences in topography and rate of population growth. The relatively compact, homogeneous municipality of 1800 had yielded to the patchwork city of 1900, a city of fragments loosely sewn into a metropolis. And as the city moved from relative homogeneity to sprawling heterogeneity, the significance of the alderman as district representative and ward emissary increased.

Thus, the role of the alderman in molding municipal policy diminished, although his function as ward advocate survived. Before the 1860s and 1870s city council committees directly supervised municipal functions, determining appointments, hiring city employees, fixing policy, and even deciding administrative details. After the 1860s and 1870s the supervisory role of these committees declined sharply, yielding to the new authority of commissioners and department chiefs. Yet the stack of constituent petitions mounted ever higher, and the alderman was kept busy fighting for his district's fair share of the municipal bounty. He no longer supervised the departments of municipal government, but he could wrest favors from them. And in the anonymous American cities of the late nineteenth century, with their hundreds of thousands of inhabitants, it was vital for each district to have a friend in city hall.

This pattern of change was not uniform throughout the nation. In many smaller cities characterized by homogeneity and governmental simplicity the city council remained the dominant force in municipal government. But in the largest urban areas a change in the role of the alderman was evident. During the last three decades of the nineteenth century his power over city appointments and finances gradually declined. City councilmen were no longer in command of the municipality. Nevertheless, they remained tribunes for the plebeians in the neighborhoods.

LIMITING ALDERMANIC AUTHORITY

Throughout the United States city councils surrendered prerogatives during the last decades of the nineteenth century, but no council suffered such a loss of power as occurred in the nation's greatest metropolis, New York City. As early as the 1850s and 1860s state lawmakers had shifted authority for New York City's health, fire protection, and police from the city council to state-appointed commissions. In 1870 the New York state legislature returned control of these functions to the municipality, but during the last three decades of the century the city fire commissioners, police commissioners, and health commissioners issued the bylaws governing their own departments. Likewise the board of park commissioners enacted rules governing the city parks; the dock commission regulated the construction, maintenance, and use of the municipal piers; and the Board of Education adopted ordinances regulating the city's schools. The health commissioners enjoyed especially broad authority to enact sanitary regulations, and in 1897 one expert on municipal government observed that "the board of health is, perhaps, a more important legislative body than the board of aldermen in the present city of New York."[2] Each of the special-function boards and commissions made its own rules and did not rely on the Board of Aldermen to determine policy.

Moreover, New York City's aldermen no longer enjoyed the power of the purse. In 1871, at the urging of the city's political boss William M. Tweed, New York's state legislature created the Board of Estimate and Apportionment. This board, as reconstituted by the charter of 1873, consisted of three executive officers—the mayor, the comptroller, and the president of the Department of Taxes and Assessments—as well as the president of the Board of Aldermen. Together these officers estimated upcoming city expenditures, drafted the municipal budget, and fixed the city tax rate. The Board of Estimate and Apportionment then submitted the proposed annual budget to the

Board of Aldermen, which could offer objections or rectifications. Finally, the budget was returned to the members of the Board of Estimate, who generally ignored the aldermen's suggestions and approved their original handiwork. Writing in 1898, the leading authority on New York City's finances observed that "nearly every one of the [aldermanic] 'rectifications' has always been overruled" by the Board of Estimate, and stated further that this board was "practically unhampered by the aldermen."[3] In 1885 the *New York Times* accurately observed that "the provisions of the charter which require the submission of the estimates . . . to the Board of Aldermen are all a solemn farce, intended to give the Aldermen the appearance without the reality of having something to do with the matter."[4] Appropriations and taxation were, then, the responsibility of the officers on the Board of Estimate, whereas executive departments and commissions determined the rules and regulations for a broad range of municipal activities.

During the late nineteenth century New York City's municipal legislature also lost its role in the selection of department officials and commissioners. Under the city charter of 1873, the mayor appointed each department head and commissioner, though the Board of Aldermen had to consent to the appointment. This veto power over appointments proved a valuable bargaining tool for the board. But in 1884, at the behest of local reformers and former Mayor William Grace, the state legislature eliminated the requirement for aldermanic confirmation and gave the mayor absolute appointing power. Young Theodore Roosevelt sponsored this reform in the state legislature, complaining that "[aldermanic liquor sellers] who from their vices should be the lowest in the social scale are allowed to rule over us." Characterized by the patrician Roosevelt as "the lowest stratum of New-York life," such men seemed unworthy of municipal authority.[5] The legislature concurred in this view, depriving the Board of Aldermen of one more prerogative.

By the 1880s and 1890s virtually the only formal power of significance left to New York City's aldermen was the power to regulate the use of city streets and sidewalks and to grant public utilities the rights-of-way along these thoroughfares. And the aldermen's exercise of this power earned them the contempt of many. As early as 1852 New York City's municipal legislators won the nickname "the forty thieves" for their sale of street railway franchises to those offering generous bribes. In 1884 the aldermen renewed their right to this title when they refused to sell a valuable franchise at auction but awarded it to a company offering the city meager compensation for the privilege. An ensuing investigation resulted in bribery indictments against twenty-two of the twenty-four aldermen. After 1888 a new force limited the aldermen's freedom to accept bribes and sell franchises, for, according to Alderman Alfred Conkling, during that year the board began taking orders from Democratic political boss Richard Croker.[6] Henceforth Croker was to sell the franchises and the aldermen were to vote as Croker wished. Croker extolled the merits of this concentration of power when he told a young reporter: "A business man wants to do business with one man, and one who is always there to remember and carry on the business."[7] In the name of concentrated authority, the political boss, like the mayor and executive officers, had stripped New York City's aldermen of their previous prerogatives.

New York City's then-independent sister city of Brooklyn pursued a similar policy of reducing aldermanic authority. Under the Brooklyn charter of 1873, the Board of Aldermen retained authority over appropriations and revenues, and the charter specified that mayoral appointments required aldermanic approval. Moreover, the board exploited the confirmation power, and according to one observer at that time, the mayor "may appoint, but the Aldermen may disappoint."[8] During the 1870s Brooklyn's municipal legislators still played a significant role in the city's government.

During the early 1880s, however, the Brooklyn Board of Aldermen suffered a severe loss of authority. In 1880 lawmakers in Albany created a Board of Estimate for the city of Brooklyn, consisting of the mayor, controller, and auditor, as well as two county officers. It was empowered to prepare the annual budget for the city and county and to determine appropriations for city and county agencies. The Board of Estimate submitted its budget recommendations to the Brooklyn Board of Aldermen, which had the authority to reduce appropriations for any item in the city budget but could not authorize any increases. Moreover, under a new charter that took effect in 1882, mayoral appointments no longer required confirmation by the Board of Aldermen. After 1882 Brooklyn's mayor had absolute power over appointments, and the aldermen ceased to enjoy leverage over the selection of executive officers. With little control over city finances and no role in the appointment of city officials, the Brooklyn board survived as a minor element in the determination of city policy.

The decline of the city council was most dramatic in New York City and Brooklyn, but in New England the same trend was evident. For example, Boston's charter of 1885 transferred all executive powers to the mayor and his appointees, denying council committees their previous authority to supervise municipal departments and to interfere in the administrative business of the city. Moreover, this charter shifted the power to nominate executive officials from the city council to the mayor, though appointments still required confirmation by the upper house of the bicameral council. The Massachusetts legislature of 1885 also denied the council its traditional authority over the city's Police Department and instead created a police commission to be appointed by the governor. And leveling still another blow at aldermanic authority, that same legislature, responding to the requests of the mayor and many property owners, imposed a ceiling on the municipal tax rate, thereby limiting the hitherto unrestrained power of Boston's council to raise revenue. Henceforth the council had little latitude in raising revenues, but each year fixed the tax rate only as high as the state legislature would permit. Loan measures paid for permanent improvements, but in 1891 the legislature granted the mayor in practice an absolute veto over loans.[9] The council still had a voice in the distribution of appropriations and loans, but it lacked the freedom of action and preeminent authority it had once commanded.

During the second half of the 1890s, Boston's council gradually lost further prerogatives. After 1895 the mayor's choice for city fire commissioner no longer required aldermanic confirmation, and in 1897 the aldermen likewise lost their power to veto the mayor's nominees to head the municipal departments dealing with penal and charitable institutions.[10] In 1898 Boston's Mayor Josiah Quincy completed the emasculation of the city council when he pushed through the state legislature a measure creating a board of estimate and apportionment modeled on that of New York City.[11] Although the Boston Board of Apportionment survived less than a year, its creation was indicative of the trend of the times. Authority over the budget and appropriations was shifting to the city's executive officers, leaving the municipal legislators a limited role in charting major municipal policy.

During the 1880s and 1890s, then, Boston's councilmen, like their counterparts in New York City and Brooklyn, lost much of their authority to make decisions vital to the city's future as a whole. The mayor usurped many of the aldermen's former powers; the state legislature, at the behest of the mayor, assumed other prerogatives; and executive commissioners also filled the void left by the declining council. Throughout the last fifteen years of the century, departmental commissioners bypassed the council and issued their own rules and regulations, with the Health Department exercising especially broad legislative powers in matters of health and the abatement of nuisances. By the 1890s the lower house of the council was being described as a "municipal debating club" unworthy of continued existence.[12] Even before 1899, when the Board of Apportionment actually assumed control of finances, the lower house was basically a do-nothing body, failing to take advantage of the limited legislative powers it did retain. According to Boston's Mayor Quincy, during the summer of 1898 the lower house "undertook to hold fifteen meetings, but was obliged to adjourn six times for want of a quorum without transacting any business . . . ; and it was only upon rare and exceptional occasions that the attendance was such . . . that the fifty votes necessary for the passage of a loan order could be secured."[13] At the beginning of the twentieth century another Boston chief executive indicted both houses of the municipal legislature when he concluded that "the achievements of the City Council in the past fifteen years, judged by our public records, and especially by our City Ordinances, are unduly slight."[14]

In one city after another the financial powers of the municipal legislature were diminishing. Indianapolis's charter of 1891 authorized the city controller to draft the municipal budget and provided that the council could reduce but never increase the controller's recommended appropriations and tax levies. And under Buffalo's charter of 1892 a two-thirds vote of all members of the bicameral council was necessary to alter the budget recommendations of the comptroller. The New York state legislature also created a Board of Estimate and Apportionment similar to the New York City board for all cities with a population of 50,000 to 250,000, including such municipalities as Albany, Rochester, and Syracuse. In 1887 the Michigan legislature likewise established a Board of Estimates for Detroit, and Baltimore's charter of 1898 conformed to prevalent fashion and assigned budget-making authority to a board of executive officers.[15]

In some cities appointive commissions virtually superseded the board of aldermen. During the late 1880s Cincinnati largely supplanted its council through the creation of a series of commissions appointed first by the governor and then, in the 1890s, by the mayor. The most powerful of these commissions was the Board of Administration, consisting of four executive appointees who were in charge of public works, health, and parks. According to one observer this board, "aside from the power vested in the police board, transacts five-sixths of the business of the city"[16] By the 1890s Cincinnati's city council survived only as a historical vestige, with little power and less prestige. Other Ohio city councils also surrendered powers to appointed commissioners. In 1891 Youngstown adopted a commission plan in which four city commissioners were appointed by the mayor and county probate judge, and these commissioners exercised virtually all the powers of city government, having charge of pubic works, public safety, and the granting of franchises. In 1893 Ohio's legislature applied this same scheme to the city of Akron.[17] Likewise, in Colorado during the late 1880s the state legislature, at the urging of local reformers, placed the city of Denver under the dual authority of a Board of Fire and Police and a Board of Public Works, both appointed by the governor. The legislature's action was a repudiation of council government in the state's largest city and a late-nineteenth-century mayor of Denver bluntly observed that "the board of public works was created to prevent the public improvement moneys being squandered by the City Council."[18]

Opposition to council rule also motivated New Jersey's legislators to adopt government by appointed commissions. By the 1890s a Board of Finance appointed by the mayor framed Jersey City's municipal budget and fixed the tax rate, whereas fire and police boards governed the public safety programs. In 1891 New Jersey's solons further created a Board of Street and Water Commissioners in both Newark and Jersey City. The mayors of the respective cities appointed the commissions, which had full charge of public works, buildings, and parks and exercised the authority to enact ordinances dealing with these areas of municipal endeavor. One observer writing in the *Commercial and Financial Chronicle* noted that the law creating the boards left the city councils of the two cities "more ornamental than useful."[19]

In Saint Louis and Cleveland, as well, the municipal assembly lost some of its previous authority over public works. The Saint Louis charter of 1876 created a Board of Public Improvements consisting of five commissioners appointed by the mayor plus a president elected by the city's voters, and this board had the exclusive authority to initiate public works ordinances. The Board of Public Improvements prepared all ordinances for the construction, repair, or sprinkling of streets; the laying of sewers and water pipes; the construction or extension of the waterworks; the improvement of the harbor and levees; the planning and maintenance of parks; and the erection or repair of municipal buildings. It submitted these ordinances to the municipal assembly, which could accept or reject the proposals but could not amend them.[20] In Cleveland a body known first as the Board of Improvements and later as the Board of Control likewise enjoyed authority to initiate measures for street and sewer construction or repairs. Without the recommendation of this board, the council could not authorize major public works. Moreover, beginning in 1891 Cleveland's Board of Control, consisting of the mayor and the department chiefs appointed by the mayor, had veto power over all city contracts involving $250 or more. In neither Cleveland nor Saint Louis could the municipal legislature adopt public works measures independent of an executive board. One Clevelander said of his city's government during the 1890s that the mayor and the Board of Control had become "by custom, perhaps even by sanction of law, the real legislative body" of the city and the "City Council was reduced to hardly more than a body of citizens with power of veto."[21]

Though the authority of the alderman was declining, in such major cities as Chicago and Philadelphia his power remained considerable. As late as 1898 a student of Chicago's city government concluded that "the municipal history of Chicago has emphasized at least one fact . . . : the supremacy of the common council during more than half a century of municipal activity."[22] Chicago's council determined appropriations without any strictures imposed by boards of estimate or finance commissions. Moreover, aldermanic confirmation was necessary for executive appointments. The Chicago council did have to share power with independent park and sewerage commissions; and the library and school boards, though formally subject to the council, did not kowtow to its authority. But the formal powers of Chicago's municipal legislature generally remained intact. Philadelphia's council likewise continued to exercise control over appropriations and retained the right to veto mayoral appointments. The Philadelphia charter of 1885 forbade the council to exercise any executive functions (though the distinction between legislative and executive functions was not clearly defined), and it also concentrated power to nominate appointive officials in the hands of the executive.[23] Yet the municipal legislators continued to exercise the right to confirm appointments and could wield the power of the purse both to influence administrative decisions and to pressure executive agencies.

An especially important figure in Chicago was the chairman of the council Committee on Finance. Usually a member with lengthy council experience and business acumen, the finance chairman cooperated with the city comptroller in drafting the municipal budget and could generally block appropriations he opposed or push through expenditures he favored. The council as a whole usually adopted the report of the finance committee without serious debate, and an effective chairman could ensure that his views were the committee's views. In the 1880s the twenty-year council veteran Arthur Dixon commanded the committee, and in the 1890s Republican boss Martin Madden was the finance czar. For these men a seat in the council was a position of power from which to guide municipal policy.[24]

Even in Chicago and Philadelphia, however, the municipal legislatures seemed increasingly willing to defer to the preeminent authority of the executive branch. In 1906, when a delegate to Chicago's charter convention referred to that municipality as "a council-governed city," former Mayor George Swift quickly rejected this description, claiming that Chicago was "an administration-governed city." According to Swift, when he was mayor in the mid-1890s he vetoed approximately three hundred orders and ordinances of the city council, and no more than 1 percent of these vetoes were overridden.[25] Chicago's aldermen had broad authority to act, and they used that authority. But politically astute mayors were generally able to check the power of the municipal legislature and force that body to obey. Likewise, in Philadelphia the council exercised power, but on questions of broad policy the executive officers seem to have held sway. In 1898 Philadelphia's director of public works told one observer of American municipal government that "there was no control exercised by the council's committee over his activities except cutting down 'appropriations' for items, or passing stray 'ordinances' about details in which particular members had a personal or political interest."[26] Similarly, Philadelphia's mayors seemed to regard the council as a hindrance or a nuisance but hardly as a threatening rival. Councilmen could prove an obstacle to executive and departmental policy, and they certainly had the power to obtain favors, but they did not chart and dictate municipal policy. By 1900 the city councils in Chicago and Philadelphia still wielded extensive authority, but the initiative in municipal government now rested with the executive.

In New York City at the close of the century there was, however, a momentary flurry of interest in reversing the course of history and enhancing aldermanic authority. Believing that a municipal assembly with enhanced powers would attract "men of the highest character and intelligence," the framers of the Greater New York charter of 1897 attempted to concentrate legislative authority in a two-house council and to limit the ordinance-making power of the executive departments.[27] Still fearful of aldermanic powers, however, the framers hedged the new municipal assembly with a series of checks. In fact, under the charter the authority to initiate legislation and propose ordinances rested primarily with the executive agencies, whereas the aldermen were left with the power to obstruct adoption of these measures, a power that they occasionally exercised to the irritation of good-government reformers. The municipal legislature failed, then, to become a major formulator of municipal policy, but instead one alderman said of the 1898–99 session that "the meetings were largely occupied with very petty matters, and but little time or attention was given to the framing or enacting of general ordinances."[28] New York City's dalliance with notions of restored aldermanic power represented a half-hearted deviation from the norm. By the close of the century many viewed the city council as a pernicious relic to be discarded as soon as possible. Writing in 1899, one reformer expressed the attitude of many when he observed: "It has yet to be shown that aldermen have ever filled a useful function in a modern American city."[29]

Gradually, then, city councils lost power to the municipal executive and to independent commissions. Moreover, city dwellers relied increasingly on the state legislatures to determine municipal policy, thereby bypassing the aldermen. Municipal corporations were creatures of the state legislatures and were subordinate to the supreme power of the state. Legislators in the state capitols granted municipal charters and could repeal or amend them in any manner, subject only to specific restrictions in the state constitutions. From the 1780s on, critics of incumbent municipal rulers had appealed to state legislators for aid in their struggle against the status quo, and especially after 1850 anyone with a pet scheme for municipal betterment or a bitter grudge toward the city council turned to the state lawmakers. Good-government reformers, petitioners for special privileges, those seeking utility franchises, and sponsors of partisan plots all found that compliant legislators might grant their requests more readily than recalcitrant city councils. In articles, editorials, and speeches, urban dwellers repeatedly decried the interference of state legislatures in local affairs, but few hesitated to elicit such interference if it was in their interest. Consequently, if appeals to the city council failed, petitions to the state legislature followed. In Massachusetts, New York, Ohio, and throughout the United States, appealing to the state legislature became one more way to skirt aldermanic authority. By the 1890s executive departments could issue regulations, independent boards or commissions could frame ordinances, and state legislatures could enact laws governing the municipality. Legislative authority over municipal questions was not concentrated in the city council, or board of aldermen, but dispersed among rival rulers of the metropolis.

Yet in most major American cities aldermen and councillors retained some role in the determination of general policy for the city. With the exception of cities in New York and New Jersey, city councils continued to enjoy varying degrees of authority over municipal appropriations and taxation. By exercising this power, the councils could veto a broad range of programs and schemes initiated by the executive departments. Moreover, in most cities municipal legislatures continued to grant public utility and streetcar franchises. This was the most controversial of the powers that the aldermen retained, and their franchise measures inspired sharp criticism not only in New York City but in urban centers across the nation. In 1894 a Philadelphia reformer commiserated that "during the past few years our City Councils have passed . . . ordinances granting to private corporations franchises worth millions" and "the very men who have been elected to protect the interests of the city have sacrificed those interests in the most shameless way."[30] Likewise, in the 1890s a corrupt pack of Chicago aldermen known as the Gray Wolves auctioned off municipal franchises to the highest briber. In response to such misdeeds, satirist Finley Peter Dunne's fictional character Mr. Dooley attended a Chicago board meeting where the aldermen granted the International Microbe Company a right to lay pipes and pump microbes throughout the city.[31] Such fictional accounts did not seem too far-fetched to city dwellers of the 1890s, for the municipal legislatures had lost much prestige, and many citizens believed that the legislatures deserved to lose their remaining powers.

THE NEIGHBORHOOD REPRESENTATIVE

Though franchise grants attracted the greatest publicity, aldermen devoted most of their time and effort to performing more menial chores. The chief work of the alderman was servicing the needs of the neighborhood he represented. In New York City, Philadelphia, Boston, Baltimore, and Chicago the councils were elected by wards or districts, as was the lower house of the bicameral municipal assembly in Saint Louis. The upper house of Saint Louis was elected at large, but the informal rules of politics required an equitable distribution of upper-house members throughout the various sectors of the city, and each generally owed his nomination to the party leaders of his ward.[32] Most aldermen, then, were ward representatives, elected by the voters of a certain ward and concerned primarily with obtaining privileges for their constituents. They carried the petitions of their neighborhood constituents to the council, and they ensured that the city answered these requests. Their focus was thus on the fragment rather than the whole, on the needs of their neighborhood rather than on those of the entire city.

Page after page of council minutes in America's major cities is filled with orders, resolutions, and ordinances dealing, for instance, with the paving of a few blocks in the Twenty-first Ward, the construction of sidewalks between Elm and Oak streets in the Eighteenth Ward, or a grocer's petition to hang a sign over a sidewalk in the Seventh Ward. General ordinances pertaining to the organization of city departments or to the provision of services to the city as a whole are relatively rare. The journals reveal the alderman not as a figure dedicated to molding city government but as a neighborhood envoy who sought to secure as many services and favors as possible from the city government and to make certain that the city served his constituents. The alderman was a conduit between the neighborhood and the executive departments with their growing corps of professional bureaucrats; he was the link connecting the ward and its constituents with the increasingly distant forces of municipal rule centered in the city hall.

New York City, as the nation's largest city, offers a prime example of a city whose aldermen, possessing little formal authority over citywide questions, were especially preoccupied with the petitions of their constituents. At each meeting aldermen would present dozens of public works proposals—for example, to erect lampposts, pave streets, or extend gas or water mains. Each alderman introduced the public works proposals for his own district, and the proposals were usually then referred to the Committee on Street Pavements or the Committee on Lamps and Gas. These committees reported back the proposals, and typically the board unanimously approved measures recommended by the committees.

Committee recommendations, moreover, depended largely on the views of the district alderman. In American municipal councils a form of aldermanic courtesy often prevailed, which meant that the board as a whole deferred to the judgment of a district's elected representative(s) on any question dealing solely with that district. For example, if a special assessment imposed on neighborhood property owners financed district paving or sewer construction, such improvements would cost the remainder of the city nothing. These public works were therefore a neighborhood concern and a matter for the district representative alone to handle. On many neighborhood questions the judgment of the district alderman was thus decisive. If he wanted a privilege granted to a person or group within his ward, the privilege would be granted. Provided a neighborhood matter had no significance for anyone outside the district, the district alderman's opinion was virtually law.

This practice of aldermanic courtesy was commonplace in New York City during the late nineteenth century. One New York City legislator of the 1890s, in recounting his years on the municipal council, observed that "generally each Alderman was allowed to exercise exclusive control over all such matters affecting his district only."[33] In 1898 on her visit to New York City's municipal legislature, the British reformer Beatrice Webb likewise found that "any ordinance affecting particular persons (for instance, trading licenses) was always referred to the Alderman of the district in which the person concerned resided for his Report."[34] Etiquette required that an alderman enjoy free rein over his own bailiwick, and others on the council generally were expected not to trespass.

Public works measures usually had to make a perfunctory trip to a committee, but as Beatrice Webb discovered, New York City's board approved permits and exemptions without even requiring this formality. For example, in 1888 Alderman McMurray introduced a resolution to permit Vito Fortounascere "to place and keep a stand for the sale of fruit, inside the stoop-line, in front of [the] northeast corner of Twenty-eighth street and Fourth avenue."[35] This sidewalk area was city property, but the Board of Aldermen immediately voted on McMurray's resolution and granted Fortounascere the privilege. Likewise, Alderman Benjamin's resolution that permission be granted Joe Lewkowitz to keep a sidewalk stand for "the sale of soda-water" was approved without delay or reference to committee, as was Alderman Barry's request that George Hodtwalker be allowed to "keep a watering-trough on the sidewalk."[36] And Alderman Hubbell won quick passage of his resolution that an exception to the fireworks ordinance be granted to the parishioners of Saint Maria of Mount Carmel so that they could celebrate their Fourth of July picnic with pyrotechnics.[37] The sidewalks of aldermanic District Eleven were Alderman McMurray's domain, just as the sidewalks of District Eight were the realm of Alderman Benjamin. Colleagues on the board did not interfere with the territory of their fellow aldermen, for aldermanic courtesy demanded that each alderman alone determine the special privileges to be bestowed on his constituents.

The granting of such favors through aldermanic courtesy was a prominent feature of each council session during the late nineteenth century. In 1879 New York City's board passed more than five hundred resolutions authorizing street obstructions such as stands, troughs, and bay windows, and this number constituted half of all resolutions adopted by the board that year.[38] In December, 1888, the city's aldermen sought to deal with street stands in one omnibus measure granting 4,000 permits to favored constituents throughout the city.[39]

New York City's aldermen may have enjoyed little or no authority over appropriations and appointments and may have played a minor role in determining public policy. But if residents wanted a street paved, a water main laid, or a street lamp erected, the alderman was the figure in city government who could realize their desires. To the people in the neighborhoods who sought services and favors from city officials downtown, the alderman was an all-powerful figure.

In fact, no matter whether he was a member of a political machine or an independent, reform-minded municipal legislator, the New York City alderman performed many of the functions traditionally associated with the ward boss. Servicing constituents and ensuring that the impersonal city authorities responded to neighborhood wishes was not only a task of the political machine's ward leader but also a vital function of the alderman. For example, Alderman Alfred R. Conkling, of New York City's Seventh District, was a Yale graduate and a Republican dedicated to good-government reform who conscientiously returned the free passes given him by streetcar companies. He was not an Irish ward boss of the Democratic Tammany organization; yet his personal journal for 1887–88 records his repeated efforts to secure employment, charity, liquor licenses, and shortened jail sentences for his constituents. On January 4, 1887, he wrote to the city commissioner of public works, asking that a constituent be hired as a laborer, and he also composed a letter of introduction to the police commissioner for an applicant seeking work as a patrolman. During the early months of 1887 he informed municipal relief agencies of indigents in his district who needed coal, and he urged the mayor to grant a "music & beer license" to a district resident. Likewise, he aided the proprietors of Gus's Wine Room by getting their bartender out of jail and exercised, as well, his magisterial power to marry neighborhood couples. He also made full use of the practice of aldermanic courtesy to ensure that the city paved the streets in his districts, erected lamps, and allowed residents to cut down trees in the sidewalk area in front of their properties.[40]

It bears emphasizing that the power of Conkling and other municipal legislators in New York City did not emanate from their position within a ruling political machine. For example, aldermen representing those conflicting factions of the Democratic party—the Tammany Democrats and the County Democrats—joined with Republicans to approve Conkling's requests for his neighborhood. Party or factional affiliation usually made no difference when the aldermen voted on neighborhood improvements or minor privileges for a district constituent. And, as stated earlier, the vote, if recorded, was almost always unanimously in favor of such measures. Authority over one's district was a prerogative inherent in the office of alderman; it was not simply a privilege won through loyalty to the ruling political organization. Moreover, it was a fiercely defended prerogative. According to a municipal legislator of the 1890s, "each Alderman fought bitterly any attempt of the Board as a whole to interfere with such matters in his district."[41] Each municipal legislator, by virtue of his office alone, had extensive power over his district, and partisan-inspired invasions of his realm were the exception, not the rule.

Aldermanic prerogatives, however, also proved a burden, for servicing a district constituency was a time-consuming task that deflected municipal legislators from the less parochial concerns of the city as a whole. A reform Republican alderman of the 1890s reported that Italians seeking permits for fruit or peanut stands "came to [his] residence at early morning and late at night, and besieged [his] office at all hours of the day . . . offering all sorts of appeals to one's sympathies, bribes, threats, tears and hysterics to secure the necessary approval." Moreover, the alderman confronted architects who "were constantly demanding permits for iron and glass awnings and other building projections over the sidewalks," and "it often took from two to five interviews of about an hour each to convince an architect that his application should not be granted." Though a reform-minded adherent of the minority party in New York City, this alderman found himself regarded as the fount of governmental favors and the guardian of his district's manifold concerns and interests. As a result of his experience, he was able to conclude that "the Alderman is next to the Tammany Hall district leader, supposed to be the principal comforter of the afflicted and the aid of the undeserving unfortunates within his district."[42]

In the nation's second most populous city, Chicago, aldermen also bore the burden of serving neighborhood constituents. As in New York City, the alderman in Chicago was the means by which local residents could obtain services and favors from city hall. And in Chicago, too, aldermanic courtesy was an unwritten rule of legislative procedure. In 1892 one of Chicago's municipal legislators explained that " 'aldermanic courtesy' is, briefly, reciprocity; it's you help me and I'll help you." According to this city father, if any members of the board of aldermen failed to vote for a neighborhood measure sponsored by a ward representative, then he would not "help them when they have some little measure that they want put through. So they vote for it without asking any questions except as to whether the courtesy will be returned."[43] Chicago aldermen had a greater voice in determining citywide policy than did their counterparts in New York City. But even in Chicago aldermen devoted the bulk of their energies to answering constituent demands and working to ensure a fair share of benefits for their neighborhoods. Laudatory sketches of individual Chicago aldermen often referred to the fact that the subject had "secured many needed improvements for his ward."[44] This was a fitting tribute for those scores of municipal legislators whose chief responsibility was the interests of the ward and not the overall welfare of the city.

In Chicago, two aldermen represented each ward and were responsible for introducing all public improvement measures for their district. Moreover, as in New York City the alderman's support for the measure was vital if it was to win the approval of the council. In 1898 Beatrice Webb claimed that at each council meeting Chicago's aldermen distributed a list of proposed improvements "and these were all voted en bloc without a word, each Alderman being allowed practically to put in the list whatever he pleased for his own ward."[45] In 1892 Chicago's street commissioner complained that "the whims of property owners on the street in question, or of the Alderman representing the district have served to determine . . . [paving] questions and the administrative branch of the City government has had no say in the matter whatever."[46] The ward representative and not the central administrative authorities determined when and how a neighborhood street was paved.

As in New York City, aldermen in Chicago also exploited the tradition of logrolling reciprocity to win less significant favors for the residents of their wards. A municipal legislator of the 1890s testified that " 'aldermanic courtesy' is responsible for the passage of the majority of the ordinances granting the lesser privileges,"[47] and the published proceedings of the city council support this contention. If an alderman submitted a request for permission to hang a sign or an awning over a sidewalk, to open a sidewalk stand, to install a streetside watering trough, or to erect any other obstruction on the city's property, the council immediately and unanimously granted the request without referring it to a committee or interfering with the alderman's prerogative to bestow minor privileges on his constituents. Thus, at their meeting of September 10, 1888, the city council approved without delay Alderman Whelan's motion that James J. Smith be permitted to erect an illuminating sign, as well as Alderman Dixon's order that Frank Fairmen receive a permit to erect an awning or canopy and Alderman Harris's petition that Coit and Company be authorized to excavate a coal vault under a city alley.[48] Two months earlier the Democratic alderman from the Fifth Ward had introduced an order permitting a neighborhood club backing Democratic presidential candidate Grover Cleveland to string a banner at the corner of Twenty-second and Grove streets. Though the Republicans controlled the council by a two-to-one margin, the alderman's order passed without delay.[49] For banners in the Fifth Ward were among the responsibilities of the fifth ward alderman, and the Republican council deferred to his request.

Anyone seeking a special privilege from Chicago's city government sought the invaluable aid of his ward aldermen. One of Chicago's reform aldermen of the 1890s complained that he and his colleagues in the municipal legislature were "expected to be unceasing, overflowing spigots for patronage and passes, never tiring in [their] willingness to run errands for [their] constituents;
. . . dispensers of every municipal privilege from bailing out drunks to signing bonds, and procuring building permits."[50] As in New York City, aldermen in Chicago did not so much govern as distribute the benefits of government. Executive officers were more significant in determining municipal policy, but legislators ensured that the city served the neighborhood and the individual constituent.

In Philadelphia, then the third most populous city, the story was much the same. Public improvements proceeded piecemeal, with city council members introducing one ordinance after another providing for one block of pavement, a few hundred yards of gas or water mains, or a short extension to the sewer system. As in New York City and Chicago, it was the ward councilman's responsibility to introduce improvement measures for his own ward and to transmit to the council the petitions of his constituents for upgraded services. For example, at the select council meeting of April 2, 1888, Councilman Patton presented five petitions from ward property owners asking for the paving of streets or the laying of sewers, and he also introduced fourteen ordinances for paving and grading streets, laying gas and water mains, and constructing sewers within the boundaries of the ward.[51] At the next meeting, Councilman McMurray introduced twenty-two measures authorizing similar improvements in his district, and the following week he presented ten more ordinances for public works benefiting his constituents.[52] Because of the municipal legislature's preoccupation with neighborhood petitions and improvements, an exasperated Philadelphia mayor of the 1890s complained that "the City as a whole, in so far as her interests are concerned, is without representation." The mayor charged that councilmen turned thumbs down when considering a measure for the general good because they "saw nothing in it for their own wards." He could only conclude that the councilmen's "loyalty is to a locality rather than to the whole City."[53]

Boston's mayors echoed this complaint and warned the city's councilmen: "You cannot legislate for the sole benefit of your Ward or District; you belong to the whole City, and your service concerns the entire population."[54] Repeatedly those in the executive branch who represented a citywide constituency urged Boston's municipal legislators to "shun sectional views, and consider the whole."[55] Yet each year the representatives from East Boston watched jealously to ensure that their district received the same share of the municipal benefits as did the neighborhoods of Charlestown or Roxbury, and South Boston's councilmen lobbied vigorously for a level of improvements equal to that awarded the Dorchester and West Roxbury neighborhoods. Boston did not rely on special assessments for the financing of most minor improvements, but instead the council annually appropriated $25,000 to each ward for street improvements, thereby attempting to maintain equity among the rival districts.[56] This preoccupation with the parts, however, seemed to undermine the welfare of the whole. Consequently, in the late 1890s Mayor Josiah Quincy successfully campaigned to limit the council's authority over appropriations, claiming that "under the pressure for local improvements, the machinery for obtaining appropriations for general purposes has practically broken down."[57] Boston's ward representatives, like their counterparts in other cities, were primarily agents of neighborhood supplicants, men dedicated to ensuring that their districts won an ample share of the municipal largesse. For members of the executive branch of city government, such as Mayor Quincy, this parochialism was intolerable.

Despite these complaints, aldermen in city after city remained primarily neighborhood emissaries charged with exploiting their prerogatives to win favors for constituents. In Buffalo, ward aldermen introduced applications for butchers' and pawnbrokers' licenses, requests for permission to install watering troughs, orders for sidewalk construction, and resolutions allowing the hanging of signs over the sidewalk or the construction of vaults under it—and the municipal legislature approved these measures without delay or dissent.[58] Ward representatives in Baltimore, Saint Louis, and Detroit similarly carried an endless stream of requests to the city hall and logrolled constituent favors through the council. Meanwhile, in Minneapolis and Saint Paul the city councils formally recognized the special prerogatives of the neighborhood representative and frequently referred proposals dealing with a single ward to a special committee consisting of the aldermen from that ward. Moreover, the council as a whole virtually always ratified without debate the recommendations of these ward "committees."[59] In all these cities, the municipal legislator was the vital link between the neighborhood and the city government, the agent for the interests of the ward.

Some aldermen, however, were not always disinterested agents, serving their constituents selflessly. Critics often alleged that municipal legislators serviced their wards in exchange for bribes, and undoubtedly some constituents had to pay for the privilege of a watering trough, an overhanging bay window, a canopy, or a fruit stand. Discussing the tradition of aldermanic courtesy, the *Chicago Tribune* in 1892 surmised that this unwritten practice had "perhaps made quite a little for some Aldermen."[60] At the close of the century the *Tribune* specifically claimed that first ward alderman "Bathhouse John" Coughlin "has had a habit of introducing . . . favors for merchants in his ward, all of which are allowed to go through without objection," and charged that Coughlin "acted more as attorney than alderman in these matters and found the practice profitable."[61] A New York City alderman likewise admitted that "there were . . . ugly accusations that some of the members required gratuities for their approval of local permits; and such charges may have been true."[62] But the general consensus in New York City was that aldermanic courtesy reaped little if any monetary reward for city legislators. The *New York Times*, though highly critical of New York City's Board of Aldermen, had to admit that the city's legislators probably earned little from the sale of minor favors. According to the *Times*, sidewalk obstructions such as "the meat rack and the awning are permitted as matters of comity, and . . . the Alderman seldom derives from them any more substantial profit than the gratitude of the applying butcher or grocer." Moreover, the *Times* explained that "there is supposed to be something in the bay window, but it is not much."[63] Public utilities may have contributed handsomely to some aldermen's purses, and a number of ward representatives may have collected small fees in exchange for permission to erect a sidewalk stand or as thanks for recommending a constituent for city employment. Nevertheless, service as errand boy for the ward was not necessarily a financially rewarding career.

In summary, whatever his motives, the alderman of the 1880s and 1890s was a formidable figure in his ward. He was the means by which residents obtained services, improvements, permits, exemptions, and, sometimes, jobs. In some cities he may have played a minimal role in the molding of municipal policy or have exercised negligible influence over the budget or executive appointments. But if a neighborhood resident wanted something from the city, the alderman was the person to see. Even if the alderman was a member of the minority party or faction, the informal tradition of aldermanic courtesy ensured that he could achieve results, for his power was inherent in his office and did not stem from any allegiance to the ruling political clique. From the perspective of the metropolis as a whole the alderman was a figure of declining significance, but within the restricted domain of his ward he remained a power.

THE PAROCHIAL AND PLEBEIAN BRANCH OF GOVERNMENT

The neighborhood was the alderman's particular realm, and most aldermen of the late nineteenth century were neighborhood figures. They typically were not men with citywide prestige or social standing who represented downtown business interests or belonged to prestigious men's clubs, but usually were persons who worked in the neighborhood they lived in and represented and who found most of their recreation and social life within a few blocks of their homes. Late-nineteenth-century aldermen were most often small-time operators, elected because they were known and liked in their neighborhood. The ward or neighborhood and not the city was their milieu and barony of power.

In 1877–78 at least 21 of the 28 members of the Saint Louis House of Delegates who claimed a place of employment both lived and worked in the ward they represented, and only 8 of the 28 listed their place of business as within the central business district.[64] And in 1889–90 at least 20 of the 28 delegates lived and worked in the same ward.[65] Seventeen of Buffalo's 25 aldermen serving in 1896 worked in the same ward in which they resided, and only 5 commuted to jobs in the central business district.[66] Similarly, that same year 23 of the 32 Detroit councilmen listed their place of business as within the ward they represented, and only 9 earned a living in downtown shops and offices.[67] In 1894–95 in Philadelphia, of the 143 councilmen with a place of business, only 36 percent worked in the city's central business district, and 48 percent were employed in the ward that they represented.[68] The percentages for Cleveland's council during the late 1880s and early 1890s were almost identical to those of Philadelphia. [69] In no major city did downtown businessmen constitute a majority of the council.

According to traditional lore, aldermen were frequently friendly neighborhood saloonkeepers who exchanged free drinks for votes and gathered a political following from among their barroom cronies. The *New York Times* reported that ten of the twenty-four New York City aldermen elected in 1882 were "keepers of gin-mills" and two were "former gin-mill keepers" so that "one-half the board . . . is composed of representatives of the bar-room portion of the community."[70] In 1883 the *Times* likewise dismissed the Board of Aldermen as "largely made up of saloon-keepers and the worst class of pothouse politicians."[71] Seven years later a Chicagoan claimed that in his city "popular sentiment is demanding that of the forty-four [aldermanic] seats to be filled . . . fourteen, or one-third, shall be filled by saloonkeepers or liquormakers." And the *Chicago Tribune* warned voters that if they were not alert the city council might be "filled with those whose only school in the arts of local government has been the whiskey shop," men who "are chiefly illiterate, uncouth, coarse-mannered, and boorish rum-sellers."[72] Repeatedly, critics characterized the aldermanic boards as little more than a gathering of bartenders.

The saloonkeeper was, in truth, overrepresented on the city councils. The corner saloon was a neighborhood headquarters for the male population, who comprised the nineteenth-century electorate, and the saloonkeeper was a neighborhood fixture. He did not commute to work out of the district but was in constant contact with the ward and its people. As such he had a natural proclivity for ward politics. Moreover, politics was worth his effort. A seat on the council might well exempt him from unwelcome police raids and other forms of official harassment so troublesome to saloonkeepers who stretched the moral codes of the city. And as an independent proprietor he could find the necessary time for serving on the board. The saloonkeeper knew the neighborhood, and his contacts and interests were largely confined to the neighborhood. Yet he could also use a friend in city hall. Thus he was a likely candidate for alderman.

The traditional stereotype of municipal legislatures as assemblies of rum sellers is, however, somewhat inaccurate. Saloonkeepers may have been overrepresented, but they were rarely in the majority and generally constituted no more than 10 percent or 20 percent of the municipal council. Other small businessmen—butchers, plumbers, contractors, real estate agents, grocers, cigarmakers, tailors, printers, druggists, and coal dealers—filled most of the remaining seats in the council chamber. Those in the building trades, such as contractors and plumbers, could exploit the influence enjoyed by an alderman to win city contracts or receive preferential treatment from city building inspectors. Butchers and grocers, like saloonkeepers, were neighborhood retailers in close contact with the ward population, and both had a strong interest in winning permission for stands and canopies over sidewalks. And real estate agents were vitally concerned with the extension of municipal services to new housing tracts. Rum sellers were thus not the only neighborhood businessmen who sought special favors or could profit from service in the municipal assembly.

The composition of several city boards illustrates the variety of occupations represented. The New York City board that was elected in 1882 included not only 12 current or former gin-millkeepers but also a jeweler, a shoe dealer, a hotelkeeper, a builder, a dealer in mason's materials, a real estate dealer, a retired real estate agent, 2 professional public officeholders, and 3 lawyers.[73] Sixteen years later New York City's board included 8 liquor dealers and an equal number of professional politicians and real estate dealers, 4 manufacturers, 3 lawyers, 3 truckmen, 2 machinists, 2 plumbers, and 20 other members of miscellaneous occupations, such as grocer, horseshoer, undertaker, carpenter, and painter.[74] Of the 50 councilmen serving in the Cincinnati municipal assembly in 1887, probably no more than 8 operated saloons. The remainder pursued a wide range of occupations, such as huckster, cigarmaker, baker, and musician. Only 3 were lawyers; 4 were full-time public employees; 2 ran street-sprinkling businesses dependent on municipal contracts.[75] In 1894–95 the Philadelphia city council had a few members of higher economic status.

Only 4 of the 160 members admitted being in the liquor trade, whereas 2 were bankers, 18 were attorneys, and 5 were physicians. The remaining contingent consisted largely of every variety of small businessman, with a number earning their living as plumbers, plasterers, bricklayers, or builders. Again, however, the leading business families in Philadelphia were absent from the list of councilmen.[76] Philadelphia's council was unusually lacking in the stereotypical rum seller, but otherwise the occupational composition generally conformed to the norm for American municipal legislatures.

Although some members of municipal councils may have occupied a higher notch on the occupational scale than others, a certain economic pattern prevailed among aldermen throughout the nation. Most were independent proprietors of small businesses located within their home wards, who were able to devote a portion of their time to the task of winning municipal favors and services for their districts. They were persons of ordinary circumstances who typified the urban median. In his valedictory address Boston's Mayor Nathan Matthews calculated the percentage of the city councilmen serving during the period 1822 to 1895 who paid property tax. He found a sharp decline in the percentage of taxpaying councilmen after 1875, but as late as 1895 29 percent of the municipal legislators were among the propertied taxpaying class, whereas only 20 percent of the registered voters paid property tax.[77] Boston's municipal legislators were certainly not a plutocratic assembly, but, as Matthews's figures indicate, they ranked slightly above the norm. Aldermen, in general, were rarely wealthy business moguls and distinguished professionals, but neither were they likely to be laborers, factory hands, or other members of the working class. Commonly they hailed from that large middling economic class between the two extremes.

Aldermen were not, then, necessarily vulgar barflies, but they also were not the urban economic elite. P. T. Sherman, a reform alderman in New York City during the 1890s, said of his colleagues that "their ability was beyond their education; but few of them represented any great experience in either politics or affairs." According to Sherman, they were not "the hard-drinking, loud-dressed men" of tradition, "but, as a body, they resembled any other aggregation of ordinary New York citizens." In his opinion, they were "average citizens—neither better nor worse than the mass of the people of the districts they represented."[78] And Chicago's reform Alderman William Kent viewed his colleagues more as likable dunderheads than scoundrels, saying that "they were kindly, tolerant souls and [he] liked them as real though highly flavored human beings."[79] Both Sherman and Kent were aldermanic anomalies hailing from the social and economic elite, and in their eyes the typical alderman was ordinary and simple rather than evil and immoral. The alderman was, indeed, a plebeian who, though lacking experience in public affairs, had won modest success within the small sphere of his ward, and a seat on the city council was the hallmark of that parochial triumph.

When ranked according to social prestige, America's aldermen also fell short of the top echelons. While they frequented ward political meetings and neighborhood fraternal lodges, most could not set foot within the fashionable downtown clubs where industry moguls and the leading professionals gathered. In the mid-1890s none of New York City's aldermen were among the members of the elite Metropolitan Club, presided over by the financier J. Pierpont Morgan, and none of Buffalo's ward representatives could claim membership in that city's fashionable Buffalo Club. By the early 1890s such Brahmin resorts as Boston's Somerset and Saint Botolph's clubs were off limits to city councilmen, as was the fashionable Algonquin Club. In Philadelphia and Chicago the Union League clubs were bastions of elite Republicanism; yet in 1895 only 2 of the 50 Republicans in Chicago's municipal legislature were Union Leaguers and only 9 of Philadelphia's 140 Republican councilmen enjoyed the social glory of Union League membership.[80] Municipal legislators, while still exercising some political power, remained outside the metropolitan social elite. The rank of alderman did not transform a saloonkeeper into a social lion.

Most aldermen were also notably absent from their city's social register (a listing of who's who in society) and from the local bluebook (a volume publishing the names and addresses of those who qualified as fashionable). New York City's social register of 1891–92 listed approximately 7,700 of the most socially prominent persons in the city, or about 2 percent of the total number of families in the metropolis. Yet, not 1 of the 30 aldermen elected to the board in 1892 won a place in the register. Moreover, of the 136 candidates who ran for alderman in the election of 1892, only 2 were scions of the social register, and both were candidates of the minor Prohibition Party and not serious contenders for a place on the board.[81] Likewise, in Boston the city council could hardly claim social distinction. In 1893 that city's bluebook, an "elite private address, carriage and club directory," included approximately 15 percent of the families in the city, and yet only 8 percent of the city councilmen achieved listing therein.[82] Thus, in both Boston and New York City, the percentage of aldermen in the social directories was lower than the percentage of the population as a whole. During the 1880s a few social notables, such as Alfred Conkling and James Van Rensselaer, had deigned to serve on New York City's board. But the social complexion of the municipal legislature was definitely not patrician.

In those cities in which aldermen exercised greater authority over citywide policy, the social prestige of the councils was higher, but in no major city did those deemed fashionable by the editors of the bluebook win a majority in the legislative bodies. In 1893 in Chicago, only 28 percent of the aldermen were in the bluebook, a volume that included approximately 13 percent of the city's families.[83] And in 1895 39 percent of Philadelphia's councilmen were in that city's bluebook, which listed about 10 percent of all families.[84] In both cities, residents of the wealthier, more socially prestigious wards generally elected aldermen from their own class who had attained a place in the social directory. If the councils continued to exercise broad powers over questions of citywide importance, as they did in Chicago and Philadelphia, then members of the upper-middle class were willing to represent their peers in the municipal legislature. They, however, remained a minority, for representatives of the humbler wards predominated.

Moreover, in virtually every major city the wards housing the poorest and least socially acceptable residents were overrepresented on the boards of aldermen. Though cities made some attempt to apportion aldermanic seats on the basis of population, the downtown wards, characterized by cheap lodging houses, brothels, and gambling dens, had fewer residents than the outlying wards, inhabited by business leaders or upstanding working-class families. In addition, the downtown wards were stable or declining in population, and as the number of inhabitants in the peripheral wards soared, the inequities became pronounced despite periodic redistricting. In 1890 the least populous wards in Boston, Philadelphia, Cleveland, Cincinnati, and Saint Louis were those in the downtown area; the downtown wards in Baltimore, Buffalo, and Chicago also had far fewer inhabitants than the average. The suburban Twenty-eighth Ward of Saint Louis, for example, had twice the population of the First and Second wards in the downtown lodging-house district. Yet each of these wards elected a single member to the municipal house of delegates. In 1890 in Boston the ratio of population of the most populous ward to the downtown ward was three to one, but each chose three councilmen. In Chicago the ratio was more than two to one, and in Baltimore it was almost two to one. And Philadelphia's dockside Sixth Ward had one-eighth the population of the fashionable outlying Twenty-fourth Ward, but each could claim only a single seat in that city's upper house of the municipal council. In city after city the votes of those inhabiting the "disreputable" districts counted at least twice as much as those in the typical residential ward. For instance, the transients, gamblers, and pimps in "Bathhouse John" Coughlin's notorious First Ward of Chicago elected the same number of aldermen as the more respectable residents of each of the West-Side wards, which had twice the population of the first. And the so-called vicious classes inhabiting the bottoms in Cincinnati enjoyed far more than their fair share of representation in the city's legislature. Thus, the "disreputable" elements of society were not only fairly represented but often disproportionately represented in late-nineteenth-century boards of aldermen.

Aldermen of the last decades of the century were, then, generally middling, neighborhood types with little social prestige but with considerable opportunity for winning favors, services, or improvements from the city government. Since the social and economic barriers to entry were low, the aldermanic seat quickly became a political embarkation point for those immigrant groups and ethnic minorities wishing to win a voice in municipal rule. Executive posts with a citywide constituency might prove difficult or impossible for an Italian, Pole, black, or even a "shanty" Irishman to attain. But if an ethnic minority constituted a substantial portion of the electorate in a ward, then this minority had the opportunity for a seat on the board of aldermen. No tradition of deference to social betters excluded ethnic newcomers from the municipal legislature. The only requirement for entry into that plebeian and democratic body was a plurality of votes in a ward.

Thus ethnic minorities quickly won representation on city councils throughout the country. The Irish and Germans who poured into American cities during the mid–nineteenth century were commonplace on boards of aldermen by the 1870s and 1880s. O'Haras, O'Briens, Callahans, and McCarthys were not strangers to the aldermanic chambers of municipalities such as Boston and New York City, and as early as 1874 at least twenty-two of Chicago's forty councilmen were foreign-born, sixteen of them Irish immigrants.[85] Alderman P. T. Sherman estimated that nearly one-half of his colleagues on the New York City Board of Aldermen in the late 1890s "were of Irish birth or parentage and the remainder were about equally divided between Germans and Americans."[86] German names also became increasingly common in the roll call of aldermen in Saint Louis, Cincinnati, and Milwaukee. By the 1880s and 1890s immigrants from southern and eastern Europe were likewise winning a place in the municipal legislatures. In 1885 an Italian secured a seat on Chicago's board, the first of his ethnic group to achieve this distinction, and a second compatriot followed in 1892.[87] In 1888 Chicago's Sixteenth Ward elected that city's first Polish-American alderman, and Scandinavians and Czechs also enjoyed representation on Chicago's board in the 1890s.[88] Not until the twentieth century did blacks win a seat on the Chicago board of aldermen, but elsewhere they, too, were exercising their voting power and securing a voice in the municipal assembly. In 1890 for the first time blacks garnered the council seat for Baltimore's Eleventh Ward, and in every council from 1895 to 1905 Baltimore's blacks won representation.[89] Moreover, by 1899 three blacks held seats on Philadelphia's council, exploiting their concentration of voting strength in the seventh ward.[90] For groups seeking their first access to political power, the city council was a golden door of opportunity. And in the late nineteenth century no lawmaking body so accurately reflected the ethnic diversity of the nation as did the municipal legislatures.

Aldermanic powers were thus rapidly being acquired by new immigrant groups and those who were far from the top rung of the social and economic ladders. In the eyes of most "fashionable" city dwellers, the municipal legislators seemed decidedly common. They smoked ill-smelling cigars and made liberal use of council cuspidors. One Chicago alderman reported that "during lulls in the voting or speech-making, you could hear the steady drip or explosive precipitation of saliva in the spittoons."[91] Municipal assemblymen fractured the English language in speeches that would drive a grammarian to his grave, and they mourned deceased colleagues with a lavish display that seemed excessive even to Victorians. At opening sessions of the council, they received elaborate floral decorations from grateful constituents, huge floral "flags, shields, arm chairs, stars, roosters, and eagles" that the *Chicago Tribune* described as "more costly than artistic and tasteful."[92] And when the dignified Lord Mayor of Dublin visited Chicago's council, some practical joker passed around exploding cigars.[93] To those denizens listed in the city's bluebook, such behavior hardly seemed worthy of men bearing the appellation "city fathers."

If municipal legislators generally could not be counted among the genteel classes, neither did they typically number among the political notables of the city, but instead were members of the partisan rank and file. Though the alderman was a power within his neighborhood while serving on the board, he usually did not retain office for more than one or two terms. Few municipal legislators built up any seniority, and most were amateurs who served uneventfully and then passed quietly into political oblivion. Some voluntarily retired and abandoned the sometimes petty chores of the job, and others lost their post through the machinations of opponents within their own political party or the rival party. Ward politics in the late nineteenth century was competitive and unstable, and there was always a multitude of candidates ready to oust the incumbent from power. Turnover on city councils was rapid, and change rather than continuity typified the municipal legislatures of the late nineteenth century.

This lack of continuity was evident in cities throughout the nation. At the beginning of each new council session, a flock of novice legislators assumed seats in the council chamber. As shown in table 1, during the 1880s and early 1890s there was an average yearly turnover rate of over 50 percent on New York City's annually elected Board of Aldermen. And there was a 70 percent to 90 percent turnover rate every two years, with only a small minority of the members serving three consecutive years. Aldermen in their fourth year of service achieved a seniority matched by few of their colleagues. Likewise, table 1 indicates that in Baltimore's annually elected lower house of the bicameral city council, holdovers were generally in the minority, and that during the 1880s and 1890s only about 15 percent served more than two consecutive terms. As further illustration, only 21 percent of Boston's councilmen for 1888 had served on the annually elected common council in both 1886 and 1887, and the member with the greatest consecutive service was in his fifth year in the municipal legislature. Of the forty members on Cleveland's annually elected board of councilmen in 1888, only 23 percent had served during both of the two previous sessions, and 68 percent were serving their first term as legislators. Chicago's aldermen were elected biennially, but in that midwestern metropolis turnover was also high. In 1893 only 36 percent of Chicago's aldermen had served on the board two years earlier. Similarly, only 29 percent

TABLE 1. Turnover of Members on Municipal Councils

Aldermanic Term	Aldermen Who Had Served in the Previous Session*	% of Total Number	Aldermen Who Had Served in the Two Previous Sessions*	% of Total Number
New York City				
1885	7	29	3	13
1886	9	38	3	13
1887	13	54	5	21
1888	10	40	4	16
1889	14	56	6	24
1890	11	44	6	24
1891	11	44	5	20
1892	17	68	7	28
Baltimore (Lower House)				
1885	11	55	2	10
1886	5	25	3	15
1887	8	40	2	10
1888	8	40	3	15
1889	14	64	4	18
1890	7	32	4	18
1891	10	45	3	14
1892	11	50	4	18

Sources: New York Tribune Almanac, World Almanac, and Baltimore Sun Almanac, 1885–92.
* For Baltimore, these numbers apply to aldermen who had served in the previous session of either house.

of the members of the Saint Louis House of Delegates for 1893–95 had served in the previous house. The turnover rate was even more striking in San Francisco, where no one member of the Board of Supervisors assuming power in either 1893 or 1895 had served on the previous board. Only once between 1885 and 1895 was there more than one holdover from the preceding term in San Francisco's twelve-member municipal legislature.[94]

Service on the municipal councils was, then, a short-term privilege. Of the 569 aldermen who served from 1836 to 1900 in Newark, New Jersey, 60 percent held office for two years or less, 29 percent continued on the board for three or four years, and only 11 percent remained aldermen for more than four years. Between 1877 and 1901 the 227 men who served in the biennially elected Saint Louis House of Delegates averaged only three years in office, with 65 percent retaining the post for two years or less and fewer than 10 percent persisting for more than four years. Of the 165 men serving on San Francisco's Board of Supervisors from 1872 to 1899, 88 percent continued in office for two years or less, and only 2 could claim more than four years as municipal legislators.[95] There were some exceptions to this pattern of limited tenure. Chicago's E. F. Cullerton was alderman every year but one from 1871 to 1892, and his seniority won him a leading position on the council's powerful finance committee. By 1900 Chicago's notorious boodler John Powers had completed twelve years of service on the council, and the colorful "Bathhouse John" Coughlin was in the ninth year of his forty-six-year stint in the municipal legislature. Likewise, by the close of the 1890s Philadelphia's Edward W. Patton had represented the Twenty-seventh Ward in the select council for a quarter of a century. Figures such as Cullerton, Powers, Coughlin, and Patton deserved the adjective *perennial*, and in most cities there was at least one grand old man of the aldermanic chamber who had logged more than a decade of service in the legislative branch. Yet in most wards no one persisted in office for long. Late-nineteenth-century aldermen generally were not life-tenure lords of their districts. They were short-term legislators lacking in governmental experience and constantly threatened with ouster. Their political glory was fleeting.

In a number of major cities, however, holders of the post of clerk of the council did ensure some continuity in the legislative proceedings. The clerk was usually elected by the council, and the post was often nonpartisan, with the incumbent serving session after session no matter which party or faction was in power. In Boston, Washington Gregg served as clerk of the city council for forty-one years, from 1843 to 1884, surviving Whig, Republican, and Democratic councils. In Philadelphia, one man served as clerk of the upper house of the council from 1873 through the 1890s, and another served as clerk of the lower house from 1865 to the close of the century. One man retained the office of council clerk in Cincinnati from 1880 to the early twentieth century, and John A. Russell assumed the post of clerk of the San Francisco Board of Supervisors in 1868 and held it for over thirty years. These longstanding officials helped to guarantee that the machinery of the board or council ran smoothly. The clerk kept the records, handled council finances, transcribed and published the ordinances, and transmitted resolutions and orders to the executive officers of the municipality. The members of the board may have been novices, but their administrative agent, the council clerk, was often an old hand whose expertise must have compensated, in part, for the ineptitude of incoming aldermen.

Aside from the council clerk, however, few old faces appeared year after year at council meetings. Since most municipal legislatures were elected annually or biennially, aldermen faced frequent election contests and many did not survive the challenge. A few moved on to higher posts, though most did not possess the necessary social and economic status or political clout to win a place among the chief officers of the city, state, or national governments. And a few paid for their political crimes with a term in prison. But the majority of aldermen neither rose to higher glory nor descended to ignominy. Instead, they continued to tend their saloon or grocery and perhaps survived as elder statesmen of their neighborhood domains.

3 THE RESPECTABLE RULERS: EXECUTIVE OFFICERS AND INDEPENDENT COMMISSIONS

 As the role of the alderman narrowed, executive officers and special-function boards and commissions assumed new significance. In the 1870s, 1880s, and 1890s these officers and boards were the ascendant elements in urban decision making, the new centers of power in American municipal government. During the first half of the century the ward-based council had dominated city government, so that representatives of the parts made policy for the whole. As plebeian elements came to control ward politics, and as municipalities embarked on giant public projects demanding citywide coordination, a gradual shift in authority occurred. Municipal policy became increasingly the responsibility of those representing a citywide constituency and of those who were isolated from the pressures of neighborhood politics. The mayor and comptroller, who were elected by voters from throughout the city, grasped the reins of authority and assumed the initiative in matters of significance for the metropolis as a whole. Moreover, special-function commissions that were largely autonomous of both the mayor and the council rose to a new place of eminence. Neighborhood complaints and demands remained the business of the alderman. Responsibility for drafting the municipal budget, laying out park networks, and establishing library systems gravitated into other hands.

Those serving in the newly powerful executive positions and on the independent boards and commissions were generally a different breed from the men occupying seats on the city councils. Downtown bankers, wholesalers, manufacturers, and lawyers dominated the offices of mayor and comptroller and held most of the places on the park commissions and library boards. Neighborhood butchers, contractors, grocers, and saloonkeepers with a following confined to a few city blocks might win positions on the city council, but they rarely garnered an executive office in city hall. Figures with a reputation for respectability who commanded citywide prestige monopolized the latter posts. During the late nineteenth century Irish ward politicos may have been winning control of the legislative branch and gaining a voice in city government. Nevertheless, some of the chief municipal offices were still off limits to those beyond the pale of "fashionable" society.

Thus the structural distribution of municipal power changed markedly during the last decades of the century as authority shifted from the council to the mayor. But the social redistribution of power was less marked, with the "respectable elements" and solid businessmen retaining considerable leverage in city government. Business and professional leaders might complain that "less desirable" persons were taking over urban government while those best-suited to rule refused to dirty their hands in the corrupt arena of municipal politics. In fact, however, structural reform perpetuated and preserved the voice of the wealthy in municipal government, leading to social balance rather than social capitulation. Old-stock, social-register Protestants had not abandoned city government to the "unwashed mob"; instead, they had carefully reserved a vital domain of power that served as their trump card in the game of urban rule.

THE MAYOR

Preeminent within the executive branch was the mayor. Before the midcentury most American mayors exercised limited control over municipal policy. Though New York City's charter of 1830 granted the mayor veto power over council ordinances, the chief executives of Boston and Philadelphia did not win veto authority until 1854, and Pittsburgh's mayor lacked this power until 1874.[1] Moreover, before the Civil War, appointment of executive officers remained largely the responsibility of the city councils. Prior to 1850 mayors enjoyed ceremonial powers that entitled them to hand out keys to the city and to cut ribbons, but they generally played only a minor role in the selection and supervision of municipal officials. The making of policy and appointments was in the hands of the aldermen and their committees.

During the last half of the century executive powers gradually increased. The mayors of all the major cities acquired the power to veto council measures, and generally only a two-thirds vote of the council could override the mayor's action. Occasionally more than a two-thirds vote was required to remove the mayoral roadblock. In New York City, for example, a three-fourths vote was necessary to override a veto involving an assessment, an expenditure, or the lease of real estate or franchises, and a four-fifths vote was required to overcome mayoral opposition to a special appropriations bill. Moreover, in most major cities mayors won the right to exercise the item veto, enabling them to strike down specific items in ordinances without invalidating the entire measure. This was a power especially significant when dealing with lengthy budget bills. Illinois's general Municipal Corporations Act of 1872 authorized item vetoes, as did the Saint Louis charter of 1876, and by the close of the century mayors throughout the nation had been granted this power.[2]

During the last decades of the century, municipal executives used the veto power effectively and decisively. Few mayors enjoyed consistently friendly and harmonious relations with the municipal legislatures. Instead, they often regarded the members of the legislative branch as improvident, incompetent, and venal. Even Chicago's Mayor Carter Harrison, Sr., who worked ably and successfully with the city's aldermen, asserted that "a majority of the Council is dishonest and corrupt."[3] Especially in the aftermath of the economic depression of the 1870s, penny-conscious mayors repeatedly vetoed city-council appropriations they deemed frivolous or unnecessary. Moreover, the mayor's veto curbed the council's power to bestow valuable public utility franchises and rights-of-way without sufficient financial return to the city. And mayors occasionally interfered with the minor favors that the aldermen granted to their constituents. For example, reform Mayor Abram Hewitt of New York City did not hesitate to veto permits for street or sidewalk obstructions if he viewed them unnecessary or harmful. In July, 1888, Hewitt vetoed a resolution giving permission for a watering trough on the sidewalk "in front of No. 2119 First avenue" because he claimed that it "would cause an unnecessary waste of water and an accumulation of water and mud in the vicinity."[4] Thus, some mayors not only voided council measures on citywide questions such as franchise grants but even violated the neighborhood prerogatives of the alderman.

Usually the mayor proved victorious in any conflict with the council. In the late nineteenth century, aldermen overrode only a small portion of the many vetoes handed down by the executive. For example, of the 920 ordinances and resolutions enacted by the New York City Board of Aldermen in 1887, Mayor Hewitt vetoed 285. Though hostile to the reform mayor, the board passed only 48 of the 285 over the executive's veto.[5] From 1882 through 1885 Seth Low served as mayor of Brooklyn, and during three of these four years he confronted a council of political foes. But during his entire administration, the council only overrode 2 of his vetoes.[6] In Chicago, as well, the mayor usually had the last say. Of the 60 vetoes handed down by Chicago mayors between 1882 and 1889, only 9 were overridden. Though Democratic Mayor Carter Harrison, Sr., faced a Republican council through much of the 1880s, Chicago's aldermen generally concurred with the executive's judgment, and most veto messages aroused opposition only among a minority of the municipal legislators.[7] And in Baltimore the executive veto proved even more effective, for a three-fourths majority of the bicameral city council was necesary to override it. Between 1882 and 1889 Baltimore's mayors sent 118 veto messages to the First Branch of the City Council, and only 8 times did that branch pass a measure in defiance of the executive's disapproval. Likewise, the mayor delivered 51 vetoes to the Second Branch, which overrode only 7 of them.[8]

At the same time that the mayor was acquiring increased control over council legislation, he was also winning new powers of appointment. New York City's charter of 1857 first concentrated the authority to appoint administrative officers in the hands of the mayor. The Saint Louis charter of 1870 copied

New York's example, as did the Illinois Municipal Corporations Act of 1872, the Brooklyn charter of 1873, and the Boston and Philadelphia charters of 1885. Moreover, in the 1880s and 1890s the mayor's appointive power became absolute in New York City and Brooklyn, as the councils lost their right to veto mayoral nominations.[9] By the 1890s selection of executive officers was solely the responsibility of the executive.

Yet mayors continued to complain about their lack of authority over executive appointees. The terms of many of these appointees did not coincide with the mayor's term, and before the 1890s few mayors had the power to remove holdovers from a previous administration. For example, in New York City the police commissioners served six-year terms, as compared with the mayor's two-year tenure. In an effort to spare incoming mayors an onslaught of job-seeking campaign workers, the Saint Louis charter of 1876 provided that each mayor appoint the commissioners of public improvements and other major administrators at the end of the second year of his four-year term. The result, however, was that every Saint Louis mayor spent the first two years in office bargaining or bickering with his predecessor's appointees. Such staggered terms limited the mayor's control over supposedly subordinate officers and caused chief executives to cry for increased powers of removal. New York City's Mayor William Grace complained that divided executive authority left the "executive office paralyzed," and his successor Mayor Hewitt concurred heartily in the criticism.[10] In the 1870s and 1880s New York City's mayors had awesome appointive authority, but they had little power to coerce antagonistic holdovers chosen by a political foe.

During the last decades of the century, however, lawmakers were seeking to ensure that the mayor was, in fact, boss of the executive branch. In many municipalities mayors demanded and received the power to remove executive officers at will, guaranteeing that the chief city administrators would be the mayor's men. As early as 1875 Illinois's legislature granted mayors in that state the power to remove executive officers, though the chief executive was required to report the reasons for removal to the city council. Thus throughout the late nineteenth century, Chicago's mayor could fire any administrative official who displeased him.[11] In 1882 Mayor Seth Low of Brooklyn told the city council that each of his appointees had assured him "personally" that he would, without delay, submit his resignation whenever the mayor asked for it.[12] Boston's charter of 1885 authorized the mayor to remove executive officers, as did the Cleveland and Indianapolis charters of 1891, Buffalo's charter of 1892, the New Orleans charter of 1896, and the Baltimore charter of 1898.[13] In 1895 incoming mayors of New York City even won the power to oust incumbents from previous administrations.[14] By the 1890s city department heads were assuming the same relationship to the mayor as that of cabinet members to the president in the national government. Department heads were agents of the mayor to be hired or fired at his pleasure.

Not only were mayors attaining supreme authority over city departments, in many cities their office entitled them to a seat on a number of vital commissions and boards. For example, in both New York City and Brooklyn the mayor was one of the four members of the Board of Estimate and Apportionment, which approved the city budget, determined appropriations, and fixed tax rates. Moreover, New York City's mayor served as one of the commissioners of the sinking fund, the body that managed the financing of the municipal debt; he served as a member of the Board of Street Openings, the body that ordered the opening of new streets in outlying parts of the city; and he also was a member of the Aqueduct Commission, which was in charge of the expansion of the city's water supply. Likewise, Philadelphia's mayor was an ex officio member of the city Board of Health, Board of Charities and Correction, Sinking Fund Commission, Board of City Trusts, park commission, and public buildings commission. And in Baltimore the mayor served ex officio as a member of the Harbor Board, the Park Commission, the Water Commission, and the Fire Commission. In each of these cities mayors not only appointed commissioners but could supervise their work firsthand by directly participating in board meetings. Through his ex officio positions, the mayor was the one figure who had intimate knowledge of what was happening in each branch of the city's government.

It was the mayor, then, who held the reins of city government. Though executives complained about interference from corrupt aldermen and bothersome boards, the mayor was, in fact, becoming the unchallenged leader of city government and the most significant figure in determining citywide policy. In many major cities aldermen might still obstruct executive policy initiatives, but even in Chicago and Philadelphia the council alone could no longer frame and execute municipal policy. The mayor could veto council actions, and only the mayor and his appointees could implement programs. If any one of the elected municipal officers could be considered in charge, it was the mayor, and the continuing trend during the 1880s and 1890s was toward concentration of supervisory authority in this single individual. Aldermen might still have clout within their neighborhood domains, and might still be the person to see if one wanted a neighborhood street paved, an awning over the sidewalk, or a petty job with the city or with a municipal contractor. Yet in most cities the mayor was the man to visit if one wanted to alter major city policies.

Thus the mayor was a figure of citywide authority, and the rules of nineteenth-century politics demanded that a person of equally broad prestige occupy this executive post. As pointed out in Chapter 2, the chief requirement for election to the post of alderman was popularity in the neighborhood, and minor tradesmen and gin-mill owners were readily able to fill this requirement. The entire city, however, elected the mayor, who had to command respect among varying segments of the urban electorate. Moreover, he had to be a successful businessman or professional, for an incompetent could mean disaster for the political party or faction that backed him. Political party leaders recognized these realities of the game of politics. In other words, the mayoral candidate could not be a neighborhood saloonkeeper who would offend "respectable" elements of the city population and steal from the municipal treasury. Instead, he had to be someone with a name capable of garnering broad support and a person with a reputation for integrity and ability.

Moreover, his ethnic background had to be acceptable to a majority of the urban electorate. The new migrants from eastern and southern Europe did not yet command the voting strength or social and economic prestige to win the highest municipal office. Nor did the black population in American urban centers. In cities with large Irish or German populations, members of these older immigrant groups occasionally rose to the mayor's office, though only if they were well assimilated into Yankee culture. "Shanty" Irish did not stand a chance in the mayoral race. Indeed, most big-city mayors were old-stock Americans, descendants of those who had migrated to the New World in the seventeenth and eighteenth centuries. Political leaders recognized that the safest candidate was a multigeneration American. An Irishman aroused the contempt of other groups, but those whose great-grandparents and great-great-grandparents hailed from Massachusetts or Virginia still enjoyed the trust and respect of a majority of urban Americans and seemed the most acceptable choice to preside over the urban melting pot.

A lingering deference to social betters among politicians also reinforced support for an old-stock, downtown business leader as mayor. Irish-American political leaders such as Richard Croker in New York City, Patrick McGuire in Boston, and Christopher Buckley in San Francisco chose to imitate elite Americans of Anglo-Saxon ancestry: Croker emphasized his supposedly aristocratic English forebears, one of whom had served as governor of Bermuda, and adopted the elite hobby of raising thoroughbred horses; McGuire allied himself with Back Bay Brahmins; and Buckley married a genteel Bostonian and established himself on a country estate. None idealized the nobility of the working class or sought to topple the wealthy or elite from their social or economic thrones. Their role models were not to be found in the tenement districts of Manhattan's lower East Side or the North End of Boston. Instead, as the Irish politicos acquired wealth they patterned themselves after the gentlemen of Fifth Avenue, the Back Bay, and Nob Hill. The Yankee business leader thus retained a prestige and reputation that commanded deference from immigrant newcomers and native-born, middle-class Americans alike.

A still-more-practical consideration further limited mayoral contenders to gentlemen of wealth and standing. In the late nineteenth century party leaders expected candidates for mayor to underwrite a large portion of the campaign expenses, and mayoral hopefuls paid thousands of dollars in campaign assessments. According to the political insider William Ivins, in the election of

1886 New York City's Mayor Abram Hewitt paid $12,000 apiece to the two leading Democratic organizations in the city, Tammany Hall and County Democracy. In 1880 millionaire Mayor William Grace paid $12,500 to the then-powerful Irving Hall faction and $7,500 to Tammany Hall. And Ivins also claimed that in the election of 1878 plutocrat Mayor Edward Cooper "practically created a party, at what cost to himself he only knows." Only those who could collect $20,000 or $30,000 from friends, relatives, or their own bank account were actually eligible for New York City's highest office.[15] In other cities, as well, the financial realities of campaign expenditures and party assessments limited the field of candidates to those with the requisite cash.

Late-nineteenth-century mayors were, then, a breed apart from the average alderman. Throughout the nation municipal executives conformed to a pattern of business success, outward respectability, and citywide influence. The mayor's office was not open to those "low-bred" aldermen so maligned by critics of city government, but was, instead, the preserve of that class of men who dominated both the social and economic life of the city.

This pattern was repeated in cities throughout the nation. In 1873 in New York City a wealthy sugar manufacturer won the mayor's seat. He was succeeded in office by two leading attorneys, two millionaire iron and steel manufacturers, the founder of one of the nation's greatest shipping lines, a produce wholesaler who had served as president of the New York produce exchange, a wealthy wholesale dry-goods merchant, and a judge. Of those serving as New York City's mayor during the period 1873 through 1901, only Thomas Gilroy, who had spent his entire career as a city employee, was not a well-to-do business figure or professional. In Brooklyn the same type of individual occupied the mayor's office. During the period 1874 to 1898 the mayors of Brooklyn included a banker, a combination banker and tobacco wholesaler, an iron manufacturer, the son of the city's leading merchant and property owner, a grocery wholesaler, a lawyer, a stockbroker and governor of the New York Stock Exchange, one of the leading manufacturers of leather belting in the United States, and an iron and spring manufacturer. In Chicago five-term Mayor Carter Harrison, Sr., was a prosperous speculator in real estate and an established figure among the city's business elite. Ferdinand Latrobe, mayor of Baltimore for thirteen years, was a lawyer and member of the greatest family of engineers in the nation. In Boston such patrician attorneys as Nathan Matthews and Josiah Quincy occupied the mayor's office during the 1890s, and virtually all their predecessors in the 1870s and 1880s had also been prominent professionals or businessmen. Almost without exception late-nineteenth-century mayors were drawn from the ranks of bankers, manufacturers, wholesale merchants, large-scale real estate developers, and lawyers.

Examples of old-stock pedigrees were also common among America's mayors. Of the twelve men serving as mayor of New York City from 1873 through 1901, ten were native-born Americans, and two were born in Ireland. Nine were at least nominally Protestant and only three were Roman Catholic. Nine men served as mayor of Brooklyn from 1874 to 1898—seven were native-born; two were born in Germany; and all were Protestant. Brooklyn's long-time political boss Hugh McLaughlin was an Irish Catholic, but none with that background could capture the mayor's office. Elsewhere, foreign-born mayors were equally rare. Between 1870 and 1900 none of Chicago's twelve mayors was European-born, and only one was Catholic. During this period all of Philadelphia's mayors were native-born Protestants, and the same is true of Baltimore's chief executives. Though Irish Catholics dominated the Boston City Council by the 1890s, only one of the city's nineteenth-century mayors was a Roman Catholic of Irish ancestry. There were occasional exceptions to the general pattern of old-stock, Protestant domination, but as late as 1900, representatives of old American families still filled the mayor's chair in major cities throughout the country. Boston's Mayor Josiah Quincy could trace his lineage in America back to 1628; New York City's Mayor Robert Van Wyck was a seventh-generation descendant of a Dutch immigrant to New Netherlands; and Chicago's chief executive Carter Harrison, Jr., was a scion of one of the first families of Virginia.[16]

Such figures also belonged to the city's finest clubs and lived at prestigious addresses. They were usually not the wealthiest men in the city, not the country's multimillionaire robber barons. Neither the Vanderbilts nor the Astors ever vied for the New York City mayor's office; nor did Potter Palmer or Marshall Field ever seek to be chief executive of Chicago. But big-city mayors were deemed worthy of entry in a city's social register or bluebook, and they were usually members of what Victorians called the "better class" of citizens. Elite Beacon Street was the home of Boston's mayors; New York City's executives resided in uptown brownstones; and Chicago's mayors lived along the city's fashionable boulevards. During the mid-twentieth century Chicago's Mayor Daley hailed from the working-class neighborhood of Bridgeport, where he lived among the blue-collar masses of the city. In the nineteenth century, rarely did anyone from such a neighborhood become mayor. Few urban chief executives were products of ethnic ghettos or neighbors of factory hands. Mayors Cooper, Grace, Hewitt, and Strong of New York City belonged to the same clubs as the Astors, the Duponts, the Morgans, and the Vanderbilts. Philadelphia's chief executives were Union Leaguers, and Boston's mayors were familiar faces to the clubmen of the Back Bay. Nineteenth-century Americans looked up the social ladder when choosing their mayors and elected those on the higher rungs. Aldermen were representative of the people, whereas mayors were representative of what the people respected and admired in their social betters.

Not only did aldermen and mayors differ in their social and economic standing, but they also were products of divergent political backgrounds. The alderman was dedicated to ward politics; he was a protégé of a neighborhood political boss or was himself the party leader of his district. Most mayors, on the other hand, had little experience in the political theater of the ward or had long since risen above the level of neighborhood politics. Of the twelve men who served as mayor of New York City between 1873 and 1901, only one had been a district alderman. Likewise, of the nine men who served as mayor of Brooklyn between 1874 and 1898, only one had had experience in the city's municipal legislature. In Chicago experience as a ward alderman also was not a prerequisite for the office of mayor. Of the eleven mayors presiding over Chicago during the period 1872 through 1900, only three had ever held a seat as ward alderman. Neither Carter Harrison, Sr., nor Carter Harrison, Jr., who occupied the Chicago mayor's office for a total of thirteen of these twenty-nine years, had ever been municipal legislators. Nor was Baltimore's longtime Mayor Ferdinand Latrobe a graduate of the city's legislative branch. In Boston the pattern was much the same, and most of that city's patrician executives never filled the office of ward councilman. In Philadelphia a higher proportion of the mayors could claim previous experience in the municipal assembly, but service as councilman was certainly not the primary stepping stone to the mayor's office. Even in Saint Louis only four of the nine men serving as mayor between 1873 and 1900 were former municipal legislators, and, similarly, in Cleveland four of the nine mayors of this period had had experience in the city council.

Most big-city mayors did not, then, begin their political careers as contestants for the plebeian prize of ward leadership, but as candidates for more reputable offices. Their social and economic prestige meant that they need not start at the bottom of the political heap, but could enter politics halfway up its slopes. In New York City, Brooklyn, and Chicago the United States Congress served as the training ground for a number of future mayors. Mayors Smith Ely and Abram Hewitt of New York City, John Ward Hunter and David Boody of Brooklyn, and Carter Harrison, Sr., of Chicago all served in Congress prior to their election as municipal chief executive. Most frequently, however, mayors began their elective careers in the state legislatures, moving from state to city government. Some had gained experience in other executive positions in city government, such as commissioner of public works or city attorney. But others had never held public office prior to election as chief executive. Such individuals relied upon their reputations as businessmen and as community leaders to secure the city's chief prize without ever scrambling up the political ladder. This was especially true of self-styled good-government reformers who viewed their own lack of political ties as a virtue rather than a shortcoming. Such mayors as William Strong in New York City, Seth Low and Charles Schieren of Brooklyn, and Edwin Fitler in Philadelphia were novices in politics who won office because of their reputation for integrity, respectability, and competence in nonpolitical endeavors and not because they had proven themselves in previous elective office.[17]

Neighborhood politics was not the natural milieu of men such as the above, nor of most big-city mayors. Some municipal executives had begun their officeholding careers as ward aldermen, and others entered public life as candidates for posts in the statehouse or in Washington, D.C.. But whatever their background, their political perspective was broader than that of the neighborhood politician. Mayors were metropolitan figures who could perceive of the city as more than a collection of wards. They were persons of broad background and distinguished experience, for whom the narrowing role of alderman held little attraction. To be sure, these nineteenth-century executives depended on neighborhood politicos for votes, and they had to associate with the ward heelers whose support was vital in any election. Yet they were more at home at the chamber of commerce than in the corner saloon.

Indeed, frequent visits to the corner saloon could prove damning to a prospective chief executive, for the mayor was expected to be a pillar of respectability, a man morally worthy of the high position bestowed upon him. Suggestions of moral taint or blemish might bring a quick halt to the candidacy of a mayoral hopeful. For example, in the winter of 1894–95 State Senator Boies Penrose, a Harvard-educated lawyer from a fine old family, seemed sure of winning the Republican nomination for mayor of Philadelphia. But the well-bred Penrose was a young bachelor with a reputation as a roué, and in the weeks before the Republican city convention rumors of his fondness for the pleasures of the brothel and the barroom swept Philadelphia, arousing protests both from women's organizations and clergymen. A group of clergy signed a petition calling for a mayoral nominee of "high personal character," and a combination of women's societies likewise petitioned "for the nomination of a candidate for Mayor whose private life shows a high moral standard." According to one newspaper, some of the petitioning women "held up both hands and almost screamed when they heard some of the stories which make Mr. Penrose out a gay and festive young man." To make matters worse, Penrose was widely perceived to be the choice of the controversial political boss of Pennsylvania, Matthew Quay. Penrose's allies objected to this "campaign of innuendo and insinuation," but their complaints were to no avail.[18] The nineteenth-century mayor's chair was a seat of respectability, and most Philadelphians did not want a playboy friend of prostitutes at the head of the executive branch. At the Republican city convention Penrose lost the mayoral nomination to the upright City Solicitor Charles Warwick, whom an acquaintance described as "a married man, with a lovely family, and a member of the Episcopal Church."[19] In the late nineteenth century the mayoralty thus went to unblemished Episcopalians and not to tarnished profligates.

Moreover, few of these Victorian mayors could be regarded as stand-ins for immigrant party bosses. In the nineteenth century, party or factional leaders rarely exercised enough authority to govern the municipality through a pliant mayor acting as a front man. Political leadership in Chicago and Boston was divided among a number of mutually hostile ward leaders, none of whom commanded loyalty throughout the city. Though the Gas House Trust gained publicity as the political machine in Philadelphia, there, too, party leadership was largely dispersed among factional or ward bosses. Saint Louis's supposed boss Ed Butler was more of a freelance political speculator who bargained for favors than a boss who dictated policy. Following the fall of the Tweed Ring in the early 1870s, New York City's Tammany Hall political organization failed to regain undisputed control of municipal government until the late 1880s, and only three or four of the twelve mayors serving from 1873 through 1901 might be classified as agents of Tammany. Brooklyn's Democratic boss Hugh McLaughlin enjoyed varying degrees of power during the last three decades of the century, and at least one of Brooklyn's nine mayors of the period seems to have been a surrogate for the boss. Yet in most cities there was no political boss to dictate policies; instead, there were only a number of neighborhood and factional leaders with whom to bargain. Most mayors were to some degree independent operators. They had to compromise with party leaders, barter with them, and grant them favors and some patronage. But they were not subject to the commands of a machine boss who had unchallenged control of the city. Nineteenth-century mayors, with a few exceptions, were not stooges but men who wielded power.

In fact, a number seemed foolishly independent, tending to ignore political realities, offending powerful components of the electorate, and generally failing to manipulate the system to their own advantage. Unfamiliar with ward-level politics and disdainful of the presumed social inferiors who made up the corps of political underlings in each party organization, many mayors proved incapable of governing effectively. New York City's Abram Hewitt demonstrated his insensitivity to immigrant groups when in 1888 he refused to attend the city's Saint Patrick's Day parade organized by Irish-Americans. This snub and the resulting furor ended his political career.[20] Similarly, in the 1890s New York City's reform Mayor William Strong offended virtually everyone by his blunt and tactless independence, and, like other reform-minded political novices, proved inept at bargaining with politicians and catering to constituents. Many mayors feuded with the district aldermen and ward politicians, who came from an environment so alien to their own. The executive and legislative branches of city government represented different elements of the metropolitan population, and conflict was thus commonplace.

Some mayors, however, proved extremely adroit combatants in the arena of late-nineteenth-century urban government. The most notable masters of municipal politics were the father-and-son team of Carter Harrison, Sr., and Carter Harrison, Jr. Though southern aristocrats by ancestry, they knew how to curry the favor of urban immigrants, and as a result each of the Harrisons won five terms as mayor of Chicago. Both carefully cultivated the favor of various ethnic groups, and according to one observer of Carter Harrison, Sr., on "St. George's Day Harrison blooms out like an English rose. St. Andrew's

Day he is stuck full of thistles. Saint Patrick's Day he looks like a clover field. He is covered from head to foot with shamrock." To the city's Bohemians the elder Harrison spoke of his travels to their homeland and observed in one speech: "What struck me most of all was the beauty of the women of Bohemia; if I had been unmarried, I certainly would have brought one of your fair sisters back to Chicago."[21] Such ethnic pandering won the Harrisons a following in the immigrant neighborhoods unequaled by most of their contemporaries in the mayor's office. Yet they also had the support and trust of downtown business interests. They were capitalists living largely off the rents from extensive real estate holdings, and they knew and understood the city's business elite. Unlike many other mayors, the Harrisons were able to span the social, economic, and ethnic range of the city, winning the devotion of enough disparate elements to ensure reelection. Moralistic clergymen opposed the Harrisons' willingness to tolerate saloons and gambling, and, like the city's Republican newspapers, thus preached against both father and son. But in election after election, the father and the son proved their knack for remaining at the city's helm.

Baltimore's Ferdinand Latrobe almost matched the Harrisons in the game of urban politics. Scion of one of Maryland's most distinguished families and linked through kinship and marriage to the state's elite, Latrobe enjoyed the respect of many in Baltimore's middle and upper classes. But like his Chicago counterparts he was a well-known figure in the ethnic neighborhoods, frequenting Italian church bazaars, Irish rallies, and German parades. This common touch won him a loyal tribe of working-class followers. With a political reach that stretched from the top to the bottom of the social ladder, Latrobe racked up seven terms as mayor of Baltimore and dominated the city's government during the last three decades of the century. Like the Harrisons he proved a master of the difficult and divided world of urban America.

In Detroit the New England-born shoe manufacturer Hazen Pingree matched the electoral success of the Harrisons and Latrobe, serving four terms as mayor. Though a Yankee Baptist, he won strong support among Polish Catholics by awarding them appointments, and was able to build a powerful political organization in immigrant wards. Like the Harrisons, Pingree offended middle-class moralists by refusing to take a tough stand against liquor, but unlike either the Harrisons or Latrobe, he alienated certain business leaders by his seemingly radical stance against the streetcar, gas, and electric companies. Each election, however, he carried both working-class and middle-class wards and proved himself unbeatable in Detroit. An amalgam of respectability and rebellion, Pingree fashioned a political style that would serve as a model for such later reform mayors as Cleveland's Tom Johnson and Toledo's Samuel Jones.[22]

Few nineteenth-century mayors remained in power for as long as Pingree, Latrobe, or the Harrisons, yet no matter who occupied the mayor's chair, the exterior portrayed was much the same. Mayors were men who served as directors of local banks, speculated in urban real estate, belonged to the First Presbyterian Church, and acted as trustees of the local home for wayward girls. They had a reputation as good, solid citizens, though in some cases the reputation might well have been a veneer masking a tarnished reality. In their outward appearance, late-nineteenth-century mayors still exemplified the Yankee ideals of respectability. They were models of upper-middle-class American success, and such men were to remain in ascendancy as the power of the mayor increased and the authority of the ward alderman narrowed.

THE COMPTROLLER, CORPORATION COUNSEL, AND OTHER EXECUTIVE OFFICERS

The mayor was not the only executive officer gaining new and unprecedented authority. Second only to the mayor in significance was the city comptroller or controller. This official was the watchdog of the city treasury, the person who audited city accounts and exerted increasing authority in the preparation of the municipal budget. In an age that rang with cries of graft and peculation in public office, the comptroller was the figure charged with exposing such venality and halting future theft. Moreover, the financial depression of the 1870s had wreaked havoc with city finances, pushing a number of major municipalities to the brink of bankruptcy. It became the responsibility of the comptroller to bolster the financial position of the city and to ensure that the municipal government would not again prove vulnerable to the dangers inherent in boom-bust economic cycles. The comptroller was, then, the person responsible for restoring municipal government to a state of honesty and financial viability.

In each of the nation's chief cities the comptroller proved a powerful public official. He had to sign all warrants authorizing expenditures, and his signature was necessary on all major contracts. All bills and vouchers passed through his hands, and he could disallow an expenditure if he thought the appropriation was for unauthorized purposes or if the department or agency involved was exceeding the budgetary limits imposed upon it. Moreover, he could reject contracts that he considered unfavorable to the city. If a paving company, construction firm, or any supplier in the city seemed to be charging above a fair market price, the comptroller could refuse to sign a contract with the party.[23]

As the guardian of the treasury, the comptroller's office also supervised the accounts of all other city agencies, prescribing the accounting forms to be used, inspecting their books, and requiring regular reports. In the largest cities the comptroller's office had broad powers to examine and inspect not only the municipal accounts but also the actual performance of the departments and the actual work of city contractors. In 1892 the auditing bureau of the New

York City comptroller's office employed eleven men to inspect all public construction and repair projects in the municipality. That year they conducted nineteen thousand inspections and reported adversely in almost three thousand cases. These auditors attempted to ensure that contractors were not employing defective supplies or materials and that they were performing the job specified in their contract with the city. In other words, the comptroller's office sought to guarantee that the city received its money's worth.[24]

Moreover, municipal comptrollers acted as the city's agent in the sale of bonds. The comptroller's office marketed municipal bond issues and ensured that the city complied with state laws restricting the issuance of such bonds. It also negotiated the sale of the securities with interested banks or bond dealers, seeking a premium from the purchaser. Thus the comptroller was responsible not only for auditing the city's expenditures but also for managing its credit.

Perhaps most important, however, was the comptroller's role in preparing the municipal budget. Preparation of the budget began when each department head drafted an estimate of his department's expenditure for the coming year. By 1900 in every American city of 200,000 or more population, except Boston, department heads submitted these estimates to the chief of the finance department, who usually bore the title of comptroller. The comptroller then revised and compiled the estimates before transmitting them to the city council or Board of Estimate and Apportionment. In New York City and Brooklyn the comptroller was a member of the Board of Estimate and Apportionment, and because of his familiarity with city finances he often enjoyed a dominant voice in the board's consideration of the budget. Chicago's comptroller worked closely with the finance committee of the city council in drafting the annual budget, and at the close of the century, Cleveland's auditor likewise prepared the municipal budget in cooperation with the council committee on appropriations.[25] But throughout the last decades of the century, the trend was toward growing discretionary power for the city comptroller at the expense of the prerogatives of the municipal legislature. By the 1890s the comptroller was definitely the figure to cajole and influence if one wanted funds from the city.

As ex officio member of municipal boards and commissions, the comptroller influenced city policy in yet another way. In New York City the comptroller was one of the five commissioners of the sinking fund who were charged with paying off the city's debt, and he also served as one of the five members of the Board of Street Openings. Likewise, in Philadelphia he was one of three sinking-fund commissioners, and in Boston the city auditor held the post of secretary to the Board of Commissioners of Sinking Funds. In Chicago the city comptroller acted as president of the board of trustees of both the police pension fund and firemen's pension fund. Whenever city funds or financing were involved, the city comptroller had a strong voice in the proceedings.

Thus, the comptroller was an influential figure in late-nineteenth-century city government, and his contemporaries recognized his ascendancy in the structure of urban rule. Writing in 1897, an observer of New York City's government went so far as to contend that the city's mayor was "of far less importance, except for his appointing power, than the Comptroller."[26] The following year a student of Chicago's government concluded that the comptroller could "be considered the most important administrative functionary below the mayor."[27] And a leading authority on Philadelphia's municipal structure stated that the comptroller was "the most important and responsible officer in the city government."[28] In city after city the authority and prestige of the office of comptroller was impressive. The comptroller acted both as financial czar of city government and as the municipal conscience. He was supposed to keep wayward politicians from pilfering, and prevent crass contractors from exploiting the vulnerable body politic. Like the mayor, the comptroller was an official rising to dominance, for the city needed some central coordination of finances, and the taxpayers wanted a central watchdog. The comptroller provided both the required coordination and the desired supervision.

New York City's comptrollers proved especially forceful in molding municipal policy and blocking expenditures. Comptroller Andrew H. Green, who served from 1871 to 1876, was an unbending guardian of the public treasury, dedicated to battling contractors with claims against the city and vigorous in his fight against municipal department heads eager for additional funds. By 1876 the president of the park commission was complaining that Green had "done all in his power to interfere with and clog the workings of the Department of Parks," and in retrospect Green's critics lambasted his "obstructive" administration and his "picayune methods of business."[29] Green's successor was Tammany leader John Kelly, who likewise pursued a policy of economy in government, and though he proved less abrasive with department heads, was more irascible in dealing with the state government. He was able to achieve a sharp reduction in the city debt and a marked improvement in the municipality's credit standing. At the close of his four-year term even the city's leading Republican newspaper characterized the administration of this Democratic mogul as "careful, conscientious and honest."[30]

New York City's comptrollers of the 1880s and 1890s did not garner as many headlines as had the controversial and sometimes ill-tempered Kelly and Green, but they remained true to the tradition of these combative predecessors. Economy was the watchword of the comptrollers, and they continued to examine city invoices and trim the municipal budget with an eye for waste or fraud. Their dedication to investigating every expenditure exasperated many of their fellow officials in the executive branch, and at one meeting of the Board of Estimate an angry mayor told an officious comptroller, "The idea that this board must refer everything to the Controller is absurd. We might as well abolish the board altogether."[31] But the comptrollers defended their right to interfere and remained a potent force in favor of economy. Each year they received the departmental budget estimates in early September, and one comptroller expressed the general sentiment of his ilk when he notified department heads that "every item included in the estimates should be reduced to the lowest amount of expenditure consistent with efficient service, in order to secure the utmost economy in the administration of city affairs."[32] Budget pruning was the comptroller's preoccupation, and requests for additional funds won an icy response from these guardians of the treasury.

At the close of the century New York City's Comptroller Bird S. Coler won special recognition for his dogged opposition to raids on the public purse and for his successful battle against the Ramapo water scheme. In 1899 a group of Tammany officials sought to commit the city to a forty-year contract with the Ramapo Company for the purchase of water at an annual cost of $5 million. Regarding the proposal as a prime example of political plundering, Coler mobilized opposition, enlisting the city's newspapers in a publicity campaign against the Ramapo Company. Coler publicly denounced the scheme as "the most outrageous proposition that was ever presented to any city in the world" and claimed that the earlier sale of streetcar franchises by bribed aldermen was "only a picayune case of shoplifting compared with this Ramapo job." The doughty comptroller vowed to reporters that "under no circumstances" would he "consent to any outside company or any other agent than the city furnishing its water." Coler was able to fulfill his promise. Unable to survive Coler's blistering criticism, the Ramapo scheme quickly fizzled.[33] It was alleged to have been a pet project of both the Tammany leadership and the Republican state machine; however, it failed to win the comptroller's approval, and in the late nineteenth century the comptroller was a person of sufficient prestige and clout to thwart the best-laid plans of political lords.

In Philadelphia, as well, the office of comptroller had become a significant check on the designs of political leaders and city officials. Before 1878 Philadelphia's comptrollers had remained faceless figures auditing the books and maintaining a quiet anonymity. But that year the Democrat Robert Pattison won election to the comptroller's office and transformed it into a scalpel exposing the questionable schemes of the city's dominant Republican politicians. According to an admiring reformer, Pattison halted the "eager and indiscriminate reaching for the contents of the treasury," and earned the opprobrium of "public contractors, who had grown rapidly rich from their frauds upon the city government," as well as the hatred of "Department-heads, who had conspired with and shared the spoils of these contractors."[34] All this reaped Pattison personal glory and catapulted him into two terms as Pennsylvania's governor. His successors had less-brilliant political futures, but they also claimed broad discretionary powers and refused to act simply as clerks or bookkeepers. Moreover, Pennsylvania's courts ratified this liberal interpretation of the comptroller's authority. In 1883 the Philadelphia Court of Common Pleas ruled that the comptroller is "of the highest importance to the welfare of the city, and he requires and is clothed by law with great powers of judgment or discretion and execution."[35] Three years later the state supreme court observed that the "office of city controller is certainly one of the gravest importance and responsibility" and upheld the authority of this officer to do whatever he might "deem needful to protect the interests of the . . . city."[36] In Philadelphia, as in New York City, the comptroller was a formidable figure who could bring ruin to filching municipal contractors or improvident department heads, and men such as Robert Pattison and Bird S. Coler could build political careers on their reputation as the taxpayer's messiah.

Not everyone, however, was suited for such a prestigious office. Nineteenth-century Americans believed that the comptroller had to be honest and upright beyond question and possess an astute business sense worthy of administering the city's millions of dollars. In terms of the necessary "business sense," that was presumably not a job for a ward politician, a corner grocer, or a saloonkeeper-turned-statesman. And such neighborhood leaders rarely rose to the rank of comptroller. As in the case of mayor, only members of the "better class" of citizens served as the city's chief financial officer, whether the comptroller was chosen by the urban electorate, as in Philadelphia, Brooklyn, Saint Louis, and New York City, or appointed by the mayor, as in Boston, Baltimore, and Chicago. During the last three decades of the nineteenth century, downtown businessmen, not ward politicos, occupied the post of comptroller just as they did the office of mayor.

New York City's notorious Comptroller Richard "Slippery Dick" Connelly brought his office into disrepute during the reign of the Tweed Ring in the late 1860s and early 1870s. But following his ouster from power, New York City's political and business leaders were more careful about who filled the post. Of the seven men who served as New York City's comptroller between 1871 and the close of the century, six were native-born Protestants and all had proven their ability in business or in the legal profession. Three were bankers and brokers, two were lawyers, one was a former president of a railroad, and one was a soapstone and grate manufacturer. Only one had ever served as a district alderman. For example, Theodore Myers, comptroller from 1888 through 1893, was a leading private banker and member of the New York Stock Exchange, whose firm had branches in Boston, Philadelphia, Baltimore, and Chicago. He had served, moreover, as president of the Business Men's Association of New York City. He was also a member of the New York Yacht Club and the Rockaway Hunt Club and was an enthusiastic art collector.[37] Similarly, Comptroller Bird S. Coler, who served from 1898 through 1901, was a partner in his father's banking and brokerage firm, which was one of the nation's leading dealers in government bonds. Such links with the financial world were among the criteria for selecting a nominee for New York City's comptroller. It was thought that a comptroller who had earned the trust and support of Wall Street would be able to secure favorable terms for municipal bond issues. By the close of the century Wall Street was the comptroller's constituency and not the lower East Side tenement district.

There was one partial exception to this general pattern of respectable downtown businessmen occupying the New York City comptroller's office. From 1877 to 1880, the earlier-mentioned John Kelly, leader of the Tammany Hall political organization, held the post of comptroller. Kelly was an Irish-Catholic politician in an office usually reserved for old-stock Protestants who never bore the title of political boss. He was, however, a successful businessman with a reputation for reforming Tammany. And, above all, he was known for his scrupulous honesty and unswerving integrity. Even his bitterest enemies acknowledged the appropriateness of his nickname "Honest John," and as comptroller he won many enemies because of his penny-pinching devotion to thrift. Only his predecessor, the previously mentioned comptroller Andrew H. Green, exceeded him in his obsessive hatred of waste. Both Green and Kelly served as watchdogs of the treasury with a snarling ferocity, but they ensured that New York City would no longer stand on the brink of bankruptcy as it had in the early 1870s.

Elsewhere this emphasis on integrity, financial acumen, and favorable ties with the banking community also strongly influenced the choice of comptroller. In Brooklyn the political parties nominated native-born, well-to-do lawyers, directors of banks, and real estate brokers. Philadelphia also chose men of irreproachable repute to fill the chief financial post in that city. Chicago's comptrollers were wholesale merchants, bankers, and prominent real estate developers whom even opposition newspapers could describe as having "always sustained a high personal character."[38] That city's leading financial journal described the younger Harrison's choice for comptroller, Robert A. Waller, as "a prominent citizen, a man of unquestionable integrity, pursuing thorough business methods in his own private affairs and in any public office he may hold, and commanding the respect of the best elements."[39] And the respect of the best elements was to pay off for the city. In 1897 Waller succeeded in selling city tax warrants at par, whereas for some years they had sold at a discount. According to Mayor Harrison, the comptroller's success was "due to his intimacy with many of the leading bankers who took the paper out of friendship for him, knowing that while he was comptroller the city would make good."[40] Waller represented the ideal comptroller, someone who could win the financial community's support for the city.

If the comptroller's office was to garner the confidence of the best elements and serve as the city's conscience, it could not be a tool of a political machine. Few comptrollers of major cities were supine servants of partisan leaders or mindless flunkies of the mayor and council. Most had had some previous political experience and had won election or appointment as a party nominee; however, partisan loyalty to the dominant political faction was not a chief

criterion for attaining the post. New York City's Comptroller Theodore Myers won reelection in 1890 with the endorsement of the Republicans, both
major factions of the Democratic party, and that year's reform alliance. Only
two minor party candidates opposed him, and Myers won 97 percent of the
votes cast. Myers was the nonpartisan, consensual ruler of New York City's
finances. His successor, Ashbel Fitch, was a Republican-turned-Democrat
who later returned to the Republican fold. He was Tammany's nominee but
hardly a machine loyalist. In 1893 Democratic Mayor Carter Harrison, Sr., of
Chicago appointed a Republican as his comptroller. The following year Harrison's successor chose as comptroller a former president of the Illinois Central Railroad, who was so apolitical that apparently he had never attended one
of the numerous local party conventions. This appointee accepted the office
only on the condition that he be "allowed to conduct the department in his
own manner and without political interferences."[41] In 1897 Carter Harrison,
Jr., a leading silverite and supporter of William Jennings Bryan, selected as his
comptroller a believer in the gold standard and a foe of Bryan. Philadelphia's
voters likewise sought to ensure that the city's comptroller was not a partisan
pawn of those he was supposed to audit, and during the 1880s they regularly
split their tickets and elected Democrat comptrollers to oversee Republican
administrations. Moreover, Boston's nonpartisan appointee James H. Dodge
held the title of city auditor from 1881 into the early twentieth century and
served under both Republican and Democratic mayors.

The career of New York City's longtime Deputy Comptroller Richard A.
Storrs demonstrates that the comptroller's office was not considered part of
the spoils of each changing city administration. Storrs served in the comptroller's office thirty-nine years, from 1857 to his death in 1896, and held the
post of deputy or assistant comptroller during most of this period. Through
the years of Tweed Ring supremacy, reform reaction, rule by the County Democracy faction, renewed victory by Tammany, and the return of reform,
Storrs was the second-ranking official in the city's Finance Department. Moreover, as deputy comptroller he was secretary of the Board of Estimate and
Apportionment and the Board of Sinking Fund Commissioners. Generally
recognized as having an "encyclopedic grasp of the city affairs," Storrs did not
hesitate to correct the members of the powerful Board of Estimate and Apportionment if they strayed from the path of fiscal responsibility. According to an
account by one of his contemporaries, at budget meetings Storrs "sat watch-
fully silent until the members had discussed each separate item of appropriation," then "at the last moment, particularly if there was a proposition before
the board to increase an annual estimate . . . , Mr. Storrs would quietly
interpose an objection based on precedent or on a mandatory law which everyone else had either forgotten or had never known."[42] Decade after decade
Storrs quietly logged his objections, and year after year he supervised the
bureaus of the Finance Department, ensuring that municipal auditors and

inspectors uncovered waste and malfeasance. He was not a loyal subject of any machine boss nor was he a saloonkeeping, immigrant flunky of Tammany Hall. Storrs was a descendant of early settlers of Long Island, a Son of the American Revolution, a director of the Christian Home for Intemperate Men, and a Methodist Sunday school teacher.[43] And he was nonpartisan. At the time of Storrs's death the city comptroller observed, "if this public servant had any politics, I . . . never learned what they were."[44] Storrs objectively and painstakingly fulfilled his duties as protector of the city's funds, and after administering hundreds of millions of dollars in public monies, he died with an estate of only $15,000.[45]

The administration of the New York City comptroller's office was, then, in large measure above politics. After Storrs's death in 1896, Tammany chief Richard Croker reportedly submitted his choice for deputy to Comptroller Ashbel Fitch, who himself had been elected with Tammany backing. The *New York Times* observed, however, that "it is not thought that Tammany can dictate this appointment," and the *Times* proved correct.[46] Fitch called a meeting of the presidents of twelve leading banks and insurance companies and with these select financiers chose the new deputy, who was a fourteen-year veteran of the finance department. In choosing the deputy comptroller, Fitch did not call a conclave of ward bosses but instead relied on the advice of financial leaders. For, according to Fitch, the new deputy must have the confidence of those who "have charge of the great financial interests which are so closely connected with the business and the credit of the city's Treasury."[47] Thus, the president of the Knickerbocker Trust Company had more of a voice in the selection of Finance Department officials than did the leader of the third ward. In New York City as in Chicago, the comptroller was the banks' man and not the boss's.

Other posts in the executive branch also attracted substantial professionals ready to wield broad authority. Throughout the last three decades of the nineteenth century the office of corporation counsel, or city solicitor, was among the most important in the municipal structure and as such could not be relegated to hack practitioners. The corporation counsel defended the municipality in the courts, condemned lands for public improvements, and prosecuted not only polluters of the water supply but delinquent taxpayers and suppliers who defaulted on their contracts with the city. In 1893 the New York City Law Department, under the leadership of the corporation counsel, initiated over 1,600 actions and proceedings, while in the smaller city of Boston the municipal Law Department brought more than 450 cases, and that same year the city attorney of San Francisco reported that his office had 325 cases pending in the courts.[48] Moreover, the corporation counsel advised the mayor, the comptroller, the municipal departments, and the city council on questions of law, informing each whether its proposed action was legal or exceeded the municipality's charter powers. In 1893 the New York City Law Department prepared

318 opinions for the city officers, with the comptroller requesting such advice most often.[49] Two years later the number of advisory opinions was up to 874, filling 7,065 printed pages.[50] Elsewhere the city solicitor was performing this same service, with Cleveland's attorney rendering 109 opinions in 1895 and Saint Louis's counselor drafting 62.[51] Reliance on the expertise of the city solicitor was frequent, and an adverse judgment by this official could prove a serious obstacle to municipal action.

This was evident, for example, in the struggle over Illinois's civil service law. In 1895 the state legislature enacted a system of civil service examinations for Chicago, but two years later, just as this merit system was in its nascent stage, Mayor Carter Harrison, Jr., appointed as corporation counsel Charles Thornton. A foe of civil service, Thornton handed down advisory opinions increasing the number of positions exempted from competitive examination, and the city's executive officers acted on this advice. In the ensuing battle with Chicago's Civil Service Commission, Thornton also argued that the civil service law was unconstitutional and thus he further encouraged disregard for the procedures. As a result, the civil service commissioners were unable to establish a merit system until a series of Illinois Supreme Court decisions finally overruled Thornton's opinions.[52] Exercising his authority as chief legal officer of the municipality, a counselor like Thornton could seriously undermine a program he deemed illegal or objectionable. Anyone seeking to implement a new proposal or policy might well find the city solicitor a valuable, if not necessary, ally.

In addition to his courtroom and advisory chores, the municipal attorney also drafted many of the bills presented to the state legislature and kept a careful eye on the actions of lawmakers in the state capital. One assistant corporation counsel in New York City's Law Department was assigned specifically to legislation, and thus attended committee hearings in Albany and represented the municipality's interests before the state solons. In 1895 he and his aides reviewed each of the forty-five hundred bills presented in the legislature to determine the impact of each on the city.[53] Boston's corporation counsel spent at least as much time working with the state legislature as with the city council. And in Cleveland the law department also furthered the municipality's interests by drafting a total of 24 legislative acts in 1895 alone.[54]

Such duties could not be left to officials whose only merit was partisan loyalty. By 1895 New York City's Law Department was the largest law office in the country, employing twenty-eight lawyers and sixty-four clerical workers.[55] By comparison, the United States Department of Justice in Washington, D.C., at the time maintained a staff of only twenty-four lawyers.[56] To manage such a legal force, New York City's mayors generally selected highly able counselors who could boast of both professional repute and party service. From 1875 to 1882 the corporation counsel of New York City was William C. Whitney, a rising lawyer who later in the century was to amass one of the largest fortunes in America, in addition to being named to the national cabinet. Whitney's assistant counsel was Francis L. Stetson, who eventually became the nation's leading corporate lawyer and personal attorney to the financier J. P. Morgan. [57] Among the other assistants during Whitney's tenure and throughout the following two decades were a score of future judges. In fact, the corporation counsel's office was an admirable place for a young attorney to begin his rise through the ranks of bench and bar.[58] And New York City was always ready to draw on this reservoir of bright young men.

During these years New York also enjoyed the services of the longstanding assistant corporation counsel David Dean, a person steeped in the law of municipal corporations and supreme in his knowledge of the legal intricacies of city government. Dean was the Law Department's counterpart to Richard Storrs, a sober, conscientious Methodist of native stock who served as an assistant corporation counsel for thirty-one years, from 1866 until his death in 1897. Unsurpassed in his expertise, at the close of his life he was chosen to draft the new charter for Greater New York. He had argued many of the city's cases during the last thirty years of the century and drafted volumes of advisory opinions.[59] It was fitting that he should also frame the fundamental law of the future consolidated municipality.

Other cities could also boast of talented lawyers on their payroll. Chicago's corporation counsels were usually respected lawyers who had won the political goodwill of the mayor. Their capability was demonstrated by the fact that on leaving the city's service they attracted such clients as Marshall Field, the Union Stockyards, Standard Oil, the Pullman Company, and Republic Steel. And in the early 1890s the acting corporation counsel of Chicago was Clarence Darrow, who was beginning his rise to fame as the nation's foremost trial lawyer.[60] Boston's corporation counsel, like its auditor, was a nonpartisan figure who offered his expertise to one administration after another, both Democratic and Republican. Daniel Webster's former law partner John P. Healy held the office of city solicitor, or corporation counsel, for twenty-six years, from 1856 to his death in 1882. Throughout this long tenure he remained among the most highly respected of Boston's lawyers.[61] In Brooklyn, Philadelphia, Saint Louis, Cleveland, and Cincinnati grand old men of the bar like Healy rarely accepted the post of city solicitor but left that office instead to younger men who dreamed of rounding out their careers with a judgeship.

Like the comptrollers, these ambitious solicitors generally were native-born Protestants who resided in the "better" neighborhoods. They were not Irish ward bosses. Of the nine men serving as New York City's corporation counsel between 1872 and 1900 six were Protestant and only three Catholic, and all were born in the United States. The five men who held the office of corporation counsel of Brooklyn between 1869 and 1897 were all old-stock Protestants. One was a member of the prominent DeWitt family, tracing his lineage in America back to 1647; another was grandnephew of the New England reformer Wendell Phillips; and a third was a descendant of a seventeenth-century founder of Springfield, Massachusetts, and an eighteenth-century chief justice of Connecticut. A few Germans and Jews interrupted the prevailing hegemony of native-born Protestants in the corporation counsel's office in Chicago, but descendants of seventeenth-century New England Puritans most often occupied the post. And the Harrisons showed a definite preference for appointing counselors who came from fine old Kentucky families like their own. Likewise, in the heavily German city of Saint Louis the city counselor's office remained a stronghold of old-stock lawyers with Anglo-Saxon names. In the leading American municipalities Yankees did not abandon the corporation counsel's office to self-trained police-court practitioners just a few years off the boat. Instead, this post, like that of comptroller, usually remained in the possession of native Protestants of some professional distinction.

In addition to the offices of corporation counsel, comptroller, and mayor, another position growing in significance was that of commissioner of public works. As chief of the public works department, the commissioner hired thousands of day laborers and negotiated construction contracts involving millions of dollars. Any occupant of this office could win many friends and possibly even the mayoral nomination in the next election. Yet an incompetent who allowed the sewers to back up and the pavements to crumble could reap much criticism and bring disgrace to his party. No political organization could afford to put a second-rate ward heeler in this post, and political leaders generally recognized this precept of survival. The public works commissioner might be ambitious, but he had to be able.

Chicago's Mayor Carter Harrison, Jr., expressed the attitude of many mayors when he confided that for the Public Works Department he wanted "a man of brains, experience, political acumen, integrity, *guts*."[62] Moreover, he acted upon his words by refusing to appoint his stalwart supporter Bobbie Burke to the office of public works commissioner. Burke was a rotund little politician who spent his life marching in Cook County Democratic parades, rounding up votes in neighborhood saloons, and handling the less respectable political chores that neither the younger Harrison nor his father could perform. No person could claim greater credit for the younger Harrison's mayoral victory in 1897, and Burke sought the public works post as a reward for his loyal labors. But the younger Harrison turned instead to a person more experienced in water supply, paving, and sewerage and less immersed in campaign maneuvering and grassroots politics. Burke was a veteran political operative who proved invaluable to the Harrisons at election time. Nevertheless the office of public works commissioner was above his station and beyond his reach.[63]

There were, however, numerous executive offices that mayors and political leaders viewed as partisan plums to be awarded to loyal party workers or devoted friends and relatives regardless of merit. Perhaps the most lucrative of these was the office of city treasurer, or chamberlain. This official had custody of the city's funds, but unlike the comptroller he had little or no voice in determining how they were spent. In fact, the post was largely clerical and not particularly arduous. Yet it could be most rewarding. In many cities during the 1870s it was legal and accepted for the treasurer or chamberlain to pocket city fees and the interest earned on city funds in lieu of any salary. By the close of the century such practices were no longer legal, but to compensate for the loss of past privileges, municipalities granted their treasurers generous salaries. In 1890 New York City was paying its chamberlain $25,000 a year, and this official also earned about $7,000 to $8,000 annually in fees for the administration of trust funds assigned to his charge by the courts. From this sum the chamberlain had to pay his office expenses, but generally he could clear $17,000 each year in net profit.[64] This was a truly munificent sum for a period when the average laborer earned no more than $500 annually. New York City's chamberlain enjoyed the second highest salary of any public official in the United States, with only the president earning more.

The man collecting this generous sum in 1890 was the Tammany boss Richard Croker. For a big-time politico like Croker the chamberlain's office was an appropriate reward. This Irish immigrant of questionable integrity did not conform to the prerequisites for mayor or comptroller. But as chamberlain he could line his pockets handsomely and legally. New York City newspapers referred to the chamberlain's post as "the fat office," a plump plum appropriate for a devoted follower or dedicated party worker.[65] And in other cities, as well, the post of city treasurer was deemed to be worthy compensation for a party loyalist who deserved financial tribute but did not merit much formal governing authority.

Lesser offices were available for other friends and minor party satraps who were worthy of special recognition but who could not be trusted with significant power. For example, in Chicago the posts of inspector of gas, inspector of oils, and city sealer of weights and measures were reserved for deserving minor politicians. These were the executive positions open to ward politicos who had worked the saloons and streets rounding up votes for the mayor. Such jobs provided the officeholder with a good salary or ample fees, yet they offered little opportunity for embarrassing the city administration. In fact, the elder Harrison bestowed the position of city sealer on that loyal ward heeler Bobbie Burke. Elsewhere an ample number of similar posts existed for the party faithful, and scores of minor executive appointments went to those who never enjoyed a listing in the social register.

The executive branch was not, then, totally off limits to ethnic newcomers in the wards, and some executive appointments were not beyond the grasp of minor retailers, small contractors, or undistinguished party loyalists. But only rarely did such small-time individuals break the social barrier and seize the highest offices in the city. The major executive officers in large measure determined policy affecting the city as a whole, and these officers were usually old-stock Protestant businessmen or professionals and not Irish neighborhood potentates. Even the old stalwarts of the executive branch, the veteran deputies like Storrs and Dean who administered departments for decades, were more likely Methodist Sons of the American Revolution than Catholic scions of Erin. Though immigrant ward politicians could force favors from the mayor and possibly even from the comptroller, as yet they did not wield the power of these offices. The Yankee pillars of respectability still commanded votes throughout the metropolis and still dominated the chief positions in city government.

INDEPENDENT BOARDS AND COMMISSIONS

As Americans revised their municipal charters and restructured their governments, they not only shifted authority from the city councils to the offices of mayor and comptroller but they also experimented with government by special-function boards and commissions. Boards of public works and fire and police commissions, for example, exercised authority in many municipalities in the 1870s and 1880s. Most of these boards were appointed by the mayor and council and were dependent on appropriations from the council or board of estimate. During the last three decades of the century, however, lawmakers created some commissions that were isolated from the politics and partisan haggling endemic in the legislative and executive branches. Those in the chambers of commerce and reform organizations who framed the laws structuring municipal government believed in protecting these boards from parties, factions, and rings and securing them for "persons of standing and character." Thus a number of boards were not subject to the appointment powers of the mayor or council, and some commissions had independent funding and taxing authority. These autonomous bodies were not agents of the executive or the municipal legislature but instead represented a third element in American city government, an element vital to urban rule in the late nineteenth century.

Among the earliest autonomous commissions were those for the government of police departments. By the 1860s independent police commissions appointed by state governors were commonplace, administering police forces in New York City, Brooklyn, Saint Louis, Baltimore, and Cleveland. After 1870 such commissions persisted in Saint Louis and Baltimore, and during the 1880s the police forces in Cincinnati and Boston also became the responsibility of state-appointed boards. In each of these cities, proponents of gubernatorial appointment claimed that such a reform would remove the police from the debilitating control of local factions or political cliques. Especially irritating to native-born critics was the hold that immigrant, ward-level politicians had on police appointments and law enforcement policy. Irish and German party leaders with a tolerance for liquor could use their political clout to ensure that the police treated saloons gently. Those of colonial ancestry who were more likely teetotalers viewed this political interference as intolerable. Thus, in 1885 Boston supporters of a state board argued that "the police should be removed from the effect of local influences, political and otherwise, which are very powerful hindrances against the execution of certain laws." Proponents of a state-appointed commission claimed that Boston's police failed to enforce the liquor laws because of the department's dependence "on the favor of a City Council representative of the vicious, criminal and corrupting classes of the community." According to these critics, what Boston needed was a police commission "independent of this demoralizing condition and uncompromised by a record of subserviency," a commission that would "be able to make the city comparatively wholesome once more."[66]

In Cincinnati the demand for an outside check on partisanship also resulted in a police board appointed by the governor. Under the Non-Partisan Police Commission Act of 1886 Cincinnati's mayor retained command of the police force, but all appointments and removals had to be approved by the state-appointed board consisting of two Republicans and two Democrats. Sponsored by the Committee of One Hundred, a reform group that according to a local newspaper comprised "all the honest and respectable men in Cincinnati," this law was intended to ensure a stalemate of partisan forces and thereby rid the police of party influence. Four years after the board's creation, its president argued that the "existing law is so framed that it is impossible . . . for the force to be the creature of the arbitrary whim or personal or political bias of either the Mayor or the Board."[67] As in Boston the "honest and respectable" elements had urged gubernatorial intervention as a check on local politicians and their partisan designs.

But enthusiasm for independent police commissions generally waned during the late nineteenth century, for the state-appointed boards were rarely effective in removing the police force from partisan politics. Instead, in cities with state-appointed commissions the police simply shifted from the partisan control of mayoral or council appointees to the political supervision of the governor's favorites. By 1870 New York City, Brooklyn, and Cleveland had already abandoned experiments with state-selected boards, and in the following decades most commentators on municipal rule opposed any return to this form of police government. During the 1880s and 1890s the law enforcement agencies in most major cities were under the control of the mayor and council, and in those cities with state-appointed commissions the police boards were the targets of repeated complaints from advocates of local self-rule. Republicans in Saint Louis strongly resented the boards appointed by the perennially Democratic governors of Missouri, and Democrats in Boston criticized the control exercised by the Republican state administrations. State police boards survived in some cities, but in the last decades of the century few municipalities chose to adopt such a scheme of outside control for their police departments.

For some municipal services, however, the autonomous board seemed more appropriate and acceptable. During the 1870s, 1880s, and 1890s a number of city park commissions, library boards, school boards, and sinking-fund commissions were at least one step removed from the pressures of the mayor and the council. Many felt that such boards should be free of local politicos and insulated from the tainted influence of the alderman and the ward politician, and that intellectual and cultural institutions, especially, such as libraries and parks, should not fall prey to the philistines. Consequently, in many of the chief municipalities the members of these commissions were not appointed by the executive or confirmed by the council, and in some cities the financing of these commissions was not dependent on the appropriations of the board of aldermen. Lawmakers erected a wall around the city's parks, libraries, schools, and sinking funds, and mayors and councilmen only had a limited right to trespass on this protected turf.

Moreover, these independent commissions often became bastions of the city's elite. The urban plutocracy viewed culture and beauty as their special domain, and service on park and library boards was a social distinction that many of the wealthy readily accepted. Money and investments were also specialties of the urban elite, so that independent sinking-fund commissions became preserves of upper-crust power as well. School boards included a broader spectrum of social types, yet by the 1880s and 1890s reformers were fighting to free these boards from political influence and to upgrade the social standing of the membership. Critics of late-nineteenth-century municipal rule repeatedly complained that the wealthiest and supposedly most-accomplished city dwellers refused to play a part in urban government. Such criticisms were well founded, if applied only to the boards of aldermen and city councils. The independent boards, however, belie such a facile generalization. Many of the greatest names in business and society did contribute to the government of the city through the less partisan forum of the independent boards. Through these governing bodies, members of the elite could administer the parks, libraries, and city indebtedness relatively free of interference from the municipal legislature or executive.

Independent park boards were especially common in the late nineteenth century. In 1869 the Illinois state legislature created three park districts in Chicago—the South Park District, the West Park District, and the Lincoln Park District.[68] Each was governed by a board of five members appointed by the governor for five-year terms, and each board enjoyed the power to lay taxes and borrow money. The boards were totally independent of the municipal corporation of Chicago, they had full authority to govern the city's major parks, and in 1879 the state legislature also granted them control of the boulevards linking the metropolitan park system. Gubernatorial appointees with the power to levy taxes and issue bonds thus laid out, maintained, and regulated the thousands of acres of parkland ringing Chicago and the miles of tree-lined, landscaped thoroughfares.

The men charged with the task of bringing sylvan beauty to the hog-butchering capital of the world were almost without exception persons from the upper strata of society. Whereas in 1893 only 28 percent of Chicago's aldermen enjoyed sufficient social prestige to win listing in the city's bluebook, that same year 93 percent of the park commissioners were among those recorded in the directory of fashionable persons. Only one of the fifteen commissioners failed to attain this social recognition.[69] In fact, year after year the park boards included substantial business and professional leaders, some of them—like millionaire landowner Potter Palmer—ranking among the most notable plutocrats of their day. Major real estate developers who could profit from the appreciation of residential properties along the parks and boulevards were prominent among the board members. For example, Paul Cornell, the developer of the Hyde Park neighborhood of Chicago, was one of the chief sponsors of the bills creating the park districts and served thirteen years on the South Park Board.

Such a lengthy term of service, however, was not unusual among the businessmen-commissioners. Of the five South Park commissioners serving in 1897, one had been on the board for twenty years, another eleven years, two for eight years, and one for three years.[70] The constant turnover that characterized the board of aldermen did not plague the South Park commissioners. Change of membership occurred more frequently on the Lincoln Park and West Park boards, but even the Lincoln Park Board could claim a commissioner who held office for twenty-four years.[71] Protected from local partisan upheaval, the park governments of Chicago proceeded under the steady hand of long-term commissioners drawn from among the leading businessmen. Writing in 1898, one student of Chicago government observed that the obvious reason for gubernatorial appointment "was the removal of the park boards from the direct control of the popular will, and local politics."[72] During the late nineteenth century, this independence allowed the so-called better elements to rule the parks relatively insulated from the bickering of local politicians.

Likewise in Philadelphia the mode of appointing park commissioners permitted a degree of independence. In 1867 the Pennsylvania legislature created a park commission consisting of six city officers serving ex officio, together with ten citizens appointed to five-year terms by the district court and Philadelphia County Court of Common Pleas. Park commission appointments were not within the power of the city council or mayor but were the responsibility of the county judges, men who were professionals serving long judicial terms and who were less responsive to political pressures than the executive and legislative officers. Unlike Chicago's commission, Philadelphia's park commission was dependent on the city council for appropriations. But the ward politicians in the legislative branch had no formal voice in the selection of those who spent the park funds.

The list of members of the Philadelphia park board reads like a who's who in business and society. Three of the five men who served as president of the Pennsylvania Railroad between 1852 and 1900 were members of Philadelphia's park board, as were the railroad's chief counsel and a number of members of its board of directors. Among the other park commissioners were a former United States minister to Great Britain and a former minister to Greece and Spain. One of the nation's largest sugar refiners, E. C. Knight, held the office of park commissioner, as did two of the greatest plutocratic art collectors of the period, the nouveau riche Peter A. B. Widener and the esteemed attorney John G. Johnson. One of the prominent commissioners at the close of the century was president of seven companies and director of twenty-five others. Union Leaguers, Rittenhouse Club members, and University of Pennsylvania trustees were commonplace on the Philadelphia park commission, and though the county judges named Republican party nabob James McManes to the commission, they refused to appoint plebeian ward politicians. Whereas less than 40 percent of Philadelphia's council members for 1895 were listed in the city's bluebook, all of the park commissioners were listed.[73]

As in Chicago, these plutocratic commissioners were not short-term appointees vulnerable to the changing popular whim. Of the ten court-appointed commissioners serving in Philadelphia in 1900, one had been in office twenty-one years, another nineteen years, two for thirteen years, and one for eleven years. In fact, the court appointees enjoyed virtual life tenure, and of the twenty-six court-appointed commissioners who completed their term of service before 1900, eighteen died in office.[74] The turnover among the ex officio members was greater, but the majority of the commissioners seemed relatively immune from the popular will. During the late nineteenth century a virtual oligarchy governed Philadelphia's parks.

An oligarchy also ruled over Baltimore's parklands. Created in 1860, Baltimore's Public Park Commission consisted of the mayor and five citizens who enjoyed life tenure. Moreover, the commission itself was responsible for filling any vacancies due to the death or resignation of its own members, though the appointments were subject to the approval of the city council. Further, the franchise agreement with the city's street railway companies provided that one-fifth of the gross receipts of the companies was to be used for park construction and maintenance. Thus the commission had an independent source of income and did not need to rely on council appropriations. And the commissioners who expended these funds could act almost entirely without regard for public opinion, since they served for life and owed their appointment to their colleagues on the commission and not to any elected official. The presence of the mayor as an ex officio member and the requirement of council confirmation of appointments ensured some popular restraint, but it was a feeble restraint. Not until 1888 did mayoral appointment supplant the system of co-option, and in 1892 two-year terms replaced life tenure.[75] Yet before the 1890s the Public Park Commission was a closed corporation of some of Baltimore's most respected citizens, who acted independently of any significant political influence.

Elsewhere, mayors and city councils also exercised little or no authority over park boards. From 1870 to 1900 San Francisco's park commissioners were gubernatorial appointees with independent authority to finance parks through taxation and borrowing. And among the San Francisco appointees were millionaires like Leland Stanford and Adolph Spreckels.[76] In Saint Louis a board of five commissioners serving five-year terms governed the city's second largest recreation ground, the Tower Grove Park. The park's benefactor, Henry Shaw, chose the original commissioners, but the Missouri Supreme Court filled all subsequent vacancies. Yet the Tower Grove Park board was actually an oligarchy of leading Saint Louis businessmen serving for life. The eleven commissioners appointed during the period 1867 to 1900 remained on the board an average of twenty-two years. They received a fixed annual appropriation from the city council for the development of the parkland and submitted an annual report to the council, but they ruled their publicly financed domain without the interference of elected officials.[77]

Cleveland's park government conformed to a similar pattern. In 1893 the Ohio legislature created a Cleveland Board of Park Commissioners consisting of the mayor, the president of the city council, and three citizens appointed by the trustees of the sinking fund, an elite body whose members were themselves chosen by co-option. In other words, a majority of Cleveland's park commissioners owed their appointment to a board of trustees, the members of which were neither popularly elected nor appointed by elected officials. Any vacancy among the trustees of the sinking fund was filled by the remaining trustees, and any vacancy on the park commission was filled by the self-elected trustees. These trustees were some of Cleveland's wealthiest residents, and they selected park commissioners from their own social class. During the 1880s and early 1890s, affluent Clevelanders had battled the city council's reluctance to finance park development.[78] Now wealthy civic leaders had their own board, removed from the pressures of the mass electorate yet empowered to borrow funds and to raise money through an independent park levy.

In some major cities park boards did not enjoy a formal, structural immunity from political or popular control but in fact, they operated largely autonomous of the mayor or council. Brooklyn's mayor appointed the members of that city's park board to three-year terms, but the board was actually dominated by Brooklyn patriarch James S. T. Stranahan, who served as president of the park commission from 1860 to 1882.[79] Stranahan fought with mayors and aldermen, but he persevered and governed the city's parks as he wished. Though appointed by the city's mayor, Buffalo's park commission was likewise under the control of leading businessmen, most notably the manufacturer Sherman S. Jewett, who was on the board for twenty-eight years, from 1869 to 1897, and served eighteen years as board president, through both Democratic and Republican administrations.[80] In Buffalo and Brooklyn as well as Cleveland, Saint Louis, San Francisco, Baltimore, Philadelphia, and Chicago, the urban business elite monopolized park government and ruled the expanding park systems with some degree of autonomy, whether formal or informal. Throughout the nation, lawmakers had protected park government from the forays of ward politicians and the urban populace.

Much the same pattern prevailed among city library boards. Again, these bodies were insulated from the influence of the aldermen and the much-maligned political leaders, and, again, they were the special responsibility of the community's social and economic lords. In some cities plutocratic benefactors dominated library government, and elsewhere trustees were subject to the benign influence of boards of education. Virtually everywhere, however, the trustees were recruited from the social register.

In both Baltimore and Pittsburgh private benefactors provided the initial funds for public libraries and also established boards of trustees chosen by co-option. In 1882 millionaire Enoch Pratt gave the city of Baltimore $833,000, with the understanding that the city council would create a perpetual annuity of $50,000 for library expenses. Pratt also stipulated that political or religious considerations should not influence the choice of library trustees and officers. To ensure that the board was to his liking, Pratt himself selected the first trustees and personally assumed the post of president of the board. The trustees enjoyed life tenure and filled, by co-option, any vacancies on the board due to death or resignation. Though the city of Baltimore was the recipient of the benefaction, Pratt guaranteed that the mayor and councilmen had virtually no control over the institution. Instead, power rested with the nine trustees named by Pratt, five of whom were millionaires and two of whom were future members of the national cabinet. These distinguished gentlemen remained in charge decade after decade, and three of the original members were still on the board in 1920, after thirty-seven years of service.[81]

In the 1890s steel baron Andrew Carnegie emulated Pratt's example and donated $1 million for the construction of a central library buildling in Pittsburgh and a system of neighborhood branches throughout the city. Carnegie did not grant a permanent endowment for operating expenses but required the city to appropriate annually not less than $40,000 for library maintenance. The millionaire also provided that he be allowed to name half of the eighteen-person library commission and that these nine Carnegie trustees have life tenure, vacancies being filled by co-option. The other half of the commission consisted of the mayor and representatives of the city council and board of education, ensuring some public control over the expenditure of the city's annual appropriation, which in 1899 amounted to $104,000. Carnegie's trustees represented the business elite, and at least five of the nine were millionaires—including the board's treasurer, the great steel manufacturer Henry Clay Frick, and the chairman of the board's Auditing Committee, the young banker Andrew Mellon.[82] Carnegie permitted greater public control than had Pratt, but in Pittsburgh, as in Baltimore, life-tenure plutocrats enjoyed the power to block any action by those responsible to the city's voters.

No single benefactor played such a dominant role as Pratt or Carnegie in the founding of municipal libraries in Philadelphia or New York City, but there, too, the public libraries were the responsibility of self-elected, elite board spending public appropriations as well as private endowments. In 1894 the Philadelphia city council created the Board of Trustees of the Free Library of Philadelphia, consisting of the mayor, the presidents of both branches of the bicameral council, one citizen elected annually by each branch of the council, and eighteen private citizens who enjoyed life tenure. All vacancies among the eighteen private citizens on the board were to "be filled alternately by the said board and by the Mayor."[83] Again, co-option and life tenure characterized the government of the municipal library, even though the preponderance of library funds came from public tax levies and city appropriations. In 1897 New York City committed itself for the first time to the large-scale financing of library facilities. Guiding the development of the New York Public Library was a self-perpetuating body of twenty-one gentlemen serving for life. During the second half of the 1890s nineteen of these twenty-one were to be found in the social register, and four were among the social arbiter Ward McAllister's "Four Hundred" leaders of New York City society. In 1899 the city comptroller did win an ex officio position on the board, as did the mayor and president of the Board of Aldermen in 1902. But in the late 1890s the New York Public Library was not publicly administered, much to the distress of the city's Mayor Van Wyck, who fumed about "this system of fostering private control of public institutions."[84]

Other cities also resorted to self-perpetuating boards for the government of publicly funded libraries. As early as 1878 the California legislature created a Board of Trustees chosen by co-option to establish and govern San Francisco's Public Library. Framers of the measure preferred an autonomous and self-elected board as insurance against political control, but they failed to provide the board with an independent tax levy and left it dependent on the appropriations of San Francisco's Board of Supervisors.[85] In 1878 Wisconsin's legislature likewise created a board of library trustees for Milwaukee and included among its members the president of the school board, the superintendent of schools, three persons appointed by the mayor from among the city councilmen, and four trustees listed by name in the statute who were to serve four-year terms. At the close of the four-year terms, the board itself was to fill the vacancies. In other words, co-option was the means of electing four of Milwaukee's nine trustees, and, as usual, these four represented the city's elite and generally remained on the board as long as they wished.[86] Similarly, in 1896 in New Orleans the city council established a public library board that was a self-perpetuating body of life-tenure directors. New Orleans's mayor was an ex officio member, but the remaining directors supervised library expenditures without fear of voter retaliation or electoral ouster.[87]

In a number of American cities, however, members of the library board were not self-elected but were chosen by the local board of education. The popularly elected members of Cleveland's Board of Education appointed that city's library board, and before 1891 Cincinnati's school board likewise named the city's library trustees. Prior to 1893 the Saint Louis Public Library was under the control of the Board of Education, and during these same years the Indianapolis school commissioners governed that city's public library. Libraries usually were not under the control of the politicized city council or mayor's office. Instead, nineteenth-century lawmakers deemed school board supervision safer and more appropriate.

In a few major cities such as Chicago and Boston, however, the library trustees were limited-tenure mayoral nominees subject to confirmation by the council. Yet even in these cities the boards enjoyed some autonomy and were not the creatures of ward politicians. Illinois's legislature authorized an independent library levy that was meant to ensure financial freedom for Chicago's trustees but that actually led to feuding between the library board and the city council. And in Boston the board, while formally responsible to the mayor and council, was, in fact, an independent body of gentlemanly bibliophiles that administered the public library and defended it against politics and the misguided will of the public. In 1877 friends of Boston's Public Library became aroused by the city council's slashing of salaries, and recognizing "the danger to which the Library is liable to be exposed by . . . the action of the City Council," a committee investigating library operations recommended that the institution "be placed upon an independent basis" through passage of an act of incorporation.[88] The following year the state legislature responded to this proposal and adopted an act of incorporation that specifically defined the authority of the library trustees and clearly granted them sole control of personnel questions. According to the superintendent of the public library, this state law "practically limited the interference of the city government to defining the gross limits of expenditures."[89] Though seemingly the agent of the mayor and council, the Boston Board of Trustees was, according to one late-nineteenth-century critic, "about as close a corporation as could well be devised . . . , composed of five excellent gentlemen, of high character and similar social position, who live near each other in the Back Bay district." Writing in 1892, this observer contended that "as the Mayor would naturally wish to appoint only such new members as would be acceptable to the older trustees, there is very little chance of new influences to get at the library."[90] In other words, the same Brahmin class of old-stock Harvard graduates with homes along fashionable Beacon Street ruled the Boston library decade after decade.

Major urban libraries were, then, governed by benevolent oligarchies. Library directors regarded the public libraries as a trust to be protected from the people for the benefit of the people. Literature and urban democracy did not yet appear compatible, and to preserve the former, lawmakers believed they might reasonably compromise the latter. Urban America would not yet allow the Callaghans and O'Haras to administer the legacy of Homer and Shakespeare. In some cases the existence of private endowments seemed to justify a degree of control by self-elected trustees. But in city after city, elite boards were expending public as well as private monies with little interference from elected officials.

In a few cities autonomous plutocratic commissions also administered the municipality's investments and sinking funds. By creating these boards, lawmakers again sought to remove a vital area of municipal business from the purview of politicians. Sinking funds used for the retirement of the municipal debt needed to be protected from money-hungry elected officials. And municipal investments and trust funds could not be left in the hands of those objects of suspicion, the ward aldermen. In the minds of many Americans financial prudence too often seemed at odds with representative government. Consequently, some cities assigned responsibility for sinking funds and investments to the wealthiest and most successful businessmen, providing yet another oligarchic check on urban democracy.

In Ohio's two leading cities, the sinking-fund commissions were independent boards with an elite membership. Cleveland's commission dated from 1862, when the Ohio legislature placed the municipality's railroad stocks and bonds in the hands of a self-perpetuating board. The act of 1862 specifically named the first members of the board, who had life tenure and could fill any vacancies due to death or resignation. They were to administer the city's stocks and bonds and use the profit from these investments to redeem the principal of the municipal debt. Throughout the last four decades of the nineteenth century, the city's holdings were in capable hands, for the men who served on the Sinking Fund Commission were well acquainted with earning profits. They were Cleveland's wealthiest citizens, and millionaire Henry B. Payne, one of the founders of the Payne-Whitney fortune, was president of the commission from 1862 until his death in 1896.[91] In 1877 Ohio's legislature created a sinking fund for Cincinnati, and again lawmakers ensured that city investments would not fall into the hands of ward politicians on the city council or anyone indebted to the council for appointment or confirmation. The judges of the Cincinnati Superior Court appointed that city's commissioners, who served five-year terms. As in Cleveland, Cincinnati's commission was a stronghold of the city's most influential businessmen and included among its members representatives of the aristocratic Longworth family and the powerful Taft clan. At the close of the century four of its five members were acknowledged millionaires.[92]

In 1880 Louisiana legislators followed the example of the Ohio cities and created a life-tenure, self-perpetuating board of prominent bankers and businessmen to administer the municipal debt of New Orleans. According to the leading authority on the New Orleans Board of Liquidation of the City Debt, the state legislature established this agency so that the "bonded indebtedness of the city should be cared for in a manner absolutely free from political considerations or influences."[93] During the following two decades this independent board, headed by a millionaire banker, refinanced the city's burdensome debt, selling the new municipal bond issues to those local banks that the board members controlled. Free from the pressures of the public or of politics, New Orleans business leaders, like their affluent brethren in Cleveland and Cincinnati, administered the municipal indebtedness in accord with their own perceptions of the public interest.

Philadelphia's municipal holdings were controlled by equally prosperous gentlemen. A commission consisting of the mayor, the comptroller, and a mayoral appointee administered Philadelphia's sinking fund, but the city was also the fortunate beneficiary of thirty-nine substantial private bequests, and these municipal funds and properties were in the hands of the Board of Directors of City Trusts. Pennsylvania's legislature created this board of directors in 1869 to ensure the proper management of these legacies, and the state lawmakers provided that the board include the mayor, the presidents of each branch of the bicameral city council, and twelve members of unlimited tenure appointed by the judges of the Pennsylvania Supreme Court, the district court, and the Philadelphia County Court of Common Pleas. As in the case of the Philadelphia park commission, the directors of the city trusts were judicial appointees and not nominees of the mayor subject to city council confirmation. And like the park commission, the city trust board was a conclave of wealth; fourteen of the fifteen members in 1895 were in the city bluebook, and most were downtown business leaders accustomed to handling large sums of money. By the 1890s these judicial appointees administered city trusts worth more than $25 million, trusts that supported a college and a hospital as well as providing funds for the poor and needy.[94]

Thus, during the late nineteenth century cities throughout the nation relied on boards or commissions protected from direct popular control, insulated from the undue influence of the city's aldermen, and dominated by those perched proudly on the top rung of the urban social ladder. These boards included representatives of such patrician families as the Biddles in Philadelphia, the Longworths in Cincinnati, and the Chouteaus in Saint Louis, but also among the board members were such ostentatiously wealthy robber barons as Peter Widener, Henry Frick, and Potter Palmer. Together these representatives of wealth, both old and new, were to play a leading role in the government of city parks, public libraries, and municipal investments. If the ward and the neighborhood were the bailiwick of the alderman, the park and the library were the millionaire's preserves.

Perhaps the most significant autonomous commissions, however, were the boards of education. Virtually everyone claimed to believe that schools, like parks and libraries, should remain free of partisan politics, and few proposed that highly politicized city councils should directly control the development of young minds. Good-government reformers feared the desecration of learning by ward bosses, and even such professional politicians as Cincinnati's Republican boss George Cox and San Francisco's Democratic leader Christopher Buckley mouthed opposition to political maneuvering among the members of the board of education. Nothing could arouse the furor of voters like charges of partisan tampering with the schools, and party bosses found excessive interference with education to be a sure path to defeat in the next election. Yet at the same time most urban Americans believed in popular control of school government and would not have accepted irresponsible self-elected boards of education modeled after the self-perpetuating library commissions. Rich and poor alike sent their children to school, and the operation of the schools personally affected the lives of an overwhelming majority of families in the city. Parents who never went to the public library and were willing to yield control of that institution to the elite did send their offspring to the neighborhood school and thus had a personal stake in public education. Similarly, those who failed to understand sinking-fund investments and were ready to abdicate supervision of that subject to financial experts did know when their child failed to learn the alphabet or suffered punishment at the hands of a teacher. School government was, then, a subject of vital concern to a broad swath of society, and the boards of education had to remain responsible to the public. What urban Americans seemed to demand in the 1880s and 1890s was nonpolitical but popular control of the schools. The people called for some say in the determination of school policy, and most urban dwellers were not willing to let politicians act as their interpreters.

The result in many cities was popular election of school boards, combined with a persistent fear of those by-products of the electoral process, the ward bosses. In New York City and Chicago the mayors appointed the boards of education, but in Boston, Saint Louis, Detroit, Cleveland, Cincinnati, Indianapolis, and San Francisco city voters elected the school boards. Baltimore's municipal council chose the commissioners of the public schools for that city, and in Philadelphia members of the central school board were appointed by the county judges, whereas the voters elected those on the ward school committees. Modes of selection differed, but lawmakers generally sought to preserve popular control. Direct election rather than appointment by the mayor or council proved the most common means for choosing school board members, and in 1897 thirty-two of the fifty-two cities in the United States with over 50,000 population elected their boards of education.[95]

Yet in most cities popular control also meant election or appointment by wards, and this supposedly opened the schoolhouse door to neighborhood politicians, a class that upper-middle-class metropolitan leaders stereotyped as venal and lowbred. Of those cities that ranked among the nation's ten largest in the late nineteenth century, all but Chicago, Boston, and San Francisco elected or appointed school board members by wards or allocated some authority over neighborhood schools to ward or district boards. New York City, Philadelphia, and Brooklyn each maintained ward or neighborhood school committees, as well as a central coordinating board for the city as a whole.[96] And in many other cities there were central school boards that, like the city councils, generally consisted of neighborhood leaders who represented the interests of their wards and were dedicated to winning favors for their bailiwicks. These ward-based school boards did not include such an elite personnel as the city park or library boards. To be sure, fewer saloonkeepers filled school board seats than aldermanic positions, and more professionals, especially neighborhood physicians, served on the boards of education than on city councils. But school boards were certainly not the realm of the patrician or the downtown business leader. Elected representatives of the less fashionable classes were present at board meetings, seeking to satisfy the demands of their constituents even though these demands might conflict with the business judgment of their social betters and the pedagogical wisdom of the growing cadre of educational experts.

By the late 1880s and the 1890s attacks on this neighborhood-based school government were rising to a shrill peak as reformers sought to ensure a centralized administration of the city's schools, one that would be dominated by those who were presumably best able to rule: the city's successful business leaders and the educational professionals. In Saint Louis a Washington University professor favored at-large election of school board members rather than ward election, because he believed members elected by the entire city electorate would enjoy freedom from that "bane of good administration of city affairs in any branch of its government—the ward politician."[97] The superintendent of schools of Saint Paul, Minnesota, claimed that in his city the "one great foe to the success of the schools has been the local interests represented by the members from the different wards" who have created a "lack of unity and the possibility of demagoguery."[98] In New York City and Philadelphia the thrust of the attack was on the ward-level committees, which had the power to appoint teachers and administer neighborhood school facilities. In 1891 a critic of Philadelphia's schools told the Pennsylvania Senate that the neighborhood boards were "made up for the most part of the worst element of ward politics." And another Philadelphian claimed that some of the ward-level board members "can scarcely read and write."[99] In 1895 Columbia University's Nicholas Murray Butler expressed much passion, if only partial truth, when he described New York City's ward trustees as "utterly unknown and insignificant persons, often active local politicians, and not always . . . above preying upon the schools."[100] Butler may have exaggerated the sinister political character of the maligned trustees, but he was generally correct in his contemptuous description of them as "utterly unknown and insignificant persons." Ward representatives were, for the most part, persons with only a neighborhood reputation and were not business figures or professionals who were known throughout the city. They were not the type who would ever win a seat on the park board, the library board, or the sinking fund commission, or ever occupy the office of mayor or comptroller. And Butler felt that they were also not the type who should play a major role in the government of city schools.

Especially upsetting to proponents of centralized school administration were the frequent accounts of petty factional squabbles among ward school directors. For example, in 1895 in Philadelphia's Fifth Ward a "lively row" developed over a proposed flag-raising ceremony. A majority of the neighborhood board wished to invite as speaker for the occasion a political leader associated with the Republican party faction led by Matthew Quay. Anti-Quay Republicans on the board opposed the move, and among the opponents was the chairman of the board's committee on property, who had charge of the flags. He said point-blank that there would be no flag raising unless the board invited anti-Quay speakers as well. Meanwhile, the Fifth Ward board also split over the question of whether to hire pro-Quay school janitors or anti-Quay school janitors.[101] Such disputes were not unusual, and in the minds of critics such as Nicholas Murray Butler this political pettiness offered evidence of the need for a change.

The days of ward power, however, were numbered, and during the 1890s foes of ward-based school government won one victory after another. In 1891 Saint Paul, Minnesota, abandoned ward representation, and in 1892 Cleveland discarded election by wards and adopted instead a seven-member school board elected at large. Five years later reformers likewise succeeded in eliminating neighborhood representation in Saint Louis and required board candidates to win the favor of a citywide electorate in at-large contests. Meanwhile, in 1896 lawmakers in Albany responded to the wishes of Nicholas Murray Butler and abolished New York City's ward trustees, thereby enhancing the authority of the mayoral appointees on the central board of education. And in 1905 Philadelphia's ward school committees finally succumbed to the forces of centralization.

As neighborhood representation disappeared, the social composition of school boards shifted, with downtown business leaders and prestigious professionals gaining greater control over school matters. Saint Paul's school superintendent noted proudly that the city's first at-large board of education consisted of "two bank presidents, men of high standing in the business community; two college presidents, two editors, and a physician."[102] In Saint Louis only one-third of the members of the ward-based school board of 1896 were among those listed in the city's bluebook, but in 1897, after the abandonment of ward representation, three-fourths of the new at-large board could claim that social distinction.[103] In the 1890s only about 10 percent of New York City's ward trustees were listed in the social register, but approximately one-third of the members of the newly powerful central Board of Education were listed there. Moreover, during the early 1890s less than 40 percent of the ward trustees lived in the more affluent residential areas north of Fourteenth Street in New York City, whereas in 1897, following the centralization of educational authority, at least eighteen of the twenty-one members of New York City's Board of Education resided in uptown neighborhoods.[104] With the abolition of the ward trustees, the populous working-class neighborhoods on the lower East Side of Manhattan no longer had a direct voice in school government. For in the 1890s, education became the responsibility of those living uptown.

Just as lawmakers progressively deprived the less fashionable ward aldermen of power and enhanced the authority of the respectable element in the executive branch, so they were also eliminating the ward representatives from school government. In city after city neighborhood power was yielding to centralization, and the ward leader was losing authority to those who claimed to speak for the metropolis as a whole. Yet in most municipalities the school board, unlike the park commission or library board, remained directly responsible to the urban electorate. Boards of education were becoming a bit more gentrified, but direct election remained the most common mode of selecting board members, and this popular check prevented the boards from becoming closed corporations with an elite personnel.

School boards thus differed from the other prominent autonomous commissions. In the case of all the various independent boards, autonomy was intended to serve as a bulwark against that much criticized practice known as politics. Yet when lawmakers created independent park commissions and library boards, they often excluded not only politics but also popular control. Boards of education, in contrast, remained responsible to the urban public. Fears of sinister schemes by ward politicians might have limited the expression of grassroots sentiment through neighborhood representatives. But the business elite did not displace the voter totally, for the electorate retained access to the ballot box.

THE BALANCED STRUCTURE OF URBAN OFFICIALDOM

The second half of the nineteenth century was a period of great change in the social and economic fabric of the American city, and it was also an era of adjustment and revision in the structure of urban government. As the compact, homogeneous city yielded to the sprawling heterogeneous metropolis, the simple council-dominated government of the early 1800s gave way to a more complex framework of redistributed authority and balanced power. The new framework of the 1870s, 1880s, and 1890s allowed for greater centralization and continuing neighborhood power, for coordination as well as fragmentation. Thus the comptroller became citywide financial czar, yet the alderman remained satrap of his ward domain. It was not a simple structure readily diagrammed by that emerging corps of political scientists dedicated to clear lines of authority and neat blueprints of rule. But it was a structure adapted to the complicated city of the late nineteenth century. This balanced structure accommodated the neighborhood while bolstering the power of the central authorities in city hall. It was, then, a system adapted to the geographical tensions of periphery versus core, east side versus west side.

Likewise, the structure of municipal officialdom was adapted to the social tensions of the age. It permitted immigrant newcomers to exercise a strong voice in the city councils and to wield authority over their own neighborhoods. Yet those native-born businessmen who had long exercised authority in urban America remained at the helm of the executive branch. Irish politicians may have been crowding these traditional leaders by the last decades of the nineteenth century, but the downtown businessman and professional definitely retained a role in the system of urban rule. And with a fickle disregard for notions of democracy, the framers of this structure were willing to grant millionaire benefactors such private domains of authority as the park commissions and library boards. Just as the system achieved geographic balance, so it maintained a careful social balance, reserving various niches of authority for the diverse social elements of the city.

Moreover, the officeholders in the municipal structure exercised real authority. Mayors, comptrollers, commissioners, and even aldermen were not necessarily marionettes dangling at the end of strings manipulated by political bosses. Many of the executive officers were independent figures who made decisions and sought to implement them. The mayor and comptroller usually were not party hacks mindlessly doing the bidding of a political organization. They were successful persons of established prestige who bargained with party leaders but generally refused to play the role of lackey. Even an alderman's power did not depend on his devotion to the dominant political faction, but rested on the tradition of aldermanic courtesy. He had power over his ward by virtue of his office and not simply because he had won the favor of a Tammany nabob. The formal officials of urban America were, then, significant figures worthy of serious consideration. They cannot be dismissed as faceless stooges, for they exercised power vital to the molding of the American city.

Yet others also participated in the government of the nation's cities. And among the leading makers of American municipal government were the state legislators. They enacted the charters that outlined the distribution of municipal authority. In addition, they heard endless requests for urban legislation and acted as the court of last resort for those frustrated by the inactivity of the mayor, the commission, or the council. The story of municipal government is incomplete without a recital of the state legislator's role in the system of urban rule.

4 STATE LEGISLATURES AND URBAN AMERICA

 State legislative interference is one of the chief bogeys in American urban history. Traditional accounts speak of the nineteenth-century heyday of special legislation as a benighted era, a dark age during which state lawmakers maliciously meddled with city government. Urban reformers of the early twentieth century, whose fervor sometimes outpaced their knowledge, wrote of state control, state "repression," "the bondage of cities," "the wilder excesses of legislative domination," and the plethora of "legislative atrocities."[1] In 1916 the most learned expert on municipal home rule denounced "the whole miserable practice of legislative 'interference,'" and virtually no one at the time would have challenged this view.[2] More recently, historians have related sad accounts of municipalities seeking added powers from state legislatures that "were hostile to the cities" and dominated by lawmakers "who were suspicious of all things urban."[3] Volume after volume has depicted this age as a period of urban thralldom preceding the liberating enlightenment of municipal home rule.

Too often, however, accounts of late-nineteenth century urban legislation have been simplistic, superficial, and incomplete. Early-twentieth-century reformers saw the horrors they wanted to see, and historians have frequently accepted reform rhetoric as absolute truth. There are enough notorious examples of the evils of legislative meddling to lend credence to the traditional account, and the principles of nineteenth-century law seem to support the concept of the enslaved city. In principle, nineteenth-century cities were creatures of the legislature and agents of the state, and in principle, lacking a constitutional provision to the contrary, state lawmakers could limit the powers of the cities, revise their charters, or destroy them at will. A long series of judicial decisions had clearly enunciated this relationship from the first half of the nineteenth century onward, and despite some rhetoric about "the inherent right of local self-government," it was the judicial rule of thumb from the 1870s through the 1890s.[4] A superficial examination of urban history, then, would tend to support the notion of cities prostrate before the feet of rural and small-town lawmakers.

Practice, however, does not necessarily accord with principle, and the realities of lawmaking often deviate from the dictates of the legal treatise. This is especially true with regard to the thousands of special laws concerning city government enacted during the late nineteenth century. For though state legislatures were potentially masters of the city, throughout much of the United States they were actually compliant servants of urban spokesmen. Legislative procedure and custom differed from state to state, but in most areas devotion to local self-rule was a powerful sentiment, and state lawmakers deferred to local representatives rather than defied them. State legislatures had the legal authority to browbeat localities, but the American tradition of localism limited their exercise of that authority. Special legislation dealing with city government was not, then, primarily a product of rural antagonism or the centralizing tendencies of the state. Instead, these laws largely reflected the needs and desires of the urban area, and at every stage of the legislative process local leaders were in control of local measures and guided their destinies. State legislation was not a strait jacket for the cities so much as a ready means of adapting to the fast-changing realities of a rapidly industrializing and urbanizing society. And urban legislators exploited this means, fashioning volumes of special urban measures.

THE LEGISLATIVE PROCESS

The first step in the lawmaking process was the framing of local legislation by local interests. Rural legislators did not write the laws that governed the city; they were lucky if they could keep abreast of legislation vital to their own constituents. Instead, city councils, city attorneys, chambers of commerce, good-government groups, and lawyers serving urban contractors or real estate speculators drafted special legislation for the urban areas. Harried state solons confronted by eight or nine hundred bills during a ninety-day session did not make law so much as enact it. The source of urban legislation was the city itself.

Charter measures were usually the product of a local body. For example, good-government reformers and a joint committee of the Philadelphia City Councils fashioned the blueprint for that city's Bullitt charter enacted in 1885.[5] Buffalo's charter of 1891 was primarily the handiwork of the good-government Citizens Association, and a charter commission authorized by the city council and appointed by the mayor drafted Baltimore's charter of 1898.[6] In Ohio, Cincinnati's charter of 1891 was modeled after a proposal made by the city's Commercial Club, and Cleveland's charter of the same year was a compromise presented by local Republicans and Democrats.[7] A municipal reform convention sponsored by the local Board of Trade drafted the framework of Columbus's charter of 1893.[8] In Wisconsin a popularly elected convention had drafted Milwaukee's charter of 1852, and in 1874 the Milwaukee City Council devised a new framework of urban rule.[9] A charter committee of the city council, headed by the city attorney, wrote Minneapolis's revised charter of 1881.[10] Saint Louis's charter of 1866 was a product of a city charter convention, and the city auditor prepared the proposed revision of 1871.[11] And in 1874 a mass meeting of Kansas City (Missouri) residents chose a committee of thirteen headed by the mayor to frame that municipality's new charter.[12] Indeed, throughout the nation, local leaders—not farmer-legislators— were assuming responsibility for drafting charter measures and other bills vital to the government of their cities.

After city councilmen or interested citizens drafted proposals for the government of Philadelphia, Saint Louis, or San Francisco, they would hand the proposal to a local assemblyman or senator for presentation to the legislature. It was an unwritten rule that the member from the locality affected introduced local bills, and amendments or suggestions from members residing elsewhere were rare. The needs of a local constituency were the responsibility of the representative of that constituency. The exact code of legislative etiquette differed from state to state, but as with the earlier-discussed tradition of aldermanic courtesy, it was generally considered improper to interfere with a local bill that did not affect one's own territory. Thus the local representative was in charge of local bills regarding his district, and it was his duty to shepherd the legislation through both houses of the legislature.

In fact, in the West and most of the Midwest, the local delegation for all practical purposes constituted a standing committee that debated, revised, and approved or disapproved local legislation. The legislature regularly referred city charter proposals and other local bills to the local delegation, and this delegation held the power of life and death over these measures. The unwritten rules of the legislature prevented outside legislators from intervening, for the locality was accorded the right to determine its own fate through its duly elected representatives.

In state after state this pattern of deference to the local delegation prevailed. During the early 1870s the Missouri legislature automatically referred all legislation dealing exclusively with the city of Saint Louis to the representatives and senators from Saint Louis County.[13] Likewise, local legislation involving Minneapolis went to the Hennepin County delegation, and the Milwaukee charter revision of 1874 "being . . . merely local . . . was referred to the Milwaukee delegation."[14] Indeed, throughout the following quarter of a century the Milwaukee delegation was the vital channel through which all Milwaukee legislation had to flow, in addition to being the body that received representatives from the city council, heard their petitions, amended their proposals, and sanctioned or defeated their schemes.[15] In Colorado, bills dealing solely with Denver went immediately to the Arapahoe County delegation. Farther west, California's legislature referred all local measures to the delegation representing the affected locality and consistently deferred to that delegation's judgment. And no delegation was so heavily burdened with local bills as was San Francisco's. Prior to the adoption of a state home-rule provision in 1879, bills affecting every aspect of San Francisco municipal government went to that city's delegation, which either amended the measures, squelched them, or recommended their passage.

The vital role of the local delegation was also evident in Ohio, with its great urban centers of Cincinnati and Cleveland. Though Ohio's legislative procedure varied somewhat during the 1870s, 1880s, and 1890s, the legislature frequently assigned consideration of Cleveland legislation to the Cuyahoga County delegation, while Cincinnati's measures went to Hamilton County's senators and representatives. For example, during the sessions of 1891 and 1892 the Ohio House of Representatives referred a total of seventy-eight local bills to the Hamilton delegation and forty-three to the members from Cuyahoga County. In 1891 when the legislature was considering new charters for both Cincinnati and Cleveland, the local delegations were given a decisive voice in determining the legal framework of their cities. The house of representatives referred Cincinnati's proposed charter to a select committee consisting of the entire Hamilton County delegation together with the Standing Committee on Municipal Affairs;[16] Cincinnati's spokesmen dominated this special committee, with nine of the sixteen members hailing from Hamilton County. Cleveland's charter proposal went to a select committee consisting of the entire Cuyahoga County delegation plus three outsiders, with the result that Clevelanders had a two-thirds majority on the committee.[17] And the senate referred Cleveland's charter bill to a select committee consisting solely of Cleveland's two senators.[18]

Even when the local delegations did not receive such a bounty of measures, Ohio's largest cities were not prostrate before the power of the small towns and rural areas. For during the 1890s, in instances when the senate failed to refer local bills involving Cleveland and Cincinnati to the local delegations, it assigned them to the Municipal Corporations Committee Number One, a standing committee that dealt solely with Cincinnati and Cleveland measures.[19] In accord with the prevailing pattern of deference to local opinion, a majority of the members of the committee was always from Cuyahoga and Hamilton counties, and the committee chairman was consistently from Cleveland or Cincinnati. Though outsiders could serve on the committee, the big cities dominated committee action, and urban interests were not subject to rural whim.

A similar situation existed in the Indiana legislature, where the house and senate standing committees on Indianapolis handled all special legislation dealing with that state's biggest metropolis. During the 1880s and 1890s the house committee included all six members of the Indianapolis delegation constituting two-thirds of the committee membership. And by the 1890s Indianapolis's four senators likewise controlled the seven-man Senate Committee on Indianapolis. Indianapolis charter amendments, bills fixing the salaries of councilmen, measures creating park boards, and legislation regulating street-car fares all went to the committees on Indianapolis, whose members had ultimate power over the proposals. Legislators from outside the city partici-pated in committee deliberations, but they represented a minority.

In like manner, Chicago's lawmakers could usually decide the destiny of legislation dealing with the municipal government of their city. The Illinois Constitution of 1870 prohibited special legislation pertaining to individual cities, and in 1872 the Illinois legislature passed a general act granting the state's municipalities unusual latitude in framing their own governments. As a result, Illinois solons enacted relatively few special measures dealing with the city government of Chicago. But when Chicago bills did appear before the legislature, Cook County representatives enjoyed the upper hand, because in every legislature from 1883 to 1899, a majority of the House Committee on Municipal Corporations hailed from Cook County. In some legislatures of this period, Cook County spokesmen held a two-to-one majority on this vital committee.[20] Thus measures dealing with the municipal government of Chi-cago almost always reflected the will of the Cook County representatives.

In the largest cities of the South the local delegation likewise controlled the legislative process for local bills. The Maryland legislature referred all such measures to the delegation from the county affected, and the delegation from the city of Baltimore was no exception. Baltimore representatives and sena-tors introduced all city bills and constituted a select committee to consider these proposals. Measures dealing with the waterworks, police, streetcars, and city parks were all the responsibility of the city delegation, and generally the city representatives and senators alone decided the fate of proposals affecting Maryland's metropolis.[21]

The same was true in Louisiana, where the legislature granted New Or-leans's elected spokesmen autocratic authority over city issues. During the late nineteenth century New Orleans measures before the Louisiana House of Rep-resentatives went either to the Committee on City Affairs or the Committee on the Liquidation of the City Debt. From 1886 to 1900 every member on both committees was an elected representative of Orleans parish. Orleans spokes-men alone considered New Orleans measures in committee, for no outsiders served on these vital committees. Similarly, in the Louisiana Senate, Orleans senators almost always constituted an overwhelming majority of the member-ship of the Committee on New Orleans, the average committee during the 1880s and 1890s consisting of six Orleans members and three outsiders. Thus local lawmakers determined whether the Orleans Levee District deserved ad-ditional taxing authority, whether reform of the New Orleans Police Board was necessary, and whether the city indebtedness was properly administered.

Even on the most vital questions, the legislature allowed Orleans members broad latitude. In 1880 the house of representatives referred consideration of a new city charter to a special committee that consisted of all twenty-three Orleans members and only five outsiders.[22] If New Orleans was to have a new charter, it would be a charter fashioned by the elected representatives of the city and not by those elected from distant rural districts. Sharp animosity between the city and rural areas was a persistent theme in nineteenth-century Louisiana history. However, this did not mean that rural lawmakers sought to rule New Orleans. Instead, each side remained responsible for its own camp, and neither invaded the other's realm. In 1901 a leading New Orleans citizen observed that the "members of the legislature from other parts of the state have never forced on New Orleans legislation opposed by the members elected by the people of the city."[23]

In the Northeast, the local delegation seemed to enjoy fewer prerogatives than in the South, West, or Midwest, but even so, urban measures were not subject to unchecked rural tyranny, and farmers and small-town residents generally had only limited opportunities to toy with the city's fortunes. Occasionally, the Pennsylvania legislature formally referred local bills to the local delegation, and legislative etiquette seems to have ensured Pittsburgh and Philadelphia legislators preeminent authority over measures affecting those cities. When a delegate to Pennsylvania's Constitutional Convention of 1873 complained of state interference with Philadelphia questions, another delegate interrupted and asked, "Does not the gentleman know that all questions affecting the interests of the city of Philadelphia are remitted absolutely to the members from this city, and that they arrange the passage or defeat of the bill?"[24] Moreover, throughout the late nineteenth century big-city senators and representatives dominated the Pennsylvania standing committees on municipal affairs. During the years 1887 through 1896, Allegheny County and Philadelphia legislators together constituted at least half the membership of both the house and senate municipal committees, even though the two counties together elected only one-fourth of the state legislators.[25] Urban representatives and senators sought appointments on those committees that most directly affected their districts, and the speaker of the house and president of the senate, who made Pennsylvania's committee assignments, recognized that urban legislators should have the most prominent voice in urban affairs.

In Massachusetts the tendency to defer to spokesmen of the locality was also evident, especially during the last decade of the century. At this time a trio of metropolitan boards governed the water, sewerage, and park systems of the Greater Boston area, and from 1895 onward all local legislation involving the metropolitan boards or the city of Boston was referred to the Metropolitan Affairs Committee of the house and senate. In accordance with the principle that local representatives should handle local issues, the Metropolitan Affairs Committee consisted solely of members from the metropolitan region. The distribution of members on the committee approximated the distribution of population in the metropolitan area, with 40 percent to 50 percent of the members coming from Boston. By the 1890s Boston legislation was, then, subject to extensive interference by suburban legislators, but was relatively insulated from the meddling of lawmakers living outside the greater metropolis.

The line between a local and a general question, however, was not always clear, and during the first weeks of its existence, hostile legislators forced Boston's Metropolitan Affairs Committee to define and defend its realm. Dispute over the new committee arose in January 1895, when the issue of an additional reservoir for the metropolitan area came before the legislature. The proposed scheme called for diversion of the Nashua River, destruction of the rural village of Boylston, and flooding of portions of other country towns. It was a question vital to the metropolis but also crucial to those residents of the Nashua River watershed living beyond Greater Boston. A number of legislators thus urged assignment of the measure to the Committee on Water Supply, claiming that the "committee on metropolitan affairs is made up only of men who live within the metropolitan district" and that the "people of the rest of the State should have something to say when the subject arises." This argument proved convincing, and the water committee initially won assignment of the plan. State house observers began to wonder whether the metropolitan committee ever should have been created, "inasmuch as it was calculated to excite the jealousy of the rural members against the city folk, and so defeat its best directed efforts." But sparring between the two committees continued, with the result that within two weeks the legislators compromised and referred the Nashua River project to both committees sitting jointly.[26] In a case such as this where the interests of an urban locality impinged on the welfare of a rural district, the simple rule of deference proved inadequate, for rural members were not willing to surrender abjectly to their urban colleagues. However, when the question clearly involved only Greater Boston, spokesmen from Lowell or Boylston would not be expected to intervene.

Even in New York, state lawmakers were willing to extend some logrolling courtesies and grant urban legislators notable influence over city measures. As early as 1846 a Brooklyn delegate to the state constitutional convention complained that the typical municipal charter "is a piece of empiricism by the wiseacres of the place where it is to be put in force," and "no one except the representative from that locality cares what it contains." As a result, said the delegate, "every city may be said to be a law unto itself; and the sovereignty of the state, instead of being exercised in . . . [the city's] behalf, is absolutely surrendered to it, to be used at its own discretion."[27] Moreover, a special committee of the New York Senate investigating municipal problems in 1891 listed first among "the chief difficulties which underlie the government of cities in [the] State" the "too frequent yielding on the part of the Legislature to the importunities of representatives of the various cities for the passage of special local bills."[28] And the following year an upstate legislator summed up the feelings of many of his rural colleagues when he commented on a New

York City bill: "It is not in good taste, I think, for a member from a country district to oppose a bill that six of the seven senators from New York vote for."[29] "Good taste" thus dictated that New York City's legislators decide whether a New York City bill passed.

The pattern of committee assignments in New York also guaranteed some protection for urban interests. As in Pennsylvania, big-city legislators dominated the assembly Committee on City Affairs. In every New York legislature from 1882 to the end of the century, the representatives of New York City, Brooklyn, and Buffalo constituted a majority of the committee, with the minority usually consisting of spokesmen from Syracuse, Rochester, Albany, and one or two small-town or rural members. New York's speaker of the house, like his counterpart in Pennsylvnia, recognized the preeminent right of city representatives to handle city questions.

Yet, New York City representatives did not enjoy the power over local bills that the San Francisco, Milwaukee, Saint Louis, or Baltimore delegations, for example, exercised. Legislators from Syracuse and Oswego headed the senate committee on cities during the 1880s and 1890s, and Senator Clarence Lexow, who represented rural Rockland County, played a much-publicized role in the history of city legislation during the 1890s. Lexow chaired a famous investigation of the New York City Police Department, headed the committee to define the boundaries of Greater New York, and drafted the bill for the consolidation of the metropolitan area. Repeatedly in New York the city delegation had to compromise with upstate Republicans or face their opposition. In New York state legislators nodded in deference to the city delegation, but they did not bow.

Generally across the nation, however, special city legislation did not lead to undue outside interference; instead, the city delegation almost always received whatever it wanted in terms of local bills. In 1891 the *Cincinnati Enquirer* testified to the power of the local delegation when it reported that "there is no question but that it lies within the power of the members from Hamilton County to pass or defeat" the charter bill.[30] And that same year State Senator David Morison of Cleveland told a reporter: "Why, certainly, the senate will pass the Cleveland bill. Senator Herrman and I will support it and that makes the delegation unanimous." According to Morison, "Usually either house passes any local measure which is unanimously agreed upon by the delegation from the locality which is affected by the law, so it will be only an act of courtesy when the senate passes the bill."[31] Senators Herrman and Morison, then, determined the fate of Cleveland bills in the Ohio Senate and not the bulk of senators from rural Ohio. Again, interference from rural members was a breach of legislative etiquette not generally tolerated. In 1874 a Saint Louis legislator reminded a rural colleague who was violating this etiquette, "that the gentleman from Schuyler had no more right to interfere in this bill than a member of the St. Louis delegation would have to interfere in a local measure from that gentleman's county."[32] Schuyler County measures were the concern of Schuyler County's representative, and Saint Louis County measures were the concern of the Saint Louis delegation.

In state after state a favorable recommendation by the local delegation was virtually tantamount to passage. The Cuyahoga and Hamilton County delegations in the Ohio House of Representatives made eighty recommendations during the legislative sessions of 1891 and 1892. Only once did the house act in direct contradiction to the delegations' recommendation, overwhelmingly defeating a minor Cleveland bill. In fifty-nine cases the house lined up unanimously in support of the delegation's judgment, and in only six instances did more than 3 of the 114 representatives refuse to accept the cue given by the spokesmen for the locality.[33]

In Indiana the recommendations of the Indianapolis-dominated committees on Indianapolis were equally influential. The house and senate committees made ninety-eight recommendations regarding bills and resolutions during the sessions of 1895, 1897, and 1899, and only four times did the house or senate defy the committees and act contrarily to their recommendations. Once the Indianapolis members, through parliamentary trickery, forced a reconsideration of a bill, achieving their ends on a second vote. Another time the Indianapolis delegation was sharply divided on a question, and still another time a majority of the Indianapolis delegation opposed the recommendation of the committee on which they served. Only once during these years did the Indiana legislature succeed in defying the clear and unanimous opinion of the representatives from Indianapolis.[34]

Elsewhere the powerful influence of the local delegation was equally evident. In 1892 Baltimore City representatives in the Maryland House of Delegates made 47 recommendations concerning local bills, and not once did the house defy any of those recommendations. Thirty-eight of the 47 times the house unanimously endorsed the delegation position, and only once did more than four members vote contrarily to the local recommendation. During the 1870s, prior to the adoption of home-rule amendments in Missouri and California, the judgment of the Saint Louis and San Francisco delegations was just as decisive. In the session of 1873–74 the San Francisco delegations of the California House of Representatives and Senate made 117 recommendations, and the house and senate accepted 112 of these. In 3 of the cases of deviation from the local cue the San Francisco delegation was sharply divided, and the house or senate sided with the minority faction of the delegation; and in both of the remaining cases the disputed measures were probably minor ones involving the widening of a street and a bill empowering the San Francisco Board of Education to pay any deficit in the school fund for the previous year.[35] The following year, in 1875, the Saint Louis delegation of Missouri's house and senate handed down 31 recommendations with regard to bills concerning the government of the city, and not once did the house or senate defy the position of the elected representatives of the city. In two-thirds of the cases the Missouri house or senate unanimously accepted the ruling of the local delegation.

Deference to local opinion was, then, basic to the legislative process in late nineteenth-century America. Legislatures of this period, for the most part, did not make policy or fashion the legal structure of municipal government. Instead, they more often simply responded to the demands of localities in accord with the cues given by the local delegation. One prominent Ohio lawmaker of the 1870s characterized the legislative tradition when he observed that local laws for the cities "have heretofore been assented to in a functory way by members from the other counties" who "merely yield out of compliance with the wishes of the delegation from Hamilton or Cuyahoga." The history of special legislation in Ohio rested on the practice of deference to the locality, and city charter amendments were approved "simply to comply with the wishes of those members of the Legislature who have been elected from the various counties in which such cities exist."[36] If the local delegation unanimously supported a local measure, then the legislature would typically follow suit.

Even the most notorious examples of legislative interference have been those sanctioned and nurtured by the local delegation. In 1886 Cincinnati's reform Committee of One Hundred, disgusted by the city's elected officials, proposed the creation of a nonpartisan board of public affairs to be appointed by the governor to regulate public works and public health in Cincinnati. The measure would have transferred much of the power of local government to a state-appointed commission and would have constituted the type of state tampering later deplored by many reformers. Yet a Cincinnati representative responded to the local reformers' demands and introduced the measure into the legislature, which referred it to the unanimously Republican Hamilton County house delegation. The Hamilton County representatives struck the nonpartisan provision from the bill and unanimously recommended its passage. Ohio's senate assigned the measure to Hamilton County's senators, and again the spokesmen for the locality unanimously favored sacrificing the powers of local government to state appointees.[37] One Cincinnati senator purportedly made the self-damning remark "that no man of ability or responsibility can be elected to office in Cincinnati" and hence the people of Cincinnati "wanted them appointed." In a "ringing appeal in behalf of an outraged city," this Hamilton County senator told his colleagues that "the people of Cincinnati actually demanded" the reform.[38] The legislature accepted the delegation's recommendation and endorsed this surrender of local authority to the Republican governor.

Legislative interference in the government of Denver conformed to the same pattern. In 1889 Denver's "inhabitants became dissatisfied with the management of local affairs by its own officers" and the general assembly was "importuned by them to protect the city against itself."[39] Thus the Arapahoe County legislators introduced a measure to transfer control over public works in the city from the city council to a governor-appointed board. In accordance with Colorado tradition, the measure was referred to the Arapahoe delegation in both the house and senate and won a favorable recommendation from the local members in both chambers. And in deference to the opinion of the local representatives, both houses passed the bill unanimously.[40] Colorado's lawmakers had thereby removed responsibility for municipal public works from the city council and created a state board to govern improvements in Denver, but they did so because this was what the local delegation wanted.

This pattern of deference not only permitted locally sponsored abdication of self-rule, it also thwarted any imposition of truly general laws. In a number of states during the second half of the nineteenth century, constitutional conventions drafted clauses that required general laws for the organization of cities, and throughout the nation legislatures evaded these mandates and allowed local representatives to obtain the unique measures they favored. For example, Ohio's constitution forbade local legislation and prescribed general statutes, but legislators devised a classification scheme that allowed every major city to have the form of government it desired. According to the scheme, the state's cities were divided into "general" classes, with only one city to each class. Cincinnati was the only city of the first class, first grade, and Cleveland the only city of the first class, second grade. During the late nineteenth century the Ohio Supreme Court approved this subterfuge, because it was necessary under the existing pattern of deference to local demands. Thus, through a system of special legislation, Ohio cities were allowed to retain a degree of independence seemingly impossible under a code of general laws, and for this reason most urban lawmakers preferred to perpetuate the tradition of local laws.

This issue arose at Ohio's Constitutional Convention of 1874 when some delegates sought to put teeth in the prohibition on special legislation by limiting the number of classes to six. This mild proposal, however, raised howls from certain urban delegates who denounced it as a violation of local self-rule. A delegate from Cincinnati claimed that general legislation "is destructive of local self-government" and "an interference with . . . proper municipal independence." He favored a return to unrestricted special legislation for Ohio cities because he "would give to every city and town in Ohio that constitution and charter which its people might seek."[41] Another presented the same argument in support of special legislation, saying that "the people ought to be permitted to have such laws passed as they deem essential for their best interest and for their well-being."[42] In the opinion of these Ohio lawmakers, special legislation was not a tool of state tyranny, but a means of maximizing the locality's control over its own structure of government.

Ohioans presented similar arguments in 1891, when both Cleveland and

Cincinnati sought new charters. At that time a few lawmakers suggested a uniform system of municipal government for the state's major cities. The proposal, however, was the object of more derision than support, for as the *Cleveland Leader* observed, "the Cincinnati people are asking for a form of government at which Cleveland people would hoot."[43] Ohio's former attorney general stated forthrightly that "he opposed trying to adopt one general measure to apply to all the cities of the state and believed it the duty of the legislature to pass the . . . bill which both political parties and the people of Cleveland generally approved."[44] In nineteenth-century Ohio, it was felt that Cleveland and Cincinnati deserved to have the form of government that each desired, irrespective of the other. And with deference to local sentiment the rule, general charter legislation was neither desirable nor possible.

Elsewhere special legislation also seemed conducive to greater independence and expanded self-rule. When Minnesota adopted a constitutional amendment prohibiting special legislation in 1892, Twin City lawmakers panicked. Minneapolis and Saint Paul had always preferred different forms of government, and this diversity had been possible under a regime of special laws. And in Colorado the state constitution of 1876 permitted cities either to retain their special charters and remain subject to special legislation or choose to accept a general-law charter enacted by the legislature. Every city in the state, including Denver, chose the special-legislation option. Special legislation permitted flexibility and laws tailor-made to the needs and desires of the locality, and this is what the Denver city fathers wanted.

Throughout most of America, special legislation survived as a much-criticized but essential means for ensuring flexibility and adaptability. And basic to the procedure for handling local bills was the tradition of deference to the local delegation. This did not mean that mayors and city councils enjoyed a carte blanche from the legislature. Indeed, the local delegation did not necessarily adhere to the recommendations of the city's officials, and conflict arose most often not between the city and the state but between the local delegation and the city government. At least two sets of locally elected officials governed the cities, and if reform groups or business interests did not obtain what they wanted from one, then they could always appeal to the other. In Cleveland, Cincinnati, Denver, and elsewhere, reformers appealed to the local delegation to revise the structure of city rule, and the legislative contingent responded in spite of hardy protests from the city council. Repeatedly the local delegation was an alternative channel for action, a means for circumventing the city officials who decried "legislative interference" and "state dictation."[45] In fact, the barriers to passage of city measures may not have been high enough. In retrospect, legislatures may have been too easily swayed by the demands of disgruntled urban elements angry at the mayor and city council, and too responsive to profit-conscious urban contractors, speculators, and streetcar companies.

PARTISAN INTERFERENCE

There are always exceptions to the rules of etiquette, and there was one major exception to the pattern of deference to local representatives. If a local bill was a partisan measure that endangered the position of one of the political parties in the locality, then members of that political party from throughout the state might rally to the aid of their imperiled comrades. In most states, of the plethora of local bills few had any partisan significance. But if a measure did affect party fortunes or if there was any suspicion of partisan chicanery, then deference to the local majority might disappear. The bill thus ceased to be a local question and it became a party question.

One reason for repeated state involvement in New York City questions was that party lines in New York conformed to geographic lines. Upstate New York was predominantly Republican or anti-Tammany Democratic, but New York City was the stronghold of the Tammany machine. Local measures sponsored by a Tammany henchman such as Senator George Washington Plunkitt immediately aroused suspicion in the minds of representatives from Buffalo or Plattsburgh. And the longstanding partisan or factional rifts between upstaters and city spokesmen weakened the system of deference common in other states. Too often in New York, local bills were party bills, and the result was conflict rather than concession.

In his famous talks on "very practical politics," Senator Plunkitt himself emphasized the partisan animosity of the Republican-dominated legislature toward the Democratic city. Plunkitt observed frankly of the Albany lawmakers: "When a Republican mayor is in, they give him all sorts of power. If a Tammany mayor is elected next fall I wouldn't be surprised if they changed the whole business and arranged it so that every city department should have four heads, two of them Republicans."[46] Tammany senators might win approval of local bills that posed no threat to Republicans and offered little advantage to Democrats. But if the upstate Republican boss Thomas Platt or the Republican legislative leadership perceived partisan designs in the efforts of Plunkitt and his party comrades, then the columns of political combat would form and logrolling courtesies would be set aside.

Considering the massive amounts of local legislation prior to 1900, this type of partisan interference was relatively rare across the nation. But it happened often enough to irritate reformers sick of partisan bickering. Partisan splits were most common when the local bill was a significant one involving the distribution of political power in the city. Such partisanship, for example, disrupted the legislative procedure in Ohio in 1890 and prevented passage of a new Cleveland charter. The unanimously Republican Cuyahoga County delegation favored one version, but the Democratic majority in the legislature and Democrats on the Cleveland City Council favored another draft. Cleveland's leading Democratic newspaper claimed that "nothing but bigoted party prejudice can explain Republican opposition" to the superior Democratic measure and also suggested that "the Republican members of the legislature . . . fear that its adoption and enforcement would become so popular that a storm of indignation would follow them for opposition, hence they are fighting against its adoption."[47] The Republicans, on the other hand, claimed that the Democratic measure was a ripper bill motivated by selfish interests. A leading Cleveland Republican contended that if the Democrat charter were adopted "about every Republican in the city holding an office would be turned out, and the entire municipal government placed at the mercy of Democrats."[48]

To secure the defeat of the Democrat measure, Cleveland Republicans seem to have resorted to bribery. A leading Republican member of the Cleveland delegation later admitted that a "sum of money was soon raised, and two wily Democrats were sent to Columbus to do missionary work" among their party brethren.[49] Money loosened the bonds of party discipline, and five Democrats joined the Republican legislators to defeat the Democrat alternative. As a result no charter was passed in 1890.

To ensure the passage of a new charter, Democrats and Republicans fashioned a compromise in 1891. Instead of referring the charter proposal to a select committee of the unanimously Republican Cleveland delegation, the Democratic house assigned it to a committee consisting of all six of the Cuyahoga representatives plus three Democrats from elsewhere in the state. If the partisan loyalties of the local delegation differed from those of the legislative majority, then some interference by outsiders might be necessary. But the three outsiders on the Cleveland charter committee did not serve as spokesmen for rural Ohio; they were not interfering in the government of Cleveland to thwart big-city power. They represented the Democratic party and served to protect local Democratic interests. The new charter thus passed.

In Minnesota party rivalry likewise led to a violation of the dominant pattern of deference to local representatives. In 1891 the overwhelmingly Democratic Hennepin County delegation introduced a charter proposal for Minneapolis drafted by Democratic State Representative W. H. Tripp of Minneapolis. The Hennepin County delegation held the usual hearings on the measure and heard some strong complaints from a few Republicans. But the Republicans in the legislature generally deferred to the judgment of the Democratic local delegation, and the Tripp charter passed the house of representatives unanimously and won the approval of all but four members of the senate.[50] So far the dominant force of localism was prevailing over the powerful force of partisanship.

Minnesota's Republican Governor Merriam, however, was not so disposed to comply with the wishes of Hennepin Democrats. Merriam vetoed the Tripp charter, noting that "under ordinary circumstances, it has been the custom of the executive office to interpose no objection to what is known as local legislation." But he claimed that "inasmuch as this is to be practically the constitution of a city, in population one-seventh of the size of the entire state," he felt impelled "to return it, believing . . . it would be wiser to submit [the] proposed charter to the people of the city for their approval or disapproval."[51] Thus the Republican governor urged further consideration of local sentiment, but in the process aroused partisan ire.

Minneapolis's legislative delegation was furious at the governor for violating the long-revered rules of lawmaking in Minnesota. Hennepin's Democratic senators argued that the veto was "a blow at the rights of every municipality in this state . . . , a blow at time honored rights and privileges, which have heretofore been secure from assault." According to the senators, "If the personal preference of private . . . individuals be allowed to prevail as against the action of lawfully elected representatives of the people in matters of local concern, every member of this body will surrender for his constituents rights which should forever remain inviolate." The delegation insisted that "the bill is a local bill . . . , having the indorsement of the local delegation." Hennepin's members further asserted: "We speak with authority for the people whom we represent, and in their behalf, we ask that they be permitted to govern themselves as they desire in matters that concern only themselves."[52] Legislative etiquette demanded that the local delegation decide local matters. When the Republican governor squared off against the Democratic Minneapolis delegation, however, the issue ceased to be a local question and became a party question. As a result, the legislators fought along partisan lines to override the governor's veto. The Democrats generally voted to override, but the Republicans voted to sustain the veto, and the governor's veto stood.[53] In this instance, the local delegation thus failed to dictate the destiny of local legislation, and Minnesota lawmakers, owing to party considerations, momentarily deviated from the general rule of local self-determination.

Throughout the late nineteenth century the relatively few breaches of the rule of deference were chiefly due to party interest. If a local bill became a party issue, then the local delegation no longer enjoyed its unchallenged authority over the question, for a party issue deserved the attention of members from throughout the state. In 1874 a Missouri representative argued that reconsideration of a Saint Louis County measure was not solely the responsibility of the Saint Louis County delegation by charging that "the bill was passed as a party measure and it was unfair for the gentleman to state that the bill was passed as a local measure."[54] Local measures were the exclusive responsibility of the Saint Louis delegation, but party measures were not solely the business of local representatives and therefore could lead to outside interference.

Occasionally, however, the distinction between a party measure and a local bill blurred, and a legislative free-for-all ensued. For example, in 1875 Kansas City's Republican representative introduced a revised municipal charter before the Missouri legislature. The bill quickly ignited a conflict in Kansas City between Republicans and reform Democrats on one side and regular Democrats on the other. Each political faction testified at length before the legislature, and it was clear that the measure was partisan and did not represent a local consensus. Yet according to newspaper reports, when opponents of the charter attempted "to hoist . . . [this] purely local measure upon Democrats as a party measure," Democratic legislators balked and the effort proved "a pitiable failure." Thus the Democratic caucus took no official stance, though representatives from throughout the state did split on the charter issue according to the Kansas City faction that seemed to them most acceptable.[55] In the case of the Kansas City charter, the cues from both the local delegation and the party caucus were mixed, confusing the charter struggle and preventing easy passage of the bill. Such a situation could prove a special nightmare for city representatives eager to obtain legislation and for rural lawmakers who did not wish to be bothered by arcane urban bills irrelevant to their constituents.

Yet the hundreds of measures enacted to permit the expansion of municipal services in San Francisco, Cleveland, or Baltimore, for example, were, for the most part, local measures that were drafted by local interests, introduced and sponsored by the local delegation, and adopted unanimously by the state legislature. Authorization of a bond issue for boulevards, establishment of a library board, and creation of a park network were usually not partisan questions, and the legislatures readily applied their rubber-stamp approval to such measures. In 1891 when Ohio's house of representatives was Democratic and the Cleveland delegation unanimously Republican, a majority of those legislators voting endorsed the delegation position ten out of eleven times and unanimously adopted the Cuyahoga recommendations in seven cases. On local questions, then, Democrats bowed to the judgment of Republicans in recognition of the right of district representatives to make laws for their special domain. Thus, the late-nineteenth-century system was not one of state dictation, supervision, or guidance, but one of state deference to the demands of the local representative. The one joker in the legal deck was the political party. But this joker only occasionally surfaced to spoil the schemes of the local delegation.

THE URBAN DELEGATION

The men who wielded the impressive prerogatives of the city's delegation were generally not members of the social or economic upper crust, but neither can they be classed with the aldermanic hoi polloi. In the eyes of their contemporaries, the urban representatives and senators ranked somewhere between— a step above the saloonkeeper but a few steps below the banker. Upper-middle-class reformers sometimes condemned city delegates to the same boodler's hell as their counterparts on the board of aldermen, but attacks on representatives and senators were less persistent and less general than those on the much-abused members of the city council. Unlike most city councilmen, the state legislators continued to exercise significant authority over municipal policy, and they were not simply neighborhood errand boys. Thus state legislative posts could sometimes attract those with ambition, professional training, and a broader metropolitan perspective. A politician whose only qualification was a loyal following at the corner saloon had a bit tougher time winning the legislative nomination than a seat on the board of aldermen.

In each of the leading cities, the legislative delegation included persons of diverse social and occupational backgrounds. Some were manufacturers and wholesale merchants, while others were clerks, shopkeepers, and livery stable owners. Such plutocratic names as William Waldorf Astor and such patrician figures as Theodore Roosevelt occasionally ornamented the roll call of New York City's legislators, but representatives of the middling elements of society prevailed in most urban delegations. The urban legislator had often achieved some business success, but he shared little beyond the title "businessman" with the Astors or Vanderbilts. Like the city's aldermen, the members of the urban delegation usually were not found in exclusive club registers or social directories. For example, in 1897 none of New York City's aldermen, senators, or representatives were members of J. P. Morgan's plutocratic Metropolitan Club. Similarly, in 1896 the Union League Club had only four of Philadelphia's forty-seven state legislators on its membership register, and the Philadelphia and Rittenhouse clubs counted no state lawmakers among their members.[56] The names of state legislators did not occur much more frequently in city bluebooks or social registers than did those of the city councilmen. Only one of New York City's thirty-one state legislators for the year 1892 appeared in the social list, as opposed to none of the aldermen. In Chicago in 1893, 30 percent of the city's representatives and senators were listed in the city's bluebook, as compared with 28 percent of the city council members. And in 1896 30 percent of Philadelphia's state legislators likewise ranked among the bluebook's listing of notables, a figure comparable to that for the city's councillors.[57] The great majority of those serving in the urban delegations, however, had neither inherited an elevated social pedigree nor won the laurels of fashion and society.

Yet city councils and urban delegations were not identical in their composition. In most cities a higher percentage of the state legislators were lawyers. At a typical session of the city council in New York City or Chicago, for instance, no more than 10 percent to 15 percent of the aldermen were attorneys, whereas during the 1890s 30 percent to 40 percent of the legislators from these cities practiced law.[58] On the average almost one-fourth of Philadelphia's delegation were lawyers, and during the 1890s 30 percent to 40 percent of a typical delegation from Minneapolis and Saint Paul were attorneys.[59] Likewise, of the sixty-six legislators serving Indianapolis's Marion County during 1880 to 1900, 39 percent had practiced law.[60] Those with professional legal training were more likely to aspire to a seat in the state legislature than a place on the city council, and members of the bar exercised disproportionate clout through their service in the urban delegation.

These attorney-legislators, however, were not usually among the most distinguished practitioners of their profession. Instead, they tended to be young ambitious lawyers who used their service in the state legislature to further their legal or political careers. In most leading cities the majority of the lawyer-legislators were under forty years of age, and a number were still in their twenties. In 1892 seven of the eleven lawyers in New York City's delegation were under forty, and four of these seven were under thirty.[61] That same year three of the four attorneys representing Newark, New Jersey, were in their thirties. In 1893, six of the eleven lawyers in the Philadelphia delegation were in their thirties, and one of the eleven was in his twenties.[62] Likewise, of the eleven lawyers representing Minneapolis-Saint Paul in 1893, nine were under forty.[63] Elsewhere the figures were much the same. At the close of the century fifteen of the nineteen lawyers in Chicago's Cook County delegation were in their twenties or thirties, and eleven of the fourteen lawyer-legislators representing Baltimore were under forty.[64]

As stated, service in the state legislature did not typically cap a lawyer's career; rather, it was a stepping stone to success. Since the state legislature was the sovereign source from which all legal blessings flowed, a young lawyer could attract an impressive clientele if he had clout in Springfield, Harrisburg, or Albany. Moreover, once he vacated his legislative seat, he might serve his clients well as a state house lobbyist. Most corporate lobbyists were former legislators, and a struggling lawyer eager for a lucrative future could recognize the long-term profitability of a few years in the assembly or senate. Those with political ambitions also appreciated the value of a sojourn in the legislature. A few terms at the state capital would allow a rising political leader to establish the statewide connections necessary to win more august offices. For a venerable leader of the bar, however, state legislative service offered much less. In fact, those who already enjoyed professional prestige and an established practice generally regarded a stint in the state legislature as a time-consuming nuisance rather than an enviable pastime.

While members of the bar may have been overrepresented on urban delegations, those who tended bar proved less prominent in the state legislature than in the city council. Of the 173 men who served in the New York City delegation from 1895 through 1899, only 2 listed their occupation in the legislative manual as liquor dealer or saloonkeeper.[65] No doubt some were reluctant to admit their dependence on the whiskey trade and may have claimed more respectable vocations, but other sources also indicate that saloon operators were more common in the council chamber than the state house. According to the biographies of legislative candidates compiled by the *New York Herald* in 1892, 21 of the 60 major-party contestants in New York City were lawyers, whereas only 3 were in the liquor trade. In contrast, the *Herald* sketches of city council candidates that year indicate that only 3 of the 61 major-party nominees were lawyers, but 12 were liquor dealers or were "hotel keepers," a common euphemism for those who operated saloons.[66] Moreover, Chicago's Cook County delegation, the Philadelphia delegation, and the legislative contingents from Cincinnati and Cleveland likewise included few representatives of the liquor trade. Angry reformers may be said to have focused undue attention on those few legislative members with ties to the saloon business, for the stereotypical rum seller-politician that so offended the moral sensibilities of many middle-class Americans was actually a minor figure in the urban delegations of the 1870s, 1880s, and 1890s.

The legislative contingents from America's great municipalities could, then, boast of fewer "gin mill" operators than the city councils, and state lawmakers could claim greater professional training. Like the councils, however, the state legislatures had an ample supply of well-known ward heelers, such as New York City's George Washington Plunkitt or Philadelphia's George Vare. Those who had loyally served their party and profited from a series of deputy clerkships in county and municipal agencies also were found among the urban senators and representatives. Elite reformers and crusading newspapers could characterize some legislators like Tammany's Timothy D. Sullivan as "preposterous," "absolutely incompetent," and "the clown of the lower house."[67] But in New York City and elsewhere state legislators never quite aroused the contempt that was heaped upon aldermen. In 1890 the *New York Times* dismissed the Board of Aldermen as "a body to which respectable people nowadays seem to give very little attention."[68] The urban legislative delegation never suffered such a severe snub, and at least it could still attract a number of ambitious young professionals to its ranks.

As in the case of city councils, the rate of turnover in the state legislatures was high, and few delegates remained in the senate or house for more than two terms. In New York, assemblymen were elected for one-year terms, whereas state senators were elected for two-year terms, and during the period 1872 through 1893 the members of New York City's delegation averaged less than two years each.[69] In 1896 only 21 of New York City's 46 representatives and senators had served a previous term in the state legislature, and in 1898 the 80-man delegation for the newly consolidated City of Greater New York included only 36 veterans of previous sessions.[70] Pennsylvania's legislators enjoyed longer terms, with house members elected for two years and state senators for four. But from 1870 to 1900 the members of Philadelphia's delegation averaged only four years of service.[71] And elsewhere the same pattern prevailed. Of the 269 men who were senators or representatives from Cincinnati or Cleveland during the period 1870 to 1900, only 61 served more than one term in the Ohio legislature, and none served more than ten years.[72] Among the members of the Chicago, Minneapolis, and Indianapolis delegations, four years of legislative experience also could earn one a place of seniority. A few urban legislators accumulated decades of service, like Philadelphia's George Handy Smith, "the Nestor of the Senate," who sat in Pennsylvania's upper house for twenty years. But such urban legislators were uncommon.

The urban delegation was, then, a body of amateur lawmakers who journeyed to the state capital for three- or four-month sessions and then returned to their law practices or livery stables. After two or three such sojourns, the typical solon would retire from legislative service, either by choice or because of political defeat. Delegates were usually not persons who had mastered the legislative process or had had extensive experience in government. During the short legislative sessions they spent most of their time pushing through mounds of urban measures, relying on the legislative tradition of deference to the locality to expedite this task. And the delegates' lack of time, experience, and expertise only enhanced the power of extralegal forces in the lawmaking process. The drafting of laws was often the task of special business interests, of chambers of commerce, good-government groups, and the party organizations. Such groups generally knew more about the special problems of municipal financing, sewerage, fire prevention, or building codes, for example, than did the elected representative. Moreover, lobbyists for these organizations usually were more familiar with legislative procedure. The public utility lobbyist might well have significantly more experience in the capitol chambers than the urban legislator, and could use this superior knowledge to benefit his clients. An overburdened, part-time body of legislative novices could be easily influenced by fast-talking individuals who wanted a measure enacted with a minimum of questions asked. The amateur state legislatures of the late nineteenth century proved that they were often vulnerable to such influence.

5 REFORMING THE CITY-STATE RELATIONSHIP

 Every January in odd-numbered years during the late nineteenth century, scores of good-government lobbyists, public utility lawyers, and city attorneys boarded trains in Philadelphia, Detroit, and Milwaukee for trips to their state capitals. During the following weeks this tide of "law seekers" engulfed the senate and house chambers, and when the supplicants receded in April they carried with them dozens of new local laws authorizing the paving of boulevards, the construction of water-works, and changes in mayoral powers. Each legislative session saw a scramble for benefits, with the local legislative delegation approving scores of projects for numerous conflicting interests. At the session's close, many of the legislators had only a vague notion of what had been enacted. The legislative process was an uncoordinated distribution of favors by harried amateur lawmakers who occasionally responded to the cues of a local political machine if such a machine existed, but who more often coped with the flood of demands as best they could.

By the last three decades of the century, an increasing number of Americans were expressing doubts about this chaotic, seemingly systemless mode of urban lawmaking. In the depression-ridden 1870s the plethora of local laws troubled economy-minded reformers who sought to protect the city from further costly public works projects. By the 1890s many viewed local laws as an open door through which transportation magnates and utility interests might proceed to their goal of unwarranted profits. And by 1900 urban reformers doubted whether the cities' elected representatives devoted enough time or possessed enough expertise to handle competently the task of lawmaking for the burgeoning metropolitan centers. Throughout these decades there were considerable misgivings. Did the legislators exercise sufficient discretion, possess sufficient "sales" resistance, or have adequate training or knowledge to enact the thousands of special laws so vital to the modern metropolis? The answer of many concerned citizens was a resounding no.

To correct the supposed structural flaws, reformers sponsored proposals aimed at limiting the lawmaking role of the local legislative delegation and the state legislature as a whole. Constitutional provisions prohibiting special legislation appeared in some state constitutions as early as the 1850s, and such clauses became increasingly common during the last half of the century. But beyond this there emerged two movements that had a limited impact in the nineteenth century, but were of vital significance after 1900. These were the much-ballyhooed municipal home-rule crusade, which sought to ensure cities the right to draft and ratify their own charters, and the movement for state administrative supervision of the cities, which favored the transfer of decision-making authority from amateur legislators to professional administrators. Each traced its origins to the late nineteenth century, and each gained adherents during the century's final decades.

On the surface, the two movements seem contradictory. Home rulers supposedly yearned for greater local control over the cities and an end to state meddling. Advocates of administrative supervision, on the other hand, demanded more systematic state control and condoned the idea of state inspectors snooping into city accounts and examining municipal services. One crusade seemingly sought less state supervision, whereas the other sought more. One emphasized more power for Philadelphia, Saint Louis, and San Francisco; the other urged more authority for Harrisburg, Jefferson City, and Sacramento.

The conflict, however, was largely illusory. Both movements were seeking the same goal—an end to the helter-skelter, uncoordinated and unchecked deluge of what amounted to "legislative interference" by those storekeepers, real estate dealers, young lawyers, and ward heelers who represented the city in the legislature. Early advocates of municipal home rule sought to liberate the city not from an unresponsive legislature but from one that was all-too-responsive, that granted too much with too little thought. Early supporters of state administrative supervision likewise wished to free the city from unthinking and uninformed legislative action and endeavored to ensure expertise and professional standards of procedure and service. Municipal home rulers did not fear state power per se, only state power in the hands of greedy contractors, political hacks, and even service-hungry citizens who mindlessly boosted the urban tax rate. State power in the hands of professional experts who valued efficiency and soberly calculated costs and benefits was deemed not only less threatening but highly attractive.

Both movements, then, endeavored to curb the interfering authority of the state legislature as exercised by the local legislative delegation. Yet they differed in approach. Municipal home rulers envisioned ending the mass of local legislation by creating an inflexible structure resistant to change and meddling, a structure that would not respond so readily to every costly demand of the urban constituency. Early advocates of state supervision were not so opposed to change but sought to ensure that government relied on the much-heralded expertise of professional accountants, educators, and engineers. Municipal home rulers endeavored to limit politicians in the state legislature through constitutional prohibitions, whereas devotees of central administration viewed professionalism as a means of "reining in" the political process. Both groups, however, regarded legislative lawmaking with the same disdain. The emergence of both movements toward the end of the nineteenth century and during the first years of the twentieth century marks an attempt to change the course of urban law, an effort to pursue a new direction in the city-state relationship.

THE ORIGINS OF MUNICIPAL HOME RULE

The first constitutional home-rule provisions were products of the depression-stricken 1870s. During the deflationary downturn of that decade cities throughout the nation suffered from the burden of debt contracted during the booming and inflationary 1860s and confronted awesome interest payments. Revenues were declining, budgets were tight, and city fathers believed they could not afford any additional financial responsibilities or public works projects foisted on them by the state legislature at the behest of certain local interests. Special legislation and a permissive system of lawmaking meant expense for the cities, and most business leaders, property owners, and civic heads opposed any further expenditure. Retrenchment was the cry of the 1870s, and this meant blocking the lawmaking channels through which flowed the deluge of special responsibilities and privileges embodied in local legislation. Many citizens during the 1870s thus sought to halt the stream of special legislation and to create an inflexible system that would discourage costly changes, block the imposition of new obligations, and prevent every interest in the city from tapping the municipal treasury for its pet project.

In many states constitutional framers intended to dam the flow of special laws by requiring that all municipal legislation be generally applicable to cities throughout the state. But this proved unsatisfactory. A system of general laws could not satisfy, after all, the peculiar needs of the largest cities—Saint Louis was not Flat River and San Francisco was not Grass Valley. Classification schemes that allowed state legislators to enact different general laws for cities in different population categories were also no solution, for the categories often included only a single city, thus permitting a thinly veiled form of special legislation. In the end, the answer lay in a system that allowed for the peculiarity of the largest cities but did not encourage frequent change, amendment, or meddling. What the first home rulers of the 1870s desired was a means for establishing a permanent but anomalous municipal framework, a tailor-made structure resistant to alteration.

The lawmakers of Missouri and California were the first to attain this goal. In the 1870s these two states pioneered the development of constitutional home rule for their cities, and in each the motive for adopting the reform was much the same. The leaders of both Saint Louis and San Francisco viewed special-interest bills and legislative jobbery as evils corrupting the city. To achieve salvation big cities had to create a structure fitted to their particular needs but that would discourage unthinking change.

The Saint Louis delegation to Missouri's Constitutional Convention of 1875 framed that state's innovative home-rule provision, and in the convention debates Saint Louis spokesmen repeatedly expressed their contempt for the transitory nature of the municipal structure and the ease with which amendments and revisions passed through the legislature. One such delegate observed that "there is scarcely an amendment made to the charter of the city from year to year that does not cost the city of St. Louis not only thousands but hundreds of thousands of dollars." Another argued that "the power of changing at any time the municipal charters has proved to be one of the greatest sources of corruption in the history of American cities." A rural delegate reiterated the arguments of the Saint Louis delegation when he contended that the object of the home-rule scheme was "to prevent the repeated attempts that have been heretofore made by parties who did not represent fairly the true interests of the city." Still another ably argued: "What we are asking for . . . is stability." According to this spokesman, constitutional home rule for Saint Louis would establish "local government upon a rock and not upon quicksand as it has been for the last twenty years, to be blown over by every wind and flood of bummerism, high fraud, and rascally speculators."[1]

Four years later the San Francisco delegates to California's Constitutional Convention of 1879 expressed much the same sentiments. One delegate told his colleagues to "look at the laws of this State, and you will find stacks upon stacks of Acts conferring additional powers upon the Boards of Supervisors," with the result that San Francisco's taxes "are greater than [those of] any other city in the United States, or in the world." Another delegate spoke of the "one hundred supplemental Acts passed by the Legislature" that "might as well be denominated one hundred raids upon the taxpayers of San Francisco, or one hundred steals out of the treasury." In the minds of such delegates, legislative amendment of the city charter was too easy, the lawmaking structure too much at the mercy of urban demands. One convention spokesman claimed that "there is not a gentleman within the sound of my voice who . . . ever knew of an amendment to the charter being defeated by the Legislature: nor did the country members ever come to the rescue of San Francisco." Instead, lobbyists "rush through the legislature those vicious measures which it would be impossible to pass through Boards directly responsible to the people." The aim of California's home-rule advocates was, then, "to stop the corruptions that flow from the Legislature" and create a lawmaking mechanism less vulnerable to the persuasions of the varied interests within the city.[2]

Thus, spokesman after spokesman at the Missouri and California conventions reiterated the view that the largest cities needed to be saved from sugar-daddy state legislatures that gave urban interests everything they asked for and in the process corrupted the cities' morals. Saint Louis and San Francisco suffered not from degrading deprivation but from corrupting excess. In the opinion of the urban delegates, the system of special legislation was too open-handed, the response of state lawmakers too ready and unthinking.

The home-rule procedure devised by constitutional framers in Missouri and California in the 1870s made the structure of lawmaking less sensitive to the manifold desires of special urban interests. Urban law under the home-rule provisions was supposed to be a law of consensus. City charters and amendments were to represent the homogeneous public interest and not the heterogeneous special interests of a polyarchic city. The original home-rule provisions, in fact, represent a nostalgic attempt to construct a consensual, immutable foundation for an urban America that was ephemeral and divided. Rapid change, it was felt, in the past had driven municipalities into financial distress. Now city fathers sought stability.

The fiery young journalist Joseph Pulitzer, one of the chief advocates of municipal home rule at the Missouri convention, expressed the desire of the Saint Louis delegation for stability in his initial resolution on the subject. Pulitzer proposed that municipalities of 100,000 or more inhabitants "shall be regulated by a fundamental constitutional charter which shall not be liable to yearly change by the Legislature, but shall remain a permanent fundamental law of the State." Amendments to this permanent fundamental law would require the approval of two-thirds of the city council, as well as the sanction of the mayor of the municipality and would have to be "endorsed by at least two-thirds of the people thereof voting at a special election." In Pulitzer's opinion, such a system would prove a formidable bastion against the perceived villains of the urban drama.[3]

The final home-rule provision adopted by the Missouri convention did not erect quite such formidable barriers to change, but it did reflect Pulitzer's wish to secure permanency and stability and to thwart those eager to expand the city's obligations or manipulate its structure. Missouri's Constitution of 1875 authorized any city with a population of more than one-hundred thousand persons to elect a board of freeholders for the purpose of drafting a city charter. These freeholders would submit their proposed charter to the city voters, and in the case of Saint Louis a majority of those voting in the election would have to approve the charter before it took effect. For any other cities that might pass the one-hundred-thousand mark, a four-sevenths majority was necessary. The ratified charter could only be amended "at intervals of not less than two years," and amendments had to win the approval of at least three-fifths of the qualified voters casting ballots in the election. The Saint Louis city charter could no longer be a bargain hammered out between various interests in legislative anterooms safe from general scrutiny. It had to suffer public exposure before adoption, and it had to prove satisfactory to a majority of the city electorate. The authors of this first home-rule provision did not fear the mass electorate so much as the backroom politician and state house lobbyist. In fact, through exercising their clout in a charter election, the city voters would, so the home-rule framers believed, save the city from such rippers and schemers. Moreover, under the home-rule procedure no bummers or speculators could add one amendment after another to the Saint Louis charter. Amendments could only be submitted once every two years, and had to win an extraordinary three-fifths majority of those casting ballots on election day.[4] Ratification was almost impossible if the city council submitted amendments for approval in a general election. For issues did not attract the voters' attention like candidates, and three-fifths of those voting for governor or president in the general election would not bother to express themselves either for or against charter amendments.

San Francisco's delegation to the California convention secured adoption of virtually this same procedure. Copying word for word from the Missouri Constitution, the Californians required an extraordinary three-fifths majority for charter amendments and permitted such changes at most once every two years.[5] In both California and Missouri, the home-rule charter was to be a permanent foundation for municipal government, amendable only at the behest of a large majority of the urban electorate. Charter changes, then, were to reflect that vague but much-vaunted concept known as the public interest; in other words, city charters were no longer to be patchwork products of every private interest in the city, but instruments of the public will.

Thus convention delegates from Saint Louis and San Francisco successfully limited the role of the overly compliant local legislative delegation and made the city electorate watchdogs against future raids on the municipal treasury. Yet state legislatures did retain some authority over the cities. Delegates from outside Saint Louis and San Francisco did not favor a total break between city and state but demanded that the city remain subordinate to lawmakers in Jefferson City and Sacramento. The result was a constitutional loophole significant to the future of municipal home rule.

At both the Missouri and California conventions, delegates expressed the fear that home rule meant secession, and they therefore sought reassurance that cities were to remain subject to the state. Though one delegate from rural Missouri wanted to remove Saint Louis "from the operations of the fickle popular breath of other portions of the State," he insisted that he would "not give [his] vote to any feature in this Constitution which in the least degree impairs the sovereign rights of the whole people of the State . . . over the city as well as the country." He feared that home rule might exempt the city from all laws governing the state, and he asked his colleagues, "Ought not any law affecting the rights of property, descent distribution and social relations and anything else, be the same in the city as in the country?"[6] When confronted by the California home-rule provision, one delegate from outside San Francisco cried, "This is the boldest kind of an attempt at secession." Another agreed and announced that he was "not in favor of allowing any part of [the] State to set up an independent empire." These spokesmen did "not object to the City of San Francisco framing its own charter, so long as it is subject to the supreme power of the State, and not superior to it."[7] They did not believe that rural legislators should interfere with city affairs, but they suspected that the innovative home-rule provision might prove too drastic a solution.

To allay such suspicions, both the Missouri and California conventions included clauses in their home-rule provisions that reasserted state supremacy. In Missouri the delegates added to the home-rule section for Saint Louis a reserve clause: "Notwithstanding the provisions of this article the General Assembly shall have the same power over the city and county of Saint Louis as it has over other cities and counties in the state." And the convention revised the section for all other cities of one-hundred thousand or more population so that their home rule charters had to be not only "in harmony with" but also "subject to" the laws and constitution of Missouri.[8] Missouri's Constitution of 1875 specifically prohibited special legislation for municipal affairs, but the convention delegates intended that Saint Louis and all other home-rule cities would remain subordinate to the general laws of the state. In California the delegates inserted a proviso requiring cities to submit home-rule charters and charter amendments to the state legislature, which could approve or reject the charter or amendment but could not alter or revise those measures endorsed by the urban electorate. This proviso guaranteed state supremacy, but would supposedly prevent a mass of special additions and amendments by over-indulgent legislators. Moreover, California's Constitution of 1879 also provided that all city charters "framed or adopted by authority of [the] Constitution, shall be subject to and controlled by general laws."[9] In both Missouri and California, then, home-rule cities were to remain subject to the general laws of those states.

The Saint Louis and San Francisco delegations did not regard these reserve clauses as a serious threat to their goals of stability and fiscal conservatism. Special laws were, after all, the object of their scorn and not legislation of general applicability. In both states most city delegates expressed no objection to the idea of home-rule municipalities remaining subject to general laws. The Saint Louis delegate chiefly responsible for drafting the Missouri home-rule provision announced that the city delegation "intended to leave [the home-rule] charters subject to any general law . . . which the General Assembly might at anytime see fit to enact," and one of his colleagues contended that the legislature would enjoy the authority to repeal any section of a home rule charter through general legislation.[10] Likewise, the chief spokesman for San Francisco clearly stated in the convention debates that the home-rule provisions "do not take from the Legislature the power to legislate by general law." Instead, he said that "the whole purpose of this article has been to take from the Legislature the power of special legislation."[11]

Special legislation was, then, the evil to be eliminated, and few from city or country showed any sympathy for unchecked legislative authority. This sentiment was especially shared by Missouri delegates. One rural spokesman from Grundy County, Missouri, insisted that the convention should "relieve the General Assembly of [the] State from that class of changes which has constantly been urged upon them from St. Louis—changes of charters." And another rural delegate concurred, stating that "if there is any one thing [he] would wish to keep out of the Legislature, it is legislation upon St. Louis affairs." Such legislation had, in his view, "created more confusion and trouble in the Legislature and . . . done more to prolong the session than anything else."[12] Home rule, so the delegates theorized, would prevent the unchecked passage of local laws and yet permit the city to enjoy a structure suited to its special needs. Inflexibility and stability were the goals of both city and country delegates, and the home-rule procedure reflected these aims.

The handiwork of the Missouri delegates was to have a notable impact on other states. California was not the only state to copy the Missouri procedures almost verbatim. In 1889 constitutional convention delegates in the new state of Washington did likewise, and seven years later, framers of Minnesota's home-rule amendment of 1896 followed suit. By the close of the century four states had thus adopted strongly similar constitutional provisions permitting cities to draft and ratify their own charters.

Washington's constitutional convention delegates did deviate somewhat from the Missouri and California procedures for altering city charters. During the convention debates, the Washington delegates removed one obstacle to amendment by changing a clause that required a two-thirds approval of all of those voting on the amendment to one requiring only a simple majority vote thereon at a general election.[13] Yet the continuing desire to block ill-considered change was evident in Seattle's charter of 1890, framed by free-holders under the home-rule provision of 1889. This charter required that an amendment twice win the approval of three-fifths of the city council and receive the mayor's sanction before being submitted to the voters. According to the charter, the proposed amendment would then have to garner the approval of a majority of the city's voters casting ballots in the general election, rather than just a majority of those voting on the amendment proposal. It was a well-known fact, however, that a majority of those voting in general elections did not even bother to look at the issues on the ballot, let alone vote on them. As the Washington Supreme Court noted in holding this charter provision to be contrary to the state constitution: "It will be safe to say that the freeholders' charter of Seattle bids fair to take rank among the famed oriental laws that never could be changed."[14]

Minnesota lawmakers also established notable barriers to change. New home-rule charters in that state required the approval of four-sevenths of those participating in the ratifying election, and as in Missouri and California, three-fifths of those casting ballots on election day would have to endorse any charter amendment before it became effective.[15] Moreover, in both Washington and Minnesota, home-rule charters were subject to the general laws of the state, and such legislation was to take priority.

In each of the four states that adopted constitutional home-rule provisions in the nineteenth century, the emphasis was not on liberating the city from the supervision or control of the state. Rather, the goal was to block ceaseless, costly change and to halt the constant amendments granted by indulgent politicians in the local legislative delegation. Home-rule advocates sought to diminish the power of political brokers and lobbyists serving special interests within the cities and to curb what they considered the irresponsible use of state lawmaking authority. The Saint Louis and San Francisco delegates to the Missouri and California constitutional conventions had few qualms about general legislation. What they resented were the special bills that endlessly passed through the legislative chambers. In 1875 a Saint Louis delegate explained that "the main object the St. Louis delegation had in view was that this interminable tinkering with charters might be stopped."[16] Drafters of the fundamental law in Missouri, California, Washington, and Minnesota framed their constitutions to achieve just this end.

CONSEQUENCES OF CONSTITUTIONAL HOME RULE

The legal stability sought by drafters of the original home-rule provisions during the late nineteenth century was largely achieved. In both Missouri and California, constitutional barriers to capricious change ended the practice of perpetual tinkering and ensured that charter revisions were relatively few and infrequent. State legislators ceased to churn out laws authorizing the paving of a certain city street or the extension of a specific local park. Moreover, voter-mandated charter changes were rare or nonexistent.

Yet the social and economic currents of change continued to propel the cities of Saint Louis and San Francisco inexorably onward. Populations soared, demands for new services increased, expectations rose, and fads in municipal reform appeared and disappeared. But whereas the needs and desires of many of the city's residents changed, the home-rule system of municipal government proved inflexible. Thus during the 1880s and 1890s some of the very citizens who had demanded an end to legislative interference found themselves yearning for additional flexibility. Occasionally they turned again to the state legislatures, seeking special laws cloaked in the garb of the general legislation. By 1900 some viewed the previously desired permanence as a form of paralysis, and realized that in a changing world stability was a close cousin of stagnation. The fathers of constitutional home rule had attempted to create a consensual and permanent legal foundation for cities beset by flux and conflicting aims. In so doing they denied the local legislative delegation its necessary role as broker among the fragmented urban interests petitioning for favors. Lacking political brokers, governmental rigidity resulted. At the close of the century it seemed to many that the constitutional framers had built the barriers to change a bit too high.

The consequences of constitutional reform were readily evident in late-nineteenth-century Saint Louis. During the decade 1865 to 1875, prior to home rule, the local legislative delegation had bestowed two new charters on Saint Louis and debated still another general revision of the city's municipal framework. The average life expectancy of a city charter at that time was four or five years. Yet the first home-rule charter of Saint Louis, adopted in 1876, survived as the fundamental law of the city with relatively few changes until 1914. Similarly, between 1863 and 1875 Missouri's legislators had ratified seventy measures broadening or amending the powers and responsibilities of Saint Louis.[17] After 1875 state lawmakers continued to amend the city's charter through "general" laws applying to cities of one-hundred thousand or more population, a category consisting solely of Saint Louis. But from 1876 through 1888 the legislature passed only six measures amending the charter, and the city's voters only approved an additional four minor changes through the home-rule amendment process.[18] Thus, the rapid structural change of 1863 to 1875 had yielded to stability bordering on ossification during the period 1876 to 1888.

Two factors contributed to this structural inflexibility: first, the hostility or indifference of the city electorate to amendment proposals; and second, the self-restraint of the state legislature. After 1894 Missouri's judiciary reinforced the second factor by occasionally reminding the legislators of the need for restraint. But during the first years of home rule it was primarily the Saint Louis voters and the Jefferson City solons who ensured that the expectations of the framers of the 1875 constitution were, in fact, realized. The framers had intended to create a less flexible, less manipulable system of lawmaking for the state's largest city, and in the 1880s the urban citizenry and state legislators worked to guarantee such a system.

No group seemed more dedicated to the status quo than did the city's electorate. Repeatedly the citizens of Saint Louis marched to the polls and vetoed charter proposals sponsored by the city council. In 1879 a joint committee of the municipal assembly submitted thirty-six proposed amendments to the voters, and not one of the thirty-six received a simple majority, let alone the extraordinary three-fifths majority required by the Missouri Constitution of 1875. The only proposal that aroused a general furor was one authorizing regulation of brothels in order to prevent the spread of venereal disease. Both the *St. Louis Globe-Democrat* and the local clergy attacked this as "an illy-disguised attempt to legalize prostitution in [the] city."[19] The other proposals, however, were mostly minor revisions that dealt with a variety of technical flaws in the original document. Yet on election day the voters defeated each of the thirty-six proposals recommended by their municipal lawmakers. Less than half the number of citizens voted on the amendments as voted for city council candidates two weeks later, and a substantial portion of the electorate in all of the wards, including both wealthy neighborhoods and immigrant slums, were so apathetic that they did not vote.[20] But the majority of those who did vote, voted no.

Undaunted, the municipal assembly in 1881 proposed thirteen amendments to the charter of 1876 and submitted these proposals to the voters in the general election. In that election thirty-seven thousand voters cast ballots for mayor, but only thirteen thousand voted on the amendments. Eleven of the thirteen amendments won the approval of at least three-fifths of the thirteen thousand, but the 1875 constitution required approval by three-fifths of all those participating in the election. Since less than two-fifths of the total participating voted on the amendments, all thirteen went down to defeat.[21]

Their expectations having been reduced, the municipal lawmakers in 1885 submitted only six proposed amendments at a special election, and finally achieved a limited victory, with the city electorate approving two of the proposals while defeating the remaining four. Of the two amendments that passed, one changed the opening date of the municipal assembly from the first to the third Tuesday in April. (City lawmakers had proposed this change in both 1879 and 1881, because every second year the first Tuesday of April was election day, with the result that the municipal assembly was to convene the same day that it was being elected.) The other amendment that was approved clarified the mayor's veto power and required him to transmit to the assembly his reasons for vetoing an ordinance. The four amendments that were defeated dealt with the vital questions of street construction and taxation.[22] The voters thus accepted a few minor structural revisions, but in general they were hostile to most change.

The voters in the 1885 Saint Louis election were, moreover, a decided minority of the urban electorate. In 1885 only about 25 percent of those who normally voted in city elections cast ballots on the amendment proposals. Voter indifference was a well-established pattern by the mid-1880s when the *St. Louis Globe-Democrat* editorialized that it would be "something of a wonder to see the St. Louis people turn out to vote on a mere question of organic law." According to the newspaper, "the 'nice people' of St. Louis will never turn out to vote; [and] the ward politicians and strikers do not care to vote where there are no offices and no campaign funds to divide." Consequently, "the organic law of the city is always left to take care of itself."[23] Contests between partisan candidates stirred emotions and enthusiasm, activated party machinery, and drew voters to the polls. But obscurely phrased proposals on dry matters such as special assessments and municipal indebtedness either bored or confused most voters, who were unsure of the meaning or significance of the small print. As a result, most voters stayed at home on special charter election days, and those who did vote generally voted no if there was any reason to believe that the arcane proposals might tax their wallets. The future of the city's government, it seemed, was in the hands of a minority of naysayers. Of the fifty-five amendments submitted to Saint Louis voters during the first decade following the adoption of the home-rule charter, only two had succeeded in the referenda.

Though two more amendments won voter endorsement in 1888 and another passed in 1891, the electorate continued to demonstrate its opposition to additions and revisions to the St. Louis city charter. In 1898 the municipal assembly submitted four amendment proposals aimed at easing charter restrictions on financing the construction of public buildings, sewers, and streets, but each suffered defeat in twenty-seven of the city's twenty-eight wards and lost by a more than three-to-one margin citywide. Suspicious of the motives of politicians in the discredited legislative branch of city government, voters refused to endorse proposals that might burden the taxpayer.[24] In the end, uncompliant urban voters would prove much more of an obstacle to the schemes of the city council or mayor than the lawmakers in Jefferson City ever had.

Although after the adoption of the 1875 home-rule provisions solons in the state capital would still be the source of some aid, even among the state legislators the traditional attitude of permissiveness no longer prevailed. The state's supreme court ruled as early as 1884 that state lawmakers could enact "general" laws applying only to the city of Saint Louis.[25] Such laws were relatively few, however, as compared to the number of local bills enacted in the 1860s and early 1870s, and most often state legislation on Saint Louis dealt with the city's judicial system, which legislators regarded as being among the county responsibilities of the independent city and not among those associated with the traditional municipality. The Missouri legislature no longer issued new charters every four or five years, and the local delegation in Jefferson City no longer could guarantee passage of special-interest or reform schemes. By the mid-1880s Missouri's state legislators were not the glad-handed dispensers of urban law they had once been.

During the first few legislative sessions following adoption of home rule, the Saint Louis delegation continued to operate as a special committee of the state legislature, determining questions relating specifically to Saint Louis. Occasionally, old-fashioned ripper bills aimed at wreaking political vengeance appeared before the delegation. For example, in 1881 opponents of Saint Louis's Mayor Henry Overstolz introduced a bill to amend the city charter so that the mayor could not serve more than four years in office. The *St. Louis Globe-Democrat* urged that nothing be "done to [the city's] Charter by Jefferson City influences," and a member of the Saint Louis municipal assembly appeared before the Saint Louis legislative delegation and "intimated that he wanted no tampering . . . or interference in local affairs." According to one reporter, "the measure did not seem to meet with much favor" among the delegation itself, and the Saint Louis legislators eventually killed the bill.[26] But the incident demonstrated that some were still willing to turn to the legislative delegation in order to achieve partisan charter revisions.

Within a few years, however, the local delegation was to lose some of its prerogatives, when the legislative tradition of deference to the locality suffered a telling blow. In 1883 the Committee on Rules of the Missouri House of Representatives recommended that "the practice of constituting the St. Louis delegation a standing committee of the House, with a special clerk, be abolished."[27] Saint Louis members succeeded in defeating the recommendation, but it foretold an end to the delegation's privileged position. Two years later, in 1885, the Saint Louis members were themselves sharply divided as to the need for such a committee. Finally recognizing the full meaning of the home-rule provision, one Saint Louis member argued that "the object of this committee is to accomplish local or special legislation, and [the committee] is unconstitutional per se." Missouri's lieutenant governor, in his role as president of the state senate, contended that the practice of establishing the Saint Louis delegation as a standing committee to handle Saint Louis legislation was "entirely unnecessary and by no means to be desired." According to this official, the adoption of home rule and the constitutional ban on special legislation meant that "now . . . there are no laws to be passed relating to St. Louis which are not of interest to the State, and all the Representatives should create them and conduct their passage."[28]

Such words marked an end to the traditional power of the local delegation in determining city legislation. In 1885 the Missouri House of Representatives proceeded to abolish the Saint Louis committee, and henceforth the speaker of the house assigned municipal legislation to the Committee on Banks and Corporations, a majority of whose members hailed from districts outside of Saint Louis. Moreover, the state senators from Saint Louis no longer exercised formal privileges with regard to local legislation that they once had enjoyed. With the adoption of home rule, local reliance on the state legislature declined and the permissive legislative practice of deference to the local will disappeared. Since special legislation was unconstitutional, all legislation was now supposedly of general interest and subject to the scrutiny of members from throughout the state. Prior to 1875 bills affecting the municipal government of Saint Louis had been the business solely of the elected spokesmen of Saint Louis. After 1885, lawmakers framed such measures as general laws and submitted them to committees consisting of men from city and country. In 1889 one Saint Louis member of the Missouri House of Representatives lamented "the existence of an element in the Assembly which is opposed to anything St. Louis wants, for no other reason than that she wants it."[29] The home-rule constitution of 1875 had outlawed special legislation and thereby limited the capacity for urban self-rule. But this was what the constitution's framers had desired, a system of lawmaking less compliant to diverse urban interests. By the mid-1880s, such a system existed.

Some who had originally sought a less flexible, less permissive structure were, however, having doubts by the 1880s. Inflexibility was admirable when it thwarted the manipulations of one's enemies. But when voter indifference or hostility teamed up with legislative restraint to block one's own schemes, the merits of the system were less obvious. As a delegate to Missouri's Constitutional Convention of 1875, Joseph Pulitzer had been an ardent foe of the constant altering of city charters and had advocated a permanent, fundamental law for the city. Yet by 1881 Pulitzer's newspaper, the *Post-Dispatch*, was actually demanding some intervention, and most notably the revision of the strict limitations imposed by the 1876 charter on the municipal taxing powers. The *Post-Dispatch* claimed that Saint Louis was "generally being choked and strangled by a hoggish Charter which seems to have been cut out for Jefferson City instead of a metropolis." According to the newspaper, "under the limited levy fixed by the Charter the city is running behind and wearing."[30] Pulitzer's rival, the *Globe-Democrat*, also decried the limitations imposed by the unrevised charter, and in 1881, following the defeat of amendments that would limit the power of private utility companies, it proclaimed that "the city is practically at the mercy of the gas companies."[31] A charter designed for the stringent times of the depression-ridden 1870s was thought inadequate for the more affluent 1880s. And citizens who sought better pavements, new sewers, and an improved water supply felt trapped by the obstacles to change imposed by home rule.

During the 1890s the situation worsened, for the state supreme court began imposing new limits on state legislative authority. In 1894 Missouri's highest tribunal invalidated a state law applying to cities of three-hundred thousand or more inhabitants, ruling that it applied only to Saint Louis and was therefore special legislation.[32] The court sporadically and inconsistently pursued this argument through the remainder of the century, limiting the authority of state lawmakers to legislate for Saint Louis. At the close of the century Saint Louis continued to operate under its charter of 1876, a document that reflected the views of the 1870s and was notably out of step with the latest reform fashions. Though municipal theorists of the 1890s were extolling strong-mayor government with power concentrated in the hands of a single executive, Saint Louis was subject to a charter that divided power between two houses of a city council, various independent department heads, a board of public improvements, and a relatively weak mayor. Those wanting to reform this structure could no longer take their cause to a permissive legislature nor could they expect to win reforms from a naysaying or apathetic electorate.

In the late 1880s Kansas City passed the one-hundred-thousand mark in population and thus was eligible to become the second home-rule city in Missouri. Though Kansas City voters were not as hostile to change as those in

Saint Louis, Missouri's second largest city also experienced the restraints imposed by the home-rule provisions of the state constitution. In 1888 Kansas City voters defeated the first home-rule charter drafted by the board of freeholders, thus indicating that voter sanction was not to be automatic in Kansas City any more than in Saint Louis.[33] The following year voters finally approved a new charter, but the Missouri courts soon curbed the state legislature's power to aid Kansas City in meeting the new demands of the late nineteenth century. In the 1890s the state supreme court twice invalidated state laws creating park commissions for Kansas City, and the second decision specifically rejected the legislative action as a violation of the home-rule provision of the state constitution.[34] In 1905 the electorate again stymied reform by rejecting a new city charter that had been drafted with the cooperation of municipal experts, and not until 1908 did Kansas City obtain a more "up-to-date" framework for municipal rule.[35]

Thus in both Kansas City and Saint Louis, the framers of the 1875 constitution largely achieved their goal. During the 1880s and 1890s the home-rule provision did raise the barriers to charter tinkering and did thwart those who sought to manipulate the structure of municipal government for their own ends. The permissive tradition of referring all Saint Louis measures to the Saint Louis delegation disappeared, and both legislative self-restraint and occasional judicial action limited the opportunities for tampering with the city's fundamental law. Home rule in Missouri ensured a more solid, stable foundation for the framework of city government, but it proved a deterrent to those who conscientiously sought additions and repairs for a faulty and aging structure.

In San Francisco home rule also produced an inflexibility in the lawmaking process that hampered those seeking change. As in Missouri, San Francisco voters, state legislators, and jurists together ensured that the structure of city rule would remain almost unchanged for twenty years after the ratification of the constitution of 1879. While new municipal services became commonplace in cities across the nation and American municipal reformers experimented with multiple schemes to purify and streamline city government, San Francisco remained trapped in the procedural web of the state's home-rule provisions—this, despite the fact that San Francisco's population rose almost 50 percent from 1880 to 1900.

Basic to the dilemma of San Francisco government was the persistent opposition of city voters to the adoption of new charters. Like their counterparts in Saint Louis, San Francisco citizens voted against such charters much more often than they voted for them. In 1880, 1883, 1887, and 1896, the handiwork of successive boards of freeholders suffered defeat. Not until 1898 did the electorate approve a new charter, which took effect in 1900, replacing that much-reviled but durable patchwork of legislative measures enacted by state solons prior to 1879.

Time and again the majority of San Francisco's electors proved apathetic or hostile to changing the structure of city government. In 1880 many denounced a provision of the proposed charter forbidding burials within the city limits and also repudiated a section threatening to lower school expenditures and teachers' salaries. The Roman Catholic archbishop attacked the charter's burial provision, claiming that "it confers a power on the Common Council the exercise of which would amount to sacrilege."[36] Voters responded by defeating the charter by a margin of better than four to one. The charter failed to win a simple majority in 136 of the city's 137 precincts, with virtually every neighborhood from Nob Hill to Chinatown rejecting the document.[37] In 1883 another freeholder's charter lost by thirty-two votes out of a total of over eighteen thousand ballots.[38] Repeating the pattern of disinterest apparent in Missouri, less than half of those who voted in the previous general election cast ballots in this charter referendum. The *San Francisco Chronicle* inferred from the results "that the class most interested in securing for the city an economical and efficient City Government were too indolent to go to the polls."[39] In 1887 opponents of still another home-rule charter attacked centralization of power and claimed that the charter would make "the Mayor a perfect autocrat."[40] Again, less than half the registered voters marched to the polls, where 60 percent rejected the proposed framework of municipal rule.[41] Nine years later, in November, 1896, indifference still prevailed when less than 40 percent of those casting votes in the presidential contest bothered to vote that same day on the fourth freeholders' charter. Since the home-rule provisions of the constitution of 1879 required approval by a majority of those voting in the election, the indifference of 60 percent of those who went to the polls automatically doomed the 1896 proposal to defeat.[42]

Finally, in 1898 in a special election, 35 percent of San Francisco's registered voters straggled into the polls, and a majority of these approved a new charter for the city.[43] The state legislature then readily and without debate sanctioned the charter in accord with the provisions of the constitution of 1879. After five attempts and nineteen years, the citizenry discarded the makeshift mass of legislative measures enacted in the 1850s, 1860s, and 1870s and adopted a new fundamental law for their municipality. The drafters of the 1879 constitution had acted in fear of frequent and precipitous revision of the governmental structure. Under the system of home rule, apathy and a negative penchant ensured that such kaleidoscopic legal change would not prevail. As was the case with Saint Louis citizens, San Franciscans were not greatly stirred by charter contests and tedious questions of governmental mechanics, and among those civic-minded souls willing to vote, change was more an object of suspicion than of hope. San Franciscans were reluctant to endorse the proposals of the board of freeholders, just as Saint Louis voters refused to sanction the schemes of the municipal assembly. The untried and unknown might prove costly and endanger the interests of Catholics, burial plot owners, school teachers, or any number of other special groups. The status quo generally seemed safer.

Reinforcing this inflexibility in the lawmaking structure was the California Supreme Court. In 1880 the state legislature enacted a "general" charter for the "government of merged and consolidated cities and counties of more than one hundred thousand population," a category that included only one municipality, the city and county of San Francisco. Opponents of the charter immediately challenged this legislative interference in the courts, and that same year the California Supreme Court voided the legislative charter as unconstitutional. First, the court held that the general intention of the new constitution "to emancipate municipalities . . . from the control of the Legislature is apparent" and that a majority of the voters of a muncipality had to approve adoption of a general law charter before it could become the fundamental law of the city. Second, the court ruled that the charter in question was not a general law but a form of special legislation in violation of the constitution. Under the constitution, state lawmakers could enact legislation applying to cities classified according to population but could not add the qualification that the legislation applied solely to merged cities and counties.[44] San Francisco was the only merged city and county in the state, and, consequently, any legislation referring exclusively to merged cities and counties was a form of special legislation. Henceforth, voter ratification was necessary for the adoption of a general-law charter, and the legislature could classify cities only on the basis of population.

This decision seriously limited the possibility of legislative tampering with San Francisco's structure of government. In 1882 the California Supreme Court did uphold the state legislature's authority to amend San Francisco's existing legislative charter without local voter ratification, but the legislature had to frame the amendment as a general law, and state lawmakers could not substitute an entirely new framework unless the voters approved.[45] State legislation dealing with the city government of San Francisco dwindled to virtually nothing in the 1880s; the legislature no longer organized the San Francisco delegation as a standing committee; and the permissive tradition of lawmaking by local representatives disappeared. In the late 1890s lawmakers in Sacramento were to churn out more San Francisco measures than during the previous fifteen years, and the city's delegation momentarily regained standing-committee status.[46] But no longer could the local representatives create, revise, and re-create the structure of local government without interference from country colleagues or city voters.

Caught between the jaws of naysaying or indifferent voters and the state's supreme court, city officials and reform groups found structural change impossible. Proponents of home-rule charters repeatedly urged the electorate to make the short trip to the polls to save the city from ruin. In 1887 the *San Francisco Chronicle* told its readers that they would have "only their own apathy and indifference to blame if . . . [the city] finally goes head under in the slime and mire of municipal misrule and corruption." Moreover, it warned that a no vote would "doom the city to another decade of stagnation, retrogression and decrepitude."[47] Nine years later the Merchants' Association called upon the voters to "awaken . . . to [the] crisis of affairs in our city" and ominously contended that "permanent progress and prosperity can never come to this muncipality under the present obsolete, defective and chaotic system of municipal government."[48] The home-rule provisions of the Constitution had blocked the traditional channels for adapting the municipal structure to the changing times. San Francisco's voters seemed dedicated either to ignoring charter questions or retaining their current ramshackle structure that was based on almost four-hundred and fifty acts of the state legislature. Consequently, the structure, powers, and responsibilities of San Francisco's city government remained virtually unchanged.

In both Saint Louis and San Francisco, then, the consequences of municipal home rule were similar. Missouri's Constitution of 1875 and California's Constitution of 1879 both marked the end of responsive, permissive, and manipulative urban lawmaking in those states. Before the late 1870s the state legislatures generally enacted whatever the local legislative delegation endorsed; a small cadre of elected representatives decided charter questions, and they were amenable to proposals for revision. Framers of home-rule procedures, however, succeeded in transferring authority from the legislator to the electorate, and urban voters proved much less sympathetic to amendments than were the legislative delegations of the past. Though other cities experienced rampant charter tampering during the late nineteenth century, the lawmaking structure remained remarkably unchanged in Saint Louis and San Francisco. Home rule had thwarted the army of charter tinkerers who sought change in the pursuit of reform, privilege, political advantage, or profit.

By the turn of the century, however, the course of municipal home rule had begun to shift as urban leaders recognized the flaws in the procedure. In both Missouri and California, constitutional amendments removed certain obstacles to the revision of charters. For example, in 1902 Missouri voters approved deletion of the clause forbidding the amendment of charters at less than two-year intervals. Moreover, such amendments henceforth needed to win the approval of only three-fifths of those voting on the proposition and not three-fifths of those participating in the election. The constitutional amendment of 1902 also stated clearly that a Saint Louis board of freeholders could propose an entirely new charter to replace the existing home-rule charter.[49] With their aversion for charter revolutions and their dream of a permanent fundamental law, the members of the convention of 1875 had failed to specify whether the home-rule provision granted Saint Louis continuing authority to draft and redraft new charters. Now Missouri's largest city had definite authorization to cast aside its handiwork of 1876 and frame a more modern instrument for urban rule.

That same year in California, state voters also approved a constitutional amendment that eliminated certain barriers to the adoption or revision of charters. The amendment changed the requirement for adoption of a charter from a majority of those voting at the election to a majority of those voting on the charter proposition.[50] This would prevent a repetition of the debacle of 1896, when the home rule charter suffered automatic defeat because less than 40 percent of those casting ballots in the presidential contest bothered to vote yes or no on the proposal. Also after 1902 only a simple majority was necessary for the approval of charter amendments, as opposed to the extraordinary three-fifths majority specified in the constitution of 1879.

Elsewhere the same trend was evident. None of the states that incorporated home-rule provisions in their constitutions after 1900 required extraordinary majorities, and each permitted citizens to initiate charter amendments through a petition signed by a specified percentage of voters. The barriers to change were falling, and constitutional framers no longer seemed so dedicated to the ideal of a permanent, consensual charter, an expression of the general will intended to serve for decades. Instead, they were opening the door to amendments and revisions.

This change in the method of adopting or altering home-rule charters reflects a change in the goals of constitutional framers. The urban delegates to the Missouri and California constitutional conventions of the 1870s had not opposed the passage of truly general laws applicable to their cities. They had attacked the continuous flow of special laws that seemed to keep city government in constant and costly flux. To halt this excess of lawmaking, they thus sought to erect barriers to legislative action and to turn the referendum process into an obstacle course.

By 1900, however, constitutional framers were less concerned about an excess of lawmaking and more concerned about who was making the law. General legislation governing municipal questions was increasingly under attack, and in 1896 Californians ratified a constitutional amendment specifically stating that "municipal affairs" were not subject to or controlled by the general laws of the legislature.[51] In many home-rule states during the early twentieth century, courts adopted this limitation on the state's lawmaking powers. In the twentieth century home-rule advocates were suspicious of state lawmakers; in the 1870s they had feared all lawmakers.

In summary, nineteenth-century home rule was a product of those who opposed excessive change, who sought stability, and who hoped to build a lasting foundation for city government. They dreamed of legal monuments in an age of jerry-built law. They were determined to block the traditional channels to structural change, and in Missouri and California they largely destroyed the adaptive mechanism of special legislation and the permissive practice of deference to the local legislative delegation. Their goal was perhaps unrealistic in light of the rapid social and economic change of the period. But they introduced a lawmaking procedure that was to assume new importance in the twentieth century.

THE ORIGINS OF STATE ADMINISTRATIVE SUPERVISION

Though home rule was much applauded by reformers at the turn of the century, the concurrent trend toward state administrative supervision of city government was perhaps of greater significance. For from the pioneer efforts of nineteenth-century administrators grew the state bureaucratic structure of the twentieth century. During the 1880s and 1890s administrative supervision was in its nascency; however, the increasing need for professional expertise and for statewide coordination of affairs spurred demands for administrative development, demands that would win a favorable response in the first decades of the twentieth century. As early as the 1890s, lawmakers were beginning to refashion the relationship between city and state by adding a new decision-making element, the central bureaucracy with coercive power to implement the orders of professionals. By 1900 city councils and urban boards of education were gradually becoming subordinated not simply to the mandates of state legislators but also to the dictates of an increasing number of state administrators.

From the midcentury on, state legislators had been creating state offices designed to aid and educate local government officials in both city and country. County tax assessors were subject to some control from state boards of equalization, and state boards of charity attempted to impose certain standards on county poor farms and almshouses. State superintendents of schools collected statistics from local school districts and disseminated information on the latest innovations in teaching among city superintendents and boards of education. In 1869 Massachusetts established the first state board of health, and during the next twenty years, twenty-nine other states followed its example. These agencies collected statistics on disease, computed birth and death rates, and investigated health conditions in localities throughout the state.

Yet the state boards of health, state superintendents, and state commissions were for the most part advisory, with authority to gather data and to inform local governments but without power to coerce localities or order action at the local level. Central administrators were especially ineffectual in dealing with city governments. Some state superintendents could impose minimum qualifications for rural teachers or devise certifying examinations for instructors of one-room schoolhouses. But during the nineteenth century the wealthier urban school districts with their professional superintendents and corps of supervisors and principals were allowed to operate relatively free of interference from the state educational authorities. In the early 1890s a student of Philadelphia city government observed that "the State Department of Public Instruction is rather [more] statistical and advisory than administrative" and the state "superintendent has little to do with Philadelphia."[52] The same could be said of nearly every state administrative agency in the nation. Each was statistical and advisory, and prior to the 1890s few had dominion over the nation's major cities.

State legislators had, of course, created state-appointed commissions to handle certain functions in individual urban centers. Gubernatorial appointees, for example, governed the police forces in St. Louis, Kansas City, and Baltimore, and other state-appointed boards controlled public works in Cincinnati and Denver. Such commissions, however, were makeshift legislative responses to local problems in certain individual municipalities and did not represent a systematic state program of administrative control. These were not agencies created to achieve expert, bureaucratic supervision or statewide coordination. Instead, they were often either partisan creations, arising from a clash of local political interests, or reform schemes designed to ensure the dominance of a local elite. Prior to 1890, state legislatures had not established departments of local government to administer each of the local units within the state, and they had not yet established a system of centralized coercion by experts. There was as yet no American tradition of central administration by state inspectors, auditors, or engineers.

However, from 1885 to 1900, a gradual increase in administrative supervision became apparent. In the areas of water supply, sewerage, education, and finance, state administrators for the first time were assuming coercive authority over urban governments. New technology, growing professionalism in engineering, and an emerging awareness of the opportunity for a healthier environment bolstered support for state administrative regulation of water resources. Meanwhile, pedagogues urged the creation of state educational bureaucracies to ensure uniform standards of schooling. And an emerging faith in statistical data and the new cult of efficiency led to increased agitation for central administrative supervision of municipal accounting. Clearly, full-blown mechanisms of central control did not arise overnight in cities like Albany, Harrisburg, or Columbus; local power was, after all, a jealously guarded asset. But by 1890 the current was moving toward centralized administration, and some state agencies were beginning to assume supervisory authority over certain municipal functions.

The change was especially evident in the area of water supply and public health. In the late 1880s and early 1890s typhoid fever continued to ravage the nation's cities, and sanitary experts recognized the link between polluted water, untreated sewage, and this dread killer of thousands. The rivers that provided drinking water and served as outlets for city sewage defied local political boundaries, flowing from county to county and city to city. Even if city officials adhered to the finest sanitary standards, the local citizenry could suffer due to the incompetence of officers many miles upstream. Americans needed statewide supervision if water supplies were to be safe and the public health protected. Americans also needed professional guidance by engineers and public health experts. Not every state legislator or city councilman understood typhoid bacilli, filtration plants, and sewage treatment. Statewide coordination and professionalism were thus necessary in the field of sanitation, and, to achieve a safer, healthier environment, legislators had to grant state-employed experts coercive authority.

At professional meetings and in professional journals, physicians and engineers repeatedly called for coercive action by state boards of health. As early as 1882 the secretary of Indiana's Board of Health, speaking before the members of the American Public Health Association, urged that "provision should be made by order of the State Board of Health for abandonment of shallow wells as sources of supply of potable water," and he insisted that improvement in health conditions would "not take place except under compulsory rules, firmly enforced."[53] In 1891 the American Water Works Association unanimously endorsed a bill in the Pennsylvania legislature providing that no water supply system "shall be constructed, enlarged, or used" when the State Board of Health "shall by its certificate in writing express its disapproval thereof as dangerous or unsafe to the public health."[54] Five years later a group of Illinois civil engineers and physicians met in the Chicago offices of the Western Society of Engineers and appointed a committee to draft a bill that would "give to some central body the power to regulate city water supplies and sewerage systems."[55] That same year the editors of the periodical *Municipal Engineering* endorsed state control of water supply and sewerage and argued "the more thorough the control the better the results." They contended that state supervision of municipal sanitation was necessary because of "the ignorance of the public in regard to engineering questions and as to competency of engineers, and the consequent certainty that much work will be done on defective plans or without plan."[56] Both physicians and engineers recognized the dangers arising from unsupervised, unprofessional local sanitation, and the solution they proposed was state administrative control by trained experts.

State legislatures soon heeded such complaints. As early as the late 1880s New York's legislature had enacted special laws requiring certain municipalities to submit their plans for sewerage systems to the State Board of Health for its approval. In 1889 New York's legislators passed a general law granting the health board veto-power over the sewerage proposals of all villages in the state.[57] Likewise in 1888 the Massachusetts legislature required all municipalities installing a system of water supply or sewerage to present their plans to the State Board of Health in order to obtain its expert advice, and ordered that "all petitions to the legislature for authority to introduce a system of water supply, drainage or sewerage shall be accompanied by a copy of the recommendation and advice of the said board thereon."[58] Massachusetts's Board of Health had no authority to order local units to change their schemes for water supply or sewerage, but the legislature always adhered to the board's "recommendation and advice" so that the judgment of the board was as good as law.[59] Massachusetts's board, in fact, became a model for the rest of the nation. During the 1890s it represented the epitome of expertise, with professors from Massachusetts Institute of Technology employed as water analysts and consulting biologists, and a graduate of the Hygienic Institute of the University of Berlin acting as a bacteriologist.

Other states sought to create similar agencies of expertise and to subject municipal water and sewerage systems to a central administrative authority. The first actually to require state board approval of all municipal water and sewerage systems was Ohio, in 1893. The Ohio Board of Health, created in 1886, sponsored the bill extending its authority and enlisted the vigorous backing of the Ohio Society of Surveyors and Civil Engineers, which unanimously endorsed the proposed measure at its annual meeting of 1892. One Ohio engineer expressed the feelings of his colleagues when he observed that many of the state's streams "are made absolutely unfit for water supply by reason of the vast amount of sewerage and refuse that find their way into these streams," and the president of the engineering society observed that the state's rivers, which had once been the natural highway of commerce, "are now the natural highway of sewerage."[60] Ohioans realized that something had to be done; state legislators could not handle the problem simply through statutory law, nor could local officials cope with it through city ordinances. Expert state administration was felt to be the answer.

The Ohio law of 1893 was supposed to provide such administration. Under this law no municipality or water company could "introduce a public water supply or system of sewerage, or change or extend" any supply or system then in use, "unless the proposed source of such water supply or outlet for such sewerage system shall have been submitted to and received the approval of the state board of health."[61] Unfortunately, niggardly funding by the legislature hampered sanitary investigations, but in 1898 the legislature did empower the board to create a laboratory for chemical and bacteriological examinations of water samples.[62] By 1899 the board had been called upon to approve plans for water and sewage systems for 142 municipalities and public institutions.[63]

During the following decade other state boards of health also exercised veto power over municipal water and sanitation schemes. In 1902 Minnesota's State Board of Health ordered municipalities to submit all plans for new waterworks and sewerage lines to the board for its approval.[64] Three years later the legislatures of Pennsylvania and Wisconsin granted similar authority to their state boards, and in 1907 Kansas adopted the Ohio model and likewise required approval by the Kansas State Board of Health for the construction or extension of water or sewerage schemes.[65] By the late 1920s at least thirty-one states required central administrative approval of waterworks and sewerage proposals, and in at least sixteen states central agencies also had to inspect and approve the operation and maintenance of existing sewage disposal systems.[66] Before the late 1880s indifferent legislators had rubber-stamped locally sponsored bills for waterworks or sewerage schemes, and usually no one other than the local legislative delegation had ever read the measures. Outside interference in municipal public works had been politically motivated and generally sporadic. In contrast, by the early twentieth century, state engineers, bacteriologists, and physicians were beginning to examine, sample, and test state waters, and were overseeing the actions of cities in such matters to an unprecedented degree. In the field of sanitation, then, systematic supervision and administrative mandates were supplementing traditional statutory law.

Although in the 1890s the emerging role of the state expert was most evident in the field of sanitation and water supply, by the close of the century state-employed pedagogues were also seeking greater coercive powers in the area of education in an attempt to ensure uniform standards. In 1894 Indiana's superintendent of public instruction recommended that the state's "school system ought to be centralized in the hands of school experts such as the State Board of Education, and all under officials should be made answerable to the State Board." Two years later a new state superintendent reiterated these sentiments and urged that Indiana's state board upgrade the quality of city superintendents by establishing mandatory qualifications for the office. In 1898 still another Indiana superintendent complained that his duties were "too largely of an advisory character."[67] Meanwhile, the state superintendent of New York was attempting to force urban school districts to accept a uniform examination for teacher certification devised by the State Department of Public Instruction. Twenty-four of the state's thirty-eight cities had voluntarily adopted the department's standard examination by 1897, but the superintendent wanted mandatory compliance and argued, "No valid reasons have yet been assigned to show that the power to determine the method of examining and licensing teachers in cities should not be vested in the State Department of Public Instruction."[68]

Though local control of schooling remained a cardinal principle of American education, by the last decade of the nineteenth century more educators were speaking of the need for statewide uniformity and for greater central authority. In 1890 the state superintendent of New Hampshire, speaking before a meeting of the National Educational Association, contended that it was necessary "for the sake of harmony and efficiency of action, that town committees and county supervisors should be responsible to the State superintendent, and in general work under his direction."[69] A leading educational figure from Ohio responded to these comments by asserting that "the State superintendent should be invested with large powers," for "unless he holds such powers there can be no unified State system of schools." A colleague from Minnesota complained that as yet there were no state systems of education, and he called for "a general, authoritative State regulation." And a member of the National Educational Association from New Jersey seconded these views and advocated "a thorough system of State supervision."[70] Although the local lay school board remained enthroned in its seat of power, the lack of systematic, expert regulation and of professional uniformity in American education was troubling an increasing number of pedagogues.

During the 1890s state superintendents or departments of education did, however, win a few victories in their struggle for greater authority. One such conquest would be claimed by New York's central administrators. In 1895 the New York legislature enacted a law forbidding city school districts to employ anyone as a teacher unless the applicant had at least three years of teaching experience or had graduated from a "high school or academy having a course of study . . . approved by the State Superintendent of Public Instruction" and had subsequently completed a course of teacher's training approved by the state superintendent.[71] In other words, every urban high school in the state had to conform to a course of study determined by a state administrator. If any high school failed to conform, none of its graduates was eligible to teach in New York schools. No longer were the city boards of education or city superintendents free from state administrative supervision in designing the high school curriculum. Following passage of the law, New York's state superintendent drafted a standard plan of study for all urban high schools, requiring a minimum of three years of English, mathematics, foreign language, history and civics, drawing, and vocal music; two years of physics and botany; and one year each of geography and physiology and zoology. These were state-dictated requirements, and school authorities in New York City, Brooklyn, and Buffalo had to accept this administrative mandate. Moreover, these cities each maintained normal schools for the training of teachers, and these, too, now had to conform to the superintendent's rulings on curriculum. During the mid-1890s New York's cities dutifully submitted to the state superintendent's course of study, and in 1897 the superintendent reported that "by the close of the present school year all will have conformed to the regulations."[72]

Elsewhere legislatures were enhancing the authority of state boards and superintendents by empowering them to determine what textbooks should be assigned. A few states had experimented with a system of centrally designated textbooks as early as the 1870s, and between 1885 and 1899 at least fifteen states adopted the scheme. Five were sparsely populated, nonurban states in the Rocky Mountain region, but Michigan, Indiana, Missouri, and California were also among those that authorized state boards to select the textbooks to be used in every school district. Thus by the close of the century, state authorities were dictating what books were to be used in the city schools of Detroit, Indianapolis, Saint Louis, and San Francisco. According to Michigan's superintendent of public instruction, the need for expert guidance in the choice of textbooks was among the reasons for the adoption of the system in his state. Instead of leaving the matter in the hands of local school board members with little knowledge of pedagogy, the Michigan law provided "for competent judges in making the selection of books."[73]

These changes during the last fifteen years of the century were but the beginning of a gradual increase in central administrative authority. Local school officials clung to their autonomy with ferocity, but the continuing desire for professionalism and uniformity eroded the independence of the township, village, and city boards in the ensuing decades of the twentieth century. A central educational bureaucracy was to develop and state administrative dictates were to supplement the mandates of the state legislature.

Demands for professionalism and uniformity were also to produce new schemes for state administrative supervision of municipal finances. Just as engineers urged expert central coordination of sanitation projects and pedagogues spoke of statewide systematization of schooling, a band of efficiency-oriented reformers emerged during the 1890s, campaigning for uniform municipal accounting procedures devised by state accountants who would conduct mandatory audits of city financial records. Eager for more streamlined, efficient government and for a body of reliable comparative data with which to evaluate city services, university professors, accountants, business leaders, and engineers increasingly advocated state-imposed uniform accounting and regular state investigation of the municipal books. By the close of the century, the seemingly dry and pedestrian subject of uniform accounting had, in fact, become one of the chief planks in the platform of the reform-minded National Municipal League. State administrative supervision of city accounts had been adopted as a reform passion.

As early as 1891, a New York legislative committee investigating municipal rule complained of the difficulty of obtaining information about the financial condition of cities in the absence of any state law requiring submission of financial statistics.[74] In 1895 the Ohio State Board of Commerce, a business-man's reform group, resolved that the state general assembly should "establish a bureau for the collection and tabulation of municipal reports, which should be prepared by municipal officers, in a uniform manner to be prescribed by the head of such bureau."[75] That same year Professor J. R. Commons of Indiana University proposed the creation of a state municipal board with an auditing department "composed of experts" that would "prescribe a system of municipal bookkeeping and . . . examine the books of city officers at any time, without notice."[76] And in 1898 Professor C. W. Tooke of the University of Illinois, writing in the pages of *Municipal Affairs*, reiterated this desire for state-imposed uniformity in municipal accounting practices.[77]

One national organization after another joined in the call for greater central oversight of the municipal purse. In 1898 the League of American Municipalities adopted resolutions strongly endorsing state action to require uniform methods of accounting, a regular state audit of all municipal accounts, and compilation and publication by state authorities of the financial statistics of municipal corporations.[78] That same year a committee of the National Municipal League reported a "Municipal Program" that included a provision requiring "financial reports to be made to some fiscal officer of the State in accordance with the forms and methods prescribed by him." And in 1900 the League resolved "to appoint . . . a committee to give special consideration to the subject of uniform municipal accounts."[79] By the end of 1900, the American Economic Association, the American Statistical Association, the American Society of Civil Engineers, the American Public Health Association, and the League of American Municipalities were among the many organizations that had appointed committees to consider the subject.[80] Resolutions on the subject were rife and discussions frequent.

During the 1890s only the frontier state of Wyoming experimented with administrative supervision of municipal finances. In 1891 Wyoming's legislature created the Office of State Examiner, and in 1895 lawmakers in Cheyenne authorized the official appointed to fill this office to supervise not only the accounts of banks and county and state institutions but also the financial records of all municipal corporations within the state. The state examiner was expected to require a uniform system of bookkeeping for all public officials, so as to facilitate examination of their accounts, and was to instruct city officials in the proper methods of accounting. Moreover, he could require a financial statement from each municipality, and upon request of the city council he was to examine the municipal accounts and report any misappropriations or malfeasance. Thus, an appointed administrative official of the state of Wyoming was to dictate to municipal corporations how to keep their books and was to ensure that the city treasurers were properly executing their jobs. Henceforth, determination of the forms and procedures of municipal bookkeeping would rest in the hands of a state administrative official, and not with the state legislature or municipal council.[81]

Wyoming's experiment encouraged other states to do likewise. In 1896 two special commissions appointed to revise the mode of government in New York's second- and third-class cities (10,000 to 250,000 population) recommended the creation of a state municipal board to prescribe uniform methods of bookkeeping and to investigate municipal finances and contracts.[82] New York's legislature, however, failed to implement the recommendation, and not until 1902 did a major urban state, Ohio, adopt a system of administrative control with a Bureau of Supervision and Inspection authorized to impose uniform accounting procedures on every municipality in the state and to conduct annual audits of city records.[83] New York did copy the Ohio model in 1905, and in 1906 Iowa's legislature also created a Municipal Accounting Department with examiners who at least once every biennium were to audit the books of all cities having a population of 5,000 or more.[84] By 1913 twelve states from Masachusetts to California had enacted provisions for the installation of uniform accounts in cities and had established an administrative apparatus to supervise local finance.[85]

In the field of urban finance, as in education and sanitation, then, the last decade of the century marked the dawn of a new era in the relationship of city and state. During the 1890s advocates of efficiency, expertise, and statewide coordination urged the expansion of state administrative control of municipal government, and in the first decades of the twentieth century state legislatures responded to their arguments. Throughout the late nineteenth century legislators enacted scores of special bills to authorize the issuance of municipal bonds or the levying of a new local tax, yet there was no systematic administrative supervision of municipal financing. State guidance remained a matter of legislative mandate rather than administrative control. By the turn of the century, however, a new pattern was developing, and in the twentieth century state solons delegated much supervisory authority to accountants and auditors. These masters of the public ledgers joined state bacteriologists and state engineers as new actors in the drama of city government. No longer were state legislators the only source of central control. Instead, the state administrator was easing toward center stage.

Thus state administrative supervision, like municipal home rule, represented a shift in decision-making authority and a redefinition of the role of the state legislature. Proponents of enhanced central administrative authority hoped to stop amateurish interference by representatives and senators on technical questions and to limit their legislative role to the formulation of broad policy. Experts, it was reasoned, should be delegated responsibility for implementing legislative policy through specific dictates and systematic supervision. Advocates of home rule endeavored to halt the flood of irresponsible special bills rushed through permissive legislatures by compliant local delegations. They hoped to eliminate legislative logrolling and to enhance the veto power of the urban electorate. Missouri and California pioneered with home rule charters and referenda, whereas Massachusetts, Ohio, and New York were among the first to grant coercive authority to engineers, physicians, and educators in administrative agencies. In each of these states, however, the message was the same. Americans were tired of the tradition of legislative rule. As a result both the electorate and the expert were to gain authority. Rampant representative rule was under attack, and both direct democracy through referenda and technocracy through administrative supervision seemed to be gaining ground.

But home rule and central administrative supervision were as yet the exceptions and not the rule. In the overwhelming majority of states, state solons or at least local legislative delegations still determined the destiny of city charters and charter amendments. And in most states at the close of the century state experts still only advised on questions of municipal sanitation, urban education, or city finances. By 1900 state legislatures had delegated very little authority. Only during the twentieth century did the reform schemes of the 1870s, 1880s, and 1890s transform city-state relations throughout much of the nation.

6 THE PROFESSIONALS

 The stereotype of a city officeholder of the late nineteenth century is a paunchy ward heeler sporting a walrus mustache, decked in a shiny suit, and crowned with a cheap derby. He gnaws on malodorous cigars, speaks with an ill-educated Irish brogue, and devotes more time to politicking than to public administration. His survival in office depends on the election returns, and he comes and goes with the passing of each political regime. Every new mayor of the correct partisan persuasion finds the ward heeler waiting in line at city hall immediately following the mayoral swearing-in, and the wait usually garners him a job. A municipal mayfly, he develops no expertise in office, but remains in a post only long enough to fill his purse. Then he passes on, supplanted by another of his ilk. This is a portrait familiar even to the novice in American history, and has been sketched repeatedly by good-government reformers of the late nineteenth and early twentieth centuries, as well as by many conventional historians.

Like most stereotypes there is some truth to this portrait. Any visitor to the city halls of New York City, Chicago, Philadelphia, or Boston in the 1880s and 1890s might well have found scores of such figures inhabiting the offices and corridors, surviving off the largess of a grateful party. Yet others of a different breed would also be found on the municipal payroll—dedicated public employees with years of experience and training in their fields; men and women who served decade after decade no matter who was mayor, public works commissioner, school board president, or chairman of the parks commission. A complete picture of city officialdom should include not only the hacks but the hundreds of persons highly proficient in their work, many with national or international reputations. Even before the adoption of the first municipal civil service laws in the 1880s and 1890s, these professionals occupied public office, year after year managing the increasingly complex operations of the expanding cities. They built the giant waterworks, planned the sewerage projects, designed the parks, organized the libraries, taught millions of urban school children, and guarded the public health and safety. They were vital elements of the structure of urban government, for, to a great extent, they made the structure work. Aldermen served only two or three years; the mayor's office changed hands every biennium. Yet many less conspicuous functionaries occupied posts for years, maintaining the quality of municipal services no matter who won electoral office.

Moreover, rising expectations and changing technology heightened the importance of the municipal professionals. The ill-educated, inexperienced political appointee could neither manage the complex functions of ever-larger cities nor fathom the mysteries of bacteriology or sanitary engineering. During the late nineteenth century municipal services were expanding, and urban residents were demanding more from their city governments. Only trained and experienced officials could provide the safety and comfort that voters expected. Professional civil servants and expert consultants were thus essential to America's city fathers, for without them services would deteriorate and voters rebel.

With the increasing need to rely on experts, a permanent urban bureaucracy burgeoned. Civil engineers, landscape architects. librarians, school teachers, physicians, firemen, and policemen all occupied niches in the structure of urban rule. In city after city they mapped their own protected baronies of power, jealously guarding their domains from intrusions by politicians, good-government reformers, and even other bureaucrats. By the close of the century, many American cities were familiar not only with the rule of ward bosses but were experiencing the clout of a new breed of department bosses, functional lords who allowed little interference from lay persons and whose primary loyalty was to their profession and not to any party or political leader. These expert civil servants and their professional colleagues who served the cities as paid consultants were among the most significant participants in urban government during the late nineteenth century, and any survey of the American municipality must include their story.

CIVIL ENGINEERS

Perhaps the most important of the new bureaucrats was the civil engineer. Basic to the improvement of the American standard of living was the construction of waterworks, sewerage systems, bridges, and urban thoroughfares. Basic also to the expansion of the rapidly growing American cities was the extension of these public works. That these endeavors were so successful during the period 1870 to 1900 is owed to the imagination and expertise of a growing body of civil engineers. They were responsible for ensuring that water flowed into the kitchens and bathrooms of urban homes, that cities did not sink in a mire, and that human waste products somehow disappeared. Boston, New York City, and Chicago each embarked on giant public works projects for the comfort, convenience, and safety of urban dwellers, and each of these cities relied on a corps of professional engineers to achieve these ends. During the last decades of the nineteenth century, American cities employed scores of such experts, including the finest practitioners in the nation.

In New England's municipalities, continuity and expertise among employees of the city engineering departments was especially noteworthy. Though Massachusetts's civil service regulations did not cover municipal civil engineers until 1897, throughout the last thirty years of the century professionalism took precedence over partisan politics in the city engineering departments. In 1872, for example, Boston's leaders were unable to agree on a candidate for city engineer and referred the question to a commission of experts, who recommended Joseph P. Davis, a veteran of the municipal engineering departments of Brooklyn, Saint Louis, and Boston. Deferring to the judgment of the distinguished commission, Boston's city council elected Davis, who served eight years before resigning to become chief engineer of the American Telephone and Telegraph Company. Esteemed by his colleagues, Davis also served as president of the Boston Society of Civil Engineers and director and vice president of the American Society of Civil Engineers.[1] In proper bureaucratic fashion, Davis was succeeded as Boston's chief engineer by his erstwhile assistant city engineer, Henry M. Wightman, a man with twenty-three years of experience in the municipal engineering corps.[2] Following Wightman's death in 1885, an incumbent assistant, William Jackson, in turn acceded to the post of city engineer, serving for twenty-five years until his death in 1910. Jackson was a product of the Massachusetts Institute of Technology and had worked fourteen years in Boston's Engineering Department prior to his appointment as city engineer. Moreover, like his predecessors, he enjoyed the nationwide respect of his colleagues, as exemplified by his membership on the board of directors of the American Society of Civil Engineers.[3]

Others in Boston's engineering corps likewise served in office for decades with distinction. For example, the superintendent of the western division of the Boston waterworks from 1873 to 1902 was Desmond FitzGerald, an old-stock Yankee descendant of Rhode Island's founder Roger Williams, who enjoyed the unique honor of serving as president not only of the Boston Society of Civil Engineers but also of the New England Water Works Association and the American Society of Civil Engineers. In addition, he was the only person during the nineteenth century to twice win the Norman Medal, an annual prize awarded by the American Society of Civil Engineers for the best paper presented in the field of civil engineering.[4] Also working with FitzGerald and the Boston Engineering Department from 1873 to 1884 was Alphonse Fteley, another Norman Medalist and future president of the American Society of Civil Engineers.[5] Boston could have hired no more highly regarded experts in waterworks technology than FitzGerald and Fteley.

Longtime employees were commonplace among Boston's engineering corps, and they designed and maintained a variety of public works. For example, the chief engineer of Boston's Board of Survey joined the municipal engineering staff in 1856 and remained a city employee for thirty-five years. Another engineer supervised the construction of the city's bridges from 1874 until his death in 1906, and assisting him was a veteran civil servant who remained ensconced in city hall for forty-five of the forty-seven years from 1874 to 1921. The man chiefly responsible for park engineering likewise retained his post with the city for four decades. Still others served more than a quarter of a century planning and constructing Boston's public works.[6] During these long decades of service in the Engineering Department and waterworks, FitzGerald, Jackson, and their colleagues saw scores of political figures come and go. After 1885 the mayor began appointing the city engineer for a term of three years and the Board of Aldermen had to confirm the appointment. During William Jackson's twenty-five years as city engineer, nine mayors, both Democratic and Republican, held office, yet every three years Jackson won reappointment. New political administration did not signal a bloodletting among the expert personnel in the waterworks or engineer's office; instead, those who had designed and supervised the city's public works in the 1870s continued to do so well into the twentieth century. At the time of William Jackson's death, one of his memorialists wrote that Jackson "stood above politics, surviving all municipal political changes."[7] The same could be said of his colleagues in the engineering corps of Boston.

In New England's less populous cities stability and expertise also characterized the municipal engineering corps. One man served continuously as engineer of bridges and harbor in Providence, Rhode Island, from 1878 to 1923, whereas the engineer in charge of planning and supervising street construction in that city remained on the payroll from 1877 to 1916. Providence's engineer in charge of sewerage also enjoyed a long tenure, from 1867 to 1916. For four decades the same trio of men thus were in charge of the sewers, streets, bridges, and harbor of Rhode Island's chief city, and by the 1890s the Providence engineering department was regarded nationwide as a model nonpolitical organization.[8] In 1902 the editor of *Municipal Journal and Engineer* found that in Springfield, Massachusetts, it has been a "time-honored custom to return a faithful administrative officer . . . to his position as long as he may desire it; the mayoralty and councilmanic offices being the only ones subject to partisan contentions."[9] Likewise in Bridgeport and New Haven, Connecticut, New Bedford and Somerville, Massachusetts, and Manchester and Concord, New Hampshire, engineers remained in office for decades.

In fact, municipal waterworks superintendents in New England seem to have enjoyed a job security and permanence of tenure equal to that of superintendents working for private water companies. According to a survey conducted by the periodical *Engineering News*, 38 percent of those serving as municipal waterworks superintendents in New England in 1883 held the same position fourteen years later, as opposed to 40 percent of private company superintendents. And 45 percent of the municipal officers held their posts ten years later, as against 42 percent of the company officials.[10] This may in part reflect the continuity of one-party control in some New England cities, yet New England was not politically static, and partisan and factional strife did exist. Despite political turnover, the engineering bureaucracy enjoyed a degree of stability and permanence.

Outside New England, civil engineers were more vulnerable to political buffeting, and especially in the smaller or medium-sized cities the municipal engineer was less likely to be a sacrosanct figure on a professional pedestal above the partisan strife. Yet in many of the largest municipalities there was continuity of service and reliance on acclaimed experts both as permanent employees and hired consultants. In New York, Pennsylvania, and Illinois, for example, as in New England, expanding municipalities were not willing to turn to inexperienced politicos or partisan practitioners for the design of their waterworks, sewerage systems, or bridges. Instead, they employed professionals.

The country's largest municipality, New York City, faced the greatest engineering challenges, and most of the leaders of the civil engineering profession were at one time on that city's payroll. Seven of the first eight presidents of the American Society of Civil Engineers were either permanent employees of New York City or did consulting work for it. The city's massive Croton Aqueduct and reservoir schemes employed much of the nation's talent, and Alfred W. Craven, fourth president of the American Society of Civil Engineers, served as chief engineer of the Croton Aqueduct Department for nineteen years, from 1849 to 1868, years otherwise marked by political upheaval and partisan strife.

This pattern of continuity and expertise in New York City's engineering corps persisted throughout the remainder of the nineteenth century. Following Craven's retirement, George S. Greene, Sr., seventh president of the American Society of Civil Engineers, assumed the post of chief engineer of the water supply. The Greene family, in fact, established a dynasty in New York City's municipal engineering corps, with George S. Greene, Jr., following his father's example and joining the ranks of the city employees, serving as chief engineer of the Department of Docks from 1875 to 1897. Horace Loomis surpassed Greene's tenure, remaining in the employ of New York City continuously from 1875 to 1914 and holding the senior engineering post in the Department of Public Works—chief engineer of sewers—from 1880 until his retirement thirty-four years later. New York's civil service laws, enacted in the 1880s, did not protect the high-level positions of Greene and Loomis, posts that theoretically remained patronage plums of the political authorities. Yet throughout the various political changes, from County Democracy to Tammany Democracy to Fusion reform, both men remained in the foremost engineering posts in their departments. They were respected experts in their fields, both having served as vice president of the American Society of Civil Engineers, and the political leaders of New York City recognized their dependence on such professionals.[11] Likewise, George W. Birdsall served twenty-seven years, from 1875 to 1902, first as assistant engineer and then as chief engineer of the New York City waterworks. During this period a new commissioner of public works assumed office about every three years, with Allan Campbell succeeding General Fitz-John Porter, H. O. Thompson supplanting Campbell, Rollin Squire replacing Thompson, and commissioners Newton, Smith, Gilroy, and Daly following Squire in rapid succession. Yet while these appointees came and went, Birdsall and Loomis remained in office.[12]

Expertise, however, was not an absolute guarantee of continuity in office, as George Greene, Jr., sadly discovered during the last decade of the century. In the winter of 1891–92 Tammany boss Richard Croker suggested to a Tammany dock commissioner that the commission replace Greene with a younger engineer more acceptable to the political leader. The commissioner rejected Croker's suggestion, but to placate the Tammany boss Greene paid Croker $125 in both 1892 and 1893. In 1895 Greene admitted having made these contributions before a reform investigatory panel seeking evidence that Croker extorted funds from city employees. Croker claimed that "George S. Greene's statement is damned nonsense" and said of the distinguished engineer, "I would not know the man if he was to walk across the corridor or if I was to meet him on the street." But the angry boss did not forget the engineer's damaging testimony, and when Tammany returned to power in 1898 Greene's long tenure came to a close.[13] Greene had committed a fatal error for a member of the emerging municipal technocracy. He had aided one partisan faction to the detriment of another, sacrificing his political neutrality and heightening his vulnerability. Professionals were vital to municipal services, but those who allowed themselves to become entangled in political feuds were expendable.

Though certain engineers might prove expendable, reliance on the profession was unavoidable. In 1884 when New York City began construction of a new Croton Aqueduct to replace the older one, municipal leaders again turned to professionals. They lured Alphonse Fteley away from Boston, and Alfred Craven's nephew also joined in the effort as division engineer. While on the project the younger Craven testified before a committee investigating suspected corruption and political interference in the construction of the Croton scheme. An angry politician told Craven, "you have done the last piece of work you will ever do on this job," and Craven replied, "I will be here when you are gone." Craven was right; he remained on the city payroll for thirty-six years.[14] Unlike Greene, Craven had aroused only a minor tempest and irritated only a minor politician, and unlike Greene he survived his transgression. For his expertise was a valued commodity among city leaders, and, like Birdsall and Loomis, he could trade this commodity for political indulgences.

The municipal engineer not only had to guard against politicians, he also had to cope with the tax-conscious public. This check on the engineer's power became apparent in the struggle over New York's aqueduct project. At the heart of the struggle was the proposed Quaker Bridge Dam, a gigantic masonry structure that would have far exceeded the size of any previous dam. Mammoth schemes like the Quaker Bridge Dam were expressions of engineering hubris and appealed to the municipal engineer's fondness for ever-greater technological triumphs. But city taxpayers proved less enthusiastic about multimillion-dollar monuments to engineering. From 1885 to 1891 business and taxpayer groups, aided by some doubting engineers, persistently opposed the plans of the aqueduct commission's expert staff and repeatedly expressed their misgivings in testimony before the lay members of the commission. Caught between the taxpaying citizenry and their own expert employees, the commissioners regularly delayed action on the Quaker Bridge project until 1891, when a slightly smaller but still grandiose dam won final approval. The *New York Times* chastised lay opponents of the Quaker Bridge proposal, arguing that matters of water supply "manifestly . . . are questions for experts."[15] Not all Americans, however, conceded the "manifest merit" of abdicating control of millions of tax dollars. Certain engineers might enjoy long tenure and the deference of lay authorities, but they could not foist giant schemes on the public without arousing protest.

Elsewhere on the East Coast other engineers retained public appointments for decades and carefully established bases of growing power. From 1855 to 1916, only three men occupied the office of chief engineer of Philadelphia, the first serving from 1855 to 1872, when he resigned to accept the post of assistant to the president of the Pennsylvania Railroad and the second holding office from 1872 until resigning in 1893, shortly before his death. The third, George S. Webster, a veteran of sixteen years in the Philadelphia municipal engineering corps, then succeeded to the position, holding it for the next twenty-three years and earning a variety of professional honors including the presidency of six engineering societies.[16] Also on the Philadelphia payroll for ten years during the 1870s and 1880s was Rudolph Hering, who established his expertise in sanitary engineering during this time and then embarked on a lucrative consulting practice. In the course of his career he helped design the sewerage systems of Philadelphia, New York City, Chicago, Los Angeles, Baltimore, Washington, D.C., Minneapolis, Montreal, Toronto, and Mexico City, and his work won him the title of "Dean of Sanitary Engineering."[17] While Hering and his erstwhile superiors managed the engineering projects of Philadelphia, Republicans and Democrats, machine candidates, and self-styled reformers exchanged control of the mayor's office and the city council, and a kaleidoscope of political faces appeared and disappeared. Yet in 1886 *Engineering News* reported that in Philadelphia's engineering departments, "though no civil service rules are in effect . . . , subordinates frequently remain through successive administrations, and sometimes rise from the lowest to the highest positions."[18] As in New York City and Boston, beneath the surface of political change in Philadelphia rested a more stable layer of municipal professionals.

To the west, in Chicago, Milwaukee, Minneapolis, and Seattle, engineers were also defining their domains and demanding deference from the political authorities. At the helm of public works projects in the booming city of Chicago from 1855 to 1879 was Ellis S. Chesbrough. Chesbrough was serving as Boston's first city engineer when, in 1855, Chicago's city fathers recruited him to assume the awesome task of draining their soggy western metropolis. During his quarter century of service the city soared in population from eighty thousand to five-hundred thousand, and through his efforts Chicago was raised from mud and mire and provided with an internationally acclaimed waterworks. More than any mayor, alderman, or other political figure, Chesbrough left his mark on the city, and his efforts won him professional admiration and the presidency of one regional and two national engineering societies.[19] Chesbrough's counterpart in Milwaukee was George H. Benzenberg, who served in the municipal engineering office for a quarter century from 1874 to 1899 and garnered such professional laurels as the presidency of the American Society of Civil Engineers, the American Waterworks Association, and the American Society of Municipal Improvements. Both Republican and Democratic mayors appointed Benzenberg to his six consecutive three-year terms as city engineer, and each reappointment won unanimous confirmation by the city council.[20] Likewise, in Minneapolis both Republican- and Democrat-dominated city councils backed Andrew Rinker for the post of city engineer, and Rinker won eleven consecutive appointments, serving in the office from 1877 to 1893.[21] In Seattle, in 1892 Reginald H. Thomson began his two decades of continuous service as city engineer. Holding office under mayors of various political persuasions, Thomson became a legend in the Washington metropolis, and by 1907 local newspapers regarded him as the city's "most powerful citizen" who could "make or unmake councilmen" and "even bring the mayor of the city on his knees, begging favors."[22] In Chicago, Milwaukee, Minneapolis, and Seattle, then, figures like Chesbrough, Benzenberg, Rinker, and Thomson maintained their own baronies of power above the strife of partisan battle.

In Saint Louis, civil engineers also were acquiring a secure position of power in government. The Saint Louis charter of 1876 created a Board of Public Improvements consisting of a president elected by the voters and five commissioners nominated by the mayor and confirmed by the municipal assembly. This board had sole authority to draft all public works ordinances, which the municipal assembly could then accept or reject but not amend. Henry Flad, who in the course of his career served as president of the American Society of Civil Engineers and was a longstanding executive of the Engineers' Club of Saint Louis, served as president of the board during its first fourteen years. The board's commissioners were also primarily leading engineers in the city and were often officers of the city's Engineers' Club. Continuity was especially noteworthy in the waterworks department, with Chief Engineer Thomas J. Whitman serving twenty years until he retired in favor of his assistant, who then served a total of twenty-two years.[23]

Such continuity, however, was not unusual among waterworks superintendents, for they managed the most complex element of the municipal public works and thus required substantial experience and expertise. In Baltimore, for instance, despite the tumult of Civil War politics and the postwar era's bitter political battles, Robert K. Martin worked continuously from 1858 until his death in 1893, planning and constructing the city's waterworks.[24] In Cleveland, John Whitelaw spent twenty-five years, from 1867 to his death in 1892, as superintendent of the city's waterworks, expanding the plant's daily capacity from eight million gallons to seventy million gallons.[25] Chicago's longtime superintendent of waterworks was DeWitt Cregier, who served for twenty-six years, from 1853 to 1879. In Minneapolis, by 1895 the chief of the city's waterworks was in his fifteenth year in office, and, in Buffalo, one man served continuously as engineer of the water supply from 1882 to the first decade of the twentieth century.[26] Likewise, in Saint Paul, John Caulfield managed the waterworks from the time it came under municipal control in 1882 throughout the remainder of the century. According to this steadfast civil servant, "politics have played no part whatever in our affairs." Caulfield ruled the water department with a personal devotion and protective jealousy that caused a Saint Paul journalist to refer to the waterworks as Caulfield's "bride as well as his pride."[27] Throughout the nation as a whole, a remarkable 23 percent of those who held the post of municipal waterworks superintendent in 1883 still occupied the same position in 1897.[28] By contrast, in 1897 only one of the mayors of the nation's forty most populous cities was a veteran of five consecutive years in office and none could claim fourteen years of experience as municipal executive.

During the 1870s Chicago's DeWitt Cregier demonstrated that the unique knowledge of the waterworks superintendent could lead to his survival despite the animosity of the mayor and sundry party operatives. In 1876 after twenty-three years in office, Cregier suffered dismissal as a result of a feud with the mayor over adoption of a "patent smoke-consumer" at the city pumping works. When word of Cregier's termination became public, indignant protests were showered upon the mayor, Board of Public Works, and city council. The *Chicago Tribune* lauded Cregier's "reputation for skill, personal honesty, competency and devotion to the public service." Fearful of fire losses due to mismanagement of the waterworks, Chicago's Board of Underwriters held an "indignation meeting" where "the unwarranted removal of Mr. Cregier was stigmatized as an outrage and a crime against the best interests of the city." Over two hundred of the city's leading businessmen likewise petitioned the city council for Cregier's reinstatement, and one alderman expressed the view of a number of his colleagues when he proclaimed that Cregier "knows his business better than all the Mayors we have ever had." Finally after a few months interval, Cregier was back on the job. According to a local newspaper, the mayor reinstated him "partly because many citizens demanded it," partly because Cregier's successor lacked self-confidence and requested the veteran engineer's return, and "partly because some of the engines of the works will soon have to undergo thorough overhauling, and it is desirable that some one who perfectly understands them should superintend the job, and Mr. Cregier probably knows more about them than does anybody else."[29] In other words, Chicago deemed Cregier indispensable. At the waterworks, politicians could not attain their every wish; they had to tolerate DeWitt Cregier, for no one knew the machinery of modern water technology as well as he.

Some cities did not hold their municipal engineers and waterworks superintendents in such high esteem, but dismissed them with each successive mayor. Especially in the largest cities, though, permanency of personnel and reliance on expertise were becoming significant characteristics of municipal engineering departments and of city government generally. Not only were there bosses in Tammany Hall, but there were now also "bosses" in the engineering offices of the major cities. In Saint Paul, for example, the water department was Caulfield's territory, and politicians trespassed at their own risk. Other appointed officers such as Chesbrough, Benzenberg, and Rinker played a more significant role in molding the history of their expanding cities than any political leader, and that Brahmin epitome of professional expertise, Desmond FitzGerald, also did not stand in the shadow of any partisan hack. Before the late 1890s few cities had effective civil service regulations for their engineering staffs, so that as yet few formal barriers protected the expert bureaucracy from political strongarming. But able, diplomatic, and forceful appointees could and did attain a position of authority secure from partisan forays. Men such as William Jackson in Boston and Horace Loomis in New York City did not need to be political, but they did need to be politic.

During the late nineteenth century, then, an engineering bureaucracy was emerging as a powerful force in the nation's urban government. By 1900 the age of the municipal engineer was not simply dawning; it was approaching high noon. For decades, engineering experts had wielded influence in the government of the nation's largest cities, and the massive public works of America's municipalities stood as monuments to their clout. In Boston, Davis, Jackson, and FitzGerald had applied their technical skills to the transformation of the metropolis. In New York City, Greene, Loomis, and Fteley had introduced the benefits of modern technology. And in Chicago, Chesbrough and Cregier had done likewise. All had demonstrated that the professional engineer was as essential an actor in urban government as the mayor or police commissioner.

LANDSCAPE ARCHITECTS AND PARK SUPERINTENDENTS

America's municipalities not only relied on experts in engineering but they also patronized the most highly respected landscape architects in the nation. Landscape architecture did not even exist as a profession in 1850, yet by 1900 it was a flourishing business. Much of this professional development was due to the patronage of cities. When the city councils and park commissioners of New York City, Chicago, Boston, and Buffalo decided to lay out giant parklands, they did not turn to the mayor's brother-in-law to design the grounds or hire Boss O'Brien from Ward Six to draft the plan. Instead, they ignored politics in favor of expertise, hiring emerging leaders in landscape architecture whose offices were in Boston and New York City. Such firms would serve municipalities throughout the country and would continue to do so despite whatever party controlled city hall.

Preeminent among this first generation of landscape architects was Frederick Law Olmsted. From 1857 to 1863 and 1865 to 1878 Olmsted worked for New York City as landscape architect and superintendent of Central Park. Together with his partner Calvert Vaux, Olmsted designed the city's huge urban parkland and inspired a movement for the development of city parks that spread throughout the country. In the course of his career, virtually every major city in the nation consulted Olmsted, and the cities of Brooklyn, Chicago, Buffalo, Boston, Detroit, Hartford, and Louisville implemented his schemes. Throughout the United States, city fathers wanted the best in park planning, and that meant turning to Frederick Law Olmsted.

Yet Olmsted's long service with New York City in the end soured his view of municipal government, so that after 1878 he worked primarily as a private consultant and not as a public servant. His experience as a civil servant illuminates, in fact, the problems confronting emerging professionals in municipal service during the 1860s and 1870s. The boundaries between political officials and their expert employees were not yet clearly defined, and civil servants like Olmsted fought interference by aldermen and commissioners, while at the same time occasionally forgetting that the parklands were public property and not private projects.

Both Olmsted and Vaux were "evangelists" of park development, Olmsted viewing the urban park as an instrument of social and moral regeneration in an industrialized society and Vaux regarding landscape architecture as an "Art," an antidote to the vulgarities of the philistines. While working for New York City they had to deal with good-government reformers like Andrew Green, the city comptroller and park board member, and also with a succession of Tammany Hall officeholders. Green was a fiscal crusader dedicated to cutting Olmsted's budget, and the Tammany men were staunch supporters of their political fraternity and devoted to providing jobs for needy Democrats.

Friction was inevitable, and tact and diplomacy were vital. Yet according to Vaux, Olmsted's diplomacy as an administrator was "very defective and impatient," and during his years of service Olmsted developed a loathing for Green and a contempt for Tammany.[30] Likewise, a friend of the two landscape architects described Vaux as "stubborn and untractable" with an "invariably uncompromising attitude" and observed, moreover, that he "disliked discussion" and "wrangling of any kind . . . made him unhappy."[31]

Though tempers flared, the political authorities deferred enough to the expertise and ability of Olmsted and Vaux to keep them on the city payroll year after year. Yet the relationship was rocky and the landscape architects regarded each cut in the park budget of the nearly bankrupt city as a personal attack. Experts such as Olmsted and Vaux could and did achieve much, as evidenced by the magnificence of Central Park. But in order to achieve their goals, they had to deal with lay persons who represented other viewpoints. The new professionals were not inviolate idols immune from the touch of mundane matters; they had to bicker, bargain, and sometimes even beg in the lively arena of nineteenth-century American city government. This was the aspect of municipal service Olmsted and Vaux disliked but for many years tolerated.

Despite conflict with a laity unschooled in the personal philosophies of Olmsted and Vaux, the profession of landscape architecture flourished, and the best in the field did not lack for municipal clients. Olmsted's one-time associate Jacob Weidenmann designed and superintended the public parks of Hartford, Connecticut. Another landscape architect who had worked with Olmsted, Horace W. S. Cleveland, helped lay out parks in Brooklyn and Chicago, though his finest work was for the cities of Minneapolis and Saint Paul. In the 1890s, Olmsted's disciple Charles Eliot was responsible for planning the regional park system of metropolitan Boston, and at the same time the young George Kessler was designing a park scheme for Kansas City, Missouri, and embarking on a notable planning career.[32] Such new professionals in regional planning and landscape architecture, together with their mentor Frederick Law Olmsted, satisfied the growing need among municipalities for expert advice.

Like Olmsted, these new leaders in the profession achieved much of their renown as private consultants working for a fee rather than as civil servants earning a salary. There were other devotees of park development, however, who became salaried employees of the cities and ensured a continuity of park management through their decades of service. For example, the longtime curator of the work of Olmsted and Vaux was Samuel Parsons, who held the offices of park superintendent or landscape architect in the New York City parks department for twenty-seven of the twenty-nine years from 1882 to 1911, and who twice served as president of the American Society of Landscape Architects. Throughout these years Parsons proved an irascible defender of

Central Park as designed by Olmsted and Vaux, and his autobiography records his repeated feuds and battles with those lay persons who seemed to threaten the artistic integrity of that sylvan domain. Parsons admitted, "the Park Commissioners would have been justified again and again . . . in discharging me." But, he observed, "apparently my honesty and knowledge of Central Park and the almost general reliance on me in Park matters by both the press and the public saved me for thirty years."[33]

When faced with a conflict between his integrity as a landscape architect and his obedience to the will of the park commissioners, Parsons loyally sided with his profession rather than his lay superiors. For example, in 1894 public protest forced the park commissioners to look for a landscape architect to design the proposed Harlem Driveway. The commissioners refused to rely on the expertise of the commission's own salaried landscape architect, the highly regarded Calvert Vaux, claiming Vaux had become "obnoxious" to the board. Yet Frederick Law Olmsted and other reputable private practitioners would not work for the park board except in cooperation with Vaux. Finally the commissioners turned to their superintendent Samuel Parsons and ordered him to draw up the plans. But Parsons joined with Olmsted in refusing to act. As a professional Parsons would not cooperate in an insult administered to a fellow landscape architect, but instead defied orders. Frustrated, the president of the park commission resigned while Parsons remained in office. In 1898 a Tammany-dominated park board did oust Parsons as superintendent, though he returned shortly thereafter to municipal service.[34] No civil service provisions protected Parsons's high-level position, and his personality and politics proved no asset. Yet the New York City park commissioners generally deferred to Parsons's experience and expertise and tolerated his occasional insubordination.

Elsewhere other park superintendents also presided over their parklands for decades, surviving in spite of the shifting partisan currents. In Buffalo, William McMillan served as superintendent of parks from the inception of the Buffalo park commission in 1870 until his retirement in 1899. Successive waves of Buffalo park commissioners served their four, five, or six years in office and then moved on, but throughout the last three decades of the century the day-to-day management of the parks remained the responsibility of McMillan. To the west the dominant force in the work of Chicago's South Park District was J. F. Foster, who began as engineer of the district in 1879, rose to the rank of superintendent, and was still in charge of Chicago's South Side parks in the 1920s. Moreover, Foster was not a puppet for politicians. According to one of Foster's contemporaries, "in the past and in the present the South Park Commissioners have performed precisely the duties of a directorate of an incorporated company," determining broad policy but remaining aloof from daily operations. The maintenance and administration of the parks was strictly Foster's realm, for he was "superintendent in fact as well as in

name."[35] In Chicago's West Park District, lay interference was more prevalent, though the distinguished landscape gardener Jens Jensen served fourteen
consecutive years with the West Parks until his dismissal in 1900, following a
dispute with his political superiors.[36]

Another veteran of the Chicago park network moved on to manage Minneapolis's park system for two decades. In 1885 the Minneapolis park commissioners were seeking a superintendent and turned for advice to their consultant in landscape architecture, Horace Cleveland. Cleveland recommended
William Berry, an experienced park administrator who had served fourteen
years with Chicago's South Park District. The commissioners thus hired
Berry, and he remained in office from 1885 until 1905, when he retired at the
age of seventy-seven.[37] Partisan politics did not lead the Minneapolis commissioners to employ this outsider from Chicago; rather, they chose him because
they wanted an experienced practitioner.

No one, however, epitomized so well the new breed of park superintendents
as did San Francisco's John McLaren. Trained as a landscape gardener at the
Edinburgh Botanical Gardens in his native Scotland, McLaren assumed
charge of San Francisco's Golden Gate Park in 1887 and transformed it from
an expanse of sand dunes into a lush oasis with an unequaled variety of trees,
shrubs, and flowering plants. His success won him near-sacrosanct status
among city employees, and not even advancing age could bring his downfall.
He remained city superintendent of parks until his death in 1943 at the age of
ninety-six, a veteran of fifty-six years on the public payrolls. Known belovedly
to San Franciscans as "Uncle John," he boasted that "the parks of San Francisco were built by gardeners and not by politicians." While McLaren was in
charge, he tolerated no interference with his parks. Once when the city board
of public works ordered the paving of a parking area at the park police station,
the defiant McLaren sent his men to shovel out the cement as quickly as the
public works employees poured it in place. The exasperated board yielded in
the face of such resistance, and as usual McLaren triumphed, planting oak
trees where the parking lot was to be. McLaren referred to himself as the boss
gardener, and the title was apt.[38]

In San Francisco, Minneapolis, Chicago, Buffalo, and New York City, the
desire for expertise was in fact nurturing a profession of boss gardeners who
were winning the respect of the political authorities. New York City's park
commissioners did not tolerate the irascible Olmsted or the combative Parsons because of whatever political persuasion these men espoused, but because the commissioners wanted the best that the emerging profession of
landscape architecture had to offer, and Olmsted and Vaux seemed best
qualified to do the job. Yet this did not mean that Andrew Green or the other
political authorities would bow to the experts' every wish or finance every
expensive request for the fulfillment of their artistic dreams. Park commissioners deferred to a degree, but the aura of nascent professionalism had not

totally blinded them. The commissioners had their own interests and ideas, and landscape architects had to recognize this blunt fact. By the close of the century, some landscape architects such as John McLaren enjoyed near dictatorial sway over their parks, but in most cases accommodation with lay persons proved necessary though often distasteful. As in the case of the engineers, the landscape architects and park administrators of the late nineteenth century played a significant role in American city government, exercising influence and wielding power. Nevertheless, they were not immune from lay supervision, and they had to expect meddling by their political superiors.

PUBLIC LIBRARIANS

Perhaps none of the new professionals in American urban government acquired greater independent authority than the public librarian. In 1850 tax-supported municipal libraries did not exist, and a few scattered bibliophiles with no sense of profession managed the existing semiprivate institutions. By 1900, however, public librarians were a feature of every major city in the nation. Moreover, they had organized nationally and regarded themselves as professionals schooled in the mysteries of a specialized art. The acquisition, care, and cataloging of books had become a science, and city governments were hiring those in the forefront of this new field. A fresh breed of professionals in American city government had thus emerged, and during the late nineteenth century librarians defined their realm of power within the governmental structure.

Throughout the nation, urban librarians asserted their authority and established their professional standing. The public librarians of the late nineteenth century were not political hacks hired by grateful fellow partisans to dust and shelve volumes of Shakespeare and Homer; on the contrary, they were seriously devoted to the task of making literature available to urban dwellers, and the library boards chose their librarians on the basis of literary predilection or expertise and not because of political beliefs. Thus, career civil servants whose ultimate loyalty was to the freshly fabricated precepts of their new profession soon captured control of urban libraries throughout the country.

In Boston some especially notable figures assumed command of the public library. The first to do so were primarily minor literary gentlemen chosen for their love of books. But each was strongly devoted to the betterment of the public library, and each expected to be treated as a respected expert. Charles Coffin Jewett served twelve years as public library superintendent, from 1856 to his death in 1868, and during his tenure Jewett's supporters bolstered his defenses against political interference. The city council had originally appointed the public library superintendent, and in 1865 some council members attempted to defeat Jewett's reappointment because they opposed his politics. Reacting to this attempt to politicize the public library, Jewett's friends on the council transferred appointment of the superintendent to the more genteel, less political library trustees. The council, however, retained authority to fix the superintendent's salary.[39]

In 1868 Boston's trustees chose Justin Winsor as Jewett's successor, and Winsor was to battle for the deference due a professional librarian. The new chief of Boston's book depository was a serious devotee of the new profession, winning a reputation as "perhaps the greatest librarian of his time" and serving in 1876–77 as the first president of the American Library Association.[40] Yet in 1877 his annual salary as library superintendent was only $3,000, as compared with $4,500 for the city engineer. Insulted by this sign of inferior status, Winsor demanded a $1,500 raise. This in turn elicited cries of protest from a few city councilmen. One argued that there were "hundreds of citizens who could fill that place after a few weeks' experience with just as much ability as Mr. Winsor," and another flatly stated, "what particular qualifications are required in cataloguing books I am not able to see." Such blasphemies against the new profession and its respected president, however, represented the minority viewpoint. The city council library committee voted ten to two to raise Winsor's salary to $4,500, and the council as a whole unanimously approved. Winsor soon resigned, however, over a petty dispute about whether his salary increase began in May or July, and he accepted the post of librarian at Harvard University.[41] But he had fought to establish the professional status of the librarian, and he had forced the city council to accept the notion that a librarian was worth as much as an engineer.

Moreover, most of the local newspapers regretted Winsor's departure and recognized the need for a nonpartisan scholar at the head of Boston's library. The *Boston Globe* viewed the Winsor incident as "a serious blunder" resulting from "the higgling of the municipal authorities" and concluded: "We await with no little interest and some solicitude for the application of the Alderman's idea of running a library." And the *Sunday Herald* hoped that the city would obtain a new librarian "not by such petty dealing as too often characterizes the action of some of our City Hall men, who seem to have not one idea inseparable from some form of political machinery, but in accordance with the broadest, soundest principles of public good."[42] Winsor had won the support of the press, and most of the newspapers as well as a majority of the aldermen believed in a library free from party politics and the taint of the spoils system. During Jewett's administration, Boston's city council had refused to allow politics to determine library appointments, and during Winsor's tenure the council had rejected arguments that denigrated the professional librarian to the place of an unskilled clerk. By the 1870s both the city's municipal leaders and its journalists were already convinced of the necessity for a professional librarian.

Less commanding figures served as Boston's chief librarian during the succeeding eighteen years, and the lay trustees assumed greater initiative. But in

1895 the library board imported Herbert Putnam, head of the Minneapolis Public Library, and during the next four years Putnam reasserted the authority formerly exercised by Justin Winsor. Putnam moved on to the post of librarian of Congress in 1899, but his tenure in Boston demonstrated that the power and authority of the public librarian depended to a great degree on the personal diplomacy, energy, and ability of the appointee. Winsor and Putnam skillfully commanded the government of the library during their years in office. Other individuals were unable or unwilling to exercise equal executive authority. As with the new urban bureaucrats in engineering and park administration, much depended on their ability to handle their lay superiors on the city boards or commissions. According to a friend, Putnam had a "clever way of keeping a guarding and controlling hand over men without offending them," and this was a trait of great value to the emerging civil servants of urban America.[43]

Aiding Putnam and his predecessors was a loyal staff of stalwarts who served the city of Boston for decades. In 1900 Boston's head librarian had had thirty-one years of service with the library; the library auditor had been on the payroll thirty-two years; the librarian in charge of the patent and newspaper departments had served for twenty-four years; the ranking librarian of the Dorchester branch had served for twenty-seven years; the head librarian in the South End branch for twenty-five; and the ranking librarians at the Jamaica Plain and West End branches twenty-three years each. There was thus a continuity and professionalism among the city's ranking library staff. The chiefs of the various departments were men and women who viewed their jobs as a career, not as a temporary appointment. Moreover, in the 1890s all staff of grades "A" or "B" (approximately 15 percent of the total in 1896), had to have knowledge of at least two foreign languages as well as some background in that new professional discipline known as library science. By the close of the century the Boston Public Library, like the city's engineering department, was a stronghold of experts.[44]

Elsewhere professionalism and continuity were also evident in municipal libraries. In Providence William E. Foster acted as director of the public library for fifty-three years, from 1877 to 1930. During his long tenure, Foster administered the library free from partisan meddling.[45] In Cleveland, William H. Brett served as chief librarian for thirty-four years, from 1884 to his death in 1918, and won a nationwide reputation, as reflected in his election to the presidency of the American Library Association in 1896. Brett's most serious dispute with members of the city library board arose over appointing non-Clevelanders to the library staff, but Brett won the right to appoint outsiders.[46] By the close of the century Brett determined the qualifications for staff appointments, and the influence of board members was limited. In Detroit, Henry M. Utley headed that city's library from 1885 to 1912 and won the presidency of the American Library Association in 1894. Though partisan politics seems to have influenced a Detroit library appointment in 1878, during Utley's tenure there was no political interference. In 1890 a fellow librarian described the Detroit Public Library as being "free from political influences" and congratulated Utley on his "stable and comfortable status."[47] Still another president of the American Library Association was Frederick M. Crunden, chief librarian of the Saint Louis Public Library from 1877 to 1909. Throughout his years of service he enjoyed the trust and respect of his lay superiors, and in 1893 the president of the board of managers of the Saint Louis library expressed the board's pride in their librarian when he proclaimed that "no name is better known in library circles from Maine to California than [that of] Frederick M. Crunden."[48]

Foster, Brett, Utley, and Crunden all served for decades, secure in their posts and in command of their institutions. Each was a pioneer in his profession and was dedicated to the cause of library science. None would tolerate lay interference that might seriously compromise his authority over library operations, an authority each equated with professionalism. These men were dedicated to establishing the preeminence of the permanent civil servant in their branch of municipal government. And each succeeded.

Likewise in Chicago, the largest midwestern metropolis, both the library board and the librarian sought to establish a tradition of expert management. When in 1873 the city opened its first public library, the members of the governing board did not appoint a local favorite as director of the infant institution but sought to hire the most distinguished librarian available in the nation. Their choice was William F. Poole, former librarian of the Boston Athenaeum and the Cincinnati Public Library and author of *Poole's Periodical Index*, one of the great library reference works of the nineteenth century. The *New York Times* commented that "Mr. Poole's name can never be pronounced without respect." From 1873 to 1887 this figure of world repute directed the Chicago Public Library and continued to lead the young profession, succeeding Justin Winsor as president of the American Library Association. Poole stepped down as public librarian in 1887 in order to organize Chicago's Newberry Library, but he was succeeded by Frederick H. Hild, a man "trained and steeped in the ideals of his venerated" predecessor, and Hild directed the city library for the following twenty-two years.[49]

Not all librarians so successfully survived the crucible of municipal government as Poole, Crunden, Utley, Brett, or Foster. One notable dropout from the public library world was Charles Evans, author of the renowned twelve-volume *American Bibliography*. Handicapped by an obstinate, offensive personality, Evans was dismissed as director of the Indianapolis Public Library after five and a half years, then served two difficult years with the Baltimore public library before being asked for his resignation, after which he resumed command of the Indianapolis library for another three years, until another battle with his lay superiors on the local school board led again to dismissal. Evans's misfortunes, however, were not due to partisan politics or flaws peculiar to city government. His relations with the board of directors of private institutions were just as unhappy, leading to forced departures from both the Newberry Library and the Chicago Historical Society.[50] Frederick B. Perkins, protégé of Justin Winsor and chief of the San Francisco Public Library, faced similar trials due to a difficult temperament. His penchant for roughing up noisy children patronizing the library and his readiness to attack the library's board of trustees earned him little popularity and led to his resignation.[51] Perkins and Evans were misfits incapable of administering a public library, and the lay boards governing municipal institutions soon tired of their behavior. These new professionals were victims not of politics but of their own personalities.

Basic, then, to the development of municipal libraries in the late nineteenth century was the emerging role of career librarians who, if competent, could serve for decades in their positions and strengthen their authority vis-à-vis the governing library board. They, like the municipal engineers and landscape architects, regarded themselves as professionals, and they demanded that the lay rulers of the city defer to their self-proclaimed expertise. Moreover, these lay rulers did, to a great extent, defer to professional judgment especially if it was sugar-coated with tact and diplomacy. By 1900 the leading professional librarians had generally won the upper hand on questions of acquisitions and hiring, although the lay persons on the library boards retained supervision of finances and acted as liaisons to the political authorities in city hall.

PHYSICIANS AND PUBLIC HEALTH OFFICIALS

In 1873, three years before the organization of the American Library Association, a group of physicians and self-styled sanitarians met to organize the American Public Health Association. Municipalities had long assumed responsibility for protection of the public health, and New York City and Philadelphia had for years maintained municipal hospitals for treatment of the poor. Prior to the late 1860s, however, municipal efforts were often half-hearted, and the municipal hospital was most frequently an ill-funded adjunct of the almshouse. The founding of the American Public Health Association, however, was indicative of a new concern. During the last three decades of the nineteenth century and especially during the 1890s, city health departments stepped up their war on disease, and throughout the final years of the century municipal hospitals expanded their services and constructed new convalescent wards, surgical theaters, and pavilions for victims of contagious disease. In the vanguard of the battle against disease was a new corps of public health professionals, physicians who accepted public health work not as a charitable obligation of their profession but as a career. In the municipal hospitals there was likewise a new generation of physicians and professionally trained nurses that expected city governments to promote medical education and research. By 1900 most big cities maintained a professional corps of public health experts devoted to preventive medicine, in addition to a municipal hospital dedicated to curing patients and training physicians and nurses. During the late nineteenth century, municipalities engaged in a two-pronged attack on disease, first through the public health department and second through the municipal hospital. And in both cases the city relied on first-rate professionals who demanded a degree of autonomy from the political authorities.

The medical staffs of the leading municipal hospitals enjoyed an especially large measure of self-government and were unusually free from the dictates of politically motivated lay citizens. Bellevue Hospital in New York City, Blockley Hospital in Philadelphia, and Boston City Hospital were all funded by municipalities and were subject to the authority of the city government. As early as the 1860s and 1870s, however, the medical staffs took the initiative in governing these institutions. It was the staff physicians who exercised the strongest voice in determining policy and appointments; the role of the political authorities was much less significant.

This was clearly evident at Boston's municipal institution, where the City Hospital trustees, chosen by the mayor, appointed new staff members who were nominated by the hospital's senior physicians. Moreover, the trustees regularly conferred with the medical staff before taking any action, and the function of the trustees was actually to transmit the requests of the medical staff to the city council and to lobby for additional funds. Boston's City Hospital had to adapt to popular sentiment more readily than did comparable private hospitals, and city aldermen could use their clout to win favors for constituents desiring medical treatment. But the medical establishment remained ensconced at the hospital, and political elections did not threaten to disrupt the hospital's administration. From 1879 to 1909 Dr. G. H. M. Rowe served an uninterrupted tenure as superintendent of the Boston hospital. Another dominant force on the medical staff from the 1860s until his retirement in 1907 was Dr. David Cheever. More than any other person, Dr. Cheever, a Harvard Medical School graduate, determined the policies of Boston's hospital, and in the process tolerated little interference from Irish politicians on the city council. Even so, he recognized the hospital's dependence on the city authorities, and at the close of his long career he commended "the unstinted liberality of the municipal government."[52] For Dr. Cheever and the medical staff at Boston City Hospital, however, the city council was more a benefactor than a governing authority, a patron who was to be humored and cajoled but not allowed to exert control over the hospital administration.

In Philadelphia the political authorities were not quite so deferential to the medical experts, and in 1889 a dispute between Mayor Edwin Fitler and the distinguished chief of surgery, Dr. J. William White, led to White's dismissal from the Blockley Hospital, together with five allies on the medical staff, all of whom, like White, were on the faculty of the University of Pennsylvania. Within a few years, however, Dr. White returned to his Blockley post, and such interference by the political authorities proved the exception at Philadelphia's municipal hospital.[53]

In New York City, Bellevue Hospital was the preserve of the city's three medical schools and also remained off-limits to politicians. The three medical colleges nominated the members of the hospital supervisory board of visiting physicians, and the city commissioner of charities perfunctorily approved the nominees.[54] In New York City, as in Philadelphia and Boston, the list of those on the medical staffs of the municipal hospitals read like a who's who of American medicine, and these eminent physicians did not expect to kowtow to ward-level potentates. For the most part the professionals ruled the city hospitals.

In fact, the government of these municipal institutions was not only by the professionals but largely for the professionals. During the late nineteenth century the municipal hospitals were as much medical training clinics as institutions for healing and treatment. Medical students observed the senior physicians and received practical instruction at Bellevue, Blockley, and the Boston City Hospital, and the opportunities for teaching and research attracted leading practitioners to the staff. Physicians were less sensitive about exposing the many charity cases in municipal hospitals to troops of medical students than they would have been about violating the privacy of more "respectable" paying patients. Also family or friends were less likely to claim the corpses of paupers, and consequently municipal hospitals had an abundance of cadavers and ample opportunity for postmortem research. The great British physician William Osler, who migrated to Philadelphia in 1884, was said to have made the move primarily because of the promise of a position on the Blockley staff. While in Philadelphia, he fulfilled his dreams, conducting scores of postmortems invaluable to his research.[55] Some physicians at municipal hospitals even seemed willing to endanger the health of patients for the sake of teaching and research. For example, in 1874 the Bellevue medical staff opposed removal of the maternity ward from the hospital, even though the rate of mortality among the confined mothers was soaring due to their proximity to those suffering other ailments. A member of the hospital visiting committee claimed that the staff opposed the move because "the obstetrical service was very important to the Medical School, and to remove the women . . . would have interfered with the [teaching] clinics."[56] According to this suspicious observer, the medical staff viewed teaching as more significant than the health of indigent mothers.

The municipal hospitals also proved a breeding ground for professionalism in the field of nursing. Each of the major city-supported hospitals pioneered programs for the training of nurses and thereby nurtured a new class of professionals on the public payrolls. The second training school for nurses in the

United States (and the first to be connected with a municipal institution) opened at New York City's Bellevue Hospital in 1873, and five years later the Boston City Hospital trustees authorized organization of a comparable program at that municipal institution. Philadelphia's Blockley Hospital followed suit in 1884. Moreover, the city fathers in these municipalities did not demand that the sisters or daughters of local ward leaders guide these programs. Instead, in the field of nursing as in library science, landscape architecture, and engineering, America's municipal institutions sought the finest personnel in the world. The first head of the Bellevue program was a trained nurse imported from Britain; Boston's original superintendent of nursing education was a student of Florence Nightingale; and the Philadelphia authorities hired another Nightingale protégé, whom they lured from her post as chief nurse of the city hospital in Birmingham, England.[57] Professionalism took priority over politics in the nation's municipal hospitals, and the chief nursing posts were not patronage positions awarded for party service.

In the municipal health departments the employees were less insulated from politics than were the hospital staffs. In fact, the development of the public health profession was hardly evident in many cities before the 1890s, and in most small and medium-sized municipalities city physicians or health commissioners were political appointees who served two or four years while their party was in power and then stepped down. They were generally capable persons and experienced physicians, but their career was not in public health. Instead, service with the city board of health was only a temporary task that provided a steady salary to supplement the fees obtained from moonlighting in private practice.

Yet in the largest cities a bureaucracy of career officers in public health was already developing by the 1870s and 1880s. The commissioners who headed New York City's Health Department periodically succumbed to the politician's ax, but below the level of commissioner there was greater stability, with several officials remaining in public service for decades. Dr. Edward H. Janes, for example, served as sanitary inspector with the Health Department from 1866 until his death in 1893 and survived the administrations of various health commissioners and agency reorganizations. Moreover, Janes was no time-serving hack clinging to public office for the salary, but instead he ranked among the most highly regarded physicians in the city, occupying the chair of hygiene at the Woman's Medical College for seventeen years and acting as secretary of the New York Academy of Medicine for several terms. He was also a founder of the American Public Health Association and secretary of that organization for two terms.[58] Dr. Charles F. Roberts, the department's sanitary superintendent at the close of the century, surpassed Janes's length of tenure, remaining with the department from 1870 to 1907. Meanwhile, Drs. John Nagle and Roger Tracy, who worked together and each headed at different times the department's Bureau of Vital Statistics, had both served the city for thirty years by the end of the century and had established the bureau's reputation as one of the finest in the world. Other respected physicians served for decades as well, and a pension program guaranteeing Health Department employees retirement benefits after only twenty years of service offered a strong incentive to remain on the job for at least two decades.

In New England's largest cities not only the staff but also the chiefs of the health departments were lifetime appointees who ruled their agencies free from constant fear of political spoilsmen. Dr. Samuel H. Durgin was health commissioner of the city of Boston from 1873 until his retirement in 1912. No political trimmer, Dr. Durgin was clearly in command of this department, and, according to a contemporary, his sense of duty and executive ability won him "the support of many who secretly have desired to use his office for political purposes." At his retirement one Bostonian observed that in confrontations between Dr. Durgin and the various mayors he served under, "the mayor has invariably retreated and the head of the Health Department has remained unmolested if not undisturbed."[59] Bolstering Dr. Durgin's authority was the respect he enjoyed not only among Boston's medical community but nationally as well. Widely acknowledged as one of the foremost pioneers in public health, he was lecturer on hygiene at Harvard Medical School for decades and enjoyed the honor of serving as president of the American Public Health Association. Boston's civil service regulations did not cover Dr. Durgin's high-ranking post, but ability and prestige ensured his continuing presence in the Health Department.

Similar figures presided over public health efforts in Providence. Dr. Edwin Snow was superintendent of health in the Rhode Island metropolis for twenty-nine years, from 1855 to 1884. Moreover, he was one of the founders of the American Public Health Association and served as its third president. Dr. Snow's successor in Providence, Dr. Charles Chapin, remained chief of the Health Department from 1884 to 1932 and won a reputation as dean of municipal health officials in the nation. A leader in public health efforts during the late nineteenth and early twentieth centuries, Dr. Chapin wrote numerous books and papers on the subject, won every prize and honor his colleagues could bestow, and represented the preeminent role model for young initiates in the emerging public health profession. Dr. Chapin was an institution not only in Providence but also nationwide.[60]

Though figures such as Drs. Durgin, Snow, and Chapin were dedicated career professionals as early as the 1870s and 1880s, the greatest advances in the public health profession occurred after 1890. During the 1890s the bacteriological breakthroughs of Louis Pasteur, working in France, and Robert Koch, in Germany, transformed municipal health departments and resulted in unprecedented programs and expanded facilities. Heading the new municipal laboratories were bacteriologists and chemists with special skills and training not shared by all medical practitioners. Before the 1890s any number of physicians with the right political credentials might fill positions in the average urban health department. Subscribing to the then-popular "filth theory" of disease transmission, most medical officers simply urged cleanliness and tacked up quarantine signs. After 1890, however, municipalities required specialists knowledgeable in the mysteries of tubercle bacilli and diphtheria antitoxin. Public health departments now sought experts in a new field, men and women dedicated to making preventive medicine and public health their lifelong career.

Although Drs. Chapin and Durgin were among the first Americans to accept the bacteriological findings of the great European scientists, New York City's Health Department led in recruiting the new breed of public health experts. Prominent among these emerging health bureaucrats was Dr. Hermann M. Biggs, who in 1892 won appointment as chief of the Division of Bacteriology and Disinfection of the Health Department. Though only thirty-three years old, Biggs was already a professor at the Medical School of New York City and had served as president of the New York Pathological Society.[61] Widely acknowledged at the time of his hiring as one of the most brilliant young practitioners in the city, during his twenty-one years with the health department Biggs attracted a corps of able and imaginative physicians dedicated to the cause of public health. For example, he appointed as director of laboratories Dr. William H. Park, who served in that position from 1894 to 1937, and assisting Park from 1895 to 1934 was Dr. Anna Williams, who had studied at the Pasteur Institute in Paris.[62] Among Biggs's staff in the bacteriological division during the 1890s were future presidents of the American Public Health Association, the Women's Medical Association, and the American Medical Association. Under Biggs, a corps of experts and career specialists became entrenched in the New York City Health Department.

The same change occurred in other municipal health departments in the 1890s. In 1892 David D. Chandler began his twenty years of service as chief health officer of Newark, New Jersey, and Chandler's chemist, chief bacteriologist, and superintendent of the Bureau of Contagious Diseases all were to remain more than thirty years with the Newark Health Department.[63] Philadelphia, Baltimore, and Chicago also hired bacteriologists, persons of no known political viewpoint whose dedication was to the laboratory and not to the party. The medical profession and public now clamored for experts, and municipal leaders had to hire the new specialists no matter whether these career civil servants had rallied in support of the Republicans or the Democrats in the last election.

This professionalization of health officials, however, created certain tensions in a number of big-city departments. The chief officer of many of these departments was still a partisan figure chosen largely for his compatibility with his political superiors. Yet the department staff members were increasingly specialists in public health who worshiped expertise and refused to bow before the altar of party politics. The problem was whether a career expert or a political administrator should command the city health department. Should the new bureaucrats rule or the old political appointees?

The solution arrived at independently in New York City, Chicago, and Baltimore was to have two chiefs, one a long-term appointee acceptable to the professionals and the other a liaison figure with the political authorities. In Chicago Dr. Frank W. Reilly, former secretary of the Illinois Board of Health, assumed the post of assistant commissioner of health in January 1895, remaining in that position until his death in 1909. Four men traded off as commissioner during these years, the incumbents changing according to which party controlled city hall. Some of the commissioners were respected physicians and others political placeholders. But throughout the period each mayor and commissioner agreed to retain Dr. Reilly, and he remained the driving force of the department.[64] Reilly's counterpart in Baltimore was Dr. C. Hampson Jones. A Republican, Jones served as city health commissioner from 1898 to 1900, bringing to the office "native talent and a real interest in public-health administration." With the return of the Democrats to power in Baltimore at the close of the century, Jones could no longer remain commissioner, but the city retained his valuable services by appointing him assistant commissioner. Until 1915 he served in that post, and, with the aid of the department bacteriologist, a career specialist who served more than a quarter of a century with the city, Jones in reality ran the municipal health corps.[65]

Likewise in New York City Dr. Hermann Biggs acted as "General Medical Officer" of the Department of Health from 1902 through 1913, with responsibility for determining the broad policies of the agency. The health commissioners who entered and exited with the changing mayoral administrations devoted themselves chiefly to routine administration and liaison activities with the Board of Estimate and mayor's office. Dr. Biggs, however, like Drs. Reilly and Jones, was the dominant figure in his department, and the achievements of the department were largely his.[66] In Chicago, Baltimore, and New York City, bulletins and communications carried the commissioner's signature but most likely they were the work of his career assistant. By the beginning of the century, longstanding public health specialists were ventriloquists speaking through commissioners who were often no more than figureheads.

Thus, career experts in public health had joined the new engineering bureaucrats, the landscape architects, and professional librarians on the payrolls of America's major cities. The political physicians of the 1870s who issued quarantine orders and exhorted against filth had yielded to career bacteriologists who dedicated themselves to the new precepts of preventive medicine. By 1900 these professionals, like their counterparts in other fields, had reached an accommodation with the political authorities and had established themselves as still another permanent fixture of the nation's complex municipal structure.

EDUCATORS

During the last half of the nineteenth century the largest body of public servants was in the field of education. In 1850, urban public education was only completing its early stage of development, but by 1900 a structure of superintendents, assistant superintendents, principals, and teachers existed in each of the leading cities. Hundreds of thousands of school children lived in municipalities such as New York City, Chicago, and Philadelphia, and a massive educational system was necessary to teach them even the basic "three Rs." In the largest cities thousands of teachers instructed these youths, and the school system had become a giant industry. Moreover, it was an industry of trained professionals, a large proportion of whom remained on the job for a lifetime. The urban school teacher of the 1890s was not a teenage novice filling in for a few months to earn some money for a dowry; nor was the teacher a young man earning extra money to pay for college or to support himself while training for a profession in law or a career in the pulpit. Such individuals had been familiar figures in urban schools of the early nineteenth century, as well as in rural schools of the 1870s or 1880s. By the 1890s, however, most teachers in city school systems regarded teaching as a profession, and educational administrators generally were men and women steeped in years of experience as career educators.

The foundation of the education bureaucracy was the school teacher. Most urban school teachers of the late nineteenth century could claim either professional training or years of practical teaching experience. Though good-government reformers repeatedly uttered anguished warnings of political influence in teaching appointments, partisan interference was the exception and not the rule. School teachers served for decades without fear of partisan politics, and there is only limited evidence of Republican or Democratic ward heelers determining appointments or promotions. Instead, by the 1880s and 1890s the urban school system was a bureaucracy, with personnel rules based primarily on professional norms and not on politics.

Urban school boards of the late nineteenth century recruited most new teachers from the graduating classes of the city normal schools. These training schools offered a one- or two-year course in teaching techniques to young women who had graduated from the city high school or had passed an equivalency examination. During the 1870s and 1880s the school system generally hired all the graduates of the local normal school, though by the late 1890s an excess of normal school graduates made this impossible. Of those who graduated from Cleveland's training institute from 1875 to 1885, 95 percent found jobs in the Cleveland public schools, and in 1892, 135 of the 142 Saint Louis normal-school graduates for 1890–91 were employed in that city's school system.[67] Seventy-four percent of the 1,368 women who graduated from Boston's normal school between 1852 and 1895 found jobs in the Boston system, with the figure rising to over 80 percent in the 1880s.[68] The school systems of Cleveland and Saint Louis almost automatically inducted all those who had passed through professional initiation at the normal school, and Detroit's schools likewise absorbed most of the local trainees.[69] In the 1870s, 1880s, and early 1890s, when there was no excess of trainees, normal-school graduates needed no political or personal influence to secure a teaching post. Their professional diplomas were their cards of entry.

To prevent the teaching staff from becoming too ingrown and parochial, many city systems refused to rely solely on the local normal school for their supply of teachers. For instance, though virtually all the new teachers in Saint Louis during the 1800s and 1890s were local normal-school graduates, in Cleveland, Boston, and Detroit normal-school alumni constituted only 60 percent to 80 percent of the new appointees.[70] In Boston's school system those with one year of teaching experience or a diploma from a state normal college could take an examination administered by the school system's Board of Supervisors and thereby qualify for certification in the city. And in other cities similar examinations allowed outsiders an opportunity to prove themselves. From the pool of normal-school graduates and nongraduates who had passed the qualifying examination, the school superintendent or a lay-dominated school board committee nominated candidates for teaching appointments, and then the lay persons on the city school board or on the ward school committees accepted or rejected the nominations.

Rumors of political interference in this process surfaced frequently during the late nineteenth century, and there was talk of politicians in clandestine meetings dictating, for example, who taught the third grade at the local primary school. Yet in most major cities partisan interference was relatively uncommon and certainly not the norm. During those years when the number of normal-school graduates approximated the number of job openings, the discretion of the lay authorities was severely limited, and in any year the appointments in the largest cities had to be made from the list of those certified by diploma or examination. In the 1890s, when there was a large backlog of trained applicants in most major cities, the discretionary powers of the lay board members may have increased. But still the judgment of the professional school superintendent often carried great weight and could prove decisive. During the 1880s Superintendent George Howland of Chicago, a classical scholar and thirty-year veteran of the city system, urged candidates for appointment to obtain letters of recommendation from their ward committeemen, but it was common knowledge that the committeemen relied on Howland to tell them which applicant to recommend.[71]

Reports by superintendents of two major school systems support the view that partisan politics played only a minor role in teacher selection. The superintendent of the Saint Paul school system observed that "the strongest demand for the appointment of incompetent teachers comes not from the politician but from the citizen who is interested in this pitiable case or in that friend."[72] And the former superintendent of Cleveland's public schools claimed that much more serious than the conflict between Republicans and Democrats in the school system was "school politics," the nonpartisan trading of favors and exercise of influence.[73] To the extent that lay persons exercised undue influence in the appointment process, they did so most often because of friendship or kinship and not because of partisan politics. A father or uncle on the school board might have been invaluable to an applicant for a teaching post. Yet in the nation's largest cities no factor was of greater significance in getting a job than the normal-school diploma or certificate of proficiency based on examination.

Moreover, tales of young women compromising their honor with lecherous school board members in order to retain a teaching job, however appealing to the popular imagination, were probably for the most part false. Once a candidate had obtained a post, he or she had little difficulty keeping it. In Boston and Saint Louis teachers had to obtain reappointment each year, and the Detroit school board appointed its teachers to six-month terms. Yet after the first few years of service, reappointment was a mere formality, and it was common for teachers to remain with a city school system for decades. Forty-four percent of the teachers on Boston's payroll in 1881 still served the school system in 1901.[74] Of the teachers employed by the Saint Louis school system in 1881, 37 percent were still on the system payroll in 1900.[75] Likewise 25 percent of Chicago's teachers of 1874 still worked for the school system in 1894.[76] Marriage was the cause of much of the turnover, since many school boards required married women to resign. Thus at the high school level, where male teachers were more common, the persistence rate was even higher. Fifty-two percent of the teachers at Chicago's public high school in 1874 were still employed by Chicago's schools twenty years later.[77] And 47 percent of those teaching at Boston's Public Latin School in 1874 still remained with the Boston school system in 1894.[78] In Boston, Chicago, Saint Louis, and other major cities as well, the urban teaching corps was a trained body of long-term career employees with years of experience. By 1900 Boston's public school teachers had an average of seventeen years of teaching experience, and more than one-sixth of the teaching corps had been on the job for over thirty years.[79] In 1892 the public school instructors of Newark, New Jersey, could boast of an average teaching experience of more than eleven years, and one Newark pedagogue had spent forty-six years behind the teacher's desk.[80]

If anything, America's urban educators had too much longevity. When Boston's William Boardman died in 1901 at the age of seventy-three, he was in his forty-seventh year of service to the city schools, and the following year Robert Swan, "the Nestor of Boston masters," died while still on the job at the age of eighty-one, having completed his sixty-fourth year of teaching.[81] In the absence of pension plans, many educators such as Boardman and Swan remained at their school desks well into old age. The system of annual reappointment made some instructors uneasy, but any competent teacher had little cause for worry. By the 1890s senility was more of a problem for the urban teaching staff than job insecurity. In 1896 a Chicago educator complained that "teachers are too secure" and the system kept "teachers in that should be out." Another teacher confessed that in his city "the rule has been, once a teacher, always a fixture, even when glaring deficiencies could not be hidden."[82]

Longstanding career professionals also occupied the administrative posts in urban school systems. Both principals and superintendents were generally persons with years of educational experience who had risen within the city system or had been imported from another urban system. New York City's superintendent from 1879 to 1898 had had over two decades of experience with the school system at the time of his appointment, having served as both a teacher and an assistant superintendent. George Howland, Chicago's superintendent from 1880 to 1891, had been principal of the city high school for twenty years before his promotion to the superintendency. And Howland's successor had previously served eighteen years as the Cook County school superintendent. In 1883 Philadelphia's school board appointed as superintendent the incumbent chief of Milwaukee's educational system, and seven years later the board selected as a successor the former principal of a state normal school. In 1880 the Saint Louis school board chose a long-time system employee, who served as superintendent until 1895, when the board elected as the system's chief administrator a man with twenty-three years of service as principal of the city's high school and normal school. Likewise in 1880 Edwin Seaver, veteran principal of Boston's English High School, began a twenty-four-year tenure as that city's school superintendent. Each of these individuals was a career figure who had devoted his lifetime to schooling and the emerging educational bureaucracy.

The clout that these professional educators exercised differed according to personality and local tradition. Until the late 1890s, the lay persons on the boards of education officially determined all significant questions of school policy, while the superintendent advised the board and supervised the teaching staff. Relations between the superintendent and the board were often uneasy, and few superintendents retired voluntarily from office. Yet some did survive for decades, and their "advice" to the school boards carried much weight. For example, Aaron Gove served as Denver's superintendent from 1874 to 1904, and he was an institution in that city by the 1890s. Enjoying nationwide esteem, he served as president of the National Education Association, and by the close of the century was acclaimed by a professional journal as "the statesman among the schoolmen of the period."[83] Gove was no mere hired hand of the school board. Unlike some of his fellow superintendents, he did, in fact, superintend the city school system. Likewise in Kansas City, Missouri, James M. Greenwood ruled the school system with a firm hand throughout his tenure as superintendent, which lasted from 1874 until his death in 1914. At the close of his career he wrote: "It has been my aim in shaping the public schools of this city to spare the members of the Board of Education as much of the specific details of school management as possible," and throughout his forty years of service the lay board members dealt primarily with fundamental policy while Greenwood directed the system.[84] To emerging professional educators throughout the nation, Greenwood was a model superintendent. Rather than suffering humiliation at the hands of lay persons, he "shaped" the public schools of his city. Greenwood was an example of the triumphant professional, a role that many less competent or less fortunate superintendents envied.

By the 1890s the rising wave of professionalism was beating against the bastions of lay power. In 1890 the superintendent of Brooklyn's schools complained that the functions of professional school officers "are at best advisory" and that "their best efforts may be nullified by those who hold the reins of authority." That same year the Committee on City School Systems of the National Educational Association observed bitterly that "instead of determining as an expert what is best to be done in his department, and then doing it in the most efficient manner possible," the city school superintendent "is required to submit his plans to those who may have neither the training nor the experience requisite to judge of their value."[85] Another leader in the education profession insisted that "the purely educational questions should be left to educational experts—to the superintending officers[;] . . . over these matters boards of education should have no control."[86] The school superintendent of Washington, D.C., summed up the feelings of many in the profession when he categorically pronounced: "The superintendent must make the school."[87] School boards consisting of amateurs were thwarting the progress of the professional educator, and the new professionals sought to do something about it.

In 1890 the Committee on City School Systems of the National Educational Association proposed a solution. It recommended reforms that would grant school superintendents full responsibility for initiating action with regard to the school curriculum, "the selection of text-books and teaching appliances . . . and last, but not least, the selection and assignment of teachers." The committee was willing to allow the school board the right to accept or reject the superintendent's proposals. Yet it sought to guarantee that the professional, and not the amateur, would be the source of teaching policy if not the final decision maker. In their report, the committee members admitted that "there are scores of city superintendents who . . . are now performing more or less fully these duties," but they wished to formalize this exercise of authority and secure "the authorization of these supervisory functions by law." They urged lawmakers to define clearly the role of the school superintendent and to tip the balance of power in the direction of the professional. In their opinion,

the superintendent "must not only be permitted to make suggestions and recommendations, but the responsibility of school progress must be laid squarely
upon him."[88]

Some superintendents felt the committee's proposal was too radical an invasion of lay prerogatives. But most professionals viewed the report's pre-
scription as a panacea for educational ills. Proponents of such reforms proved
successful in the 1890s and early twentieth century. In 1892 the Ohio legislature was in the vanguard of the movement to enhance the powers of educational professionals when it reorganized the Cleveland Board of Education
and broadened and defined the authority of the superintendent. Cleveland's
lay board was to fix teachers' salaries and it controlled the construction and
repair of school buildings, but the superintendent was wholly responsible for
hiring and firing the professional staff.[89] In 1897 the Missouri legislature likewise adopted a reform charter for the Saint Louis school board that granted
the superintendent sole authority to initiate actions concerning appointments,
promotions, curriculum, textbooks, or student discipline. According to the
charter, the lay board might in some cases veto the decision of the superintendent, but policy initiative rested with the professional.[90] And in 1901 New
York's legislature adopted a similar plan when it reorganized the New York
City Board of Education. Under the reorganization scheme, a board consisting of the superintendents from each of New York City's boroughs initiated all
actions concerning textbooks, teaching apparatus, methods of instruction,
appointments, and qualifications for employment.[91]

The result in Cleveland, Saint Louis, and New York City was added authority for the professional educator and a clearer understanding of the realm and
domain of the expert. In 1897 a Saint Louis newspaper commented that the
school superintendent was now "supreme . . . [,] a pedagogic Pope, absolutely infallible, unamenable to anyone or anything."[92] In education as in engineering, landscape architecture, library science, and public health, then,
those who claimed professional expertise were on the rise. As early as the
1870s and 1880s, the normal school was turning out trained professionals,
many of them women who spurned marriage and presided over classrooms for
decades. By the 1890s the professional educator was conquering new territory
and assaulting the prerogatives of the lay amateurs on the boards of education. During the late nineteenth century the urban educational bureaucracy
had matured into a force of formidable authority that would determine the
future course of American schooling.

FIRE FIGHTERS

In 1850 urban fire companies were volunteer bands of part-time amateurs
who devoted as much time to the political advancement of their leaders as to
fire fighting and who periodically brawled with members of competing fire
companies. The fire brigades were politicized, violent, and often lacking in the

expertise or professional sense of responsibility that accompanies full-time career service. They were the very antipathy of the spirit of professionalism that would emerge in the late nineteenth century and were in sharp contrast to the ideal of the nonpartisan career specialist.

By 1900 the role of the fireman had changed radically. In the 1850s, 1860s, and 1870s the nation's major cities disbanded the volunteer companies of the past and supplanted them with brigades of full-time paid employees. Moreover, by the 1890s civil service regulations in such leading municipalities as New York City, Brooklyn, Buffalo, Boston, Chicago, and Milwaukee gave firemen some job security and protection from dismissal on political grounds. By the close of the nineteenth century, most urban firemen were career employees who served year after year on the force no matter what party or faction controlled city hall. The department officers and chiefs of the 1880s and 1890s were likewise career men who had won their rank after years of service on the force and had climbed the rungs of the fire department bureaucracy. Political influence certainly might help one rise to the top in the fire department, but it was not a substitute for the requisite experience demanded of each chief engineer or brigade commander. No mayor's son fresh out of a bank teller's cage assumed the post of fire chief in any major city of the 1880s or 1890s. That post went to men who had answered many alarms and dowsed many fires.

Vital to the development of the career fire fighter was the influence of fire insurance underwriters. Uncontrolled blazes in the nation's largest cities could destroy millions of dollars of property and drive fire insurance companies into bankruptcy. The continued existence of the insurance underwriters thus was dependent on a capable, effective fire department, and the underwriters worked to ensure the finest protection possible. Underwriters were largely responsible for the creation of New York City's paid force in the 1860s and could claim credit for the force's survival in the 1870s. Moreover, these underwriters were the first to protest if Tammany or any other political organization attempted to substitute a collection of inexperienced, incompetent political hacks for the incumbent fire fighters. As early as the 1870s a leading underwriter testified that fire commissioners "know they have got one hundred and fifty insurance companies behind them, and if they don't do their business well, they know there will be such a noise and howling . . . that they will be driven from their places."[93] The professional journal of insurance underwriters similarly reported that New York City's fire chiefs of the 1880s and 1890s "effectively warded off attempts to introduce politics and political methods into the uniformed force, by emphatic statements that any such attempts would arouse the insurance interests of the city to vigorous and determined action."[94] Professional fire protection meant money in the pockets of fire insurance companies, and those in the fire departments who sought to protect themselves against interference from politicians found a formidable ally in the underwriters.

Across the nation the professionalization of fire departments was evident.

In the major cities, firemen were not short-term public employees hired by one mayor and fired by the next. According to a survey of fire departments conducted by the National Association of Fire Engineers, in 1889 50 percent of the noncommissioned firemen had at least ten years of experience with their departments and 36 percent had fifteen or more years of service.[95] Commissioned officers, lieutenants, or battalion captains generally had ten or fifteen years of experience, and by the beginning of the twentieth century thirty-year veterans were not uncommon. In 1900, the ranking deputy chiefs for Manhattan and Brooklyn, for example, both had been with the local fire department for over three decades.[96]

Heading the fire brigades of America's largest cities were career men who often survived as chief for years regardless of the changes in political party fortunes. In Boston Louis P. Webber served as chief of the Fire Department for seventeen years, from 1884 to 1901, and accumulated a total of thirty-eight years with the force. His memorialist noted that "without the aid or influence of friends or powerful influences, step by step he worked his way to the highest position in the department, filling every position from private to Chief."[97] The claim of unaided triumph may be viewed skeptically as postmortem fantasy, but Webber's climb through the fire department bureaucracy during a lifetime of service was a verifiable fact and was typical of urban fire chiefs. Command was a reward bestowed on those who gave their entire careers to the force and dutifully rose through the ranks.

In New York City the pattern was much the same. Eli Bates, who was chief from 1873 to 1884, retired because of ill health after forty-four years with the volunteer and paid forces. His successors were also veterans. The appointment in 1899 of Edward Croker as fire chief, however, testified to the continued significance of political influence in Fire Department promotions. Croker was a career man who joined the force at the age of twenty-one and had served for fifteen consecutive years. Moreover, he was highly regarded by the men in the fire corps. Yet he was also the nephew of Tammany boss Richard Croker, and there was no question that his relatively rapid rise to chief was largely due to his uncle. He served ably as chief and won national recognition in his profession, gaining the honor of being the first New York City chief to be elected president of the International Association of Fire Engineers. Further, and rather surprisingly, the fire insurance interests claimed that he "fought politics continually in the department, and succeeded in keeping the uniformed portion free from such influences."[98] He was, then, a combination of the old and the new, the political appointee and the professional.

In the nation's second largest city, Chicago, no political leader was able to install a nephew or son in a position of authority in the Fire Department, for that agency was the domain of a veteran of many blazes, Chief Denis J. Swenie. Swenie began his career as a fire fighter in 1849 at the age of fifteen and remained in the fire corps for fifty-two years, serving as chief from 1879 to

1901. Though an acknowledged Democrat, Swenie refused to allow party politics to influence the management of the Fire Department, but insisted that merit govern appointments and promotions. His longtime assistant reported that Swenie established "the idea of a merit system before the merit system was even seriously discussed by anybody," operating the department "without regard for political considerations." His sole interest was the quality of his department and contemporaries claimed that "he ate and slept fire" and that his "only hobby was fire fighting." Revered by Republicans and Democrats alike, Swenie was, in fact, a Chicago institution, and each year the newspapers respectfully reported the anniversary of his appointment as chief. All agreed that Swenie determined policy in the Fire Department, and even good-government reformers ever-conscious of political interference admitted that this agency of municipal rule was "out of politics."[99]

Throughout the last two decades of the nineteenth century, Chicago mayors rarely dared to cross Swenie. In the 1890s a Republican mayor swept Democrats from appointive office but spared the Fire Department. According to a leading politician of the period, Swenie's "underlings were as hand-picked as the sturdy old fire fighter could make them" and the mayor "lacked the nerve to touch them." The next mayor, a Democrat, may have faulted Swenie for believing "himself absolutely indispensable," but this mayor also retained the bluff old chief. Civil service provisions did not protect such a high-level position as fire chief, yet Swenie's reputation and prestige proved a more formidable defense against the politicians than did any law.[100]

Swenie was, in the eyes of the emerging corps of fire fighting professionals, the model chief and Chicago's department the model professional bureaucracy. Officers rose gradually through the ranks; tenure depended on good behavior, and able, physically fit fire fighters could serve in the corps for decades. As late as 1900 there were still thirty-nine firemen on the payroll who were veterans of the city's Great Fire twenty-nine years earlier. The chief determined personnel questions, and no ward alderman could override Swenie's judgment. According to contemporary accounts, the only one who could influence Swenie was his wife who "often interceded with him and made him promise to go easy with the boys who had done wrong." In Chicago wayward firemen turned not to political headquarters but to the mercies of Mrs. Swenie.[101]

After the disastrous Great Fire of 1871 the willingness of Chicago politicians to defer to the professional chief was perhaps natural. Chicagoans knew that they needed the best fire brigade possible. Yet elsewhere professional fire fighters were also gaining greater independence, and long-term chiefs were seeking to minimize interference by political authorities. In Cleveland James W. Dickinson was chief of the Fire Department for two decades, from 1880 to 1900, and in the first year of his administration he joined with two members of the civilian Board of Fire Commissioners to define the requirements for promotion to the rank of officer. Beginning in 1882, years before Ohio lawmakers introduced civil service examinations for other municipal positions, Dickinson and the two commissioners appointed officers "according to their average standing at the examinations held." Similarly in Milwaukee in 1885, two years after James Foley began his twenty-year service as department chief, that city also initiated a system of competitive examinations. And in Kansas City, Missouri, throughout his service as fire chief from 1884 to 1902, George C. Hale sought to limit political interference and to ensure what he perceived as professional standards.[102]

Swenie, Dickinson, Foley, and Hale were all representatives of the career men who were managing the largest fire brigades of late-nineteenth-century America. In some cities, each political change of command at city hall still meant a new fire chief. And in many cities a politician might still reward a loyal follower with a job in the fire department. Yet by the close of the century a permanent, career personnel headed by longtime veterans staffed most major city fire departments, and the surest route to the post of fire chief was up the bureaucratic pyramid. Swenie, Dickinson, Foley, and Hale were all succeeded by their first assistant chiefs, men who had waited for years for the retirement or removal of their esteemed superiors and who had then with mechanical predictability climbed up the last level to the pinnacle of power in the department. Command belonged to those who had proven themselves within the profession and had moved from lieutenant to captain, from second assistant chief to first assistant chief. In 1850 fire fighting was the sport and hobby of amateurs. By 1900 it was the job of a professional bureaucracy.

THE POLICE FORCE

The most politicized branch of the emerging municipal bureaucracy was the police force. A career staff was to develop later in the police department than in any other agency of city government, and politicians interfered with the police force more persistently than with any other municipal department. The police force, in fact, largely conformed to the stereotype of the nineteenth-century civil service. In most cities there was political harassment within the police force, little continuity of leadership, and often little deference to those with experience and knowledge. By the close of the century, a new corps of professionals was beginning to assume command, but as yet the distinction between the partisan and the professional remained unclear.

Underlying the politicization of the police force were the moral and economic conflicts of the late nineteenth century. Unlike the other branches of municipal service, the police were at the very heart of the great clashes within urban America. Labor versus capital and teetotaler versus saloonkeeper, these were the chief battles in late-nineteenth-century urban America, and the police were central to both. Employers expected the police to suppress labor agitation, and foes of liquor, gambling, and prostitution expected the guardians of the law to squelch "sin." Workers felt the police should act as public servants and not as tools of capital. And immigrants from Ireland, Germany, and eastern and southern Europe opposed police suppression of Sunday drinking as a violation of their personal liberties. If the police force combatted Sabbath breakers and strikers, it aroused the animosity of labor and the drinking public, who might in turn decide the next municipal election. If it failed, however, to battle liquor and labor, management and moralists screamed police corruption and demanded that the political authorities cleanse the department of wrongdoers. No matter which way the police force turned, it incurred political opposition. In contrast, if the waterworks superintendents, landscape architects, librarians, public health physicians, school teachers, or firemen performed their duties conscientiously, they generally aroused little animosity. There might be controversy over the means employed by such professionals, but there was usually consensus about the ends to be achieved, as virtually everyone approved of abundant water, beautiful parks, uplifting literature, good health, a little learning, and the dowsing of fires. The civil servants charged with realizing these aims might involve themselves in a political mare's nest, but such trouble was not inevitable. With the policeman, however, the very nature of his job forced him into the political battle.

In some cities the police were quite literally central to the political contest. In New York City, for example, the Bureau of Election was a branch of the Police Department, and the police commissioners defined election districts, appointed poll clerks and inspectors of election, chose polling sites, and ordered ballots printed. The Police Department kept the voter-registration lists, guarded the polls, and counted the votes at each of the polling locations. In New York City, the Police Department was the agency that supervised the electoral process, and any party or faction that sought control over that process endeavored to make the police their political tool.

Further hampering police professionalism was a widespread failure to recognize that a police officer might require special skills. Every able-bodied man seemed fit to patrol the city streets. In contrast, few could understand how water made its way through the city mains and out the faucets of urban homes, or knew anything about bacilli or the disease process. And it took some skill and training even to operate a steam fire engine or the other apparatus of fire fighting. Thus political leaders had to defer to competent civil engineers, rely on trained bacteriologists, and nurture a career fire brigade. Too often, though, city officials seemed to believe that anyone with the correct political credentials was able to swing a billy club. Police work was not yet deemed a profession or even a skilled craft.

Moreover, police brigades, unlike the other emerging professions, had few loyal and respected friends to lobby for their betterment. Fire underwriters exerted pressure to protect the fire department and enhance skill in fire fighting. And though local physicians were occasionally uncooperative with public health officials, a health officer like Boston's Dr. Samuel Durgin had powerful friends in the medical community to rally in behalf of his authority. Likewise the mass of concerned parents could bolster the cause of the professional educator. Yet the police enjoyed few such supporters. Moralists might support the department so long as the police cracked down on vice, and saloonkeepers might prove friendly so long as the police failed to act. But if the police deviated from the desires of either group, a host of foes appeared ready to attack the guardians of law and order. Insurance companies had little to lose from barroom brawls, gambling, or Sunday drinking, and no theft of the period was so great an insurance catastrophe as the Great Chicago Fire.

The urban police, then, far from enjoying special support or deference, suffered much antagonism. In a nation that maintained only a skeletal professional army, the concept of professional defenders of the law developed slowly. The police were symbols of authority in a libertarian nation. They rounded up strikers and sinners, enforcing laws that half the citizenry did not want enforced; or they failed to enforce laws that another half wished enforced, earning the opposition of employers and teetotalers. Whatever their actions, they were likely to become ensnared in the economic and ethnocultural traps that pockmarked the political landscape of the city. They were caught between Yankees and immigrants, Protestants and Catholics, labor and management, Republicans and Democrats. They were victims of an unfavorable social and cultural climate, a climate that did not nurture police professionalism. The police were, in short, umpires of urban conflict, and nobody likes the umpire.

Exemplifying the political forces so common in the 1870s and 1880s was the Philadelphia Police Department. Before 1887 all Philadelphia policemen were personal appointees of the mayor and as such were his loyal political servants. In 1869 when a Democrat became mayor he dismissed virtually the entire department, all of them appointees of Republican mayors. And when in 1872 a Republican replaced the Democrat the new mayor in turn fired almost the entire corps of seven hundred Democrat appointees. A broad-minded Democrat elected in 1881 with the support of reform Republicans ended the cycle of firings and hirings by retaining the Republican force of his predecessor. Yet throughout most of the 1880s politics determined the majority of police appointments.[103]

Moreover, experience was not a prerequisite for appointment to command posts. Two of the four men who served as Philadelphia police chief between 1869 and 1887 had no experience with the police force prior to their appointment. The chief from 1869 to 1872 was a Civil War general who, upon stepping down from the force, became an artist in Paris. In 1884 Philadelphia's mayor appointed another Civil War officer who had spent fifteen years as head of a local mercantile house. Of the five captains on the Philadelphia force in 1887, two had no police experience prior to their appointment to the captaincy. The captain of the third division had served four years as a member of the state house of representatives and had held clerkships in the municipal gas office and registry of wills. But he had never been a policeman. The captain of the police patrol service was a longtime wholesale and retail dealer in wines and groceries but without experience on the force. Six of the twenty-eight police lieutenants likewise had never served as policemen prior to their appointment as command officers. Another had three months experience, and still another had once been a temporary patrolman during an emergency.[104]

Even those who had served many years with the Philadelphia police department often attained their position due to their dedication to the Republican party. The captain of the first division during the late 1880s had twice served as his ward's representative on the Republican city committee, and for four terms he was chairman of the Republican executive committee in the ward. The commander of the Delaware Harbor Police had been alderman in the Fourth Ward, and others were veterans of various partisan clerkships.[105] By the late 1880s wholesale partisan firings such as occurred in 1869 and 1872 were a phenomenon of the past, and policemen had a degree of job security. But inexperienced partisans continued to occupy command posts, and party loyalty was as strong a force among the men as any devotion to a professional ideal.

In the smaller city of Denver, politics played an even greater role in the Police Department's history. Few policemen survived the political tumult of Colorado's capital city, and police chiefs rose and fell in rapid succession. Between 1877 and 1897 sixteen men served as Denver's chief of police, their tenures ranging from four years to one day. Thirteen of the sixteen had never served with the police department prior to their selection as chief, and in each case the appointment was partisan. Undertakers, mining engineers, butchers, labor leaders, and florists all briefly donned the uniform of chief. Rapid turnover was also characteristic of the lower ranks. Some career men remained on the job one administration after another, winning promotions from the Republicans and demotions under the Populists. But each change of personnel on the civilian Board of Police Commissioners could mark a reshuffling of the police ranks. Denver's Police Department was a toy of the political authorities and was commanded by party men rather than career experts.[106]

Elsewhere political authorities also retarded the development of a professional police corps. In a number of cities the rate of turnover among police force commanders rivaled that of Denver. Eight chiefs served in Buffalo between 1879 and 1894; seven men occupied the chief's chair in Cincinnati between 1878 and 1886; and nine commanders moved in and out of office in Chicago between 1879 and 1897.[107] In contrast, during this same eighteen-year period, only one man, Denis Swenie, a lifelong career man who devoted himself uncompromisingly to upgrading the quality of fire protection, headed Chicago's Fire Department. While good-government reformers of the 1890s could diagnose Denis Swenie's Fire Department as free of political influence, they ridiculed the Police Department as "the football of politics."[108] As late as 1897, a new Democratic chief of Chicago's force dismissed or demoted hundreds of Republican police officers. This happened in a city where political authorities had long before deferred to such pioneer professional leaders as Ellis Chesbrough, William Poole, and Denis Swenie.

This same phenomenon was in evidence elsewhere in the nation. Political authorities did not yet defer to experts in the police field, and relatively few police officers had any right to claim expertise. Civilians commanded the corps in a number of cities. In 1897 in Kansas City, Missouri, a lawyer with no police experience accepted the post of police chief. In contrast, George Hale, a twenty-six-year veteran of the Fire Department, commanded that city's brigade of fire fighters. That same year in Portland, Oregon, a bank president became police chief. In Kansas City and Portland, as in Denver, amateurs continued to command the police corps at the close of the century.[109]

This, however, was not the case in every city. By the 1880s and 1890s seniority and experience were significant criteria for advancement and command in many of the largest urban areas. For example, in New York City extensive police experience was a prerequisite for command positions, and the city's police force was a body of career men led by veteran officers. In 1885 more than half of all New York City policemen had ten years or more consecutive service with the department, and 12 percent had been on the force at least twenty years. Of the thirty-five captains, nineteen had twenty years or more experience and thirty-two had at least fifteen consecutive years on the force. None had served less than ten years.[110] Even a defender of New York's force in the 1880s admitted that "nearly every appointment is made through personal or political influence."[111] But politics alone could not win a man a command post on the police force; seniority and experience were vital. With both political clout and fifteen years of service a police sergeant could become a captain. If he lacked either influence or seniority, he probably would remain a sergeant.

New York City's department was, then, a politicized career force, and amateurs did not command as they did in Denver, Kansas City, or Philadelphia. Nor were New York City's police chiefs satisfied cogs in the political machine. George W. Walling, chief from 1874 to 1885, resented civilian meddling and expressed his contempt for the political authorities in his memoirs when he wrote of the typical alderman as a "ward heeler" and "tough" and claimed that the city officials ruled "by brute force rather than by intellect." According to Walling, New York City suffered under a "a government by the politician, of the politician, and for the politician."[112] A successor of Walling, Chief Thomas Byrnes, also expressed resentment toward political superiors who interfered with his prerogatives. When a Tammany leader who headed the police commission ordered the police to arrest troublesome federal marshals attempting to ensure honesty at the polls, Byrnes announced that if anyone obeyed the Tammany chieftain's order, he "would take the buttons off him."[113] Men like Walling and Byrnes tolerated Tammany, but they were no worshipful adherents of the Democratic organization. Both served almost four decades on the police force, and the Police Department was their life. But although they endeavored to create a department subject to their preeminent authority and not the authority of civilians, neither was strong enough to establish an independent domain. And by the end of the century, the New York Police Department was being attacked by good-government reformers.

In a few cities at the close of the nineteenth century, police chiefs did succeed in creating a department of career men commanded by experienced officers who operated relatively free of undue political tampering. For example, John T. Janssen served as Milwaukee chief of police from 1888 to 1921, and during this thirty-three-year tenure he commanded his department without yielding to the pressures of the various parties and factions who controlled the mayor's office and council chambers.[114] Chief Richard Sylvester of Washington, D.C., likewise sought to create a professional, rather than a partisan, department. In fact, Sylvester worked to upgrade departments throughout the nation, serving from 1901 to 1914 as president of the International Association of Chiefs of Police.[115] Janssen and Sylvester, however, were exceptional figures. Such chiefs were not common in the late nineteenth century.

Instead, partisan leaders continued to manage and exploit urban police forces, and politicians and the general public failed to show the same deference for police officers as they showed for other professionals in the emerging municipal bureaucracy. In the 1880s one supporter of the New York City Police Department observed that the popular conception of the policeman was that of a "bloated, drunken, brutal fellow, who depends on craft and political influence to retain his sinecure situation, and who perfunctorily does his 'sixty minutes to the hour,' from pay day to pay day, and from one blackmailed rumhole to another."[116] The state legislature's partisan-inspired investigations of the New York City Police Department further tarnished the reputation of these guardians of the law. And by the close of the century, good-government reformers regarded the police department in general and New York City in particular as the prime example of municipal corruption. Civil engineers, landscape architects, librarians, physicians, teachers, and firemen were exploiting the public's growing respect for experience and expertise and defining domains of professional power within the municipal structure. Police officers enjoyed less respect and remained instruments of the political authorities.

THE PROFESSIONALIZATION OF MUNICIPAL GOVERNMENT

In summary, as late as 1840 American cities had few if any professional civil servants on their payrolls. There were no police forces, no paid fire fighters, no municipal librarians, no park superintendents or municipal landscape architects, and the engineering profession was only just emerging. Some schoolmasters did draw a salary from the municipal treasury, but superintendents, assistant superintendents, supervisors, and the other levels of the educational bureaucracy were not yet among the city's employees. A local physician received a stipend as city health officer, but his staff was small or nonexistent. In general, cities relied on volunteers, contracted laborers, or untrained clerks and menials to perform the tasks of local government.

Within sixty years, however, all this had changed. The second half of the nineteenth century witnessed the professionalization of municipal government, the appearance of career experts as integral elements of the governmental structure. Adapting to changing technology and rising expectations, America's cities hired some of the finest practitioners of the new professions that arose in the last decades of the century. Rather than resisting innovation, the municipal fathers more often embraced it, and America's municipalities actually served as leading patrons of the new professions. Together with the railroads and the United States Army, American municipal governments nurtured the first generation of professional engineers in the nation, and the patriarchs of the profession perfected their skills and made their fame working on municipal water supply and sewerage projects. Though Frederick Law Olmsted accepted commissions from such private patrons as the Vanderbilts, America's city governments were the true Medicis of the modern art of landscape architecture, and most of the early leaders in the field served municipal clients. Similarly, the breeding ground of the professional librarian was not the nation's colleges and universities but its municipal libraries. And municipal hospitals provided the practical training acquired by thousands of physicians and nurses.

Political leaders and lay persons were not always willing to accept the professional pretensions of this new corps of experts, and the engineer, librarian, and physician had to shove aside those partisan meddlers who threatened to trespass on their bureaucratic turf. Adding, though, to the leverage of the new career civil servants were the rising demands of such special interests as the fire underwriters, who lobbied for modern services that only the expert could provide. Fierce party rivalry and intraparty factionalism left the political authorities ever-vulnerable to popular unrest. The political leaders could not complacently ignore cries for water, sewers, parks, and first-rate fire fighters. If they did, they might well find themselves in the loser's column the next election day. By 1900 expertise had become a necessity for American municipalities, and the political authorities recognized their dependence on the professional.

This recognition did not shield the expert from all political pressure. By the 1890s, however, the professionals were gaining a formal reserve of protection through the passage of municipal civil service laws. Together with the informal pattern of deference to expertise, these laws promised to secure the influence of the career civil servant. In some cities, the role of the new professional was especially formidable; Boston and Providence provided unusually hospitable environments for career experts with decades of experience. Elsewhere the political climate was less favorable to the new professionals, but everywhere they were gaining some foothold and moving toward the front ranks of municipal government.

During the late nineteenth century, then, a new department-based contingent of combatants entered the arena of municipal government. Together with the ward-based politicians, the downtown-based metropolitan leaders, and the civic league-based reformers, they grappled for the upper hand. And from 1870 to 1900 the professionals scored their share of victories. By the early twentieth century some such as Denis Swenie and John McLaren had established themselves as virtual dictators of autonomous realms. Others such as New York City's Dr. Hermann Biggs and Boston's chief engineer William Jackson had worked out an accommodation with the political authorities. As the new century opened the professionals had established themselves as vital components of American city government.

7 BOSSES AND BUSINESSMEN: EXTRALEGAL MOLDERS OF MUNICIPAL RULE

Nineteenth-century city charters typically were lengthy documents with dozens of sections and subsections framed in page after page of small print and convoluted legal prose. These detailed documents not only described the responsibilities of the formal agencies of urban rule—the council, the executive, the commissions—but provided authorization for the appointment of the professionals who managed the waterworks, parks, and health agencies. Yet city charters did not present the complete cast of performers in the pageant of municipal government. In every major city extralegal agents existed, whose wheedling, bargaining, bullying and scheming were vital to the development of the municipal structure in late-nineteenth-century America. Political party bosses and partisan clubs, reform leagues and boards of trade, and such diverse special interests as fire insurance underwriters, builders, architects, real estate brokers, sculptors, and physicians each exerted an influence on municipal policy, often molding legislation or determining appointments. The council, mayor, comptroller, park commission, and board of health represented the legal skeleton of the city, but extralegal associations added much flesh to the municipal body politic.

From Boston to San Francisco the influence of extralegal forces was evident. Political party organizations provided most of the personnel for city offices, nominating the candidates for mayor and council and suggesting worthy party loyalists for appointment. Extralegal partisan leaders largely determined who would operate the system described in the charter. Business groups and reform clubs provided the impetus for many of the changes in municipal structure and policy, drafting new laws and lobbying for their passage in the state capital. The municipal charters themselves were largely the handiwork of private associations; representatives of special business and professional interests, for example, wrote the specific provisions of the electrical codes and building laws—provisions incomprehensible to the saloonkeepers and corner grocers on the city councils and their counterparts in the state legislatures. Throughout the late nineteenth century private organizations and leaders performed tasks such as these that were necessary to the operation of municipal government. They were as much a part of the story of urban rule as the mayor or the waterworks superintendent.

POLITICAL PARTIES, FACTIONS, AND LEADERS

According to traditional literature on nineteenth-century city government, no organization was more important than the political machine, and no person held such sway as the party boss. In fact, many Americans during the nineteenth and early twentieth centuries believed that the boss and his machine were the very sources of the evils befalling the city and the leading causes for the conspicuous failure of municipal government. One author after another during the 1880s and 1890s viewed the party leader and his organization as the twin banes of city government—powerful, malignant cancers destroying the health and vitality of urban rule. In 1883 a foe of "bossism" in Philadelphia claimed that "unscrupulous speculators who dealt in local politics as a trade and who grew fat upon the spoils of office" had forged the fetters of the political machine, and "neither sex, age, nor condition provoked the pity or stayed the hand of the despoilers."[1] Similarly, the distinguished British observer James Bryce, though warning his European readers that the boss was "not a demon," wrote of the "sordid beginnings" and "noxious trade" of the urban political leader and described these partisan potentates as men to whom "ideas of honour and purity are . . . strange."[2] And New York City's leading Presbyterian preacher and moral reformer, Charles Henry Parkhurst, scaled the peak of passion and rhetorical flourish when he described the political boss as "the most sagaciously devised scheme ever originated for the purpose of crushing out, weakening, and drying up in the individual all manly personality."[3] "Dictatorial," "despotic," and "tyrannical" were words frequently found in nineteenth-century accounts of the boss and his machine, and critics repeatedly issued warnings about the malefic power of the party organization.

Yet the purple-prose image of evil, omnipotent party machines distorts the reality of nineteenth-century politics. For factionalism and localism, not unity or central control, characterized urban politics of the 1870s, 1880s, and 1890s, and even the few citywide machines that did dominate for more than a few years were usually fragile and makeshift alliances rather than dictatorial tools of command. In fact, the term *machine*, with its connotations of impersonal efficiency and effortless, automatic production seems ill-suited to the tentative network of alliances linking party leaders in the city. Urban party organizations are more aptly described as confederations or coalitions than machines. Likewise, the word *boss* seems misleading when applied to the party leaders who bartered and bargained to ensure some semblance of order in the political confederations. Few men actually wielded the power necessary to boss a citywide organization that commanded loyalty throughout every neighborhood.

"Broker" better describes the role of the major party leaders than does the pejorative "dictator." Urban politics, was, then, a divisive arena of competition and rivalry presided over by party brokers who sought to create coalition in the place of conflict.

The very structure of party government was fragmented, for the foundation of the party organization was not the city central committee but the many city wards. Though central supervision by citywide party leaders developed in some municipalities, in every major urban area the ward or legislative district remained the base of the party framework from 1870 to 1900. The nomination process began at the ward level, with the primary election or caucus. At this neighborhood poll, party loyalists nominated the candidate for district alderman and elected delegates to the city convention. This convention in turn chose the nominees for such offices as mayor and comptroller. The neighborhood was thus a recognized unit of the party structure and played a significant initial role in the selection of city officers.

Even within the ward, rivalry and competition fragmented the party organization: Poles fought with Irishmen for political dominance; one precinct captain sought to oust another; and an ever-ready body of rising statesmen sought opportunities to topple the established ward leadership. Primary contests reflected these divisions, and violence often accompanied neighborhood elections. In 1887 in Chicago's Eighth-Ward Republican primary, a slate of "anti-gang delegates" challenged the list of delegates sponsored by ward leaders Christopher Mamer and John Lussem. At the polling places several brawls ensued, one of which left Lussem with knife wounds over one eye and in his shoulder. Meanwhile, in the Thirteenth-Ward Republican primary, "a gang of young toughs whose language and general behavior were scandalous" tried to rough up those who sought to deny their favorite the nomination. And in the Fourteenth Ward the Young Republican Club vied with the Hertz-Knopf faction for supremacy within the neighborhood Republican ranks, amid accusations of fraudulent voting by known Democrats.[4] Chicago's Democratic ward primaries suffered similar dissension and mayhem. In 1893 two neighborhood factions battled for the Democratic aldermanic nomination in the city's Seventh Ward, and, according to the *Chicago Tribune*, every few minutes during the polling "the monotony of the wrangling was varied by the sound of a scuffle." That same year in the Thirty-third Ward, Poles, Irish, and Germans met in pitched combat during a Democratic primary in which representatives of each of the nationalities were seeking the ward's aldermanic nomination. According to the city's leading Republican newspaper, "lots of gore was flowing" on primary day in the Thirty-third Ward and "blood and riot" reigned.[5]

Elsewhere factional splits at the ward level were also common. In 1889 in Boston intraparty feuds divided the Democratic caucuses in wards Twelve, Thirteen, Nineteen, and Twenty-two, with the minority factions in each of these wards bolting the regular organization and nominating their own list of delegates. The badly fragmented forces of Democracy in Ward Nineteen produced three tickets, each committed to one of the rival neighborhood chieftains.[6] In 1890 the *Boston Globe* reported that the Ward Twelve Democratic caucus degenerated into a brawling match, "and despite the strenuous efforts of the police the disturbance could not be quelled." Fortunately, however, "aside from a general shaking up and slight bruises, no one was seriously hurt."[7] In equally faction-ridden Cleveland a newspaper covering the ward contests of 1893 reported that "as usual there was a dispute in the Twenty-eighth ward," and commented that "a rumpus there is non-partisan, non-sectarian, and a customary feature of every caucus."[8] Two years later in this same ward five candidates fought for the Democratic council nomination, and a wrangle at the polls again predictably ensued. Challengers representing each of the candidates surrounded the voting booth and "the voter who cast his ballot was forced to run a perfect gauntlet of questions and abuse."[9] In 1887 in Saint Louis's Fourth Ward the McGarry-Lane Democratic faction battled incumbent ward committeeman James Moore and sought to deny him the opportunity on primary day to install election judges and clerks favorable to his own cause. According to a local newspaper, the McGarry-Lane partisans seriously discussed a plan to kidnap Moore on the morning of the primary, spirit him away to East Saint Louis, and lock him in a boxcar until night.[10] Two years later factional fights among Saint Louis Republicans resulted in a fierce credentials contest at the municipal convention, with rival ward delegations battling for recognition in nine of the city's twenty-eight wards.[11]

In New Orleans bitter factional feuds over ward leadership likewise made the primary elections rowdy and raucous events. According to the *Daily Picayune*, the municipal primary of 1888 passed "with less than the usual excitement," yet in a number of wards fistfights, shootings, and near-riots accompanied the canvassing of the vote. In the Tenth Ward, where Peter Farrell and M. J. Sheehan were battling for ward command, "about a dozen men . . . engaged in a general fight, during which pistols were drawn and a general fusillade of shots were fired." The Eleventh Ward primary was equally violent, with two neighborhood statesmen, McGeehan and McDonald, fighting for supremacy. During the primary, "a notorious hoodlum named Tug Wilson, one of McGeehan's friends, . . . seized one of the voters in line by the throat and choked him." Finally, "the man's friends came to his rescue and beat Wilson unmercifully." According to the local newspaper account, in both the Tenth and Eleventh wards "the toughs made themselves felt and were not backward in showing their weapons and brandishing them in the air."[12] In New Orleans, as in Saint Louis, Cleveland, Boston, and Chicago, no citywide boss squelched competition and ensured party harmony at the ward level. Instead, in the urban neighborhoods party leaders were vulnerable and factional divisions often sharp.

Sometimes the ward-level factional feuds were so severe that they caused party divisions not only in the primary but in the general election. In Boston, Philadelphia, and Saint Louis three- or four-way races for city council were not uncommon in the general elections, in which the regular Republican candidate sometimes faced an independent Republican and the organization Democrat confronted a renegade Democrat. In Boston's volatile Sixth aldermanic District, regular Democratic and independent Democratic tickets repeatedly competed for office in the general elections of the early 1890s.[13] The losers of Philadelphia's ward primaries often proceeded to contest the regular nominee in the general election, and in 1887 there were especially severe factional battles among Republicans in the First, Fifth, Eighteenth, and Twenty-ninth wards.[14] That same year in Saint Louis, Democrats who claimed their primary opponents had cheated them of the nomination through ballot-box stuffing likewise continued in the race, posing a serious challenge to the regular candidates in two of the city's aldermanic districts.[15]

In some cases, however, ward leaders were able to ensure greater unity within the neighborhood organization, and a lone ward boss was able to name the aldermanic candidates and convention delegates without opposition. Often only a small minority of the voters were concerned about ward nominations, and in the late 1880s less than 10 percent of New York City's electorate participated in the district primaries. If the turnout was small, ward bosses could dominate the primaries or caucus by relying on those hardcore party stalwarts known derisively as bummers. The bummers always participated in the primaries and were willing to follow the cues of the neighborhood captains, especially if promised a few drinks at a nearby saloon. Not every neighborhood party leader could count on the combined forces of voter apathy and bummer activism to ensure unchallenged control of his district. But some ward bosses did grasp political power and rule their neighborhood as a private barony.

Often these neighborhood bosses were also ward aldermen who could use the prerogatives of their office and their ability to win favors from public utility franchises to build a loyal clientele willing to obey commands. In Chicago, Alderman Johnny Powers of the Nineteenth Ward granted jobs, permits, and exemptions to his constituents and thereby created an obedient following, which made him invincible within his neighborhood stronghold. Likewise, in Chicago's First Ward, "Bathhouse John" Coughlin and his colleague on the board of aldermen Michael "Hinky Dink" Kenna were securing political control of their neighborhood during the closing years of the century.[16] Kansas City's Jim Pendergast used his position as alderman to consolidate his power as boss of the First Ward.[17] In Boston during the late 1880s and early 1890s Martin Lomasney and his brother exploited their membership on the city council and tightened their grasp over the neighborhood.[18] And Philadelphia's William Vare strengthened his family's position in their home ward through service on the city council.[19] Men like Powers, Coughlin, Kenna,

Pendergast, Lomasney, and Vare were political masters of their neighborhoods by the close of the century, and they wielded strict control over the ward primaries. They could march into the city conventions with a handpicked delegation ready to vote according to orders. Such neighborhood leaders thus enjoyed power within the party. These men were not lackeys of a centralized city machine but exemplified the power of the ward boss in the fragmented system of nineteenth-century politics.

In many major American cities the political parties were, in fact, nothing but a collection of ward or factional satraps, many of whom only temporarily clung to power within their neighborhoods. No one in Chicago during the late nineteenth century could legitimately claim the title of city boss, and no centralized machine effectively governed either party in that city. By the late 1890s the Republican leader William Lorimer had been able to win control of the party organization in eight of the city's thirty-five wards and could rightfully claim the crown as boss of the West Side. But at least five other Republican "bosses" ruled over their share of Chicago's political turf and owed no allegiance to Lorimer.[20] Likewise, in Boston no central political czar dictated to ward leaders, but rather each ward organization jealously preserved its prerogatives. And in Cleveland a variety of leaders with neighborhood strongholds shared political leverage: Charles P. Salen led the Ninth Ward; William Crawford dominated the Fourth councilmanic District; and "Czar" Harry Bernstein could deliver the votes of his neighborhood's Russian Jews, Italians, and blacks. But none was supreme in the citywide party.[21] In nineteenth-century Philadelphia, decentralization and a political free-for-all also prevailed in sharp contrast to that city's Republican machine of the early twentieth century. Philadelphia's William Vare noted that at the beginning of his career in the late 1880s, "instead of a central organization, there were various factions within the party, and the bickerings between these elements, along with their weakened alignments against the Democracy of that period, furnished the political strifes of the times."[22] James McManes assumed the title of "King" of Philadelphia Republican politics in the 1870s and 1880s, but he actually was only king of the Seventeenth Ward and of the city gasworks with its hundreds of patronage jobs. Republican Mayor William Stokeley and his followers vied with McManes for political clout, and numerous ward leaders and neighborhood notables held the balance of power. No absolute monarch pulled the strings of Philadelphia politics.

Similarly, Saint Louis's notorious Colonel Ed Butler did not have a firm hold on that city's Democratic party organization, but was actually a free-lance political operator with a neighborhood power base. Butler controlled his home territory, the Nineteenth Ward, and his son commanded the Democratic forces in the First Ward. Using this base, together with his loyal body of political rowdies known as the "push," the colonel influenced city nominations and elections, but his power was never such that he could walk into a

Saint Louis municipal convention and name the complete ticket. In the 1887 municipal election Butler's force was one of three powerful factions within the Democratic party, and early in the campaign a local newspaper described his tactics when it reported that "just now he is contenting himself with making arrangements to be found on the winning side, as usual."[23] That year Butler secured the leadership of the Democratic campaign committee, but the Democrats proved not to be the winning side. At the city convention of 1889 Butler's influence was at a low ebb, and every time he spoke it was a "signal for tumultuous shouting to drown his voice, ribald jests and hisses."[24] By the mid-1890s he had made a comeback, yet he bolted the Democratic city convention of 1897 and helped nominate an independent candidate for mayor who had begun his campaign as a foe of bossism and boodling.[25] Throughout his long public life, Butler remained chiefly a political manipulator, a factional and ward leader who tried to make the most of his limited clout. No one person bossed Saint Louis politics, and in 1897 a local reformer admitted that "St. Louis always has been a party city, but it has not suffered from political bossism."[26]

In some cities neighborhood leaders guaranteed a semblance of order by creating an effective central council of ward bosses. For example, the Democratic party leaders of New Orleans's seventeen wards formed the caucus of seventeen, which controlled the nomination of municipal officials and the distribution of city patronage. In each election the caucus decided on a slate of candidates and submitted it to the city nominating convention, which mechanically approved the caucus selection by a unanimous vote.[27] At the caucus meetings strife among the neighborhood lords was common, as each sought to win more offices for loyal Democrats from his ward. According to one of the party chieftains Martin Behrman, some leaders, "due to heavy votes in their wards or greater personal activity (and sometimes due to good luck) [,] are always more powerful than others." During the 1880s and 1890s, however, no single boss established clear supremacy.[28] The caucus was basically a council of equal neighborhood lords who cooperated in controlling Democratic party politics in the city.

The world of ward politics in New Orleans, Philadelphia, Chicago, and New York City was a forum open to all, the immigrant masses no less than the Yankee middle class. Irish and German newcomers readily seized control of politics in their wards, and by the close of the century Slavs and Italians exercised growing clout in neighborhood caucuses. The neighborhood party organization was a prize well within the reach of the enterprising immigrant, and during the last decades of the century foreign names unknown to earlier American politics appeared ever-more-frequently among the list of ward committeemen and party block captains. Middle-class wards with native-born majorities might continue to select old-stock party leaders. But now such natives had to share power with those of foreign stock.

As the social and ethnocultural background of neighborhood party chiefs changed, native-born reformers and plutocratic downtown businessmen grew increasingly contemptuous of the office of ward leader. In 1886 Theodore Roosevelt, the scion of a fine old New York family, wrote that in the tenement district of lower Manhattan "where there is a large vicious population, the condition of politics is often fairly appalling, and the boss is generally a man of grossly immoral public and private character."[29] Teetotalers were especially critical of the moral status of the neighborhood politician. Just as ward aldermen were frequently products of the tavern, so ward committeemen were often saloonkeepers or habitués of the local bar. James Bryce found that in 1884, 633 of the 1007 political primaries and conventions conducted in New York City took place in local saloons.[30] Elsewhere, ward boss Jim Pendergast of Kansas City was a neighborhood saloonkeeper, as was his counterpart in the First Ward of Chicago, Michael "Hinky Dink" Kenna. Most ward party leaders were small neighborhood businessmen like Philadelphia's Vare brothers, who during their early years in politics operated a door-to-door produce route and small-scale contracting business in their South Side ward. Some of the ward politicians were indeed members of Roosevelt's "vicious" class; many others were simply too common and vulgar for the patrician taste. In general, ward politicians were men of narrow vision who were less concerned about the city as a whole than about the twenty or thirty blocks that formed their bailiwick.

In most cities, then, party politics was a ward-based battle among factional leaders who rarely achieved that illusory goal of citywide supremacy. Few bosses could individually command a city convention and name their personal favorites to municipal posts. Sometimes the various ward leaders on the city central committee would agree on a slate of candidates before the convention met and then would win the delegates' quick and harmonious approval of the slate. But just as often the leaders would not agree, or the delegates would break the slate and nominate their own favorites. In fact, some conventions were scenes of total chaos, both unruly and unbossed. At the Saint Louis Democratic city convention of 1897 two conflicting factions each elected their own convention chairman, refused to recognize the objections of the opposing side, and hooted down their foe's leader every time he attempted to speak. Violence ensued as each faction stormed the convention platform and tried to remove the opponent's chairman. Alarmed by the mayhem, the chief of police turned in a riot call, summoning all police to the district of the convention hall.[31] Other examples of pandemonium were common in urban politics of the late nineteenth century, and in most cities no one boss successfully established anything approaching permanent order. Citywide party dictators were not necessary to nineteenth-century city government; for the most part they did not even exist.

In some cities, however, a single political strategist was able to rise to a position of supremacy over the ward leaders and secure recognition as *the* boss. For example, New York City's Richard Croker bossed the Tammany Hall machine and stood at the helm of the citywide Democratic party organization during the late 1880s and the 1890s. When Croker presented a slate of nominees to a Tammany convention, it was a certainty that no delegate would object. In Cincinnati George B. Cox was the acknowledged leader of that city's Republican organization during the 1890s. At the city convention of 1894 Cox stood before the chairman's platform, signaling the delegates when to make a motion or a nomination, and the whole business, including seven nominations, was completed in a record fifty-eight minutes.[32] Boss Hugh McLaughlin likewise was the recognized leader of Brooklyn Democrats throughout most of the late nineteenth century, and in Baltimore, Isaac Freeman Rasin ruled that city's Democratic coalition. Similarly, on the West Coast San Francisco's Christopher A. Buckley won the title of city boss of the Democratic party during the 1880s.

These figures did exercise citywide authority and each imposed some degree of unity on the faction-ridden, ward-based parties. The most powerful and successful of these political leaders were men who truly deserved the epithet of boss. Richard Croker in his heyday reigned supreme over New York City politics, doling out nominations and patronage to those who enjoyed his favor. In the late 1890s during the administration of Mayor Robert Van Wyck, Croker wielded power known to few party bosses. Even a Tammany loyalist admitted that Van Wyck "entirely surrendered himself into the hands of Croker and acted exactly as though the latter held him under a hypnotic spell."[33] In 1897 young George McClellan, Jr., a Tammany backer and future mayor of New York City, went to Croker to ask that Tammany politico Charles Murphy be appointed city dock commissioner. Croker asked McClellan, "Did you speak to Bob Van Wyck about Murphy's appointment?" McClellan replied, "No, was it necessary?" And the Democrat party boss answered, "No, it was not at all necessary, but it might have flattered him if you had consulted him."[34] At the close of the century party leader Croker was the person in charge of mayoral appointments and not the man elected to the mayor's office. In the case of Croker, the term *boss* was appropriate.

Yet four years after the interview with McClellan, Richard Croker was toppled from his throne and relegated to political exile in Great Britain. His fate was indicative of the infirm foundation underlying the citywide boss; the forces of factionalism, competition, and divisiveness were so great that few persons retained a tight grasp on city politics for long. Those citywide machines and coalitions that did exist seemed forced to engage in a perpetual struggle to maintain their supremacy. After the fall of the Tweed Ring in the early 1870s Tammany Hall did not regain secure control of the Democratic party in New York City until the late 1880s, and only in the 1890s was Tammany Hall synonymous with the Democratic Party in the city. Tammany was just one of the factions competing for power in the 1870s and 1880s, and neither it nor the rival Irving Hall organization or the County Democracy could justifiably claim to be the one, true Democratic machine. In 1880 Tammany was in such a weak position that the Democratic mayor of New York City was able to oust Tammany's leader John Kelly from the office of comptroller. In both the mayoral elections of 1880 and 1882 Tammany had to cooperate with the rival Democrat factions, and Kelly chose the mayoral candidate for 1880 from a list submitted by the Irving Hall Democrats. Moreover, two-term Democratic Mayor William Grace was openly hostile to Kelly and his organization, cutting off the opportunities for patronage that the mayor's office could amply offer. New York City politics was thoroughly fragmented, and no one after Tweed would honestly claim to be boss of a ruling party organization except for Richard Croker in the 1890s.

In other municipalities across the country, citywide bosses also proved vulnerable to the shifting quicksands of party factionalism and rebellion. Cincinnati's George Cox commanded his Republican coalition from 1891 until he was temporarily unseated in 1897 following defeat at the polls. Cox returned to power by the close of the century, but the 1897 election proved that a drubbing by the voters was sufficient to upend the boss's throne. San Francisco's Christopher Buckley presided over an even shakier confederation, surviving as boss only eight years. During his tenure he faced opposition within his own party from Anti-Boss Clubs and from a rival organization known as the Precinct and County Democracy.[35] Brooklyn's Hugh McLaughlin was renowned for his longevity as party leader, and was a dominant influence in the city's Democratic politics for over thirty years. Yet he, too, faced repeated revolts, with important Democrat leaders bolting in 1875, 1878, 1880, and 1893, and he was forced to deal with the rival Jefferson Hall faction during the early 1880s. Setbacks led to occasional spells of retirement, and by 1894 he had already retired from politics three times.[36] McLaughlin proved much more durable than Buckley, but in Brooklyn, San Francisco, and Cincinnati alike the party organizations were uneasy coalitions preserved with difficulty and readily disrupted.

Not only did party factions threaten the city boss, but the boss also faced dangerous competition from the rival party. In contrast to the one-party Democrat-dominated cities of the mid- and late twentieth century, most nineteenth-century cities were arenas of serious two-party battle. One party might have an edge, but the other usually felt that victory and power were possible. Democrats generally filled the mayor's office in New York City, but a Republican elected on a Fusion ticket served as chief executive during the mid-1890s. In Chicago, power shifted back and forth between Republicans and Democrats, and the same was true in Brooklyn. Philadelphia was predominantly Republican, but in the 1870s and 1880s Democrats still constituted an effective opposition, and two Democrats served as mayor between

1870 and 1900. In Boston and Saint Louis both parties also held the reins of authority intermittently during the last three decades of the nineteenth century. And even in predominantly Democratic Baltimore the Republicans assumed control of the city government in the 1890s. In not one of the nation's largest cities did a single party hold the mayor's office throughout the last three decades of the century. Hugh McLaughlin may have been boss of Brooklyn's Democrats, but during part of his reign he was ruling a body of outs. Buckley's dominance of San Francisco's Democrat party similarly proved a hollow triumph between 1884 and 1886, when the Republicans swept their foes from the city's Board of Supervisors. Control of the party did not mean control of the government.

Thus even in municipalities where a single boss held dominion, the party leader's power was hardly secure, for both internal challenges and tough external rivalries had to be faced. Ward leaders, for example, could prove restive. In Brooklyn the Democratic boss of the Gravesend district remained largely independent of Hugh McLaughlin, and New York City's Tim Sullivan, Democratic leader of the Bowery area, felt only perfunctory loyalty to Boss Croker. Antiboss factions in New York City organized within each party as those disgruntled with their share of patronage and power sought to unseat the object of their discontent. In 1891 the Steckler brothers and their powerful organization in the Tenth Assembly District seceded from Tammany partially because Alfred Steckler did not receive the judgeship he had been promised and partially because of differences over Governor Hill and Lieutenant Governor Jones. Such a rebellion could mean loss of the Tenth District and possibly loss of the city, for there was always the opposition party to defeat, a task that could prove trying.[37] Citywide bosses were not dictators or czars; rather, they enjoyed a mandate from party loyalists and indirectly from the voters. One defeat at the polls could topple their organization as rivals sought to snatch victory from the wreckage of the leader's defeat. As in the case of Richard Croker during the mayoralty of Robert Van Wyck, the boss could wield great authority. But he remained vulnerable.

Not only did internal and external rivalries limit the power of a party leader but so also did the political game rules. If a leader violated this informal constitution of the political system, he might well find himself a retired elder statesman. For example, the rules dictated who should fill what offices and exercise what authority. According to these rules, the mayor generally was to have been a respectable businessman or professional, and the comptroller a man of integrity who enjoyed the confidence of the city's business community. The park board was to consist of social-register types, whether of the nouveau riche or old-patrician variety, as was also true of the library board and sinking fund commission. Any wise boss dealt carefully with the fire department, for fear of retribution from the fire insurance interests, and approached the city finance department cautiously in order to placate banking houses and municipal bond holders. Certain city employees with long experience and technical expertise had to be tolerated, for without them the structure of city services might collapse, bringing inevitable defeat to the boss at the next election. A boss was most successful if he understood whom he had to satisfy, accept, and recognize.

During his heyday in the early 1890s, Richard Croker exemplified a boss who was aware of the political and governmental realities of his position. He knew whom he had to placate and he knew how to do so. His favorite mayoral candidate was Hugh Grant, a wealthy Roman Catholic of Irish ancestry with a reputation for personal integrity, a gentleman who fit "the mayoral mold," but also a man whose ethnicity and religion appealed to the Tammany rank-and-file and to voters in the working-class wards. Croker's comptroller candidates were independent business or professional leaders of untarnished reputation. Moreover, he did not allow politics to undermine the Fire Department, thereby satisfying the insurance interests, and his superintendent of the building department generally enjoyed the support and respect of the builders, realtors, and architects. Croker furthermore retained most of the valuable members of the city engineering corps. Yet even Croker could not satisfy everyone. Moral reformers critical of corruption in the Police Department, of drinking on the Sabbath, prostitution, and gambling lambasted the Tammany organization and joined forces with the Republicans and with renegade Democrats dissatisfied with their allotment of the spoils under Croker's regime. Together they defeated Croker in 1894, though the boss returned to power in the 1897 election. In his prime, however, Croker was as much a master of the rules of urban politics as any person living in the late nineteenth century, and only by mastering the conventions and realities of partisan conflict in the municipal arena did he achieve political dominance in New York City.

Still another limitation on the power of a party leader such as Croker was his inability to exercise the formal authority of the chief municipal offices, combined with the political independence of those who did. Unlike Chicago's Mayor Richard Daley, who in the twentieth century exercised the formal authority of the city's executive office as well as the informal power of party chieftain, Croker, Cox, Buckley, McLaughlin, and Rasin never held the highest posts in the city and never directly pulled the levers of government. They had to act through others, often those respectable gentlemen who chafed under the party leader's suzerainty and refused to play errand-boy for a product of the immigrant-saloon-ward culture. Few were so fortunate to have for mayor a stooge like Croker's Robert Van Wyck. In Baltimore the long-term patrician mayor Ferdinand Latrobe enjoyed a personal base of popularity both among ward politicians and business leaders and proved independent of city Democratic boss Isaac Rasin. Latrobe might often cooperate with Rasin, but he did not kowtow to him. Christopher Buckley's mayors in San Francisco were likewise independent individuals, and though Mayor Edward B.

Pond, a prominent merchant, won office with Buckley's backing, he was anti-boss and known to be hostile to his own party's satrap. Likewise, in New York City Tammany-sponsored officials could prove indifferent or antagonistic to the will of the Democratic organization. Comptroller Theodore Myers, a Democrat of wealth and business renown, was no servant of Richard Croker, and the Tammany-backed Comptroller Bird Coler clashed sharply with Croker's stand-in Mayor Van Wyck. Even the usually compliant Tammany mayor of the early 1890s, Hugh Grant, could be defiant as when he refused to name as fire commissioner a close Croker friend whose criminal record included a charge for murder. According to the *New York Times*, the boss's friends, in reviewing the names of Grant's appointees, complained that there was "not much of a showing in the list for Richard Croker."[38]

One of the ironies of late-nineteenth-century urban politics was that bosses often had to rely on "unbossed" or "antiboss" candidates to win victory for the party organization. In 1898 one observer of New York City government wrote of the municipality's chief elective offices: "No party quite dares to put up for these positions mere ward heelers."[39] A reputation as a tool of the bosses could prove a serious liability to a candidate for mayor or comptroller and would provide campaign mudslingers with plenty of ammunition. This phenomenon resulted in the nomination of persons who were not always responsive to the will of the party leader and who did have minds of their own. For example, Bird Coler, the Tammany candidate for comptroller and Boss Hugh McLaughlin's favorite for mayor of the newly consolidated Greater New York, was hardly a devotee of boss rule. At the close of the century Coler wrote a book on municipal government in which he announced that the "corrupt political machine of to-day, controlled by a boss, is contrary to the American system of government" and "is the most complete political despotism ever known."[40] Men such as Coler and Myers in New York City and Latrobe in Baltimore were the type that figures such as McLaughlin and Croker often had to rely on to govern the city. Upright and independent, "unbossed" candidates could bring the party electoral success but they would not hand control of the city to the boss.

Thus throughout the United States, party leaders proved influential in municipal government but were not tyrannical figures with unlimited power. In a majority of the largest cities power was shared among ward or district leaders. The most prominent municipal officials might have to bargain or cooperate with these neighborhood lords, but no single party nabob was capable of dictating to the officials chosen in a citywide election. Elsewhere bosses with citywide authority seized power and proved formidable figures on the political scene, but factionalism, competition, the unwritten rules of politics, and the independence of many in the municipal executive branch undermined the boss's regime. Even during the prime of that most powerful of bosses, Richard Croker, his grasp on the city was looser and less secure than was portrayed by sensation-seeking journalists. Throughout 1873 to 1898, with the exception of the years 1889 to 1891, the city's powerful Board of Estimate and Apportionment included at least one foe of Tammany, and even during 1889 to 1891 one of the Tammany members was not a staunch defender of Boss Croker. Unanimous approval by the board was necessary for passage of the annual appropriation bill, and thus the city's financial measures virtually always depended on bargains struck between Tammany and its foes.[41] Neither Croker nor his organization's mayors had absolute authority; instead, they had to dicker. The party leader was one of the actors in the drama of municipal government, but the drama was not a one-man show.

In city after city the party leaders were influential but hardly totalitarian. They dominated the nomination process, and candidates for office were obligated to ward bosses or citywide machines for their place on the ballot. After election day, the party leaders could collect on the candidates' obligations and secure the desired patronage and favors. Depending on their political clout and the amenability of the mayor, party leaders might determine only a few or virtually all of the appointments for public office. But few mayors were surrogates for bosses, and few party leaders decided municipal policy unless it seriously affected the economic interests of party loyalists and backers. In 1892 Cincinnati's George Cox told an interviewer that all he demanded in return for his support was that "the men who made possible the nomination should be first considered when favors were passed around."[42] The boss usually did not expect to govern; he simply intended to ensure that he and his supporters benefited from government. Similarly, Boss Buckley did not dictate how San Francisco's Democratic supervisors should vote on every municipal issue before the board. Buckley's supporters could differ sharply on policy issues presented before the supervisors. Yet he was willing to use his influence for the benefit of himself and his organization. Men like Cox, Buckley, Croker, and their less-potent counterparts in the wards of Boston and Chicago used their role in the nomination and election of officials to make city government work for them.

BUSINESS ORGANIZATIONS AND REFORMERS

While plebeian party workers were using their clout to win jobs and favors, downtown business leaders were exerting their influence to fashion a government conforming to middle-class ideals. During the last decades of the nineteenth century, members of the upper middle class recognized the emerging power of the working-class wards and realized that immigrants and the "unwashed majority" were gaining ground in the city councils and the party organizations. To counter this erosion of authority and guarantee that the social balance of power continued to tip toward the "better elements" of society, business leaders and professionals turned to extralegal organizations as alternate organs of expression and influence. Such groups as the chamber of commerce, the board of trade, and the good-government club became instruments for ensuring that the voice of "respectable" citizens was heard as loud and clear as ever. These organizations initiated campaigns for new municipal programs and improved city services. They drafted legislation and lobbied for its passage in the city council chambers and state capitals. And many of the upper-middle-class reform groups even interfered in the electoral process, endorsing candidates and infringing on the party organization's traditional power over elected officers and municipal personnel. The urban businessmen's clubs and middle-class civic groups were, in fact, among the most significant participants in municipal government, and the form and functions of urban rule reflected the demands of these organizations.

Upper-middle-class business leaders and professionals expressed their demands through two distinct types of organizations: First, there were the chambers of commerce or boards of trade, organizations founded to promote and regulate trade, but which often gravitated toward municipal reform at the close of the century. These groups were permanent associations with long histories of activity centering on the supervision of commercial exchanges and the arbitration of business disputes. Chambers of commerce and boards of trade usually avoided interfering in the nomination or electoral processes, eschewing endorsement of specific candidates. But they could be active in promoting legislation or programs to upgrade the quality of municipal services and thereby make the city a more profitable and attractive site for existing trade and new business. Comprising the second category of associations were the good-government clubs and civic leagues, which proved less hesitant about invading the party machine's traditional domain. Like the chambers of commerce, these groups advocated new programs and reforms in the structure of government, but most of the civic associations were also willing to endorse candidates for public office. Consisting primarily of upper-middle class business leaders and professionals, these civic leagues sought to rob the plebeian ward boss of his power and restore selection of candidates to the control of the city's respectable citizenry, the "better element" of the population. Downtown business leaders and professionals thus expressed their extralegal influence through both trade-oriented groups that sought to remain aloof from the electoral process and through civic groups that dealt solely with municipal matters and were not so reluctant to venture into the political thicket.

Of the two groups, the first enjoyed the greater seniority and spoke with the higher authority. This was because the chambers of commerce and boards of trade were longstanding bodies and their members were many of the most distinguished and powerful business leaders in the city. As early as 1768 a group of twenty New York City merchants organized the first chamber of commerce for the purpose of "promoting and encouraging commerce, supporting industry, adjusting disputes relative to trade and navigation, and procuring such laws and regulations as may be found necessary for the benefit of trade in general."[43] Merchants in other cities followed New York's lead, with Philadelphians organizing a Chamber of Commerce in 1801 that merged with the local Board of Trade in 1845. And businessmen in the emerging cities of the Midwest and West created similar bodies during the nineteenth century. In each of these cities the original purpose of the chambers of commerce or boards of trade remained consistent with the aims stated by the New Yorkers in 1768. The groups were commercial and not political, and before the 1880s and 1890s they were usually hesitant to enter the municipal arena or to influence policy or the appointment of officials. In 1873 the executive committee of New York's Chamber of Commerce urged the rejection of a proposed resolution calling for the retention of Andrew H. Green as city comptroller. Though Green was the businessman's ideal official, the executive committee "deemed it not to be within the province of the Chamber to interfere in matters of this character."[44] The organization was still very much a chamber of commerce and not a chamber for the determination of municipal policy.

In the last twenty years of the century, however, the distinction between commerce and civic improvement became increasingly blurred. Though chambers of commerce and boards of trades usually remained chary about making any commitment for or against candidates for public office, these commercial organizations issued a growing body of resolutions to the city councils and mayor's offices and organized a string of committees to draft municipal legislation or lobby for change in municipal policy. Realizing that superior municipal services and commercial prosperity were intrinsically linked, the chambers and boards applied their traditional booster spirit to the cause of good government and became potent forces in the development of municipal rule.

By the 1890s one of the most active commercial organizations was the venerable New York Chamber of Commerce. Few associations could claim such plutocratic distinction as the New York chamber, with its membership limited to 1,000 of the leading business figures in the metropolitan area. In 1896 its president and eleven of the twelve vice presidents were millionaires, one of the vice presidents being the great financier J. P. Morgan. John Jacob Astor, John D. Rockefeller, and Cornelius Vanderbilt were among its members, and its roll call included all the demigods in the capitalist pantheon.[45] Such a conclave could speak with a powerful voice, and the resolutions that issued from chamber meetings during the last decade of the century carried weight with lawmakers.

During the 1880s and 1890s New York's Chamber of Commerce entered the municipal fray as advocate of a wide variety of measures. In 1888, for example, the chamber joined the campaign for the consolidation of Brooklyn, New York City, and surrounding suburban communities because the group perceived that metropolitan disunity was detrimental to municipal services and consequently unfavorable to local business. During the following decade, the chamber also applied pressure on the municipal government to repave the streets and rebuild the city's wharves, and the commercial leaders further lobbied for ballot reform and a restructuring of the Police Department.[46] One member denounced the chamber resolution calling for police reform, arguing that he was "opposed to the Chamber discussing political subjects."[47] Such sentiments, however, were becoming outmoded in the 1890s, and in 1895 New York's chamber even went so far as to take sides in the city's electoral struggles. The chamber resolved that its Committee on Municipal Reform, consisting of five millionaire businessmen, should join with the other anti-Tammany forces in the city to organize a committee of fifty charged with nominating a slate of candidates to oppose the Democratic machine ticket. The chamber strongly recommended that its members "co-operate with other associations and citizens . . . to the end that corrupt government, which has heretofore soiled the good name of our City, may never again be possible."[48]

At no other time in the late nineteenth century did New York's Chamber of Commerce take such a blatantly political stance; instead, it focused more on municipal policies and programs than on candidates and parties. In fact, its most notable contribution of the 1890s was as author and advocate of the city's rapid-transit program. By 1890 surface streetcars proved woefully inadequate to handle the hundreds of thousands of commuters in metropolitan New York, and the city's elevated railroads only supplied modest relief for the congested trolley lines. Talk of an underground system had circulated for decades, and in the 1890s, largely through the efforts of the New York Chamber of Commerce, dreams of subway travel approached realization. By early 1894 plans for a rapid-transit system seemed stalled, and in February of that year the chamber appointed a committee to investigate. Not only did the committee review the problems confronting any future subway program, it proceeded to draft a bill creating a new rapid-transit commission that was authorized to issue city bonds to finance tunnel construction. The bill provided that the commission consist of the mayor, the comptroller, the president of the Chamber of Commerce, and five citizens specifically named in the measure, four of whom were millionaire members of the chamber. Moreover, the commission was to be self-perpetuating, the surviving members filling any vacancies due to death or resignation.[49]

The chamber's committee on rapid transit submitted the bill to the state legislature in March 1894; the state lawmakers approved the measure the following month, and the governor affixed his signature in May. New York's legislators altered the handiwork of the chamber by adding a provision requiring a popular referendum in New York City to decide whether the municipality should construct the rapid-transit line. But beyond this, the bill remained intact, and the will of the Chamber of Commerce became law.[50] Thus, a chamber committee had drafted the law and named the commissioners, and chamber members had a five-to-three majority on the commission. Though municipal bonds funded the construction of New York City's subways, the Chamber of Commerce was actually in charge of the project. Its representatives on the rapid-transit commission were to select the plans for the network and to let the contracts for construction.

Elsewhere chambers of commerce and boards of trade were also participating in municipal government by campaigning for improvements and proposing and planning upgraded services. In the early 1880s the Philadelphia Board of Trade pressured the council to squelch a proposal for elevated railway lines to handle commuter traffic; petitioned municipal lawmakers to dredge the city docks; and campaigned for a more adequate water supply in the downtown business wards.[51] In the late 1880s and early 1890s Philadelphia's board successfully arbitrated a dispute between the city and the Reading Railroad over the location of a new railway terminal; lobbied on behalf of a city ordinance authorizing construction of a beltline railway; urged repavement of thoroughfares; and met with the city director of public works on behalf of a proposal for the construction of a grand boulevard linking the city hall and Fairmount Park.[52] In Newark, New Jersey, the local Board of Trade played an even more active role in civic affairs. During 1894 alone it agitated against municipal plans for a new reservoir; realized its proposal for a public park system; reviewed the state of Newark's pavements; requested construction of sewers in the East End; urged an extension of the municipal restrictions on flammable wooden structures; and battled the street railways. Throughout the late 1880s and early 1890s the Newark board was the chief proponent of public parks and sponsored the bill creating a park commission. Appropriately, the chairman of the Board of Trade's park committee became the first president of the new commission.[53]

Commercial organizations also helped mold municipal policy in the growing cities of the Midwest. In 1893 Cleveland's Board of Trade reincorporated as the Cleveland Chamber of Commerce and expanded its activities beyond simply regulating and promoting trade to include a wide range of civic endeavors. It fought for improved street pavements and lighting, urged civil service reform, investigated school finances, and reviewed the work of the city's park commission.[54] In 1897 the chamber's secretary could report that "nearly all of the important propositions for [public] improvements were submitted to the Chamber for consideration and approval," and "with rare exceptions the legislative representatives, city officials and members of the Chamber labored unitedly" on behalf of state legislation aiding the city of Cleveland.[55] In Columbus, Ohio, by 1887 the wide-ranging activity of that city's Board of Trade was causing critics to claim that the board bore "the same relation to Columbus that Paris does to France." The organization's perpetual involvement in civic improvements and its efforts in drafting legislation seemed to justify the taunt that "the Board of Trade is Columbus."[56] In Indianapolis the Commercial Club played a similar role. Under the guidance of the pharmaceutical tycoon Eli Lilly, this association sought to "stimulate business activity and enterprise, combat extreme and retrogressive conservatism, and promote the general welfare of the community." And in pursuit of these ends it took the lead in drafting the Indianapolis charter of 1891; organized a joint committee of club members and city officials to frame legislation creating a park commission; paid for preliminary surveys of the park system; and hired engineers to examine the city's sewers and present proposals for a drainage network.[57]

Farther west, business groups were also taking action. In Minneapolis the local Board of Trade sponsored the creation of the city's park system, despite opposition from the municipal authorities. In 1883 the Minneapolis City Council opposed a municipal park network, but the Board of Trade ignored the council's views and together with the Chamber of Commerce drafted a park bill that the state legislature approved. Moreover, in the text of the bill the board and chamber named the first members of the city park board, thereby ensuring initial control by leading businessmen.[58] The Chamber of Commerce of nearby Saint Paul investigated the city school system; studied local garbage collection, recommended the pavement of major thoroughfares; and lobbied in favor of bills to reorganize municipal government.[59] And in the 1890s the Merchants' Association of San Francisco, though eschewing party politics, claimed notable victories on behalf of cleaner and better-paved streets. In 1897 a leading member of the group testified that "scarcely a week passes without some beneficial interchange of ideas and suggestions between the Merchants' Association and the Mayor, the Board of Supervisors or the various heads of the departments of the city government."[60]

Boston's commercial organizations, however, could claim the most innovative arrangement for influencing city policy. In 1896 Mayor Josiah Quincy outlined his plan for a Merchants' Municipal Committee, an informal advisory body of representatives from the six leading commercial organizations in the city. During the next four years these representatives of commerce met regularly, submitted recommendations to the mayor, and drafted bills for submission to the state legislature. The assembled leaders of such groups as the Boston Associated Board of Trade, the Boston Chamber of Commerce, and the Boston Merchants' Association drafted a tax reform measure, and, like the Philadelphia Board of Trade, attempted to arbitrate differences between railroad corporations and the city over track relocation and the construction of a terminal. Boston's Merchants' Municipal Committee was, however, only an informal body without legal authority. Moreover, its members confined their advice to municipal matters strictly related to the well-being of Boston's business community. Partisan politics was not their concern, and at their first meeting the merchant leaders unanimously agreed that none of the committee members should publicly endorse a candidate for office.[61]

Boston's Merchants' Municipal Committee, Cleveland's Chamber of

Commerce, Philadelphia's Board of Trade, and New York's Chamber of Commerce all were dedicated to mustering business clout for the betterment of municipal government. And each of these groups proved to be a powerful influence in its community. Each drafted legislation, lobbied for its passage, arbitrated disputes between business interests and the municipality, and generally sought to ensure municipal government conducive to commercial expansion. Yet each usually avoided any partisan affiliations and the endorsing of candidates. Even in 1894, when many members of New York's Chamber of Commerce issued the call for a citizens' movement to oust Tammany Hall from power, a chamber leader announced that "in any . . . political matter [the Chamber's members] are acting as individuals," for "the Chamber of Commerce takes no part in politics."[62] The following year the chamber did officially join in support of the anti-Tammany forces, but this was an exception. Boards of trade and chambers of commerce were dedicated primarily to business and not politics. Increasingly in the 1880s and 1890s leading urban businessmen used their commercial organizations as instruments for forcing plebeian city councils to respond to their demands and for cajoling the compliant state legislatures to take action. But these associations did not challenge the Republican or Democratic organizations by fielding their own slate of nominees, and the focus of their endeavors remained commerce.

In order to achieve more direct political action and exert greater pressure on municipal authorities, disenchanted upper-middle-class business leaders and professionals had to turn to still other organs for extralegal pressure. And during the late nineteenth century, especially the 1890s, good-government committees and civic leagues provided a political refuge for these discontented pillars of respectability. In the eyes of the upper middle class the political system seemed tarnished, badly in need of the polish that only persons of "character" and social distinction could apply. Commercial organizations refused to devote themselves wholeheartedly to "cleansing" the city. Consequently, businessmen and professionals founded reform committees, societies for civic improvement, and good-government leagues devoted wholly to righting civic wrongs and placing "good men" in office.

Exacerbating this tension between reformer and party chieftain were the ethnic animosities rife in late-nineteenth-century America. In New York City and Boston, Irish Catholics quickly gained an upper hand in Democratic ward organizations, forcing native-born Protestants to bestow favors and patronage on the newcomers. Elsewhere, foreign-born politicians with an alien tolerance for Sunday drinking and a desire to distribute jobs among their compatriots likewise divested the upper-middle-class Yankee of his preeminence within party circles. Party caucuses once dominated by native-born Protestants had become a babel of foreign accents, so many old-stock Americans felt more at home in the good-government committees and civic leagues.

During the 1870s and 1880s businessmen reformers acted most often through elite committees consisting of substantial but dissatisfied citizens. For example, the Committee of Seventy, a plutocratic and patrician coalition in New York City, overthrew the Tammany organization of William Tweed in the early 1870s. In 1885, discontented Cincinnati respectables organized the Committee of One Hundred to purify city government, and that same year a group of leading New Orleans citizens founded their own Committee of One Hundred. Meanwhile, in Philadelphia a series of such committees came and went during the two decades following the Civil War. In 1874 the powerful and well-heeled members of the Union League Club appointed a Committee of Fifty-eight to urge the nomination of exemplary persons for municipal office. The following year the same group created a Committee of Sixty-two to ensure that "only the best men of the Republican Party be placed in nomination."[63] During the early 1880s those dissatisfied with the Republican organization ruling Philadelphia formed the Committee of One Hundred and succeeded in winning the mayor's office. Leading downtown business figures residing in the fashionable neighborhoods dominated the movement, and 41 percent of those serving on the Committee of One Hundred between 1880 to 1883 were members of the Philadelphia Board of Trade, whereas two-thirds were in the society directory.[64] Through the Board of Trade these gentlemen worked for municipal improvements related to the commercial health of the city. But via the Committee of One Hundred they could influence not only municipal policy but also the selection of municipal personnel.

During the last fifteen years of the century, short-lived committees of select business leaders and professionals yielded command of good-government efforts to a new body of organizations seeking to cleanse municipal rule. In the late 1880s and the 1890s the numerous municipal leagues and civic clubs so typical of urban reform first became fixed features of American government. These groups were not momentary political alliances endeavoring to remedy a temporary malady in the body politic by ousting the ruling party faction. Instead, they were incorporated bodies, often with ward or neighborhood branches, and with salaried directors or executive secretaries whose full-time career was fighting party bosses, corrupt councilmen, indifferent voters, and grasping public utilities. These groups were dedicated to the broad task of improving municipal government in all of its aspects, both through new programs and through the election of new officials. By working for improved municipal services, these civic associations supplemented the efforts of the chambers of commerce and boards of trade. And by intervening in the nomination and election process, they trespassed on the traditional domain of the party organizations. Through their concern for both policy and personnel, however, they exercised an influence that earned them a significant position as extralegal participants in America's municipal government.

Urban residents organized a long list of civic organizations during these last years of the century, all of them dedicated to upgrading the quality of city rule.

In the nation's largest municipality, the City Club of New York was among the most active and durable of the upper-middle-class reform organizations, whereas the Civic Federation of Chicago led reform forces in America's second largest city. Many Philadelphia gentlemen relied on the Municipal League of Philadelphia to serve as their mouthpiece on civic issues, and the Municipal League of Boston flourished in New England's principal metropolis. Likewise, in Baltimore a number of businessmen and professionals allied themselves with the Reform League. Most of these groups attempted to conduct a wide range of programs, and many maintained committees on health, charities, and education—subjects often neglected by the commercial organizations, with their interest in more business-oriented issues such as transportation. Some groups seemed dedicated primarily to self-publicity and talk. But the civic associations of the 1890s did exert pressure on the municipal authorities, and they were responsible for concrete proposals, innovative ordinances, and aggressive new programs. For example, the Civic Federation of Chicago hired Pinkerton detectives who raided the city's gambling halls, forcing municipal officials to act against those notorious establishments. The federation also investigated the local school system, encouraged monthly meetings between parents and teachers, and sponsored a movement for vacation schools. And together with the Chicago Real Estate Board it pushed through the legislature reforms in the procedure for assessing taxes.[65] Pittsburgh's Civic Club of Allegheny County, founded in 1895, lobbied for a purer water supply, for smoke abatement, and for an ordinance against spitting on sidewalks or in streetcars. In addition, it pioneered the summer playground program and secured city financing for this recreation scheme, and it won city approval for the construction of a municipal hospital.[66]

Yet many of the civic associations sought more dramatic achievements than the passage of antispitting ordinances. Most of these groups intended to work toward the overthrow of bossism and the plebeian ward machines and to redeem the city councils. In its annual report of 1893 the City Club of New York warned that "if nominations shall be made upon the . . . principle of rewarding party service, then this Club will not be content and will use its influence to nominate and elect fit candidates, instead of merely political candidates."[67] Each member of Chicago's Civic Federation pledged to "take an active interest in and attend" the ward primary elections and to "work and vote only for delegates whom [the member] believe[d], after investigation, to be honest, capable men."[68] The Municipal League of Philadelphia also pledged itself to endorsing honest and capable candidates in lieu of party hacks, and the constitution of the Municipal League of Boston similarly dedicated the society "to secure the nomination and election of municipal officers solely on account of their fitness for the office."[69] Each of these groups intended to play a role in the electoral process and to use its influence to undermine allegiance to the party organization as a criterion for nominations to municipal office.

During the 1890s the civic associations implemented their plans, establishing organizations that reached down to the wards and challenged the two traditional parties for control of the nomination and election process. The City Club of New York financed the creation of Good Government Clubs in every aldermanic district in the city, and together these groups were instrumental in the ouster of Tammany Hall in the municipal election of 1894. Both the City Club and the district-based Good Government Clubs worked for the anti-Tammany candidate for mayor, contributing poll watchers on election day to guard against Tammany ballot frauds. In an effort to ensure continued victories, the City Club and its Good Government affiliates sponsored ballot-reform bills in the state legislature and urged the holding of municipal elections on a different day than state and national contests, in the hope of limiting the influence of state and national politics on local contests.[70]

Reform leagues elsewhere took much the same action. In Chicago in 1896 the Civic Federation organized the meeting that led to the creation of the Municipal Voters' League, a group dedicated to defeating the boodlers on Chicago's city council. Like the City Club, the Municipal Voters' League relied on neighborhood organizations and worked to establish committees in every ward to report on local conditions and advise the central organization as to which aldermanic candidates deserved league endorsement. This reform machine heavily publicized the wrongs of those it opposed, attacking a plebeian party regular like "Bathhouse John" Coughlin as "uneducated and coarse in conduct; the friend of toughs and thugs; a disgrace to his ward and city."[71] And in most cases the attacks achieved results. Of the thirty aldermanic candidates receiving the league's recommendation in 1896, twenty-five won election; in 1897 the league won seventeen of thirty contests; and in 1898 its record was twenty-three victories and eight losses.[72] In the state capital, the Civic Federation furthered the cause of political reform by securing passage of a new primary election law that imposed strict penalties on those who resorted to fraud in order to capture their party's nomination.[73] Meanwhile, Baltimore's Reform League also established ward-level good-government clubs, and the self-styled reform forces won control of that city in 1895.[74] Further, by 1894 the Municipal League of Philadelphia had organized in the wards and was claiming "substantial results in the defeat of bad candidates and the election of competent representatives to the local legislature."[75]

Like the committees of the 1870s and the 1880s, the civic league machines of the 1890s were organs of a business and professional elite. New York's City Club was an elite body of many of the city's wealthiest citizens, and included among its members such plutocrats as John Jacob Astor, J. P. Morgan, and Cornelius Vanderbilt, as well as gentlemen bearing such old patrician names as Roosevelt, Stuyvesant, and Van Cortlandt. Approximately 60 percent of the club's members were listed in the city's social register, and according to the *New York Times* its Fifth Avenue clubhouse contained "the usual accessories which pertain to a club situated in the fashionable part of the city and suited to the tastes of men of comfortable circumstances." The neighborhood-based good-government clubs were less distinguished socially, yet in 1895, of the forty-two members of the confederated councils coordinating the various clubs throughout New York City, over one-third enjoyed a place in the social register. Moreover, the clubs with the largest memberships were located in the elite districts of midtown Manhattan whereas those in the less-affluent reaches of lower Manhattan had a skeleton crew of officers, but few members.[76]

In other cities, the pattern was similar. The executive committee of Chicago's Municipal Voters' League was no band of saloonkeepers or petty politicos. Successful businessmen and professionals dominated the committee, though a token labor representative was among the original members. In 1900 the eight members of the executive committee included five lawyers, one architect, one businessman, and one warden of a social settlement.[77] Baltimore's Reform League likewise consisted chiefly of successful representatives of business and the professions. In 1895 the Baltimore social register listed only about one thousand of the city's ninety-five thousand families, yet two-thirds of the sixty-seven members serving on various league committees were among those in the society directory. Baltimore's neighborhood good-government clubs included groups that were not as elite, with slightly less than half of the members of the Eighth Ward club, for example, winning recognition in the social register. Yet as in New York City, the clubs in the most fashionable wards attracted the most members, whereas only two concerned citizens attended the organizational meeting for the ward club in working-class East Baltimore.[78] Moreover, the boss of Baltimore reform was the millionaire attorney Charles Bonaparte, a grandnephew of the Emperor Napoleon, whose patrician arrogance won him the nickname "the Peacock of Park Avenue."[79]

Groups such as the City Club, Municipal Voters' League, and the Reform League were elite alternatives to the traditional dominance of the political parties, which had fallen into the coarse hands of politicians of humble origin and common manners. Foreigners with a culture alien to old-stock urbanites were assuming seats on party committees and were leading the delegations to political conventions. The so-called respectable citizenry still dominated through their control of the executive branch and the independent commissions; but they no longer monopolized power, for both the ward-based party organization and the neighborhood aldermen had slipped from their grasp. By the 1890s the "respectable element" had become alienated from the party organizations, and the civic associations were their response. Through neighborhood reform clubs and committees, they were creating rival channels for the selection of candidates, channels safely controlled by kid-gloved hands.

Having met with some electoral success, these elite political organizers felt encouraged to embark on still-more-ambitious schemes. By the close of the century, they had organized a cooperative, nationwide campaign for good government. In 1894 civic groups across the nation joined to form the National Municipal League in order to "combine the forces of all who realize that it is only by united action and organization that good citizens can secure the adoption of good laws and the selection of men of trained ability and proved integrity for all municipal positions."[80] Each year the league held a conference at which local civic leaders and university professors presented papers diagnosing the common maladies of municipal government and prescribing supposed cure-alls. By 1900 the disparate ills of New York City, Chicago, and Philadelphia had become a national urban problem that merited permanent study and treatment by the growing corps of municipal reform experts on college campuses and in the offices of civic organizations.

Indicative of this new perception of the common plight of cities was the drafting of the Municipal Program of 1898 by a committee of the National Municipal League. This program was a blueprint for reform, a description of what the committee viewed as the ideal structure of municipal government.[81] It was, in fact, a national codification of diverse reform panaceas, but it marked a new departure especially significant for the twentieth century. National civic organizations were now beginning to supplement the efforts of local groups, and much of the impetus for the restructuring of municipal government in the twentieth century would come from these nationwide organizations and from self-styled experts on municipal rule who served no single city but peddled their ideas throughout the United States. During the early twentieth century the local business elite would have to share the good-government limelight with a new character in the municipal drama, the professional reformer.

SPECIAL BUSINESS AND PROFESSIONAL INTERESTS

Throughout the late nineteenth century a broad range of diverse business and professional groups displayed a special concern for the excellence of municipal services and the merit of city officials. Such businesses as fire insurance underwriting, the construction industry, and real estate had an enormous financial stake in the competence and quality of municipal government. And emerging professionals such as artists and physicians also felt a need to assert their standing and demand a hearing from those in city office. If the waterworks were inadequate and the fire brigade inept, conflagration could mean bankruptcy for the fire insurance companies. If framers of building codes misunderstood the principles of construction or the city inspectors proved obstinate, ignorant, or dilatory, builders and their suppliers could find themselves hamstrung by the law. Similarly, if property assessments soared and city officials refused to extend services to suburban tracts, real estate developers might face ruin. And, if municipalities displayed the handiwork of second-rate sculptors or appointed medical quacks to public office, these actions could prove a blow to artists and physicians attempting to establish and maintain standards in their respective fields. For each of these diverse groups and many others as well, municipal actions could prove significant if not vital. Therefore, surveillance of municipal officials was necessary and intervention in the making of municipal policy was essential. Through lobbying, the issuance of ultimatums, and virtual blackmail, these business and professional interests were among the many extralegal molders of municipal law and practice.

Perhaps the most active were the fire underwriters. Few businesses depended so heavily on the quality of city services, and few suffered so greatly if services proved inadequate. Rampaging urban fires not only wiped out block after block of dwellings, shops, and factories, they forced insurance underwriters into bankruptcy. The Chicago fire of 1871 destroyed an estimated fifteen thousand buildings, devastated three and one-half square miles in the heart of the city, and drove sixty-eight insurance companies into liquidation. Though small by comparison, the Boston fire of 1872 obliterated seven hundred and fifty buildings, ravaged sixty-five acres of the central business district, and ruined additional companies. Such disasters had to stop if the fire insurance business was to survive. And to prevent future conflagrations municipalities had to maintain an abundant supply of water, a sufficient hydrant pressure, and a large, well-trained, well-equipped body of firefighters. An antiquated waterworks or a politicized fire brigade of ward heelers and saloon loafers manning outdated or defective engines could spell doom for the fire underwriter. Therefore, to ensure profit and stave off bankruptcy, insurance agents lobbied, coaxed, and coerced cities into adopting fire prevention measures and upgrading those services vital to firefighting.

During the 1850s and 1860s fire insurance companies and their agents had proved instrumental in the fight to replace volunteer fire companies with professional fire departments, and throughout the last three decades of the century they were to continue their fight for improved services. Leading the struggle in city after city were the local boards of underwriters that were established in the 1860s and 1870s primarily to halt cutthroat competition and rate wars between rival agents. But not only did these local boards seek to fix minimum levels for premiums, they also demanded the best fire protection the taxpayer's money could buy. As early as 1857 agents in San Francisco organized the Board of Fire Insurance, superseded four years later by the Board of Fire Underwriters of San Francisco; in 1867 New York City insurance interests formed the New York Board of Fire Underwriters; and in 1872 Saint Louis agents founded a similar board for their city.[82] These and comparable bodies in other cities were to act as watchdogs of municipal water and fire services.

The work of the Saint Louis Board of Fire Underwriters was typical of the insurance industry's efforts to ensure optimum fire protection. Throughout the early 1880s Saint Louis agents were critical of the city's Fire Department, and prominent local underwriters warned: "We are receiving letters from our companies every day saying they can not stand the severe losses they sustain here and some [are] threatening to withdraw unless we can get a better Fire department." One Saint Louis agent received a letter from the manager of his New York-based company complaining of Saint Louis's "superannuated fire marshal, . . . [the city's] played out hose, and the inefficiency generally of what is called by courtesy the Fire Department," and again there was the threat that the company would refuse to issue policies unless improvement ensued.[83] Finally in 1884 the local underwriters forced the city government into action. The president of the Board of Fire Underwriters delivered an address on the Fire Department's shortcomings, and one of the city's leading newspapers printed the speech verbatim. Responding to the exposé, the chief of the Fire Department summoned the president of the board and proposed joint action by the department and the underwriters in securing additional fire extinguishing equipment for the city. The board president agreed, secured the cooperation of other leading business groups, and won the support of the city comptroller, whose backing was vital if the fire department was to obtain an extraordinary appropriation. Moreover, at the behest of business interests and the comptroller, a committee of the Board of Fire Underwriters investigated fire conditions and reported its findings to the city council, which then adopted the board's recommendations. Additional firehouses, personnel, hydrants, and water mains were forthcoming as a result of the underwriters' campaign.[84]

Elsewhere, local boards also rallied public opinion through investigations of existing conditions, and advised lawmakers. In 1872 New York City's Board of Fire Underwriters appointed a committee to convince the governor of the need for an increased municipal water supply, and the board was instrumental in the expansion of the city's Croton reservoir system.[85] Likewise in San Francisco the local Board of Fire Underwriters fought proposals to alter the city's fire limits and to permit the construction of flammable frame buildings within the most heavily populated portion of the city. In dire tones reminiscent of their colleagues in Saint Louis, San Francisco's underwriters warned of the withdrawal of insurance companies from the San Francisco market and threatened policy cancellations if the city did not act to improve fire protection. In 1883 during a quarrel between the city's Board of Supervisors and the privately owned company providing the municipal water supply, fire underwriters demanded a quick settlement, and one after another they announced that any interruption of the water supply "means a cancellation of policies and retiring from business."[86] Similarly in 1873 fire underwriters threatened Boston's city fathers, announcing that if the city did not "choose to apply the remedies" suggested by the underwriters, then the insurance companies would "cancel their policies and discontinue business in Boston."[87] Thirteen years later a committee of the Boston Fire Underwriters' Union opposed reappointment of the city's incumbent fire commissioners and lobbied successfully against their confirmation by the Board of Aldermen.[88]

Throughout the 1870s, 1880s, and 1890s the efforts of local, state, and regional boards were supplemented by the emerging clout of the National Board of Fire Underwriters. Founded in 1866 to fix uniform rates nationwide and to oppose state legislation hostile to insurance interests, the national board also was to pressure municipalities into upgrading their firefighting forces, increasing their water supplies, adopting building codes that prohibited flammable construction, and enacting ordinances outlawing fire hazards. Though it suffered a period of dormancy in the mid-1880s, by the close of the 1890s the national board had assumed such authority that it virtually dictated the standards for fire protection and prevention in America's municipalities.

During the 1870s the chief object of the national organization's ire was the city of Chicago, site of the catastrophic blaze of 1871 that realized the underwriters' worst nightmares. Fearful that history might repeat itself, in June, 1874, the national board sent a special committee to visit Chicago and report on conditions. The committee found political interference with the Fire Department, poor discipline among those on the force, blocks of flammable frame buildings, and abundant industrial hazards. Incensed by this negligence, the national board forwarded six demands to the Chicago City Council, the most important demand being "the complete reorganization of the Fire Department, the eradication of political influence, the establishment of discipline, and the improvement of equipment." If the city did not meet these terms by October 1, 1874, the member companies of the national board pledged to discontinue business in Chicago.[89]

Chicago's municipal authorities hesitated, and by October 2, forty of the leading insurance companies had refused to insure any further properties in the city. Aroused by the action of the companies, the Citizen's Association, consisting of leading Chicago businessmen, moved quickly to force improvements. It convinced the city council to acquiesce to a reorganization of the Fire Department under the guidance of New York City's fire commissioner, who received a fee of $10,000 paid jointly by the Citizen's Association and the Board of Fire Underwriters. Moreover, the council extended the area in which construction of frame buildings was prohibited, and committees of the Citizen's Association, the insurers, and the city council cooperated in drafting a new building law. By December the *Chicago Tribune* could report that "the reorganization of the Fire Department has been determined upon, and the water-service will be enlarged with the return of warm weather," and, more importantly, "the people have learned the danger of playing with fire, and the municipal authorities the danger of trifling with the people." In the face of some improvements and promises of further change, in December the national board lifted its sanctions on Chicago. "Blackmail" had thus proved an effective weapon of the insurance interests, and during the remainder of the century Chicago's fire brigade enjoyed a reputation as one of the best equipped and most efficient forces in the world.[90]

Not until the late 1880s did the national board embark upon a more systematic program of investigation and correction. In 1889 the board hired the assistant chief of Brooklyn's fire brigade to inspect and examine the "present condition and needs of the fire departments and fire facilities throughout the country," and thereby initiated a permanent program of supervision.[91] Moreover, in 1892 the board sponsored the drafting of the National Board Electrical Code, a body of rules governing the installation of electric wiring and lighting. For the next decade the national organization sought to pressure municipalities into adopting the code. By 1901, 125 municipalities were enforcing the board's code as law, though the electrical departments in some cities such as Chicago devised a few additional rules "made to apply to local conditions."[92] In 1896 the national board likewise sought to impose uniform building standards on the nation's cities and voted to frame a model building law.[93] By the close of the century, many of the rules, regulations, and ordinances enforced by municipalities in an effort to limit fire hazards were in fact creations of the insurance interests. Underwriters for the great insurance companies were safeguarding their risks by encouraging municipal governments to adopt uniform standards of prevention and protection fixed by the industry's national board.

Just as party leaders played a vital role in the selection of officials, and civic associations in the drafting of city legislation, so the fire underwriters were overseeing the quality and competence of municipal public safety programs. They complained if the city authorities seemed lax, and even sought to coerce municipalities through concerted threats. Their rate schedules provided a positive incentive for improved water systems and fire departments, and they endeavored to guide municipalities through the framing of model codes. No citizen's league or party boss had greater influence over the development of municipal efforts to prevent and extinguish fires than did the fire underwriters.

Insurance companies, however, were not the only organizations interested in municipal safety regulations or building codes. Rules governing construction that were aimed at ensuring a safe, healthy environment were equally of interest to builders, architects, real estate developers, and suppliers of building materials. Each of these groups was vitally concerned with the drafting and administration of building codes, because such codes struck at their purses and could seriously affect their livelihood. Consequently, they, like the fire underwriters, assumed a major role in determining municipal codes and regulations. The rules governing the construction of American cities in the late nineteenth century were largely the product of joint action by the parties to be regulated.

This was especially evident in New York City, whose building legislation became a model copied by other municipalities in the United States and worldwide. During the late nineteenth century builders, architects, and developers not only played an extralegal role in the formulation of this code, but also enjoyed certain formal legal powers. The New York state legislature did not hesitate to bestow formal regulatory power on representatives of private interests. In that city, private organizations not only helped to administer the law but lobbied, pressured, and petitioned for legal change.

In 1860 legislators in Albany enacted the first separate building law for New York City, which provided for a department of building manned by a superintendent, deputy superintendent, and eight inspectors. Selection of these officials, however, was not to rest with the political authorities; instead, three persons chosen by the American Institute of Architects and three members of the Mechanics' and Tradesmen's Society were to meet with three representatives of the Fire Department, and together these nine were to nominate the officers of the city building department. Two years later the legislature granted the mayor the power to appoint the superintendent of buildings, but before appointment the mayor's nominee had to pass an examination conducted by a committee of the American Institute of Architects. Thus the city's leading architects retained the power to veto the mayor's choice.[94]

To permit some flexibility and allow variance in the building code, in 1874 the New York legislature authorized the creation of a Board of Examiners consisting of one representative elected by the New York Board of Fire Underwriters; one spokesman chosen by the American Institute of Architects; two members of the Mechanics' and Traders' Exchange—one a master mason and the other a master carpenter; and the superintendent of buildings. Amendments to the building law in 1885 and 1892 added four new members to the Board of Examiners, one chosen by the Society of Architectural Iron Manufacturers, one selected by the Real Estate Owners and Builders' Association, one from the New York Real Estate Exchange, and the fourth was the chief of the city's Fire Department. These seven spokesmen of private organizations, together with the two city officials, had the power to vary or modify the building code in special cases where strict application would prove detrimental to the purpose of the law or when no provision of the code specifically applied. In other words, representatives of the builders, architects, and real estate developers were to have broad discretionary authority to make exceptions to the rules.[95]

Besides this formal delegation of authority, New York City's private organizations also assumed certain extralegal tasks not specified by statute. Those serving on the Board of Examiners repeatedly undertook without statutory authorization the responsibility of drafting proposed revisions of the city's building law for submission to the state legislature. In 1883 spokesmen for the building, architectural, and insurance organizations drafted a new law requiring safer construction of theaters and the use of fireproof building materials for structures exceeding eighty-five feet in height. Another revision followed in 1887, and two years later representatives of the Board of Fire Underwriters, the New York Chapter of the American Institute of Architects, the Mechanics' and Traders' Exchange, the Society of Architectural Iron Manufacturers, and the Real Estate Owners and Builders' Association again decided to frame amendments to the existing law, which had proven "too stringent" and suffered from "loose and ungrammatical wording." During November, 1889, these groups held meetings for two hours every Monday, Wednesday, and Friday, conducted open hearings, and heard testimony from those with suggestions for change, before submitting their final proposed amendments. Two years later the procedure was repeated, and another new draft of the city's building law emerged. The state legislature obliged these private organizations and enacted their handiwork. In December 1895 an enlarged committee including delegates from the Architectural League of New York, the Association of Master Plumbers, the Master Carpenters Association, and the Masons and Builders Association embarked on still another round of meetings and hearings.[96] Throughout these decades the private organizations, not the Board of Aldermen, the mayor, or the state representatives, took the initiative in writing the city's building code. Building law in New York City was a compromise among the various interested private organizations and reflected their views and demands.

During the late nineteenth century, then, experts from the private sector exercised a formidable influence on municipal building regulation in New York City. They drafted the law and sanctioned variations and modifications of the statutory specifications. Moreover, they attempted to ensure nonpolitical and professional administration of the building department, and by the late 1880s they were claiming some success. In 1887 the New York Chapter of the American Institute of Architects boasted that it was entitled to "some credit for the introduction and growth of a faithful professional animus in the Building Bureau of New York City, contrasting strongly with the old-time prevalent spirit of mere self-seeking political placemen."[97]

Yet the builders' and architects' influence did not always supplant the power of politics, and reformers as well as Tammany loyalists could become the focus of their ire. For example, in 1895 reform Mayor William Strong decided to remove the Tammany-appointed superintendent of the building department despite petitions supporting the incumbent from the city's most prominent architects and builders. In place of the Tammany official, Strong named a conscientious superintendent who soon antagonized the construction industry by examining applications for building permits too carefully, thereby delaying and sometimes halting construction. Architects who had previously complained of extortion by building inspectors now spoke nostalgically of "the old regime of liberal douceurs [that] . . . had at least the merit of hastening examinations and securing the promptness architects, builders and owners desired."[98] Though the building interests might talk of a municipal building department that best served the public interest, they actually sought to achieve a department that was attentive to the sometimes conflicting private interests of insurers, builders, architects, and manufacturers of building materials. The organizations that drafted the building laws and served on the examining board did not want a department whose ultimate loyalty was to Tammany or to reform; rather, they sought to create a municipal agency whose first love was the agency's clientele, those private parties with a vested interest in building. During the late nineteenth century they only partially achieved this end.

Meanwhile, in other cities those engaged in building also helped fashion municipal construction codes and influenced the administration of the city building departments. For example, in 1891–92 the executive committee of the Chicago Chapter of the American Institute of Architects cooperated with a city council subcommittee in writing an ordinance restricting the height of structures, and the chapter also joined with the council in revising the municipal building ordinances. During the 1890s the Chicago City Council further stipulated that applicants for the job of city building inspector first pass an examination before a board appointed by the Chicago Builders' and Traders' Exchange, the local Fire Underwriters' Association, the Building and Trades Council, and the local chapter of the American Institute of Architects. Chicago politicians seemed dedicated to evading this requirement, but the private organizations were determined to ensure that the city building department conformed to the standards of builders, architects, and insurance companies.[99] In 1891–92 a committee of the Philadelphia Chapter of the American Institute of Architects helped the city council revise the building code, and in Baltimore the city's new building law was the product of a committee consisting of the president and the secretary of the local chapter of professional architects, delegates from the builders' exchange, and representatives of the municipal government.[100] Likewise, in 1890 architects in Indianapolis framed that city's building ordinance, though by the end of the year they found that "the entire ordinance is 'more honored in the breach than in the observance.' "[101] Moreover, in 1892 Massachusetts lawmakers copied the New York model and created a board of appeal for approving variances and modifications of Boston's building statute. And as in New York City, Boston's three-man board was to be an expert panel, including one architect appointed by the Boston Society of Architects.[102]

Throughout the nation architects and builders as well as fire underwriters were assuming the lead in the drafting of building ordinances and were seeking to ensure professional implementation of the codes. It was in their self-interest to ensure that this area of municipal regulation did not fall subject to political hacks or priggish reformers who lacked training or experience in construction. The fire underwriter wanted protection for his risks through stringent regulation, whereas the builder and architect favored regulation that was not too stringent and a group of inspectors whose first loyalty was to the building industry and not to a political party. The members of the Society of Architectural Iron Manufacturers sought to ensure that regulations permitted use of new building materials such as iron and steel beams. Each group pursued different and sometimes conflicting goals, but all agreed that experts in the private sector should frame the building code and that the elected aldermen or representatives merely approve it. Each group was dedicated to exercising a strong voice in the determination of municipal regulations.

Among this chorus of private voices were the local real estate exchanges. Urban real estate agents, who were represented on the examining board of New York City's building department, feared construction codes detrimental to their business. But municipal policy affected them in still other ways. As speculators in urban real estate and managers of large landholdings, these agents viewed high property taxes and burdensome assessments as a special threat and misery. Inexpensive, efficient municipal rule thus was a notion especially dear to their pocketbooks. Yet municipal government offered promises for profit as well as threats of taxation. If the municipal council voted, for example, to extend transit lines, it would open outlying acreage to development. And if municipal park commissioners agreed to create a new park or tree-lined boulevard, it would add thousands of dollars to the value of adjoining lots and bring financial joy to many real estate brokers. During the last decades of the nineteenth century, real estate exchanges sought to realize such potentially profitable schemes, while at the same time limiting the grim realities of taxation.

Year after year the local boards or exchanges lobbied for improvements that would benefit both the city and the real estate industry. Few groups matched the persistence of the New York Real Estate Exchange in its pursuance of the construction of a rapid-transit system in New York City. Exchange committees representing uptown property holders met with the mayor, lobbied state legislators, proposed schemes, and drafted resolutions. When the city finally embarked on a subway scheme it was with the full support of those members of the Real Estate Exchange who were eager to subdivide the relatively inaccessible upper reaches of Manhattan.[103]

Chicago's Real Estate Board was equally active in pressuring the municipal authorities. In 1884, for example, the board considered such issues as the construction of boulevards and the elimination of livery stable nuisances.[104] And in 1890 the board created a permanent Public Service Committee, whose chief purpose was to secure a favorable hearing for board-sponsored measures at both the state and local levels.[105] The following year board members lobbied in Springfield on behalf of the city's massive sewerage project and in support of the West Park District.[106] During the last years of the century, the board also backed the growing movement for small neighborhood parks and urged the Board of Education to purchase an extra acre adjoining each school for playground purposes.[107]

Boston's Real Estate Exchange was organized later than those of New York City and Chicago, but by the early 1890s it, too, was urging stepped-up municipal improvements. In 1891 the exchange's president called for state legislation authorizing a city commission to plot the streets and sewers in outlying areas prior to private development. Expressing his faith in the clout of the real estate brokers, the president argued that the exchange "will carry to the State House a force and a character which will compel consideration" of the improvement measure. The exchange leader proved correct. That session the legislature responded to the combined pressure of the mayor and the exchange, creating a Board of Survey to formulate plans for undeveloped lands within the city limits.[108]

Yet the real estate industry was not an unquestioning supporter of municipal improvements, especially when those improvements might increase the tax burden on the property holder. Low real estate taxes were, in fact, sacred to urban land speculators and property managers. In 1889 the legislative committee of New York's Real Estate Exchange embarked on a plan to secure absolute home rule for the city and thereby relieve it of the burdensome expenses imposed in Albany. The exchange did not think "that Albany rule for New York was ever wise or can ever be profitable to the taxpayers of this city."[109] Chicago's Real Estate Board battled for years to abolish the various sets of township assessors responsible for valuing property within the city. In 1898 the real estate brokers succeeded in ridding Chicago of this system, which had permitted some sections of the city to be assessed more heavily than others. The board also backed reforms in the system of special assessment and fought vigorously against increases in the tax rate. Though it supported the city's park and sewerage schemes, it lobbied against property tax increases designed to pay for these services. To the members of the Real Estate Board, license fees or poll taxes seemed preferable means for raising additional revenue.[110]

Although real estate exchanges were active participants in the governmental arena, they generally avoided politics, refusing to take sides in the battle between parties or factions. In the municipal election of 1894 New York's Real Estate Exchange did drop its impartial stance and organized an Honest Government Club to combat Tammany;[111] but such action was rare. In 1899 the president of Chicago's Real Estate Board summed up the standard position when he advised his colleagues: "Keep our board out of politics; . . . don't expect to secure good laws and to pound the lawmakers at the same time; keep in the line of real estate work."[112] Real estate organizations fought for the interests of their own industry first and foremost and only secondarily for honest, good government.

At the same time that real estate brokers, builders, and underwriters were seeking to tailor municipal policy to their needs, a number of professional groups were also attempting to establish a foothold in city hall. Typical of the groups engaged in such efforts were the artists and physicians. These emerging professionals sought to ensure that city officials both bowed to their expertise and pursued a policy that enhanced not only the public interest but also their private welfare. Like other special interests, they had a stake in municipal endeavors, and they were determined that their voices be heard. If municipalities were to decorate parks with sculpture and public buildings with murals, the artistic community felt that city officials should defer to those who knew best about such subjects. Similarly, if cities were to battle disease, physicians felt they should assume command positions.

Leading the efforts of the artistic community in New York City were two organizations founded in 1893, the Municipal Art Society and the National Sculpture Society. Consisting of architects, painters, sculptors, and friends of the arts, the Municipal Art Society was dedicated to providing "adequate sculptural and pictorial decorations for the public buildings and parks in the city of New York."[113] Guided by its president, the distinguished architect Richard Morris Hunt, the founding members of the society were especially concerned about the poor quality of sculpture in the city's parks. One of the society's original officers had nothing but contempt for the commemorative statue of Simon Bolivar in Central Park, and he observed of the Garibaldi statue in Washington Square that it gave "one the idea that Garibaldi had spent a hilarious night."[114] The National Sculpture Society seconded these views. Under the leadership of such eminent sculptors as John Q. A. Ward, Daniel Chester French, and Augustus Saint-Gaudens, this group also sought to prevent any further marble or bronze monstrosities from finding their way into the city parklands. Thus, one of the clearly expressed aims of the National Sculpture Society was to give advice to local authorities engaged in selecting designs for monuments and statuary.[115] Both groups intended to encourage municipal patronage of the arts, but they also advocated that professional experts be consulted in municipal decision making in order to maintain aesthetic standards.

By the close of 1893 the two societies had joined forces in the controversy over the landscaping of New York's Harlem River driveway and were already pressuring municipal officials to defer to professional landscapists. The various art organizations in the city petitioned the park commission and mayor not to depart "from the established policy of creating [the city's] public parks under the direction of trained professional skill and cultivated taste."[116] The battle raged for over a year, and finally in December, 1894, Saint-Gaudens and Stanford White representing the National Sculpture Society and the Municipal Art Society, together with Richard Morris Hunt, Daniel Chester French, Childe Hassam, and other artists of distinction, petitioned for the removal of the park commissioners.[117] The following month the president of the park commission resigned, owing, in part, to the harsh criticism of the artists who he claimed "did not know what they were talking about."[118] In 1895 a reconstituted park commission satisfied the troublesome artistic community by turning for advice to the city's landscape architect Calvert Vaux. The sculptors, architects, and painters had thus won the first round in their fight for a public policy that recognized the special talents of the aesthete.

Soon the National Sculpture Society was expanding its influence even further. In 1895 New York City's park commission requested the society to examine existing statues in the municipal parks and report "any changes which may be deemed advantageous." The commission further asked the society to judge the merit of statues and monuments offered to the city for the decoration of public areas.[119] One proposed gift was a monument of the German poet Heinrich Heine, offered by some of his German-American admirers. The society recommended that the city refuse the monument, and the park board accepted this judgment. Thus the official body deferred to its extralegal advisors.[120] In the past municipal authorities had readily accepted statues honoring heroes of every nationality, with the result that bronze liberators and bards cluttered open spaces throughout the city. These statues had been political and ethnic monuments, sops to the national origins and political predilections of the city's residents. Now under the aegis of the National Sculpture Society, statuary was no longer to be regarded as a political gesture to a polyglot population. Statuary was art, and as such fell within the realm of the expert connoisseur and the artist.

But the city's Board of Aldermen still tended toward the earlier view. Deferring to German voters rather than American sculptors, this popularly elected, neighborhood-based body seemed ready to accept the Heine memorial. New York's aesthetes were aghast, and the sculptor Augustus Saint-Gaudens spoke for his colleagues when he argued that the city "should not be made a laughing stock for the artistic world."[121] Alert to the danger, the Fine Arts Federation, a newly formed body representing all the major artistic societies in New York City, secured passage of a law creating a Municipal Art Commission consisting of the mayor, the president of the Board of Aldermen, the president of the National Sculpture Society, and the president of the Municipal Art Society. According to the new law, before the city erected any statue or monument, the proposed work of sculpture had to win the approval of all four of these commission members.[122] And the presidents of the artistic societies soon exercised their power, blocking such important projects as a soldiers and sailors monument planned for the plaza at Fifty-ninth Street and Fifth Avenue.[123] Thus the sculptors, painters, architects, and connoisseurs no longer were only extralegal advisors; they now possessed a legal veto over statuary in the nation's largest city.

In few municipalities were artists and friends of the arts so well organized as in New York City, but by the close of the century local art organizations were beginning to gain influence in a number of city halls. As early as 1871 a Philadelphia group dedicated to statuary had founded the Fairmount Park Art Association, a private organization that assumed responsibility for acquiring and placing sculpture in that city's mammoth public park. Headed by the wealthy Anthony J. Drexel, the group consisted mainly of amateur connoisseurs rather than practicing sculptors, but it was dedicated to ensuring aesthetic quality in the embellishment of the city.[124] In 1894 a number of the leading artists and collectors in Cincinnati organized a municipal art society "to provide appropriate sculptural, pictorial or other decorations for the public buildings and parks in the city . . . , and otherwise to encourage high artistic standards."[125] This body assumed responsibility for the interior decoration of the new city hall, and a professional panel headed by the city's most notable painter, Frank Duveneck, judged the submitted mural designs.[126] By 1899 the Municipal Art Society of Baltimore was offering to aid in the funding of murals for that city's new courthouse and was hosting a conference on municipal art attended by interested citizens from throughout the country.[127] At the same time, then, that insurance underwriters were seeking to determine the fire protection policies of the major cities, municipal art groups were equally intent on playing the chief role in deciding the aesthetic future of their communities. Municipal art societies were to assume greater importance in the first decade of the twentieth century. But already in New York City, Philadelphia, and Cincinnati private bodies were playing a significant role in the public decoration of the city.

Equally eager for a larger role in municipal decision making were the local medical societies. As in the case of the sculptors, the underwriters, and the builders, the urban physicians sought a firmer grasp over municipal policy both in order to further the public welfare and to enhance their professional fortunes and standing. In an age abounding with medical quacks, osteopaths, and Christian Scientists, many physicians were defensive about the prestige and public standing of their profession. These medical leaders firmly believed that only physicians trained in correct medical schools should determine public health policy. Moreover, they favored the appointment of public health administrators who would understand the interests of the medical profession and avoid treading on the toes of private practitioners. Through imposition of quarantines, requirements for reporting diseases, and distribution of antitoxins, city health departments interfered with the doctor-patient relationship, a relationship held sacred by individual practitioners who did not want an officious public health bureaucrat challenging their diagnoses or prescriptions. In the opinion of the medical societies, health officers should, then, represent the medical establishment and act in a manner acceptable to the city's respected practitioners. Furthermore, lay officials were expected to defer to the judgment of the professional medical organizations. For mayors or aldermen to ignore the advice of medical societies was an insult to the medical profession and a sure sign of incompetent and irresponsible rule.

In city after city the local boards of health sought the support and cooperation of the medical societies, and the societies in turn were ready with proposals for reform. The public health section of New York City's Academy of
Medicine studied municipal garbage disposal, investigated the city's water
supply, debated the Health Department provisions of the new charter for
Greater New York, and lobbied on behalf of Health Department optical examinations for school children. Together with the County Medical Society, it
also pressured the Board of Education to improve sanitary conditions in the
public schools. And to ensure that its influence was felt, the academy appointed advisory committees to consult with the municipal board of health.[128]
The Chicago Medical Society urged improvement of the city's water supply
and sewerage and applied its chastening hand to the municipal Health Department if that body faltered. For example, when Chicago's health officials
wrongly challenged a private practitioner's diagnosis, the medical society was
quick with a reprimand.[129] In Boston the Suffolk District Medical Society
maintained close relations with the board of health and generally bolstered the
efforts of that board's respected president Dr. Samuel Durgin. For example,
in 1884 the society appointed a committee to cooperate with the board of
health and the municipal milk inspector in formulating a scheme for protecting the purity of the city's milk supply. In 1890 the society likewise appointed a
committee to join with the board of health in urging the city government to
improve its street-cleaning services.[130]

Occasionally the local medical societies collided head-on with municipal
authorities, and an accommodation between the city and the disgruntled professionals proved necessary. In 1897 New York City's health authorities issued
an order defining tuberculosis as communicable and requiring all physicians
to report cases of the disease. This violation of the prerogatives of private
practice was met with loud protests by physicians. Though prominent leaders
of the Academy of Medicine's public health section supported the city's action, the medical profession as a whole condemned the "offensively dictatorial
and defiantly compulsory character" of the ruling. A special committee of the
academy suggested a compromise whereby the board of health "might wisely
delay the enforcement of compulsory notification," and the city health officers
unofficially recognized the wisdom of cautious implementation. Hesitant enforcement thus became the prevailing pattern in the last years of the 1890s,
during which the municipal authorities and medical profession parried and
feinted in a match of accommodation.[131] With hostilities continuing, in 1898
the County Medical Society unsuccessfully sponsored a bill in the state legislature to limit the power of the municipal board of health.[132] Diplomatic over-
tures from both the city and profession, however, gradually quieted the
controversy.

Throughout these years the medical societies were clearly seeking to make
municipal health departments their domain, and nothing aroused the practi-

tioners' wrath so much as lay officials who refused to concede control to the profession. For example, New York City doctors complained vigorously about the state law that specified that only a lay person could serve as president of the board of health. In 1887 in a paper delivered before the County Medical Society, one prominent New York City practitioner, commenting on the municipal Health Department, urged that "a bill be drawn up making it essential for the head of that department to be a regularly qualified physician," and he denounced the existing law as "a gross political outrage."[133] Two years later the New York Academy of Medicine sought a change in the law so that "never again will it be within the province of a Mayor to place a stockbroker in a position which belongs to the guardian of public health." And, according to one newspaper, physicians associated with the Academy of Medicine, the County Medical Society, "and bodies of similar dignity" had decided "that they should claim some right to recognition in a board which has so much to do with their profession."[134]

In leading midwestern cities medical societies were uttering similar complaints, reflecting a growing desire on their part to determine municipal health policy and appointments. Chicago's physicians seethed with anger when in 1895 Mayor George Swift ousted the professionally acceptable incumbent city health commissioner and appointed in his stead that lowest of political animals, an ex-alderman without any medical training. At a meeting of the Doctor's Club, one physician contended that this sad situation was "the fault of the physicians themselves in not organizing and asserting a greater influence in the community." A colleague concurred saying, "We must organize as politicians. . . . Not until then will we cease to be the football of rotten politicians." Some members urged doctors to "utterly ignore the department" and to "understand that there is no such thing as a health commissioner, and [not to] recognize the layman in office." And the club as a whole resolved that "the appointment of a non-medical man as chief health officer of the city is to be condemned as unnecessarily jeopardizing the lives and health of the citizens."[135]

Cincinnati's leading physicians were voicing much the same opinions. Frustrated by the fact that laymen on the city's Board of Administration determined policy for the Health Department, one prominent Cincinnati physician in 1891 urged his fellow practitioners: "Assert our prerogative and be heard upon all matters of a sanitary nature. . . . We have the right to interfere, and it is our duty to do so." And the local medical societies exploded with outrage in 1897 when the mayor appointed as city health officer an unlicensed practitioner who advertised quick cures in the newspapers. The editor of the prestigious local medical journal referred to the health officer as "a notorious advertising quack" and viewed the appointment as "a travesty upon justice, decency and everything else that goes to make a respected and respectable community!" The Cincinnati Academy of Medicine likewise deprecated the choice as "an insult to the profession and a menace to public health."[136] In Cincinnati, then, as in Chicago and New York City, leading physicians expected the municipal authorities to conform to the standards dictated by the local medical societies. Often politics seemed to demand that city officials do otherwise, but such deviation led to sharp censure by the city's medical overlords.

As the century waned the medical societies seemed to be making headway. Throughout the late nineteenth century one of the four seats on New York City's board of health was unofficially reserved for a member of the Academy of Medicine, and in the 1890s two of the academy's presidents were former board members. Under Dr. Hermann Biggs, the New York City Health Department aroused the ire of some practitioners, but professionalism was clearly dominant. In fact, the conflict over the compulsory reporting of tuberculosis was largely a fight between research bacteriologists in the vanguard of the medical profession and rank-and-file practitioners dedicated to treating measles and flu. Likewise, the appointment of the ex-alderman as Chicago's health commissioner did not conform to the prevailing trend toward professionalism in the public health administration of that city. And by 1900 Cincinnati's physicians had succeeded in installing a highly respectable medical doctor in the post of city health officer.[137] In most cities, the local medical societies proved less successful at dictating health policy than the insurance underwriters were at determining fire protection standards. Yet in the last decade of the century the clout of the urban medical societies was growing. Few municipal health officers could ignore the advice or demands of the medical profession.

Physicians, sculptors, fire underwriters, builders, architects, and real estate developers all imposed standards on the city in an effort to protect their own interests. Each group felt it had much to lose if the municipal leaders proved lax, ignorant, incompetent, or dishonest, and therefore each chose to participate in the determination of municipal policy as a safeguard. Other private groups also exerted pressure, lobbied, and coaxed. Neighborhood improvement associations battled for pavements and sewers, better police protection, and additional fire stations. Labor unions urged shorter hours and better wages for those employed by municipal contractors. Bankers and municipal bondholders demanded improved accounting techniques, honest financial management, and limits on public indebtedness. Streetcar, gas, and electric companies bribed public officials and appealed to state legislators in order to achieve better franchise deals. And saloonkeepers conducted a perpetual battle against enforcement of the Sunday closing laws and other regulations that might limit their "ill-gotten" gains. The extralegal, if not illegal, efforts of the public utility franchises and the saloon and gambling elements were, in fact, among the chief complaints of the reform crusaders of the 1890s, and the role of these much-vilified groups in the formation of municipal policy and practice fills pages of good-government literature.

These private interest groups were among the facts of political life, and overreaching politicians had to beware of their opposition. In 1891 Saint Louis's Mayor Edward Noonan learned his lesson when he nominated a new fire chief who was unacceptable to the fire underwriters and selected, moreover, his brother-in-law as health commissioner without sufficiently considering the reaction of reputable physicians. The Board of Fire Underwriters and the medical profession backed Noonan's opponents in the city council, and neither appointment received confirmation. A councilman frankly confessed to reporters that the nominee for health commissioner "was rejected on the ground that his appointment did not satisfy the medical fraternity." And the insurance interests together with the real estate brokers, bankers, and wholesale merchants ensured defeat of the mayor's nominee for fire chief.[138] Thus, even though the mayor and a majority of the council were of the same political party, Noonan could not push through appointments offensive to powerful private interests. In the factionalized politics of Saint Louis, party unity quickly crumbled under the pressure of insurance agents and bankers.

Moreover, in the last ten years of the century, special interests throughout the country seemed to gain new energy and force. As the economic interests of the metropolis grew more diverse and the functions of the municipal corporation expanded, an increasing number of trade associations, occupational groups, and business guilds were to muster their influence in campaigns to determine municipal policy. By the 1890s such professionals as physicians, sculptors, and architects had become increasingly self-conscious about their status and had organized to demand an unprecedented degree of control over their own areas of expertise. National bodies were also beginning to bolster the authority of their local representatives, thereby stiffening the pressure applied to local officials. The National Board of Fire Underwriters, for example, was finally imposing uniform standards throughout the country after two decades of only sporadic success. In the future, municipal programs and proposals might issue not only from the city itself or from the state capital but from a distant national organization headquarters.

Thus by the final years of the century, aldermen, mayors, bosses, and civic reformers all had to recognize that they were not the only figures writing urban law. The cast of lawmakers included names not found in the directory of city officials, the membership rolls of Tammany Hall, or the dues-paying list of the good-government club. It included a motley lot of insurance underwriters, builders, bankers, real estate speculators, public utility magnates, and labor union officials. These all numbered among the decision makers in American municipal government.

II THE FUNCTIONS AND FINANCES OF URBAN GOVERNMENT

8 THE TRIUMPH OF TECHNOLOGY

In 1830 Chicago was a frontier trading post with a few log structures, a few muddy paths, and a few dozen inhabitants. Seventy years later it was a city of 1.5 million people, with a waterworks pumping 500 million gallons of water to its residents each day and a drainage system with over 1,500 miles of sewers. More than 1,400 miles of paved streets lighted by 38,000 street lamps crisscrossed the prairie, and 925 miles of streetcar lines carried hundreds of millions of passengers each year. A fleet of 129 fire engines protected lives and property, and over 2,200 acres of city parkland and a public library of 300,000 volumes offered recreation and a means for self-improvement. In a single lifetime Chicago residents had transformed a prairie bog into one of the greatest cities in the world, and during this short period the governmental authorities, with remarkable energy and daring, had provided migrants to the metropolis with a level of public services rarely equaled in the world of the late nineteenth century. In the 1850s the city council had ordained that the level of the swampy city be raised ten feet, and it had been done. In later decades the municipal authorities had ordered that the flow of the Chicago river be reversed, and so it was reversed. The achievements of government in Chicago at times rivaled the feats of the Old Testament God.

Moreover the Chicago experience was representative of what was happening throughout the nation. In Boston, New York City, Saint Louis, and San Francisco urban rulers faced the awesome challenge of a spiraling population and an ever-changing technology, and they met that challenge at least as ably as urban leaders in any other nation of the world. During the last half of the nineteenth century American city governments sponsored feats of engineering never before attempted, provided comforts and conveniences previously unknown to urban dwellers, and initiated a range of municipal services of unprecedented breadth. By 1900 the city governments of the United States, those conspicuous "failures" of American life, provided the most extensive, most advanced public services known to urban residents.

To better understand the scope and quality of American city services, one can apply James Bryce's own tests for "practical efficiency." In 1888 this great critic of American municipal rule argued that urban government could best be evaluated if one asked two vital questions: "What does it provide for the people, and what does it cost the people?"[1] What, then, were the benefits of American city government, and what were the costs? In this and the following chapter, I will apply the first half of Bryce's test and examine the benefits of urban rule in the United States. In Chapter 10 I will turn to the second half of the test, the question of municipal finance and taxation. To measure the relative achievement of American municipalities, major cities in the United States are compared with the much-vaunted European cities of the period. Late-nineteenth-century critics of the American municipality repeatedly pointed to European cities, and especially the cities of Great Britain and Germany, as models that the failed metropolises of the New World could emulate. Reform literature of the period cited the supposed efficiency of Glasgow and Breslau and the reputed good governments of Birmingham and Berlin as yardsticks against which the trumpeted shortcomings of the American city could be measured. Did the American city in fact rank so poorly as a purveyor of services as compared with the municipalities of Great Britain or Germany? How did America's parks, public libraries, schools, water and sewerage systems, streets, public transportation, fire and police services measure up when juxtaposed with those of London and Birmingham or Berlin and Leipzig? Such an analysis reveals the strengths and weaknesses of American urban rule, its characteristics and peculiarities. It also demonstrates that reform-minded Americans were not forced by abominable urban conditions to denigrate their cities but chose to emphasize the bad and overlook the good. The "failure" of the American city was a matter of subjective perception and not objective fact. Many middle-class Americans of the late nineteenth century simply refused to view a municipality governed in part by ward-heeling Irish politicians as worthy of praise.

Nowhere was the actual magnitude of American municipal achievement more evident than in the area of technology. American cities were the most "modern" in the world, adopting the newest technological advances more readily than their European counterparts. A Frenchman visiting Chicago in 1886 expressed the view of many Europeans when he reported to his Old World compatriots that "none of the new inventions (which our own cities fail to adopt) are lacking here."[2] Throughout the United States municipalities employed the latest engineering techniques to create ambitious water and sewerage projects; quickly applied electricity to street lighting, transportation, and fire alarm systems; and pioneered the development of bacteriological laboratories. By the close of the century the city governments of Boston, New York City, Philadelphia, and Chicago had ensured their residents technological superiority in public services. Assuredly, there were shortcomings. Some schemes failed, and the municipal fathers often had to proceed by trial and error. Those who sought to criticize the American city could justifiably identify problems and faults. But at the same time such critics ignored the monumental achievements of systems that by and large did work and did provide services unsurpassed in the world.

WATER AND SEWERAGE

One of the most vital functions of local government is to provide water and sewer services, and in this field the late-nineteenth-century rulers of urban America achieved considerable success. As indicated in table 2, America's largest cities constructed hundreds of miles of water and sewer lines, and by the last decade of the century they maintained the most extensive such systems in the world, far surpassing the mileage of systems in German cities, for example. In the early 1890s New York City could boast of 660 miles of water lines and 464 miles of sewers, whereas the somewhat more populous Berlin could claim only 424 miles of water lines and 365 miles of sewers. Similarly, the city of Cleveland had constructed 301 miles of water mains and 146 miles of sewers, yet Dresden, with a slightly larger population, possessed only 104 miles of water mains and a sewerage system stretching only 93 miles. On the whole, American cities averaged two to three times as much mileage in water and sewer lines as did German cities of comparable population. Only backward Baltimore had a woefully inadequate system of sewerage (28 miles), which compared unfavorably with its European counterparts.

Moreover, as seen in table 3, American cities expanded their systems markedly during the 1890s, with the length of water and sewer lines nearly

TABLE 2. Sewer and Water Mains, 1889–92

American Cities				German Cities			
City	Population	Mains (mi.)		City	Population	Mains (mi.)	
		Water	Sewer			Water	Sewer
New York	1,515,301	660	464	Berlin	1,578,794	424	365
Chicago	1,099,850	678	525	Hamburg	569,260	253	186
Philadelphia	1,046,964	930	376	Leipzig	357,122	89	59
Brooklyn	806,343	416	380	Munich	349,024	123	72
Saint Louis	451,770	336	328	Breslau	335,186	102	150
Boston	448,477	631	291	Cologne	281,681	88	33
Baltimore	434,439	407	28	Dresden	276,522	104	93
San Francisco	298,997	342	193				
Cincinnati	296,908	271	98				
Cleveland	261,353	301	146				

Sources: Statistisches Jahrbuch Deutscher Städte—Zweiter Jahrgang (Breslau: Wilh. Gottl. Korn, 1892), pp. 81, 90; Report on the Social Statistics of Cities in the United States at the Eleventh Census: 1890 (Washington, D.C.: U.S. Government Printing Office, 1895), pp. 68–86.

TABLE 3.   Sewer and Water Mains, 1902

City	Population	Mains (mi.)		City	Population	Mains (mi.)	
American Cities				German Cities			
		Water	Sewer			Water	Sewer
New York	3,623,160	1,706	1,467	Berlin	1,888,326	629	576
Chicago	1,815,445	1,918	1,529	Hamburg	705,738	339	247
Philadelphia	1,343,043	1,419	951	Munich	499,959	285	150
Saint Louis	599,932	709	522	Leipzig	455,089	255	187
Boston	583,376	727	582	Breslau	422,738	171	148
Baltimore	523,861	634	44	Dresden	395,349	210	192
Cleveland	403,032	577	330	Cologne	372,229	209	153
Buffalo	371,731	501	434				

Sources: Statistisches Jahrbuch Deutscher Städte—Dreizehnter Jahrgang (Breslau: Wilh. Gottl. Korn, 1906), pp. 78, 130; Bureau of the Census—Statistics of Cities Having a Population of over 25,000, 1902 and 1903 (Washington, D.C.: U.S. Government Printing Office, 1905), pp. 65, 105, 127.

tripling in Chicago between 1890 and 1902 and almost doubling in Saint Louis and Cleveland. At the beginning of the twentieth century the wide gap between American cities and German cities persisted with the American systems remaining two or three times longer than those of the German municipalities. American systems were so extensive in large part because American municipalities, with the exception of New York City, were less densely populated than those of Europe, and the inhabitants were dispersed over a wider area. In spite of this dispersion, the cities of the United States were able to service urban residents through the creation of mammoth networks for water and drainage. In the United States urban residents could enjoy single-family dwellings and suburban lawns, yet still receive the services available in the tightly packed European centers.

Not only were American water networks far more extensive than those of Germany, but the quantity of water supplied to American urban dwellers was far greater than that piped to residents of Old World cities. As seen in table 4, in the mid-1890s the average per capita daily consumption of water in the major municipalities of the United States was over 130 gallons, whereas in British and German cities the per capita figure generally ranged between 20 and 40 gallons. European water systems were on a small scale compared with the operations of American cities. Berlin's waterworks pumped only 18 gallons per capita, as compared with Philadelphia's 162 gallons per capita; the municipality of Sheffield, England, ensured its residents a daily supply of 21 gallons per capita, yet the city government of Cleveland was able to meet a daily demand of 142 gallons per person. During the late nineteenth century hundreds of millions of gallons of water flowed into American cities each day,

TABLE 4. Per Capita Water Supply, 1895–97

American Cities		British Cities		German Cities	
City	Per Capita Daily Water Supply (U.S. gal.)	City	Per Capita Daily Water Supply (U.S. gal.)	City	Per Capita Daily Water Supply (U.S. gal.)
New York	100	London	42	Berlin	18
Chicago	139	Glasgow	65	Hamburg	52
Philadelphia	162	Liverpool	34	Munich	38
Brooklyn	89	Manchester	40	Leipzig	16
Boston	100	Birmingham	28	Breslau	23
Saint Louis	98	Leeds	43	Dresden	24
Baltimore	94	Sheffield	21	Cologne	45
Cleveland	142				
Buffalo	271				

Sources: James H. Fuertes, *Waste of Water in New York and Its Reduction by Meters and Inspection* (New York: Merchants' Association of New York, 1906), pp. 222, 225; F. F. Turneaure and H. L. Russell, *Public Water Supplies* (New York: John Wiley & Sons, 1901), pp. 23, 32; Allen Hazen, "Notes on European Water Supplies," *Journal of the New England Water Works Association* 9 (1894–95): 121; Columbus O. Johnson, *Water Supply and Prevention of Waste in Leading European Cities* (New York: Merchants' Association of New York, 1903), pp. 3, 79–80; J. J. Cosgrove, *Sewage Purification and Disposal* (Pittsburgh: Standard Sanitary Mfg., 1909), p. 189.

Note: Figures for the United States are for 1895 with the exception of those for Baltimore, dated 1890. Figures for Great Britain are for 1896–97 with the exception of those for Glasgow, dated circa 1902. Figures for Germany are for 1895 with the exception of those for Cologne, dated circa 1892.

far exceeding that supplied by the industrialized metropolises of western and northern Europe.

The extensive water and sewer systems in American cities enabled many urban residents to enjoy bathroom facilities of a type known only to the European elite. For example, flush toilets and bathtubs were much more common in the United States than in Great Britain or Germany. At the close of the nineteenth century, Manchester, England (population 544,000) had one hundred thousand privies and facilities known as pail closets, where human excrement accumulated in containers collected periodically by the city, but this same city could claim only thirty thousand flush toilets. Nearby in the city of Oldham (population 148,000) only 10 percent of the dwellings had flush toilets, whereas 90 percent relied on the more primitive, less sanitary dry-closet system. In Nottingham (population 239,000) there were only about ten thousand flush toilets and forty thousand dry closets, and in Dresden, Germany, only 15 percent of the houses had flush toilets.[3] In contrast, as early as 1893 in the United States, 51 percent of the tenement residents of New York City lived in houses having flush toilets, and 32 percent of the slum dwellers of Philadelphia lived in buildings having such facilities. Of the tenement buildings under construction in Manhattan in 1900, 61 percent provided a private flush toilet for each family in the dwelling.[4] And by the end of the century the flush toilet was standard equipment in the middle-class American home, as was the bathtub. In 1890 the imperial capital of Berlin could boast of only one bathtub for every seventy-nine residents, whereas in 1893 in provincial Springfield, Massachusetts, there was one tub for every nine inhabitants.[5] European water and sewer systems were not large enough to service hundreds of thousands of flush toilets and bathtubs. Only American municipalities with their massive water and sewer networks could meet this challenge.

While Americans enjoyed water in abundance, some Old World metropolises could not even meet the modest requirements of their bathless society. For example, water famines were commonplace in London, especially in the working-class East End. From August through October, Britons in this section of London often had water service only four hours a day, due to the low level of the reservoirs. During the water shortage of 1898, London church pulpits rang with popular indignation, and the city's press deplored the fact that a "great portion of London must go unwashed, and its thirst unslaked, and its drains unflushed." One East End vicar reported to the *Times* that "there has been no water whatsoever for four days in the bath-room or lavatories" of his vicarage, and "to-day we have "to go without vegetables, as we cannot afford the water to clean and boil them." Another clerical correspondent observed that "the suffering and discomfort caused to poor consumers in the mean streets of the East-end have during the week been aggravated in certain districts by the water only being on for an hour, and even half an hour per day. In Hackney this is often a mere dribble." And during the shortage the management of the Cyclone Grinding Works complained that "yesterday not a drop of water came into our works from 6 A.M. until 8 P.M. and we were in consequence compelled to stop work, having no water for our engine."[6]

Other European capitals experienced similar water problems. Before the 1890s the supply of potable water for the city of Paris was woefully inadequate, necessitating the use of polluted water from the Seine River throughout the year but especially during the dry summer months. Even with the river water, there was not sufficient pressure to supply the upper floors of the houses in two-thirds of the city. In 1886 an English sanitarian studying the French capital could only conclude that "no water supply for domestic purposes that is worthy of the name exists in the greater part of Paris."[7]

Such conditions were unheard of in New York City. During an occasional rainless spell New York City authorities might warn of diminishing water supplies and urge conservation. For example, in the unusually dry autumn of 1891 the commissioner of public works fruitlessly exhorted consumers to practice economy and levied fines on householders who wasted water hosing off their sidewalks and windows.[8] But water famines of the type common to London were unknown in America's largest city. Twenty-four-hour service remained the rule, and municipal governments successfully kept ahead of the giant demand, creating new reservoirs and thereby forestalling shortages.

Moreover, most American cities refused to pursue a policy aimed at slowing the ever-growing desire for water. German cities installed water meters in households and charged users according to the amount of water consumed. But American municipalities generally levied a flat rate on each household regardless of quantity used, and consequently urban dwellers had no financial motive for limiting consumption. Further, American city councilmen were dedicated to reducing the water rate imposed on constituents even though reduced rates could mean greater waste. Some cost-conscious reformers favored adoption of water meters, yet city leaders were not willing to impose any permanent constraints aimed at conservation. Instead, in the American municipality the answer to growing demand was growing supply. American urban leaders sought to satisfy the thirst of the citizenry with abundant water and not to discipline the populace with restrictions. Huge reservoirs typified American cities whereas water meters represented the European approach.

Thus American cities fulfilled demands for water of a magnitude unknown in the Old World. American wastefulness and inefficiency may account in part for the inflated consumption figures for New World municipalities, but these consumption figures also reflected the prevalence of modern comforts and conveniences. Americans demanded flush toilets, bathtubs, a private tap for each family, and water for sprinkling their lawns. The American city, unlike London or Paris, met these demands. Far from failing to provide services, the municipalities of the United States offered a level of water supply and sewerage that ensured American city dwellers, especially middle-class residents with the latest bathroom fixtures, the highest standard of living in the world.

Underlying America's success in this area was a series of ambitious engineering schemes admired throughout the world. As early as the 1830s New York City's authorities began construction of the Croton Aqueduct, which would carry water thirty miles into the city. It became the greatest project in water engineering since the Roman Empire. By 1885, however, the city required more water, and again the organs of government reacted by embarking on another colossal engineering program, a second Croton aqueduct that a British observer would acclaim as "the most enormous ever projected."[9] When completed in 1893 the new aqueduct conveyed over 300 million additional gallons of water daily to New York City. It far surpassed European aqueducts in capacity, the water flowing through a tunnel with a height and breadth of thirteen feet six inches. Moreover, in order to increase the size of the reservoir supplying the system, the city constructed the New Croton Dam, the highest masonry dam in the world at the time of its completion. The New Croton Aqueduct was costly not only in terms of money but also in human lives; ninety-two men died working on the dangerous tunnel project. But the dividends were impressive. By the 1890s New York City reservoirs held 42 billion gallons of water, more than four times the capacity of the municipal system at the beginning of the 1880s.[10]

Baltimore's water system did not equal the magnitude of New York City's, but it did rival the Croton network as an engineering achievement. To supplement the water supply of the Maryland metropolis, the city's water commission during the 1870s embarked on a project to dam the Gunpowder River and conduct the river's water into a seven-mile tunnel drilled through a range of hills separating the Gunpowder valley and the city. At the time of its construction the Gunpowder tunnel was the longest in the country, and much of it was through hard rock. Boring through this rock proved so difficult that at times workers could progress only two feet every twenty-four hours. Yet by 1881 an army of 1,500 laborers and miners had succeeded in completing the project, which contemporaries believed would supply Baltimore "for generations to come with all the water for ordinary purposes that can be used or wasted."[11]

Boston likewise kept pace with the continually increasing demand for water. By the late 1860s the city's leaders realized that the Cochituate Water Works, constructed in the 1840s, was already inadequate. To supplement this source, Boston built the seventeen-mile Sudbury Aqueduct, which was completed in 1880. But the demand for new water sources continued, and in 1895 Boston and its suburbs jointly embarked on a project to tap the south branch of the Nashua River, thirty-three miles to the west of the city. Included in this project was construction of Wachusett reservoir, which surpassed all American and European reservoirs in size, having double the capacity of New York City's New Croton reservoir.[12]

Meanwhile, Boston's leaders had not neglected the problems of sewerage. Prior to the 1870s Bostonians had constructed hundreds of miles of sewers, but there was no coordination to their efforts. In fact, there were thirty-two distinct drainage districts within the city, each with a separate outlet depositing raw sewage on the populated shores of Boston harbor. To deal with this pollution problem, the city council appointed a sewerage commission composed of three experts of national distinction. These consultants recommended construction of an intercepting sewer that would draw sewage from each of the existing drainage districts and carry it far from the city shores to an island in Boston harbor, where it would be released into the Atlantic at high tide. Boston's municipal leaders accepted the scheme and by 1884 it was in successful operation, a model comprehensive system that elicited praise from the engineering profession. Five years later a newly created metropolitan commission initiated construction of intercepting sewers throughout the Greater Boston area, and at the close of the century a comprehensive system served both central city and suburbs.[13] The American standard of living demanded ever-increasing quantities of water, and American sensibilities demanded freedom from filth and noxious odor. Boston's municipal authorities realized both demands in their grand schemes of engineering.

Chicago's water and sewerage systems were also public works projects of awesome scale and ingenuity. Lying on the shores of freshwater Lake Michigan, Chicago, unlike New York City or Boston, had a ready supply of drinking water at its front door. But the water near the city's lakefront was too polluted for human consumption, and thus Chicagoans sought to tap the water miles out from shore. In 1864 under the guidance of the municipal engineer Ellis Chesbrough, the city began work on a masonry tunnel sixty feet beneath the lake's surface that would stretch two miles into Lake Michigan and convey unpolluted water to the booming metropolis. It was an elaborate undertaking, and at the time of its construction was regarded as "one of the grandest triumphs of modern engineering."[14] In the late 1850s Chesbrough also designed a sewerage system for Chicago, one of the first comprehensive municipal drainage systems in the world. Since Chicago's flat topography was unfavorable to sewer construction and proper drainage, the city adopted as part of Chesbrough's scheme a plan to raise the grade of city streets an average of ten feet. Chicago successfully implemented the project, and as early as 1871 the municipality could boast of 140 miles of sewers draining into the Chicago River. A British visitor to Chicago in the 1870s exclaimed that "so far as water supply and drainage are concerned, Chicago has achieved wonders."[15]

Yet Chesbrough's handiwork was imperfect, for the sewage-laden river occasionally backed up and began flowing into Lake Michigan, fouling the city's water supply. To protect Chicago residents from this danger, further engineering feats were necessary. In 1892 the city completed another intake tunnel for the water supply, this one extending four miles from the shore in the hope of escaping lakefront pollution. In addition, in the early 1890s Chicago engineers began construction of the Sanitary and Ship Canal, which would ensure that the Chicago River and its sewage flowed southward into the Illinois and Mississippi rivers and not eastward into Lake Michigan. Over thirty million cubic yards of earth were excavated from the giant canal ditch leading southwest of Chicago, making this the largest earth-removal project in municipal history.[16]

In Chicago, Boston, and New York City the story was the same. Municipal officials were employing the latest engineering technology to create systems of water supply and drainage of unrivaled size. American municipalities administered a larger network of mains than any other governing body in the world; they provided a greater supply of water than any other city worldwide; and they sponsored unmatched schemes of engineering. The waterworks and sewer systems of America were objects worthy of pride.

One group that testified to the engineering achievements of the largest cities was the suburban electorate living just beyond the municipal limits. Time and again they voted in favor of annexation in order to share in the benefits of big-city water and drainage. In the 1870s voters in East Cleveland sacrificed independence for the sake of Cleveland's water, and the need for water and sewerage likewise led West Roxbury's residents to embrace consolidation with Boston. During the following decade the citizens of suburban Hyde Park and

Lake View found the water and sewerage systems of Chicago so tempting that they cast their ballots for annexation. And in the 1890s residents in Queens and Staten Island expressed their admiration for New York City's relatively cheap and abundant water supply by choosing to unite with the metropolis.[17] None of these suburban communities could match the public works of their central cities, and consequently the electorate chose to forfeit suburban autonomy. Neither the American suburb nor the European metropolis could equal the technological accomplishments of New York City, Chicago, or Boston.

American systems of water supply did, however, suffer some shortcomings. Water was plentiful in the nation's cities, but the water flowing into American homes was unfiltered and at times unsafe for drinking. Especially in Philadelphia there was repeated discussion of the need for filtration and a purer supply of water. In 1895 a Philadelphia newspaper reported that the city's water suffered from a "disagreeable, sickening smell carrying with it suggestions of dank, dark caverns and miasmatic gases" and that it tasted "very much like a solution of gum boots and coal tar."[18] In 1893 a special inquiry commissioned by the British medical journal *Lancet* found Chicago's water supply free from sewage pollution and of a superior softness and chemical purity to that of London. Yet the British sanitarians also discovered considerable inorganic suspended matter in Chicago's water and strongly recommended that visitors to the Illinois metropolis only drink water that had passed through a household device known as a Pasteur filter. If a Pasteur filter was not in use, *Lancet* advised visiting Britons to avoid Chicago's water.[19]

Such warnings were not uncommon, and in the area of water filtration the United States was certainly a bit backward. At the close of the century, London, Liverpool, and Birmingham in Britain, and Berlin, Hamburg, and Breslau in Germany all employed sand filters for the purification of their water supplies, whereas Albany (population 95,000) and Denver (population 134,000) were the largest American cities to have installed a filtration system. A number of smaller American cities had filtration schemes, but the enormous volume of the water supplied by the largest American municipalities made purification a difficult and costly process for these major metropolises. Moreover, most American engineers continued to believe, with some justification, that water from rural reservoirs uncontaminated by urban pollution did not require filtration. As a consequence, in 1900 only 6 percent of the urban population of the United States was supplied with filtered water.[20]

Likewise, sewer lines did not extend to all areas of the American city, and the largest city having a sewage purification plant at the close of the century was Worcester, Massachusetts (population 118,000). Untreated sewage flowed into rivers and lakes, often contaminating municipal water supplies. The result was a relatively high incidence of typhoid fever and other diseases associated with polluted water. Berlin and London consistently had lower death rates from typhoid than did New York City and Chicago, and Pittsburgh suffered a scandalously high incidence of the disease. The American climate may have been more conducive to the spread of typhoid, but the unhealthy quality of municipal water supplies also contributed to the prevalence of this serious illness.

Thus the commissioners and engineers in charge of water supply and sewage disposal continued to confront formidable problems. Through the application of the latest technology they had achieved much, but their work was not flawless. They had met America's vast demand for water, yet they had not eliminated the threat of pollution. Much remained on the municipal agenda for the engineers of the twentieth century.

STREETS AND BRIDGES

Just as the expanse of American water and sewer lines was unequaled in European cities, so also was the magnitude of American street construction and paving. Because of the relatively low density of American municipalities and their extensive acreage, the area of paved streets in the largest cities of the United States was much greater than in European cities of comparable population. As seen in table 5, by the turn of the century Chicago could claim more than three times the paved area of Berlin, and the expanse of pavement in Buffalo was almost double that in equally populous Cologne. The area paved by the city of Saint Louis was more than twice that of Hamburg and about equal to that of Paris, a city with more than four times the population of Saint Louis. In New York City the paved streets extended almost 1,800 miles; those of Chicago stretched over 1,400 miles; and over 1,100 miles of improved streets crisscrossed the city of Philadelphia. As in the case of water and sewerage, American cities were confronted with the problem of a relatively dispersed population, and they met that challenge by maintaining public

TABLE 5.   Street Paving, 1902

American Cities			German Cities		
City	Area of Paved Streets (sq. yds.)	% Asphalt	City	Area of Paved Streets (sq. yds.)	% Asphalt
New York	30,952,870	21.4	Berlin	7,331,480	32.8
Chicago	26,197,000	11.0	Hamburg	4,424,722	4.1
Philadelphia	17,259,228	29.5	Munich	4,095,463	2.6
Saint Louis	10,748,696	3.9	Leipzig	3,536,333	7.7
Boston	9,116,932	3.6	Breslau	1,723,316	6.2
Baltimore	7,276,886	6.7	Dresden	3,349,039	7.8
Cleveland	4,237,738	6.6	Cologne	3,657,966	3.5
Buffalo	6,908,168	62.8			

Sources: Statistisches Jahrbuch Deutscher Städte—Zwölfter Jahrgang (Breslau: Wilh. Gottl. Korn, 1904), pp. 69–70; *Bureau of the Census—Statistics of Cities Having a Population of over 25,000, 1902 and 1903* (Washington, D.C.: U.S. Government Printing Office, 1905), p. 114.

works on a scale unknown in European municipalities. At the close of the century many thoroughfares within American city limits remained unpaved. But these were generally minor residential streets and even more often were little-traveled roads in the semirural periphery of America's sprawling cities. Thousands of miles of well-traveled streets and avenues were surfaced.

The quality of American pavements, however, varied greatly. During the late nineteenth century, city fathers in both Europe and America suffered through trial and error experimentation with a wide variety of paving materials. Wood block pavements rotted too quickly, though they muffled the noise of nineteenth-century traffic. By contrast, the sound of horseshoes on granite or brick pavements could be deafening. Granite was also slippery and thus doubly objectionable. The question before city officials in the late nineteenth century was basically which material was least offensive, and often they could find no satisfactory answer. Chicago relied heavily on inexpensive cedar-block pavements, many of which rotted within a few years. In 1878 the professional journal *Engineering News* commented that "there are some hundreds of miles of wooden block pavement in Chicago . . . but at present there is hardly a dozen miles . . . in the city that is fit to travel upon, although laid only three to five years ago." This journal concluded that the "wooden pavement of Chicago is a standing disgrace to everybody concerned in them."[21] Elsewhere poorly laid cedar and pine block also sank into the mire of the thoroughfares. And in almost every major American city harsh climatic extremes, unknown in London or Paris, cracked and buckled pavements, adding to the street superintendent's nightmares.

In fact, during the 1870s and 1880s the pavements in many American cities were supporting evidence for accusations of municipal failure. European travelers frequently complained of the poor pavements, and a French visitor of the 1880s noted that New York City's "streets are horribly paved. From my windows, which looked on Madison Square, the carriages appear to rise and fall as if on a troubled sea."[22] A British traveler likewise wrote of a carriage ride through New York City "over the rough stones of the not too good pavements" and complained of the "horrid jolts and jerks" experienced during the journey. And still other foreigners also reported on "the horrors of bad pavements and filthy ways."[23] Some were less critical, lauding certain American thoroughfares such as the boulevards linking Chicago's park system.[24] But the foreign indictments were serious. During the 1870s and 1880s American cities failed to find a superior paving material that would upgrade the quality of their streets.

By the 1890s, though, the problem was a bit less perplexing, for Trinidad asphalt was gaining favor among the world's paving experts. It was quiet, durable, clean, and not prohibitive in cost. Asphalt thus seemed an answer to the paving dilemma, and during the last decade of the century the increasingly powerful corps of municipal engineers joined forces with the growing army of bicycle enthusiasts in urging the use of this smooth and superior surfacing.

Throughout the last decade of the nineteenth century bicycling was the great fad of the American middle class, and hundreds of thousands of men and women joined cycling clubs that lobbied vigorously for asphalt pavements. In 1892 cyclists in Brooklyn formed the Good Roads Association, and five years later they could count among their members Brooklyn's mayor, comptroller, and commissioner of public works. With such friends the cycling group was able to achieve its wishes, and the result was miles of freshly asphalted Brooklyn streets.[25] Chicago's Associated Cycling Clubs maintained a Good Streets Committee that likewise sought improved pavements, and the New York City chapter of the League of American Wheelmen did not hesitate to demand more asphalt surfacing on Manhattan's thoroughfares. As in the case of water and sewerage, the pressure of a demanding public and the influence of a respected engineering corps combined to push America into the technological vanguard.

American cities varied in their reliance on asphalt (see table 5), but the United States generally took the lead in applying this paving material. In 1902 almost 63 percent of the pavements in Buffalo were asphalt, as were 61 percent of the pavements in Washington, D.C. (not shown in table), and during the late 1890s these two urban centers won laurels as the best-paved cities in the world.[26] Likewise, at the beginning of the twentieth century 61 percent of the pavements in San Francisco (not shown in table) were asphalt, as were 58 percent of the street surfaces in Kansas City (not shown in table). By contrast, in Berlin, which was usually regarded as the best-paved German city, less than 33 percent of the pavements were asphalt, and at the turn of the century other German cities could claim relatively few thoroughfares that benefited from this form of surfacing. Of course, not all asphalt thoroughfares were models of paving perfection. In 1895, for example, the Committee on Political Action of New York City's Associated Cycling Clubs complained that the chuckhole-ridden asphalt pavement on Eighth Avenue was in a "bone-racking, wheel-straining, and thoroughly wretched condition."[27] Yet asphalt was generally winning the favor of American street superintendents, while Old World cities retained their granite block surfacing. At the turn of the century no European city had as smooth or as quiet pavements as Buffalo, for no German or British municipality had responded so rapidly to the introduction of Trinidad asphalt. Many of the cities of Germany were well paved, and some European thoroughfares were the envy of American paving experts. But street surfaces in the best-paved American cities could at least match those of Germany.

In the field of street lighting the American municipalities enjoyed an even-more-commanding lead over their European counterparts. Gas lighting was the prevailing form of street illumination throughout the late nineteenth century, but by the 1880s and 1890s American cities were introducing the more brilliant electric arc lamps. Powerful electric arc lamps were better suited to the central business districts of American cities than the dim gaslights, and as early as 1879 the city of Cleveland authorized inventor Charles Brush to install electric street lights around the public square. It was a daring move by the Cleveland authorities, and the first lighting of the lamps drew a curious crowd eager to witness the spectacle. According to a local newspaper, when the lamps were lit "a dazzling glory filled the park" and some of the spectators "wore smoked glasses to protect their eyes from the glare."[28] The following year New York City and San Francisco also tested this wondrous innovation in street illumination, as did Philadelphia in 1881. Within a few years the electric street lamp was commonplace in the largest cities, and in 1887 a visiting British journalist wrote of "the brilliancy of the electric lights in and around" New York City's Madison Square, "making the night almost as bright as day."[29] By 1890 electric street lamps supplemented gaslights in urban areas throughout America, and New York City, Brooklyn, Philadelphia, Buffalo, Rochester, and Saint Louis each could brag of more than one thousand electric street lights.

Meanwhile, European municipalities retained the older, less brilliant gaslights, only slowly recognizing the merits of electricity. By the beginning of the twentieth century Chicago alone could claim more than double the combined total of electric street lamps existing in the seven largest German cities (see table 6). Chicago had twelve times as many electric street lights as Berlin, and Boston had over fifty times the number of electric lamps in Leipzig. British cities (not shown in table) also compared unfavorably with American municipalities. Glasgow maintained 814 electric street lamps in 1904, but Leeds had only 122, and Manchester a mere twenty-nine.[30] European cities did compare favorably with American municipalities in number of gaslights, and thousands of street lamps lined the thoroughfares of Britain and Germany. But Chicago was more brilliantly illuminated than Berlin because Chicago more readily exploited the new technology of electricity.

TABLE 6. Street Lighting, 1903

American Cities			German Cities		
City	Street Lamps		City	Street Lamps	
	Electric	Gas		Electric	Gas
New York	16,668	42,777	Berlin	735	23,478
Chicago	8,820	24,855	Hamburg	399	22,900
Philadelphia	9,977	21,218	Munich	1,291	7,342
Saint Louis	1,745	13,260	Leipzig	74	8,500
Boston	3,742	9,481	Breslau	46	7,593
Baltimore	1,873	6,771	Dresden	492	12,471
Cleveland	1,119	6,520	Cologne	342	10,376
Buffalo	2,741	5,736			

Sources: *Statistisches Jahrbuch Deutscher Städte—Dreizehnter Jahrgang* (Breslau: Wilh. Gottl. Korn, 1906), p. 108; *Bureau of the Census—Statistics of Cities Having a Population of over 25,000, 1902 and 1903* (Washington, D.C.: U.S. Government Printing Office, 1905), p. 106.

One argument against electric lights was that they necessitated a mass of ugly overhead wiring. By the mid-1880s a heavy web of telegraph, telephone, and electric lighting wires shrouded the main thoroughfares of the largest American cities, offending the aesthetic sensibilities of many and posing a safety hazard. A clamor arose for some remedy, and the leading municipalities responded with yet another technological solution. As early as 1882 the city of Chicago required an electric company to lay its line underground, and during the 1880s Chicago's municipal electrician, J. P. Barrett, was in the forefront of developments in underground wiring. In 1890 the Illinois metropolis already could claim 169 miles of subterranean electric light cables, and at the close of the century utility poles had disappeared altogether from downtown Chicago and were becoming less common in outlying neighborhoods as well.[31]

New York City also took measures to eliminate the danger and eyesore of overhead lines. In 1885 the New York state legislature created a municipal board of commissioners to plan a system of underground wiring for New York City, but private electric companies resisted the action and moved slowly to comply with the reform. By 1889 a series of deaths due to poorly insulated above-ground wires had brought the public's temper to a boil. For example, in October, 1889, a Western Union lineman was "roasted on a wire gridiron" within plain view of City Hall and his dead body dangled from the faulty overhead lines for more than an hour, a grisly sight for thousands of passing New Yorkers.[32] Such gruesome spectacles could not continue, and New York City's mayor ordered the immediate removal of all dangerous overhead lines. When the companies delayed, the city took decisive action. To the applause of the citizenry, municipal employees within a two-week period cut down more than one million feet of lines and toppled almost eight hundred utility poles. This audacious move won results from the private companies, and by 1893 there were about seven hundred and fifty miles of electric light cables running beneath New York City.[33] Electricity had its drawbacks, but in leading urban centers such as New York City and Chicago municipal authorities proved able to cope with the liabilities as well as the assets of the new technology.

Yet there was still another problem that city street superintendents had to face, the awesome task of street cleaning. In the era of horse-drawn transportation the amount of manure accumulating on city streets each day was enormous, and one expert with a penchant for quantification estimated that "one thousand horses will, in every working day of eight hours, deposit about 500 gallons of urine and 10 tons of dung upon the pavement."[34] Throughout the world disgusted urban dwellers deplored their dirty streets, but European travelers claimed that American pavements were among the filthiest. A British visitor of the early 1880s noted that the "very first thing" that struck him on the day after landing "was the neglected and dirty state of many of the New York streets, a state of which an English market-town would certainly be ashamed."[35] Another Briton catalogued Chicago's street filth: "refuse in masses by the kerbstones, orange and apple peels, pea-nuts, oyster shells, feathers, paper, mud, dirt" on the pavements. This visitor could only conclude from a walk through the city "that the authorities did not turn much of their attention to sanitary measures."[36]

In fact, street cleaning did not rank among the great successes of the American municipality. Though American cities made some use of sweeping machines, street cleaning was primarily a labor-intensive service in which men with brooms and shovels played a more important role than machinery. Rarely did cities in the United States achieve superiority in such services. New York City hired thousands of sweepers, but such cities as Chicago, Saint Louis, and Baltimore were unwilling to pay for a huge army of street cleaners to collect all the trash and manure along the hundreds of miles of thoroughfares in these sprawling municipalities. Moreover, little dedication to duty inspired American street sweepers, for most were political "bummers" employed as a partisan favor. European cities could recruit a mass of impoverished rag pickers to work at a wage unthinkable in the United States. But in America frugal city fathers only rarely appropriated funds sufficient to pay for an adequate street-cleaning force.

The most notable exception to this pattern of relative failure was New York City's street-cleaning department during the reform administration of Mayor William Strong. In 1895 Strong appointed as commissioner of street cleaning the noted sanitarian George E. Waring, Jr. Waring reformed the municipal street-cleaning force, increased the number of street sweepers, imposed discipline, and sought to eliminate political influence in the making of appointments. Dressed in neat white uniforms and bearing the nickname "white wings," New York City's street sweepers became a model to the rest of the nation and proved unusually successful at their job.[37] When Waring traveled to Europe in the summer of 1896, he found that New York's streets were generally cleaner than those of Vienna and London and that "New York is as clean and at least as tidy as Paris." He admitted that America's largest city could learn some lessons from Berlin and Birmingham, but he found European capitals struggling with the problem of litter and rubbish just as the urban centers of the United States.[38]

Most municipal observers conceded that Waring had raised New York City to a new level of cleanliness, but to finance Waring's army of street sweepers the city had to pay a sum most American municipal comptrollers would have refused to appropriate. In the mid-1890s the per capita appropriation for cleaning in New York City was more than four times the per capita figure for Chicago, and two and one-half times that of Boston.[39] Waring's reforms also entailed a cut in patronage that few politicians applauded. American cities could have been cleaner, but politically and financially the price was too great. Street sweeping was not high enough on the list of American municipal priorities to warrant the sacrifices necessary to keep the nation's cities clean.

Of much higher priority was the more dramatic business of bridge building. Manure and trash may have stymied urban authorities, but rivers and ravines only stimulated the ingenuity of ambitious municipal engineers. And nowhere was this so evident as in New York City. Begun in 1869, the city's Brooklyn Bridge took fourteen years to complete and ranked among the wonders of the nineteenth century. A private corporation backed by municipal funds from both Brooklyn and New York City originally had charge of the project. But in 1875 dissatisfaction with the supposed mismanagement of the company resulted in a transfer of control to a board of trustees appointed by the mayors and comptrollers of the two cities. Henceforth the project was under municipal supervision, and the twin cities along the East River could take credit for realizing the giant scheme. When opened in 1883, the Brooklyn Bridge claimed the longest span of any bridge in the world, and was one of the great attractions for travelers to the metropolis.[40] A British civil engineer visiting America in the 1880s described this monument to modern technology as "a magnificent structure" and "the finest piece of bridge engineering" he had ever seen.[41] Ten years later a fellow countryman spoke of the structure as "beautifully poetic" and claimed that "one cannot say too much in eulogy of a construction that is so noble, useful, and beautiful."[42] Though conflict among the trustees and charges of corruption were rife during its years of construction, the final product was, according to an observer of the time, a "great landmark which characterizes and dominates the city as St. Peter's from across the Campagna dominates Rome, and the Arc de Triomphe the approach to Paris."[43]

Yet just as the growing demand for water necessitated ever-grander aqueducts and tunnels, the soaring traffic between New York City and Brooklyn led to the construction of still other engineering monuments spanning the East River. By the mid-1890s forty-four million passengers each year were taking the cable railway across the Brooklyn Bridge, and millions of others were crossing by foot or in wagons or carriages.[44] Another bridge was needed, and in 1895 the state legislature authorized creation of a second East River bridge commission, to be appointed jointly by the mayors of New York City and Brooklyn. Construction of this additional link, known as the Williamsburg Bridge, began the following year, and in 1903 the structure opened to traffic. Though less highly touted and less impressive in appearance than its illustrious predecessor, the Williamsburg Bridge stole the record as the longest suspension bridge in the world, its main span being four and one-half feet longer than that of the Brooklyn Bridge.[45] Moreover, by the turn of the century, the newly consolidated city of Greater New York was already considering the creation of two additional bridges linking Manhattan and Long Island.

Other American cities did not face such formidable challenges as the bridging of the East River, but in Boston and Philadelphia the municipal authorities and their engineering staffs also proved capable of spanning the waterways. Desirous of beautifying their riversides, the cities of Boston and Cambridge embarked on a campaign to replace the antiquated wooden pile bridges across the Charles River. According to the mayor of Cambridge, these bridges were "unsightly structures, utterly inadequate to the daily demands made upon them and grotesquely inconsistent with the present plans for the future of the river." Through a joint commission, the two municipalities first constructed the masonry Harvard Bridge from 1887 to 1891, and in 1898 the cities won authorization from the state legislature for the even-more-monumental and ambitious Cambridge Bridge.[46] Meanwhile, Philadelphia's city government built spans across the Schuylkill River, above railroad tracks, and over the numerous streams draining the vast city. Between 1891 and 1895 the city Bureau of Surveys constructed a total of thirty-six bridges vital to the unimpeded flow of urban traffic.[47] The bridges of New York City, Boston, and Philadelphia may not always have been so aesthetically pleasing as the celebrated bridges of Paris. But no European municipality attempted a bridge project of such magnitude or engineering bravado as that of the Brooklyn Bridge, and even the lesser spans across the Schuylkill and Charles proved functional if not so inspiring as the New York wonder.

By the close of the nineteenth century, then, the American record with regard to streets and bridges was a mixture of success and failure. American city streets suffered certain serious flaws, but similar drawbacks plagued many municipalities throughout the world. Paving techniques were imperfect, and in some American cities the street surfaces were deplorable—though in others they were superb, testifying to the latest advances in paving technology. American avenues were generally well lit and probably more brilliantly illuminated than thoroughfares anywhere else in the world. Yet at the same time city streets in the United States were often filthy, a woe common to the horse-drawn society of the 1880s and 1890s. In the construction of bridges, however, the American municipalities took top honors, and New York City ranked as the premier patron of this branch of engineering. On the whole, American city officials had made considerable advances, having paved, lighted, and cleaned thousands of miles of streets and bridged scores of streams. And in the process they had adopted the latest technology more readily than the lord mayors, aldermen, and burgomasters of Europe.

MASS TRANSPORTATION

Perhaps the most controversial public service of the late nineteenth century was mass transit. In the United States, municipalities contracted with private companies for the provision of streetcar services, whereas by the turn of the century many European cities had purchased local transit lines and operated them as a municipal enterprise. A number of vocal and frustrated Americans admired the European alternative of municipal ownership, and they repeatedly fought local franchise grants. For these Americans Europe had solved the urban transportation dilemma, while the United States continued to suffer the tyranny of monopolistic streetcar interests. Dedicated to curbing the private power of the traction magnates, critics of the system of franchise grants never failed to publicize the imperfections of American streetcars.

A comparative examination of American and European streetcar systems, however, indicates that the much-maligned companies of the United States were not so derelict in their duty and that American cities were not suffering from unusually backward or deficient transit services. At the beginning of the twentieth century American cities could claim far more extensive streetcar systems than the urban centers of Great Britain or Germany, and American streetcar networks carried many more passengers per capita than the tramway lines of European metropolises (see table 7). Chicago had almost two and one-half times the trackage of the Berlin metropolitan area (and, incidentally, transported 66 million more persons each year). Baltimore had eight times the trackage of Birmingham, England, and over twice the rides per inhabitant. Buffalo had five times the trackage of Leeds or Breslau, and the Buffalo lines also accommodated millions more passengers each year. In the major German cities there were approximately 0.10-to-0.30-miles of trackage per 1,000 residents, whereas in major American cities the miles of trackage per 1,000 residents ranged from about 0.35 to 0.85. Baltimore's streetcar company operated about 1,500 cars, but equally populous Munich had only 281 cars. Cleveland's companies maintained 941 trolleys, whereas Dresden operated 487.[48] There was no lack of streetcar transportation in the American metropolis. In American municipalities there were more cars, more trackage, and heavier business than in European urban centers. In fact, the streetcar systems of the United States, like the water, sewer, and street systems, were on a scale that dwarfed networks in comparable European municipalities.

During the 1870s and 1880s European cities were especially slow in developing streetcar transportation, and most Old World urban residents still relied on their feet as the chief means of locomotion. As late as 1890 in the leading cities of both Great Britain and Germany the yearly number of fares per capita averaged only 56, as compared with 233 for Greater New York City and 225 for Boston and its suburbs.[49] Accustomed to the slow pace of their own walking cities, European visitors to America expressed amazement and some horror at the mass of streetcar lines bisecting American city streets, carrying closely packed cargoes of humanity from one side of the metropolis to the other. In 1880 a British visitor told his fellow countrymen that the horse-drawn "street-car system is . . . a great feature of American city life; nowhere [else] is it carried out in such perfection." According to this observer, horse-drawn "cars are running incessantly from morn to night" stuffed with passengers.[50] And a Frenchman in Chicago in 1886 exclaimed that the city

TABLE 7. Streetcar Service, 1901–2

American Cities			British Cities			German Cities		
City	Streetcar Track (mi.)	Rides per Inhabitant	City	Streetcar Track (mi.)	Rides per Inhabitant	City	Streetcar Track (mi.)	Rides per Inhabitant
New York	1,299	266	London	188	47	Berlin	436	131
Chicago	1,036	232	Glasgow	89	222	Hamburg	175	125
Philadelphia	518	256	Liverpool	112	155	Munich	68	105
Saint Louis	396	211	Manchester	139	129	Leipzig	132	143
Boston	452	246	Birmingham	45	91	Breslau	64	75
Baltimore	365	190	Leeds	63	112	Dresden	140	186
Cleveland	237	201	Sheffield	46	129	Cologne	67	83
Buffalo	320	176						

Sources: Statistisches Jahrbuch Deutscher Städte—Zwölfter Jahrgang (Breslau: Wilh. Gottl. Korn, 1904), pp. 134–39; *Bureau of Census Special Reports—Street and Electric Railways, 1902* (Washington, D.C.: U.S. Government Printing Office, 1905), pp. 24, 151, 153.

Note: The British reported only the length of streetcar lines instead of the length of trackage. Yet many lines had double trackage. To make the British data comparable with that of Germany and the United States, the author has increased the British figures for length of lines by 67.5 percent. See: John P. McKay, *Tramways and Trolleys* (Princeton: Princeton University Press, 1976), p. 72; *Bureau of Census Special Reports—Street and Electric Railways, 1902* (Washington, D.C.: U.S. Government Printing Office, 1905), p. 151.

possessed "a net of streetcars like nowhere else."[51] Other foreign visitors complained that the streetcar rails cut up the thoroughfares, and carriage traffic suffered from having to bounce over the protruding tracks. But the great British writer Matthew Arnold correctly observed that "the inconvenience is for those who use private carriages and cabs, the convenience is for the bulk of the community who but for the horse-cars would have to walk."[52] The horse-drawn cars of the 1870s and 1880s were crowded and their rails were the bane of cabs and carriages occupied by the wealthy, but the alternative, and the only option open to many Europeans, was walking.

Moreover, as in the case of water engineering and street lighting, American technology in the field of mass transit was far ahead of Europe. The electric trolley was first adopted in the United States, and Europe was ten to fifteen years behind America in the acceptance of this vital innovation. Electric trolleys were cleaner than the horse-drawn cars with their by-product of manure. They could also carry more passengers than the small horse-drawn cars, and they were faster, traveling about ten miles an hour as compared with five miles an hour for the horsecar. With the advent of electrification one could commute farther in less time and escape the congestion of the central city.

The first city to adopt an all-electric system of streetcars was Montgomery, Alabama, in 1886. But other American cities were not far behind. By 1890 there were over nine hundred miles of electric lines in the United States, representing almost 16 percent of the total streetcar mileage in the nation. During the following few years electrification swept the country, and at the close of 1895 84 percent of the streetcar lines in the United States were electrified. In contrast, in 1890 all of Europe could claim only fifty-eight miles of electric streetcar lines. Five years later 23 percent of all German streetcar lines were electrified, but only 6 percent of British lines. By 1902 Germany had caught up with the United States, but in Great Britain still only 38 percent of the streetcar lines were electrified, as compared with 97 percent of the lines in American cities. Likewise, as late as 1901 half the streetcars of Paris were still horse-drawn.[53] While the people of Birmingham, Manchester, London, and Paris were still riding antique horsecars, Americans were traveling farther and faster, enjoying the most advanced streetcar systems in the world. A French visitor of the 1890s told his fellow countrymen that compared with mass transit in New York City or Chicago, "Parisian transportation seems a pitiful and exasperating thing."[54]

The United States also kept pace with Europe in the development of other forms of mass transit. An elevated railroad began service in New York City in the 1870s, Brooklyn's overhead rapid transit system opened in 1885, and Chicago's famous elevated network first transported customers in 1892. Though most viewed the elevated railroad as an aesthetic blot on the city, prior to the 1890s it was generally regarded as the premier form of rapid transit. Its elevated tracks kept light and air from reaching the avenues below, but it also carried more people faster than any other means of urban transportation existing in the 1870s and 1880s. Moreover, it was usually regarded as superior to the steam-powered underground railway of London with the latter's smoke-filled tunnels and asphyxiated passengers. In 1883 a British visitor to America testified that the "upstairs railway at New York is far more pleasant to the stranger than the underground railway in London," and four years later a correspondent for the *Times* of London reported that the elevated trains of New York, "smoothly and swiftly gliding through and over the great city," gave "more real enjoyment for less money than any other entertainment in the usually costly metropolis."[55] Other Britons also believed the New York elevated system superior to anything London could offer, and one boldly claimed that "the most perfect system of transportation in the world is the New York Elevated Railways."[56]

With the application of electricity to transportation in the 1890s, the option of underground transit seemed more attractive. Smokeless electric trains traveling underground could carry as many passengers as quickly and as comfortably as the elevated lines and yet spare the city the ugliness and noise of overhead tracks. Again American cities soon recognized the merits of the new technology of electric-powered rapid transit, and during the 1890s the largest municipalities initiated planning or construction of underground lines. Since private entrepreneurs proved unwilling or unable to finance and construct the costly subway projects, the city governments of Boston and New York City took direct control of the creation of underground systems. Thus the original American subways were owned by government agencies that leased the completed lines to private transit companies. The first of these American subway systems was opened for passengers in Boston in 1897, and only the underground railways of London, Glasgow, and Budapest predated that of the Massachusetts capital. At the turn of the century New York City's subway was under construction, and by 1905 an underground transit line ran from Battery Park at the southern tip of Manhattan to Harlem at the island's northern end.[57] Boston and New York City had responded readily to the new technology of underground electric transit, more readily than such cities as Hamburg or Vienna, and coordinating the response were local government agencies. The city fathers of these American municipalities did not abjectly surrender when private enterprise failed to ensure city residents the latest in transportation technology. Instead, the public sector stepped in to guarantee the development of the most advanced forms of rapid transit.

Despite their transportation achievements, American city authorities heard endless complaints about the streetcar companies, most centering on the cost of streetcar travel and the unwarranted profits of streetcar entrepreneurs. In many cities during the early 1890s competing streetcar companies merged in order to share the costs entailed by electrification. Control of mass transit in a typical city thus came to rest in the hands of one or two companies that seemed to be taking advantage of their monopoly of a vital service. Adding to the suspicions of reformers and the general public were the relatively high fares charged by the streetcar companies. In 1902 the average fare charged by surface streetcars in the United States was 4.94¢ (4.82¢ in urban centers of over half a million population), as compared with 2.26¢ in Great Britain and from 2.1¢ to 2.6¢ in Germany. The standard American fare was 5¢, but by the turn of the century in many cities one could purchase six streetcar tickets for 25¢, and the streetcar companies of Boston, Saint Louis, San Francisco, and Denver charged only 2.5¢ for school children.[58] Most European cities had fares graded on the basis of distance traveled, so one could ride one-half mile for only 1¢ or go to the end of the line for as much as 7¢. On the average, however, the European fare was half that of the American, and foes of the American traction interests felt the difference was largely due to excess profits reaped by corporate magnates. The cry of many urban reformers was for a 3¢ streetcar fare.

American streetcar companies may not have been eleemosynary organizations, but the discrepancy between European and American fares was not as suspicious as many supposed. First, the general cost of living was higher in the United States than in European nations, with the cost of various consumer items averaging 50 percent higher in America than in Great Britain or Germany.[59] Second, the average wage of conductors and motormen on American streetcars was as much as double the wage of the their counterparts in Sheffield or Glasgow, and wages represented 57 percent of the cost of streetcar operation.[60] Third, the average wage of all American workers was 70 percent to 80 percent higher than the wage of British workers, and about 140 percent greater than the wage of the average German laborer.[61] In short, the costs of operating anything were much greater in the United States than in Europe and especially the labor costs of streetcar transit. And the 2.4¢ paid by the German worker represented a larger portion of his total wage than did the 4.9¢ paid by the American worker. Further, the passenger-trackage ratio was lower in the United States than in Europe because of the dispersion of population in American urban areas. The consequence was additional overhead expenditures for the American streetcar company.

Given the differences in costs and wages, American streetcar fares were not so prohibitive or inflated. Mass transit was no more of a burden for the American worker than the German, though the European system of graded fares would definitely have benefited working-class Americans who lived closer to the urban core and traveled shorter distances on the trolleys. America's middle class in the suburbs was the chief beneficiary of ungraded fares. White-collar professionals and businessmen could travel to the city outskirts for five cents, when in Europe it might cost six or seven cents. Those who could best afford the price of streetcar transportation received the greatest bargain.

In fact, America's streetcar system spawned middle-class suburbia. The unusually extensive transit networks of metropolitan America, with their relatively speedy electric trolleys and ungraded fares, encouraged low-density settlement unknown in Europe. Americans could have single-family dwellings, lawns, gardens, and trees, and still travel into the urban core each day for an average of 4.9 cents. Such suburbanization was not possible in European cities, with their short lines and delayed technology. But in the United States the mass transit system afforded this luxury.

Thus the consequences of municipal franchise grants were not all dire and grim. Traction magnates and their political allies certainly reaped fortunes from the streetcars, and no doubt the public paid in part for the shady dealings among transit companies, party leaders, and city councils. Moreover, many Americans at rush hour suffered the discomfort of having to stand in a packed trolley half the journey home, unable to rest their weary legs after a long day at work. But the advantages of the American system of urban transport were impressive. It was up-to-date, rapid, and extensive, and it relieved the congestion of the urban core and transported millions each day to outlying residential districts. America's municipalities had not failed in their responsibility for transporting the urban citizenry.

FIRE PROTECTION

In no field of municipal endeavor was American superiority more evident than in fire protection. Throughout the late nineteenth century American fire departments were larger and better equipped than any in comparable European cities. By 1890 New York City had ninety-one steam fire engines, as compared with the eight owned by equally populous Berlin. During the early 1890s major German cities like Munich and Cologne had only one steam engine each, whereas Boston and Saint Louis could each boast of more than thirty. And American departments averaged twice the number of fire fighters as the German municipal brigades.[62]

During the following decade, moreover, the United States maintained this advantage. At the turn of the century, European departments were primitive in comparison to American fire-fighting forces (see table 8). The city of Chicago owned 129 fire engines, as compared with the Berlin fire brigade's 27 engines, and the Chicago squad could claim 30 percent more professional firemen than its counterpart in the German capital. On the average, American fire departments still had more than twice the personnel of the fire departments in German cities of comparable population. And British fire departments were often even smaller and had less apparatus than comparable German or American cities. London's metropolitan fire brigade maintained 99 fire engines, whereas the New York City Fire Department owned over two hundred. Birmingham's fire squad had one-tenth the fire engines and less than one-sixth the full-time fire fighters of equally populous Baltimore. In every

TABLE 8. Fire Departments

American Cities (1899)			British Cities (1899)			German Cities (1902)		
City	Fire Engines	Full-time Firemen	City	Fire Engines	Full-time Firemen	City	Fire Engines	Full-time Firemen
New York	208	2,404	London	99	1,115	Berlin	27	847
Chicago	129	1,100	Liverpool	14	55	Hamburg	64	496
Philadelphia	52	764	Manchester	10	100	Munich	23	169
Saint Louis	73	506	Birmingham	6	61	Leipzig	27	213
Boston	74	730				Breslau	24	224
Baltimore	57	396				Dresden	34	181
Cleveland	31	401				Cologne	38	121
Buffalo	38	430						

Sources: *Statistisches Jahrbuch Deutscher Städte—Dreizehnter Jahrgang* (Breslau: Wilh. Gottl. Korn, 1906), pp. 113–15; "Report from the Select Committee on Fire Brigades . . . ," *British Sessional Papers, House of Commons, 1899* (London: Her Majesty's Stationery Office, 1899), 9: 246–47, 286, 290–91, 489; "The London Fire Brigade," *Municipal Journal and Engineer* 10 (May 1901): 184–85; *Bulletin of the Department of Labor, 1900* (Washington, D.C.: U.S. Government Printing Office, 1900), p. 936.

Note: Figures for London are for 1901.

category of equipment, American departments outranked those of Europe. Birmingham owned 4 hose carts, and Berlin could claim 15. But Baltimore possessed 43 hose wagons, and Chicago boasted of more than one hundred. In terms of size, the American fire departments had no equals in the Old World.

The technology of American fire brigades was also far superior to that of fire fighters in Germany or Britain, and American departments introduced most of the major innovations in nineteenth-century fire protection. In 1851 Boston's city council appropriated $10,000 for the first fire alarm telegraph, which provided instantaneous communication between street-corner alarm boxes and the municipal fire department. Philadelphia installed a similar system in 1855 and Saint Louis followed suit in 1858. But not until 1878 did a British city initiate a fire alarm telegraph system.[63] Before the 1880s urban Britons generally had to run or ride to the nearest station to notify the fire brigade of a blaze. Meanwhile, fire alarm systems were becoming commonplace in the New World, and by the close of the century every American municipality worthy of the title of "city" maintained an alarm network. In 1902 the United States could claim electric fire alarm systems in 764 cities, and almost forty thousand miles of wiring linked alarm boxes with local fire stations.[64]

American cities pioneered other innovations as well, and fire departments experimented with a plethora of new devices during the last half of the nineteenth century. In 1872 the Boston Fire Deparment purchased the first boat built expressly for fighting fires, and at the close of the century every major American port city had a fleet of such vessels. In 1879 New York City's fire brigade introduced the first water tower, a device to aid fire fighting in tall buildings.[65] New contraptions for the split-second harnessing of fire horses were among the American brigades' equipment, and every advance in hoses and nozzles found a ready market in the fire departments of American municipalities. During these same years, America's modern brigades replaced the primitive hand-pumped fire engines with steam engines, and by the turn of the century only three of the devices for pumping water by hand remained in use in New York City and four in Chicago. In Germany, however, almost one-half of Dresden's fire engines were manual, as were three-fourths of those in Cologne, and in Britain one-third of Birmingham's engines were hand-operated.[66] In Dresden, Cologne, Birmingham, and Manchester, no brigade could match the advanced equipment of the American municipal departments.

Sometimes American fire fighters may have been a bit too eager to experiment with new equipment, risking their physical safety in pursuit of ever-more-advanced devices. For example, in 1875 New York City purchased a combination aerial ladder and hose carrier from Mary Belle Scott-Uda, who was described in fire department annals as "a fascinating woman."[67] Her fascination, however, proved lethal, for when tested before Scott-Uda and department officials the ladder collapsed, hurling three firemen ninety feet to their death. Others were injured at the scene of the disaster, including Scott-Uda who, "frenzied by the calamity," jumped on a streetcar "which was running at full speed, and fell senseless on the platform." A coroner's inquest ordered a halt to use of the Scott-Uda aerial ladders, closing an episode in the history of experimentation.[68] But other aerial ladders followed, and one new device after another tempted American fire chiefs who were always eager to extinguish blazes as quickly and as efficiently as possible. Nowhere in the world were municipalities so ready to harness the mechanical ingenuity of the late nineteenth century to the task of fighting fires as in America.

The disparity between European fire protection and that of America's cities was not, however, indicative of municipal negligence in Britain or Germany but reflected differing conditions in the Old World and the New. London and Berlin did not need such large and elaborate fire squads as New York City and Chicago because the threat from fire was much less in Europe than America. Inexpensive but flammable lumber was a popular building material in the United States, unlike in most of Europe, and drought and extreme heat were more common in Chicago than in Glasgow or the other cool, damp cities of northern Europe. Building conditions and climatic factors in the United States were much more conducive to the outbreak and spread of fires, and large fire brigades and advanced equipment were vital for the public safety.

Confronted with the awesome challenge of protecting the fire-prone cities of the United States, American fire departments performed as efficiently and effectively as anyone could reasonably expect. The number of urban fires increased throughout the late nineteenth century as the urban population soared, but by the 1880s and 1890s America's first-rate municipal fire brigades were able to contain blazes and limit damage. The result was a sharp drop in property loss per fire. During the period 1866–70 the average loss per fire in New York City was $5,043, whereas by 1895–99 this figure had fallen to $1,015.[69] Likewise, the average loss per fire in Chicago during the late 1860s was $4,548, but only $551 for the period 1895–99.[70] In the 1880s and 1890s American cities did not suffer another uncontrollable blaze of the magnitude of Chicago's fire of 1871. Only a natural disaster in the form of an earthquake in San Francisco in 1906 disrupted fire protection sufficiently to permit a conflagration rivaling, though not matching, that of Chicago. The age of catastrophic urban fires was coming to a close owing largely to the efforts of America's municipal fire departments.

Many foreign observers testified to the quality of these departments, citing their efficiency and technological preeminence. Even the hypercritical British municipal reformers Sidney and Beatrice Webb had to admit that the fire protection "is good in all American cities."[71] And a writer with greater expertise than the Webbs in fire fighting, the editor of the British trade journal *The Fireman*, lauded "the splendid departments" of the United States, "with the size and highly organized constitution of which we in England have nothing that can for a moment be compared."[72] The chief of the Dublin, Ireland, fire brigade also praised the efforts of American municipalities to ensure the public safety. Following an inspection tour of the United States in the mid-1890s, he reported that American stations were "generally perfectly constructed with a view to practical utility and maintained regardless of cost." He could not praise too highly American fire boats, remarking, "I cannot conceive any more effective protection to important manufacturing or business sections of a large city." And he found that "the American alarm system is a long way ahead of any arrangement for this purpose in Europe."[73]

The Dubliner's judgments reflected those of other Europeans as well, and a visit to an American fire station was a must for many prominent travelers from the Old World. In 1877 in his account of a tour of America, Jacques Offenbach, the French composer and musician, wrote: "To go to New York and not to see how fires are put out in America would be a most unpardonable neglect." The amazed Frenchman described the rapid response of New York City's fire fighters to an alarm as "real magic."[74] On a visit to Chicago during the 1880s the British actor Henry Irving witnessed a similar display of fast-paced fire-fighting action, which he described as "sufficiently theatrical in its effect to make the fortune of an Adelphi drama." Irving was convinced that the "fire service at Chicago is, no doubt, the finest and most complete organization in the world."[75] Visiting noblemen and clerics likewise expressed glowing admiration for the American brigades, and during the 1880s and 1890s even the harshest critics of American cities conceded the quality of the fire departments.[76]

Many Americans joined this chorus of praise and exuded an arrogance about fire fighting that put Europeans on the defensive. American newspapers observed confidently that "the United States is far ahead of all other countries in fighting fire," and a British expert on the subject noted peevishly that "some of our American friends, when describing English fire brigades, treat them almost entirely in terms of good-humored banter, as if there were no points in them deserving the attention of serious men."[77] In 1893 a select corps of Kansas City's firemen, most of them ex-acrobats recruited from circuses, demonstrated American fire fighting prowess at the International Fire Brigades Congress in London. With a showy bravado they scaled the walls of buildings for the amusement of Europeans and set a world's record for the hitching of fire horses, completing the task in one and two-fifths seconds.[78] Such stunts were indicative of the professional pride of American firemen and exemplified their sense of superiority. In this one area of municipal service, Americans generally believed themselves to be the best and they were not hesitant to flaunt their talents.

The municipal fire department was, then, an object of pride for many American cities. Fire posed an unusually serious threat in the New World, and insurance interests may have wished for even better results from the municipal brigades. But the technology of American fire fighting was superior to that of any European nation. The American fire alarm systems were the most advanced in the world, as were American engines, hoses, hydrant systems, and fire boats. At the close of the century the municipal fire departments of the United States were the prime authorities on the art of fire protection. Europe could teach American municipalities very little about extinguishing blazes.

PUBLIC HEALTH

Measured by international standards, municipal public health programs in late-nineteenth-century America deserve many laurels and a few brickbats. Throughout the Western world, late-Victorian cities continued to suffer the scourges of typhoid, diphtheria, and smallpox. Moreover, tuberculosis preyed on urban dwellers in Britain, Germany, and the United States, dispatching hundreds of thousands to a premature grave. By late-twentieth-century standards, the "advanced" cities of the world were unsanitary and dangerous pestholes of contagious disease. Yet great strides were being made as knowledge of bacteriology increased and city authorities stepped up programs of sanitation. In the vanguard of public health developments were the American municipalities. Nineteenth-century Great Britain pioneered the public health movement, but by 1900 American health authorities had won the respect and admiration of their counterparts in industrialized Europe.

Throughout the Western nations, the urban mortality rate gradually declined during the second half of the nineteenth century, and the death rates in the cities of the United States were, on the average, no greater than those in the northern European nations. As seen in table 9, at the close of the 1880s the death rate in the cities of Britain, Germany, and the United States ranged from Saint Louis's inordinately low 17.4 per 1,000 individuals to Munich's 30.4 per 1,000. Rates in the low 20s were general throughout the industrialized nations, and the United States conformed to this pattern, with only New York City exceeding the 25 per 1,000 figure. By the end of the 1890s the mortality rates had dropped notably in cities of the United States and Germany and remained approximately the same in Great Britain. Buffalo, Cleveland, and Chicago could claim the lowest death rates among the major cities in the three nations, and during the 1890s American urban boosters advertised their cities as the healthiest in the world. Such boasts may have been exaggerated, but American cities certainly were not inordinately unhealthy or unusually disease-ridden. All of the cities of the industrial world still suffered the ravages of contagious disease, but in general American cities were no worse than the others and possibly better.

City fathers, however, were not satisfied with death rates of 20 or 25 per 1,000, and during the late nineteenth century urban Americans benefited from new programs initiated by municipal boards of health. In 1866 the creation of

TABLE 9. Death Rates

American Cities	Death Rate (per 1,000)		British Cities	Death Rate (per 1,000)		German Cities	Death Rate (per 1,000)	
City	1890	1899	City	1889–90	1899–1900	City	1889	1899
New York	26.5	19.0	London	18.8	19.3	Berlin	23.4	18.8
Chicago	19.1	15.0	Glasgow	25.0	21.6	Hamburg	23.9	17.4
Philadelphia	21.3	19.0	Liverpool	22.6	26.0	Munich	30.4	23.9
Saint Louis	17.4	17.4	Manchester	28.7	24.4	Leipzig	20.8	20.0
Boston	23.4	19.9	Birmingham	19.7	22.2	Breslau	29.4	25.4
Baltimore	22.9	20.0	Leeds	22.4	19.6	Dresden	21.7	19.5
Cleveland	20.2	14.6	Sheffield	22.9	22.4	Cologne	22.5	23.1
Buffalo	18.4	13.9						

Sources: *Journal of the Royal Statistical Society* 53 (Mar. 1890): 180; *Journal of the Royal Statistical Society* 63 (Mar. 1900): 162; *Journal of the Royal Statistical Society* 54 (Mar. 1891): 192; *Journal of the Royal Statistical Society* 63 (Mar. 1900): 162; *Journal of the Royal Statistical Society* 64 (Mar. 1901): 168; *Sanitarian* 24 (Mar. 1890): 272; *Sanitarian* 44 (Mar. 1900): 276–77; *Report on Vital and Social Statistics in the United States at the Eleventh Census: 1890. Part II. Vital Statistics, Cities of 100,000 Population and Upward* (Washington, D.C.: U.S. Government Printing Office, 1896), pp. 5–9; *Bulletin of the Department of Labor, 1900* (Washington, D.C.: U.S. Government Printing Office, 1900), p. 952.

New York City's Metropolitan Board of Health marked the beginning of a new era in municipal public health. One year later the city of Chicago reorganized its health board and hired a sanitary superintendent and sixteen inspectors. Boston followed suit in 1872, restructuring its board of health and initiating a program of smallpox vaccinations and meat inspection. In 1870 New York City's health board had also begun a door-to-door campaign of free vaccinations, and in 1874–75 physicians working for this city agency performed over 126,000 vaccinations.[79] From the 1870s onward, employees of the New York City board inspected the slaughterhouses, markets, and tenements of the metropolis in an attempt to protect the public from tainted foodstuffs, faulty plumbing, and inadequate ventilation. Throughout these years, however, city health departments suffered from both lack of staff and lack of money.

Conditions improved in the 1890s as urban health departments intensified their efforts and ushered in the heyday of public health. By the close of the decade, New York City employed 353 sanitary inspectors, compared with 260 in London. At the same time Baltimore employed 12 sanitary inspectors and Cleveland 26, compared with the 19 inspectors on the payroll of the city of Sheffield.[80] In 1898 New York City's 50 food inspectors conducted over a million inspections, condemned 9.6 million pounds of food, and conducted over forty-two hundred chemical analyses. In 1898 the Boston health department examined over thirteen thousand samples of milk, and the health inspectors of Chicago analyzed more than twenty thousand samples of milk and water. The city health authorities of New York City and Boston had the power to examine children in the public schools. Accordingly, in 1898 New York City inspectors conducted physical examinations of almost 140,000 pupils, and Boston officials gave checkups to over fifty thousand students.[81] Plumbing inspectors, meat inspectors, milk examiners, and scores of other officials were investigating the health of the cities to a degree unknown in previous decades. Still, their efforts were often inadequate, and public health authorities acknowledged that meat inspection in the cities of the United States and Great Britain could not match the thoroughness of the Berlin health department, where 240 inspectors conducted scrupulous examinations of the carcasses in municipal slaughterhouses.[82]

Yet at the same time American municipalities were making headway against epidemic disease. Exemplifying the success of American health authorities was the defeat of cholera in the 1890s. Cholera had been the most serious epidemic disease of the mid–nineteenth century, when it swept through the world with deadly consequences for both Europe and America. In 1892 it reappeared in Hamburg, Germany, killing eight thousand persons, and that summer immigrant ships carried the cholera infection to New York City. But New York City's authorities acted quickly to prevent spread of the disease. Through bacteriological examinations, city health officials were readily able to identify the disease in its early stages and to quarantine victims. Moreover, New York City's health board divided the tenement-house neighborhoods into cholera districts and assigned to each a corps of physicians, nurses, and special disinfectors, who were to report any outbreak of the illness and disinfect those areas exposed to contagion. The precautions paid off, and in 1892 New York City reported only nine deaths from cholera. In contrast, over five thousand New Yorkers had succumbed to the cholera epidemic of 1849, and in the 1866 cholera epidemic more than five hundred died despite broad and effective action by the newly created Metropolitan Board of Health. By 1892 American municipal health authorities could do more than limit cholera to a few hundred victims. They could prevent an epidemic altogether.[83]

The experiences of 1892 not only testified to the vigilance of New York City's board of health, they also clearly demonstrated the value of bacteriological examinations in combating disease. Bacteriology was a new area of medicine that arose in large measure from the discovery of the tubercle bacillus and cholera bacillus by the great German physician Robert Koch. By the late 1880s, due to the work of Koch, Louis Pasteur, and other Europeans, the bacteriological revolution in medicine was well underway. Yet it was the Americans who first applied this new knowledge on a broad scale through municipal health programs. In 1888 Charles Chapin, the pioneering city health officer of Providence, Rhode Island, established America's first municipal bacteriological laboratory, using it primarily to analyze local water supplies.[84] Not until the creation of the New York City Health Department Laboratory in 1892 did American city health officials exploit the discoveries of Koch and Pasteur in bolder and more innovative programs that were to earn American municipal health departments world acclaim.

Guiding the work of the New York City municipal laboratory was Dr. Hermann Biggs. Assisted by Drs. William Park and Anna Williams, Biggs embarked on unprecedented programs to ensure the public safety. He quickly recognized the value of the bacteriological laboratory in aiding in the early diagnosis of diphtheria, and by 1896 the New York City Health Department was conducting more than twenty-five thousand diphtheria tests annually for this purpose and also to identify carriers of the disease.[85] But New York City health authorities did more than simply identify the disease; they also embarked on a program to limit its lethal power. While traveling in Europe to gather information on the latest achievements in medical research, Dr. Biggs learned of Emile Roux's method for producing diphtheria antitoxin and immediately cabled Dr. Park to prepare for production of the life-saving serum. In 1895 the New York City Health Department began manufacture of this antitoxin, improved its quality through experimentation, and distributed it without charge to all public institutions and to all indigent patients. During the year 1896 the city issued almost seventeen thousand vials of the antitoxin, and within two years the mortality from diphtheria dropped almost 40 percent.[86] By 1898 as eminent an authority as the laboratory chief of the renowned Pasteur Institute in Paris had proclaimed the New York City antitoxin the strongest and most effective in the world, and he observed that "with the work of Park and Williams a great advance has been accomplished in the production of diphtheria toxin."[87]

Meanwhile, Dr. Biggs and his laboratory analysts also sought to curb the deadly power of other diseases. They embarked on a campaign against tuberculosis and examined thousands of specimens of sputum from those suspected of suffering from the fatal illness. In 1895 the New York City laboratory began experimentation with a tetanus antitoxin, and the following year the health department sent Dr. Williams to the Pasteur Institute to work on the development of a streptococcus antitoxin and to learn the latest advances in the fight against rabies. Moreover, the municipal bacteriologists engaged in research in typhoid during the last years of the century. As the work of the municipal laboratory expanded, so did its staff, and by 1897 the scientific personnel in New York City's bacteriological division included twenty-five physicians, two veterinarians, a chemist, and numerous laboratory assistants.[88]

Knowledge of Dr. Biggs and his efforts spread quickly, and other muncipalities soon emulated New York City. Philadelphia created a division of bacteriology in 1895, and to head this new agency the municipal authorities imported a Baltimore bacteriologist who had studied under the renowned Robert Koch.[89] That same year Newark, New Jersey, also established a municipal bacteriology laboratory, as did Baltimore in 1896 and Boston in 1898. In 1899 the Newark Board of Health estimated that the diphtheria antitoxin manufactured by the city had saved 321 lives that year, and elsewhere throughout the nation municipal health officials claimed similar successes.[90] Boston's mortality rate for diphtheria dropped 60 percent between 1897 and 1898, and in October, 1898, a local newspaper reported that "one remarkable feature of the mortality report for Boston this week is that it shows diphtheria to be almost stamped out." The *Boston Medical and Surgical Journal* attributed the "unprecedentedly low mortality from diphtheria" to three factors: "the early diagnosis of the disease by the bacteriological examination, the introduction of antitoxin, and the excellent facilities for treatment afforded by the contagious department of the City Hospital."[91] Antitoxin and the municipal laboratory also proved valuable to the city of Chicago, where the assistant health commissioner, Dr. Frank W. Reilly, sought to apply discoveries in bacteriology to public health practice. During the three-year period following the introduction of antitoxin in Chicago, there were 43 percent fewer deaths from diphtheria than during the previous three years, a fact well publicized in Reilly's widely admired health bulletins.[92] In Cincinnati, Saint Paul, and Detroit as well as Chicago, Boston, and New York City analysts employed by the municipal government were conducting thousands of tests for diphtheria, tuberculosis, and typhoid, identifying those who were in the early stages of illness and those who carried the contagion.[93] Advances in bacteriology had transformed medicine, and American municipalities readily adapted to this change.

In fact, American health authorities exploited the new knowledge more willingly than the municipal fathers of European cities. As early as 1894 Robert Koch admitted that the New York City Health Department was considerably ahead of the German authorities in the practical management of diphtheria and told Hermann Biggs, "You put us to shame in this work." By the turn of the century Koch was "urgently recommending Dr. Biggs's organization to the study and imitation of all municipal authorities." And a few years later he exclaimed to Biggs and his colleagues at the New York City Health Department that "we in Germany are years and years behind you" in the practical application of bacteriological discoveries.[94] Just as American cities quickly exploited the advantages of electricity and asphalt, so they recognized and applied the medical discoveries of Europeans more readily than the Europeans themselves.

Thus during the last years of the nineteenth century American municipal officials were aggressively combating disease and conducting bold and innovative programs. American health authorities and city fathers were negligent in some areas. Some American municipal water supplies were polluted, resulting in higher typhoid fever rates than in most German or British cities. And no American city of comparable size maintained a force of sanitary inspectors equal to Glasgow's or meat inspectors equal to Berlin's. Many American health departments were, moreover, understaffed and underfinanced, but so were many of the departments of Europe. Contagious disease swept through American cities, but European urban centers suffered the same fate. By the close of the century American municipal health departments were hardly conspicuous failures, and in the area of bacteriological analysis and experimentation they had won fame. With largely justified pride, the *New York Sun* observed in January, 1897, that "all in all, there is probably no more thoroughly well managed and more useful concern in any city of the world than our Health Department."[95] And when invited to speak before the British Medical Association, Dr. Hermann Biggs could boast to the gathered physicians "that there is no great city in the world to-day which . . . is cleaner and healthier than New York."[96] Problems persisted, but municipal authorities were advancing, not only in their assault on disease but in numerous other areas as well.

9 CREATING A HUMANE AND ORDERED ENVIRONMENT

Nothing impressed visitors to New York City or Chicago so much as the frenzied pace and bustling vitality of America's urban hubs. These were cities of kinetic energy with streetcars passing every few seconds, elevated railroads roaring overhead, and a mercenary citizenry perpetually hustling to make a dollar. Chicago butchered more hogs in less time than any other city in the world, and all humanity seemed to rush up and down New York City's Broadway in a single day. American cities were new, fast-paced, and technologically up-to-date. They epitomized all the mechanical ingenuity and commercial assertiveness of the nineteenth century.

For some who dreamed of a more genteel past, however, America's cities too often appeared vulgar and coarse, mechanistic dynamos enclosed in an ugly mesh of wires, rails, pipes, and mains. Even the city fathers sensed that enormous water aqueducts, glaring electric lights, smooth asphalt pavements, and clanging fire engines did not add up to decent urban living. No inventor or engineer could manufacture a utopian city out of asphalt, wires, and steel. The latest technological triumphs were not enough, and during the late nineteenth century city leaders refused to be satisfied with the merely mechanical. Instead, they sought to create a more humane and ordered environment characterized not simply by speed, noise, and machinery but by beauty, learning, humanity, and discipline.

To achieve this end American municipalities devoted millions of dollars to the development of parks, libraries, schools, welfare institutions, and law enforcement agencies. These public services were as much a part of the municipal agenda as were the great engineering projects or the innovative health programs. City leaders relied on these services to blunt the dangerous, sharp edges of nineteenth-century urbanization, to limit the suffering, ignorance, and crime endemic to the city. Green, open spaces would supposedly quiet the jangled nerves of victims of urban mayhem, and the natural beauty of parklands would strengthen the moral spirit of those who otherwise might fall prey to the evils of street and saloon. Public libraries would supposedly enlighten the urban populace and uplift the underprivileged, bringing literature and learning to the harried city. The public schools also were dedicated to creating a better social order through the teaching of vital skills and middle-class American values. And municipal charities were to sustain the poorest in society, whereas the police were to curb those "vicious elements" among the poor. Each of these functions was among the responsibilities of America's municipalities, and through these programs the leaders of New York City, Chicago, Philadelphia, and Boston sought with some success to make urban life a safer, more pleasant, and more humane experience.

European cities, likewise, endeavored to fashion a more ordered, humane environment, but as in the case of water, sewers, lighting, and fire protection, German and British efforts often seemed modest when contrasted with those of American municipalities. Especially in the development of parks and public libraries few questioned that the major American cities took high honors when compared with those of Europe. Only in the areas of paternalistic supervision of the poor and suppression of social deviants were American municipal institutions less highly developed than those of continental European cities. American policemen were a somewhat sloppy, indifferent crew as compared with the efficient, strutting police of the German Empire. And American municipal governments intervened little in the lives of the poor and were relatively unimaginative in creating programs aimed specifically for the needy. Yet America's municipal institutions of pleasure and learning were among the wonders of the nineteenth century, and they testify conspicuously to the success of American urban rule.

PARKS

The American city made especially impressive progress in the field of parks and recreation, and urban experts of the time generally acknowledged that American city parks were equal, if not superior, to any in the world. In the 1870s and 1880s many of the leading German cities had set aside only small preserves for public use, and their park projects were minor as compared with the ambitious schemes of the New World municipalities. By the early 1890s Philadelphia had almost four times the park acreage of Berlin, and the city of Boston maintained over eleven hundred acres of parks as compared with 270 in Munich. The city of Hamburg reserved only 235 acres of parklands, whereas Saint Louis owned over two thousand acres, and Dresden only reported 54 acres of parks in contrast to the 540 acres in equally populous Cincinnati.[1]

By the turn of the century German cities were claiming some additional acreage in parkland, but American urban centers retained their lead over the municipalities of both Germany and Great Britain. The imperial capital of London, with its extensive royal preserves, did surpass New York City in park acreage, but this was the exception to the rule. As seen in table 10, the park commissions of industrial Chicago administered a system of public grounds

TABLE 10. Public Parks, 1900–1901

American Cities		British Cities		German Cities	
City	Park Area (acres)	City	Park Area (acres)	City	Park Area (acres)
New York	6,730	London	13,000 (approx.)	Berlin	1,147
Chicago	2,151	Glasgow	1,039	Hamburg	289
Philadelphia	3,671	Liverpool	785	Munich	402
Saint Louis	2,183	Manchester	405	Leipzig	634
Boston	2,620	Birmingham	360	Breslau	428
Baltimore	1,250	Leeds	726	Dresden	860
Cleveland	1,438	Sheffield	330	Cologne	569
Buffalo	1,026				

Sources: Statistisches Jahrbuch Deutscher Städte—Zwölfter Jahrgang (Breslau: Wilh. Gottl. Korn, 1904), p. 80; Thomas De Courcy Meade, "Address before the Conference of Engineers and Surveyors to County and Other Sanitary Authorities," Journal of the Sanitary Institute 21 (Oct. 1900): Appendices A and B; John A. Fairlie, Municipal Administration (New York: Macmillan Co., 1901), p. 266; Bulletin of the Department of Labor, 1901 (Washington, D.C.: U.S. Government Printing Office, 1901), p. 876.

that was almost twice as extensive as that of the elegant German capital. Hamburg had double the population of Buffalo but less than one-third the park acreage. Baltimore had almost four times the park acreage of more populous Birmingham. And Sheffield maintained only 330 acres of parks, whereas Cleveland with an equal population operated a park system of more than fourteen hundred acres. Boston administered more than twenty-six hundred acres of parks and Manchester and Munich only about four hundred each. In terms of size, American municipal park systems generally were unparalleled.

The quality, as well as the size, of American parks won many tributes from foreign visitors. Central Park in New York City was a must for all tourists visiting the metropolis, and in 1873 the young Lord Rosebery, future prime minister of Great Britain, exclaimed that it was "by far the finest public park" he had ever seen "in variety of scenery."[2] Many Europeans added similar accolades during the following decades, and by the 1890s New York City's newly developed Riverside Park was also winning praise. One visiting Briton reported that there was "nothing in London—and I have seen nothing elsewhere—in the same class of scenery, so attractive . . . as the New York river-side park."[3] Philadelphia's Fairmount Park won equal laurels from Europeans, who regarded it as the chief wonder of Pennsylvania's metropolis. In 1876 a member of the British Parliament traveling through Philadelphia heaped lavish praise on this "most attractive and wonderful public park," saying that "it is impossible that there can be anything like it in the world."[4] Two years later another visiting member of Parliament proclaimed Fairmount Park "the most lovely and extensive Park, so far as I know, of which any city in the world can boast."[5] And a French visitor of the 1870s observed that "it is impossible to imagine anything finer or more picturesque" than Fairmount Park.[6] During the 1880s a London journalist wrote of Fairmount Park's "unrivalled advantages in delicious natural scenery," and in the 1890s Europeans were still testifying that the pleasure ground's "natural beauties are indeed unsurpassed."[7]

Parklands in other American cities also elicited the enthusiastic applause of travelers from the Old World. A Frenchman visiting Chicago in 1886 described that city's Lincoln Park as "a wonderland, a paradise," and he admitted that "nowhere in Europe" had he seen "anything to compare with it."[8] The following year a correspondent for the *Times* of London said of Chicago's parks that "art has planted abundant foliage with little lakes and miniature hills, ornamented by beautiful flower gardens and shrubbery, large sums being spent upon their care and steady development."[9] While visiting the Illinois metropolis, Sidney and Beatrice Webb, the great municipal reformers of Britain, likewise expressed their admiration for the city's pleasure grounds. Though the Webbs disliked almost everything American and had few kind words for the cities of the United States, they had to admit that Chicago had a "great system of parks and connecting boulevards," which "are excellently laid out and kept." Moreover, with uncharacteristic enthusiasm Beatrice Webb positively gushed about the management of parks in Boston. In her diary she recorded that Boston's Park Department "with its playgrounds and bathing places, its open spaces and gardens, seems almost ideal."[10] Another British visitor summed up the feelings of many Europeans when she wrote that in "no country in the world are there such extensive and delightful public parks and pleasure-grounds as in America."[11]

Given the beauty and expanse of American parks, such praise was understandable. In New York City, Brooklyn, and Boston the municipal parks included a wide range of attractions and facilities for the enjoyment of urban residents. Frederick Law Olmsted's Central Park, laid out from 1857 onward, was a botanical wonderland, and the city planted an estimated 4 million to 5 million trees, shrubs, and vines within the park's bounds during the first sixteen years of its existence. In 1873 New York City's sylvan preserve included over four hundred species of deciduous trees and shrubs and 230 species of evergreens, all handsomely interspersed among picturesque waterfalls, grottoes, and pavilions.[12] Brooklyn's Prospect Park, begun in 1866, was another Olmsted project that included not only the scenic delights of nature but also a children's playground complete with a pool for sailing toy boats, a maze, and a summer house. Elsewhere in Brooklyn's municipal pleasure-ground a music pagoda for band concerts graced the shores of a large pond equipped with a "circular yacht," a floating merry-go-round propelled by sails and oars.[13] To the north in Boston, Olmsted also laid out a chain of parks that drew thousands of visitors each weekend. In 1886 Boston began work on one of Olmsted's finest creations, Franklin Park, which was designed as an English deer park with broad meadows and pastoral scenery. It had nineteen miles of walks, two miles of bridle paths, and ten miles of driveway. In a nearby area Boston, in cooperation with Harvard University, also maintained Arnold Arboretum, 155 acres of woods and plantings. And in South Boston along the bayshore, the city laid out Marine Park, complete with waterfront paths; a long pier for promenades; a park service fleet of rowboats, canoes, sailboats, and steam launches; and a "medieval German" cafe for seaside luncheons.[14]

Philadelphia was not able to boast of any such seaside retreats, but its parklands also deserved the praise they received. That city's Fairmount Park, established in 1867, covered almost twenty-seven hundred acres along the Schuylkill River and included a botanic garden, the first zoo in the United States, and handsome glades and meadows that inspired one German visitor to proclaim it "the most beautiful garden that one could imagine."[15] Skating and sleighing were popular winter diversions in Fairmount Park, whereas summer visitors enjoyed band concerts and boating on the Schuylkill. A special event in autumn was "nutting day," a gala occasion when Philadelphia's school children descended on the pleasure-ground and harvested the fruit of the park's thousands of nut-bearing trees. According to a guidebook of the 1870s, on nutting day "the whole Park becomes a moving panorama for miles of happy, singing, romping, laughing children."[16]

Midwestern and western cities also could boast of fine park systems that inspired superlatives and offered delights for youngsters bent on play. In Chicago the park commissioners transformed a tract of sand dunes into Lincoln Park, a three-hundred-acre preserve complete with lagoons, conservatories, floral displays, and bicycle and bridle paths. During the first ten years of Lincoln Park's history, the commissioners purchased 50,000 yards of black soil for the creation of lawns, and by the close of the century the park gardeners were setting out a quarter of a million plants annually for the decoration of the grounds. Between 1870 and 1900 nearly twenty thousand deciduous trees, ten thousand evergreens, and fifteen thousand shrubs were purchased for the beautification of the parkland. Baseball diamonds, tennis courts, a zoo, a palm house, a fernery, and outdoor band concerts were added attractions at the park.[17] In San Francisco the park authorities likewise performed the marvelous feat of turning sand dunes into lawns and gardens. In the 1860s the site of San Francisco's Golden Gate Park was a sandy waste, but by 1900 the city's giant recreation ground claimed the usual lakes, groves, drives, and conservatories as well as such unusual attractions as a Japanese tea garden and a herd of grazing buffalo.[18] In cities throughout the nation the story was much the same. Local government agencies were transforming the landscape and creating parklands of a quality unsurpassed in European cities of comparable size.

In fact, the idea of a coordinated system of interrelated parklands was basically an American invention. Parks in the cities of Britain and Germany, with the possible exception of London and Berlin, were largely the product of haphazard development. Private benefactors donated stray parcels of land, and occasionally the municipal authorities purchased some acreage. But there were no preconceived metropolitan plans for an integrated system of public open spaces linked by parkways nor were there any regional schemes for preserving local beauty spots. In the United States the pattern was different. As early as the late 1860s Chicago's park commissioners purchased extensive tracts at the edge of the city to ensure the creation of an encircling system of parks connected by landscaped boulevards. By 1892 the commissioners had realized their plan, having laid out a network of eight large parks, twenty-nine smaller parks or squares, and thirty-five miles of parkways.[19] Similarly, in 1883 the park board of Minneapolis sought to create a comprehensive, integrated system of parks and hired Horace W. S. Cleveland to design such a network. Within the next ten years the Minneapolis board implemented Cleveland's scheme, acquiring almost fifteen hundred acres of parkland.[20] In 1893 Kansas City, Missouri, followed Minneapolis's example and retained the young landscape architect George Kessler to draft a comprehensive blueprint for a system of parks and boulevards. During the following decade the Kansas City authorities carried out Kessler's plans and earned their city a reputation for urban beautification.[21] Meanwhile, in the metropolitan area of Newark, New Jersey, a park commission was acquiring tracts in an effort to preserve the scenic landmarks of the region and create a "series of picturesque breathing spots" linked by handsome boulevards.[22]

The landscape architect Charles Eliot, however, deserves credit for the most notable scheme of comprehensive metropolitan park planning. During the early 1890s he joined with the journalist Sylvanus Baxter in a campaign for a metropolitan park system for the greater Boston area. In 1893 the Massachusetts legislature acquiesced to the petitions of Eliot and Baxter, creating the Metropolitan Park Commission. This commission soon adopted Eliot's plan for a giant suburban network of public preserves, and between 1893 and 1902 it purchased approximately fifteen thousand acres of open land, including ten miles of seashore, over twenty miles of right-of-way for parkways, and thirty miles of river frontage. During the 1890s, then, the Boston area pioneered in regional planning, creating not simply a few city parks but a suburban system of forest preserves, beaches, and scenic corridors.[23] By the first decade of the twentieth century Boston's parkland was a model to the rest of the world, drawing envious praise from reform-minded Parisian officials and pioneering German urban planners.[24]

Though these great American parklands attracted millions of visitors annually, the work of Olmsted, Cleveland, and Eliot did not benefit all urban residents equally. Most major parks in both Europe and America were distant from the poorest sections of the city and beyond the walking range of slum dwellers, who could not afford to waste money on unnecessary streetcar trips.

For example, Central Park was a four-mile walk from the lower East Side, and not many inhabitants of the latter area made the journey from Hester Street to Fifty-Ninth Street and Fifth Avenue. The poet Walt Whitman observed the passing of persons and vehicles through Central Park on a fine afternoon in 1879, describing it as a procession of "Private barouches, cabs, and coupés, some fine horseflesh—lap-dogs, footmen, fashions, foreigners, cockades on hats, crests on panels—the full oceanic tide of New York's wealth and 'gentility.' "[25] Fashion and finery filled the park, untainted by the intrusion of indigents or urchins. Likewise, Olmsted's handiwork in the Back Bay and West Roxbury area was miles from the Boston slums, and Charles Eliot's suburban forest preserves were even more remote from the congested hub of the city. Philadelphia's enormous Fairmount Park was similarly removed from many of the poorest neighborhoods. Even though Chicago maintained a widespread system of parks, in the 1890s one investigator claimed that between 30 percent to 35 percent of that city's population lived more than a mile from a major park.[26] In Chicago and New York City, as in Paris and Manchester, poverty and parklands did not coincide.

By the 1890s, however, American municipal authorities were beginning to recognize the need for more small, neighborhood parks in the poorer districts, and some park commissions were taking action. Leading the effort was the city of Boston, which in 1889 converted a ten-acre strip bordering a tenement house district into a recreation ground known as Charlesbank. Charlesbank was not simply a green swatch of breathing space for slum dwellers. Aside from the usual walks it included two open-air gymnasiums, which the Park Department hoped would provide the poor with some opportunity for athletics. By 1897 Boston had also created neighborhood parks in Charlestown and along the shore adjacent to the densely populated immigrant area of the North End.[27] Other cities were beginning to act as well. As early as 1887 the New York state legislature passed a measure drafted by Mayor Abram Hewitt that authorized New York City to spend $1 million a year for the creation of small parks. Delays stymied full implementation of the act, but by the late 1890s New York City had laid out Mulberry Bend Park in the heart of the congested lower East Side and was in the process of constructing Seward Park in the same neighborhood. The Philadelphia city council made its first appropriation for neighborhood playgrounds in 1895, and in 1899 Chicago's council and park boards created a joint Special Park Commission to plan the creation of small parks and playgrounds in crowded districts.[28] By the turn of the century, however, most slum dwellers had yet to benefit from the good intentions of park planners and municipal authorities in the nation's largest cities.

Middle-class urbanites and their prosperous working-class cousins were, on the other hand, profiting greatly from the efforts of park commissions. These city dwellers could readily afford the price of streetcar fare to the immense municipal pleasure grounds, and thus they could take full advantage of the wonders of Central Park or Fairmount Park. For them the great parks were accessible refuges from the drabness of the city, and thousands flooded the municipal preserves each weekend, testifying to the success of American park programs.

PUBLIC LIBRARIES

For those urban Americans who desired not only the beauties of nature but also the wonders of literature, American cities provided excellent public libraries. As in the case of parks, American public libraries were more than comparable to the best municipal-supported European institutions. In fact, only the cities of the British Empire rivaled America's municipalities in the size and quality of their collections. Even before the philanthropist Andrew Carnegie donated the bulk of his fortune to public libraries in Great Britain and the United States, these two nations led the field. By the turn of the century the principal cities in Britain and the United States administered public collections of hundreds of thousands of volumes (see table 11). Chicago, Philadelphia, Baltimore, Buffalo, Manchester, Liverpool, and Birmingham all maintained libraries having from 200,000 to 300,000 volumes. Meanwhile, New York City, London, and Boston, each could claim a collection of more than 700,000 books.

Throughout the late nineteenth century the British and the Americans alone vied for supremacy in the public library field, and each deserved some laurels. The circulation of library books was greater in Britain, partly because of the British public's greater predilection for reading and partly because Americans

TABLE 11. Public Libraries

American Cities (1900)		British Cities (1900)		German Cities (ca. 1896–99)	
City	Volumes in Library	City	Volumes in Library	City	Volumes in Library
New York	1,342,259	London	830,224	Berlin	100,520
Chicago	306,601	Glasgow	None*	Hamburg	None
Philadelphia	234,221	Liverpool	207,218	Munich	27,743
Saint Louis	150,000	Manchester	279,957	Leipzig	15,000
Boston	771,968	Birmingham	242,218	Breslau	15,084
Baltimore	204,397	Leeds	194,177	Dresden	42,186
Cleveland	170,123	Sheffield	120,327	Cologne	13,000
Buffalo	232,982				

Sources: Thomas Greenwood, ed., *British Library Year Book, 1900–1901* (London: Scott, Greenwood & Co., 1900); "Statistics of Education in Central Europe," *Report of the Commissioner of Education for the Year 1899–1900*, 2 vols. (Washington, D.C.: U.S. Government Printing Office, 1901), 1: 772–73; *Bulletin of the Department of Labor, 1901* (Washington, D.C.: U.S. Government Printing Office, 1901), p. 889.
*In 1900 Glasgow was in the process of organizing a public library.

could better afford to purchase their own books. In any case, British librarians could claim greater success in encouraging use of the public collections. But American libraries were more innovative and until the 1890s enjoyed an unequaled reputation for intelligent and efficient administration. American public libraries introduced the modern card catalog, open stacks, the juvenile library, and the traveling library for maximum distribution of volumes. All of these innovations were copied by admiring British institutions, and in 1894 a leading British expert could write, "in library economy and administration we can learn many lessons from our progressive cousins on the other side of the Atlantic." Even the one notable British critic of American public libraries readily admitted that "both Britain and the United States have much to learn from each other."[29]

Indeed, by the 1890s the American municipal library was a model to cities throughout the world. During the nineteenth century, the emphasis in continental Europe was on scholarly libraries, not popular institutions open to the mass of people. Only in the final years of the century did the Bücherhallenbewegung (Public Libraries Movement) produce the beginnings of change in Germany. One of the chief leaders of the movement was Constantin Nörrenberg, who had visited American libraries during a trip to the Chicago World's Fair of 1893 and who strove thereafter to imitate the American example. Another leading advocate of free popular libraries in the German-speaking world was the Viennese professor Eduard Reyer, who traveled in both the United States and Britain, examining the model institutions of those nations.[30]

Yet at the turn of the century, German cities fell far short of American municipalities in the provision of public library services. The total number of volumes in public libraries in German cities of 100,000 or more population was about 350,000, less than half the number in the Boston Public Library alone. As indicated in table 11, the people's library of Berlin contained only 100,000 volumes, whereas Dresden's popular library could boast of only 42,000 volumes and Munich's possessed fewer than 28,000 books. German public libraries were generally open only three hours every weekday evening and on Sunday afternoons, whereas major American public libraries were open from morning until night six days a week and half a day on Sunday.[31] In 1896 the total annual circulation of all the popular libraries in German cities of 100,000 or more inhabitants was 1.7 million, whereas the home circulation of the Chicago public library was 1.2 million and that of Boston was 1 million.[32]

In other continental European nations public libraries were also primitive by American standards, and public library advocates looked to the United States for inspiration and ideas. In Scandinavia, small parish libraries dotted the countryside during the late nineteenth century, but nothing existed comparable to the municipal institutions of America. By the 1890s, however, northern Europeans were becoming aware of American efforts, and during the early twentieth century Scandinavian converts to the cause of the public library viewed the libraries of Boston, Cleveland, and Chicago with a professional reverence. They made pilgrimages to the United States, studied American library techniques, and returned home dedicated to copying the American example. In the eyes of Germans, Swedes, Danes, and Norwegians, the public libraries of America's great cities were far from conspicuous failures. Instead, they were models worthy of emulation.[33]

A number of American libraries drew the praise of these Europeans, but perhaps none was so impressive as the Boston Public Library. Until the turn of the century it ranked as the largest public library in the world, and its famous director Justin Winsor had been the founding father of the library profession. In the 1870s a British editor traveling in the United States compared Boston's collection with the public libraries of Liverpool and Manchester and concluded that the efforts of these British cities "sink into insignificance when compared with the princely liberality" of Boston's municipal government, which had enabled that city's library "to rank with the most extensive Libraries in America, and to present an aggregate of issues unapproached by any."[34] During the 1870s library advocates in Paris also cited the Massachusetts metropolis as a model and compared the generosity of the Boston authorities with the "truly regrettable" stinginess of the rulers of the French capital.[35] In the opinion of book lovers in London and Paris, as well as New York City and Chicago, the Boston Library appeared without parallel.

To house the hundreds of thousands of volumes in Boston's collection, the city lavished still more princely sums on the construction of an opulent central repository that was a monument to the public library movement. In 1895 this library palace opened its bronze doors and revealed an interior complete with classical sculpture, allegorical murals, a courtyard patterned after a Renaissance palazzo, and a grand marble staircase. Panels filled with figures of the Greek muses lined the stairway, woodwork from a French château embellished the trustees' room, and a frieze depicting the quest of the holy grail overlooked the circulation desk. Electric-powered baskets delivered books from the stacks to the patrons, and a communication network of pneumatic tubes established the institution's supremacy in the field of library technology. Designed by the distinguished architectural firm of McKim, Mead, and White, this municipal palace was the finest public library building in the world, and housed the world's finest public library collection.[36] The pride of Boston, it elicited pages of tributes. The *Boston Evening Transcript* declared that "the veriest hoodlum . . . may come into this palace of the people and drink of its gentle influences and breathe in its sweetness and light as if he were a prince of the blood."[37] An article in *New England Magazine* described the great public reading room as "one of the most important rooms architecturally in the world."[38] Another commentator wrote of the building as "feeding the most careless or unconscious eye with the food of high artistic loveliness."[39]

Characterized by the press as a "magnificent literary casket," this library was a grandiose symbol of the municipality's devotion to learning and literature.[40]

But in their pursuit of opulence, Boston's library trustees did not totally overlook the practical needs of the reading public in the neighborhoods. By 1900 Boston's municipal system included ten branch libraries, each containing an average of sixteen thousand volumes, and five additional branch reading rooms. Supplementing the branches were fourteen delivery stations, where the library dispatched books specially ordered by neighborhood residents; twenty-three fire stations scattered throughout the city also received books on deposit. Even the societal misfits at the municipal House of Reformation received a collection of volumes from the library authorities.[41] With its extensive collection, magnificent main repository, and string of neighborhood outlets, Boston's municipal library was the greatest among the great urban libraries of America, and through much of the late nineteenth century it was an example of efficiency and professionalism for the entire world.

Elsewhere in the nation, however, other cities were also expending funds to create notable public collections. Boston's library, founded in 1852, was the first municipal library in a major American city, but Cincinnati followed suit in 1856, as did Detroit and Saint Louis in 1865, Cleveland in 1868, and Chicago in 1873. Each of these public collections contained over 150,000 volumes by the turn of the century and maintained branches or delivery stations serving the neighborhoods. In 1900 Chicago administered six branch reading rooms and sixty delivery stations, the delivery stations alone issuing over 1.1 million books that year.[42] Between 1892 and 1897 Cleveland constructed four branches, each containing from 10,000 to 16,000 volumes by the close of the century. By 1900 the Cleveland public library also operated four additional sub-branches containing small collections of books for circulation, and Cleveland's library authorities also assigned some volumes to nineteen deposit stations located in schools, factories, and settlement houses throughout the city.[43] Meanwhile, in 1900 Saint Louis maintained forty delivery stations, chiefly in corner drug stores.[44] Cincinnati and Detroit were slower in implementing a plan of neighborhood service, but in 1897 the Michigan metropolis established its first branch, and by 1900 Cincinnati operated thirty-three delivery stations.[45] In each of these cities and in others throughout the nation, municipalities were purchasing thousands of books and seeking to put them into the hands of the public.

Moreover, in the 1890s many municipalities found it necessary to step in where privately funded libraries had failed. In some eastern cities subscription libraries or privately endowed institutions had precluded the need for municipal libraries during the 1870s and 1880s. By the last decade of the century, however, these institutions lacked sufficient funds for further expansion. Library advocates in Philadelphia, Buffalo, and New York City all sought help from the municipal authorities, and in each case the city governments responded favorably. In 1892 the city of Philadelphia established the first free public library in that metropolis, an institution that soon ranked among the nation's busiest. At the beginning of the twentieth century, it had a circulation of over 1.9 million, maintained twelve branches, a children's library, a library for the blind, and a system of traveling libraries to distribute books throughout Philadelphia.[46] In 1897 the city of Buffalo assumed financial responsibility for a private subscription library and transformed it into the Buffalo Public Library.[47] That same year marked the beginning of municipal support for the New York Public Library, an institution that was soon to nudge Boston's library from its traditional place of preeminence.[48] Thus, owing to the willingness of Philadelphia, Buffalo, and New York to come forth with adequate resources, citizens in these rapidly expanding cities were able to realize their dream of a free library system.

The urban populace, however, shared unevenly from this municipal initiative. Though librarians hoped to uplift the poor through literature, it was the better-educated middle class or upper middle class who found the public libraries most helpful and enjoyable. Circulation statistics of the period show that residents in all areas of cities took advantage of the public libraries, but more library card holders hailed from prosperous wards than from slum neighborhoods. In Saint Louis at the close of the century the well-to-do western neighborhoods contributed the most card holders, and in Boston during the late 1890s about 30 percent of the residents of fashionable Back Bay and Beacon Hill had library cards, whereas only 4 percent of those living in a nearby tenement ward had availed themselves of this privilege. Likewise, occupational statistics reveal that far more card holders were professionals or business entrepreneurs than were common laborers. For example, of those males over twenty-one years of age holding library cards in Boston during the years 1897 through 1900, 20 percent were professionals, 54 percent were businessmen, but only 4 percent were laborers.[49] As in the case of public parks, prosperous urban dwellers were again the chief beneficiaries of municipal largesse, and the municipality proved especially responsive to their wants and desires. For those who wished to read, American cities provided among the best public collections in the world, and no group benefited more from the exemplary libraries than the urban middle class.

SCHOOLS

One of the most challenging and costly of American municipal services during the late nineteenth century was public education. Throughout the nation city boards of education administered thousands of schools that trained millions of children in the "three Rs" and offered secondary instruction to many more. As in every period since the advent of public education, there were vehement critics of American schooling, and as always, debate raged over the proper means and ends of education. During the 1890s Joseph Rice, a combination physician and freelance journalist with no practical experience in the classroom, led the self-appointed flagellators of American schooling, attacking the emphasis on recitation and the mechanical methods of urban teachers.[50] But others rejoined in defense of the nation's urban schools, for the record of schooling in the cities was in many ways impressive. Children of every social and economic rank did learn the basic skills of reading, writing, and arithmetic free of charge, and American school systems adapted to the new demands of the urban populace, expanding the curriculum and upgrading the professional training of teachers. The task was difficult, and no one in either America or Europe identified or implemented an ideal educational scheme. Yet the school systems of urban America had not abandoned the search for this ideal, and European educators recognized the merits of the American effort.

By the 1880s and 1890s the largest American school systems were giant organizations employing thousands of teachers and educating hundreds of thousands of children. In 1890 New York City schools enrolled 198,000 pupils, and by 1899 the Greater New York system was responsible for 544,000 students. Likewise, in Chicago the enrollment figures soared from 136,000 in 1890 to 242,000 in 1899. And Philadelphia's school system educated 162,000 in 1890 and 206,000 by 1899.[51] These figures were at least equal to, and usually greater than, the enrollment figures for European cities of comparable size, and in terms of sheer numbers, the American city school systems certainly matched the public schools of European urban centers. If nothing else, America's largest cities, like their European counterparts, were processing a mass of young minds, providing the expanding population of urban children with free instruction.

Moreover, American cities could claim at least one notable educational distinction when judged by international standards: The United States was the only nation in the world that provided tuition-free secondary education in addition to free elementary schooling. Whereas British, French, and German secondary school pupils had to pay for the privilege of an advanced education, none of the cities of the United States charged for high-school instruction. Only a small proportion of urban Americans of high-school age availed themselves of this free service, however, either because economic need forced them to work or because high school education did not seem a necessary step on the road to success. Yet by the close of the century more than twenty thousand students attended the public high schools of New York City, and more than ten thousand were students in Chicago's secondary institutions.

In both European and American cities, however, the public schools were crowded and inadequate by late-twentieth-century standards. Throughout the Western world classes were large, teaching staffs were overworked, and instruction was en masse. In 1890 there were fifty-four pupils for every teacher in the New York system, in Chicago the pupil-teacher ratio was forty-nine to one, and in Saint Louis it was forty-seven to one. Even in Boston's public schools, generally regarded as the best in the nation, the ratio was forty-two to one.[52] But the number of pupils per instructor was equally awesome in the much-touted city schools of the German kingdom of Prussia. In 1890 in Berlin there were fifty-five students for every teacher, and in Düsseldorf each instructor was responsible for an average of seventy pupils. Likewise in Britain and France classrooms of forty to sixty pupils were standard during the last decades of the century.[53] The children of Chicago and Philadelphia could receive only limited individual attention in the large classes of late-nineteenth-century America, but the pupils in Berlin and Paris suffered the same plight. Nowhere in the Western world did urban school systems employ enough teachers to permit classes of less than forty pupils, and few major cities in the world could match the relatively low student-teacher ratio of the prestigious school system of Boston.

Rising enrollment not only resulted in overflowing classes; it also necessitated an ever-increasing number of new school buildings. In each of the major cities of the Western world school authorities engaged in feverish building programs to keep pace with the soaring number of students. But in some American cities the supply of buildings fell behind the demands of the population, and the authorities were forced to resort to half-day schools. Such half-day sessions were common practice in the overcrowded schools of rural Prussia, but much less common in German and British cities. The American failure to provide enough classrooms therefore elicited unfavorable comments from some foreign observers. The distinguished British educator R. E. Hughes, in a comparative survey of British, French, German, and American schools at the close of the century, observed that "the deficiency of school accommodation in many of the largest of American cities is simply appalling." According to this critical schoolmaster, there was "the extraordinary spectacle of some of the richest cities in the world, such as New York, Chicago, Minneapolis, and Washington, actually resorting to the system of half-day schools, which is only tolerated in the poorest provinces of Europe."[54]

Yet American city school boards were not, for the most part, unusually stingy or negligent in the provision of facilities. In 1895 the Australian educator W. Catton Grasby wrote a comparative study of schools in the United States, Britain, and Australia based on his personal investigation of educational institutions on three continents. According to Grasby, "the American schoolhouse is architecturally more pretentious; and, internally, more elegantly and comfortably finished and furnished than the English, French, German, or Australian Elementary School." It was also "the best lighted, ventilated, and warmed," having "elaborate and apparently complicated machinery for heating and ventilation."[55] In his comparative study of education in the "civilized countries," the French pedagogue Emile Levasseur seconded Grasby's views. Writing in 1897, Levasseur described the schools in American cities as "sometimes luxurious monuments, almost always grandly laid out, comfortably furnished, [and] provided with ample teaching material." According to the Frenchman, Europeans regarded the school facilities of New York City, Chicago, and Boston as models, and few Old World cities could boast of school buildings as imposing as those in urban America.[56] Though the British educator R. E. Hughes condemned the lag in construction of schools in America, he reiterated the judgment of Grasby and Levasseur when he noted that "the furniture and fittings generally of the American classroom are considered by many observers to be superior to those of England or Germany." Moreover, he lauded the "internal arrangements" of American secondary schools and noted that some European educators had claimed that the American schoolroom is "as far superior to those of the European school as the Pullman car is ahead of the third-class European railway-carriage."[57]

Foreign educators sent by their governments to attend the Chicago World's Fair of 1893 expressed similar views about American school facilities. The Italian dignitaries commented on the "well-constructed, well-ventilated, and well-aired" American school buildings, and a leading Swedish educator exclaimed: "When visiting an American schoolroom, decorated with mural tablets, photographs, large charts, wall pictures, and bookcases, I found myself desiring to become a student."[58] Even the usually critical German pedagogues commented admiringly on the provision of blackboards in American schools and the supply of reference books for student use. Charts, maps, pianos, blackboards, and pictures were all more common in the American classroom than in the European. And the American penchant for libraries was evident in the prevalence of school libraries. Some Europeans, such as the Germans, may have questioned American teaching methods and criticized the preponderance of women in the American teaching corps, observing that "the lower degree of physical power of resistance in woman causes a lower degree of executive ability."[59] But very few foreign visitors would have characterized American urban schools as conspicuous failures. On the basis of his study of school systems in Europe and the United States, R. E. Hughes could conclude that the American city school "is, in many respects, admirable, and comparable with the best European schools."[60]

To achieve this admirable level of performance, American cities of the late nineteenth century initiated a number of programs, one of the most important of which involved the training of teachers. School authorities in the largest cities refused to rely on unprepared instructors, yet the supply of teachers graduating from state-supported institutes proved inadequate. Therefore, municipalities created their own normal schools for the instruction of prospective teachers in the latest techniques of the profession. In 1848 the controllers of public schools in Philadelphia established the first municipal normal school, and from 1848 to 1892 almost fifty-eight hundred graduated from the institution. In 1852 the Boston City Council followed the example of Philadelphia's controllers, creating the Boston Normal School. And in 1870 New York City's Board of Education opened a normal college to train teachers for that city. As early as 1886 there were twenty-two normal schools supported by city school boards across the country, and by the beginning of the twentieth century 80 percent of the American cities with a population of 100,000 or more maintained teacher's training programs.[61] These municipal colleges taught courses in the principles of education, psychology, hygiene, teaching methods, and kindergarten instruction and maintained model schools where novices could observe actual classroom experiences and practice what they had learned in their methods courses. America's great cities were not so indifferent to the quality of education as to ignore the professional preparation of their teachers. Instead, they supported not only elementary and secondary institutions but also teachers colleges that trained thousands of instructors during the years 1870 to 1900.

Meanwhile, American city school boards were also attempting to upgrade urban education through curricular reforms. For the youngest scholars, urban school systems of the late nineteenth century introduced the kindergarten. As early as 1870 Boston's school board had established an experimental kindergarten, but in 1873 authorities in Saint Louis founded the first permanent publicly supported kindergarten in the United States. Previously, children under the age of six had remained unschooled, and as a consequence the less affluent youngsters supposedly suffered premature exposure to the physical and moral dangers of the city streets. Now the Saint Louis school board provided instruction and supervision for these youngsters, and by 1880 the city's public kindergartens enrolled almost eight thousand refugees from preschool ignorance and idleness.[62] Gradually other city school boards adopted the Saint Louis scheme, with Philadelphia incorporating kindergartens into the public school system in 1887, Boston doing likewise in 1888, New York City in 1893, Cleveland in 1897, and Buffalo in 1898. By the turn of the century, the kindergarten was a standard feature of American city school systems.

The other major curricular reform of the period was the advent of manual training. Prior to 1880 the exclusive focus of American public schools was book learning and the development of intellectual faculties rather than manual skills. As early as the 1860s Boston's public schools had introduced instruction in sewing, but this was a rare exception to the usual curriculum of mathematics, science, languages, history, and geography. Yet "practical" learning rather than intellectual abstractions appealed to many urban dwellers, and by the last decades of the century school authorities faced increasing pressure to offer courses in carpentry, metal work, and drafting, as well as cooking and sewing. City school boards responded to these pressures, and the result was a proliferation of classes in the manual arts. In 1884 Baltimore's board of education founded the first public manual training high school; a year later the Philadelphia school system inaugurated a similar secondary institution; and in 1886 Cleveland began financing a manual arts high school. By 1890 thirty-seven cities of 8,000 or more population offered courses in the manual arts. During the 1890s the movement for practical training gained momentum, and at the close of the century school systems in 169 cities maintained courses in such subjects as woodworking and machine tools.[63] Cicero's orations and Caesar's commentaries were gradually yielding their place of educational preeminence to the lathe and the stove as American city school boards expanded course offerings in accordance with their perceptions of the changing needs of the community.

Yet the chief beneficiaries of manual training programs were not necessarily those poor immigrants who did most of the manual work in the city. At the close of the century, public school training in carpentry and cooking usually began no earlier than the fifth, sixth, or seventh grades. The poorest urban children, however, often dropped out of school when they reached this level, and their families could rarely afford for them to remain unemployed long enough to attend the newly created manual high schools. These schools were for students with a mechanical bent who sought an economic role of greater prestige than factory lathe operator. Many students, in fact, were middle-class youths preparing for a university education and a career in engineering. In 1895 the headmaster of Boston's Mechanic Arts High School wrote that his institution would arouse in boys "an ambition to continue their studies in a higher institution" and boasted that it offered "the best possible preparation for the higher scientific and technical schools."[64] It was, then, a feeder to the Massachusetts Institute of Technology and not a breeder of skilled factory workers. Moreover, its roll call of students included the names of very few of Boston's Italian immigrant families.[65] Similarly, an occupational survey conducted in 1894 of all those who had graduated from the Baltimore Manual Training School during its ten years of existence revealed a large contingent of engineers, draftsmen, teachers, and college students and a total absence of carpenters or metal workers. Approximately three-quarters of the Baltimore graduates held white-collar positions, with only a quarter holding such blue-collar jobs as machinist.[66] And in 1899 36 percent of the graduating class of Chicago's English High and Manual Training School intended to enroll in college, a percentage surpassed by only one of the city's thirteen traditional high schools. By contrast, only 13 percent of those graduating from Chicago's Northwest and Lake high schools were planning a college career.[67] In Chicago as in Baltimore and Boston, manual training high schools were not the molders of a skilled working class. Instead, they nurtured a middle-class technocracy.

Both the manual training high schools and the normal schools represented an expansion of the urban educational curriculum beyond the basic academic subjects taught for centuries. But, as stated, neither of these schools extended educational opportunities to that economic class for whom secondary schooling was traditionally unfeasible. Instead, the manual training high schools offered those affluent enough to remain outside the labor market during their teenage years an alternative to the traditional emphasis on languages and literature. And the normal schools offered young women who could afford to remain jobless until nineteen or twenty years old a vocational supplement to the standard curriculum. The city boards of education provided the poor with elementary learning, and many of the largest cities maintained evening schools for the continuing education of those who needed to work during the day. But financial necessity often forced those at the bottom of the economic heap to find their secondary schooling on the streets or in the shop.

Though the benefits of municipal programs may not have been distributed equally to every level of society, still American urban school authorities were not dormant. They did not suffer from debilitating indifference to the will of the majority; nor were they expending all their energy playing partisan tricks or stealing from the public till. For better or worse, they were responding to new demands, attempting to upgrade the quality of the teaching staff and revising the course offerings of the public schools. Certainly there were problems and complaints: The economic status of the school teacher in Germany and Britain relative to the average wage earner was higher than the relative status of the teacher in the United States, where female instructors earned no more than streetcar motormen. Moreover, the truancy rate in American cities was generally higher than in European cities, and in those states with compulsory attendance laws, urban authorities often seemed unwilling or unable to enforce these statutes. Shortage of classrooms remained a problem as well, and some teachers undoubtedly were tyrants or bores. Yet at the same time American urban schools had won the respect of observers throughout the world. The Australian educator W. Catton Grasby found American schools admirable and concluded that the complaints of American critics, "like patent medicine, should be taken with discretion." According to Grasby, "their ideal must be so high, that what I considered good, by comparison with work done elsewhere, is very much below their conception of possible excellence."[68] The high goals of such educational idealists may have remained elusive, but when weighed against the comparative scale of the rest of the late-nineteenth-century world, much had been attained.

CHARITY AND THE URBAN POOR

Hundreds of thousands of paupers and indigents inhabited the cities of late nineteenth-century America, and in the 1880s and 1890s, as in every period of urban history, poverty was a serious problem. Tenements lined slum streets, and shantytowns ringed the American metropolis. Thousands of individuals wandered urban thoroughfares, frequented cheap flophouses, and wrenched a meager living from the harsh city. American municipal leaders did not forget these losers of the economic game—they provided some institutions and some programs specifically for the poor. Yet by international standards, American municipalities were not nearly so innovative or bold in the area of charity and welfare as in the fields of library science, water technology, or public health. The late-nineteenth-century American municipality was not a stronghold of paternalistic compassion, nor did American city fathers feel that social control of the urban masses necessitated programs as innovative as those sponsored by private charitable groups. Action was taken to care for indigents and to ensure their sustenance; but the focus of American municipal endeavor was on servicing the prosperous and not the poor.

During the 1870s, 1880s, and 1890s the mainstay of the municipal response to poverty was the almshouse. Almshouses had existed in North America since colonial times, and throughout the nineteenth century local authorities continued to operate these institutions, which were dedicated to sheltering the poorest of the poor. At the close of the century, New York City, Philadelphia, Saint Louis, Boston, Baltimore, and Cleveland all maintained municipal almshouses, and Chicago's dependent poor were the responsibility of the Cook County authorities. The number of inmates in the New York City and Philadelphia almshouses averaged about four thousand, and the institutions in Saint Louis and Baltimore each housed over one thousand souls.[69]

Many cities also provided hospitals and asylums for less affluent residents in need of medical care. Philadelphia, Saint Louis, and Boston each maintained municipal insane asylums, and such municipal hospitals as Philadelphia's Blockley Hospital, New York City's Bellevue Hospital, and Boston's City Hospital were renowned institutions that provided free medical care to the city's populace. The municipal hospital staffs included some of America's most distinguished physicians, but quality of treatment often depended on whether the patient's disease fit the research or teaching interests of the medical corps. An indigent patient with a classic malady useful in the training of the hospital's medical students might receive much attention, but the many common drunks suffering from alcoholism would find themselves relegated to city jail or the municipal almshouse. On the whole, though, the free medical treatment provided by America's municipal hospitals was equal to that received by indigents anywhere in the world.

Not only did American cities maintain almshouses and charity hospitals, some also donated money to private charitable organizations dedicated to helping the needy. By the late 1890s New York City annually appropriated more than $3 million for 220 private charitable societies. The largest portion of this money went to institutions for the care of pauper children, but virtually every charity in the city received a handout from the municipality, including such diverse organizations as a group dedicated to clothing shipwrecked sailors and another for the support of indigent actors. But New York City's philanthropy was unusually generous. No other major American municipality appropriated over $250,000 for private charities, and many, such as Boston, Cleveland, Cincinnati, and Milwaukee, contributed nothing. American cities maintained almshouses, but most municipalities preferred to avoid expenditures for charity and leave that responsibility to the private sector. In New York City during the 1890s 79 percent of the money spent for the support of dependent children came from the public treasury, but in Philadelphia, the City of Brotherly Love, the public sector contributed only 3 percent of the cost of caring for indigent minors.[70] Throughout the United States city fathers were willing to allow much of the burden of charity to fall on churches and private organizations.

The almshouse, the asylum, the charity ward—those traditional dumping grounds for the urban poor—were, then, the chief municipal institutions for the care of indigents. After 1875 New York City provided coal, but no relief money or groceries, for impoverished persons outside these institutions, and in 1878 Brooklyn cut off all aid to the noninstitutionalized poor, as did Philadelphia the following year. Boston continued to offer some public funding for those unwilling to accept the humiliation of a sojourn in the almshouse. But cities like Baltimore and San Francisco joined New York City, Brooklyn, and Philadelphia in accepting the notion that only the institutionalized should benefit from municipal funds.[71] Thus in most major cities the almshouse remained the focus of municipal charity work. According to many commentators of the late nineteenth century, the dole and the handout undermined the independent spirit of the poor, sapping their will to succeed and weakening their determination to support themselves. Such public generosity supposedly did nothing but nurture pauperism and begging. Moreover, it was felt that relief payments to those outside the almshouse would force the more affluent to pay higher taxes. To build determination, encourage self-reliance, and keep money in the pockets of taxpayers, municipalities thus left indigents to fend for themselves or to turn to private groups for help.

Throughout the late nineteenth century the most notable developments in charity work were, in fact, the result of private, and not public, initiative. Such groups as the Charity Organization Society, the Children's Aid Society, and the Salvation Army were in the vanguard of efforts to help the poor. New ideas and new initiatives arose from the private sector, from concerned citizens like Charles Loring Brace, who sought to help the children of the slums, or from women like Josephine Shaw Lowell, who sent middle-class ladies to visit among the poor. Jane Addams created her famous Hull House and thus sparked the social settlement movement as a privately fueled endeavor. Other private individuals who founded settlement houses in other cities—with their nurseries, clubs, and middle-class amenities for the uplift of the poor— likewise did not rely on the municipal government for sustenance. The municipality did provide schools and libraries, which supposedly would help the poor help themselves. But for the most helpless in society, America's cities primarily pursued the traditional course of the almshouse and charity ward.

When compared with European cities, American municipalities appear somewhat unimaginative in their approach to poverty. The American city may have led in the use of electricity, the application of asphalt, the construction of fire alarm systems, the planning of parks, and the organization of public libraries, but when dealing with the poor, such municipal initiative was absent. American city fathers mastered the latest technology, applying it for the welfare of the middle class. Paupers, the unemployed, and slum dwellers were not so well served, however, by the formal organs of urban government. The informal government of the party machine and political boss might distribute turkeys at Christmas and coal for the winter; and the ward boss might occasionally find a job for those out of work. Yet the welfare functions of the formal agencies were relatively limited in comparison with those offered by some of the other cities of the Western world.

German cities, for example, provided a wide range of institutions to aid the needy and supervise their behavior. Munich, Leipzig, Stuttgart, Berlin, Hamburg, and Dresden either operated or subsidized labor bureaus to find jobs for the unemployed. In 1895 Hamburg's bureau secured positions for 38,000 applicants, and Stuttgart placed 7,500 who were out of work. In the United States some states established employment agencies in a few of the large cities, but there was nothing to rank with the paternalistic system of Germany. American cities likewise failed to establish municipal loan offices or pawnshops of the type existing in Germany and continental Europe. Such public loan offices or pawnshops protected the poor from the evils of private usury and aided the police in recovering stolen goods.[72] Again the machinery for paternalistic supervision was more highly developed in German cities than in American municipalities.

Municipalities in both Germany and Great Britain were also more active in establishing shelters for the homeless poor. In 1870 Glasgow opened two municipal lodging houses for indigents, and within ten years the Scottish metropolis had established seven such institutions. In Germany, Berlin, Munich, Leipzig, Breslau, and Cologne all maintained municipal lodging houses that provided free shelter to the able-bodied but homeless unemployed and also enabled the authorities to keep closer surveillance on those elements of society who might prove dangerous to the ruling elite. By the 1890s London and Paris had followed suit, extending the paternalistic supervision of the municipality to the transient poor.[73]

In American cities police stations offered temporary shelter, and during the 1880s New York City stations yearly accommodated an average of 139,000, while Chicago's police provided shelter for about 30,000 individuals yearly. But the police stations usually offered the homeless no more than a hard floor to sleep on and possibly a handout of bread. One British journalist visiting a

Chicago police station found impoverished refugees from the street sleeping on the stone floor packed together "like herrings in a barrel."[74] Such makeshift arrangements did not match the lodging houses provided by European cities. But despite the complaints of the police and the urgings of charitable societies, few cities in the United States were willing to copy the Old World example. As early as 1879 Boston's overseers of the poor did establish the Wayfarers' Lodge, where those without funds could receive a bath, a night's sleep in a bed, and a breakfast in exchange for a few hours labor. The public authorities in Washington, D.C., established a similar lodging house, and in December, 1896, after more than ten years of debate, New York City finally opened its version of the Boston institution.[75] No other major American city, however, took such action, and municipalities from Baltimore to San Francisco relied instead on the police stations and the private mission houses. According to a foreign observer, the American city, "like a stony-hearted step-mother provided for her children nothing but shelter, warmth and a stone bed."[76]

The reluctance of New York City's municipal leaders was, in fact, more typical of New World attitudes than the paternalism of Boston's overseers. As early as 1886 the state legislature authorized New York City to establish a system of four municipal lodging houses, but year after year the city's charity commissioners and executive officers refused to act. In 1891 a committee representing various private charities appeared before the city Board of Estimate, urging an appropriation of $15,000 for a lodging house, but the board obstinately refused to assume a new municipal function. The president of the municipal Department of Charities and Corrections feared the altruism of the lodging-house advocates and claimed that they did not understand "what effect it would have on tramps and vagrants who swarm into the city." And New York City's Mayor Hugh Grant insisted "that the board could do nothing until the Commissioners of Charities and Correction asked for the money." The commissioners said point blank that they would not ask for it, and Mayor Grant responded, "that settles it."[77] Not until the reform overthrow of Tammany in the mid-1890s did the idea of a municipal lodging house win official favor in New York City, and throughout the rest of the nation lodging-house proposals attracted the support of few mayors or commissioners.

The American record with regard to public bathhouses for the poor was equally unimpressive. European cities acted forcefully to ensure the cleanliness of the less affluent, whereas American municipalities responded slowly and reluctantly. By the close of the century almost 90 percent of British cities of over 50,000 residents maintained municipal bathhouses with showers or bathtubs for the many urban dwellers who could not afford the luxury of a private bathtub. London could claim more than thirty such bathhouses, Manchester nine, Liverpool eight, and Glasgow seven. Over 70 percent of German cities of 50,000 or more inhabitants also operated municipal bathhouses, as did many of the largest cities elsewhere in Europe.[78] By comparison, relatively few American municipalities maintained year-round indoor public baths, with Chicago operating four, Milwaukee two, and Boston and Buffalo one each at the close of the century. New York City did supervise fifteen bathing areas in the East and Hudson rivers during the summer months, but these outdoor watering spots were so polluted that they won the nickname "sewer baths."[79] During the late nineteenth century the municipal authorities in the nation's largest city thus failed to maintain any indoor baths comparable to those of Europe.

Some urban sanitarians and charity leaders in the United States did, however, belatedly crusade to imitate the European example. The bathtub was commonplace in middle-class American households, unlike in European homes, but reformers in Chicago and New York City insisted that public baths were necessary for the unwashed poor. Jane Addams claimed that in 1892 there were only three bathtubs in the one-third square mile adjacent to her Chicago settlement house, and in 1894 the New York Tenement House Committee found that "only 306 persons out of a total of 255,033 whose living conditions were carefully examined by its investigating staff, had access to bathtubs in their homes." Moreover, in 1901 a committee investigating tenements in Chicago found that only 3 percent of the slum population surveyed had private bathtubs.[80] Such figures were appalling to reformers who sought to uplift the poor by inculcating in them the middle-class virtue of cleanliness. In the minds of Jane Addams and the members of the various investigating committees, the municipality needed to take action.

Yet American municipal leaders resisted the burden of the public bath just as they did the responsibility of maintaining lodging houses. As early as 1885 a state tenement-house commission recommended that New York City establish indoor public baths in slum districts, and in 1891 a private charitable organization opened a model bathhouse that was supposed to inspire New York City's municipal authorities to construct such facilities. The New York City board of health was willing to embark on such a program, but Mayor Hugh Grant opposed this extension of the city's services. An advocate of the movement concluded that the mayor "will not act in the matter, unless pushed to it by an overwhelming public sentiment." In 1892 the state legislature authorized New York City to erect public baths, but still the local authorities opposed the creation of this new service for the poor. In 1893 a leading proponent of public baths won an interview with Grant's successor, Mayor Thomas Gilroy, but Gilroy answered the petitioner's pleas by claiming that "there was no public sentiment in favor of such baths."[81]

Undaunted, the proponents of cleanliness turned again to the New York legislature, which passed a statute in 1895 requiring cities of 50,000 or more population to erect bathing facilities. Still there was no municipal action. Mayor William Strong appointed a special committee, which recommended the construction of a bathhouse on Tompkins Square, but residents of the area protested such a sacrifice of their precious neighborhood parkland, and the city dropped its plans. In December 1897 New York City finally broke ground for the construction of its first municipal bathhouse, yet three years later the structure remained unfinished.[82] In Philadelphia, Baltimore, Saint Louis, and throughout the nation municipal authorities were equally reluctant to create public baths.[83] By the close of the century only the city governments of Chicago and Milwaukee had moved beyond the experimental stage in this area of municipal service.

This situation existed despite the fact that extensive municipal waterworks were pumping hundreds of millions of gallons into Philadelphia and New York City every day for the convenience of middle-class urbanites who enjoyed the most modern plumbing in the world. American slum dwellers were not provided private bathing facilities, however, and the municipal fathers were slow to alter this fact. As one proponent of public baths observed, New York City had "the most meagre bathing facilities of any great city in the civilized portion of the world while possessing the most magnificent water supply."[84] American municipal governments ensured that middle-class city dwellers enjoyed an uninterrupted flow of water for their up-to-date bathroom fixtures, but they did not match European cities in the construction of public baths for the poor.

Some European city governments were also more aggressive in their fight against blighted slum housing. In Great Britain, for example, the governments of London, Glasgow, Liverpool, and Birmingham all engaged in major slum clearance projects and constructed municipal housing for the "laboring classes." Glasgow had long suffered a reputation for urban blight, and its narrow lanes and congested working-class neighborhoods were notorious throughout the world. From 1866 to the close of the century, however, the municipality cleared eighty-eight acres of slums inhabited by 50,000 people, reconstructed and widened streets through the district, and built new housing for the poor. In 1876 Birmingham embarked on a similar scheme, expropriating and clearing ninety acres in the city center, and during the last three decades of the century Liverpool's city council ordered the demolition of 33,000 unsanitary dwellings and consequently constructed new housing blocks for laborers on the site of these former slums. Between 1875 and 1900 the Metropolitan Board of Works and London County Council likewise initiated thirty-two schemes of clearance and reconstruction in Britain's capital city.[85] Such schemes often were of limited effectiveness in combating the slum problem, but they reflected a degree of concern for unsanitary and defective housing that did not exist among the city fathers of America's municipalities. During the 1890s New York City began clearing a few small slum tracts for minor parks and playgrounds, and in the last decades of the nineteenth century private groups constructed a few model tenements in American cities. Yet there was no public commitment to municipal slum clearance equal to that in Great Britain.

America's municipalities, however, did attempt to upgrade housing through building regulations. Beginning with the Tenement-House Law of 1867, the New York state legislature imposed certain sanitary and safety restrictions on urban tenements, and during the following four decades lawmakers in New York toughened these standards. By the 1890s, the New York code included sanitary and safety provisions that regulated the condition of tenement cellars; required windows, transoms, and ventilators in tenement rooms; specified the minimum height of rooms and the minimum cubic feet of air per occupant; regulated fire escapes and stairways; and governed the supply of water to dwellings and the construction of flush toilets. In addition, the code restricted the percentage of each lot that could be covered by buildings and thus sought to limit congestion. Inspectors from the municipal building and health departments were responsible for implementing these regulations, but due to understaffing and possible corruption or negligence, violations of the building code were common. According to a special state tenement commission, only 15 of 333 new tenements under construction in Manhattan in 1900 fully complied with every provision of the building code.[86] Yet New York's building codes were not totally ignored, and they did have some beneficial effect in upgrading housing. Moreover, cities in both the United States and Europe emulated New York's example. In 1893 an early expert on urban slum housing wrote that New York City "has the honor of being far in advance of any other city in respect of sanitary regulations, and has, indeed, become a standard for other cities throughout the country and in many of the European capitals."[87]

American cities did, then, seek to ensure the safety of the poor. Yet American municipalities were not as dedicated to paternalistic intervention or social control as the city fathers of Europe. American lawmakers imposed negative restrictions such as building codes but shied away from positive action such as municipal-owned housing. City officials provided institutions for the absolutely destitute and hospitals for the infirm, yet the bulk of the poor had to fend for themselves or rely on the help or interference of private charity workers. Urban Americans of the late nineteenth century showed concern about the problem of poverty, but they expressed this concern through private endeavor and not municipal action. Money, ingenuity, and expertise created fine public facilities for the prosperous. The poor, by comparison, were neglected.

POLICE PROTECTION

Perhaps the most maligned municipal service of nineteenth-century America was the police force. Journalists, reformers, and preachers in their pulpits repeatedly attacked the police as corrupt and immoral. State legislative investigations unearthed lurid tales of bribery, brutality, and gross indifference to duty. Captain Alexander "Clubber" Williams and Chief William "Big Bill" Devery of the New York City police were known for their extortion rackets, which earned them a notoriety equal to that of the criminals they arrested. And the reputation of the cop on the beat was not much better. Moralists constantly blamed the police for the sin and license prevalent in the city, and stories of patrolmen and police chiefs receiving cash from prostitutes, gamblers, and saloonkeepers were commonplace. Partisan politics purportedly determined police appointments and promotions, and nowhere did political influence seem so dominant as in the police department.

Much of this criticism, unfortunately, seems justified. The American municipal police department did not compare as favorably with European law enforcement agencies as American fire departments, waterworks, or public libraries compared with their Old World counterparts. In the less densely populated American cities there was a larger area to patrol, yet American police forces were no greater in size than those of Europe. At the turn of the century metropolitan London had one policeman for every 396 inhabitants, whereas New York City could claim only one for every 450 residents. Paris enjoyed the protection of one policeman for every 357 residents, Berlin one for every 400, Liverpool one for every 361, and Manchester one for every 544. Chicago's municipal fathers, however, maintained only one patrolman for every 551 inhabitants, in Saint Louis the figure was one per 458 residents, in Boston one per 451, in Baltimore one per 621, and in Cleveland one per 994.[88] Though American municipalities outranked European cities of equal population in mileage of paved streets, length of sewer and water lines, extent of streetcar trackage, and size of fire departments, in the field of law enforcement American police forces were average or below average when measured by European standards. Chicago could boast of street mileage far in excess of that in Berlin, as could Saint Louis and Boston. Yet in these extensive American cities there were fewer police than in the compact German capital, and the cop on every corner was much more a reality in Europe than in the United States.

Though American police forces were at best of average size, the American crime rate seems to have dwarfed that of advanced European nations. Rate-of-arrest figures exist for twenty-three of the twenty-seven largest cities in late-nineteenth-century America, and throughout the period 1870 to 1900 the arrest rate for all offenses in these cities averaged three times the arrest rate for all offenses in London. In other words, there were three times as many arrests per thousand population in the leading American cities as in the British capital.[89] Even if one eliminates arrests for such petty offenses as loitering, vagrancy, and drunkenness and concentrates on crimes against property and crimes of violence, the American rate far exceeds that of Britain or other northern European nations. During the 1890s the murder and manslaughter rate in Philadelphia seems to have been three to five times as great as that of London.[90] Crime, like fire, was a problem of unusual magnitude in the American city, yet the response of municipalities to the need for crime deterrence was not nearly so vigorous as was their response to the need for fire protection. American municipalities had more acreage to patrol than their European counterparts and seemingly more crime to suppress; but American police brigades were of average size and did not enjoy the international prestige of American fire departments.

The arrest figures cited above, however, not only imply a higher crime rate in America; they also indicate a higher rate of activity among American policemen. For every one offender a London bobby apprehended, his American counterpart was arresting at least three. If nothing else, the American police seem to have been prolific in the production of arrests, and possibly they spent less time socializing at the precinct station and more time capturing criminals than their British brethren. Moreover, the arrest figures perhaps indicate that London's police corps was wastefully overstaffed in comparison to the lean American squads. Yet the fact remains that given the crime problem in American cities, the police departments were by international standards underdeveloped.

This is also evident from the recruitment procedures of American forces. The prerequisites for service as a policeman in the United States were minimal as compared with the standards demanded of recruits in continental Europe. Though American cities specified certain height, weight, and health requirements, short, puny, sickly candidates with political connections could find jobs in the nation's police departments. Literacy requirements and civil service examinations also posed no obstacle for semiliterate job-seekers who had served their party well. In Great Britain standards were not much higher, and police recruits were generally brawny country louts willing to work cheap. But in Germany and Austria-Hungary applicants for police work had to have served in the army and achieved a rank comparable to corporal. Berlin required six years army service and Dresden twelve. Likewise, most Paris policemen were former soldiers who had risen to the rank of sergeant, then opted for duty on the boulevards of the French capital rather than military service at a colonial outpost. The continental policeman was a disciplined military veteran who served his nation in the streets of the city as he had in the field of battle. Continental police departments also pioneered the creation of police training academies, the first having been founded in Paris in 1883. By the early twentieth century Vienna led the world in the thoroughness of its police training program. When compared with his continental counterpart, the American policeman seemed an amateur.[91]

Any comparison with continental police forces, however, is somewhat misleading, because the role of the police in continental Europe was broader than in the English-speaking nations. Kaiser Wilhelm's Germany and Franz Joseph's Austria were nations of limited freedom, and urban police kept a careful eye on all forms of behavior, especially if it seemed disruptive to the political status quo. Press censorship, examination of passports, and suppression of political movements all fell within the range of responsibilities entrusted to the German and Austrian police. Even in France under the Third Republic surveillance of potential enemies of the state was among the police duties, and secret dossiers filled the files of the Paris police. Moreover, in Paris and Berlin the police maintained strict watch over the "suspicious" transient class, and hotels and boarding houses transmitted to the authorities information on all lodgers. The privacy and liberty typical of the English-speaking world was absent in much of continental Europe, and the extensive police forces were empowered to maintain a strict scrutiny over urban residents. In the 1890s an American journalist reported that private guests and hotel arrivals had to provide German police "with an amount of information of a strictly personal nature that American or English travelers always find amusing."[92] Such police supervision might have been "amusing" to Americans when traveling, but it was certainly not acceptable at home.

Commenting on continental police practices with regard to transients, Chief Inspector Thomas Byrnes of the New York Police Department observed: "In our country nothing of that sort would be tolerated. We have multitudes of strangers arriving here all the time, but they wear no collar and carry no tag." Moreover, he admitted: "I have not men enough to watch all the avenues of travel to and from the city if I wanted to."[93] American city officials occasionally used the police to combat labor radicals, and brutal clubbing of "undesirables" was not uncommon in New York City or Chicago. But the municipalities of the United States never intended to establish efficient forces of government surveillance similar to those of France or Germany. The military professionals guarding the streets of Berlin were alien to the American political tradition and would have proved unacceptable in American cities. In the United States a corrupt and sometimes violent amateur was preferable to a systematic, trained autocrat.

Many middle-class Americans, however, would have preferred the police to adopt a firmer stance toward certain deviants. In a city such as Chicago, gamblers and prostitutes suffered only intermittent raids from the police, for periods of tough enforcement alternated with long spells of indifference. Systematic suppression of vice was, in fact, the exception rather than the rule, much to the disgust of middle-class moralists eager for an upright, chaste society. Likewise, systematic repression of paupers and indigents was not common. In every major city the police arrested thousands for vagrancy or suspicious behavior, but they also opened their station houses indiscriminately to any homeless wretch in need of a night's shelter. Private charity workers favored registration and investigation of vagabonds to determine whether they were "deserving" or "undeserving." Yet American police never applied the "scientific" techniques of modern charity work in an attempt to sort out the supposedly dangerous and shiftless class of indigents. Ambiguity and inconsistency, rather than systematic suppression and reform, characterized American police relations with both the vagabond and wayward elements of the urban underlife.

Despite the relative inferiority of the American police as a tool for social control, municipal forces in the United States could claim some achievements. American police departments, like American fire departments, kept pace with all the innovations in their field. They organized detective bureaus, made use of photography for identifying those with a criminal record, and won special recognition by maintaining the most extensive and advanced alarm systems in the world. As early as the 1850s the New York City police force had adopted a telegraph system linking precinct stations, and in 1880 Chicago's Police Department introduced the first network of telephone communication between street-corner call boxes and station houses. Milwaukee followed Chicago's lead in 1883, and Brooklyn and Philadelphia did likewise in 1884. By 1893 Chicago could boast of 1,000 street boxes throughout the city providing instantaneous communication. And nine years later 148 cities in the United States had similar alarm systems, which enhanced the effectiveness of law enforcement agencies.[94] In part, these alarm networks compensated for the lack of patrolmen. There may not have been a patrolman on every block, but in every section of the city there was a means of communicating quickly with the police.

Thus American police departments might well have merited some praise, and yet in the area of police protection New York City, Chicago, Philadelphia, and Saint Louis did not maintain inordinately thorough or professional services. Police officers did round up desperadoes, and they occasionally earned glory from some thrilling arrest. But the American police won only limited laurels from contemporaries and reaped volumes of blistering criticism. Moral reformers complained that the police failed to close saloons on the Sabbath, refused to suppress prostitution, and generally profited from a cut of the vice receipts. If officers did enforce Sunday closing statutes, saloonkeepers attacked them for violating the personal liberty of the citizenry, and disgruntled drinkers soon exerted political pressure to halt such conscientious devotion to the law. And no matter what the police did with regard to urban vice, Republicans lambasted Democrat-dominated police forces, and Democrats showed no mercy in their assaults on Republican brigades. By the 1890s the municipal police force was the pride of few American cities.

CREDITING AMERICAN MUNICIPAL SUCCESS

America's police may have been the subject of jibes, and America's poor inadequately served, but overall there was ample reason for pride in American municipal achievement. By the close of the century, American public libraries and parks were the largest in the world; the public health laboratories, fire departments, and transit systems were the most advanced; the street lights were the brightest; the asphalt pavements the smoothest; the water and sewer lines the most extensive; and the water supplies the grandest. An impartial observer judging by the contemporary standard of Britain and Germany could have entered at least as many credits in the ledger of American municipal rule as debits. And local boosters in New York City, Chicago, Philadelphia, and Boston, with excusable exaggeration, could have preached the glory of their hometown governments. For those who wanted to recognize the positive, the triumphs of American city government were at least as evident as the failures.

In the realm of technology the American municipality proved especially progressive when compared with Old World urban centers. New York City, Chicago, Boston, and Buffalo repeatedly anticipated the European metropolises in the application of the latest scientific and engineering advances. They hired the best technical experts money could buy, and the impact of this expertise was evident in the waterworks, fire brigades, and health departments of America's cities. The Brooklyn Bridge was perhaps the most striking testament to the engineering programs of the New World municipality. Yet even in the heating and ventilation of schoolrooms and the construction of police alarm systems, foreign observers noted the technological superiority of American municipalities. The high wage levels that prevailed in the United States discouraged optimum development of such labor-intensive services as street cleaning. But in the mechanized areas of municipal endeavor, American cities stood in the vanguard.

The advances in American public services should have been especially apparent to those middle-class urban dwellers who so often complained of the municipal structure and cried for reform. These comfortable citizens, together with the prosperous and skilled contingent within the working class, were the chief beneficiaries of late-nineteenth-century municipal programs. They owned the flush toilets and bathtubs that flowed with ample supplies of municipal water; they were the bicyclists who benefited from the fresh asphalt pavements; and they also rode the lengthy streetcar lines to suburban neighborhoods for a price equal to that paid by inner-city commuters for shorter journeys. Because of the extensive network of municipal services, middle-class citizens were able to enjoy a home in suburbia complete with the convenience of urban water, sewerage, and fire protection. They frequented the public libraries and the giant pleasure-grounds encompassing the cities and made full use of these monuments to municipal enterprise; their children attended the tuition-free secondary schools; and their offspring benefited most from the new normal colleges and manual training high schools. There may have been cause for middle-class dissatisfaction with some services—for example, when weak or corrupt police departments failed to enforce middle-class morality and squelch drunkenness, gambling, and prostitution. But on the whole, the deck of municipal services was stacked in favor of the manager, the professional, and the skilled artisan.

Prosperous American urban dwellers thus enjoyed the highest standard of living in the world, and this was as much due to the success of the municipal corporation as to the achievements of the much-glorified business corporation. The late-nineteenth-century city did not suffer from a blundering, buffoonish public sector that attempted little and achieved less. Instead, the public sector conceived and implemented grand schemes for the improvement of urban life. Occasionally it even had to come to the rescue of a faltering private sector. As early as the mid-nineteenth century, municipalities began purchasing investor-owned water companies when those agents of private enterprise no longer proved able to serve the city adequately. In the 1870s the municipalities of New York City and Brooklyn bought out private investors and assumed responsibility for completing the Brooklyn Bridge. And twenty years later public agencies in New York City had to intercede to construct a rapid-transit system, after private parties found the task too overwhelming. Meanwhile, private libraries in Buffalo and New York City turned to the public sector in order to expand their service to the city. Foes of public enterprise often claimed that municipal governments were too bungling or corrupt to assume new responsibilities such as the direct operation of transit lines. In actuality, however, the organs of city government generally proved competent to shoulder the heavy burdens imposed upon them and sometimes proved more competent than the private sector.

Not all citizens, however, shared equally in the achievements of municipal enterprise. While America's large middling class received much, the poor experienced relative neglect. By the late 1890s American municipalities were turning their attention to the need in slum neighborhoods for small parks, playgrounds, and public baths. Moreover, throughout the late nineteenth century the public schools and libraries were intended to be the bootstraps by which those on the bottom of the social heap could pull themselves to the top. Yet the poor would not or could not take full advantage of these institutions, and they could expect few other handouts from the city authorities. Even in Europe, programs for the poor tended to be token or repressive. But in America municipal paternalism was especially limited. Niggardly almshouses remained the municipal solution for indigence, though municipalities also provided hospital care for the poor. Beyond this, most cities did little, leaving charity to the private sector. The comfortable majority was the focus of municipal endeavor and not the indigent minority. Chicago, Boston, and Baltimore readily spent fortunes on giant engineering projects for the convenience of the prosperous, but bathhouses for the uplift of the poor were an afterthought.

Perhaps the weakest elements in American urban government were those agencies dedicated to blatant social control. American police forces were not inordinately large, nor were they inordinately respected; school truant officers were relatively few in number and sometimes ineffective; and in many cities the corps of health, sanitary, and building inspectors was understaffed and insufficient. The cities of the United States did not maintain Prussian standards of enforcement, and the American urban populace did not goose step to the beat of a policeman's club. American municipalities were much more successful at supplying comforts, conveniences, and pleasures than at imposing restrictions. New York City could build an engineering masterpiece that carried millions of gallons of water each day to the metropolis, but the municipal leaders were unwilling or unable to impose controls on wasteful consumption of water and thereby forestall the necessity for further expansion of the waterworks. The city hospitals ministered to the ailing poor free of charge, but city police were unwilling or unable to emulate Germany and monitor the movement of the lower classes. And the nation's cities provided magnificent parks and libraries for moral and uplifting entertainment and pleasure, but they proved unwilling or unable to suppress the "immoral" alternatives of the saloon, the brothel, and the gambling den. The American city gave much, yet it was reluctant to impose. It could master the natural environment, conquer diphtheria, span waterways, and transform sandy wastes into lush gardens. But it was unable or unwilling to master the social environment through the imposition of stringent codes of morality or vast ameliorative schemes for the reformation of the pauper. It planned and harnessed the inanimate; it was less systematic and overpowering in its response to the animate.

American municipal government was, then, much more of a sugar daddy than a stern Victorian father, a better provider than a regulator. By international standards, social comfort, and not social control, was the strong suit of the American municipality. Foreign observers frequently noted the Americans' love of comfort, their penchant for well-heated if not overheated rooms, their fondness for the luxury of a well-padded chair, and their devotion to a hot tub. Yet equally prominent was their contempt for heavy-handed governmental authority and their reluctance to accept public restraints. These traits were evident in the pattern of American urban rule. American city governments excelled as servants of the needs of the majority; they failed, however, as masters of morality. Their powers of coercion were less highly developed than their powers of service.

10 BOOM, BUST, AND URBAN RULE: FINANCING CITY GOVERNMENT

 When in 1888 James Bryce condemned American city government, he argued that one must judge a municipal regime in terms of what it achieved and how much it cost. American municipalities could clearly claim to have done much, paving thousands of miles of streets, constructing mile after mile of water and sewer mains, developing vast tracts of parkland, and building well-stocked public libraries. But what was the cost of all this to the taxpayers? What was the burden on the city resident, and how sound were the finances of the city? These were questions asked by many urban dwellers of the period, and quite often the answers they supplied were diatribes against the American system of municipal rule. During the 1870s, 1880s, and 1890s, critics of American urban government repeatedly condemned the waste, extravagance, and inefficiency of city administrations. Bosses and their cronies in city hall supposedly were pilfering the pockets of respectable middle-class taxpayers and leading the metropolis to financial ruin. Candidates in every election campaign ritualistically levied charges of corruption and waste, and the most niggardly city administration could suffer criticism as a spendthrift regime. Complaints were rife, and campaign rhetoric abounded in unfavorable testimony.

Certainly some of the criticisms were justifiable, for municipalities never achieved financial nirvana, and in the 1870s many cities appeared on the brink of bankruptcy. Yet the chief foe of municipal solvency was neither the corrupt politician nor the wasteful alderman but, instead, the boom-bust economic cycle of the late nineteenth century. During the last three decades of the century America's economy rose and fell in an erratic pattern that threatened ruin for business and municipal corporations alike. Expansive programs begun during good times and predicated on the prospect of growing assessed valuations and easy credit could prove serious burdens for cities caught in the throes of unexpected economic depression. And municipal debts incurred during a period of high price levels but maturing in a period of deflationary downturn could cripple city government. These were harsh facts that America's municipalities discovered in the wake of the Panic of 1873. Municipal contractors might pilfer thousands with the help of venal politicians, but these peculations never posed a threat to the city treasury equal to that of a shrinking bond market or a rising rate of tax delinquency. In the late nineteenth century economic panic proved a greater danger to municipal government than did crooked politicians.

Yet during the 1880s and 1890s American municipalities scored some successes in combating the boom-bust threat. In the quarter century following the devastating depression of the 1870s, municipal financial policy was largely dedicated to insulating city government from the worst effects of the severe economic climate. American cities pursued a conservative policy, wary of additional indebtedness, high tax rates, and soaring expenditures. As a result America's municipalities weathered the Panic of 1893 and ensuing depression with their credit ratings unblemished, with tax rates stable, and without suffering any serious setbacks in services. While major railroad corporations were falling into the hands of receivers, municipal corporations pursued their business relatively undisturbed. The 1890s did not witness a repeat of the municipal debacle of the 1870s, but instead it inaugurated a new era of financial confidence for city governments.

The last quarter of the nineteenth century was, then, a period of fiscal conservatism for cities, during which indebtedness remained under control and tax rates were kept as low as possible. It was not, despite the claims of campaign rhetoric, an era of spendthrift financing, of high debts, and of high taxes. In reaction to earlier excesses, municipal leaders adopted a cautious fiscal policy, one wary of the political and economic pitfalls of excessive expenditure. By the 1890s a new willingness to spend was evident. But comptrollers, mayors, and aldermen, still recalling the depression of the 1870s, proceeded prudently and carefully. If American municipalities erred financially in the period after 1875, they more likely sinned on the side of thrift than on that of extravagance.

MUNICIPAL INDEBTEDNESS

Looming over the city ledgers of the late nineteenth century was the persistent shadow of municipal indebtedness. Bonded indebtedness was an obligation the municipalities could not honorably repudiate, and throughout the period this obligation strongly influenced financial policy. Each of America's largest cities sought to preserve its credit and retain the goodwill of the financial community. And each also sought to curb its debt and reduce its interest payments, thereby freeing tax dollars for current expenditures. In New York, Chicago, Boston, and New Orleans alike, officials endeavored to ease the inherited burdens of debt in order to better finance the immediate needs of the community. This was basic to the fiscal strategy of American cities, and in the nation's major municipalities the comptrollers, mayors, and aldermen largely succeeded in achieving this goal.

The debt problem was basically a legacy of the late 1860s and early 1870s. During these years the nation suffered from a speculative mania common to nineteenth-century boom periods, and America's municipalities readily joined in the spending spree. Urban governments throughout the nation embarked on massive projects costing millions of borrowed dollars. New York City funded the development of Central Park, Brooklyn laid out Prospect Park, Philadelphia opened Fairmount Park, and Chicago's park districts purchased the ring of preserves surrounding that city. Construction of waterworks in Milwaukee, Pittsburgh, Baltimore, and Cleveland added substantially to the debt of those cities. Some municipalities such as Cincinnati and Baltimore invested heavily in railroad construction in the hope of enhancing their commercial fortunes. And Boston borrowed millions for street improvements, while Cleveland constructed a two-million-dollar viaduct linking the east and west sides of the city. Municipalities found the nation's money market receptive to borrowing, and the result was massive public improvements and soaring indebtedness.

In one major city after another, the municipal debt skyrocketed. Between 1868 and 1873 the net bonded debt of New York City tripled, and between 1867 and 1871 the bonded indebtedness of Chicago likewise increased three-fold.[1] Boston experienced a tripling of its municipal debt during the years 1868 to 1874; Cincinnati's bonded obligations rose fivefold between 1868 and 1876; and Cleveland's net debt soared 1,200 percent during the decade 1867 to 1877.[2] By comparison, the relatively provident city of Philadelphia only doubled its debt over this ten-year period.[3] Everywhere, however, the story was basically the same. The leading banking journal in America reported that the combined debt of the twenty cities having 100,000 or more population increased 176 percent from 1866 to 1876.[4] In New York City the beleaguered citizenry blamed Boss Tweed and his cronies for the soaring debt, while in New Orleans Democrats attributed the mounting indebtedness to corrupt carpetbagger rule. The phenomenon, however, was not a local one arising from the malfeasance of certain venal bosses. It was a nationwide trend, reflecting the city fathers' excessive confidence in the financial future and their inordinate willingness to mortgage the municipality for the purchase of expensive improvements. It was, in large measure, an expression of a boomtime mentality that was prevalent throughout the nation in both the private and the public sectors.

The bust came in 1873. That year Jay Cooke's banking firm failed, initiating a chain reaction of bankruptcies and six years of economic depression. Price levels, which had been falling since the Civil War, now plummeted, and the result was a heavier burden for debtors. Debts and interest obligations incurred during a period of high price levels now fell due in an era of sharp deflation. Moreover, the financial resources of municipalities dwindled as the assessed valuation of taxable property dropped throughout the country. In Chicago the total valuation fell one-third during the late 1870s; in Boston it dropped more than 20 percent; and in Philadelphia and Cincinnati the assessed value of property plummeted 10 percent. Likewise, in Cleveland and New York City the total value of urban property dipped about 5 percent.[5] Thus it became increasingly difficult for municipalities to raise the tax revenues necessary for current expenditures and interest payments, and deficits threatened to further boost the debt level. At the close of each year cities across the nation recorded floating debts, a product of the gap between income and outlays. Caught in the vise of financial contraction, American cities began to repent of their earlier spendthrift ways.

In the midst of this financial crisis some cities suffered the humiliation of having to default on their interest payments. Pittsburgh defaulted in 1877, as did Elizabeth, New Jersey, in 1879. Elizabeth bore an extraordinary debt burden, with the indebtedness amounting to more than 40 percent of the assessed valuation of all properties in the community. The desperate city resorted to borrowing funds to pay the interest on the debt, but finally the municipal government had no choice but to default.[6] Memphis, however, won dubious distinction as the most notable municipal bankruptcy of the 1870s. In both 1873 and 1878 the Tennessee metropolis failed to meet its interest payments, and much of the 1870s was devoted to haggling between the city administration and bondholders. After a devastating yellow fever epidemic in 1878 struck its deathblow to the already ailing city, the state of Tennessee intervened and took command. Tennessee's legislature repealed the city's charter and established the city as a taxing district. The state drew up the annual budgets for the community and collected the taxes, and the governor appointed half of the commissioners who were to administer the city, the other half being elected by the Memphis voters.[7] Bankrupt and hounded by creditors, the city of Memphis surrendered to the paternal guidance of the state, and the local voter was left with only a limited voice in determining the community's destiny.

None of the largest cities in the nation suffered the humiliation of Memphis or Elizabeth, but many comptrollers were kept busy devising financial maneuvers necessary to stave off default. For example, at one point New Orleans was at the very brink of bankruptcy and only its unique "premium bond" plan saved it from this fate. Under this plan the city enticed bondholders to trade in their old bonds for lower-interest premium bonds, using as bait a lottery scheme whereby certain lucky premium bondholders could win up to $5,000 at periodic drawings.[8] Other cities were not so imaginative, but throughout the nation municipal officials saw in the experiences of the defaulting communities a lesson not to be forgotten.

In one city after another, the comptrollers, auditors, and mayors sermonized on the wayward financial habits of the recent past and on the necessity for relying on taxation rather than on borrowing as a source of income. In 1874 New York City's Comptroller Andrew Green announced that the nation's largest metropolis could escape its debt problems if all departments kept "within the rule of 'paying as we go.' "[9] Two years later Cleveland's auditor warned that if America's cities continued to engage in a "race for incurring debt for supposed necessary public improvements," by the close of the century "nearly all of them would be irredeemably bankrupt." Hence, he believed that "there must be, necessarily, a cessation, or at least a suspension, of this apparently reckless expenditure."[10] That same year Boston's Mayor Samuel Cobb described debt as "a treacherous, as well as an oppressive master of cities as of individuals." And drawing on the Puritan imagery of Boston's founder John Winthrop, Cobb proclaimed that "a great city, absolutely clear of debt, and determined to incur none, would in this age be indeed a city set on a hill . . . , a wonderment to all its sister cities, an object of pride to its inhabitants, and almost the paradise of taxpayers."[11] The more prosaic mayor of Baltimore summed up neatly the view of most city officials of the late 1870s when he said: "To 'pay as you go,' as a general rule, is a common sense proposition."[12] The common sense of the late 1870s was to rely on taxation for revenues and to eschew the snares of indebtedness. "Pay as you go" was the phrase heard in city halls from the Atlantic to the Pacific.

Moreover, those in the private sector heartily agreed with this new policy of fiscal conservatism. Throughout the late 1870s and early 1880s the leading financial journals called for a sharp curb on municipal borrowing and had no kind words for the financial adventures of a decade earlier. In 1875 the *Commercial and Financial Chronicle*, a leading organ of the financial community, observed that "there has sprung up everywhere of late years a wonderful recklessness in issuing bonds," and it urged limits on the power of municipalities to contract debts. According to the *Chronicle*, "If the power of city officials to increase debt is not closely guarded and absolute limits placed upon it, we cannot expect either prudence or honesty to prevail."[13] *Bradstreet's*, another major financial periodical, reiterated these views even more strongly, announcing forcefully that "the most insidious foe of healthful local politics in the United States has been the extravagance and demoralization proceeding from . . . abuse of the borrowing power." Repeatedly it attacked "loose borrowing" by municipalities and the "demoralizing influence of the credit system." And the editors of *Bradstreet's* believed that "the obvious remedy is to deprive municipal officers, by constitutional enactment, of the power of mortgaging the estates of taxpayers." Both of the nation's leading financial periodicals accepted the view that "local government officers should not be intrusted with the demoralizing privilege of credit in the loan market."[14]

With both city officials and business community leaders calling for a curb on municipal authority to borrow, state legislatures and constitutional conventions moved to impose restrictions. During the 1870s and 1880s one state after another adopted constitutional provisions checking the authority of municipalities to incur debts. Illinois's Constitution of 1870 limited municipal indebtedness to 5 percent of the city's assessed valuation, and during the following decade Wisconsin and Missouri likewise imposed a 5 percent ceiling. In 1873 Pennsylvania restricted municipal borrowing to 7 percent of the valuation of the city; Indiana and Michigan imposed a 2 percent limit; and in 1884 New York adopted a constitutional provision forbidding cities and counties to incur a debt greater than 10 percent of the assessed value of property.[15] Moreover, to eliminate the floating debts of Philadelphia, Pennsylvania's legislature of 1879 passed the "pay-as-you-go act," which forbid the city to spend in excess of its estimated revenues. According to the act, any expenditure or appropriation in excess of the city council's annual estimate of municipal revenue was void.[16] Thus, no longer would spending outrun income, leaving unpaid bills at the end of the year. According to Philadelphia's controller, the pay-as-you-go plan safeguarded that city from "the chaos of the past, where debt was piled on debt without any adequate return . . . as though a reckoning day was never to come."[17] Philadelphia's officials and all the wise counsels of the late 1870s and early 1880s agreed that the profligacy of the past had to cease.

The result was retrenchment and a leveling off or slow decline in municipal indebtedness. New York City's bonded debt peaked in 1876 and then declined every year through 1886, falling 25 percent during this ten-year period. Chicago's debt reached its high point in 1871 and then gradually fell until 1889, dropping 11 percent. In Philadelphia the debt continued to mount until 1878 and then began a steady and consistent drop, declining one quarter by 1894. And between 1878 and 1884 Cleveland's municipal debt likewise fell 25 percent. Prudent Detroit, however, could claim the prize for paring municipal indebtedness. Its net debt had risen 160 percent between 1866 and 1875, but from 1875 to 1885 it plummeted from $961,000 to only $12,000.[18] Boston, Baltimore, Cincinnati, and Saint Louis did not substantially reduce their debts during the early 1880s, but their level of indebtedness generally remained static as city officials adhered to the "pay-as-you-go" policy. Everywhere the principle of retrenchment prevailed.

Moreover, throughout the 1880s and 1890s American cities could substantially relieve their inherited burden by refinancing indebtedness at lower rates of interest. Interest rates dropped steadily during the last two decades of the century, and the growing financial stability of municipalities meant that they could obtain especially favorable terms by the 1890s. For example, two-thirds of the debt incurred by New York City from 1872 to 1874 bore interest payments of 7 percent. In 1880 the average rate of interest on New York City's obligations was 6.1 percent. Yet by 1895 the average rate was only 3.9 percent.[19] Similarly, in the 1870s Baltimore was forced to borrow money at 6 percent; twenty years later the standard rate in that city was 3.5 percent.[20] Before 1875 Cleveland found it necessary to issue bonds bearing a 7 percent interest rate. Cleveland bonds issued after 1893, however, bore at most 4 percent.[21] By the 1890s municipal comptrollers and mayors throughout the country were boasting of the favorable terms they were able to negotiate. Early in 1895 Baltimore's mayor claimed that "no better evidence of the good credit of our city and the confidence of the community, in fact that its government is reasonably well conducted, can be given than the high price which its securities command in that most sensitive of all institutions, . . . the money market."[22] Two years later Buffalo's mayor proudly reported the sale of municipal securities at 3.3 percent interest, "a showing surpassed by few, if any, cities in the country."[23] And in 1899 Milwaukee's comptroller claimed that "there were many inquiries for Milwaukee city securities, and bond buyers said that if the city were to issue 3 percent bonds they would bring a satisfactory premium."[24]

During the Panic of 1893 city officials could be justifiably proud of the policies they had followed. While municipalities foundered in the Panic of 1873 and the ensuing economic depression, twenty years later, conservative fiscal policy saved them from a second debacle. Amid the financial disorder of the third quarter of 1893, municipalities did have some difficulty marketing their securities, but this setback was temporary. In fact, during the economic depression of the mid-1890s the credit of city governments remained unimpaired, with investors expressing their confidence in municipal finances. With investment in the private sector becoming increasingly risky, those with money put their funds into municipal securities, stimulating a boom in bond sales. Early in 1895 the *Commercial and Financial Chronicle* noted that "during the past year investors have manifested greater interest in municipal securities than ever before." According to the journal, the "eager and active demand" for municipal bonds was due to the fact "that there is no better security than a city bond." In the depression year of 1894 the volume of municipal bond sales was at least 40 percent higher than in the prepanic year of 1892.[25] And in August, 1894, the *Chronicle* reported that "the majority of American cities can place their long-time loans to better advantage at present than they have ever been able to do before."[26] In July, 1894, the city of Brooklyn was marketing long-term 4-percent bonds at a premium of 8.5 percent above par, and one month later, in sharp competition, nineteen investment banking firms bid for long-term 3.5 percent Baltimore bonds that sold at a 2 percent premium. By October, 1894, Boston was marketing 4-percent bonds at a 13.5 percent premium, and New York City was able to sell long-term 3-percent bonds at 3 percent above par.[27]

The economic depression of the 1870s had been a nightmare for both the business corporation and the municipal corporation. In contrast, the panic of the 1890s was only a business depression. Municipalities never enjoyed such a favorable market for their securities, for by the 1890s no investment was as sound as a municipal bond. No major city defaulted on its debt obligation between 1888 and 1900, and in the Panic of 1893 no municipality suffered the financial tribulations that Elizabeth and Memphis experienced in the 1870s. During the 1880s and 1890s, America's municipalities succeeded in establishing financial stability, and the rewards were decreasing interest rates and ready sales above par.

With interest rates declining and the level of municipal indebtedness remaining relatively steady, the annual cost of debt maintenance dropped sharply during the last two decades of the nineteenth century. At the close of the 1870s interest payments consumed a large proportion of all municipal tax dollars, cutting into the funds available for fire and police protection, street lighting and drainage, and public schooling. By the turn of the century, however, debt payments had become a much-less-significant item in the municipal budget. In 1880 28 percent of New York City's expenditures went for interest payments on the municipal debt, but by 1899 interest payments accounted for only 7 percent of New York City's disbursements. In 1880 Baltimore, too, allocated a hefty 24 percent of its budget to interest on its obligations, and interest payments also accounted for 21 percent of Cleveland's expenditures. Nineteen years later 11 percent of Baltimore's budget went for this purpose and less than 8 percent of Cleveland's disbursements.[28] Saint Louis levied a separate tax to finance its municipal debt charges, and the declining rate of this tax reflected the easing of the debt burden. In 1877 the tax stood at 90¢ on $100 valuation; during most of the 1880s it was 75¢; in 1888 it fell to 50¢; in 1892 it dropped to 40¢; and in 1899 it fell to 30¢.[29] Thus by the close of the century the municipal debt burden on Saint Louis taxpayers was only one-third of what it had been two decades before.

In the late 1870s city officials, reformers, and financial analysts condemned municipal indebtedness for draining the city coffers and imposing a yoke of heavy taxation on the citizenry. By the late 1890s, however, city government leaders had brought the situation under control. America's municipalities had survived a second economic depression relatively unscathed, with credit intact and confidence unimpaired. And they had reduced debt costs, freeing money for current expenditures. In 1880 heavy debt obligations limited the capacity of America's cities to finance services, since much of the city budget was reserved for interest payments. At the close of the century, however, hundreds of thousands of dollars formerly earmarked for bondholders were now available for everything from almshouses to zoos. Through retrenchment and refinancing, the nation's cities had seemingly made amends for their borrowing mania of the late 1860s and early 1870s and had realized the dreams of those dedicated to fiscal caution and conservatism.

By the end of the century, critics could not justifiably label America's largest cities as debt-ridden or extraordinarily prodigal. By international standards, the per capita debt figures of the leading American cities were not inordinate. Comparisons are difficult because some city governments, such as that of Chicago, exercised a limited range of duties, whereas others, like New York

City, were responsible for the full list of local services. As seen in table 12, however, in 1898–99 the per capita debt of the nation's largest cities ranged from $17 for Chicago to $105 for Boston. In Great Britain, Manchester's city fathers had saddled the citizenry with a per capita municipal debt of $150, while the figure for London was only $54. And in the major German cities the per capita municipal debt ranged from $27 for Dresden to $55 for Munich. Due to the costly improvements of Baron Haussmann and Emperor Napoleon III during the midcentury, Paris bore one of the most awesome debt burdens in the Western world, with a per capita obligation of $160. It should be remembered that Americans of the 1880s and 1890s were better able to bear such a heavy debt. The per capita income of American city dwellers far exceeded that of Europeans, and wage levels in the United States were approximately double those in Europe. The municipal debt of Breslau, Germany, represented a much larger portion of the total income of the community than the municipal debt of Cleveland or Philadelphia. All three cities had a per capita debt of $32, but $32 per person was a heavier burden in Germany than in Ohio or Pennsylvania.

At the close of the century some even felt that American municipal debts were too low. Given the favorable terms of credit prevailing and the continuing need for public improvements, it seemed a propitious time to embark again on a policy of borrowing and spending. In 1896 Cleveland's Mayor Robert McKisson boasted that "probably no other city of any considerable size in the State has as small a relative indebtedness or has been administered on more safe and conservative financial lines." Yet he also noted that the public was demanding new bridges, extension of the sewer system, and a network of parks and boulevards, improvements requiring massive expenditure. Mayor McKisson thus believed that the time had come to discard fiscal conservatism, declaring that "Cleveland can safely go forward with this work . . . and need not be bound by a limit upon indebtedness, such as exists at the present time."[30] In 1898 Chicago's Comptroller Robert Waller reported that

TABLE 12. Per Capita Municipal Debt, 1898–99

American Cities		British Cities		German Cities	
City	Per Capita Debt	City	Per Capita Debt	City	Per Capita Debt
New York	$73	London	$54	Berlin	$37
Chicago	$17	Glasgow	$59	Munich	$55
Philadelphia	$32	Liverpool	$90	Leipzig	$40
Saint Louis	$33	Manchester	$150	Breslau	$32
Boston	$105	Birmingham	$86	Dresden	$27
Baltimore	$64			Cologne	$29
Cleveland	$32				

Source: John A. Fairlie, *Municipal Administration* (New York: Macmillan Co., 1901), p. 332.

the "one great drawback to the proper administration and growth of the city is in the fact that the funded or bonded debt is limited to an insignificant sum compared with the resources of the municipality and its necessities." He specifically renounced the "pay-as-you-go" dogma when he argued that "all permanent improvements of the city should be paid for from the proceeds of bond sales[,] as they benefit not only the present but future generations who, in justice and equity, should bear their proportion of the expense."[31] In 1900 New York City's Comptroller Bird Coler urged an amendment of the state's constitutional restriction on municipal indebtedness, on the grounds that the 10 percent limit was hampering the development of the city. According to Coler, the constitutional limitation "should not be made a fetish to be worshipped blindly at the expense of really necessary progress." It was "wholly admirable at the time it was written," but Coler believed it was "not altogether adapted to modern requirements."[32] Saint Louis's Mayor Cyrus Walbridge also believed that times were changing, and he proposed an amendment to Missouri's constitution that would authorize the city to increase its bonded indebtedness by $10 million.[33] Likewise, in 1899 Philadelphia's Mayor Charles Warwick claimed that those who opposed an $11-million increase in that city's indebtedness were "dead to every public sentiment, actuated and controlled by spiteful, unreasonable, factional or sordid motives." Such opponents, he said, have "held the City by the throat like highwaymen and have checked her progress at every step."[34]

In Philadelphia opponents of borrowing were able to keep the level of municipal debt from rising during the 1890s. And in Chicago, Saint Louis, and Cincinnati constitutional restrictions or municipal policy also kept debt levels relatively constant throughout the last decade of the century. Other cities, however, responded to the favorable terms of credit and the cries for public improvements and chose to follow the advice of McKisson, Waller, and Coler. But the increase in municipal debt did not match that in the late 1860s and early 1870s. Municipalities turned again to the benevolence of a favorable bond market. Yet they proceeded with greater caution than in the years following the Civil War, for they knew that the favorable terms of today might become the awesome obligations of tomorrow. Thus, although indebtedness increased in some cities, it rose gradually, and city officials kept a much more careful eye on the ratio between debt and assessed valuation than they had in the late 1860s and early 1870s.

Boston proved the most willing and able borrower of all the major cities. In 1875 Massachusetts had imposed a statutory, rather than constitutional, debt limit on its largest city, and during the 1890s the state legislature repeatedly made exceptions to the restriction, allowing Boston to contract obligations "outside the debt limit." As a consequence, Boston's net funded debt rose 88 percent between 1890 and 1900.[35] Buffalo began the decade with a debt far below the sum permitted under New York's constitutional restriction, and like

Boston it thus had the opportunity to borrow. The result was a 60 percent rise in its bonded debt during the 1890s.[36] In 1890 Milwaukee's debt also was well below the constitutional ceiling, and during the following decade its indebtedness climbed 60 percent as well.[37] Likewise, during the last decade of the century Cleveland's municipal debt increased 70 percent.[38] And from 1890 through 1896, New York City's net debt rose by one quarter.[39] Each of these cities was able to take advantage of favorable conditions in the bond market in order to finance much-needed improvements that had been delayed during the retrenchment of the 1880s.

Thus America's cities had recovered from the financial embarrassments of the 1870s, had restored their credit, and were regaining their belief in borrowing as a means of funding permanent improvements. At the turn of the century, the municipal bond market was enjoying a golden age, and during the following decade more cities would turn to this source of cash. Civic reformers were publicizing the idea of the city-beautiful, a city of lavish appointments comparable to Paris. And municipal bonds seemed an appropriate means for financing these dreams of magnificent civic centers, boulevards, and parks. Between 1898 and 1908 the annual value of all municipal bond sales in the nation rose threefold, from $103 million to $314 million.[40] The fiscal conservatism of the last quarter of the century had established America's municipalities as a good investment. On the basis of this reputation for financial stability and strength, city leaders would fund the expanded services and upgraded public facilities of the late 1890s and the first decade of the twentieth century.

TAXATION

"Pay-as-you-go" was one pillar of the late-nineteenth-century policy of fiscal conservatism. The other was low taxes. Just as the economic depression of the 1870s produced an outcry against the burdens of indebtedness, it also nurtured a revolt against high levels of taxation. Americans facing hard times had little use for the municipal revenue collector, and their representatives in the state legislatures and constitutional conventions expressed this aversion by adopting statutory or constitutional ceilings on local tax rates. Even when some prosperity brightened the economic horizon in the 1880s, the bitter memories of grandiose public spending remained, discouraging officials from digging deeper into the pockets of taxpayers. Throughout the last two decades of the century, tax limits, together with debt ceilings, kept municipalities on a relatively frugal financial diet. The lush days of the late 1860s and early 1870s thus yielded to the thrifty 1880s and 1890s.

No period served as a better object lesson for teachers of fiscal conservatism than the 1870s. With municipalities committed to public improvement schemes and saddled with mounting interest payments, property tax rates reached new peaks during this decade. Especially following the Panic of 1873, as assessed valuations dropped and tax delinquencies rose, officials sought to compensate for lost revenues by hiking the rate of taxation. New York City's property tax rate rose to $2.94 on $100.00 valuation in 1875, a figure not to be equaled in the remaining years of the nineteenth century. Philadelphia's property tax rate peaked in 1877 and Baltimore's in 1878. In Boston and Cincinnati property tax rates soared and dipped erratically throughout the 1870s, both before and after the panic, and not until 1884 did the Massachusetts metropolis reach its tax apogee.[41] Throughout the country the 1870s marked a period of relatively high taxation, a fact that drew little applause from depression-ridden urban dwellers.

By the late 1870s and early 1880s, however, the call for retrenchment was growing, and this meant not only an end to borrowing but also lower taxes. In 1878 Cincinnati's mayor told the city council that "the extreme financial troubles throughout the length and breadth of the land . . . ought to teach us the greatest economy; all unnecessary expenses should be lopped off at once; we should live strictly within our means, expenses so curtailed that a reasonable rate of taxation would meet all demands."[42] That same year Saint Louis's comptroller argued that "the large debt of the City, the depreciation in values, and the stagnation in nearly every branch of business, all serve to urge economy, reduction of indebtedness and taxation."[43] Boston's auditor likewise reminded the city council that "excessive taxation . . . is paralyzing to the industry of a community."[44] And on assuming the mayor's office in 1879 Chicago's Carter Harrison, Sr., contended that the city's "heavy load of taxation . . . stifles energy, deters investment, and will, unless checked, dry up the sources of revenue."[45] Mayors and financial officers throughout the nation warned that it was not the time to embark on major public projects or engage in wild spending. Instead, municipalities were to abstain from borrowing and to keep taxes to a minimum.

To ensure that city governments did conform to this policy of thrift, lawmakers in a number of states established ceilings on municipal tax rates. Missouri's Constitution of 1875 specified a maximum property tax rate of $1 on $100 valuation for all cities over 30,000 population, thus curbing any tendencies to gouge the taxpayers in Saint Louis and Kansas City. This limit did not apply to taxes raised to fund debt obligations nor did it include school taxes, which were not to exceed 40¢ on $100 valuation.[46] Ohio's legislature first imposed a tax limit on Cleveland in the 1840s, but the limit was so generous that in 1881 the Cleveland City Council petitioned the legislature to lower the ceiling. The state's lawmakers readily obliged, and in 1888 the Cleveland council requested the legislature to retain the same limit rather than allowing greater taxing latitude.[47] In 1881 a tax-conscious committee of 100 Milwaukee citizens pushed a tax-limit bill through the Wisconsin legislature.[48] And four years later Boston joined the list of cities with tax ceilings when Mayor Hugh O'Brien urged the legislature to impose a maximum limit on municipal levies.

O'Brien argued that "there is no doubt that a high rate of taxation interferes with the growth and business prosperity of the city, and our expenditures should be based only on actual necessities." He contended that a ceiling on tax rates was essential in order to "stand in the way of reckless expenditure by any future City Government."[49] Tax limits also restricted the governments of Chicago, New Orleans, and San Francisco, binding them to a policy of moderate levies. No legal ceilings limited the taxing powers of some municipalities, such as New York City and Philadelphia. But in most of the nation's leading cities restrictive laws reinforced the rhetoric of thrift and curbed taxation.

The result was a decline in property tax levels in the 1880s and a generally stable rate of taxation in the 1890s. Although New York City's property tax rate equaled $2.80 or more per $100.00 valuation for four years during the 1870s, between 1882 and 1896 it never rose above $2.40, and it averaged $1.92. From 1872 to 1876 the Cleveland city property levy ranged between $1.85 and $1.88 per $100.00 assessed valuation, but from 1881 to 1899 it fluctuated between $1.315 and $1.615. After the adoption of a tax ceiling for Boston in 1885, the tax rate dropped from the earlier peak of $1.70 per $100.00 valuation and varied from $1.26 to $1.36 during the succeeding fourteen years. In Saint Louis the property tax rate for current municipal expenditures remained fixed at the constitutional maximum of $1.00 per $100.00 valuation every year from 1877 through 1900, and in New Orleans the city expense levy likewise was constant at $1.00 per $100 valuation from 1883 until the end of the century. Public pressure rather than state law kept the property tax rate down in Philadelphia. The rate had been above $2.00 every year from 1872 through 1880, but it remained a constant $1.85 from 1883 through 1903.[50]

To estimate the actual level of taxation, however, it is necessary to consider the trends in assessed valuation. Municipal officials might, after all, maintain fixed rates but radically raise assessed values and thereby squeeze additional revenue from the taxpayer. Actually, city officials did just the opposite. For example, in Cincinnati the tax rate remained stable from 1871 to 1900, but there was a growing tendency to undervalue property. Though the city's population increased 50 percent, the total assessed valuation rose but 15 percent, and the per capita valuation thus fell from $830 to $630. There is no reason to believe that Cincinnati residents suffered such a drastic decline in their wealth during these years. Instead, it is evident that assessors were growing more lenient, assessing property at a lower percentage of its true value. As a result, the effective tax rate, as opposed to the official tax rate, dropped in Cincinnati during the last three decades of the century.[51] The same was true for Baltimore. Despite increased wealth, Maryland authorized no general revision of valuations between 1877 and 1895, and Baltimore's total assessed valuation rose only 15 percent, whereas its population climbed more than 50 percent. There was no long-term rise in the city's tax rate, so the consequence was a decline in the per capita burden on the taxpayer.[52]

In none of the nation's major cities did the ratio of assessed value to actual value increase markedly during the last two decades of the century. It either remained relatively stable or it declined. City officials did not impose a hidden tax increase through juggling assessment figures. Instead, the effective tax rates were generally either steady or fell slightly, and the municipal exactions of the 1880s and 1890s were clearly less burdensome than those during the 1870s.

Thus city dwellers were not suffering from an increasing level of taxation. The prevailing policy of fiscal conservatism dictated both a reduction of indebtedness and lower taxes. Good times during the late 1890s encouraged some loosening of the restraints, but state laws and constitutional provisions safeguarded the cities from a repetition of the spending spree that characterized the years following the Civil War. Assessors were lax about raising valuations, city councils and boards of estimate were unable or unwilling to hike tax rates, and comptrollers were cautious about municipal debt levels. Economy, not expenditure, was the watchword of the age.

In some cities the sources of revenue were so restricted that the municipal authorities skimped and schemed in an effort to maintain public services. This was especially true of Chicago, where a statutory tax ceiling, a constitutional debt limit, and a tradition of ridiculously low assessments combined to starve the city government. The Illinois Constitution of 1870 restricted Chicago's debt to 5 percent of the assessed valuation, and in 1879 the legislature limited Chicago's property tax rate to 2 percent of the assessed worth of the city. Yet while Chicago's population soared, its assessed valuation and tax receipts increased only moderately. Between 1875 and 1897 the size of the city's area increased fivefold and its population rose 300 percent, but the valuation of property climbed just 34 percent. Year after year the gap between market value and assessed value grew as assessors kept the tax duplicate to a minimum. Assessors who were eager to please taxpayers and thereby win reelection made a concerted effort to undervalue property. In 1896 a tax commission of leading businessmen reported that the real estate in the central business district was assessed at only about 9 percent of its true market value. For example, the Chamber of Commerce Building, with an estimated value of $2,611,000, was assessed at only $230,000, and the Chicago Stock Exchange Building, with an estimated worth of $2,557,000, was assessed at $223,000. Throughout the city, assessment of property at 9 percent or 10 percent of the actual value was standard.[53]

The result was straitened circumstances for the city government. In 1897 a University of Chicago economist observed that the "people of Chicago have had a very cheap government" through the pursuit of a "parsimonious, penny-wise policy." The economist also observed that "the cheapest government is not always the best."[54] And Chicago was proof of this precept. Expenditures were low, but as a result the streets remained filthy and the garbage uncollected. Chicago's fire department and public library rivaled any in the world, but the city's niggardly financial policy prevented Chicago from equaling such a well-financed city as Boston in the full range of its services.

To supplement its receipts from property taxes, a needy city such as Chicago could turn to other sources of revenue. For example, every major American municipality other than Boston relied heavily on special assessments to help finance street improvements. The municipality levied this assessment on the owners of property abutting the street or sidewalk to be paved, and those cities with inordinately strict debt and tax limits found special assessments extremely useful, since such assessments were not considered taxes subject to the tax ceiling. Thus Chicago relied extensively on special assessments to fund the laying of water pipes and sewer mains as well as the paving of streets, alleys, and sidewalks. During the 1880s the receipts from Chicago's property tax averaged $5 million a year, whereas the bureau of special assessments annually collected an average of $3 million for public improvements.[55] Amid the mania for improvements in the late 1860s and early 1870s, New York City levied record special assessments, raising $5 million to $10 million annually between 1869 and 1876. During the frugal 1880s the city's special levies dropped to a yearly average of $1.5 million, equaling about 5 percent of the total city appropriations, and by the mid-1890s this average had risen to $4 million, or 10 percent of the municipal budget.[56] Likewise, in Cleveland the period 1873–75 marked the heyday of special assessments, with more than 20 percent of the city's receipts being derived from that source. By the late 1890s special assessments accounted for only 10 percent of the municipality's income, but they remained basic to the financing of public improvements.[57] In Cleveland, as in New York City and Chicago, the system of special levies allowed municipal authorities to grade streets and pave sidewalks even when revenues from the general property tax were far from adequate.

Also aiding municipal finances were a number of license fees and excise taxes on everything from dogs to shooting galleries. The most significant was the tax on liquor and saloons, which in part filled the financial gap left by the lower property levies. Foes of alcohol believed that saloonkeepers should pay an especially heavy exaction as wages for their sins, and during the late nineteenth century the liquor tax became a source of income for cities throughout the nation. In 1875 the Massachusetts legislature authorized a license fee on dramshops, and by the mid-1880s this fee was producing 4 percent of Boston's revenues. In 1886 Ohio's lawmakers passed "an act to provide against the evils resulting from traffic in intoxicating liquors" that levied an annual fee of $250 on establishments selling alcohol in Cleveland, and during the 1890s receipts from this tax accounted for approximately 7 percent of that city's income. In Milwaukee the fee for a liquor license rose from $30 in 1873 to $50 in 1874 to $75 in 1883 and finally to $200 in 1885. By 1888 this was producing almost 10 percent of the brewing capital's municipal receipts. In 1890 Maryland's Gen-

eral Assembly authorized an annual tax of $250 on liquor retailers in Balti-
more, and this tax immediately became second only to the general property
tax as a source of revenue for the city. New York City's receipts from an excise
on liquor sales doubled as a result of the passage of the Raines liquor tax law
in 1896. During the first year under the Raines law, the excise tax reaped
almost $4 million for the city government, or 8 percent of the total municipal
revenues. And in Saint Louis, dramshop licenses also accounted for a growing
portion of the city's receipts, rising from an average of 3 percent to 4 percent of
the municipal income in the late 1870s and early 1880s to 10 percent in the late
1890s.[58]

Nowhere was the liquor tax of greater importance than in Chicago. In 1883,
amid great controversy, temperance advocates secured the state legislature's
approval of a "high license" bill raising the license fee for Chicago saloons
from $103 to $500. Pitting native-born foes of alcohol against the disproportionately foreign-born defenders of drink, the high-license battle was not
simply a contest over revenues but another episode in the longstanding ethnocultural feud over liquor. A majority of Chicago's city council opposed the
increased levy, and Mayor Carter Harrison, Sr., argued that "it is unfair, un-
just, and unconstitutional to single out any particular class of the community
to bear the burden of taxation." Friends of the measure responded by describing opponents of the high license as "a rabble of rumsellers and renters of low
doggeries, whisky-soaks, hoodlums, and thieves."[59] The measure, however,
survived the rhetorical clash and proved a boon to the city treasury. In 1898
Chicago's general property tax raised less than $13 million whereas the city
comptroller estimated that miscellaneous sources, primarily saloon licenses,
enriched the municipal coffers by $3,553,000. By the 1890s, the saloon levy
produced over 15 percent of Chicago's receipts.[60] "Respectable" citizens might
complain about the involvement of the saloon element in city government, but
in Chicago the rumsellers were paying more than their fair share of the municipal bill.

Municipalities not only profited from whiskey, however, they also reaped
revenues from the more sober class of Americans addicted to the benefits of
water. For water was not a commodity provided free of charge. Instead, urban
dwellers paid water rents that financed the operation and expansion of municipal pumping plants and largely funded the extension of water mains. By the
early 1890s the rents paid for New York City's water amounted to more than
$3 million annually, while total property tax receipts ranged from $30 million
to $35 million per annum. During this same period Philadelphia's water re-
ceipts equaled over $2 million each year as compared with the city's yearly tax
receipts of $12 million. And in Saint Louis water revenues amounted to $1.2
million annually, whereas the property tax receipts averaged $5.5 million to $6
million yearly.[61] Moreover, no state ceilings or restrictions limited revenues
from this source. As a result the waterworks department was generally the
branch of city government that worried least about funding. In fact, water

departments occasionally were able to finance maintenance, repairs, and expansion and earn a profit as well. In 1895 Philadelphia's Department of Public Works happily reported an excess of collections over expenditures for the previous four years amounting to $2,160,000.[62] It was this steady stream of cash in the form of water rents that ensured American superiority in the supply of water. Other branches of municipal service had to rely on the pinched resources derived from the general property tax, but the waterworks enjoyed an independent source of income that paid for the expansive network of mains reaching to the urban fringe.

Sale of water may have brought millions of dollars into the municipal coffers, but one item was notable for the lack of revenue it produced. Although municipalities throughout the nation awarded valuable franchises to streetcar, gas, electric, and telephone companies, they received little cash in return. The reluctance of city councils to require public utilities to pay adequate remuneration to the municipality was, in fact, a subject of bitter complaint during the final decades of the century. In 1896 New York City's streetcar companies contributed only about $300,000 in franchise taxes, a sum equal to less than 1 percent of the municipal revenues. Four years later Chicago's street railways paid a little more than $100,000 in franchise fees, and during the last years of the century Saint Louis likewise averaged only $100,000 in special franchise levies.[63] As early as 1859 Baltimore included in its franchise agreement with the street railway a provision requiring the company to pay a percentage of its gross receipts to the city treasury. Yet through appeals to the state legislature, the company whittled down the percentage due the municipality, and during the 1880s and 1890s the street railway franchise tax only contributed an average of 2 percent to 3 percent of the city's receipts.[64] By the turn of the century franchises faced increasing pressure to pay a larger share of municipal expenses, but over the preceding three decades their contributions had been insignificant.

Water rents, liquor levies, special assessments, and even paltry franchise fees all helped finance municipal enterprise, but it was the general property tax that continued to be the mainstay of city finances throughout the late nineteenth century. Property taxes were the source of 70 percent to 80 percent of New York City's receipts during the last three decades of the century, and 75 percent of Boston's revenues likewise were derived from property taxes. In Baltimore property tax revenues amounted to two-thirds of the city's receipts, and in Cleveland and Saint Louis the property tax produced 50 percent to 60 percent of the municipal revenues. Even in tax-poor Chicago such taxes remained the single most important source of municipal income. This tax was, then, the chief means for exacting cash from the citizenry. Miscellaneous revenues aided cities caught in the tightening noose of tax and debt restrictions, but the property levy chiefly determined the fortunes of the American municipality.

By the close of the century, however, the property tax was the subject of considerable complaint. Criticism focused not so much on the level of taxation but on the question of who was having to pay the levies. Were those individuals best able to shoulder this tax paying their just proportion? Or was the incidence of taxation skewed to the detriment of certain groups? Municipal finance rested largely on the foundation of the general property tax. But who provided the brick and mortar for that foundation?

By the 1890s it was clear that large holders of personal property were not contributing adequately. The general property tax was theoretically a tax on both real estate and personal property, and each year assessors loyally reported the taxable value of both categories of wealth. Yet in every major city household goods, jewelry, machinery, inventories, stocks, bonds, and cash—all the forms of wealth included in the category of personal property—bore a dwindling portion of the tax burden. In the 1860s over 40 percent of the taxable property in New York City was characterized as personal property, whereas by the 1890s only a little more than 20 percent was in this class. Personal property averaged 34 percent of Boston's valuation during the years 1870–74, but by 1895–99 the average was down to 21 percent. In Cincinnati the proportion of the assessed valuation in personal property dropped from 34 percent in 1870–74 to 20 percent in 1895–99. By the close of the century personalty accounted for only 5 percent to 6 percent of Buffalo's total valuation, and in 1897 only 5 percent of Brooklyn's valuation was likewise in the form of personal property.[65] In Baltimore and Cleveland there was a comparable decline in the reliance on personal property as a source of revenue, while in Chicago personalty remained radically underassessed throughout the last quarter of the century.

There is no evidence that this proportionate decline in personal property reflected the actual trends in property holding. The late nineteenth century was a period of industrialization and corporate development. The percentage of capital invested in machinery was rising, and stocks and bonds were assuming unprecedented importance in the nation's economy. The new fortunes of the Vanderbilts and Rockefellers were as much in corporate securities as real property, but much of this escaped the municipal tax collector. Thus, as personalty grew in economic significance, its importance as a source of municipal revenue declined.

This was largely due to widespread evasion. Taxpayers did not declare their personal property, and assessors were not aggressive in uncovering such wealth. Intangible personalty in the form of stocks, bonds, and cash proved especially difficult to assess, since it was more easily hidden from the prying eyes of the local tax authorities than were grand pianos or expensive carriages. At the time of his death, the taxable personal property in the estate of New York City's William Vanderbilt was valued at $40 million, but during his lifetime he had been paying taxes on only $500,000.[66] New York City's authorities could tax the personal property in probated estates with officially ascertained values, but otherwise personalty proved elusive. "We only catch the widows and the orphans," admitted the city's tax commissioner in 1891 before a state investigating committee.[67] Elsewhere the story was the same. In 1883 in Cleveland a city council committee found that sixteen of the city's twenty-three millionaires listed no cash holdings for taxation, and thirteen reported no investments in securities.[68] This revelation, however, did not remedy the problem of evasion in Cleveland. In 1896 Cleveland's banks had $70 million in cash on deposit, but the tax rolls showed only $1.7 million declared for taxation.[69] Three years later Cincinnati's mayor said of personalty that it was a "well-known fact that only from ten to fifteen per centum of that kind of property is reached by the taxgatherers."[70] In 1894 Chicago's assessors listed only $44,000 in the hands of state banks, brokers, and stock jobbers, even though the state auditor's office recorded nearly four hundred times that amount in the city's state banks. According to the tax rolls for 1894, the total value of bank shares in Chicago's Cook County was only $357,000, whereas the state bureau of labor statistics estimated the market value of all such shares at $56 million.[71]

Reports of absurdly undervalued personal property were commonplace, and evasion seemed to be the national pastime. According to the Taxpayers' Defense League of Chicago, "one of the largest and most profitable of the department stores, making fully $1,000,000 a year profit, and carrying probably $2,000,000 of stock" had its personal property assessed at $45,000. Similarly, "a very wealthy banker and coal merchant, who is able to spend $13,000 for a rare Bible, and thousands of dollars for art, is assessed at his office at $400 of personal property, while the assessor finds nothing whatever at his home."[72] Such undervaluations were in part due to the negligence or corruption of assessors. But just as culpable was the property owner. Writing in 1898, Edward Dana Durand, the leading student of New York City finances, explained that assessors "regularly place on the rolls at the outset nearly double the number of names, and from six to ten times the amount of property ultimately retained." After the initial listing, however, New York allowed disgruntled taxpayers to correct or "swear off" their personal property assessments. In other words, citizens regularly perjured themselves, thereby reducing their tax burden. As one New Yorker noted, "swearing off one's personal taxes has become a fine art," with the tax on personalty practically becoming a "tax on conscience."[73]

Ohio's legislature sought to combat such evasion with a tax inquisitor scheme. In 1885 it authorized the county officers in Cincinnati and Cleveland to hire persons charged with discovering property not on the tax rolls, and the "inquisitors" would reap as compensation 20 percent of all the taxes recovered due to their efforts. This, however, proved both obnoxious and ineffective, an invasion of privacy that won the municipalities little added revenue. By the 1890s many regarded the tax on personal property as a farce that raised little cash but nurtured much deceit. In 1893 the Ohio Tax Commission concluded that "the system as it is actually administered results in debauching the moral sense[;] . . . it is a school of perjury."[74]

Some states obviated the need for perjury by legally exempting certain categories of personal property from taxation. In Pennsylvania horses and mules were the only personal property taxed by local governments. The state collected a levy on money, stocks, bonds, carriages, and wagons, but all other personalty was exempt. Manufacturing corporations were specifically exempt from all but real estate levies.[75] Likewise, in 1880 at the behest of Mayor Ferdinand Latrobe the Maryland General Assembly exempted Baltimore's manufacturing plants and equipment from municipal levies in order "to encourage the development of manufactures and manufacturing industry in the city of Baltimore."[76] Thus in Philadelphia, Pittsburgh, and Baltimore, the machinery, equipment, and inventories basic to industry were not subject to the municipal tax collector. Andrew Carnegie's steel mills and Philadelphia's giant locomotive works escaped local taxes legally.

With personal property contributing a dwindling portion of tax revenues, real estate naturally became the chief object of municipal exactions. And nineteenth-century Americans frequently complained about the assessment of land and buildings. Supposedly those with political connections won special treatment from the assessor, and always there were rumors of bribery and payoffs. Such charges are difficult to prove, but it does seem that assessors favored certain types of property. In 1894 the Illinois Bureau of Labor Statistics estimated that Chicago's downtown commercial property was assessed at 9.67 percent of its value; "choice" residences costing $20,000 or more were valued for taxation at 7.78 percent of their market worth; and "cheap" residential property selling at $4,000 or less was assessed at 15.9 percent of actual cost.[77] In 1898 the mayor of Cincinnati claimed that a similar malapportionment of taxes was prevalent in his city. He observed that "it does not require much scrutiny of [the city's] tax duplicates to see that the owners of small houses pay the bulk of our taxes on realty, and that, by some hocus-pocus, stately business houses and flat-buildings in the heart of the city are taxed much lighter, comparatively, than are the homesteads of the poor and middle classes."[78] The economist Edward Bemis added his support to this position when he noted that "throughout the country the people who are able to employ the most powerful attorneys and who growl the loudest, secure the lowest assessment, altho usually able to bear the highest."[79] In 1898, Edward Durand, the expert on New York City finances, likewise reported that "districts inhabited by small taxpayers and those where real estate transfers are least numerous, are, it is declared, rated too high in proportion."[80]

Given that assessment is by its nature a subjective procedure, and there is no sure means for ascertaining market value without actually selling the property, there will always be complaints against the system. But in the late nineteenth century the subjective process seemed especially detrimental to the owners of cheaper residences. Thrifty working-class families who purchased modest dwellings were less able to force a reduction in assessment than the wealthier classes, and thus they were probably more at the mercy of the assessor. In any case, the incidence of local taxation seems to have fallen more heavily on their shoulders.

In contrast, among the property most favored by assessors was unimproved land and land held for speculation in the suburban areas of the city. Short-sighted assessors usually did not assess vacant land according to its potential worth if developed, and thus such property was often grossly undervalued. In its survey the Illinois Bureau of Labor Statistics discovered that Chicago assessors valued vacant lots at less than five percent of their market worth.[81] The economist Richard Ely testified that "there is a common and iniquitous practice, which I observed everywhere in my investigations, of undervaluing land held for a rise, and not used at all."[82] Moreover, in some cities, less highly developed suburban land was subject to a lower tax rate than real estate in the urban core. Philadelphia's city limits encompassed 129 square miles, much of it rural or suburban. In 1868 the Pennsylvania legislature provided that Philadelphia's suburban property pay only two-thirds the tax rate levied on the built-up portion of the city and farms needed to pay only one-half. When Saint Louis expanded its boundaries in 1876, it agreed that the newly annexed area would shoulder a lower tax rate than the older portion of the city. Thus while the municipal rate for the heart of the city was $1 per $100 valuation, real estate along the suburban fringe paid only 40¢. Likewise, in 1888 the city of Baltimore more than doubled its area by annexing seventeen square miles of adjoining territory, but the law authorizing the consolidation provided that until 1900 the tax rate for the annexed zone should not exceed 60¢ on $100 and that the city should not increase the existing assessments of annexed property until the turn of the century. Whereas the older portion of the city was paying a tax rate of $1.90, the newly-annexed suburban wards paid a rate of $.60 on outdated assessments made prior to the development of the area.[83] In other words, in Philadelphia, Saint Louis, and Baltimore, smart speculators could hold land on the verge of urban development that appreciated markedly every year and yet pay tax rates far below those levied on depreciating slum properties in the urban core.

The municipal tax burden, then, was not strictly distributed according to wealth or ability to pay. Personalty, and especially intangible personalty, largely escaped the tax collector. In Philadelphia, Pittsburgh, and Baltimore manufacturing concerns received favored treatment, and in a number of cities commercial properties and the homes of the wealthy seem to have been assessed at a lower percentage of their true value than modest residences. And everywhere assessors were inordinately kind toward vacant land held for speculation. Those who paid the most taxes proportionate to their total wealth were working-class owners of cheaper dwellings who held no stocks or bonds and who frequented the corner saloon and through the increased price of drinks indirectly paid for the high license levied on the proprietor. Those who paid the least were the sober, well-to-do business leaders who eschewed the rum seller and invested in extensive intangible holdings, speculative suburban properties, and tax-exempt factories. It was, then, the members of the "respectable" business class, the "better element" of urban society, who enjoyed "most-favored" status under the municipal tax structure of the late nineteenth century. They might complain of waste and extravagance in city government, but municipalities trod lightly in their midst. The local tax burden was not mounting during the last two decades of the century, and those who belonged to the chamber of commerce, the board of trade, and the city club benefited from disproportionately low taxes.

Thus the late-nineteenth-century municipality did not exact extraordinary sacrifices from the business community. Tax assessment proved a subjective process liable to corruption and prejudice, and it would remain so in the twentieth century. But business leaders perhaps had the least reason to complain. During the 1870s taxes had soared at the same time that the economy tumbled, squeezing hard on some entrepreneurs. Yet the cost of municipal services during the last two decades of the century hardly imposed an onerous burden on the leading merchants, manufacturers, and real estate developers. Municipal license fees purportedly forced the closing of thousands of small dramshops. But municipalities provided members of the respectable class with water, sewers, parks, and libraries at a price that left plenty of cash in their pockets.

THE ECONOMIC MORALITY OF CITY GOVERNMENT

In 1890 over one hundred outraged New York City preachers signed an address urging voters "to overthrow the rule of falsehood and fraud that now disgraces our city." According to these irate clergymen, "the immense income of the city is fearfully squandered, and under pretense of urban improvement jobs are created which never realize the improvements, but put thousands of dollars in plunder into the pockets of contractors and their governmental allies." The preachers believed that the waste was so extensive that "it is estimated that the city of New York could be maintained in all its present condition for three quarters of the sum annually expended."[84] Similar claims and complaints appeared in editorials and petitions across the country. In Philadelphia, Cincinnati, and Saint Louis, for example, critics never failed to allege that self-seeking politicians were robbing the citizenry and plundering the public treasury. Throughout the nation many complained that citizens were not getting their money's worth from municipal government.

Such charges are difficult to prove or disprove. One could argue endlessly over what constituted an "honest" price for a square yard of asphalt pavement, or over what was the optimum number of city employees, whether this street cleaner spent the day leaning on his broom or that deputy clerk devoted his afternoons to the race track. It is clear, however, that actual embezzlement of city funds was relatively uncommon. In 1901 Frederick Clow, a New York City reformer and the leading student of financial administration in American municipalities, observed that "it is rare that money in the possession of a city treasurer is lost, and outright stealing by a treasurer is almost unknown."[85] In 1893 Minneapolis's treasurer was found to have loaned city money to private parties without the approval of the comptroller. A year earlier the assistant treasurer of Saint Louis squandered $63,000 of city funds, then set fire to the office of the treasurer in order to hide his theft, and, finally in desperation shot himself through the head. Likewise, in 1876 Chicago's collector of taxes embezzled at least $100,000 in municipal revenue, lavished it "on gamblers and card-playing friends," and then skipped town.[86] Yet such skulduggery was much more common in banks and business corporations than in city offices. And during the last quarter of the century, embezzlement was not a serious drain on any city treasury. Comptrollers, auditors, and commissioners of accounts imposed too many safeguards to allow anyone to steal very much for very long.

Subtler forms of pilfering seem to have been much more common. Padding of payrolls, favoritism in the awarding of contracts, and leaks of inside information were commonly cited problems, and some politicians frankly admitted profiting from politics in a manner that outraged those on the reform committees. In his well-known talks on practical politics, Tammany State Senator George Washington Plunkitt boasted: "I seen my opportunities and I took'em," and he boldly described how he profited from political connections and participated in what he termed "honest graft."[87] In 1899 a member of a legislative investigating committee asked Tammany boss Richard Croker, "Then you are working for your own pocket, are you not?" He answered bluntly, "All the time; the same as you."[88] Moreover, the fact that a number of leading politicians held stock in asphalt companies and street railways lends credence to the charge of corrupt alliances between businesses and city government. Few politicians were as open about their "honest graft" as was Plunkitt, but few Americans denied the existence of such practices.

Yet during the 1880s and 1890s graft did not lead America's cities to bankruptcy nor did it result in rapidly mounting tax burdens. Instead, tax levels remained stable and municipal credit improved while city services increased and public facilities expanded. In other words, graft remained at an economically tolerable level, a level that did not seriously disrupt the prevailing fiscal conservatism of the nation's cities. It may have existed, but it did not drive investment bankers to eschew municipal securities or force city governments into the arms of receivers. It may have tapped municipal treasuries of some of their resources, but American cities still provided many services equal to those offered elsewhere in the industrialized world and at the same time reduced their debts and kept their tax levels within state limits.

Dishonesty did, however, have a notable impact on the incidence of taxation. Bribed aldermen excused public utility franchises from levies that might have relieved the burden on other taxpayers. Even more important was the widespread evasion of taxes on personal property. For every bribed alderman there were twenty perjured members of the chamber of commerce who lied about intangible properties and thereby increased the proportionate tax load of those whose holdings were primarily in the form of real estate. Tax evasion proved a greater drain on the potential resources of the municipality than padded expense accounts or bloated payrolls. Yet this form of corruption was as much the fault of the citizenry as the city assessors. It was not a question of the people getting their money's worth from the municipality; it was a question of the municipality getting its money's worth from the people.

But what really troubled many Americans were the moral implications of corruption and graft. During the late nineteenth century graft was more a moral problem than an economic one. It had less effect on the bond market than it did on the content of Sunday's sermons. It was a symbol of the moral, rather than the financial, bankruptcy of urban society. The scores of clergymen who signed the address of 1890 cared little about New York City's ledgers. For them "this waste of money is the least evil." What troubled them was that "dishonesty in many forms pervades the community and loses its disgraceful stigma."[89] New York City may have been constructing a magnificent water supply system, a superb network of parks, the world's grandest suspension bridge, and other wonders of municipal enterprise, but in the process it seemed to be selling its soul to the devil. The books in the comptroller's office balanced and city bonds were selling well above par, but questionable figures crowded the council chambers and the nominating conventions. And the saloon seemed to have a larger role in politics than the church.

Even though city leaders pursued a policy of fiscal conservatism and kept indebtedness and taxes within the limits fixed by the state legislatures and constitutions, many believed the moral tone of municipal business was seriously deteriorating. In dollars-and-cents terms the American municipality had to a large degree triumphed over the serious financial problems it faced in the 1870s. By the 1890s it was no longer so vulnerable to economic fluctuations, and heavy interest payments no longer depleted the treasury of funds needed for current expenditures. Yet such facts made few headlines, and popular perceptions of municipal finances remained tarnished by tales of corruption and moral decay. The moral image of city government remained bleak even while the municipal ledgers told a different story.

11 TRIUMPH WITH THE TASTE OF DEFEAT

 On May 24, 1883, amid pomp and ceremony the cities of Brooklyn and New York officially opened the Brooklyn Bridge. The nation's president, Chester A. Arthur, five of his cabinet members, and New York Governor Grover Cleveland were among the dignitaries who rode in a grand procession leading to the magnificent bridge, where they heard three hours of oratory praising this latest wonder of modern engineering. The speakers at the dedication pronounced the bridge a "wonderful creation of genius," "a triumph of faith," "the sum and epitome of humane knowledge," and "a monument to the moral qualities of the human soul."[1] On that day of festivities all agreed that the world's largest suspension bridge was a triumph of American skill and ingenuity and a magnificent tribute to the wealth and creativity of the two cities that fathered the project. A century later it remains, along with Frederick Law Olmsted's parks and the Croton water system, one of the grandest achievements of municipal enterprise in New York City.

Yet those who attended the opening ceremonies in 1883 also knew that the triumph was tainted by a history of bitter conflict, supposed corruption, and political wrangling. Among the early sponsors of the bridge had been the notorious Boss Tweed, and accompanying his fall from power were revelations of questionable dealings among the bridge trustees. During the 1870s rumors of graft were commonplace, and feuding was constant, with new trustees allying against old ones. The board's chief engineer Washington Roebling fought year after year with troublesome officials, most of whom he deemed either ignorant or corrupt. Indeed, the "politics" of the project was among the factors undermining Roebling's health, leaving him an invalid during the final years of construction. At the completion of the bridge Roebling expressed his bitterness about the project when he wrote: "It took Cheops twenty years to build his pyramid, but if he had a lot of Trustees, contractors, and newspaper reporters to worry him, he might not have finished it by that time. The advantages of modern engineering are in many ways over balanced by the disadvantages of modern civilization."[2]

There was, then, a sour note in the litany of triumph raised in honor of the

Brooklyn Bridge. The cities of Brooklyn and New York had succeeded, but honors and laurels were not to be heaped upon their municipal governments. In fact, Abram Hewitt, the chief speaker at the dedication, devoted the final third of his oration to the subject of municipal misrule. Though he claimed that "no money was ever stolen . . . from the funds of the Bridge," he did assert that New York City had "not yet learned to govern itself."[3] Brooklyn and New York City had carried out one of the greatest engineering feats in human history, creating a monumental bridge far surpassing those built by any other muncipalities. In that age of high-flown rhetoric, few orators spared any praise when speaking of the civic glory of the nation. Yet on such a heady occasion for Brooklyn and New York City the speaker felt compelled not to laud municipal rule but to recognize its shortcomings. There were to be no kudos for municipal rule.

Hewitt's response was typical of American attitudes during the last three decades of the century. American cities achieved much, but they won the ignominious label of "conspicuous failure." Members of the upper middle class who complained loudest about the quality of urban rule benefited from an especially long list of municipal services. Abundant water, extensive sewerage systems, transportation to outlying residential tracts, great suburban parks, amply stocked libraries, and a free high school education, all these were due to the efforts of local government. And for those such as Hewitt with large intangible assets the financial burden was light. American municipalities distributed their services and benefits unequally, providing more for the prosperous than for the impoverished. But the achievements were manifold and many of the services were unsurpassed elsewhere in the world. The grandeur of the Brooklyn Bridge was symbolic of what America's city governments could and did create.

Yet for Hewitt and others the failure of municipal government in the United States was as obvious as the magnificence of the great bridge spanning the East River. Despite the splendid bridges and beautiful parks, America's municipal governments won little praise and less glory. Newspapers and reformers chose to publicize every fault or rumor of fault, and tales of corruption, whether true or false, made the headlines while evidence of exemplary service lay buried in the back pages. Throughout the period Americans refused to bestow unqualified praise on the municipal structure. Instead, the triumphs of city government were tinged with the taste of defeat.

Basic to this nagging dissatisfaction was the balanced system of municipal decision making. This system achieved magnificent ends, but too often the means seemed questionable. American city government at the time was a system of compromise and accommodation, a balancing act among elements of society that shared no mutual respect. Patricians, business leaders, engineers, librarians, partisan ward bosses, grocers, and saloonkeepers, all had their niche in urban government, and any major project or achievement involved a meeting of two or more of these diverse and sometimes hostile elements. Moreover, the making and implementation of policy often resulted from a bitterly negotiated truce between the various forces within the heterogeneous system. No single group or person pulled the strings of city government. The "better element" did not rule unchallenged nor did any party boss hold sovereign sway over the destiny of municipal government. Urban rule was a tug-of-war, with virtually everyone pulling for his or her own interests or schemes in a sometimes unseemly battle for victory. The poorest element of society, the station house lodgers and almshouse indigents, were generally not among the contestants, and thus they reaped the least rewards. But vendors seeking permission for a sidewalk stand, insurance agents battling for a better fire department, municipal engineers urging ever-larger projects, and chambers of commerce seeking more businesslike government (i.e., government by businessmen), all these individuals were playing the game of city government.

And each had to tolerate the other, like it or not. As Washington Roebling bitterly observed, the Egyptian potentate Cheops did not have to deal with trustees, contractors, and newspaper reporters, but in nineteenth-century New York no divine pharaoh ruled, nor could a civil engineer claim technocratic immunity from the nuisance of laymen. Roebling had to battle with lawyers and merchants on the bridge's board of trustees who knew nothing of tensile strength or structural stress, and had to ward off bothersome reporters who were more interested in the fabrication of scandals than the construction of bridges. The trustees, in turn, had to work with a civil engineer who knew how to span waterways but seemed oblivious to the political problem of exceeding estimated expenditures by millions of dollars. Meanwhile, newspaper reporters had to tolerate an engineer who knew nothing of the demands of a city editor. Thus, all of these individuals were forced to work with each other, yet none found it an altogether pleasant experience. It was, according to Roebling, a situation in which "the disadvantages of modern civilization" outweighed "the advantages of modern engineering."

Other experts knew well the irritation Roebling felt. A corrupt political boss who probably did not know the difference between a transit and a T square fired the highly distinguished George S. Greene from his post as chief engineer of New York City's dock department. Ignorant Boston aldermen who knew nothing of the literary classics challenged the request of the eminent librarian Justin Winsor for a higher salary. New York park commissioners whose aesthetic sense extended only to the beauties of black ink on the account books questioned the costly schemes of the preeminent landscape architect Frederick Law Olmsted and refused to work with the moody but brilliant Calvert Vaux. Pedagogues who wrote articles on all manner of educational theory had to listen to ward school trustees who still smelled of their butcher shops and livery stables. All these experts were members of emerging professions that claimed superior knowledge of their own special realms. Yet in the heterogeneous, representative government that characterized "modern civilization," each had to suffer lay interference.

Upper-middle-class leaders in the executive branch felt this same irritation. The millionaire businessman Abram Hewitt won the New York City mayor's office only with the cooperation of the Irish-born party boss, Richard Croker. While serving as mayor, Hewitt also had to tolerate the petty tradesmen on the Board of Aldermen, most of whom could not have gained entry through the front door of Hewitt's home. Throughout the country the nominating process was in the hands of common ward leaders, ill-educated "bummers" at neighborhood caucuses, and frequenters of saloons. "Gentlemen" might still win the leading executive posts in the city, but they did so only by working with those from the "lower element" of society. The old-stock Yankee Josiah Quincy of Boston, the pedigreed Carter Harrisons of Chicago, and Baltimore's distinguished Latrobe clan, all wielded power in late-nineteenth-century city government. All, however, relied on support not only from the districts populated by members of their own social stratum but also from the immigrant working-class wards. Businessmen and professionals might still dominate the vital executive posts, but they could only survive if they developed a flexibility that enabled them to appeal to the vast range of urban society. Unbending Victorian gentlemen dedicated to rigid upper-middle-class notions of morality and rectitude might at best win only one term in office. Thus gentlemen of principle often yielded to gentlemen of pragmatism, much to the dismay of those who could not adjust to the heterogeneity of urban life.

Not only did officeholders have to strike convenient bargains, so did business and professional groups seeking action beneficial to their interests. The chambers of commerce and boards of trade might exert a powerful influence over municipal policy, but they had to engage in the give-and-take of politics, for their views could only become law if they worked with state legislators and city councilmen who were themselves often creatures of a plebeian ward organization. The nation's leading physicians could only determine public health policy through cooperation with political figures, and even the likes of the sculptor Augustus Saint-Gaudens and the architect Richard Morris Hunt had to come down from the Olympian heights of artistic fame and petition common Tammany officials if they were to ensure the aesthetic integrity of New York City.

Bargains, compromises, and accommodations—all mainstays of politics—became a vital if unwelcome part of late-nineteenth-century urban rule. Government by an unchallenged social elite no longer existed. Nor had the emerging experts established unquestioned authority. Instead, power was dispersed among various interests, neighborhoods, and classes, each with its share of clout. Abram Hewitt could not govern solely according to the dictates of his conscience, nor could Washington Roebling be spared the intervention of politicians and the press in the construction of his bridge. Both had to accept the prospect of deals, accords, and compromises.

Such a system, however, grated against the Victorian sense of principle. It seemed a far cry from the unsullied republican virtue glorified in the schoolbooks of nineteenth-century America, and hardly accorded with the high moral standards preached from Protestant pulpits on Sundays. To prove successful as mayor, one had to distribute minor posts to partisan ward heelers and look tolerantly on German beer gardens and Irish saloons. In short, one had to play the game of urban politics, a game that violated traditional standards of rectitude and honor. For the urban system of compromise and accommodation was a product of necessity rather than principle; it was the bastard offspring of an uneasy union between the diverse elements of the expanding American cities.

Similarly, the ideology of the new professions offered meager support for the system. The societies of civil engineers, librarians, educators, and public health specialists inculcated in their members a belief in expertise and a contempt for interference by those not initiated into the mysteries of the profession. To hire someone on the basis of party loyalty rather than professional affiliation counted, in the eyes of the new experts, among the most serious of sins. By the 1890s expert civil servants had generally imposed standards of professionalism on the largest American cities, but occasional deviations demonstrated the essential flaws in the system.

For all their supposed flaws, however, American city governments did work. The Brooklyn Bridge was completed, a marvel of municipal enterprise unmatched elsewhere in the world. Likewise, water flowed through the city mains, fire brigades extinguished blazes with increasing efficiency, health departments prevented the spread of cholera and lessened the dangers of diphtheria, and urban parks provided recreation for millions. At the same time per capita municipal indebtedness declined and the tax burden remained within state limits. Amenable state legislatures readily responded to requests for change, maximizing the flexibility of the system and allowing it to remain elastic in an age of soaring population and new technology. Overall, prosperous Americans enjoyed public facilities at least equal to any in the world, and an especially well-governed city such as Boston probably surpassed all those in Europe in quality of services. Boston could boast of the world's largest and grandest public library, as well as a park system designed by Frederick Law Olmsted, the first subway in America, an innovative system of intercepting sewers, renowned public schools, and of course a typically American abundance of water. Moreover, it was one of the few American cities to provide public baths, municipal lodging houses for the indigent, and relief payments to the noninstitutionalized poor. Its low-interest bonds sold well above par, while state law ensured that its taxes remained within reason. Despite the rhetoric about failure and incompetence, cities like Boston successfully met the challenges of the age. Certainly there were problems: Chicago's system of taxation and assessment was ridiculous; Baltimore needed a sewerage system; slum neighborhoods throughout the country lacked parks and playgrounds; typhoid fever was too prevalent; and public utility franchises paid little into the city coffers. But if America's city governments fell far short of perfection, they were far from dismal failures in the provision of services and facilities. In the eyes of the citizenry, municipal rule often may have appeared an unholy accommodation, yet it produced results beneficial to the urban standard of living.

Moreover, this successful accommodation generally prevailed through the early twentieth century. Despite the efforts of progressive reformers, the balance was largely maintained. Good-government advocates of the period 1910 to 1930 sought to enhance the role of the expert in municipal administration through the establishment of city manager regimes, but the largest American cities rejected such plans. Whereas smaller municipalities hired civil engineers or full-time administrators as city managers to ensure professional guidance of local government, New York City, Chicago, Philadelphia, Boston, and Saint Louis never ceded such control to hired nonpolitical experts. In the largest cities experts remained vital to the administration of the metropolis, but they generally were subordinate to partisan boards or politically appointed department heads. Likewise, twentieth-century reformers often failed to eliminate the role of the political party in city government. In some cities, such as Cleveland and Chicago, twentieth-century municipal elections were officially nonpartisan, but the parties remained in charge of the nomination process and the ward leader and precinct committee member remained vital participants in the government of the municipality. Reformers also failed to undermine the influence of special interests, and petitioners for preferential treatment multiplied during the first decades of the twentieth century. The continuing trend toward centralization did weaken the neighborhood's role in the balanced formula of city government; however, ward representation survived in many large cities. And home rule provisions placed some limits on the state legislatures' role in the scheme of local government. Yet to a large degree the late-nineteenth-century system of accommodation persisted.

Despite its malodorous reputation, the framework of urban rule that was forged during the last decades of the nineteenth century succeeded and, in some measure, survived. It was no one's dream system of municipal government. It did not ensure absolute control by pure Anglo-Saxon Protestants who would govern with much-vaunted businesslike efficiency; nor did it give the Washington Roeblings, Frederick Law Olmsteds, and Justin Winsors free rein to apply their beneficent expertise to a docile public; or even give an Irish politician like George Washington Plunkitt all that he wanted in terms of patronage and party rule. Rather, it balanced the elements within society and provided the services vital to citizens in the industrialized world of the late nineteenth century. For persons of principle and gentlefolk who prized honor it seemed a failure, a system that violated the standards they valued. And yet American municipal government left as a legacy such achievements as Central Park, the New Croton Aqueduct, and the Brooklyn Bridge, monuments of public enterprise that offered new pleasures and conveniences for millions of urban citizens.

Notes

1. TRUMPETED FAILURES AND UNHERALDED TRIUMPHS

1. James Bryce, *The American Commonwealth*, 3 vols. (London: Macmillan & Co., 1888), 2:281.

2. Andrew D. White, "The Government of American Cities," *Forum* 10 (Dec. 1890): 357.

3. Edwin Godkin, "The Problems of Municipal Government," *Annals of the American Academy of Political and Social Science* 4 (May 1894): 882.

4. Jacob H. Dorn, *Washington Gladden: Prophet of the Social Gospel* (Columbus: Ohio State University Press, 1966), p. 303; Charles H. Parkhurst, *Our Fight with Tammany* (New York: Charles Scribner's Sons, 1895), p. 2.

5. Joseph D. McGoldrick, *Law and Practice of Municipal Home Rule, 1916–1930* (New York: Columbia University Press, 1933), p. 1.

6. Arthur M. Schlesinger, Sr., *The Rise of the City, 1878–1898* (New York: Macmillan Co., 1933), pp. 120, 391.

7. Bessie Louise Pierce, *A History of Chicago*, 3 vols. (New York: Alfred A. Knopf, 1957), 3:380.

8. Ernest S. Griffith, *A History of American City Government: The Conspicuous Failure, 1870–1900* (New York: Praeger Publishers, 1974), p. 283.

9. Sam Bass Warner, Jr., *The Private City* (Philadelphia: University of Pennsylvania Press, 1968), p. 98.

10. Paul Goldberger, *The City Observed: New York, A Guide to the Architecture of Manhattan* (New York: Random House, 1979), p. 27.

11. See, for example: Louis P. Cain, *Sanitation Strategy for a Lakefront Metropolis: The Case of Chicago* (DeKalb: Northern Illinois University Press, 1978); Stanley K. Schultz and Clay McShane, "To Engineer the Metropolis: Sewers, Sanitation, and City Planning in Late-Nineteenth-Century America," *Journal of American History* 65 (Sept. 1978): 389–411; Joel A. Tarr, "The Separate vs. Combined Sewer Problem: A Case Study in Urban Technology Design Choice," *Journal of Urban History* 5 (May 1979): 308–39; Clay McShane, "Transforming the Use of Urban Space: A Look at the Revolution in Street Pavements, 1880–1924," ibid., pp. 279–307.

2. NEIGHBORHOOD POWER: THE CITY COUNCIL

1. *New York Daily Tribune*, 8 Apr. 1890, as quoted in Frederick Shaw, *The History of the New York City Legislature* (New York: Columbia University Press, 1954), p. 3; J. R. Commons, *Proportional Representation* (New York: Thomas Y. Crowell & Co., 1896), p. 2. Others expressed similar sentiments. James Parton in "Outgrown City Government," *Forum* 2 (Feb. 1887): 542, 544, refers to the "little gang of dummy aldermen" and claims that "the general sentiment of intelligent New York now is, Let us have no more aldermen!" Alfred Conkling in *City Government in the United States* (New York: D. Appleton, 1894), p. 8, likewise wrote of aldermen as the

"worst class of public officers." See also E. S. Nadal, "The New York Aldermen," *Forum* 2 (Sept. 1886): 49–59.

2. Delos F. Wilcox, *The Study of City Government* (New York: Macmillan Co., 1897), pp. 209–10.

3. Edward Dana Durand, *The Finances of New York City* (New York: Macmillan Co., 1898), pp. 259, 261.

4. *New York Times*, 3 Jan. 1885, p. 4.

5. Ibid., 6 Feb. 1884, p. 4. See also ibid., 3 Jan. 1884, p. 4; 11 Feb. 1884, p. 4; 6 Mar. 1884, p. 1.

6. Conkling, *City Government*, p. 48.

7. Lincoln Steffens, *Autobiography of Lincoln Steffens* (New York: Harcourt, Brace & Co., 1931), p. 236.

8. *Brooklyn Union*, 30 Mar. 1875, as quoted in Harold Coffin Syrett, *The City of Brooklyn, 1865–1898: A Political History* (New York: Columbia University Press, 1944), p. 88.

9. Nathan Matthews, Jr., *The City Government of Boston* (Boston: Rockwell & Churchill, 1895), p. 169.

10. Charles Phillips Huse, *The Financial History of Boston* (Cambridge: Harvard University Press, 1916), pp. 245, 248.

11. "Address of Josiah Quincy," *Annual Report of the Executive Department of the City of Boston for the Year 1897* (Boston: Municipal Printing Office, 1898), p. 19; "Inaugural Address of Josiah Quincy," *Annual Report of the Executive Department of the City of Boston for the Year 1898* (Boston: Municipal Printing Office, 1899), pp. 15–19; *Boston Globe*, 2 Mar. 1898. p. 5; 3 Mar. 1898, p. 7; 9 Apr. 1898, p. 6. See also "Notes on Municipal Government—Boston," *Annals of the American Academy of Political and Social Science* 14 (July 1899): 142.

12. "Address of Josiah Quincy," *Report of the Executive Department of Boston for 1898*, p. 26; Moorfield Storey, "Municipal Government in Boston," *Proceedings of the National Conference for Good City Government Held at Philadelphia* (Philadelphia: Municipal League, 1894), p. 68.

13. "Address of Josiah Quincy," *Report of the Executive Department of Boston for 1898*, p. 26.

14. "Inaugural Address of Thomas N. Hart," *Annual Report of the Executive Department of the City of Boston for the Year 1900* (Boston: Municipal Printing Office, 1901), p. 5.

15. Jacob Piatt Dunn, *Greater Indianapolis*, 2 vols. (Chicago: Lewis Publishing Co., 1910), 1:314; *Manual of the Common Council Containing a Sketch of Buffalo* (Buffalo, 1896), pp. 74–75; Frederick R. Clow, *A Comparative Study of the Administration of City Finances in the United States* (New York: Macmillan Co., 1901), pp. 40–43. *Manual of the Common Council and Other City Departments of the City of Detroit, 1896–97* (Detroit: Thomas Smith Press, 1896), pp. 25–26; Donald D. MacLaurin, "Municipal Conditions of Detroit," *Proceedings of the Second National Conference for Good City Government* (Philadelphia: National Municipal League, 1895), pp. 382–83; *The New Charter for Baltimore City* (Baltimore: Guggenheimer, Weil & Co., 1898), pp. iv–vi.

16. Charles B. Wilby, "Municipal Condition of Cincinnati," *Proceedings of the Second National Conference for Good City Government* (Philadelphia: National Municipal League, 1895), p. 315.

17. W. E. Young, "The Commission Plan of Municipal Government," *City Government* 6 (Feb. 1899): 24–27.

18. Platt Rogers, "Municipal Condition of Denver," *Proceedings of the Second National Conference for Good City Government* (Philadelphia: National Municipal League, 1895), p. 426.

19. Isaac N. Quimby, "Municipal Condition of Jersey City," *Proceedings of the Second National Conference for Good City Government* (Philadelphia: National Municipal League, 1895), pp. 353–57; "New Jersey's New Street and Water Commissioners," *Commercial and Financial Chronicle* 53 (21 Nov. 1891): 770.

20. "The Management of Municipal Public Works in St. Louis," *Engineering News* 27 (23 Jan.

1892): 76–77; Robert Moore, "Municipal Engineering in St. Louis," *Journal of the Association of Engineering Societies* 11 (Mar. 1892): 124–33; Frederick W. Dewart, "The Municipal Condition of St. Louis," *Proceedings of the Louisville Conference for Good City Government and of the Third Annual Meeting of the National Municipal League* (Philadelphia: National Municipal League, 1897), pp. 225–27.

21. Harry A. Garfield, "The Municipal Situation in Ohio," *Proceedings of the Detroit Conference for Good City Government and the Ninth Annual Meeting of the National Municipal League* (Philadelphia: National Municipal League, 1903), p. 171.

22. Samuel E. Sparling, "Municipal History and Present Organization of the City of Chicago," *Bulletin of the University of Wisconsin Economics, Political Science, and History Series* 2 (May 1898): 140.

23. Edward P. Allinson and Boies Penrose, *Philadelphia, 1681–1887* (Philadelphia: Allen, Lane & Scott, 1887), pp. 294–96.

24. *In Memoriam: Arthur Dixon* (Chicago, Privately printed, 1919); Edgar Weston Brent, *Martin B. Madden, Public Servant* (Chicago: n.p., 1901).

25. *Proceedings of the Chicago Charter Convention* (Chicago, 1906), p. 249.

26. David A. Shannon, ed., *Beatrice Webb's American Diary, 1898* (Madison: University of Wisconsin Press, 1963), pp. 45–46.

27. Henry DeForest Baldwin, "Municipal Problems," *Municipal Affairs* 3 (Mar. 1899): 9. The most notable defense of increased aldermanic powers was Edward Dana Durand, "Council Government versus Mayor Government," *Political Science Quarterly* 15 (Sept., Dec. 1900): 426–51, 675–709.

28. P. Tecumseh Sherman, *Inside the Machine: Two Years in the Board of Aldermen, 1898–1899* (New York: Cooke & Fry, 1901), p. 31.

29. Baldwin, "Municipal Problems," p. 11.

30. George Gluyas Mercer, "Municipal Government of Philadelphia," *Proceedings of the National Conference for Good City Government Held at Philadelphia* (Philadelphia: Municipal League, 1894), p. 99.

31. Barbara C. Schaaf, *Mr. Dooley's Chicago* (Garden City, N.Y.: Anchor Press/Doubleday & Co., 1977), pp. 121–23.

32. See: *St. Louis Post-Dispatch*, 24 Mar. 1889, p. 3; *St. Louis Globe-Democrat*, 15 Mar. 1891, p. 21; 4 Mar. 1893, p. 2; 8 Mar. 1893, p. 2. Until 1884 Boston's upper house was elected at-large, but the parties ensured that their upper-house slates included a distribution of candidates from each of the city's districts. See, for example: *Boston Evening Transcript*, 6 Dec. 1876, p. 8; 29 Nov. 1879, p. 2; 5 Dec. 1879, p. 2; 29 Nov. 1882, p. 2; 5 Dec. 1882, p. 1. Boston also experimented with an at-large upper house in the mid-1890s. The upper house was elected by districts from 1884 through 1892 and again beginning in 1899.

33. Sherman, *Inside the Machine*, p. 67.

34. Shannon, ed., *Webb's Diary*, p. 63.

35. *Proceedings of the Board of Aldermen of the City of New York from July 2 to September 25, 1888* (New York: Martin B. Brown, 1888), p. 37.

36. Ibid., pp. 100, 115.

37. Ibid., p. 34.

38. *New York Times*, 14 Jan. 1880, p. 3.

39. Ibid., 14 Dec. 1888, p. 4.

40. Harold J. Jonas, "An Alderman in New York City, 1887–8: As Seen in His Journal," *New York History* 29 (Apr. 1948): 192–200.

41. Sherman, *Inside the Machine*, p. 70.

42. Ibid., pp. 68, 69, 71.

43. *Chicago Tribune*, 4 Apr. 1892, p. 4.

44. See, for example, the sketches in Fremont O. Bennett, comp., *Politics and Politicians of Chicago, Cook County, and Illinois* (Chicago: Blakely Printing Co., 1886), pp. 503, 538, 571, 581.

45. Shannon, ed., *Webb's Diary*, p. 104.

46. *Mayor's Annual Message and Seventeenth Annual Report of the Department of Public Works* (Chicago, 1892), p. 2.

47. *Chicago Tribune*, 4 Apr. 1892, p. 4.

48. *Chicago City Council Proceedings, 1888-89* (Chicago, 1889), pp. 325, 326, 339.

49. Ibid., p. 289.

50. Elizabeth T. Kent, *William Kent, Independent: A Biography* (Mimeographed by author, 1950), p. 126.

51. *Journal of the Select Council of the City of Philadelphia from April 2, 1888 to September 27, 1888* (Philadelphia: Dunlap & Clarke, 1888), pp. 13-17.

52. Ibid., pp. 28-31.

53. *Fourth Annual Message of Charles F. Warwick* (Philadelphia: Dunlap Printing Co., 1899), pp. xxxvii, xxxviii.

54. *Inaugural Address of Thomas N. Hart* (Boston: Rockwell & Churchill, 1890), p. 5.

55. "Inaugural Address of Thomas Hart," *Annual Report of the Executive Department of Boston, 1900*, p. 4.

56. "Report of the Superintendent of Streets," *Annual Report of the Executive Department of the City of Boston for the Year 1897* (Boston: Municipal Printing Office, 1898), p. 8.

57. "Mayor's Address," *Annual Report of the Executive Department of the City of Boston for the Year 1897* (Boston: Municipal Printing Office, 1898), p. 19.

58. See, for example, *Proceedings of the Common Council of Buffalo from January 1, 1895 to December 31, 1895* (Buffalo: James D. Warren's Sons, 1895), pp. 696-701, 779-84.

59. See, for example: *Proceedings of the City Council of the City of Minneapolis from January 7, 1889 to January 1, 1890* (Minneapolis: City Council, 1889), pp. 68-70, 77, 79-80, 84, 91-92, 96, 214-15; *Proceedings of the Common Council of the City of Saint Paul . . . for the Year 1889* (Saint Paul: Globe Job Office, 1890), pp. 57-58, 62-63, 79, 133, 139-40.

60. *Chicago Tribune*, 4 Apr. 1892, p. 2.

61. As quoted in Lloyd Wendt and Herman Kogan, *Lords of the Levee: The Story of Bathhouse John and Hinky Dink* (Indianapolis: Bobbs-Merrill Co., 1943), p. 200.

62. Sherman, *Inside the Machine*, p. 28.

63. *New York Times*, 11 May 1892, p. 4.

64. List of names and addresses in *Journal of the House of Delegates, St. Louis, from April 1877 to April 1878* (Saint Louis: Woodward, Tiernan & Hale, 1878); no page numbers in original.

65. List of names and addresses in *Journal of the House of Delegates, Saint Louis, April 1889 to April 1890* (Saint Louis: David Edwards & Co., 1890); no page numbers in original.

66. *Manual of the Council of Buffalo*, pp. 50-55.

67. *Manual of the Council of Detroit, 1896-97*, pp. 20-21.

68. List of names and addresses in *Manual of City Councils of Philadelphia for 1894-95* (Philadelphia: George F. Lasher, n.d.), pp. 3-10.

69. List of names and addresses in *Annual Reports of the Departments of Government of the City of Cleveland for the Year Ending December 31st, 1888* (Cleveland: Cleveland Printing & Publishing Co., 1889), no page number on the material; *Annual Reports of the Departments of Government of the City of Cleveland for the Year Ending December 31, 1889* (Cleveland: Cleveland Printing & Publishing Co., 1890); no page numbers in original.

70. *New York Times*, 10 Nov. 1882, p. 8.

71. Ibid., 7 Apr. 1883, p. 4.

72. *Chicago Tribune*, 26 Mar. 1890, p. 7; 1 Apr. 1890, p. 4.

73. *New York Times*, 10 Nov. 1882, p. 8.

74. Sherman, *Inside the Machine*, pp. 22-23.

75. Based on information from *Williams' Cincinnati Directory* (Cincinnati: Cincinnati Directory Office, 1887).

76. *Manual of Councils of Philadelphia*, pp. 3-10. For the occupations of Chicago's aldermen

of 1887 see *Chicago Tribune*, 6 Mar. 1887, p. 20. For the occupations of a typical group of Saint Louis councilmen, see *St. Louis Globe-Democrat*, 20 Jan. 1879, p. 8. The *Boston Globe*, 10 Dec. 1890, p. 1; 16 Dec. 1891, p. 1, lists the occupations of Boston's councilmen. See also *Boston Evening Transcript*, 11 Dec. 1899, p. 6.

77. Matthews, Jr., *City Government of Boston*, 171; John A. Fairlie, "American Municipal Councils," *Political Science Quarterly* 19 (June 1904): 243.

78. Sherman, *Inside the Machine*, pp. 22, 29, 30.

79. Kent, *William Kent*, p. 129.

80. See *Metropolitan Club of the City of New York . . . Constitution, By-Laws, and List of Officers and Members* (New York, 1897), pp. 39–69; *The Buffalo Club Constitution, Rules of the Club House and of the Board of Directors* (Buffalo, 1895), pp. 48–63; *Clark's Boston Blue Book* (Boston: Edward E. Clark, 1893), pp. 373–83, 441–53; *The Union League Club of Chicago* (Chicago, 1895), pp. 45–67; *Boyd's Philadelphia Blue Book* (Philadelphia: C. E. Howe Co., 1896), pp. 686–99.

81. *Society-List & Club Register for the Season of 1891–92* (New York: Society-List Publishing Co., 1891).

82. *Boston Blue Book*.

83. *The Chicago Blue Book . . . For the Year Ending 1893* (Chicago: Chicago Directory Co., 1892).

84. *Philadelphia Blue Book*.

85. For biographies of Chicago's aldermen of 1874, see M. L. Ahern, *The Great Revolution, A History of the Rise and Progress of the People's Party in the City of Chicago and County of Cook* (Chicago: Lakeside Publishing & Printing Co., 1874), pp. 205–49.

86. Sherman, *Inside the Machine*, p. 23.

87. Humbert S. Nelli, *Italians in Chicago, 1880–1930: A Study in Ethnic Mobility* (New York: Oxford University Press, 1970), p. 113.

88. Edward R. Kantowicz, *Polish-American Politics in Chicago, 1888–1940* (Chicago: University of Chicago Press, 1975), pp. 45–48.

89. Suzanne Ellery Greene, "Black Republicans on the Baltimore City Council, 1890–1931," *Maryland Historical Magazine* 74 (Sept. 1979): 203–22.

90. W. E. B. DuBois, *The Philadelphia Negro: A Social Study* (Philadelphia: Publications of the University of Pennsylvania, 1899; new ed., New York: Schocken Books, 1967), pp. 382–83.

91. Kent, *William Kent*, p. 120.

92. *Chicago Tribune*, 10 Apr. 1894, p. 1. For other descriptions of the garish floral displays at the opening session of city council, see: *Chicago Tribune*, 9 Apr. 1895, p. 1; *Philadelphia Evening Bulletin*, 2 Apr. 1894, p. 2; 3 Apr. 1899, pp. 1–2; Kent, *William Kent*, p. 116.

93. Kent, *William Kent*, p. 120.

94. *Municipal Register of Boston* (Boston: Rockwell & Churchill, 1890), p. 323; *Ordinances of the City of Cleveland* (Cleveland: Forman-Bassett-Hatch Co., 1897), pp. 1125–28; *Proceedings of the City Council of the City of Chicago for 1900–1901* (Chicago: John F. Higgins, 1901), pp. xlix–lii; *The Revised Code of St. Louis* (Saint Louis: Samuel F. Myerson Printing Co., 1907), pp. xvi–xvii; *San Francisco Municipal Reports for 1898–99* (San Francisco: Hinton Printing Co., 1899), pp.667–69.

95. Fairlie, "Municipal Councils," pp. 236–37; *Code of St. Louis*, pp. xiii–xviii; *San Francisco Reports for 1898–99*, pp. 664–70.

3. THE RESPECTABLE RULERS: EXECUTIVE OFFICERS AND INDEPENDENT COMMISSIONS

1. Edwin A. Greenlaw, "Office of Mayor in the United States," *Municipal Affairs* 3 (Mar. 1899): 38, 40, 51; James M. Bugbee, "The City Government of Boston," *Johns Hopkins University Studies in Historical and Political Science* 5 (Mar. 1887): 27; Edward P. Allinson and Boies

Penrose, *Philadelphia, 1681–1887: A History of Municipal Development* (Philadelphia: Allen, Lane & Scott, 1887), p. 157; *Boston Evening Transcript*, 7 Nov. 1854, p. 2; 14 Nov. 1854, p. 2.

2. Alfred Conkling, *City Government in the United States* (New York: D. Appleton, 1894), p. 38: Samuel E. Sparling, "Municipal History and Present Organization of the City of Chicago," *Bulletin of the University of Wisconsin Economics, Political Science, and History Series* 2 (May 1898): 92–93; King v. Chicago, 111 Ill. 63 (1884); Marshall S. Snow, "The City Government of Saint Louis," *Johns Hopkins University Studies in Historical and Political Science* 5 (Apr. 1887): 23; *The Scheme of Separation between St. Louis City and County and the Charter of the City of St. Louis* (Saint Louis: Daly Printing Co., 1888), p. 63.

3. *Chicago Tribune*, 1 Apr. 1883, p. 4.

4. *Proceedings of the Board of Aldermen of the City of New York* (New York: Martin B. Brown, 1888), p. 86.

5. Conkling, *City Government*, p. 39.

6. Ibid.; Harold C. Syrett, *The City of Brooklyn, 1865–1898: A Political History* (New York: Columbia University Press, 1944), p. 136.

7. See *Chicago City Council Proceedings* for 1882 through 1889.

8. See the journals of the proceedings of the first and second branches of the Baltimore City Council for 1882 through 1889.

9. Greenlaw, "Office of Mayor," pp. 48–49, 50, 53, 54; Bugbee, "Government of Boston," pp. 39, 45; Allinson and Penrose, *Philadelphia*, p. 350; *New York Times*, 21 Feb. 1884, p. 5; 25 Mar. 1884, p. 4.

10. Allan Nevins, *Abram S. Hewitt, with Some Account of Peter Cooper* (New York: Harper & Bros., 1935), p. 480.

11. Sparling, "Municipal History of Chicago," p. 86.

12. Syrett, *Brooklyn*, p. 109.

13. Greenlaw, "Office of Mayor," pp. 47, 59; Bugbee, "Government of Boston," p. 45.

14. *New York Times*, 1 Jan. 1895, p. 2; 3 Jan. 1895, p. 2; 6 Feb. 1895, p. 8; 7 Feb. 1895, p. 1.

15. William M. Ivins, *Machine Politics and Money in Elections in New York City* (New York: Harper & Bros., 1887), p. 56.

16. For biographical data on mayors, see Melvin G. Holli and Peter d'A. Jones, eds., *Biographical Dictionary of American Mayors, 1820–1980* (Westport, Conn: Greenwood Press, 1981).

17. Ibid.

18. *Philadelphia Press*, 22 Dec. 1894, p. 2; 7 Jan. 1895, p. 2; *New York Times*, 30 Dec. 1894, p. 2; John Lukacs, *Philadelphia: Patricians and Philistines, 1900–1950* (New York: Farrar, Straus, Giroux, 1981), p. 65.

19. *Philadelphia Press*, 9 Jan. 1895, p. 1; 10 Jan. 1895, p. 2.

20. Nevins, *Hewitt*, pp. 510–14.

21. *Chicago Tribune*, 29 Mar. 1885, p. 10; Claudius O. Johnson, *Carter Henry Harrison, I: Political Leader* (Chicago: University of Chicago Press, 1928), pp. 189, 195.

22. For information on Pingree, see Melvin G. Holli, *Reform in Detroit: Hazen S. Pingree and Urban Politics* (New York: Oxford University Press, 1969).

23. Frederick R. Clow, *A Comparative Study of the Administration of City Finances in the United States* (New York: Macmillan Co., 1901), pp. 73–83; Senior Class in the Wharton School of Finance and Economy, *The City Government of Philadelphia: A Study in Municipal Administration* (Philadelphia: University of Pennsylvania, 1893), pp. 74–79.

24. Clow, *Administration of City Finances*, pp. 79–80.

25. Ibid., pp. 38–43; Edward Dana Durand, *The Finances of New York City* (New York: Macmillan Co., 1898), pp. 264–65.

26. Henry DeForest Baldwin, "The City's Purse," *Municipal Affairs* 1 (June 1897): 349; Henry DeForest Baldwin, "Municipal Problems," ibid. 3 (Mar. 1899): 15.

27. Sparling, "Municipal History of Chicago," p. 101.

28. Allinson and Penrose, *Philadelphia*, p. 285.

29. *New York Tribune*, 14 Oct. 1876, p. 2; 14 Dec. 1880, p. 4. See also, John Foord, *The Life and Public Services of Andrew Haswell Green* (Garden City, N. Y.: Doubleday, Page & Co., 1913), pp. 114–73.

30. *New York Tribune*, 11 Dec. 1880, p. 4.

31. *New York Times*, 12 Dec. 1889, p. 9.

32. Ibid., 4 Aug. 1893, p. 8.

33. *New York Herald*, 17 Aug. 1899, pp. 3, 5; 18 Aug. 1899, pp. 3, 6, 8; 19 Aug. 1899, p. 6; 20 Aug. 1899, p. 6; 22 Aug. 1899, p. 3; *New York Evening Journal*, 24 Aug. 1899, p. 1; 26 Aug. 1899, p. 4; 30 Aug. 1899, pp. 1–2; 31 Aug. 1899, p. 4.

34. George Vickers, *The Fall of Bossism* (Philadelphia: Press of A. C. Bryson, 1883), p. 31.

35. Commonwealth *ex rel.* List v. Page, 13 Weekly Note of Cases 533 (1883).

36. Dechert, City Controller, etc. v. The Commonwealth, *ex rel.* Smart, 113 Pa. 239 (1886).

37. *New York Times*, 21 Mar. 1918, p. 13.

38. *Chicago Tribune*, 14 May 1879, p. 4.

39. *Economist* (Chicago) 17 (17 Apr. 1897): 412–13.

40. Carter H. Harrison, Jr., *Stormy Years: The Autobiography of Carter H. Harrison, Five Times Mayor of Chicago* (Indianapolis: Bobbs-Merrill Co., 1935), p. 134. For information on Waller's background, see *Chicago Tribune*, 18 Feb. 1899, p. 1.

41. *Chicago Tribune*, 30 Dec. 1893, p. 4; 31 Dec. 1893, p. 2.

42. *New York Times*, 12 May 1896, p. 9.

43. Ibid.; *New York Tribune*, 12 May 1896, p. 7.

44. *New York Times*, 13 May 1896, p. 9.

45. Ibid., 27 May 1896, p. 9.

46. Ibid., 19 May 1896, p. 8.

47. *New York Tribune*, 24 May 1896, p. 13; *New York Times*, 24 May 1896, p. 9; 6 June 1896, p. 9.

48. *City of New York Law Department—Report for Year Ending December 31, 1893* (New York: Martin B. Brown, 1894), pp. v–vi; "Annual Report of the Law Department," *Annual Report of the Executive Department of the City of Boston for the Year 1893* (Boston: Rockwell & Churchill, 1894), p. 2; *San Francisco Municipal Reports for the Fiscal Year 1892–93* (San Francisco: James H. Barry, 1893), pp. 265–66.

49. *New York Law Department Report for 1893*, p. ix.

50. *City of New York Law Department—Report for the Year Ending Dec. 31, 1895* (New York: Martin B. Brown, 1896), p. viii–ix.

51. *Annual Report of the Departments of Government of the City of Cleveland for the Year Ending December 31, 1895* (Cleveland: Brooks Co., 1896), p. 775; *The Mayor's Message, with Accompanying Documents* (Saint Louis: Nixon-Jones Printing Co., 1897), p. 40.

52. *Opinions of the Corporation Counsel and Assistants from April 5, 1897 to April 10, 1905* (Chicago: City of Chicago, 1905), pp. 7–11; Adolf Kraus, *Reminiscences and Comments* (Chicago: Toby Rubovits, 1925), pp. 116–17, 120–21; *Chicago Tribune*, 20 Apr. 1897, p. 7; Joseph Bush Kingsbury, "Municipal Personnel Policy in Chicago, 1895–1915" (Ph.D. dissertation, University of Chicago, 1923), pp. 58–59; The People v. Kipley, 171 Ill. 44 (1897); The People v. Loeffler, 175 Ill. 585 (1898).

53. *New York Law Department Report for 1895*, p. xv.

54. *Annual Report of Cleveland for 1895*, p. 775.

55. *New York Law Department Report for 1895*, pp. ix–x.

56. *Register of the Department of Justice* (Washington, D.C.: U.S. Government Printing Office, 1895), pp. 5–9. In 1893 Philadelphia employed eighteen attorneys in its law department. Senior Class of Wharton School, *Government of Philadelphia*, p. 84.

57. Mark D. Hirsch, *William C. Whitney: Modern Warwick* (New York: Dodd, Mead & Co., 1948), pp. 94–96; W. J. K. Kenny, "William C. Whitney," *World's Work* 4 (May 1902): 2109–10.

58. For information on New York City's corporation counsels and their assistants, see John H.

Greener, *A History of the Office of the Law Department of the City of New York* (New York, 1912).

59. *New York Tribune*, 12 Jan. 1897, p. 7; *New York Times*, 12 Jan. 1897, p. 12.

60. Kevin Tierney, *Darrow: A Biography* (New York: Thomas Y. Crowell Co., 1979), pp. 51–57.

61. "Memoir of John P. Healy," *Municipal Register for the Year 1882* (Boston: Rockwell & Churchill, 1882), pp. 255–76.

62. Harrison, Jr., *Stormy Years*, p. 122.

63. Ibid., pp. 122–23.

64. *New York Times*, 10 Apr. 1889, p. 4.

65. Ibid., p. 8.

66. *Boston Evening Transcript*, 6 Feb. 1885, p. 4; 7 Feb. 1885, p. 4; 13 Feb. 1885, p. 1; 25 Feb. 1885, p. 1; 28 Feb. 1885, p. 4; 23 Mar. 1885, p. 2; 16 Apr. 1885, p. 4; 17 Apr. 1885, pp. 3, 4.

67. *Cincinnati Enquirer*, 23 Mar. 1886, p. 1; 27 Mar. 1886, p. 4; 28 Mar. 1886, pp. 4, 12; 30 Mar. 1886, pp. 1, 4; *General and Local Acts Passed and Joint Resolutions Adopted, 1886* (Columbus, Ohio: Myers Bros., 1886), pp. 47–60; 237–39; *Annual Reports of the City Departments of the City of Cincinnati for the Year Ending December 31, 1889* (Cincinnati: Commercial Gazette, 1890), p. 205.

68. Glen E. Holt, "Private Plans for Public Spaces: The Origins of Chicago's Park System, 1850–1875," *Chicago History* 8 (Fall 1979): 173–84.

69. *The Chicago Blue Book . . . for the Year Ending 1893* (Chicago: Chicago Directory Co., 1892).

70. *Municipal Code of the South Park Commissioners* (Chicago: E. B. Myers & Co., 1897); no page numbers in original.

71. *Report of the Commissioners and A History of Lincoln Park* (Chicago: Lincoln Park Commissioners, 1899); *Report of the Commissioners of Lincoln Park from December 1, 1886 to January 1, 1893* (Chicago: George E. Marshall & Co., 1893), p. 3.

72. Sparling, "Municipal History of Chicago," p. 148.

73. *Boyd's Philadelphia Blue Book* (Philadelphia: C. E. Howe Co., 1896).

74. *Sixth Report of the Commissioners of Fairmount Park, December 31, 1899* (Philadelphia, 1900), pp. 4–6.

75. J. H. Hollander, *The Financial History of Baltimore* (Baltimore: Johns Hopkins Press, 1899), pp. 247–49.

76. *Fifty-fourth Annual Report of the Board of Park Commissioners* (San Francisco, 1924), p. 56; *Fortieth Annual Report of the Board of Park Commissioners of San Francisco for the Year Ending June 30, 1910* (San Francisco: Dickinson & Scott, 1910), pp. 17–27.

77. *Ninetieth Annual Report of the Board of Commissioners, Tower Grove Park* (Saint Louis, 1959), pp. 4–7.

78. John W. Perrin, *A History of the Cleveland Sinking Fund of 1862* (Cleveland: Arthur G. Clark Co., 1914), pp. 37–38; William G. Rose, *Cleveland: The Making of a City* (Cleveland: World Publishing Co., 1950), pp. 543–44.

79. *Annual Reports of the Brooklyn Park Commissioners, 1861–1873* (Brooklyn, 1873), pp. 11–19; *Thirty-sixth Annual Report of the Department of Parks of the City of Brooklyn for the Year 1896* (Brooklyn: Eagle Press, 1897), pp. 213, 219–22; Syrett, *Brooklyn*, p. 142. In 1882 the new Brooklyn charter placed the Board of Park Commissioners under the direct control of the mayor. This ended Stranahan's dominance.

80. See annual reports of Buffalo park commissioners 1869 through 1897; Walter S. Dunn, Jr., *History of Erie County, 1870–1970* (Buffalo: Buffalo & Erie County Historical Society, 1972), p. 95.

81. See annual reports of the librarian to the board of trustees of the Enoch Pratt Free Library for the years 1887 to 1900; *The Enoch Pratt Free Library of Baltimore City: Thirty-sixth Annual Report of the Librarian to the Board of Trustees for the Year 1921* (Baltimore, 1922), p. 6; Philip

A. Kalisch, *The Enoch Pratt Free Library: A Social History* (Metuchen, N.J.: Scarecrow Press, 1969), pp. 53–54.

82. William B. Shaw, "The Carnegie Libraries," *Review of Reviews* 12 (Oct. 1895): 429–33; *Third Annual Reports to the Board of Trustees of the Carnegie Library of Pittsburgh for the Year Ending January 31, 1899* (Pittsburgh, 1899), pp. 4, 6.

83. *The Free Library of Philadelphia, Eighth Annual Report, 1903* (Philadelphia, 1903), p. 36.

84. Phyllis Dain, *The New York Public Library: A History of Its Founding and Early Years* (New York: New York Public Library, 1972), pp. 80, 175, 178, 230.

85. Ray E. Held, *The Rise of the Public Library in California* (Chicago: American Library Association, 1973), pp. 3–7, 9–10.

86. *Eighteenth Annual Report of the Milwaukee Public Library, 1895* (Milwaukee: Board of Trustees, 1895), pp. 54–55; W. F. Poole, "The Milwaukee Library Law," *Library Journal* 3 (July 1878): 190–91.

87. *Fisk Free and Public Library of New Orleans: Historical Sketch, By-Laws* (New Orleans: L. Graham & Son, 1897), p. 10.

88. Horace G. Wadlin, *The Public Library of the City of Boston, A History* (Boston: Trustees of the Library, 1911), p. 75.

89. Ibid., pp. 76–79; Walter Muir Whitehill, *Boston Public Library: A Centennial History* (Cambridge: Harvard University Press, 1956), pp. 110–11.

90. C. C. Soule, "The Boston Public Library," *Library Journal* 17 (Mar. 1892): 92. For a list of the trustees and their years of service on the board, see *Fifty-sixth Annual Report of the Trustees of the Public Library of the City of Boston, 1907–1908* (Boston: Municipal Printing Office, 1908), pp. 99–100.

91. Perrin, *Cleveland Sinking Fund*, p. 7. The Cleveland City Council had to confirm those elected to vacancies on the sinking-fund board, but this did not prove a significant check on the independence of the trustees.

92. For the names and terms of service of those on the Cincinnati sinking-fund board, see *Thirtieth Annual Report of the Board of Trustees of the Sinking Fund* (Cincinnati: Commercial-Gazette, 1907).

93. Horace P. Phillips, *History of the Bonded Debt of the City of New Orleans, 1822–1933* (New Orleans, 1933), p. 6. For information on the creation of the board of liquidation, see *New Orleans Daily Picayune*, 21 Feb. 1880, p. 4; 7 Mar. 1880, p. 2; 7 Apr. 1880, p. 3.

94. For the names and terms of service of the directors of city trusts, see *Thirty-first Annual Report of the Board of Directors of City Trusts of the City of Philadelphia for the Year 1900* (Philadelphia: Allen, Lane & Scott, 1901), pp. 467–68; Senior Class of Wharton School, *Government of Philadelphia*, pp. 226–29.

95. T. H. Watkins, "Selection of School Boards: A Comparison of Methods in Operation," *National Education Association Journal of Proceedings and Addresses of the Thirty-Sixth Annual Meeting* (Chicago: University of Chicago Press, 1897), pp. 988–90; James C. Boykin, "Organization of City School Boards," *Educational Review* 13 (Mar. 1897): 232–45.

96. Joseph M. Cronin, *The Control of Urban Schools* (New York: Free Press, 1973), pp. 44–52.

97. *St. Louis Post-Dispatch*, 19 Feb. 1887, p. 4; Elinor Mondale Gersman, "Progressive Reform of the St. Louis School Board, 1897," *History of Education Quarterly* 10 (Spring 1970): 4.

98. C. B. Gilbert, "Discussions: Large School Boards or Small?" *Educational Review* 4 (Sept. 1892): 181.

99. William H. Issel, "Modernization in Philadelphia School Reform, 1882–1905," *Pennsylvania Magazine of History and Biography* 94 (July 1970): 365; *Philadelphia Press*, 6 Jan. 1895, p. 4.

100. Diane Ravitch, *The Great School Wars: New York City, 1805–1973* (New York: Basic Books, 1974), p. 147.

101. *Philadelphia Press*, 4 Oct. 1895, p. 3.

102. Gilbert, "Large Boards or Small?," p. 179.

103. Gersman, "St. Louis School Board," pp. 7, 15.

104. See *World Almanac, 1897* (New York: Press Publishing Co., 1897), p. 492.

4. STATE LEGISLATURES AND URBAN AMERICA

1. See Frank Parsons, *The City for the People* (Philadelphia: C. F. Taylor, 1901), chap. 3; Robert T. Crane, "Municipal Home Rule in Michigan," *Proceedings of the Fourth Annual Convention of the Illinois Municipal League* (Urbana, Ill., 1917), p. 61; Walter Tallmadge Arndt, *The Emancipation of the City* (New York: Duffield & Co., 1917), p. 15.

2. Howard Lee McBain, *The Law and the Practice of Municipal Home Rule* (New York: Columbia University Press, 1916), p. 28.

3. Samuel P. Hays, *The Response to Industrialism, 1885–1914* (Chicago: University of Chicago Press, 1957), p. 107. See also: Charles N. Glaab and A. Theodore Brown, *A History of Urban America*, 2nd ed. (New York: Macmillan Co., 1976), pp. 163–64; Zane L. Miller, *The Urbanization of Modern America, A Brief History* (New York: Harcourt Brace Jovanovich, 1973), pp. 54–55; Bayrd Still, *Urban America, A History with Documents* (Boston: Little, Brown & Co., 1974), p. 327.

4. For expression of this view by the highest court in the land see: United States v. Baltimore & Ohio R.R. Co., 17 Wall. (U.S.) 322, 329 (1873); Barnes v. District of Columbia, 91 U.S. 540, 544–46 (1876); Board of County Commissioners of Laramie County v. Board of County Commissioners of Albany County, 92 U.S. 307, 308 (1876); Mount Pleasant v. Beckwith, 100 U.S. 514, 524 (1880); Meriwether v. Garrett, 102 U.S. 472, 511 (1880). Thomas M. Cooley's doctrine of the inherent right of local self-government enunciated in People *ex rel.* LeRoy v. Hurlbut, 24 Mich. 44 (1871) represents an abortive attempt to reverse the trend of legal development.

5. Edward P. Allinson and Boies Penrose, *Philadelphia, 1681–1887: A History of Municipal Development* (Philadelphia: Allen, Lane & Scott, 1887), pp. 267–69.

6. Brenda K. Shelton, *Reformers in Search of Yesterday: Buffalo in the 1890s* (Albany: State University of New York Press, 1976), pp. 48–53; J. H. Hollander, *The Financial History of Baltimore* (Baltimore: Johns Hopkins Press, 1899), pp. 356–58.

7. *Cincinnati Enquirer*, 6 Feb. 1891, p. 5; *Cleveland Plain Dealer*, 4 Jan. 1891, p. 4; 5 Jan. 1891, p. 8; 31 Jan. 1891, p. 4; 17 Feb. 1891, p. 4.

8. Michael Sheppard Speer, "Urbanization and Reform: Columbus, Ohio 1870–1900" (Ph.D. dissertation, Ohio State University, 1972), pp. 106, 112–18.

9. Laurence Marcellus Larson, *A Financial and Administrative History of Milwaukee* (Madison: University of Wisconsin, 1908), pp. 53–54, 104–05.

10. Jessie McMillan Marcley, *The Minneapolis City Charter, 1856–1925* (Minneapolis: University of Minnesota, 1924), p. 13.

11. Thomas S. Barclay, *The Movement for Municipal Home Rule in St. Louis* (Columbia: University of Missouri, 1943), pp. 31–33, 39; *Missouri Democrat*, 1 Feb. 1871, p. 1.

12. James W. S. Peters, "Home Rule Charter Movements in Missouri With Special Reference to Kansas City," *Annals of the American Academy of Political and Social Science* 27 (Jan. 1906): 156–57.

13. For accounts of some typical Saint Louis delegation meetings, see *Missouri Democrat*, 9 Feb. 1871, p. 1; *St. Louis Republican*, 17 Feb. 1875, p. 1; 11 Mar. 1875, p. 1.

14. *Milwaukee Daily Sentinel*, 6 Feb. 1874, p. 1.

15. For accounts of typical Milwaukee delegation business, see ibid., 12 Feb. 1874, p. 1; 13 Feb. 1874, p. 1; 26 Feb. 1874, p. 5.

16. *Journal of the House of Representatives of the State of Ohio, 1891* (Columbus: Westbote Co., 1891), p. 338. The legislative committee that investigated Cincinnati government prior to the proposal of legislation, however, consisted largely of outsiders. *Journal of the House of Representatives of the State of Ohio for the Extraordinary Session of . . . 1890* (Columbus: Westbote Co., 1890), p. 42.

17. *Journal of House of Representatives of Ohio, 1891*, p. 154.

18. *Journal of the Senate of the State of Ohio, 1891* (Columbus: Westbote Co., 1891), p. 224. For an account of a typical weekly delegation meeting, see *Cleveland Plain Dealer*, 28 Feb. 1894, p. 2.

19. The Ohio Senate organized the Municipal Corporations Committee Number One in 1890, and it existed throughout the remainder of the century.

20. For the membership of the Illinois House Committee on Municipal Corporations, see: *Chicago Tribune*, 24 Jan. 1883, p. 7; 25 Feb. 1885, p. 2; 22 Jan. 1887, p. 9; 19 Jan. 1889, p. 9; 18 Mar. 1891, p. 6; 20 Jan. 1893, p. 3; 30 Jan. 1895, p. 2; 6 Feb. 1897, p. 6; 20 Jan. 1899, p. 5.

21. This practice persisted in Maryland well into the twentieth century. For a description of legislative procedure in the 1920s, see C. I. Winslow, *State Legislative Committee: A Study in Procedure* (Baltimore: Johns Hopkins Press, 1931), pp. 48–49, 116–18.

22. *Official Journal of the Proceedings of the House of Representatives of the State of Louisiana, 1880* (New Orleans: New Orleans Democrat, 1880), p. 161.

23. B. R. Forman, "Notes on Municipal Government—New Orleans," *Annals of the American Academy of Political and Social Science* 17 (Mar. 1901): 352.

24. *Debates of the Convention to Amend the Constitution of Pennsylvania*, 9 vols. (Harrisburg: B. Singerly, 1873), 3: 121.

25. Based on information in *Smull's Legislative Hand Book, and Manual of the State of Pennsylvania* for 1887 through 1896.

26. *Boston Evening Transcript*, 8 Jan. 1895, p. 3; 9 Jan. 1895, p. 2; 19 Jan. 1895, p. 13; 21 Jan. 1895, p. 2; 26 Jan. 1895, p. 13. Rural interference seems to have been limited, nevertheless, and in 1897 one leading Bostonian testified that "the cry of 'hayseed domination' is rarely heard." Robert C. Brooks, "Business Men in Civic Service: The Merchant's Municipal Committee of Boston," *Municipal Affairs* 1 (Sept. 1897): 501.

27. *Debates and Proceedings in the New-York State Convention, for the Revision of the Constitution* (Albany: Albany Argus, 1846), pp. 738–41.

28. *Testimony Taken before the Senate Committee on Cities Pursuant to Resolution Adopted January 20, 1890*, 5 vols. (Albany: J. B. Lyon, 1891), 5: 10.

29. *New York Times*, 23 Mar. 1892, p. 8.

30. *Cincinnati Enquirer*, 14 Mar. 1891, p. 1.

31. *Cleveland Plain Dealer*, 22 Feb. 1891, p. 3.

32. *St. Louis Democrat*, 6 Feb. 1874, p. 1.

33. In two instances, favorably recommended bills failed to pass because an insufficient number of legislators were present, and the ayes consequently did not constitute a "constitutional majority" even though they represented a majority of those voting.

34. In this one case of defiance in Indiana, non-Indianapolis legislators, contrary to the will of the Marion County delegation, forced through an amendment to a provision for the taxing and licensing of liquor wholesalers in Indianapolis. A Marion County member then moved that the enacting clause be stricken, and this motion passed. *Journal of the House of Representatives of the State of Indiana, 1899* (Indianapolis: Wm. B. Burford, 1899), pp. 1753–54.

35. The fact that there was no record of ayes and nays on either of the two bills indicates that both bills were probably trivial. In the absence of a record of the votes on these measures, it is not possible to discover whether the local delegation was divided on them. *Journal of the Assembly of the Legislature of the State of California, 1873–74* (Sacramento: G. H. Springer, 1874), pp. 905, 1008.

36. *Official Report of the Proceedings and Debates of the Third Constitutional Convention of Ohio*, 2 vols. (Cleveland: W. S. Robison & Co., 1874), 2:1304–05.

37. *Journal of the House of Representatives of the State of Ohio, 1886* (Columbus: Westbote Co., 1886), pp. 806, 841–42; *Journal of the Senate of the State of Ohio, 1886* (Columbus: Myers Bros., 1886), pp. 565, 584.

38. *Cincinnati Enquirer*, 15 May 1886, p. 1; *Cincinnati Commercial Gazette*, 15 May 1886, p. 5.

39. People v. Sours, 31 Colo. 369 (1903); Clyde L. King, *The History of the Government of Denver, with Special Reference to Its Relations with Public Service Corporations* (Denver: Fisher Book Co., 1911), p. 125; Platt Rogers, "Municipal Condition of Denver," *Proceedings of the Second National Conference for Good City Government* (Philadelphia: National Municipal League, 1895), pp. 424–31.

40. *Journal of the House, General Assembly of the State of Colorado, 1889* (Denver: Collier & Cleaveland Lith. Co., 1889), pp. 1409–10, 1414, 1461–62; *Senate Journal of the General Assembly of the State of Colorado, 1889* (Denver: Collier & Cleaveland Lith. Co., 1889), pp. 375–76, 869.

41. *Debates of Third Constitutional Convention of Ohio*, 2:1300, 1302.

42. Ibid., 2:1310.

43. *Cleveland Leader and Morning Herald*, 18 Feb. 1891, p. 1.

44. *Cleveland Plain Dealer*, 18 Feb. 1891, p. 1.

45. See also the opposition of the Cleveland City Council to the charter bill sponsored by the Cleveland legislative delegation. *Cleveland Leader and Morning Herald*, 14 Feb. 1891, p. 8; *Cleveland Plain Dealer*, 5 Feb. 1891, p. 4; 12 Feb. 1891, p. 2.

46. William L. Riordon, *Plunkitt of Tammany Hall* (New York: E. P. Dutton & Co., 1963), p. 24.

47. *Cleveland Plain Dealer*, 16 Apr. 1890, p. 8; 17 Apr. 1890, p. 4; 22 Apr. 1890, p. 4. See also the sharp partisan battle over the municipal structure in Cincinnati during the special session of 1890. *Journal of Ohio House, Extraordinary Session 1890* (Columbus; Westbote Co., 1890); *Journal of the Senate, of the State of Ohio, for the Extraordinary Session of 1890* (Columbus: Westbote Co., 1890).

48. O. J. Hodge, *Reminiscences* (Cleveland: Imperial Press, 1902), pp. 178–79.

49. Ibid., p. 179.

50. Marcley, *Minneapolis City Charter*, p. 22; *Journal of the Senate of the Twenty-seventh Session of the Legislature of the State of Minnesota* (Saint Paul: J. W. Cunningham, 1891), p. 662.

51. *Journal of Senate of Minnesota, 1891*, p. 744.

52. Ibid., p. 820.

53. Marcley, *Minneapolis City Charter*, p. 25; *Journal of Senate of Minnesota, 1891*, p. 822.

54. *St. Louis Democrat*, 6 Feb. 1874, p. 1.

55. *St. Louis Republican*, 2 Mar. 1875, p. 5; 6 Mar. 1875, p. 1; 11 Mar. 1875, p. 1. Thomas S. Barclay, "The Kansas City Charter of 1875," *Missouri Historical Review* 26 (Oct. 1931): 19–39; W. H. Miller, *The History of Kansas City* (Kansas City: Birdsall & Miller, 1881), pp. 160–61.

56. *Metropolitan Club of the City of New York . . . Constitution, By-Laws, and List of Officers and Members* (New York, 1897); *Boyd's Philadelphia Blue Book* (Philadelphia: C. E. Howe Co., 1896), pp. 645–48, 657–61, 686–99.

57. *Society-List & Club Register for the Season of 1891–92* (New York: Society-List Publishing Co., 1891); *The Chicago Blue Book . . . for the Year Ending 1893* (Chicago: Chicago Directory Co., 1892); *Philadelphia Blue Book*.

58. For occupations of legislators, see: Will L. Lloyd, *The Red Book, An Illustrated Legislative Manual of the State* (Albany: James B. Lyon, 1892), pp. 390, 411; *Manual for the Use of the Legislature of the State of New York, 1895* (Albany: Argus Co., 1895), pp. 489–90, 528–36; *Manual for the Use of the Legislature of the State of New York, 1896* (Albany: Weed-Parsons Printing Co., 1896), pp. 470, 509–17; *Manual for the Use of the Legislature of the State of New York, 1897* (Albany: Weed-Parsons Printing Co., 1897), pp. 472, 511–19; *Manual for the Use of the Legislature of the State of New York, 1898* (Albany: Brandow Printing Co., 1898), pp. 437–38, 477–85; *Manual for the Use of the Legislature of the State of New York, 1899* (Albany: Brandow Printing Co., 1899), pp. 441–42, 486–94; *List of Members of the Thirty-eighth General Assembly of the State of Illinois* (Springfield: H. W. Rokker, 1893), pp. 3, 5–6; *List of Members and Officers of the House of Representatives of the Fortieth General Assembly of the State of Illinois* (Springfield: Phillips Bros., 1897), pp. 18–33, 69–73; *List of State Officers of the State of Illinois* (Springfield: Phillips Bros., 1900), pp. 26–33.

59. See biographical sketches in *Smull's Legislative Hand Book, and Manual of the State of Pennsylvania* for 1889 through 1897. For occupations of Minnesota legislators, see the legislative manuals of Minnesota for the 1890s.

60. Based on biographical information in *A Biographical Directory of the Indiana General Assembly* (Indianapolis: Indiana Historical Bureau, 1980).

61. Based on biographical sketches in Lloyd, *The Red Book.*

62. *Manual of the Legislature of New Jersey, 1892* (Trenton: T. F. Fitzgerald, 1892), pp. 205, 223-28. *Smull's Legislative Hand Book, and Manual of the State of Pennsylvania, 1893* (Harrisburg: E. K. Meyers, 1893), pp. 773-807.

63. *The Legislative Manual of the State of Minnesota* (Saint Paul, 1893), pp. 110-11, 113-15.

64. *Official Directory of the Forty-first General Assembly of Illinois* (Springfield: Illinois State Register, 1899); *Maryland Manual, 1900* (Baltimore: Wm. J. C. Dulany Co., 1900), pp. 199-201, 209-13.

65. Based on list of occupations in legislative manuals of New York for 1895 through 1899. *Manual for Legislature of New York, 1895,* pp. 489-90, 528-36; *Manual for Legislature of New York, 1896,* pp. 470, 509-17; *Manual for Legislature of New York, 1897,* pp. 472, 511-19; *Manual for Legislature of New York, 1898,* pp. 437-38, 477-85; *Manual for Legislature of New York, 1899,* pp. 441-42, 486-94.

66. *New York Herald,* 8 Nov. 1892, pp. 13-14.

67. *New York Times,* 2 Nov. 1890, p. 12.

68. Ibid., 6 Nov. 1890, p. 4.

69. Lloyd, *The Red Book,* pp. 401-02, 446-51.

70. *Manual for Legislature of New York, 1896,* pp. 527-28; *Manual for Legislature of New York, 1898,* pp. 491-92.

71. *Smull's Legislative Hand Book, and Manual of the State of Pennsylvania, 1902* (Harrisburg: Wm. Stanley Ray, 1902), pp. 837-62.

72. Based on the list of members in Elliot Gilkey, *The Ohio Hundred Year Book* (Columbus: Fred J. Heer, 1901), pp. 238-320.

5. REFORMING THE CITY-STATE RELATIONSHIP

1. Isidor Loeb and Floyd C. Shoemaker, eds., *Debates of the Missouri Constitutional Convention of 1875,* 12 vols. (Columbia,: State Historical Society of Missouri, 1944), 12:449, 462, 468, 470-71.

2. *Debates and Proceedings of the Constitutional Convention of the State of California,* 3 vols. (Sacramento: State Printing Office, 1881), 3:1407; *San Francisco Chronicle,* 18 Jan. 1879, p. 3.

3. Loeb and Shoemaker, eds., *Debates of Missouri Convention,* 1:501.

4. Howard Lee McBain, *The Law and the Practice of Municipal Home Rule* (New York: Columbia University Press, 1916), pp. 118-22.

5. Ibid., pp. 202-03.

6. Loeb and Shoemaker, eds., *Debates of Missouri Convention,* 12:454, 455, 465.

7. *Debates of Convention of California,* 2:1061, 1062.

8. Loeb and Shoemaker, eds., *Debates of Missouri Convention,* 12:481-82, 495-96.

9. *Debates of Convention of California,* 3:1408.

10. Loeb and Shoemaker, eds., *Debates of Missouri Convention,* 12:452, 457.

11. *Debates of Convention of California,* 2:1063; 3:1406.

12. Loeb and Shoemaker, eds., *Debates of Missouri Convention,* 12:481, 495.

13. Beverly Paulik Rosenow, ed., *The Journal of the Washington State Constitutional Convention, 1889* (Seattle: Book Publishing Co., 1962), p. 726.

14. State *ex rel.* Wiesenthal v. Denny, 4 Wash. 135 (1892); McBain, *Home Rule*, pp. 411–12.

15. William A. Schaper, "The City Charter Problem With Special Reference to Minnesota," *Papers and Proceedings of the Third Annual Meeting of the Minnesota Academy of Social Sciences* (Index Press, 1910), pp. 49–50; McBain, *Home Rule*, pp. 457–58.

16. Loeb and Shoemaker, eds., *Debates of Missouri Convention*, 12:468.

17. Computed from the published laws for the state of Missouri passed at each session from 1863 through 1875.

18. Computed on the basis of *The Scheme of Separation Between St. Louis City and County and the Charter of the City of St. Louis, with all Amendments and Modifications to August 1, 1888* (Saint Louis: Daly Printing Co., 1888).

19. *St. Louis Globe-Democrat,* 9 Mar. 1879, pp. 4, 9; 10 Mar. 1879, p. 8.

20. Ibid., 15 Mar. 1879, p. 8; 2 Apr. 1879, pp. 1, 3.

21. Ibid., 8 Apr. 1881, p. 4; 16 Apr. 1881, p. 12; 20 Apr. 1881, p. 10.

22. Ibid., 3 Oct. 1885, p. 4; 5 Oct. 1885, p. 4; 7 Oct. 1885, p. 19; Frederick C. Ault, "A History of Municipal Government in St. Louis," *City Journal* 20 (29 Mar. 1938); no page numbers in original.

23. *St. Louis Globe-Democrat,* 1 Oct. 1885, p. 6; 4 Oct. 1885, p. 6.

24. Ibid., 7 July 1898, p. 11; 9 July 1898, p. 11; 10 July 1898, p. 16; 11 July 1898, p. 6; 13 July 1898, p. 14.

25. Ewing v. Hoblitzelle, 85 Mo. 64 (1884); McBain, *Home Rule*, pp. 141–43.

26. *St. Louis Globe-Democrat,* 13 Jan. 1881, p. 2; 14 Jan 1881, p. 2; 20 Jan. 1881, p. 2; 28 Jan. 1881, p. 2; 5 Feb. 1881, pp. 4, 6.

27. Ibid., 10 Jan. 1883, p. 5.

28. Ibid., 7 Jan. 1885, p. 3; 9 Jan. 1885, p. 2; 13 Jan. 1885, p. 3; 14 Jan. 1885, p. 3; *Journal of the House of Representatives of the Thirty-Third General Assembly of the State of Missouri 1885* (Jefferson City: Tribune Printing Co., 1885), p. 7.

29. *St. Louis Globe-Democrat,* 21 Jan. 1889, p. 10.

30. *St. Louis Post-Dispatch,* 19 Aug. 1881, p. 4; 22 Aug. 1881, p. 4; Julian S. Rammelkamp, *Pulitzer's Post-Dispatch, 1878–1883* (Princeton: Princeton University Press, 1967), pp. 239–40.

31. *St. Louis Globe-Democrat,* 17 Apr. 1881, p. 4.

32. Murnane v. City of St. Louis, 123 Mo. 479 (1894); McBain, *Home Rule*, pp. 123–24. The doctrine in the Murnane case was, however, repudiated in State *ex rel.* McCaffrey v. Mason, 155 Mo. 486 (1899).

33. According to a local newspaper, only one-sixth of the eligible voters cast a ballot in the charter contest of 1888. For coverage of the contest, see: *Kansas City Star,* 25 Jan. 1888, pp. 1, 2; 28 Jan. 1888, p. 2; 30 Jan. 1888, p. 1; 31 Jan 1888, p. 2; James W. S. Peters, "Home Rule Charter Movements in Missouri, with Special Reference to Kansas City," *Annals of the American Academy of Political and Social Science* 27 (Jan. 1906): 158–59; Roy Ellis, *A Civic History of Kansas City, Missouri* (Springfield, Mo.: Elkins-Swyers Co., 1930), pp. 58–59; Isidor Loeb, "Municipal Home Rule in Missouri," *Proceedings of the Fourth Annual Convention of the Illinois Municipal League* (Urbana, 1917), pp. 53–54.

34. Kansas City *ex rel.* North Park District v. Scarritt, 127 Mo. 642 (1894); McBain, *Home Rule*, pp. 156–60; William H. Wilson, *The City Beautiful Movement in Kansas City* (Columbia: University of Missouri Press, 1964), pp. 33, 55.

35. *Kansas City Star,* 5 Mar. 1905, pp. 1, 13; 6 Mar. 1905, p. 1; 7 Mar. 1905, p. 1; Peters, "Home Rule," pp. 162–67; Ellis, *History of Kansas City,* pp. 59–60; Loeb, "Home Rule in Missouri," *Illinois Municipal League,* pp. 54–55.

36. *San Francisco Chronicle,* 1 Sept. 1880, p. 2; 3 Sept. 1880, p. 2; 4 Sept. 1880, p. 2; 5 Sept. 1880, pp. 1, 4, 8; 6 Sept. 1880, p. 2; 7 Sept. 1880, p. 2; 8 Sept. 1880, pp. 2, 3.

37. Ibid., 9 Sept. 1880, pp. 2, 3.

38. Ibid., 2 Mar. 1883, p. 2; 3 Mar. 1883, p. 2; 4 Mar. 1883, p. 8.

39. Ibid., 4 Mar. 1883, p. 4.

40. Ibid., 28 Mar. 1887, p. 4; 6 Apr. 1887, p. 4; 10 Apr. 1887, p. 6; 11 Apr. 1887, p. 4; 12 Apr. 1887, p. 4.

41. Ibid., 13 Apr. 1887, p. 6.

42. Ibid., 8 Oct. 1896, p. 6; 9 Oct. 1896, p. 6; 12 Oct. 1896, p. 6; 21 Oct. 1896, p. 11; 28 Oct. 1896, p. 6; 5 Nov. 1896, p. 16.

43. Ibid., 25 May 1898, p. 6; 26 May 1898, p. 6; 27 May 1898, p. 8.

44. Desmond v. Dunn, 55 Cal. 242, 250 (1880); McBain, *Home Rule*, pp. 232–33.

45. Staude v. Election Commissioners, 61 Cal. 313 (1882); McBain, *Home Rule*, pp. 234–36.

46. For examples of the San Francisco delegation serving as a standing committee during the second half of the 1890s, see: *Journal of the Assembly of California, 1895* (Sacramento: A. J. Johnson, 1895), pp. 63, 65, 68, 145, 180, 196, 197, 208, 231, 240, 291, 294; *Journal of the Assembly of California, 1897* (Sacramento: A. J. Johnson, 1897), pp. 27, 51, 72, 77, 84, 88, 98, 109, 129, 143, 155, 157, 178, 181, 221, 226, 299.

47. *San Francisco Chronicle*, 6 Apr. 1887, p. 4; 10 Apr. 1887, p. 6.

48. Ibid., 24 Oct. 1896, p. 11.

49. Loeb, "Home Rule in Missouri," *Illinois Municipal League*, pp. 49–50.

50. McBain, *Home Rule*, p. 224.

51. Ibid., p. 252.

52. Senior Class in the Wharton School of Finance and Economy, *The City Government of Philadelphia: A Study in Municipal Administration* (Philadelphia: University of Pennsylvania, 1893), p. 53.

53. Thad. M. Stevens, "A History of Health-Work in Indiana," *Papers and Reports Presented at the Eighth Annual Meeting of the American Public Health Association . . . 1882* (Boston: Rockwell & Churchill, 1883), p. 67.

54. *Report of Proceedings of the Eleventh Annual Meeting of the American Water Works Association, 1891* (Philadelphia, 1891), p. 121.

55. "Public Sanitation in Illinois," *Municipal Engineering* 11 (Sept. 1896): 179; Jacob Harman, "Proposed State Supervision of Water Supply and Sewage Disposal," *Thirteenth Annual Report of the Illinois Society of Engineers and Surveyors* (Peoria: Nixon Printing Co., 1898), pp. 114–30.

56. "By Way of Comment—State Control of Water Supply and Sewerage Systems," *Municipal Engineering* 11 (Nov. 1896): 315.

57. John A. Fairlie, "The Centralization of Administration in New York State," *Columbia University Studies in History, Economics and Public Law* 9 (1898): 541, 547–48; *Laws of the State of New York, Passed at the One Hundred and Ninth Session of the Legislature, 1886* (Albany: Banks & Bros., 1886), p. 867; *Laws of the State of New York, Passed at the One Hundred and Tenth Session of the Legislature, 1887* (Albany: Banks & Bros., 1887), pp. 490, 820; *Laws of the State of New York, Passed at the One Hundred and Eleventh Session of the Legislature, 1888* (Albany: Banks & Bros., 1888), pp. 536, 541; *Laws of the State of New York, Passed at the One Hundred and Twelfth Session of the Legislature* (Albany: Banks & Bros., 1889), p. 501.

58. *Acts and Resolves Passed by the General Court of Massachusetts in the Year 1888* (Boston: Wright & Potter Printing Co., 1888), pp. 343–44.

59. George Chandler Whipple, *State Sanitation: A Review of the Massachusetts State Board of Health* (Cambridge: Harvard University Press, 1917), pp. 127, 134. Special laws, enacted during the late 1880s and early 1890s provided that the board not only give advice but also required board approval of plans prior to construction. See, for example, *Private and Special Statutes of the Commonwealth of Massachusetts for the Years 1889, 1890, 1891, 1892, 1893* (Boston: Wright & Potter Printing Co., 1895), pp. 414, 501–02, 1217.

60. *Thirteenth Annual Report of the Ohio Society of Surveyors and Civil Engineers* (Sandusky, Ohio: I. F. Mack & Bro., 1892), p. 120.

61. *General Acts Passed and Joint Resolutions Adopted by the Seventieth General Assembly* (Norwalk, Ohio: Laning Printing Co., 1893), p. 95.

62. *General and Local Acts Passed and Joint Resolutions Adopted by the Seventy-third General Assembly* (Columbus: J. L. Trauger, 1898), pp. 259–60.

63. C. O. Probst, "The Duty of the State in Protecting Sources of Public Water Supplies,"

Reports of Proceedings of the Nineteenth Annual Meeting of the American Water Works Association (New York: Secretary of the American Water Works Association, 1899), p. 124.

64. H. M. Bracken, "Sewage Purification Made Compulsory by the Minnesota State Board of Health," *Engineering News* 51 (11 Feb. 1904): 138; Philip D. Jordan, *The People's Health: A History of Public Health in Minnesota to 1948* (Saint Paul: Minnesota Historical Society, 1953), p. 290.

65. F. Herbert Snow, "Administration of Pennsylvania Laws Respecting Stream Pollution," *Proceedings of the Engineers Society of Western Pennsylvania* 23 (June 1907): 278–83; *Laws of the General Assembly of the Commonwealth of Pennsylvania, Passed at the Session of 1905* (Harrisburg: Wm. Stanley Ray, 1905), pp. 260–63; *Twenty-First Report of the State Board of Health of Wisconsin* (Madison: Democrat Printing Co., 1908), p. 131; *The Laws of Wisconsin . . . Passed at the Biennial Session of the Legislature, 1905* (Madison: Democrat Printing Co., 1905), pp. 749–51; *Engineering News* 57 (13 June 1907): 648; *Session Laws, 1907, Passed at the Thirty-Second Regular Session . . . of the Legislature of the State of Kansas* (Topeka: State Printing Office, 1907), pp. 548–51.

66. Schuyler C. Wallace, *State Administrative Supervision over Cities in the United States* (New York: Columbia University Press, 1928), pp. 133, 135.

67. *Fortieth Report of the Superintendent of Public Instruction* (Indianapolis: Wm. B. Burford, 1895), pp. 70–71; *Forty-second Report of the Superintendent of Public Instruction* (Indianapolis: Wm. B. Burford, 1896), pp. 20–21; *Department of Public Instruction, Nineteenth Biennial Report of the State Superintendent* (Indianapolis: W. B. Burford, 1898), p. 440.

68. *Forty-second Annual Report of the State Superintendent*, 2 vols. (Albany: Wynkoop Hallenbeck Crawford Co., 1896), 1:xvi–xx; *Forty-third Annual Report of the State Superintendent*, 2 vols. (Albany: Wynkoop Hallenbeck Crawford Co., 1897), 1:xxii–xxiii.

69. J. W. Patterson, "State Supervision: What Plan of Organization and Administration is Most Effective?," *Journal of Proceedings and Addresses: National Educational Association, 1890* (Topeka: Kansas Publishing House, 1890), p. 436.

70. "Discussion," *Journal of Proceedings and Addresses: National Educational Association, 1890* (Topeka: Kansas Publishing House, 1890), pp. 440, 441.

71. *Forty-third Annual Report*, p. xviii; Fairlie, "Centralization in New York," p. 465.

72. *Forty-third Annual Report*, pp. xix–xx.

73. *Sixty-second Annual Report of the Superintendent of Public Instruction of the State of Michigan for the Year 1898* (Lansing: Robert Smith Printing Co., 1899), pp. 55, 60; William Clarence Webster, "Recent Centralizing Tendencies in State Educational Administration," *Columbia University Studies in History, Economics and Public Law* 8 (1897): 191–201; *Twelfth Report of the Superintendent of Public Instruction of the State of California* (Sacramento: James J. Ayers, 1886), pp. 33–38.

74. *Testimony Taken before the Senate Committee on Cities Pursuant to Resolution Adopted January 20, 1890*, 5 vols. (Albany: J. B. Lyon, 1891), 5:10.

75. Allen Ripley Foote, *Public Policy Editorials*, 3 vols. (Chicago: Public Policy Publishing Co., 1901), 1:140.

76. J. R. Commons, "State Supervision for Cities," *Annals of the American Academy of Political and Social Science* 5 (May 1895): 879.

77. C. W. Tooke, "Uniformity in Municipal Finance," *Municipal Affairs*, 2 (June 1898): 195–206.

78. M. N. Baker, "Progress Towards Uniform Municipal Statistics in the United States," *Papers and Proceedings of the Thirteenth Annual Meeting of the American Economic Association* (New York: Macmillan Co., 1901), p. 278.

79. *Proceedings of the Indianapolis Conference for Good City Government and Fourth Annual Meeting of the National Municipal League* (Philadelphia: National Municipal League, 1898), p. 8; *Proceedings of the Milwaukee Conference for Good City Government and Sixth Annual Meeting of the National Municipal League* (Philadelphia: National Municipal League, 1900), pp. 52–53.

80. Other organizations that appointed committees to investigate the possibilities of uniform municipal accounts were: American Gas Light Association, American Society of Municipal Improvements, Central States Water Works Association, National Electric Light Association, New England Water Works Association, and New Jersey Sanitary Association.

81. *Session Laws of the State of Wyoming, 1890–91* (Cheyenne: Daily Sun Publishing House, 1891), pp. 358–62; *Revised Statutes of Wyoming in Force December 1, 1899* (Laramie: Chaplin, Spafford & Mathison, 1899), pp. 120–26; Tooke, "Uniformity in Municipal Finance," pp. 200–02; Baker, "Progress Towards Uniform Municipal Statistics," *American Economic Association*, pp. 268–69.

82. *New York Times*, 31 Jan. 1896, p. 14.

83. Harvey S. Chase, "Progress of Uniform Municipal Accounting in Ohio," *Proceedings of the Detroit Conference for Good City Government and the Ninth Annual Meeting of the National Municipal League* (Philadelphia: National Municipal League, 1903), p. 287; *General and Local Acts Passed . . . by the Seventy-fifth General Assembly* (Columbus: Fred. J. Heer, 1902), pp. 511–15; *General and Local Acts Passed . . . by the Seventy-sixth General Assembly* (Springfield: Springfield Publishing Co., 1904), pp. 271–74.

84. *Laws of the State of New York, Passed at the One Hundred and Twenty-eighth Session of the Legislature*, 2 vols. (Albany: J. B. Lyon Co., 1905), 2:2005-7; *Annual Report of the Auditor of the State to the Governor of Iowa, 1906* (Des Moines: Bernard Murphy, 1906), p. xi; *Acts and Resolutions Passed at the Regular Session of the Thirty-first General Assembly of the State of Iowa* (Des Moines: Bernard Murphy, 1906), pp. 24–26.

85. F. H. Irwin, comp., "State Supervision of Municipal Accounts, Under Existing Legislative Enactments Prior to 1913," *National Municipal Review* 2 (July 1913): 522–25. The twelve states were: California, Indiana, Iowa, Louisiana, Massachusetts, Minnesota, New York, Ohio, Washington, West Virginia, Wisconsin, and Wyoming.

6. THE PROFESSIONALS

1. Frederic P. Stearns and Edward W. Howe, "Joseph Phineas Davis," *Papers and Discussions of Boston Society of Civil Engineers* 4 (Dec. 1917): 437–42.

2. William Jackson, Eliot C. Clarke, and Fred. Brooks, "Henry Morse Wightman," *Proceedings of American Society of Civil Engineers* 12 (Dec. 1886): 124–25.

3. Frederic H. Fay, "William Jackson," *Transactions of the American Society of Civil Engineers* 74 (Dec. 1911): 504–05; Frederic H. Fay, "William Jackson," *Journal of the Association of Engineering Societies* 46 (Feb. 1911): 148–50.

4. George F. Swain, C. Frank Allen, and William E. Foss, "Desmond FitzGerald," *Transactions of the American Society of Civil Engineers* 92 (1928): 1656–61; "Early Presidents of the Society—Desmond FitzGerald," *Civil Engineering* 8 (Aug. 1938): 557–58.

5. William Jackson, Joseph P. Davis, Charles S. Gowen, and Charles Warren Hunt, "Alphonse Fteley," *Transactions of the American Society of Civil Engineers* 54 (June 1905): 509–12; Joseph P. Davis, Frederic P. Stearns, and George S. Rice, "Alphonse Fteley," *Journal of the Association of Engineering Societies* 31 (Dec. 1903): 213–25; "Early Presidents of the Society—Alphonse Fteley," *Civil Engineering* 8 (July 1938): 493–94.

6. Frank O. Whitney, "Samuel Clarence Ellis," *Transactions of the American Society of Civil Engineers* 87 (1924): 1334; George F. Swain, E. D. Leavitt, and Frederic H. Fay, "John Eugene Cheney," *Transactions of the American Society of Civil Engineers* 59 (Dec. 1907): 537–39; George F. Swain, E. D. Leavitt, and Frederic H. Fay, "John Eugene Cheney," *Journal of the Association of Engineering Societies* 38 (June 1907): 334–36; Edward W. Howe, Desmond FitzGerald, Frederic H. Fay, and J. K. Berry, "In Memory of Samuel E. Tinkham," *Papers and Discussions of the Boston Society of Civil Engineers* 8 (Oct. 1921): 291–309; "Samuel Everett Tinkham," *Transactions of the American Society of Civil Engineers* 86 (1923): 1704–6; Edgar S. Dorr and Frank O. Whitney, "Edward Willard Howe," *Journal of the Boston Society of Civil Engineers* 19 (June 1932): 362–64; John C. Chase and Charles W. Banks, "Frederic Irving Winslow," *Transactions of*

the American Society of Civil Engineers 89 (1926): 1708–9; Charles W. Kettell, W. H. Bradley, and Edgar S. Dorr, "Charles William Folsom," *Journal of the American Association of Engineering Societies* 33 (Nov. 1904): 329–30; Frank S. Hart and Frederic I. Winslow, "Charles Edwin Haberstroh," *Papers and Discussions of the Boston Society of Civil Engineers* 9 (June 1922): 137–40.

7. Fay, "William Jackson," p. 148.

8. Herbert E. Sherman, Elmer W. Ross, and Robert L. Bowen, "William Dexter Bullock," *Transactions of the American Society of Civil Engineers* 88 (1925): 1356–57; Herbert E. Sherman, "Justus Vinton Dart," ibid., pp. 1381–82; William D. Bullock and Irving S. Wood, "Otis Francis Clapp," *Papers and Discussions of the Boston Society of Civil Engineers* 5 (Feb. 1918): 139; George H. Leland, Samuel M. Gray, and Frank E. Winsor, "Irving Sparrow Wood," *New England Water Works Association* 34 (Mar. 1920): 90.

9. "The Story of a New England City," *Municipal Journal and Engineer* 12 (Jan. 1902): 1.

10. *Engineering News and American Railway Journal* 35 (4 Nov. 1897): 296.

11. "George Sears Greene, Jr.," *Transactions of the American Society of Civil Engineers* 88 (1925): 1392–93; Charles Warren Hunt, "Horace Loomis," ibid., pp. 1416–17; *New York Times*, 9 Mar. 1925, p. 17.

12. Edward Wegmann, *The Water-Supply of New York, 1658–1895* (New York: John Wiley & Sons, 1896), p. 81; *New York Times*, 24 Jan. 1911, p. 9.

13. *New York Tribune*, 31 Oct. 1895, p. 1; 1 Nov. 1895, p. 3; 4 Jan. 1898, p. 11; *New York World*, 31 Oct. 1895, p. 3; 4 Jan. 1898, p. 5; *New York Herald*, 31 Oct. 1895, p. 5; 1 Nov. 1895, p. 5; 4 Jan. 1898, p. 8; *New York Times*, 31 Oct. 1895, p. 8; 1 Nov. 1895, p. 3; 2 Nov. 1895, p. 4; 4 Nov. 1895, p. 4; 4 Jan. 1898, p. 6; 8 Jan. 1898, p. 6.

14. Robert Ridgway, "Alfred Craven," *Transactions of the American Society of Civil Engineers* 94 (1930): 1506–7.

15. *New York Times*, 28 Nov. 1885, p. 2; 24 Dec. 1885, p. 5; 4 Jan. 1886, p. 2; 8 Jan. 1886, p. 3; 14 Jan. 1886, p. 8; 17 Jan. 1886, p. 3; 2 Feb. 1886, p. 8; 20 Nov. 1888, pp. 4, 8; 22 Nov. 1888, p. 4; 27 Nov. 1888, p. 4; 4 Dec. 1888, p. 8; 11 Dec. 1888, p. 2; 19 Dec. 1888, p. 5; 22 Dec. 1888, p. 8; 9 Oct. 1890, pp. 4, 9; 28 Oct. 1890, p. 9; 22 Jan. 1891, p. 8; 23 Jan. 1891, p. 8; 24 Jan. 1891, pp. 4, 8; *New York Herald*, 4 Dec. 1885, p. 5; 19 Dec. 1888, p. 4; 24 Dec. 1885, p. 9.

16. J. Thomas Scharf and Thompson Westcott, *History of Philadelphia, 1609–1884*, 3 vols. (Philadelphia: L. H. Everts & Co., 1884), 3: 1748–49; G. S. Webster and Russell Thayer, "Samuel Lightfoot Smedley," *Proceedings of American Society of Civil Engineers* 21 (Mar. 1895): 88–90; Samuel T. Wagner, Henry Quimby, and Charles Stevens, "George Smedley Webster," *Transactions of the American Society of Civil Engineers* 95 (1931): 1423–28.

17. George W. Fuller, T. J. McMinn, John C. Trautwine, Jr., and Charles W. Baker, "Rudolph Hering," *Transactions of the American Society of Civil Engineers* 87 (1924): 1350–54; Alfred D. Flinn and Robert S. Weston, "Rudolph Hering," *Papers and Discussions of the Boston Society of Civil Engineers* 11 (May 1924): 228–32.

18. "Municipal Engineering: Paper No. 4—Philadelphia, Pa.," *Engineering News and American Contract Journal* 16 (25 Dec. 1886): 416.

19. "Ellis Sylvester Chesbrough," *Proceedings of the American Society of Civil Engineers* 15 (Nov.–Dec. 1889): 160–63; "Early Presidents of the Society," *Civil Engineering* 6 (Nov. 1936): 773–75; Louis P. Cain, "Raising and Watering a City: Ellis Sylvester Chesbrough and Chicago's First Sanitation System," *Technology and Culture* 13 (July 1972): 353–72.

20. John W. Alvord, C. F. Loweth, and T. Chalkley Hatton, "George Henry Benzenberg," *Transactions of the American Society of Civil Engineers* 89 (1926): 1550–51; *Engineering News and American Railway Journal* 41 (30 Mar. 1899): 200; F. C. Winkler, "Municipal Government of Milwaukee," *Proceedings of the Second National Conference for Good City Government* (Philadelphia: National Municipal League, 1895), p. 120.

21. "In Memoriam: Andrew Rinker," *Bulletin of the Affiliated Engineering Societies of Minnesota* 3 (May 1918): 109; D. F. Simpson, "Municipal Government of Minneapolis," *Proceedings*

of the Second National Conference for Good City Government (Philadelphia: National Municipal League, 1895), pp. 100–01.

22. R. H. Thomson, *That Man Thomson* (Seattle: University of Washington Press, 1950), p. 4.

23. "Early Presidents of the Society—Henry Flad," *Civil Engineering* 7 (July 1937): 529–31; *The Engineers' Club of St. Louis Mo., Sixtieth Anniversary Year Book* (Saint Louis, 1928), pp. 18–19; "The Management of Municipal Public Works in St. Louis," *Engineering News and American Railway Journal* 27 (23 Jan. 1892): 76–77; Robert Moore and Henry Flad, "Thomas Jefferson Whitman," *Proceedings of the American Society of Civil Engineers* 18 (Apr. 1892): 103–04; Edward Flad, Baxter Brown, and James C. Travilla, "Minard LaFever Holman," *Transactions of the American Society of Civil Engineers* 89 (1926): 1630–31.

24. Clayton C. Hall, "Robert Kirkwood Martin," *Proceedings of the American Society of Civil Engineers* 20 (Jan. 1894): 43–45; J. Thomas Scharf, *History of Baltimore City and County* (Philadelphia: Louis H. Everts, 1881), pp. 220–22.

25. L. Herman, M. W. Kingsley, M. E. Rawson, and Chas. H. Strong, "John Whitelaw—A Memorial," *Journal of the Association of Engineering Societies* 11 (Nov. 1892): 538–39.

26. William Sooy Smith, "DeWitt C. Creiger," *Journal of the Western Society of Engineers* 4 (Feb. 1899): 121–23; Simpson, "Minneapolis," *Second National Conference for Good City Government*, p. 101; Emile Low, "Louis Henry Knapp," *Transactions of the American Society of Civil Engineers* 87 (1924), pp. 1371–72; George W. Fuller and Alfred D. Flinn, "Louis Henry Knapp," *New England Water Works Association* 38 (March 1924), pp. 97–98. In 1900 the engineers in Buffalo's Department of Public Works averaged eleven years on the payroll. *Annual Report of Public Works of the City of Buffalo, N.Y., for . . . 1900* (Buffalo: Wenborne-Sumner Co., 1900), pp. 313–18.

27. John Caulfield, "About a Municipal Water Plant," *City Government* 3 (Oct. 1897): 131; "A Compliment to 'Our John,' " ibid. 4 (Jan. 1898): 18; *City Government* 2 (Feb. 1897): 57; "Make It Business, Not Politics," ibid. 6 (Jan. 1899): 12; "St. Paul Water Board Election," ibid. 8 (Feb. 1900): 37.

28. *Engineering News*, 4 Nov. 1897, p. 296.

29. *Chicago Tribune*, 7 Apr. 1876, p. 8; 8 Apr. 1876, pp. 4, 8; 9 Apr. 1876, p. 16; 6 May 1876, p. 8; 16 May 1876, p. 8; 23 May 1876, p. 1; 30 May 1876, p. 1; 13 June 1876, p. 7; 7 Oct. 1876, p. 8.

30. Laura Wood Roper, *F.L.O.: A Biography of Frederick Law Olmsted* (Baltimore: Johns Hopkins University Press, 1973), p. 292.

31. Mabel Parsons, ed., *Memories of Samuel Parsons* (New York: G. P. Putnam's Sons, 1926), pp. 11–13.

32. Norman T. Newton, *Design on the Land: The Development of Landscape Architecture* (Cambridge: Harvard University Press, 1971), pp. 307–36.

33. Parsons, ed., *Samuel Parsons*, pp. 89–90; "Samuel Parsons, A Minute on His Life and Service," *Transactions of the American Society of Landscape Architects, 1922–1926* (Augusta, Me.: Charles E. Nash & Son, 1927), pp. 92–94.

34. *New York Times*, 24 Nov. 1894, p. 9; 29 Dec. 1894, p. 6; 30 Dec. 1894, p. 3; 12 Jan. 1895, p. 9; 23 Jan. 1898, pp. 12, 18; 21 Feb. 1898, p. 5; Parsons, ed., *Samuel Parsons*, pp. 44–45.

35. Alexander Dow, "The Position of the Engineer in Municipal Service," *Journal of the Association of Engineering Societies* 27 (Sept. 1901): 107.

36. Leonard K. Eaton, *Landscape Artist in America: The Life and Work of Jens Jensen* (Chicago: University of Chicago Press, 1964), pp. 13–18; Malcolm Collier, "Jens Jensen and Columbus Park," *Chicago History* 4 (Winter 1975–76): 225–34.

37. Theodore Wirth, *Minneapolis Park System, 1883–1944* (Minneapolis: n.p., 1946), pp. 46, 205.

38. *San Francisco Chronicle*, 13 Jan. 1943, pp. 1, 7; Katherine Wilson, *Golden Gate: The Park of a Thousand Vistas* (Caldwell, Ida.: Caxton Printers, 1947), pp. 25–35; Writers' Program of Works Project Administration, comp., *San Francisco, The Bay and Its Cities* (New York: Hastings House Publishers, 1947), pp. 330–31.

39. Joseph A. Borome, *Charles Coffin Jewett* (Chicago: American Library Association, 1951), pp. 158–60; Joseph A. Borome, "The Life and Letters of Justin Winsor" (Ph.D. dissertation, Columbia University, 1950), pp. 245–46; Walter M. Whitehill, *Boston Public Library: A Centennial History* (Cambridge: Harvard University Press, 1956), pp. 70, 104.

40. Wayne Cutler and Michael H. Harris, eds., *Justin Winsor: Scholar-Librarian* (Littleton, Colo.: Libraries Unlimited, 1980); Borome, "Justin Winsor;" Bohdan S. Wynar, ed., *Dictionary of American Library Biography* (Littleton, Colo.: Libraries Unlimited, 1978), p. 184.

41. Cutler and Harris, eds., *Justin Winsor*, pp. 28–30; Borome, "Justin Winsor," pp. 246–55; Whitehill, *Boston Library*, pp. 104–08; "The Change at Boston," *American Library Journal* 1 (31 July 1877): 401–02.

42. As quoted in *American Library Journal* 1 (31 July 1877): 409–10.

43. Whitehill, *Boston Library*, p. 165.

44. *Annual Report of the Trustees of the Public Library of the City of Boston, 1899* (Boston: Municipal Printing Office, 1900), pp. 99–105; *Annual Report of the Trustees of the Public Library of the City of Boston, 1895* (Boston: Rockwell & Churchill, 1896), p. 104.

45. Wynar, ed., *American Library Biography*, pp. 184–86; Harry Lyman Koopman, "William Eaton Foster—An Appreciation," *Library Journal* 55 (15 March 1930): 282–83.

46. Linda A. Eastman, *Portrait of a Librarian: William Howard Brett* (Chicago: American Library Association, 1940), p. 41.

47. As quoted in Frank B. Woodford, *Parnassus on Main Street: A History of the Detroit Public Library* (Detroit: Wayne State University Press, 1965), pp. 127, 131–32.

48. *Annual Report of the St. Louis Public Library, 1891–92* (Saint Louis: Mekeel Press, 1893), p. 42; Bertha Doane, "Frederick M. Crunden, Library Statesman," in John D. Marshall, comp., *An American Library History Reader* (Hamden, Conn.: Shoe String Press, 1961), pp. 195–204. Crunden defeated his political opponents early in his career at the Saint Louis Public Library. See, *Library Journal* 5 (Apr., May 1880): 106, 139, 155.

49. As quoted in Wynar, ed., *American Library Biography*, pp. 404–12; *The Chicago Public Library, 1873–1923* (Chicago: Board of Directors of Chicago Public Library, 1923), pp. 25–26; William L. Williamson, *William Frederick Poole and the Modern Library Movement* (New York: Columbia University Press, 1963), pp. 65–91; Gwladys Spencer, *The Chicago Public Library: Origins and Backgrounds* (Chicago: University of Chicago Press, 1943), pp. 352–53; *Proceedings of the Board of Directors of the Chicago Public Library from July 10, 1886, to June 23, 1888* (Chicago, 1888), pp. 135–36.

50. Wynar, ed., *American Library Biography*, pp. 162–67.

51. Ibid., pp. 393–94.

52. David W. Cheever, "A Reminiscence of My Professional Life," *Boston Medical and Surgical Journal* 165 (28 Sept. 1911): 487. For more on Boston City Hospital, see Morris J. Vogel, *The Invention of the Modern Hospital: Boston 1870–1930* (Chicago: University of Chicago Press, 1980).

53. Agnes Repplier, *J. William White, M.D.* (Boston: Houghton Mifflin Co., 1919), pp. 67–68.

54. Homer Folks, "The City's Health—Public Hospitals: With Special Reference to New York City," *Municipal Affairs* 2 (June 1898): 274.

55. John F. Marion, *Philadelphia Medica* (Philadelphia: Smith Kline Corp., 1975), p. 85; Frederick P. Henry, ed., *Founders' Week Memorial Volume* (Philadelphia: City of Philadelphia, 1909), p. 491; Harvey Cushing, *The Life of Sir William Osler*, 2 vols. (Oxford: Clarendon Press, 1925), 1: 251–53.

56. Elizabeth Christopher Hobson, "Founding of the Bellevue Training School for Nurses," *A Century of Nursing* (New York: G. P. Putnam's Sons, 1950), p. 165.

57. Mary M. Riddle, *Boston City Hospital Training School for Nurses* (Boston, 1928), pp. 92–95; Henry, ed., *Founders' Week Volume*, pp. 498–99; Franklin H. North, "A New Profession for Women," *Century Magazine* 25 (Nov. 1882): 38–47; Hobson, "Bellevue Training School,"

Century of Nursing, pp. 156–57. The Bellevue school was governed by a private board of directors but used public facilities and relied on the cooperation of the New York City commissioner of charities and corrections.

58. "Obituary—Edward Houghton Janes," *Sanitarian* 30 (Apr. 1893): 380–81.

59. C. V. Chapin, "Doctor Samuel H. Durgin," *American Journal of Public Health* 2 (May 1912): 357–58; George A. Babbitt, "Retirement of Dr. Samuel H. Durgin from the Boston Board of Health," ibid., pp. 384–85.

60. James H. Cassedy, *Charles V. Chapin and the Public Health Movement* (Cambridge: Harvard University Press, 1962).

61. Charles-Edward Amory Winslow, *The Life of Hermann M. Biggs* (Philadelphia: Lea & Febiger, 1929).

62. Wade W. Oliver, *The Man Who Lived for Tomorrow: A Biography of William Hallock Park, M.D.* (New York: E. P. Dutton & Co., 1941).

63. Stuart Galishoff, *Safeguarding the Public Health: Newark, 1895–1918* (Westport, Conn.: Greenwood Press, 1975), p. 16.

64. Arthur R. Reynolds, "Three Chicago and Illinois Public Health Officers: John H. Rauch, Oscar C. De Wolf, and Frank W. Reilly," *Bulletin of the Society of Medical History of Chicago* 1 (Aug. 1912): 113–34; *History of Medicine and Surgery and Physicians and Surgeons of Chicago* (Chicago: Biographical Publishing Co., 1922), pp. 103–05, 345.

65. William Travis Howard, Jr., *Public Health Administration and the Natural History of Disease in Baltimore, Maryland, 1797–1920* (Washington D.C.: Carnegie Institution, 1924), pp. 159–60.

66. Winslow, *Hermann Biggs*, pp. 184–85.

67. *Forty-ninth Annual Report of the Cleveland Board of Education for . . . 1885* (Cleveland: Publishing House of the Evangelical Association, 1886), p. 108; *Thirty-sixth Annual Report of the Board of Presidents and Directors of the St. Louis Public Schools for . . . 1890* (Saint Louis: Continental Printing Co., 1891), p. 37; *Thirty-seventh Annual Report of the Board Presidents and Directors of the St. Louis Public Schools for . . . 1891* (Saint Louis: Nixon-Jones Printing Co., 1892), pp. 41, lix–xcii.

68. *Annual Report of the School Committee of the City of Boston, 1895* (Boston: Rockwell & Churchill, 1896), p. 6.

69. *Forty-eighth Annual Report of the Board of Education of the City of Detroit for . . . 1891* (Detroit: Thomas Smith Printing Co., 1891), p. 67.

70. *Annual Report of the School Committee of the City of Boston, 1899* (Boston: Municipal Printing Office, 1899), p. 49; *One Hundred Years: The Story of the Detroit Public Schools, 1842–1942* (Detroit: Board of Education, 1942), p. 30.

71. Mary J. Herrick, *The Chicago Schools: A Social and Political History* (Beverly Hills: Sage Publications, 1971), p. 56.

72. "Discussion—Who Shall Appoint Teachers, and on Whose Nomination?," *Proceedings of the International Congress of Education . . . 1893* (New York: National Educational Association, 1894), p. 82.

73. "Discussion—Report of the Committee on City School Systems," *Journal of Proceedings and Addresses of the Thirty-Fifth Annual Meeting of the National Educational Association* (Chicago: University of Chicago Press, 1896), p. 470.

74. *Manual of the Public Schools of the City of Boston, 1881* (Boston: Rockwell & Churchill, 1881), pp. 58–79; *Manual of the Public Schools of the City of Boston, 1901* (Boston: Municipal Printing Office, 1901), pp. 103–40.

75. *Twenty-seventh Annual Report of the Board of Presidents and Directors of the St. Louis Public Schools for . . . 1881* (Saint Louis: Slawson & Co., 1882), pp. 91–115; *Forty-fifth Annual Report of the Board of Education of the City of St. Louis, Mo., for . . . 1899* (Saint Louis: Nixon-Jones Printing Co., 1900), pp. 317–66.

76. *Twentieth Annual Report of the Chicago Board of Education for . . . 1874* (Chicago: Bryant, Walker & Co., 1874), pp. 206–44; *Thirty-ninth Annual Report of the Chicago Board of Education for . . . 1893* (Chicago: George K. Hazlitt & Co., 1894), pp. 278–361.

77. *Report of the Chicago Board of Education, 1874*, p. 206; *Report of the Chicago Board of Education, 1893*, pp. 278–361.

78. *Annual Report of the School Committee of the City of Boston, 1874* (Boston: Rockwell & Churchill, 1874), p. 551; *Annual Report of the School Committee of the City of Boston, 1894* (Boston: Rockwell & Churchill, 1894), pp. 156–58.

79. *Annual Report of the School Committee of the City of Boston, 1900* (Boston: Municipal Printing Office, 1900), p. 57.

80. *Annual Report of the Board of Education . . . of New Jersey . . . 1892* (Trenton: John L. Murphy Publishing Co., 1893), p. 59.

81. *Annual Report of the School Committee of the City of Boston, 1901* (Boston: Municipal Printing Office, 1901), p. 23; *Annual Report of the School Committee of the City of Boston, 1902* (Boston: Municipal Printing Office, 1902), pp. 58–59.

82. F. W. Atkinson, "The Case of the Public Schools," *Atlantic Monthly* 77 (Apr. 1896): 538; "Confessions of Public School Teachers," ibid. 78 (July 1896): 108.

83. "Men of '75 and '99," *Journal of Education* 50 (7 Dec. 1899): 371; C. W. Bardeen, *Note Book of the History of Education* (Syracuse: C. W. Bardeen, 1901), p. 254.

84. Ben Blewett, "In Memoriam—James M. Greenwood," *Journal of Proceedings and Addresses of the Fifty-third Annual Meeting of the National Education Association* (Ann Arbor: National Education Association, 1915), p. 537. For one account of the development of the school superintendency, see David B. Tyack, "Pilgrim's Progress: Toward a Social History of the School Superintendency, 1860–1960," *History of Education Quarterly* 16 (Fall 1976): 257–94.

85. "Report of the Committee on City School Systems—School Superintendence in Cities," *Journal of Proceedings, and Addresses: National Educational Association, 1890* (Topeka: Kansas Publishing House, 1890), p. 312.

86. "Discussion—Report on City School Systems," *Proceedings of Thirty-fifth Meeting of National Educational Association*, p. 470.

87. "Discussion—Appointment and Tenure of Office of Superintendents," *Proceedings of the International Congress of Education* (New York: National Educational Association, 1894), p. 78.

88. "Report of Committee on City School Systems," *Proceedings: National Educational Association, 1890*, p. 313.

89. William J. Akers, *Cleveland Schools in the Nineteenth Century* (Cleveland: W. M. Bayne, 1901), pp. 258–62; "Cleveland School System," *Ohio Educational Monthly* 41 (Apr. 1892): 178–79; *Fifty-seventh Annual Report of the Board of Education for . . . 1893* (Cleveland: W. M. Bayne Printing Co., 1893), pp. 11–13, 22–23.

90. Selwyn K. Troen, *The Public and the Schools: Shaping the St. Louis System, 1838–1920* (Columbia: University of Missouri Press, 1975), pp. 215–19; Elinor Mondale Gersman, "Progressive Reform of the St. Louis School Board, 1897," *History of Education Quarterly* 10 (Sept. 1970): 3–21.

91. A. Emerson Palmer, *The New York Public School* (New York: Macmillan Co., 1905), pp. 298–302.

92. As quoted in Troen, *The Public and the Schools*, p. 219.

93. *Report and Evidence on the Reorganization of the Fire Department* (Boston, 1873), p. 128.

94. "The Condition in New York," *Insurance Engineering* 4 (Oct. 1902): 405.

95. *Proceedings of the Seventeenth Annual Convention of the National Association of Fire Engineers, 1889* (Cincinnati: Keating & Co., 1889), p. 151.

96. *Report of the Fire Department of the City of New York for the Year Ending December 31, 1899* (New York: Martin B. Brown Co., 1900), pp. 43, 94. In 1890 41 percent of the officers in New

York City's department had over twenty years on the force. *Report of the Fire Department of the City of New York for the . . . Year Ending December 31, 1889* (New York: Martin B. Brown Co., 1890), p. 59.

97. *Proceedings of the Thirty-second Annual Convention of the International Association of Fire Engineers, 1904* (1904), p. 68.

98. "Condition in New York," *Insurance Engineering*, p. 405. Edward Croker wrote that "politics and the fire department . . . should be as widely separated as the poles . . . , and it is the duty of every city to see that politics is kept out of this department as rigidly as may be." Edward F. Croker, *Fire Prevention* (New York: Dodd Mead & Co., 1912), p. 282.

99. *Chicago Tribune*, 16 Feb. 1903, p. 1; 17 Feb. 1903, p. 4; Franklin MacVeagh, "Municipal Government of Chicago," *Proceedings of the National Conference for Good City Government . . . 1894* (Philadelphia: Municipal League, 1894), p. 82.

100. Carter Harrison, Jr., *Stormy Years: The Autobiography of Carter H. Harrison* (Indianapolis: Bobbs-Merrill Co., 1935), pp. 108–9, 121.

101. *Chicago Tribune*, 16 Feb. 1903, p. 1; 17 Feb. 1903, p. 6; *Proceedings of the Seventh Annual Meeting of the Illinois Firemen's Association . . . 1895* (Chicago: Western Fireman, 1895), pp. 68–70; *Proceedings of the Fifteenth Annual Meeting of the Illinois Firemen's Association . . . 1903* (Bushnell, Ill.: Charles C. Chain, 1903), p. 109; "Chicago Veterans," *City Government* 9 (Nov. 1900): 119.

102. *History of the Cleveland Fire Department* (Cleveland: Firemen's Relief Association, 1897), p. 61; Winkler, "Government of Milwaukee," *Proceedings of Second Conference for Good City Government*, pp. 120–21. George C. Hale did finally lose his post as fire chief, owing to a feud with Kansas City's mayor. See "Fire and Police Personals," *Municipal Journal and Engineer*, 12 (June 1902): 275.

103. Howard O. Sprogle, *The Philadelphia Police, Past and Present* (Philadelphia: Howard O. Sprogle, 1887), pp. 166–68.

104. Ibid., pp. 138, 229–31, 337–38, 388–91.

105. Ibid., pp. 326, 620.

106. See: A. Kaufmann, *Historic Supplement of the Denver Police* (Denver, 1890); Eugene Frank Rider, "The Denver Police Department: An Administrative, Organizational, and Operational History, 1858–1905" (Ph.D. dissertation, University of Denver, 1971).

107. Robert M. Fogelson, *Big-City Police* (Cambridge: Harvard University Press, 1977), p. 23.

108. MacVeagh, "Government of Chicago," *Proceedings of Conference for Good City Government . . . 1894*, p. 82.

109. *City Government* 2 (Jan. 1897): 25; *City Government* 2 (April 1897): 115.

110. Based on information in Augustus E. Costello, *Our Police Protectors* (New York: Augustus E. Costello, 1885), pp. 527–59.

111. Ibid., p. 467.

112. George W. Walling, *Recollections of a New York Chief of Police* (New York: Caxton Book Concern, 1888), p. 598.

113. James F. Richardson, *The New York Police: Colonial Times to 1901* (New York: Oxford University Press, 1970), pp. 231–32.

114. William G. Bruce, *A Short History of Milwaukee* (Milwaukee: Bruce Publishing Co., 1936), p. 86; Winkler, "Government of Milwaukee," *Proceedings of Second Conference for Good City Government*, pp. 120–21.

115. Samuel Walker, *A Critical History of Police Reform: The Emergence of Professionalism* (Lexington, Mass.: D. C. Heath Co., 1977), pp. 48, 56–57; Gene E. Carte and Elaine H. Carte, *Police Reform in the United States: The Era of August Vollmer, 1905–1932* (Berkeley: University of California Press, 1975), pp. 13–14.

116. Costello, *Police Protectors*, p. 466.

7. BOSSES AND BUSINESSMEN: EXTRALEGAL MOLDERS OF MUNICIPAL RULE

1. George Vickers, *The Fall of Bossism* (Philadelphia: A. C. Bryson, 1883), pp. iv, vi.

2. James Bryce, *The American Commonwealth*, 3 vols. (London: Macmillan & Co., 1888), 2: 455, 456, 459.

3. William Howe Tolman, *Municipal Reform Movements in the United States* (New York: Fleming H. Revell Co., 1895), p. 36.

4. *Chicago Tribune*, 19 Mar. 1887, pp. 1–2.

5. Ibid., 15 Mar. 1893, p. 2; 16 Mar. 1893, p. 3.

6. *Boston Globe*, 15 Nov. 1889, Extra ed. p. 2.

7. Ibid., 20 Nov. 1890, p. 6.

8. *Cleveland Leader*, 21 Mar. 1893, p. 8.

9. *Cleveland Plain Dealer*, 15 Mar. 1895, p. 2.

10. *St. Louis Globe-Democrat*, 15 Mar. 1887, p. 8.

11. *St. Louis Post-Dispatch*, 23 Mar. 1889, p. 1.

12. *New Orleans Daily Picayune*, 23 Mar. 1888, p. 8.

13. *Boston Globe*, 18 Nov. 1890, p. 3; 9 Dec. 1890, Extra ed., p. 7; 14 Dec. 1891, Extra ed., p. 2; *Boston Herald*, 22 Nov. 1892, p. 2.

14. *Philadelphia Evening Bulletin*, 9 Feb. 1887, p. 6; 14 Feb. 1887, p. 6; 15 Feb. 1887, p. 6. See also ibid., 17 Feb. 1891, p. 1.

15. *St. Louis Globe-Democrat*, 4 Apr. 1887, p. 6.

16. See Lloyd Wendt and Herman Kogan, *Lords of the Levee: The Story of Bathhouse John and Hinky Dink* (Indianapolis: Bobbs-Merrill Co., 1943).

17. Lyle W. Dorsett, *The Pendergast Machine* (New York: Oxford University Press, 1968), pp. 11–21.

18. Harold Zink, *City Bosses in the United States* (Durham, N.C.: Duke University Press, 1930), pp. 71–72.

19. William S. Vare, *My Forty Years in Politics* (Philadelphia: Roland Swain Co., 1933), pp. 62–65.

20. *Chicago Tribune*, 6 Mar. 1899, p. 2; Joel A. Tarr, *A Study in Boss Politics: William Lorimer of Chicago* (Urbana: University of Illinois Press, 1971).

21. James B. Whipple, "Municipal Government in an Average City: Cleveland, 1876–1900," *Ohio State Archaeological And Historical Quarterly* 62 (Jan. 1953): 3–5.

22. Vare, *Forty Years*, p. 46.

23. *St. Louis Globe-Democrat*, 14 Mar. 1887, p. 7.

24. *St. Louis Post-Dispatch*, 27 Mar. 1889, p. 2.

25. Ibid., 20 Mar. 1897, pp. 1–2; 21 Mar. 1897, pp. 4, 9–10.

26. Frederick W. Dewart, "The Municipal Condition of St. Louis," *Proceedings of the Louisville Conference for Good City Government* (Philadelphia: National Municipal League, 1897), p. 231.

27. *New Orleans Daily Picayune*, 25 Mar. 1884, p. 2; 25 Mar. 1888, p. 7; 12 Apr. 1892, p. 3; 8 Apr. 1896, pp. 1, 8; 14 Apr. 1896, pp. 1, 6.

28. John R. Kemp, ed., *Martin Behrman of New Orleans: Memoirs of a City Boss* (Baton Rouge: Louisiana State University Press, 1977), p. 20.

29. Theodore Roosevelt, "Machine Politics in New York City," *Century* 33 (Nov. 1886): 81.

30. Bryce, *American Commonwealth*, 2: 460.

31. *St. Louis Post-Dispatch*, 20 Mar. 1897, pp. 1–2; 21 Mar. 1897, pp. 9–10.

32. *Cincinnati Enquirer*, 2 Mar. 1894, p. 8; *Cincinnati Tribune*, 2 Mar. 1894, pp. 1, 4.

33. Harold C. Syrett, ed., *The Gentleman and the Tiger: The Autobiography of George B. McClellan* (Philadelphia: J. B. Lippincott Co., 1956), p. 158.

34. Ibid., p. 161.

35. William A. Bullough, *The Blind Boss and His City* (Berkeley and Los Angeles: University of California Press, 1979), pp. 153–80.

36. Zink, *City Bosses*, pp. 183–86.

37. *New York Herald*, 22 Apr. 1891, p. 7; *New York Times*, 3 June 1891, p. 5.

38. *New York Times*, 21 May 1891, p. 1; 24 May 1891, p. 9; 30 May 1891, p. 8; 31 May 1891, p. 9; 25 June 1891, p. 1.

39. Edward Dana Durand, *The Finances of New York City* (New York: Macmillan Co., 1898), p. 270.

40. Bird S. Coler, *Municipal Government* (New York: D. Appleton & Co., 1900), pp. 189–90.

41. Durand, *Finances of New York*, pp. 271–72.

42. Zane L. Miller, *Boss Cox's Cincinnati* (New York: Oxford University Press, 1968), p. 92.

43. Kenneth Sturges, *American Chambers of Commerce* (New York: Moffat, Dard & Co., 1915), pp. 12–13.

44. *Fifteenth Annual Report of the Corporation of the Chamber of Commerce of the State of New-York for the Year 1872–73* (New York: Press of the Chamber of Commerce, 1873), p. 73.

45. *Thirty-eighth Annual Report of the Corporation of the Chamber of Commerce, of the State of New York, for the Year 1895–96* (New York: Press of the Chamber of Commerce, 1896), p. 137.

46. *Thirty-fourth Annual Report of the Corporation of the Chamber of Commerce, of the State of New York, for the Year 1891–92* (New York: Press of the Chamber of Commerce, 1892), p. 109; *Thirty-sixth Annual Report of the Corporation of the Chamber of Commerce, of the State of New-York, for the Year 1893–94* (New York: Press of the Chamber of Commerce, 1894), pp. 76–78.

47. *New York Times*, 26 Jan. 1894, p. 3; *Thirty-sixth Report of the Chamber of Commerce of New York, 1893–94*, pp. 77–78.

48. *Thirty-eighth Report of the Chamber of Commerce of New York, 1895–96*, pp. 27, 31.

49. *Thirty-fourth Report of the Chamber of Commerce of New York, 1891–92*, pp. 16–19; *Thirty-sixth Report of the Chamber of Commerce of New York, 1893–94*, pp. 135–37; *New York Times*, 2 Feb. 1894, p. 3; 11 Mar. 1894, p. 9; 13 Mar. 1894, p. 8.

50. *New York Times*, 16 Mar. 1894, p. 3; 27 Apr. 1894, p. 5.

51. *Forty-seventh Annual Report of the Philadelphia Board of Trade* (Philadelphia: Chandler Printing House, 1880), pp. 25–27; *Forty-eighth Annual Report of the Philadelphia Board of Trade* (Philadelphia: Chandler Printing House, 1881), pp. 15–16, 33–35, 36–37.

52. *Fifty-seventh Annual Report of the Philadelphia Board of Trade* (Philadelphia: Burk & McFetridge, 1890), pp. 35–38; *Fifty-ninth Annual Report of the Philadelphia Board of Trade* (Philadelphia: Burk & McFetridge, 1892), p. 47.

53. *The Board of Trade of the City of Newark, N.J., The Twenty-fifth Annual Report* (Newark, 1895), pp. 28–29, 34, 49, 51–55, 61–62, 78, 82–88; *The Board of Trade of the City of Newark, N.J., The Twenty-fourth Annual Report* (Newark: John E. Rowe & Son, 1893), pp. 20–21, 33–38.

54. *The Cleveland Chamber of Commerce, Reports and Proceedings: 46th Annual Meeting, April 17th, 1894* (Cleveland, 1894), p. 33; *The Cleveland Chamber of Commerce, Reports and Proceedings: 47th Anniversary, April, 1895* (Cleveland, 1895), pp. 52, 55–57; *The Cleveland Chamber of Commerce, Forty-eighth Year, April, 1896* (Cleveland: J. B. Savage, 1896), pp. 91–92, 94–95.

55. Ryerson Ritchie, "Commercial Organizations and Municipal Reform," *Proceedings of the Louisville Conference for Good City Government* (Philadelphia: National Municipal League, 1897), p. 125.

56. *Annual Report of the Directors and Secretary of the Columbus Board of Trade for the Year Ending December 31, 1887* (Columbus: Ohio State Journal, 1888), p. 9.

57. *Annual Report of the Commercial Club of Indianapolis for the Fiscal Year Ending January 31, 1891* (Indianapolis: Baker-Randolph Lith. and Eng. Co., 1891), pp. 8, 12–15; *The Com-*

mercial Club, Fifth Year Reports of Officers (Indianapolis: Carlon & Hollenbeck, 1895), pp. 17–19.

58. Theodore Wirth, *Minneapolis Park System, 1883–1944* (Minneapolis: n.p., 1946), pp. 19–24.

59. *St. Paul Chamber of Commerce Annual Report, January, 1896* (Saint Paul, 1896), pp. 7–11.

60. J. Richard Freud, "Civic Service of the Merchant's Association of San Francisco," *Municipal Affairs* 1 (Dec. 1897): 711.

61. Robert C. Brooks, "Business Men in Civic Service: The Merchants' Municipal Committee of Boston," *Municipal Affairs* 1 (Sept. 1897): 491–508.

62. *New York Times*, 29 Aug. 1894, p. 8.

63. Howard F. Gillette, Jr., "Corrupted and Contented: Philadelphia's Political Machine, 1865–1887" (Ph.D. dissertation, Yale University, 1970), pp. 226–27.

64. Ibid., p. 238.

65. Douglas Sutherland, *Fifty Years on the Civic Front* (Chicago: Civic Federation, 1943), pp. 10–11, 18–20.

66. *Fifteen Years of Civic History: Civic Club of Allegheny County* (Pittsburgh, 1910), pp. 12–18, 33.

67. "Brief Statements Concerning the Objects and Methods of Municipal Reform Organizations in the United States," *Proceedings of the National Conference for Good City Government Held at Philadelphia* (Philadelphia: Municipal League, 1894), p. 317.

68. Ibid., p. 322.

69. Ibid., p. 333; Tolman, *Municipal Reform Movements*, p. 119.

70. *The City Club of New York, Annual Report of the Secretary* (New York, 1895), pp. 8–12, 14–20.

71. Sidney I. Roberts, "The Municipal Voters' League and Chicago's Boodlers," *Journal of the Illinois State Historical Society* 53 (Summer 1960): 141.

72. Edwin Burritt Smith, "Council Reform in Chicago: Work of the Municipal Voters' League," *Municipal Affairs* 4 (June 1900): 356–57.

73. William A. Giles, *Report on Reform Legislation* (Chicago: R. R. Donnelley & Sons Co., 1899), p. 5.

74. James B. Crooks, *Politics and Progress: The Rise of Urban Progressivism in Baltimore, 1895–1911* (Baton Rouge: Louisiana State University Press, 1968), pp. 13–45.

75. "Statements Concerning Municipal Reform Organizations," *National Conference for Good Government*, pp. 333–34.

76. *New York Times*, 10 Feb. 1895, p. 2.

77. Roberts, "Municipal Voters' League," p. 136; Smith, "Council Reform," p. 349.

78. Crooks, *Politics and Progress*, pp. 14, 29.

79. Ibid., p. 15; Eric F. Goldman, *Charles J. Bonaparte, Patrician Reformer* (Baltimore: Johns Hopkins Press, 1943).

80. Tolman, *Municipal Reform Movements*, p. 123.

81. *A Municipal Program* (New York: Macmillan Co., 1900); Clinton Rogers Woodruff, "The Nationalization of Municipal Movements," *Annals of the American Academy of Political and Social Science* 21 (Mar. 1903): 100–108.

82. Archibald MacPhail, *Of Men and Fire: A Story of Fire Insurance in the Far West* (San Francisco: Fire Underwriters Association of the Pacific, 1948), pp. 132–33; *The New York Board of Fire Underwriters, 1867–1967* (New York: Pacific Printing Co., 1967), pp. 9–10; James A. Waterworth, *My Memories of the St. Louis Board of Fire Underwriters, Its Members and Its Work* (Saint Louis: Skaer Printing Co., 1926), pp. 48–49.

83. *St. Louis Post-Dispatch*, 25 Aug. 1881, p. 8.

84. Waterworth, *Memories*, pp. 84–87.

85. *New York Underwriters*, p. 13.

86. *San Francisco Chronicle*, 5 Apr. 1879, p. 2; 18 Feb. 1883, p. 5.

87. "The Difficulty in Boston and the Remedy Proposed," *Chronicle, An Insurance Journal* 11 (19 June 1873): 388.

88. *Weekly Underwriter: An Insurance Newspaper*, 6 Feb. 1886, pp. 94–95; 13 Feb. 1886, p. 110.

89. *Chronicle, An Insurance Journal* 14 (30 July 1874): 65–69; Robert S. Critchell, *Recollections of a Fire Insurance Man* (Chicago: By the Author, 1909), pp. 103–04; Harry Chase Brearley, *Fifty Years of a Civilizing Force* (New York: Frederick A. Stokes Co., 1916), pp. 41–45; A. L. Todd, *A Spark Lighted in Portland: The Record of the National Board of Fire Underwriters* (New York: McGraw-Hill Book Co., 1966), pp. 27–28.

90. *Chicago Tribune*, 1 Oct. 1874, pp. 1, 2, 4, 8; 2 Oct. 1874, pp. 2, 4; 3 Oct. 1874, p. 2; 4 Oct. 1874, p. 8; 6 Oct. 1874, p. 4; 12 Nov. 1874, p. 5; 2 Dec. 1874, pp. 4, 7; *Chronicle, An Insurance Journal* 14 (1 Oct. 1874): 209–11; ibid., 22 Oct. 1874, pp. 257, 259; 3 Dec. 1874, p. 356; 10 Dec. 1874, p. 370; 17 Dec. 1874, pp. 389–90; 31 Dec. 1874, p. 421; Critchell, *Recollections*, pp. 104–06.

91. *Pioneers of Progress* (New York: H. Wolff, 1941), p. 123; Todd, *A Spark Lighted*, p. 34.

92. *Pioneers of Progress*, pp. 124–25; Todd, *A Spark Lighted*, pp. 37, 39; *Rules and Ordinances of the Department of Electricity of the City of Chicago* (Chicago: Halliday Witherspoon, 1900); no page numbers in original.

93. *Pioneers of Progress*, p. 124; Todd, *A Spark Lighted*, pp. 35–36.

94. *A History of Real Estate, Building and Architecture in New York City During the Last Quarter of a Century* (New York: Real Estate Record Association, 1898), pp. 289–90; John P. Comer, *New York Building Control, 1800–1941* (New York: Columbia University Press, 1942), pp. 9–11; *Laws of the State of New York Passed at the Eighty-third Session of the Legislature* (Albany: Weed, Parsons & Co., 1860), pp. 924–25.

95. *History of Real Estate in New York City*, p. 290; Comer, *New York Building Control*, pp. 15, 17–18; *Laws of the State of New York Passed at the Ninety-seventh Session of the Legislature* (Albany: Hugh J. Hastings, 1874), pp. 737–38.

96. *New York Times*, 14 Nov. 1889, p. 9; 19 Nov. 1889, p. 8; 21 Nov. 1889, p. 8; 30 Nov. 1889, p. 8; 26 Nov. 1891, p. 8; 28 Nov. 1891, p. 3; 3 Dec. 1891, p. 6; 19 Dec. 1891, p. 10; 21 Dec. 1895, p. 9; "Revision of Building Laws," *Architecture and Building* 15 (21 Nov. 1891), p. 259.

97. "Annual Report of the New York Chapter," *Proceedings of the Twenty-first Annual Convention of the American Institute of Architects* (New York: American Institute of Architects, 1888), pp. 45–46.

98. "The Building Department and the Architects," *Architecture and Building* 23 (19 Oct. 1895), p. 183.

99. "Annual Report of Chicago Chapter," *Proceedings of the Twenty-sixth Annual Convention of the American Institute of Architects* (Chicago: American Institute of Architects, 1893), pp. 88–89; *American Architect and Building News* 48 (22 June 1895), p. 118; ibid. 42 (9 Dec. 1893), p. 120. See also ibid. 23 (24 Mar. 1888), p. 136.

100. "Annual Report of the Philadelphia Chapter," *Proceedings of the Twenty-sixth Annual Convention of the American Institute of Architects* (Chicago: American Institute of Architects, 1893), p. 78; "Annual Report of Baltimore Chapter," *Proceedings of the Twenty-fifth Annual Convention of the American Institute of Architects* (Chicago: American Institute of Architects, 1892), p. 98.

101. "Annual Report of Indianapolis Chapter," *Proceedings of the Twenty-fourth Annual Convention of the American Institute of Architects* (Chicago: American Institute of Architects, 1891), p. 158.

102. "Annual Report of the Boston Chapter," *Proceedings of the Twenty-sixth Annual Convention of the American Institute of Architects* (Chicago: American Institute of Architects, 1893), p. 80.

103. *New York Times*, 10 Feb. 1889, p. 14; 16 May 1889, p. 8; 5 Feb. 1891, p. 8; 4 Jan. 1893, p. 2.

104. *Chicago Tribune*, 15 Jan. 1885, p. 8.

105. Ibid., 9 Jan. 1890, p. 6.

106. Ibid., 14 Jan. 1892, p. 10.

107. Ibid., 6 Jan. 1899, p. 12.

108. *Boston Globe*, 6 Jan. 1891, p. 6; *Boston Herald*, 6 Jan. 1891, p. 6; *Boston Evening Transcript*, 6 Jan. 1891, p. 6; 6 Feb. 1891, p. 1; 10 Feb. 1891, p. 5; *Acts and Resolves Passed by the General Court of Massachusetts in the Year 1891* (Boston: Wright & Potter, 1891), pp. 880–88.

109. *New York Times*, 20 Jan. 1889, p. 14.

110. *Chicago Tribune*, 1 Jan. 1897, p. 18; 1 Jan. 1898, p. 17; 13 Jan. 1898, p. 12; *Economist* (Chicago) 15 (2 May 1896): 541; ibid., 9 May 1896, p. 574; 23 May 1896, p. 637; 13 June 1896, p. 729.

111. *New York Times*, 30 Oct. 1894, p. 5.

112. *Chicago Tribune*, 6 Jan. 1899, p. 12.

113. *New York Times*, 20 Apr. 1893, p. 6; 25 Apr. 1893, p. 2; Lillie H. French, "Municipal Art," *Harper's Weekly* 37 (22 Apr. 1893): 371; "Public Art in American Cities," *Municipal Affairs* 2 (Mar. 1898): 8; Jon A. Peterson, "The City Beautiful Movement: Forgotten Origins and Lost Meanings," *Journal of Urban History* 2 (Aug. 1976): 417.

114. *New York Times*, 20 Apr. 1893, p. 6.

115. "The National Sculpture Society," *Year Book of the Art Societies of New York, 1898–1899* (New York: Leonard Scott Publication Co., 1899), pp. 108–09.

116. *New York Times*, 7 Dec. 1893, p. 8; 4 Jan. 1894, p. 9; 19 May 1894, p. 4.

117. Ibid., 27 July 1894, p. 3; 9 Aug. 1894, p. 9; 22 Dec. 1894, p. 9.

118. Ibid., 2 Jan. 1895, p. 3.

119. Ibid., 4 Apr. 1895, p. 16; 1 May 1895, p. 4.

120. Ibid., 4 Apr. 1895, p. 16; 1 May 1895, p. 4; "Public Art in American Cities," p. 9.

121. *New York Times*, 11 Mar. 1896, p. 9; 13 Mar. 1896, p. 9.

122. Ibid., 5 Mar. 1896, p. 3; 14 Mar. 1896, p. 1; "Public Art in American Cities," pp. 9–10.

123. *New York Times*, 24 Nov. 1897, p. 1; 15 Dec. 1897, p. 5; "Public Art in American Cities," p. 9.

124. *Fairmount Park Art Association, An Account of Its Origin and Activities, from Its Foundation in 1871* (Philadelphia: Fairmount Park Art Association, 1922).

125. *Cincinnati Tribune*, 1 June 1894, p. 5: *Cincinnati Enquirer*, 1 June 1894, p. 8.

126. "Public Art in Cincinnati," *Harper's Weekly* 41 (10 July 1897): 696.

127. Charles H. Caffin, "Baltimore Municipal Art Conference," *Harper's Weekly* 43 (30 Dec. 1899), p. 1332; Joseph Lauber, "Report of Civic Buildings Committee—National Society of Mural Painters," *Year Book of the Art Societies of New York, 1898–1899* (New York: Leonard Scott Publication Co., 1899), p. 152.

128. *New York Times*, 21 June 1889, p. 5; 7 Feb. 1891, p. 2; 2 Mar. 1893, p. 8; 10 Mar. 1893, p. 3; 6 Dec. 1894, p. 6; 5 Mar. 1897, p. 9; 19 Mar. 1897, p. 7; H. D. Chapin, "Report of Committee on Croton Supply," *Transactions of the New York Academy of Medicine* (New York: Academy of Medicine, 1894), pp. 196–209; *Annual Report of the Board of Health of the Health Department of the City of New York for . . . 1890* (New York: Martin B. Brown, 1891), p. 4; *Annual Report of the Board of Health of the Health Department of the City of New York for . . . 1891* (New York: Martin B. Brown, 1892), p. 4; John Duffy, *A History of Public Health in New York City* (New York: Russell Sage Foundation, 1974), pp. 116, 128, 170, 217.

129. "The Chicago Health Office," *Chicago Medical Recorder* 2 (Dec. 1891): 343. Bessie Louise Pierce, *A History of Chicago*, 3 vols. (New York: Alfred A. Knopf, 1957), 3:396.

130. "Preliminary Report of the Committee Appointed to Take Into Consideration the Milk Supply of Boston," *Boston Medical and Surgical Journal* 111 (31 July 1884): 111–13; Vincent Y. Bowditch, "The Condition of the Streets of Boston, and the Public Health," ibid. 122 (12 June 1890): 579–80, 582–85.

131. *New York Times*, 22 Jan. 1897, p. 12; Philip Van Ingen, *The New York Academy of Medicine* (New York: Columbia University Press, 1949), p. 264; Daniel M. Fox, "Social Policy and City Politics: Tuberculosis Reporting in New York, 1889–1900," in Judith Walzer Leavitt and

Ronald L. Numbers, eds., *Sickness and Health in America* (Madison: University of Wisconsin Press, 1978), pp. 415–31. For the reaction of Philadelphia's medical establishment to a municipal program of registering tuberculosis victims, see "Discussion on the Advisability of the Registration of Tuberculosis," *Transactions of the College of Physicians of Philadelphia* 16 (Philadelphia: College of Physicians, 1894): 1–27.

132. *New York Times*, 23 Jan. 1898, p. 5; 24 Jan. 1898, p. 5; 27 Jan. 1898, p. 5; 3 Feb. 1898, p. 6; Duffy, *Public Health in New York City*, pp. 241–42.

133. *New York Times*, 25 Jan. 1887, p. 2.

134. Ibid., 27 June 1889, p. 5.

135. "The Chicago Department of Health, the Mayor, et al.," *Chicago Medical Recorder* 9 (July 1895), pp. 37–39; *Chicago Tribune*, 29 June 1895, p. 2; 30 June 1895, p. 12.

136. As quoted in Alan I. Marcus, "Professional Revolution and Reform in the Progressive Era: Cincinnati Physicians and the City Elections of 1897 and 1900," *Journal of Urban History* 5 (Feb. 1979): 188, 196, 197.

137. Ibid., p. 197.

138. *St. Louis Post-Dispatch*, 2 May 1891, p. 4; 3 May 1891, p. 5; 6 May 1891, pp. 3, 4; 7 May 1891, p. 1; 8 May 1891, p. 5; 9 May 1891, p. 6; 23 May 1891, p. 2; 15 July 1891, p. 2; 19 July 1891, p. 17; *St. Louis Globe-Democrat*, 2 May 1891, p. 6; 6 May 1891, p. 9; 9 May 1891, p. 3; 10 July 1891, p. 4; 15 July 1891, p. 5.

8. THE TRIUMPH OF TECHNOLOGY

1. James Bryce, *The American Commonwealth*, 3 vols. (London: Macmillan & Co., 1888), 2: 278.

2. Georges J. Joyaux, trans., "A Frenchman's Visit to Chicago in 1886," *Journal of the Illinois State Historical Society* 47 (Spring 1954): 49.

3. "Disposal of Sewage and Garbage in Foreign Countries," *Special Counselar Reports*, vol. 17. (Washington, D.C.: U.S. Government Printing Office, 1899), pp. 55–57, 152, 155, 165; Shena D. Simon, *A Century of City Government, Manchester, 1838–1938* (London: George Allen & Unwin, 1938), pp. 169–83.

4. In the Bronx, 95 percent of the new tenements in 1901 provided a water closet for each family, and in Brooklyn the figure was 90%. Carroll D. Wright, *Seventh Special Report of the Commissioner of Labor—The Slums of Baltimore, Chicago, New York, and Philadelphia* (Washington, D.C.: U.S. Government Printing Office, 1894), p. 94; Robert W. DeForest and Lawrence Veiller, eds. *The Tenement House Problem*, 2 vols. (New York: Macmillan Co., 1903), 1: 24, 247, 250, 254.

5. James E. Fuertes, *Waste of Water in New York and its Reduction by Meters and Inspection* (New York: Merchants' Association of New York, 1906), pp. 30, 198.

6. *Times* (London), 23 Aug. 1898, p. 8; 24 Aug. 1898, p. 4; 25 Aug. 1898, p. 8; 29 Aug. 1898, p. 6; 2 Sept. 1898, p. 8; 5 Sept. 1898, p. 10; 6 Sept. 1898, p. 7; 12 Sept. 1898, p. 6; 16 Sept. 1898, p. 8; 17 Sept. 1898, p. 10; 19 Sept. 1898, p. 9; 26 Sept. 1898, p. 10; Milo Roy Maltbie, "A Tale of Two Cities: Water Supply in London and Philadelphia," *Municipal Affairs* 3 (June 1899): 199; Major Greenwood, "The London Water Supply," *Sanitary Record* 18 (4 Sept. 1896): 191–92; G. Shaw Lefevre, "The London Water Supply," *Nineteenth Century* 44 (Dec. 1898): 980–90.

7. D. J. Ebbetts, "The Sanitary State of Paris," *Sanitary Record* 8 (16 Aug. 1886): 54, 55. See also, "The Paris Water Supply—Startling Revelations," *Surveyor and Municipal and County Engineer* 17 (6 Apr. 1900): 378.

8. *New York Times*, 1 Oct. 1891, p. 9; 10 Nov. 1891, p. 9; 17 Nov. 1891, p. 8; 18 Nov. 1891, p. 9.

9. *Times* (London), 6 Sept. 1887, p. 13.

10. Charles H. Weidner, *Water For a City: A History of New York City's Problem from the Beginning to the Delaware River System* (New Brunswick, N.J.: Rutgers University Press, 1974), pp. 48–117.

11. "The Permanent Supply Water Works of Baltimore," *Engineering News* 4 (19 May 1877): 128–29.

12. "Water Supply of American Cities –Boston," *Engineering News* 5 (3 Jan. 1878): 4–5; ibid., 10 Jan. 1878, pp. 12–13; 17 Jan. 1878, p. 21; 24 Jan. 1878, pp. 28–29; 31 Jan. 1878, pp. 37–38; 14 Feb. 1878, p. 52; 21 Feb. 1878, pp. 61–62; 7 Mar. 1878, p. 78; 21 Mar. 1878, pp. 95–96; 28 Mar. 1878, pp. 102–03; 4 Apr. 1878, pp. 111–12; 11 Apr. 1878, pp. 117–20; 18 Apr. 1878, pp. 125–28; 25 Apr. 1878, pp. 134–36; 16 May 1878), p. 160. J. A. Stewart, "Waterworks Expansion in Boston," *Scientific American* 81 (4 Nov. 1899): 292–94; Fletcher Osgood, "How Boston Gets Its Water," *New England Magazine* 14 (June 1896): 389–409.

13. "The Sewerage of Boston," *Engineering News* 3 (19 Feb. 1876): 58–59; ibid., 26 Feb. 1876, pp. 66–67; B. G. Underwood, "Metropolitan Sewerage System Surrounding Boston," *Scientific American* 67 (17 Dec. 1892): 390–91; *Main Drainage Works of Boston and Its Metropolitan Sewerage District* (Boston: Wright & Potter Printing Co., 1899): pp. 2–31.

14. Harold M. Mayer and Richard C. Wade, *Chicago: Growth of a Metropolis* (Chicago: University of Chicago Press, 1969), p. 97.

15. John Leng, *America in 1876* (Dundee, Scotland: Dundee Advertiser Office, 1877), p. 82; Louis P. Cain, *Sanitation Strategy for a Lakefront Metropolis: The Case of Chicago* (DeKalb: Northern Illinois University Press, 1978), pp. 20–58.

16. Robert Isham Randolph, "The History of Sanitation in Chicago," *Journal of the Western Society of Engineers* 44 (Oct. 1939): 227–40; Cain, *Sanitation Strategy*, pp. 59–76; Ellis L. Armstrong, *History of Public Works in the United States, 1776–1976* Chicago: American Public Works Association, 1976), pp. 227–28; John L. Wright, "The Chicago Drainage Canal," *Lippincott's Monthly Magazine* 60 (Sept. 1897): 410–14.

17. For a fuller account of annexation campaigns of the late nineteenth century, see Jon C. Teaford, *City and Suburb: The Political Fragmentation of Metropolitan America, 1850–1970* (Baltimore: Johns Hopkins University Press, 1979), pp. 32–63.

18. *Philadelphia Press*, 24 Feb. 1895, p. 3; Edwin F. Smith, "Filtration of City Water Supplies—Abstract of an Argument for Filtration, with Special Reference to Philadelphia," *Sanitarian* 36 (May 1896): 425–34.

19. "Report of the Lancet Special Sanitary Commission of Inquiry Concerning the Water-Supply of Chicago, U.S.A.," *Lancet*, vol. 1 for 1893 (8 Apr. 1893): 832–48. For the American medical profession's response to the *Lancet*'s investigation, see: "Sanitary Council of the Mississippi Valley Association," *Sanitarian* 30 (May 1893): 463–64; "Water Supply of Chicago," *North American Practitioner* 5 (July 1893): 332–33.

20. Allen Hazen, *The Filtration of Public Water-Supplies* (New York: John Wiley & Sons, 1900), pp. 221–315; George C. Whipple, *Typhoid Fever: Its Causation, Transmission, and Prevention* (New York: John Wiley & Sons, 1908), pp. 228–66.

21. "The Wooden Pavements of Chicago," *Engineering News* 4 (20 Oct. 1877): 287; E. A. Fox, "The Wooden Pavements of Chicago," ibid. 5 (10 Jan. 1878): 14–15; 17 Jan. 1878, p. 22.

22. Max O'Rell and Jack Allyn, *Jonathan and His Continent* (New York: Cassell & Co., 1889), p. 31.

23. *Times* (London), 29 Aug. 1887, p. 4; W. H. Russell, *Hesperothen: Notes from the West*, 2 vols. (London: Sampson Low, Marston, Searle, & Rivington, 1882), 1: 19; Gaétan Desaché, *Souvenir de mon voyage aux Etats-Unis et au Canada* (Tours: Paul Bouserez, 1877), p. 29; Archibald Sutter, *American Notes, 1881* (Edinburgh: William Blackwood & Sons, 1882), pp. 4, 31; Charles E. Lewis, *Two Lectures on a Short Visit to America* (London: Blades, East & Blades, 1876), p. 24; Leng, *America in 1876*, p. 155.

24. O'Rell and Allyn, *Jonathan and His Continent*, p. 44; H. Panmure Gordon, *The Land of the Almighty Dollar* (London: Frederick Warne & Co., 1892), pp. 176–77.

25. A. H. Godfrey, "Cycling Clubs and Their Spheres of Action," *Outing* 30 (Aug. 1897), pp. 489–90. See also: *New York Times*, 15 Aug. 1894, p. 3; 12 May 1895, p. 15; 2 Aug. 1896, p. 13; *Chicago Tribune*, 24 Mar. 1897, p. 8; 2 Apr. 1897, p. 3.

26. According to John A. Fairlie, a leading student of municipal government both in America and abroad, Buffalo and Washington, D.C. were "better paved than any other cities in the world," and Boston and the borough of Manhattan "compare favorably with the best-paved of the foreign cities." John A. Fairlie, *Municipal Administration* (New York: Macmillan Co., 1901), p. 235.

27. *New York Times,* 7 May 1895, p. 6.

28. As quoted in Mildred M. Hickman, *Electrical Manufacturing in Cleveland* (Cleveland: Board of Education, 1930), p. 11.

29. *Times* (London), 29 Aug. 1887, p. 4.

30. "Glasgow Municipal Electricity Supply," *Electrical Review* 57 (17 Nov. 1905): 816; "Leeds Municipal Electricity Supply," ibid. 8 Dec. 1905, p. 940; "Manchester Municipal Electricity Supply," ibid., 10 Nov. 1905, p. 774.

31. *Rules and Ordinances of the Department of Electricity of the City of Chicago, with an Historical Appendix* (Chicago: Halliday Witherspoon, 1900), pp. 93, 159; Bessie Louise Pierce, *A History of Chicago,* 3 vols. (New York: Alfred A. Knopf, 1957), 3: 329–30.

32. *New York Herald,* 10 Oct. 1889, pp. 5, 6; 11 Oct. 1889, p. 3; 12 Oct. 1889, p. 3; *New York Tribune,* 10 Oct. 1889, p. 1; 11 Oct. 1889, p. 1; 12 Oct. 1889, p. 5; 13 Oct. 1889, p. 1; 15 Oct. 1889, pp. 1–2; 16 Oct. 1889, p. 2; 17 Oct. 1889, p. 6; S. S. Wheeler, "Overhead and Underground Wires in New York," *Proceedings of the National Electric Association at Its Eighth Convention. . . 1888* (Boston: Modern Light & Heat, 1888), pp. 92–119.

33. *New York Times,* 14 Dec. 1889, p. 4; 15 Dec. 1889, p. 5; 29 Dec. 1889, p. 16; 30 Dec. 1889, p. 8; 31 Dec. 1889, p. 2; W. H. Brown, "Underground Conduits and Conductors and the Experiences of Electric Lighting Companies of New York City," *Sixteenth Convention of National Electric Light Association* (New York: James Kempster Printing Co., 1893), pp. 305–16, 328–31. For developments in Baltimore see: *Report of the Electrical Commission of Baltimore City to the Mayor and City Council* (Baltimore); *Report of the Chief Engineer to the Electrical Commission of Baltimore for the Years 1898–1905* (Baltimore, 1906), pp. 3–5.

34. Lawrence H. Larsen, "Nineteenth-Century Street Sanitation: A Study of Filth and Frustration," *Wisconsin Magazine of History* 52 (Spring 1969): 245.

35. Edward A. Freeman, *Some Impressions of the United States* (New York: Henry Holt & Co., 1883), p. 228.

36. Russell, *Hesperothen,* 1: 175–76; Lady Duffus Hardy, *Through Cities and Prairie Lands* (New York: Worthington Co., 1890), p. 67. In 1893, Baedeker's travel guide to the United States listed "the dirt of the city streets" among the "chief physical discomforts" confronting English travelers. Karl Baedeker, ed., *The United States, with an Excursion into Mexico* (New York: Da Capo Press, 1971), p. xxxviii.

37. Martin V. Melosi, *Garbage in the Cities: Refuse, Reform, and the Environment, 1880–1980* (College Station: Texas A & M University Press, 1981), pp. 51–77; Martin V. Melosi, " 'Out of Sight, Out of Mind': The Environment and Disposal of Municipal Refuse, 1860–1920," *Historian* 35 (Aug. 1973): 621–33; Fairlie, *Municipal Administration,* pp. 258–59; S. H. Agnew, "Street Cleaning in New York," *City Government* 1 (Aug. 1896): 1–2.

38. George E. Waring, Jr., *Street Cleaning* (New York: Doubleday & McClure Co., 1899), pp. 119, 136, 158; George E. Waring, Jr., "Observations on Street-Cleaning Methods in European Cities," *Municipal Affairs* 2, supplement (June 1898): 9–77.

39. J. W. Howard, "The Street Cleaning Problem," *Municipal Engineering* 13 (Nov. 1897): 291; Fairlie, *Municipal Administration,* pp. 255–60. Even before Waring assumed charge of street cleaning, New York City spent far more per capita for this service than any other major American municipality, though the money seems to have been poorly spent. See F. W. Hewes, "Street-Cleaning," *Harper's Weekly* 39 (9 Mar. 1895): 233–34.

40. "The Brooklyn Bridge," *Harper's New Monthly Magazine* 66 (May 1883): 925–46; David McCullough, *The Great Bridge* (New York: Simon & Schuster, 1972).

41. Sutter, *American Notes,* pp. 91–92.

42. Gordon, *Land of the Almighty Dollar,* p. 38.

43. "Brooklyn Bridge," p. 946.

44. *Report of the Trustees of the New York and Brooklyn Bridge for . . . 1896* (New York, 1896), pp. 5–6.

45. Edward Hungerford, *The Williamsburg Bridge* (Brooklyn: Eagle Press, 1903).

46. *Report of the Cambridge Bridge Commission* (Boston: Municipal Printing Department, 1909), pp. 14–35, 42–43; *Harvard Bridge* (Boston: Rockwell & Churchill, 1892); "The Harvard Bridge," *Harper's Weekly* 34 (26 Apr. 1890): 331–32.

47. *Fourth Annual Message of Edwin S. Stuart, Mayor of the City of Philadelphia, with Annual Reports of James H. Windrim, Director of the Department of Public Works* (Philadelphia: Dunlap Printing Co., 1895), p. xviii.

48. *Bureau of Census Special Reports—Street and Electric Railways* (Washington, D.C.: U.S. Government Printing Office, 1903), pp. 110, 118; *Statistisches Jahrbuch Deutscher Städte— Dreizehnter Jahrgang* (Breslau: Wilh. Gottl. Korn., 1906), pp. 134, 138.

49. John P. McKay, *Tramways and Trolleys: The Rise of Urban Mass Transport in Europe* (Princeton: Princeton University Press, 1976), p. 197.

50. James Burnley, *Two Sides of the Atlantic* (London: Simpkin, Marshall & Co., 1880), p. 215.

51. Joyaux, trans., "Visit to Chicago," p. 48.

52. Allan Nevins, ed. *American Social History as Recorded by British Travellers* (New York: Henry Holt & Co., 1923), p. 505.

53. *Census Reports—Street and Electric Railways, 1902,* (Washington D.C.: U.S. Government Printing Office, 1905), pp. 8, 155; McKay, *Tramways and Trolleys,* pp. 71–73.

54. Henry de Varigny, *En Amerique: Souvenirs de voyage et notes scientifiques* (Paris: G. Masson, 1894), pp. 52–53.

55. Freeman, *Impressions of the United States,* p. 230; *Times* (London), 6 Sept. 1887, p. 13.

56. Gordon, *Land of the Almighty Dollar,* p. 39; Lewis, *Short Visit to America,* p. 33; Sutter, *American Notes,* p. 90.

57. Charles W. Cheape, *Moving the Masses: Urban Public Transit in New York, Boston, and Philadelphia, 1880–1912* (Cambridge: Harvard University Press, 1980), pp. 70–101, 126–53; James Blaine Walker, *Fifty Years of Rapid Transit, 1864–1917* (New York: Law Printing Co., 1918), pp. 123–61.

58. *Census Reports—Street and Electric Railways, 1902,* pp. 39–40, 150, 153.

59. E. H. Phelps Brown with Margaret H. Browne, *A Century of Pay: The Course of Pay and Production in France, Germany, Sweden, the United Kingdom, and the United States of America, 1860–1960* (London: Macmillan & Co., 1968), pp. 46, 54.

60. *Census Reports—Street and Electric Railways, 1902,* pp. 94–99; H. Keeble Hawson, *Sheffield: The Growth of a City, 1893–1926* (Sheffield: J. W. Northend, 1968), pp. 235–36; W. J. Clark, "British Tramways," *Municipal and Private Operation of Public Utilities,* 3 vols. (New York: National Civic Federation, 1907), 1: 454–55.

61. Brown with Browne, *A Century of Pay,* pp. 45–46.

62. *Statistisches Jahrbuch Deutscher Städte—Zweiter Jahrgang* (Breslau: Wilh. Gottl. Korn., 1892), p. 98; *Report on the Social Statistics of Cities in the United States at the Eleventh Census: 1890* (Washington, D.C.: U.S. Government Printing Office, 1895), pp. 118, 124.

63. Joseph W. Stover, "Telegraphic Systems for the Facilitation of Fire and Police Service," *City Government* 3 (Oct. 1897): 122; *Bureau of the Census Bulletin—Municipal Electric Fire Alarm and Police Patrol Systems* (Washington, D.C.: U.S. Government Printing Office, 1904), pp. 18–23; C. V. Blackstone, *A History of the British Fire Service* (London: Routledge & Kegan Paul, 1957), p. 244.

64. *Census Bulletin—Electric Fire Alarm and Police Patrol Systems,* p. 8.

65. John G. Morse, "Apparatus For Extinguishing Fires," *Popular Science Monthly* 47 (Aug. 1895): 495–96; (Sept. 1895): 603–04; Lowell M. Limpus, *History of the New York Fire Department* (New York: E. P. Dutton & Co., 1940), p. 269.

66. *Statistisches Jahrbuch Deutscher Städte—Dreizehnter Jahrgang*, p. 14; "Report from the Select Committee on Fire Brigades . . . ," *British Sessional Papers, House of Commons, 1899* (London: Her Majesty's Stationery Office, 1899), 9:246–47; *Bulletin of the Department of Labor, 1900* (Washington, D.C.: U.S. Government Printing Office, 1900), p. 936.

67. Limpus, *New York Fire Department*, p. 264.

68. *New York Times*, 15 Sept. 1875, p. 8; 24 Sept. 1875, p. 2; *New York Tribune*, 15 Sept. 1875, p. 10; 24 Sept. 1875, p. 8.

69. Fire loss data from *The World Almanac and Encyclopedia, 1921* (New York: Press Publishing Co., 1920), p. 559.

70. Fire loss data from *Chicago Daily News Almanac and Year-Book For 1923* (Chicago: Chicago Daily News Co., 1922), p. 869.

71. David A. Shannon, ed., *Beatrice Webb's American Diary, 1898* (Madison: University of Wisconsin Press, 1963), p. 106.

72. *Proceedings of the Seventeenth Annual Convention of the National Association of Fire Engineers, 1889* (Cincinnati: Keating & Co., 1889), p. 160.

73. Thomas P. Purcell, "American and European Fire Departments," *Proceedings of the Ninth Annual Meeting of the Illinois Firemen's Association . . . 1897* (Chicago: Western Fireman, 1897), p. 51; Thomas P. Purcell, "European and American Fire Systems," *City Government* 2 (Mar. 1897): 82–83.

74. Jacques Offenbach, *Offenbach in America* (New York: G. W. Carleton & Co., 1877), pp. 186, 197.

75. Joseph Hatton, *Henry Irving's Impressions of America* (Boston: James R. Osgood & Co., 1884), pp. 435, 437.

76. Russell, *Hesperothen*, 1: 35–37; S. Reynolds Hole, *A Little Tour in America* (London: Edward Arnold, 1895), pp. 262–64.

77. *New York Times*, 28 May 1893, p. 17; *Proceedings of Convention of National Association of Fire Engineers, 1889*, pp. 159–60; "Fire Department Notes," *City Government* 3 (Dec. 1897): 213.

78. *New York Times*, 28 May 1893, p. 17; "World's Champion Fire Horse," *City Government* 3 (July 1897): 22–23.

79. John Duffy, *A History of Public Health in New York City, 1866–1966* (New York: Russell Sage Foundation, 1974), pp. 55, 70–71; Charles F. Bolduan, *Over a Century of Health Administration in New York City* (New York: New York City Department of Health, 1916), p. 19; Fairlie, *Municipal Administration*, pp. 165–66; Thomas Neville Bonner, *Medicine in Chicago, 1850–1950* (Madison: American History Research Center, 1957), pp. 181–85; *History of Medicine and Surgery, and Physicians and Surgeons of Chicago* (Chicago: Biographical Publishing Corp., 1922), pp. 344–45.

80. W. H. Grigg, "The Status and Duties of a Sanitary Inspector in England," *Journal of the Sanitary Institute* 21 (Oct. 1900): 550; Hawson, *Sheffield*, p. 41; *Bulletin of the Department of Labor, 1900*, p. 959.

81. Fairlie, *Municipal Administration*, pp. 168–71.

82. E. Parkes, "Municipal Authorities and Public Slaughter-Houses," *Sanitarian* 42 (Feb. 1899): 97–105; Leonard Pearson, "Methods of Meat Inspection," *Papers and Reports Presented at the Twenty-fifth Annual Meeting of the American Public Health Association* 23 (1897): 332–36.

83. Wade O. Oliver, *The Man Who Lived for Tomorrow: A Biography of William Hallock Park, M.D.* (New York: E. P. Dutton & Co., 1941), pp. 65–81; Charles-Edward Amory Winslow, *The Life of Hermann M. Biggs* (Philadelphia: Lea & Febiger, 1929), pp. 92–99; Duffy, *Public Health in New York City*, pp. 95–96; Bolduan, *Over a Century of Health Administration*, p. 25.

84. James H. Cassedy, *Charles V. Chapin and the Public Health Movement* (Cambridge: Harvard University Press, 1962), pp. 55–57.

85. Hermann M. Biggs, "Preventive Medicine in the City of New York," *Medical News* 71 (11

Sept. 1897): 321; Hermann M. Biggs, "Preventive Medicine in the City of New York," *Sanitarian* 39 (Nov. 1897): 390.

86. Biggs, "Preventive Medicine," pp. 321, 325; Biggs, "Preventive Medicine," *Sanitarian*, pp. 390, 409; Oliver, *The Man Who Lived for Tomorrow*, pp. 82–125; Winslow, *Hermann Biggs*, pp. 101–30; Duffy, *Public Health in New York City*, pp. 97–102; Bolduan, *Over a Century of Health Administration*, pp. 25–26.

87. "The Remarkable Success of the New York Board of Health in Producing Diphtheria Antitoxin," *Medical News* 72 (5 March 1898): 308–09.

88. Biggs, "Preventive Medicine," *Sanitarian*, p. 390; Oliver, *The Man Who Lived for Tomorrow*, pp. 134–38, 141–52, 155–57; Duffy, *Public Health in New York City*, p. 105.

89. *Philadelphia Press*, 27 Feb. 1895, p. 4.

90. Stuart Galishoff, *Safeguarding the Public Health; Newark, 1895–1918* (Westport, Conn.: Greenwood Press, 1975), pp. 23–29; William Travis Howard, Jr., *Public Health Administration and the Natural History of Disease in Baltimore, Maryland, 1797–1920* (Washington, D.C.: Carnegie Institution, 1924), p. 167; "The Report of the Boston Health Department for 1898," *Boston Medical and Surgical Journal* 141 (26 Oct. 1899): 427.

91. *Boston Evening Transcript*, 29 Oct. 1898, p. 6; excerpt from *Boston Medical and Surgical Journal*, as quoted in "Diphtheria in Boston," *Philadelphia Medical Journal* 2 (12 Nov. 1898): 986; see also, "Report of Boston Health Department," p. 427.

92. William Jaques, "Diphtheria Work Done by the Health Department of Chicago," *Chicago Medical Recorder* 16 (Feb. 1899): 134–35; W. K. Jaques, "Municipal Control of Diphtheria," *Journal of the American Medical Association* 30 (12 Mar. 1898): 596–600; *Philadelphia Medical Journal* 3 (1 Apr. 1899): 681–82; "Antitoxin Treatment of Diphtheria," *Journal of the American Medical Association* 32 (1 Apr. 1899): 731; Arthur R. Reynolds, "Three Chicago and Illinois Public Health Officers: John H. Rauch, Oscar C. DeWolf, and Frank W. Reilly," *Bulletin of the Society of Medical History of Chicago* 1 (Aug. 1912): 122; Bonner, *Medicine in Chicago*, p. 186.

93. Fairlie, *Municipal Administration*, p. 170.

94. Winslow, *Hermann Biggs*, pp. 108, 179, 217; Oliver, *The Man Who Lived for Tomorrow*, p. 99. The eminent British physician Joseph Lister wrote Biggs commending the "zeal and efficiency" in Biggs's department in New York, which he said, he "should be glad indeed to see emulated here." Winslow, *Hermann Biggs*, pp. 120–21.

95. Duffy, *Public Health in New York City*, p. 109; Winslow, *Hermann Biggs*, p. 130.

96. Biggs, "Preventive Medicine," *Medical News*, p. 325; Biggs, "Preventive Medicine," *Sanitarian*, p. 411.

9. CREATING A HUMANE AND ORDERED ENVIRONMENT

1. *Statistisches Jahrbuch Deutscher Städte—Zweiter Jahrgang* (Breslau: Wilh. Gottl. Korn., 1892), p. 80; *Report on the Social Statistics of Cities in the United States at the Eleventh Census: 1890* (Washington, D.C.: U.S. Government Printing Office, 1895), p. 35.

2. A. R. C. Grant with Caroline Combe, eds., *Lord Rosebery's North American Journal—1873* (Hamden, Conn.: Archon Books, 1967), p. 32. For similar praise by visiting foreigners, see: S. Reynolds Hole, *A Little Tour in America* (London: Edward Arnold, 1895), pp. 75–84: *Times* (London), 6 Sept. 1887, p. 13; Archibald Sutter, *American Notes, 1881* (Edinburgh: William Blackwood & Sons, 1882), p. 90; Max O'Rell and Jack Allyn, *Jonathan and His Continent* (New York: Cassell & Co., 1889), p. 31; Lady Duffus Hardy, *Through Cities and Prairie Lands* (New York: Worthington Co., 1890), pp. 64–65; Gaétan Desaché, *Souvenir de mon voyage aux États-Unis et au Canada* (Tours: Paul Bouserez, 1877), p. 35; Jacques Offenbach, *Offenbach in America* (New York: G. W. Carleton & Co., 1877), p. 97.

3. Hole, *Tour in America*, p. 91.

4. Charles E. Lewis, *Two Lectures on a Short Visit to America* (London: Blades, East & Blades, 1876), p. 37.

5. H. Hussey Vivian, *Notes of a Tour in America* (London: Edward Stanford, 1878), p. 59.

6. Offenbach, *Offenbach in America*, p. 155.

7. *Times* (London), 19 Sept. 1887, p. 4; Hardy, *Through Cities and Prairie Lands*, p. 300.

8. Georges J. Joyaux, trans., "A Frenchman's Visit to Chicago in 1886," *Journal of the Illinois State Historical Society* 47 (Spring 1954): 50.

9. *Times* (London), 21 Oct. 1887, p. 4. See also: John Leng, *America in 1876* (Dundee, Scotland: Dundee Advertiser Office, 1877), p. 82; Sutter, *American Notes*, p. 32.

10. David A. Shannon, ed., *Beatrice Webb's American Diary, 1898* (Madison: University of Wisconsin Press, 1963), pp. 78, 106.

11. Hardy, *Through Cities and Prairie Lands*, pp. 300–301.

12. Henry Hope Reed and Sophia Duckworth, *Central Park: A History and a Guide* (New York: Clarkson N. Potter, 1972), pp. 30–31; Frederick Law Olmsted, Jr., and Theodora Kimball, eds., *Frederick Law Olmsted: Landscape Architect, 1822–1903* (New York: Benjamin Blom, 1970); Albert Fein, ed., *Landscape into Cityscape: Frederick Law Olmsted's Plans for A Greater New York City* (Ithaca: Cornell University Press, 1968), pp. 63–88 .

13. Clay Lancaster, *Prospect Park Handbook* (New York: Walton H. Rawls, 1967), pp. 53, 60–61; *Thirty-sixth Annual Report of the Department of Parks of the City of Brooklyn . . . for the Year 1896* (Brooklyn: Eagle Press, 1897), pp. 210–18; Leonard J. Simutis, "Frederick Law Olmsted's Later Years: Landscape Architecture and the Spirit of Place" (Ph.D. dissertation, University of Minnesota, 1971), pp. 119–31; Norman T. Newton, *Design on the Land: The Development of Landscape Architecture* (Cambridge: Harvard University Press, 1971), pp. 275–87; Fein, ed., *Landscape into Cityscape*, pp. 91–164.

14. Edwin M. Bacon, *Walks and Rides in the Country Round About Boston* (Boston: Houghton, Mifflin & Co., 1897), pp. 303, 388–89, 397; Simutis, "Olmsted's Later Years," pp. 161–74; Newton, *Design on the Land*, pp. 290–306.

15. Stewart A. Stehlin, trans. and ed., "Philadelphia On the Eve of the Nation's Centennial: A Visitor's Description in 1873–74," *Pennsylvania History* 44 (Jan. 1977): 35.

16. Charles S. Keyser, *Fairmount Park, Sketches of Its Scenery, Waters, and History* (Philadelphia: Claxton, Remsen & Haffelfinger, 1872), pp. 114–16; Esther M. Klein, *Fairmount Park: A History and a Guidebook* (Philadelphia: Fairmount Park Commission, 1974), pp. 22–27; Theo B. White, *Fairmount, Philadelphia's Park: A History* (Philadelphia: The Art Alliance, 1975).

17. I. J. Bryan, comp., *Report of the Commissioners and a History of Lincoln Park* (Chicago: Commissioners of Lincoln Park, 1899), pp. 48, 86, 112.

18. Katherine Wilson, *Golden Gate: The Park of a Thousand Vistas* (Caldwell, Ida.: Caxton Printers, 1947); *Fortieth Annual Report of the Board of Park Commissioners of San Francisco for . . . 1910* (San Francisco: Dickinson & Scott, 1910).

19. Glen E. Holt, "Private Plans for Public Spaces: The Origins of Chicago's Park System, 1850–1875," *Chicago History* 8 (Fall 1979): 173–84; Bessie Louise Pierce, *A History of Chicago*, 3 vols. (New York: Alfred A. Knopf, 1957), 3: 314.

20. Theodore Wirth, *Minneapolis Park System, 1883–1944* (Minneapolis: n.p., 1946), pp. 26–34, 39–64; Newton, *Design on the Land*, pp. 308–17.

21. William H. Wilson, *The City Beautiful Movement in Kansas City* (Columbia: University of Missouri Press, 1964).

22. *New York Times*, 11 Mar. 1896, p. 15.

23. Charles W. Eliot, *Charles Eliot: Landscape Architect*, 2 vols. (Boston: Houghton, Mifflin & Co., 1902); Newton, *Design on the Land*, pp. 318–36.

24. J. C. N. Forestier, *Grandes Villes et systèmes de parcs* (Paris: Hachette et Cie., 1906), pp. 25–28; Anthony Sutcliffe, *Toward the Planned City: Germany, Britain, the United States, and France, 1780–1914* (Oxford: Basil Blackwell, 1981), pp. 197–98.

25. Walt Whitman, *Autobiographia or Story of a Life* (New York: Charles L. Webster & Co., 1892), p. 155.

26. Charles Zueblin, "Municipal Playgrounds in Chicago," *American Journal of Sociology* 4

(1898): 146–47; Michael P. McCarthy, "Politics and the Parks: Chicago Businessmen and the Recreation Movement," *Journal of the Illinois State Historical Society* 65 (Summer 1972): 159.

27. F. L. Olmsted, Jr., "Neighborhood Pleasure-Grounds in Boston," *Harper's Weekly* 41 (25 Dec. 1897): 1290–91; *Boston Evening Transcript*, 23 Jan. 1895, p. 5; 29 Jan. 1895, p. 3.

28. *Report of the Special Park Commission to the City Council of Chicago* (Chicago, 1904), pp. 27–32; Charles Zueblin, *American Municipal Progress* (New York: Macmillan Co., 1902), pp. 278–87; Stoyan Vasil Tsanoff, "Children's Playgrounds," *Municipal Affairs* 2 (June 1898): 293–303.

29. Thomas Greenwood, *Public Libraries: A History of the Movement and a Manual for the Organization and Management of Rate-Supported Libraries* (London: Cassell & Co., 1894), p. 524; James D. Brown, "American and British Libraries—Mr. Brown's Reply," *Library* 6 (1894): 114; Peter Cowell and James D. Brown, "American and British Libraries," *Library* 5 (1893): 277–90. See also Lord Balcarres, "Public Libraries at Home and Abroad," *Library Association Record* 3 (Feb. 1901): 80–86.

30. Eduard Reyer, *Entwicklung und Organisation der Volksbibliotheken* (Leipzig: Wilhelm Engelmann, 1893), pp. 41–66; C. Nörrenberg, "Offentliche Bibliotheken in America," in Eduard Reyer, *Handbuch Des Volksbildungswesens* (Stuggart: J. G. Cotta'schen Buchhandlung, 1896), pp. 180–202; "The German Library System," *Report of the Commissioner of Education for the Year 1900–1901*, 2 vols. (Washington, D.C.: U.S. Government Printing Office, 1902), 1: 80–84; Aksel G. S. Josephson, "Library Progress in Germany," *Public Libraries* 3 (Apr. 1898): 126–28; Gisela Von Busse and Horst Ernestus, *Libraries in the Federal Republic of Germany* (Wiesbaden: Otto Harrassowitz, 1972), pp. 44–45; Alfred Hessel, *A History of Libraries* (New Brunswick, N.J.: Scarecrow Press, 1965), pp. 111–12.

31. "Progress of the Public Library in Germany," *Public Libraries* 4 (Apr. 1899): 174–75. For other reports on the short hours of German libraries, see: Mary W. Plummer, "Some Continental Libraries," *Nation* 59 (25 Oct. 1894): 305–06; "German Library System," *Report of the Commissioner of Education, 1900–1901*, 1: 82.

32. "Statistics of Education in Central Europe," *Report of the Commissioner of Education for the Year 1899–1900*, 2 vols. (Washington, D.C.: U.S. Government Printing Office, 1901), 1: 772–73; *Twenty-eighth Annual Report of the Board of Directors of the Chicago Public Library, June, 1900* (Chicago: Chicago Public Library, 1900), p. 33; *Annual Report of the Trustees of the Public Library of the City of Boston, 1896* (Boston: Municipal Printing Office, 1897), p. 99.

33. Helle Kannila, "A General View of Scandinavian Public Libraries," *Scandinavian Public Library Quarterly* 1 (1968): 5–6; Gert Hornwall, "Valfrid Palmgren, 1877–1967: Portrait of a Pioneer," in ibid. 3 (1970): 65; Preben Kirkegaard, *The Public Libraries in Denmark* (Copenhagen: Det Danske Selskab, 1950), pp. 7–8.

34. Leng, *America in 1876*, p. 236.

35. Emm. D. Saint-Albin, *Les Bibliothèques municipales de la ville de Paris* (Paris: Berger-Levrault et Cie., 1896), p. 286; "Paris Libraries," *Library Journal* 3 (Sept. 1878): 258.

36. Frank H. Case, *The Boston Public Library: A Handbook to the Library Building, Its Mural Decorations and Its Collections* (Boston: Association Publications, 1926); Walter M. Whitehill, *Boston Public Library: A Centennial History* (Cambridge: Harvard University Press, 1956), pp. 131–63; William A. Coffin, "Sargent and His Painting, with Special Reference to His Decorations in the Boston Public Library," *Century Magazine* 52 (June 1896): 163–78; *Boston Evening Transcript*, 26 Apr. 1895, p. 5.

37. *Boston Evening Transcript*, 11 Mar. 1895, p. 4.

38. C. Howard Walker, "The Boston Public Library," *New England Magazine* 12 (May 1895): 265.

39. Lindsay Swift, "The New Public Library in Boston, Its Artistic Aspects," *Century Magazine* 50 (June 1895): 262.

40. *Boston Evening Transcript*, 1 Feb. 1895, p. 3.

41. *Annual Report of the Trustees of the Public Library of the City of Boston, 1899* (Boston: Municipal Printing Office, 1900), pp. 6, 56.

42. *Twenty-eighth Report of the Chicago Public Library, 1900*, pp. 25–26, 28.

43. *Thirty-second Report, Cleveland Public Library, September 1st, 1899, to December 31st, 1900* (Cleveland: Forman-Bassett-Hatch Co., 1901), pp. 12, 49–61; C. H. Cramer, *Open Shelves and Open Minds: A History of the Cleveland Public Library* (Cleveland: Press of Case Western Reserve University, 1972), pp. 75–77; Zueblin, *Municipal Progress*, pp. 186–87.

44. *Annual Report of the Board of Directors of the St. Louis Public (Free) Library, 1899–1900* (St. Louis: Freegard Press, 1902), pp. 14–15.

45. Frank B. Woodford, *Parnassus on Main Street: A History of the Detroit Public Library* (Detroit: Wayne State University Press, 1965), pp. 154–61; *Annual Report of the Board of Trustees of the Public Library of Cincinnati, Ohio* (Cincinnati, 1900), pp. 116–19.

46. Zueblin, *Municipal Progress*, p. 186.

47. *First Annual Report of the Buffalo Public Library, 1897* (Buffalo: Public Library, 1898), pp. 48–52; Arthur Goldberg, *The Buffalo Public Library* (Buffalo: Privately printed, 1937), pp. 112–20.

48. Phyllis Dain, *The New York Public Library: A History of Its Founding and Early Years* (New York: New York Public Library, 1972), pp. 171–81.

49. *Report of Directors of St. Louis Public Library, 1899–1900*, pp. 9–10; *Report of the Public Library of Boston, 1896*, pp. 96–97; *Annual Report of the Trustees of the Public Library of the City of Boston, 1897,* (Boston: Municipal Printing Office, 1898), pp. 113–14; *Annual Report of the Trustees of the Public Library of the City of Boston, 1898* (Boston: Municipal Printing Office, 1899), pp. 131–32; *Report of Trustees of Public Library of Boston, 1899*, pp. 89–90.

50. J. M. Rice, *The Public-School System of the United States* (New York: Century Co., 1893). For a thoughtful contemporary review of Rice's book, see *Educational Review* 6 (Dec. 1893): 498–503.

51. *Report on Education in the United States at the Eleventh Census: 1890* (Washington: U.S. Government Printing Office, 1893), pp. 134, 137, 139; *Bulletin of the Department of Labor, 1900* (Washington, D.C.: U.S. Government Printing Office, 1900), p. 964.

52. Figure for New York City computed on basis of data in *Report on Education in the United States, 1890*, p. 137. Other figures based on data in: *Thirty-ninth Annual Report of the Chicago Board of Education for . . . 1893* (Chicago: George K. Hazlitt & Co., 1894), pp. 29–30; *Forty-fourth Annual Report of the Board of Education of the St. Louis Public Schools for . . . 1898* (Saint Louis: Woodward & Tiernan Printing Co., 1898), p. 47; *Annual Report of the School Committee of the City of Boston, 1890* (Boston: Rockwell & Churchill, 1890), p. 5.

53. "Education in Central Europe," *Report of the Commissioner of Education for the Year 1893–94*, 2 vols. (Washington, D.C.: U.S. Government Printing Office, 1896), 1: 215, 267; "Education in France," *Report of the Commissioner of Education for . . . 1905*, 2 vols. (Washington, D.C.: U.S. Government Printing Office, 1907), 1: 72; A. Tolman Smith, "Elementary Education in London and Paris," *Report of the Commissioner of Education for the Year 1889–90*, 2 vols. (Washington, D.C.: U.S. Government Printing Office, 1893), 1: 271.

54. R. A. Hughes, *The Making of Citizens: A Study in Comparative Education* (London: Walter Scott Publishing Co., 1902), p. 145.

55. W. Catton Grasby, *Teaching in Three Continents: Personal Notes on the Educational Systems of the World* (Syracuse: C. W. Bardeen, 1895), pp. 244, 266–67.

56. Emile Levasseur, *L'Enseignement primaire dans les pays civilisés* (Paris: Berger-Levrault et Cie., 1897), pp. 362–63.

57. Hughes, *Making of Citizens*, pp. 173, 279–80.

58. A. Ghisleri, "Education in the United States," *Report of the Commissioner of Education for the Year 1892–93*, 2 vols. (Washington, D.C.: U.S. Government Printing Office, 1895), 1: 617; E. Osterberg, "Observations Concerning American Education," *Report of the Commissioner of*

Education for the Year 1892–93, 2 vols. (Washington, D.C.: U.S. Government Printing Office, 1895), 1: 626.

59. Emil Hausknecht, "The American System of Education," *Report of the Commissioner of Education for the Year 1892–93*, 2 vols. (Washington, D.C.: U.S. Government Printing Office, 1895), 1: 526, 529.

60. Hughes, *Making of Citizens*, p. 161.

61. M. A. Newell, "Contributions to the History of Normal Schools in the United States," *Report of the Commissioner of Education for the Year 1898–99*, 2 vols. (Washington, D.C.: U.S. Government Printing Office, 1900), 2: 2447–53; *Annual Report of the School Committee of the City of Boston, 1895* (Boston: Rockwell & Churchill, 1896), pp. 6–7; A. Emerson Palmer, *The New York Public School* (New York: Macmillan Co., 1905), pp. 327–31; A. R. Taylor, "Report of the Committee on Organization, Courses of Study, and Methods of Instruction in the Normal Schools of the United States," *Journal of Proceedings and Addresses of the National Educational Association, Session of the Year 1886* (Salem: Observer Book & Job Print, 1887), p. 393.

62. *Annual Report of the School Committee of the City of Boston, 1887* (Boston: Rockwell & Churchill, 1888), pp. 18–19; Selwyn K. Troen, *The Public and the Schools: Shaping the St. Louis System, 1838–1920* (Columbia: University of Missouri Press, 1975), pp. 99–115; *Forty-fifth Annual Report of the St. Louis Board of Education . . . 1899* (Saint Louis: Nixon-Jones Printing Co., 1899), pp. 54–56.

63. C. M. Woodward, "The Rise and Progress of Manual Training," *Report of the Commissioner of Education for the Year 1893–94*, 2 vols. (Washington, D.C.: U.S. Government Printing Office, 1898), 1: 890, 893; Charles Alpheus Bennett, *History of Manual and Industrial Education, 1870 to 1917* (Peoria, Ill.: Charles A. Bennett Co., 1937), pp. 374–76; James C. Boykin, ed., "Typical Institutions Offering Manual or Industrial Training," *Report of the Commissioner of Education for the Year 1895–96*, 2 vols. (Washington, D.C.: U.S. Government Printing Office, 1897), 2: 1001–1152; "Manual and Industrial Training," *Report of the Commissioner of Education for the Year 1899–1900*, 2 vols. (Washington, D.C.: U.S. Government Printing Office, 1901), 2: 2438; William J. Akers, *Cleveland Schools in the Nineteenth Century* (Cleveland; W. M. Bayne Printing House, 1901), pp. 225–31; *Fifty-first Annual Report of the Cleveland Board of Education for . . . 1887* (Cleveland: Plain Dealer Publishing Co., 1888), pp. 25–27; Marvin Lazerson, *Origins of the Urban School: Public Education in Massachusetts, 1870–1915* (Cambridge: Harvard University Press, 1971).

64. *Annual Report of the School Committee of Boston, 1895*, p. 319.

65. See, for example, the names of the graduates of Mechanic Arts High School in *Annual Report of the School Committee of the City of Boston, 1896* (Boston: Rockwell & Churchill, 1897), pp. 303–04. (For course of study at Mechanic Arts High School, see page 107.)

66. Woodward, "Rise of Manual Training," *Report of Commissioner of Education, 1893–94*, 1: 949.

67. *Forty-fifth Annual Report of the Chicago Board of Education for the Year Ending June 23, 1899* (Chicago: John F. Higgins, 1900), p. 168. For information on the admission of English High and Manual Training School graduates to universities, see *Thirty-ninth Annual Report of the Chicago Board of Education for the Year Ending June 30, 1893* (Chicago: George K. Hazlitt & Co., 1894), p. 122.

68. Grasby, *Teaching in Three Continents*, pp. 183–84.

69. *Bulletin of the Department of Labor, 1900*, p. 970.

70. Bird S. Coler, *Municipal Government* (New York: D. Appleton & Co., 1900), pp. 26–109; Homer Folks, *The Care of Destitute, Neglected, and Delinquent Children* (New York: Macmillan Co., 1902), pp. 115–31; John A. Fairlie, *Municipal Administration* (New York: Macmillan Co., 1901), p. 190.

71. Seth Low, "The Problem of Pauperism in the Cities of Brooklyn and New York," *Proceedings of the Sixth Annual Conference of Charities . . . 1879* (Boston: A. Williams & Co., 1879), pp. 200–10; Homer Folks, "Municipal Charities," *Municipal Affairs* 3 (Sept. 1899): 517–19; Ho-

mer Folks, "Report of the Committee on Municipal and County Charities," *Proceedings of the National Conference of Charities and Corrections . . . 1898* (Boston: George H. Ellis, 1899), pp. 114–32; Edward T. Devine, "Public Outdoor Relief," *Charities Review* 8 (May 1898, June 1898): 129–37, 186–99.

72. Fairlie, *Municipal Administration*, pp. 192–96; Milo Roy Maltbie, "Municipal Functions: A Study of the Development, Scope, and Tendency of Municipal Socialism," *Municipal Affairs* 2 (Dec. 1898): 649–50.

73. "Glasgow: Its Municipal Administration," *City Government* 3 (Aug. 1897): 53; Albert Shaw, "Municipal Lodging-Houses," *Charities Review* 1 (Nov. 1891): 20–26; Maltbie, "Municipal Functions," pp. 647–48; Helen Zimmern, "The Parisian Municipal Refuge for Working-Women," *Charities Review* 2 (Feb. 1893): 226–32.

74. *Statistics of Cities of the United States, 1890*, pp. 128, 131: William T. Stead, *If Christ Came to Chicago* (New York: Living Books, 1964), p. 23.

75. *New York Times*, 12 Mar. 1886, p. 8; 4 Apr. 1886, p. 8; 28 May 1886, p. 8; 10 Mar. 1896, p. 6; 12 Mar. 1896, p. 8; 29 May 1896, p. 9; 13 Nov. 1896, p. 2; Homer Folks, "Lodging of Homeless Men in New York City," *Charities Review* 8 (Mar. 1898): 22–25; Amos G. Warner, "The New Municipal Lodging-House in Washington," ibid. 2 (Mar. 1893): 279–82.

76. Stead, *If Christ Came to Chicago*, p. 23.

77. *New York Times*, 7 Mar. 1891, p. 8; 25 Mar. 1891, p. 4; 6 June 1891, p. 8; 9 June 1891, pp. 3, 4; 10 June 1891, p. 8.

78. Maltbie, "Municipal Functions," pp. 685–87; Fairlie, *Municipal Administration*, pp. 260–61; William H. Tolman, "Public Baths, or the Gospel of Cleanliness," *Yale Review* 6 (May 1897): 56–58.

79. Robert DeForest and Lawrence Veiller, eds., *The Tenement House Problem*, 2 vols. (New York: Macmillan Co., 1903), 2: 35–43; "A New Public Bath-House," *Charities Review* 8 (Nov. 1898): 391–92; Charles Zueblin, *American Municipal Progress*, 2nd ed. (New York: Macmillan Co., 1916), p. 308; Harvey E. Fisk, "The Introduction of Public Rain Baths in America," *Sanitarian* 36 (June 1896): 487–90; *Boston Evening Transcript*, 15 Oct. 1898, p. 11; *New York Times*, 29 April 1900, p. 25; David Glassberg, "The Public Bath Movement in America," *American Studies* 20 (Fall 1979): 7; Moreau Morris, "More About the Public Rain Baths," *Sanitarian* 37 (July 1896): 7–8; Marilyn Thornton Williams, "New York City's Public Baths: A Case Study in Urban Progressive Reform," *Journal of Urban History* 7 (Nov. 1980): 54.

80. Jane Addams, *Twenty Years at Hull House* (New York: New American Library, 1961), p. 221; Lawrence M. Friedman, *Government and Slum Housing: A Century of Frustration* (Chicago: Rand McNally & Co., 1968) p. 30; Robert Hunter, *Tenement Conditions in Chicago: Report by the Investigating Committee of the City Homes Association* (Chicago: City Homes Association, 1901), p. 108.

81. Morris, "More about Public Rain Baths," pp. 8, 10; Fisk, "Introduction of Public Rain Baths," pp. 490–94; *New York Herald*, 14 Mar. 1893, p. 5; Glassberg, "Public Bath Movement," pp. 10–11; Williams, "New York City's Public Baths," pp. 58–61.

82. *New York Times*, 28 May 1896, p. 8; 14 Feb. 1897, p. 7; 11 May 1897, p. 12; 4 June 1897, p. 3; 5 June 1897, p. 6; 7 June 1897, p. 6; 29 Apr. 1900, p. 25; DeForest and Veiller, eds., *Tenement House Problem*, 2: 46–51; Tolman, "Public Baths," pp. 53–56; Fisk, "Introduction of Public Rain Baths," pp. 494–97; Williams, "New York City's Public Baths," pp. 64–67.

83. Glassberg, "Public Bath Movement," p. 11; "Public Baths," *Philadelphia Medical Journal* 1 (23 Apr. 1898): 705–06. The city government of Baltimore would not appropriate money for the construction of public baths, so bath advocates turned instead to a private benefactor, Henry Walters. Anne Beadenkopf, "The Baltimore Public Baths and Their Founder, Rev. Thomas M. Beadenkopf," *Maryland Historical Magazine* 45 (Sept. 1950): 201–14.

84. *New York Times*, 29 Apr. 1900, p. 25.

85. Lettice Fisher, "Municipal Housing in British Cities," *Municipal Affairs* 6 (Fall 1902): 357–74; DeForest and Veiller, eds., *Tenement House Problem*, 2: 174–80; P. J. Smith, "Planning

as Environmental Improvement: Slum Clearance in Victorian Edinburgh," in Anthony Sutcliffe, ed., *The Rise of Modern Urban Planning, 1800–1914* (London: Mansell, 1980), pp. 99–133; Fairlie, *Municipal Administration*, pp. 178–79; "Glasgow: Its Municipal Administration," *City Government*, pp. 52–55.

86. DeForest and Veiller, eds., *Tenement House Problem*, 2: 257.

87. Marcus T. Reynolds, *The Housing of the Poor in American Cities* (Baltimore: American Economic Association, 1893), p. 9.

88. J. M. Hart, *The British Police* (London: George Allen & Unwin, 1951), p. 34; Maltbie, "Municipal Functions," p. 619; Fairlie, *Municipal Administration*, pp. 134–35; "Report from the Select Committee on Fire Brigades," *British Sessional Papers, House of Commons, 1899* (London: Her Majesty's Stationery Office, 1899), 9: 522–23; Arthur Redford and Ina S. Russell, *The History of Local Government in Manchester*, 3 vols. (London: Longmans, Green & Co. 1940), 3: 15, 17; *Bulletin of the Department of Labor, 1900*, pp. 928, 934.

89. Eric H. Monkkonen, *Police in Urban America, 1860–1920* (Cambridge: Cambridge University Press, 1981), pp. 70–73, 169; Ted Robert Gurr, Peter N. Grabosky, and Richard C. Hula, *The Politics of Crime and Conflict: A Comparative History of Four Cities* (Beverly Hills: Sage Publications, 1977), p. 112.

90. Roger Lane, *Violent Death in the City: Suicide, Accident, and Murder in Nineteenth-Century Philadelphia* (Cambridge: Harvard University Press, 1979), p. 60; Gurr, Grabosky, and Hula, *Politics of Crime and Conflict*, pp. 115–17. See also: Erik Ekelund, "Criminal Statistics: The Volume of Crime," *Journal of Criminal Law and Criminology* 32 (1941–42): 540–47; Elwin H. Powell, "Crime as a Function of Anomie," *Journal of Criminal Law, Criminology and Police Science* 57 (June 1966), pp. 161–71; Sam Bass Warner, *Crime and Criminal Statistics in Boston* (Cambridge: Harvard University Press, 1934), pp. 135–47.

91. Raymond B. Fosdick, *European Police Systems* (New York: Century Co., 1915), pp. 204–07, 213; Philip John Stead, *The Police of Paris* (London: Staples Press, 1957), pp. 147–48.

92. Albert Shaw, *Municipal Government in Continental Europe* (New York: Century Co., 1895), p. 321; Maltbie, "Municipal Functions," p. 625; Marcel Le Clere, "La Police politique sous la IIIe Republique," in *L'Etat et sa police en France (1789–1914)* (Geneva: Librarie Droz, 1979), pp. 103–13; Stead, *Police of Paris*, pp. 137–52. For a typical British reaction to the German police of the 1860s, see Edward Wilberforce, *Social Life in Munich* (London: W. H. Allen & Co., 1863), pp. 338–41.

93. Fales Curtis, "Chief Inspector Thomas Byrnes," *Harper's Weekly* 33 (9 Feb. 1889), p. 112.

94. V. A. Leonard, *Police Communication Systems* (Berkeley: University of California Press, 1938), pp. 1–15; *Bureau of the Census—Municipal Electric Fire Alarm and Police Patrol Systems* (Washington, D.C.: U.S. Government Printing Office, 1904), pp. 23–32; William J. Bopp and Donald O. Schultz, *A Short History of American Law Enforcement* (Springfield, Ill.: Charles C Thomas Publisher 1972), pp. 66–67.

10. BOOM, BUST, AND URBAN RULE: FINANCING CITY GOVERNMENT

1. Edward Dana Durand, *The Finances of New York City* (New York: Macmillan Co., 1898), p. 375; *Forty-sixth Annual Report: Finances of the City of Chicago* (Chicago, 1903), p. 179.

2. Charles P. Huse, *The Financial History of Boston* (Cambridge: Harvard University Press, 1916), pp. 378–79; *Annual Reports of the City Departments of the City of Cincinnati for 1901* (Cincinnati: Commercial-Gazette, 1902), p. 829; Charles C. Williamson, *The Finances of Cleveland* (New York: Columbia University Press, 1907), pp. 256, 259.

3. *Fifty-first Annual Report of the City Controller . . . of the City of Philadelphia* (Philadelphia: George F. Lasher, 1905), pp. 257–58.

4. Horace Secrist, *An Economic Analysis of the Constitutional Restrictions upon Public Indebtedness in the United States* (Madison: University of Wisconsin, 1914), p. 56.

5. *Forty-sixth Report: Finances of Chicago*, p. 179; Huse, *Boston*, p. 377; *Fifty-first Report of Controller of Philadelphia*, p. 258; *Reports of Cincinnati, 1901*, p. 829; Williamson, *Cleveland*, p. 227; Durand, *New York City*, p. 373.

6. William L. Raymond, *State and Municipal Bonds* (Boston: Financial Publishing Co., 1923), pp. 340, 342, "City Debt," *New Jersey Law Journal* 2 (Mar. 1879): 90-92.

7. Gerald M. Capers, Jr., *The Biography of a River Town, Memphis: Its Heroic Age* (Chapel Hill: University of North Carolina Press, 1939), pp. 203-04; Raymond, *Municipal Bonds*, p. 341.

8. Horace P. Phillips, *History of the Bonded Debt of the City of New Orleans, 1822-1933* (New Orleans, 1933), pp. 5-6.

9. Andrew H. Green, *Municipal Debt of the City of New-York* (New York, 1874), p. 20.

10. *City Auditor's Financial Report for the Fiscal Year Ending Dec. 31, 1875* (Cleveland: Robison, Savage & Co., 1876), p. 3.

11. *The Inaugural Address of Samuel C. Cobb* (Boston: Rockwell & Churchill, 1876), p. 13.

12. *Message of Joshua Vansant, Mayor, to the First and Second Branches of the City Council of Baltimore* (Baltimore: John Cox, 1875), p. 8.

13. "Municipal Indebtedness Restricted by Law," *Commercial and Financial Chronicle* 20 (10 Apr. 1875): 346; "City Burdens," ibid. 20 (15 May 1875): 464.

14. "Debt and Taxation in New Jersey," *Bradstreet's* 2 (5 May 1880): 4; "New Orleans Finance and Municipal Borrowing," ibid. 22 May 1880, p. 4; "The Evening Post on Municipal Finance," ibid. 4 (17 Sept. 1881): 178; *Bradstreet's* 5 (18 Mar. 1882): 161.

15. Secrist, *Restrictions upon Public Indebtedness*, pp. 54-83.

16. Edward P. Allinson and Boies Penrose, *Philadelphia, 1681-1887: A History of Municipal Development* (Philadelphia: Allen, Lane & Scott, 1887), pp. 242-44.

17. *Third Annual Message of Samuel G. King, with the Accompanying Documents for the Year 1883* (Philadelphia: Dunlap & Clarke, 1884), p. 12.

18. Durand, *New York City*, p. 375; *Forty-sixth Report: Finances of Chicago*, p. 179; *Fifty-first Report of Controller of Philadelphia*, pp. 258-59; Williamson, *Cleveland*, p. 259; *Annual Reports of Officials and of the Several Municipal Departments of the City of Detroit for the Year 1900-1901* (Detroit: Richmond & Backus Co., 1902), pp. 213-14.

19. Durand, *New York City*, pp. 321-22.

20. J. H. Hollander, *The Financial History of Baltimore* (Baltimore: Johns Hopkins Press, 1899), pp. 348-49.

21. Williamson, *Cleveland*, pp. 214-15.

22. *The Mayor's Message and Reports of the City Officers . . . for the Year 1894* (Baltimore: William J. C. Dulany Co., 1895), p. 21.

23. *Annual Message of Edgar B. Jewett, Mayor* (Buffalo: Wenborne—Sumner Co., 1897), p. 13.

24. *Report of the Comptroller of the City of Milwaukee for . . . 1898* (Milwaukee: Edw. Keogh Press, 1899), p. 13.

25. "Municipal Bonds—Sales and Investments," *State and City Supplement of the Commercial and Financial Chronicle* 60 (13 Apr. 1895): 3.

26. "Municipal Bond Sales in July," *Commercial and Financial Chronicle* 59 (11 Aug. 1894): 243.

27. Ibid.; "Municipal Bond Sales in August," *Commercial and Financial Chronicle* 59 (15 Sept. 1894): 485; "Municipal Bond Sales in October," ibid., 10 Nov. 1894, p. 844.

28. Durand, *New York City*, p. 376; *Bulletin of the Department of Labor, 1900* (Washington, D.C.: U.S. Government Printing Office, 1900), pp. 989, 997; Hollander, *Baltimore*, p. 381; Williamson, *Cleveland*, pp. 243, 253.

29. *Report of the Comptroller of the City of St. Louis for Fiscal Year 1886-87* (Saint Louis: Daly Printing Co., 1887), appendix p. iii; *Report of the Comptroller of the City of St. Louis for Fiscal Year 1887-88* (Saint Louis: Daly Printing Co., 1888), p. 12; *Report of the Comptroller of the City of St. Louis for Fiscal Year 1891-92* (Saint Louis: Daly Printing Co., 1892), p. xii; *Report*

of the Comptroller of the City of St. Louis for Fiscal Year 1898–99 (Saint Louis: Woodward & Tiernan, 1899), p. xii.

30. *Annual Report of the Departments of Government of the City of Cleveland for . . . 1895* (Cleveland: Brooks Co., 1896), pp. lxxx, lxxxi.

31. *Forty-first Annual Statement of the Finances of the City of Chicago, 1897* (Chicago: John F. Higgins, 1898), pp. 16–17.

32. Bird S. Coler, *Municipal Government* (New York: D. Appleton & Co., 1900), p. 122; Bird S. Coler, "Amend the Debt Limit," *Municipal Affairs* 5 (Sept. 1901): 664–69.

33. *Report of the Comptroller of the City of St. Louis for Fiscal Year 1899–1900* (Saint Louis: Woodward & Tiernan, 1900), p. xvii.

34. *Fourth Annual Message of Charles F. Warwick* (Philadelphia: Dunlap Printing Co., 1899), p. xi.

35. Huse, *Boston*, pp. 321–27, 371.

36. *Report of the Comptroller of the City of Buffalo for the Fiscal Year Ending June 30, 1905* (Buffalo: Baker, Jones & Co., 1905), insert G.

37. Laurence M. Larson, *A Financial and Administrative History of Milwaukee* (Madison: University of Wisconsin, 1908), pp. 152–54, 171.

38. Williamson, *Cleveland*, p. 259.

39. Durand, *New York City*, p. 375.

40. Secrist, *Restrictions upon Public Indebtedness*, p. 119.

41. Durand, *New York City*, p. 373; *Fifty-first Report of Controller of Philadelphia*, p. 258; Hollander, *Baltimore*, p. 384; Huse, *Boston*, p. 377; *Reports of Cincinnati, 1901*, p. 829.

42. *Annual Reports of the City Departments of the City of Cincinnati for the Fiscal Year Ending December 31st, 1877* (Cincinnati: Times Book & Job Printing, 1878), p. 8.

43. *Report of the Comptroller of the City of St. Louis for the Fiscal Year 1877–78* (Saint Louis: Times Printing House, 1878), p. 9.

44. *Auditor of Accounts' Annual Report of the Receipts and Expenditures of the City of Boston* (Boston: Rockwell & Churchill, 1878), p. 11.

45. Willis J. Abbot, *Carter Henry Harrison, A Memoir* (New York: Dodd, Mead & Co., 1895), p. 96.

46. Frederick N. Judson, *A Treatise upon the Law and Practice of Taxation in Missouri* (Columbia, Mo.: E. W. Stephens, 1900), p. 68.

47. Williamson, *Cleveland*, pp. 77–79.

48. Larson, *Milwaukee*, pp. 124–25.

49. *Boston Evening Transcript*, 5 Jan. 1885 pp. 2, 4.

50. Durand, *New York City*, p. 373; Williamson, *Cleveland*, p. 228: Huse, *Boston*, p. 377; *Comptroller's Report . . . of the City of New Orleans, . . . 1905* (New Orleans: Jos. A. Boucher, 1905), pp. 209–13; *Fifty-first Report of the Controller of Philadelphia*, pp. 258–59. See annual reports of the comptroller of Saint Louis, 1877–1900.

51. Based on data in *Reports of Cincinnati, 1901*, p. 829.

52. Hollander, *Baltimore*, pp. 257, 384.

53. *Economist* (Chicago) 15 (2 May 1896): 535; ibid., 9 May 1896, pp. 572–73; 16 May 1896 ("Real Estate Valuation Supplement"); 23 May 1896, p. 630; 6 June 1896, p. 697.

54. Robert H. Whitten, "The Assessment of Taxes in Chicago," *Journal of Political Economy* 5 (Mar. 1897): 177. Edward D. Durand likewise blasted Tammany's policy of low taxes, claiming that it was a "policy of delusive economy" and that "the public schools especially had been seriously crippled." Durand, *New York City*, pp. 275–76.

55. *Mayor's Annual Message and the Twenty-fifth Annual Report of the Department of Public Works* (Chicago: P. F. Pettibone & Co., 1901), p. 239.

56. Durand, *New York City*, pp. 201–20, 373.

57. Williamson, *Cleveland*, pp. 90–98, 233. For a typical list of special assessments levied, see *Report of the Cleveland Department of Accounts, 1895* (Cleveland, 1895), pp. 205–25. For figures on special assessments in Saint Louis, see *Annual Report of the President of the Board of*

Public Improvements . . . 1894 (Saint Louis, 1894), p. 317. See also, Victor Rosewater, *Special Assessments: A Study in Municipal Finance* (New York: Columbia University, 1898).

58. Huse, *Boston*, pp. 213–14; *Report of Cleveland Department of Accounts, 1895*, p. 18; Williamson, *Cleveland*, pp. 100, 233; Larson, *Milwaukee*, pp. 126–27; Hollander, *Baltimore*, pp. 274–75; Durand, *New York City*, pp. 182–84; J. Raines, "The Raines Liquor-Tax Law," *North American Review* 162 (Apr. 1896): 481–85; *Report of the Comptroller of the City of St. Louis for Fiscal Year 1903–1904* (Saint Louis: Lambert, Deacon, Hull Printing Co., 1904), appendix, p. 6; *Report of Comptroller of St. Louis, 1886–87*, appendix p. vi.

59. *Chicago Tribune*, 18 June 1883, p. 4; 19 June 1883, p. 7. See also ibid., 16 June 1883, pp. 2, 4; 17 June 1883, p. 6.

60. *Forty-first Statement of Finances of Chicago, 1897*, p. 20.

61. *Report of the Department of Public Works of the City of New York for . . . 1895* (New York: Martin B. Brown Co., 1895), p. 165; *Fourth Annual Message of Edwin S. Stuart . . . with Annual Reports of James H. Windram, Director of the Department of Public Works* (Philadelphia: Dunlap Printing Co., 1895), p. 503; *Annual Report of the President of the Board of Public Improvements for . . . 1895* (Saint Louis, 1895), p. 508. See also: *Annual Reports of the Department of Public Works of . . . Buffalo for . . . 1900* (Buffalo, 1901), p. 338; *Annual Report of the Department of Public Works of the City of Cleveland, O. for . . . 1898* (Cleveland: Cleveland Printing & Publishing Co., 1899); no page numbers in original.

62. *Fourth Annual Message of Edwin S. Stuart*, p. 502.

63. Durand, *New York City*, p. 239; Hiram B. Loomis, "Franchise Taxation in Illinois," *Municipal Affairs* 5 (June 1901): 388–400; Milo Roy Maltbie, "Street Railways of Chicago: Analysis of Financial Operations," *Municipal Affairs* 5 (June 1901): 441–83; *Report of Comptroller of St. Louis*, 1903–1904; no page numbers in original.

64. Hollander, *Baltimore*, pp. 276–83, 381.

65. Durand, *New York City*, p. 191; Huse, *Boston*, pp. 376–77; *Annual Reports of Cincinnati 1901*, p. 829; *Report of Buffalo Comptroller, 1905*, Insert G; Lawson Purdy, "Taxation of Personalty," *Municipal Affairs* 2 (June 1899): 302; *Taxes and Assessments in the City of New York: Report of the Commissioners, 1897* (New York: Martin B. Brown Co., 1897), pp. 17–18.

66. Durand, *New York City*, p. 194.

67. Ibid.

68. Williamson, *Cleveland*, pp. 68–69.

69. E. A. Angell, "The Tax Inquisitor Law in Ohio," *Independent* 50 (3 Feb. 1898): 6; Lawson Purdy, "Municipal Taxation," *Proceedings of the Chicago Conference for Good City Government* (Philadelphia: National Municipal League, 1904), p. 301.

70. *Annual Reports of the City Departments of the City of Cincinnati, for . . . 1898* (Cincinnati: Commercial Gazette, 1899), p. ix.

71. *Eighth Biennial Report of the Bureau of Labor Statistics of Illinois, 1894* (Springfield: Ed. F. Hartman, 1895), pp. 30–34, 39–43.

72. Edward W. Bemis, "The Taxation Problem in Chicago," *Bibliotheca Sacra* 54 (Oct. 1897): 751–52.

73. Durand, *New York City*, pp. 192–94; Edwin R. A. Seligman, "The Three Fundamental Evils—Suggested Remedies," *Independent* 50 (3 Feb. 1898): 3.

74. *Report of the Tax Commission of Ohio of 1893* (Cleveland: J. B. Savage, 1893), p. 22; Angell, "The Tax Inquisitor Law," pp. 6–7; Purdy, "Taxation of Personalty," pp. 310–12.

75. John R. Commons, "Taxation in Chicago and Philadelphia," *Journal of Political Economy* 3 (Sept. 1895): 446–48.

76. Hollander, *Baltimore*, pp. 265–66.

77. *Report of Bureau of Labor Statistics of Illinois, 1894*, pp. 76–81, 88–89, 92–94, 102–103; Whitten, "Assessment of Taxes," pp. 179–80.

78. *Annual Reports of the City Departments of the City of Cincinnati For . . . 1897* (Cincinnati: Commercial Gazette, 1898), p. xiv.

79. Edward W. Bemis, "Evils of Tax Administration," *Independent* 50 (3 Feb. 1898): 4.

80. Durand, *New York City*, p. 195.

81. *Report of Bureau of Labor Statistics of Illinois, 1894*, pp. 94–99, 102–03; Whitten, "Assessment of Taxes," pp. 179–80.

82. Richard T. Ely, *Taxation in American States and Cities* (New York: Thomas Y. Crowell & Co., 1888), p. 248.

83. Commons, "Taxation in Chicago and Philadelphia," pp. 434–35; Allinson and Penrose, *Philadelphia*, pp. 238–39; Hollander, *Baltimore*, p. 266; *Annual Report of the Executive Department of the City of Boston For . . . 1889–90* (Boston: Rockwell & Churchill, 1890), p. 290; *Report of Comptroller of St. Louis, 1886–87*, appendix, p. iii.

84. "New York Preachers' Address on Municipal Misrule," *Our Day: A Record and Review of Current Reform* 6 (Nov. 1890): 370.

85. Frederick R. Clow, *A Comparative Study of the Administration of City Finances in the United States* (New York: Macmillan Co. 1901), p. 73.

86. *St. Louis Globe-Democrat*, 20 Dec. 1892, p. 1; 21 Dec. 1892, p. 7; *Chicago Tribune*, 13 May 1876, pp. 1, 4; 21 May 1876, p. 13.

87. William L. Riordon, *Plunkitt of Tammany Hall* (New York: E. P. Dutton & Co., 1963), p. 3.

88. Lothrop Stoddard, *Master of Manhattan: The Life of Richard Croker* (New York: Longmans, Green & Co., 1931), p. 125.

89. "New York Preachers' Address, p. 371.

11. TRIUMPH WITH THE TASTE OF DEFEAT

1. *Opening Ceremonies of the New York and Brooklyn Bridge, May 24, 1883* (Brooklyn: Brooklyn Eagle, 1883), pp. 32, 33, 47, 55.

2. David McCullough, *The Great Bridge* (New York: Simon & Schuster, 1972), p. 552.

3. *Opening Ceremonies of Brooklyn Bridge*, pp. 64, 74.

Index

Jon C. Teaford is associate professor of history at Purdue University. He is the author of *City and Suburb: The Political Fragmentation of Metropolitan America, 1850–1970* (also published by Johns Hopkins), and *The Municipal Revolution in America: Origins of Modern Urban Government, 1650–1825.*